P9-BTO-814

Other books by the author:

HEARTS
RICHIE
LOST!*

*A Dell Book

BLOOD AND MONEY

THOMAS THOMPSON

A DELL BOOK

*This is for my brother
Larry D. Thompson—a good
friend and a good lawyer.*

Published by
DELL PUBLISHING CO., INC.
1 Dag Hammarskjold Plaza
New York, N.Y. 10017

Dell ® TM 681510, Dell Publishing Co., Inc.

ISBN: 0-440-10679-6

Reprinted by arrangement with
Doubleday & Company, Inc.

Printed in the United States of America
First Dell printing—October 1977
Second Dell printing—October 1977
Third Dell printing—October 1977
Fourth Dell printing—November 1978
Fifth Dell printing—April 1979
Sixth Dell printing—July 1979

book one
JOAN

". . . Behold a pale horse . . ."

1

During the night an early spring rain washed the city and now, at dawn, the air was sweet and heavy. Remnants of fog still held to the pavements of Houston, rolling across the streets like cobweb tumbleweeds, and the windshields of early commuters were misted and dangerous. The morning seemed sad, of little promise.

In his bed, the old man sweated and tossed. This night had been worse than most. He had awakened over and over again, and each time he checked the clock. He was impatient for the new day to commence so that he could order the flowers. One hundred perfect yellow roses would surely please his daughter. Not until he saw her laugh again would he sleep well.

Once, during the long darkness, he turned on the light and looked at the photographs which surrounded his bed. Above his head was Joan from a quarter century ago, when she was a child in best white organdy, her knee saucily crossed. To his right, on the wall, was Joan in her late teens, her beauty frozen by soft focus, her features glazed, the classic debutante. And to his left, on the old Grand Rapids dresser, was Joan in recent years, her face ablaze with the triumph of yet another win in the show ring. There were a thousand like these in the big house, filling the walls, pasted into scrapbooks, stuffed into drawers, spilling out of closets. Joan and her horses had become favorite subjects of photographers across the land, and the old man's home was a museum of her image.

But even these familiar suspensions of time could not push away the scene from the night before. Each time he bolted awake, sitting up in bed, throwing a hand across his face to smear the dampness from his eyes, it was still there in all the torment.

"Joan, honey?" He had crept a few steps into the hospital room. It smelled of sterile potions and pain. Two nurses were busy about his daughter with tubes and medical contraptions.

"Pa?" she answered weakly. Normally her voice could boom clear across a cornfield. Her pillow was slightly raised, and on it her hair spilled thin and lifeless, no longer silver white and electric like a noon sun.

"They won't let me stay, honey," he said, fumbling for comfort. "You hurry up and get well, now, and tomorrow morning when you wake up I'm gonna fill your room with yellow roses."

Joan tried to smile. "I'd like that, Pa," she murmured.

"Daddy's gonna do that, Joan," he said. "You know Daddy's gonna do that."

Then one of the nurses pushed expelling hands toward him and he left the room. He stopped for a moment outside and leaned his heavy body against the wall. His heart pumped in alarm. Hadn't the doctors said she would be all right? They had, he reassured himself. He went in search of another one just to hear the words again. . . .

When the door chimes rang just before 6 A.M., the old man heard them. For an instant, in his bed, he opened his eyes and wondered who could be seeking entrance to his home so early, so unexpectedly. But he was weary, not yet ready to wake, and when he heard Ma stirring, he closed his eyes and fell back.

The old woman padded to the front door and opened it with good will. Perhaps, she thought, a neighbor is in distress. But when she saw the people with the gray and tragic faces standing at her threshold, looming out of the mist and fog, her knees buckled. They did not have to speak a word. She knew. She knew exactly what they had come to tell her.

"Oh, my God," the old woman managed as she fell. Pitifully she began to retch, throwing up the whiskey that had helped her find sleep the night before. Her son-in-law, John Hill, watched, but he did not reach down to pick her up. Although a doctor, he lacked the will at this terrible moment. One of the friends who had come with him, another physician, knelt to help Ma. He grasped her gently and lifted her and walked her to the living room. There she fell, breathing hard, onto the sofa. John Hill watched her for a few moments, then he took a tentative step toward the back bedroom where the old man was sleeping. Clearly he dreaded to make this short journey.

It was not Ma's nature to command anyone, for she was a woman who lived an obedient step or two behind her husband and her daughter. Her world was their shadows, and drawn blinds. But now she threw out her hand with an edict.

"Don't wake Pa," she said urgently. "For God's sake, let him sleep. This is the last night he ever will."

And they all sat and waited, fearfully, for Pa to wake and rise and hear the news.

2

He was a paradox, the old man, Pa. With one clenched fist rising in the direction of the beyond, he cursed God, for he had no tolerance for the foolishness of religion. Yet with the other he touched—in wonder—one of his most beloved possessions, an ivory Madonna that Christian warriors had borne through the Crusades, her back smoothed and worn from the frightened kisses of those seeking divine blessing. With one breath he scoffed at the notion of an afterlife. "An awful lot of SOBs sit on the front row of the church house," Pa often said, "and if I had to spend eternity with them, you couldn't drag me into heaven with six mules!" But with the next, he likely as not would tell of his fascination for the ancient royal houses of Egypt and his knowledge of their elaborate preparations for the journey to the other side.

When Joan was tiny she often sat in Pa's lap and heard him speak of Radames and Nefertiti and Tutankhamen: "They tell me that old King Tut was buried in a coffin that weighs twenty-four hundred pounds and is pure solid gold. Imagine that, Joanie! Solid gold! We'll see it someday. You and me are gonna see it all!" Across the map of Egypt marched his twin fingers, strong and gnarled from the rocks and earth of the fields he explored in search of oil, whisking father and daughter across the seas.

Now if you stood the man against the wall and measured him, he was, on surface viewing, the stereotypic model of the Texas oil creature from the wide-brimmed felt hat down to the gleaming black Lincoln automobile he drove at hurtling speeds about the freeways of Houston, a cassette of Eddie Arnold's country melodies soothing him from the tape deck. A quail had slight chance if it flew past the sights of his shotgun, nor did many wide-mouthed bass swim on if they chanced to nibble at his line. His

politics veered to the right of Calvin Coolidge, and liberal
Democrats, to his thinking, were as dangerous as a snake
in his swimming pool. He would not invite a black man to
sit at his dinner table, or even enter the house through the
front door, but should one arrive with a load of earth to
freshen his azalea beds, he might sit in the sun and talk
for hours of children and creaking bones and browning
blossoms, like a life of rich promise so suddenly going
away. He began most every morning with several cups of
strong hot coffee and an hour or two of spirited talk with
a table full of affluent cronies, in assemblage at the Houston Club, a *Klatsch* of elderly men whose breast pockets
might contain, side by side, the report of a new East Texas
gas well, the photograph of a grandson, and the vial of
digitalis. But there was more to Pa than gold and vinegar.
There were secrets he kept from the others. Had he faced
a firing squad and been told that his life would be spared
only if he could quote from memory great chunks of Long-
fellow and Keats **and** Shakespeare, then he would walk
away free and alive. He could read a little Greek, and
Latin, and might hold his own in the company of scholars.
But Pa insisted on presenting himself as a robust buccaneer, and he would never admit to the others at the coffee
table that *Evangeline* could still make him weep.

He was a strong, fine-looking Southern colonel kind of
man, even at seventy, with a head of thick white hair and
a muscled body that had stayed well shaped until the years
broke down his belly and pushed it out and over his belt.
Only his eyes betrayed him. They were not the eyes of a
man content with his lot. Bewilderment lived in the tired
and yellowing eyes, as did furtiveness, and suspicion, and an
occasional flash of pain, the kind that comes to a man
when he realizes that nobody—save his wife and child—
will really give a good god damn when he dies.

His name was Ash Robinson. And though its very
sound held flair, conjured visions of romantic novels, his
life for seven decades had not been one that veered from
the ruts of the ordinary road. Nor would he have seemed
in the winter of his life to be a man around whom tragedy
would break and swirl.

This is not to mean that Ash courted, as some men do,
the anonymity of shadowed places, or that he had accommodated himself to a place in the crowd, as most men
eventually do. Because he had believed, from the earliest

years of his memory, that Ash Robinson was *special*, that he possessed the talent and breeding and drive to climb somehow up the summit and once there claim a place in history. But though his life for seventy years had been an interesting and occasionally vivid one, there was nothing notable enough to set it aside for other men to mark and examine. But then came the misted March morning in 1969 when they arrived to tell him the news of Joan.

Always Ash had drawn nourishment from his money and his blood. He was the child of Southern aristocracy, both reigning and deposed. His mother, he liked to say, was "a great beauty and very possibly a genius." She was a gentle, kind young woman named Eunice Olive Davis, one of whose antecedents signed the Declaration of Independence. Her father was master of Sunnyside Plantation, south of Alexandria, Louisiana, a place where thousands of acres obediently bore sugar cane and cotton. Not even the Civil War drastically altered the orderly pattern of life at Sunnyside or ravaged the coffers of the family wealth. As the daughter of rich and doting parents, Eunice Olive journeyed to boarding school at the proper St. Mary's Episcopal Academy in Dallas where she won gold medals for scholarship, music, and manners.

Ash's father was less fortunate in his legacy. He would have been heir to another great plantation, a few hundred miles east of Sunnyside, at a place called Robinsonville, Mississippi, so named because only one white family, the Robinsons, lived on that particular slice of the bounteous delta. They were owners of a huge slave population which they considered well treated. But after the Civil War those former slaves who had not run away linked hands with the carpetbaggers to ravage Robinsonville, stripping it in the late months of 1865 as bare as a pecan tree in the path of locusts.

Sherwood Robinson, dauphin to a suddenly destroyed kingdom. left his ancestral home and went in search of a new life. In Louisville, Kentucky, he enrolled in medical school, paying for his tuition and keep by summoning one of the graces of plantation life, writing calling cards in elaborate script. His flourishes were in demand by the *nouveau riche*, eager to purchase his handiwork at twenty-five cents the dozen. With diploma in hand four years later, Dr. Sherwood Robinson wandered about the South, looking for a place to practice general medicine. New Orleans and Baton Rouge both were flush with physicians, but north, near Alexandria, he found the village near Sunnyside Plantation bereft. Not long after hanging out his shingle he received a summons from the largest house in the region. The owner's daughter, Miss Olive, was ill with influenza. In the best tradition of crinoline and magnolia blossoms, the young doctor not only treated his patient, he married her.

And in 1898 on the birthday of Abraham Lincoln, their first child, a son, was born. He was named Davis, after his mother, and Ashton, after a neighboring family who owned another sugar cane plantation across the way. Early in life Davis Ashton Robinson demanded that he be called Ash.

Dr. Robinson moved his wife and fast-growing family, soon to number three sons, across the border into Texas, a state that at the turn of the century was heavy with promise. Its Gulf Coast was attracting thousands of rice farmers and cattlemen and they were earning money enough to pay for a doctor. The Robinsons by-passed Houston, for it was a dirty, swampy place pestered by the foulest heat and mosquitoes, settling instead in Eagle Lake, sixty miles west. There the family prospered; Dr. Robinson became the pre-eminent physician for a hundred miles around.

In the manner especially peculiar to Southern men, Ash was drawn to the earth. He wanted to own land, study it, peel back the layers of time and speculate on the creatures that had walked therein. "If I had it all to do over again," he often said, well after he had passed seventy years and was semi-retired from a successful career in the pursuit of oil and gas, "I'd be an archaeologist."

Ash was a loner and a dreamer. And something of a schemer. He pretended to enjoy the medical books his father gave him to peruse. But Ash only skimmed across an occasional page, absorbing a fact here or there, enough to win the five dollars his father would occasionally award for a bit of scholarship tossed out at the dinner table. In secret he was going to the school library and finding books that told of ancient Egypt, shutting his eyes and fantasizing of how he would someday cruise the Mediterranean in search of the ruins of lost civilizations.

When it was time for college, Ash went to Tulane where he easily studied the liberal arts program. And, in a move which he would never fully understand, he enrolled to study dentistry. "I suppose it was a compromise for my father," he would say in later years. "I didn't give a damn about pulling teeth, but it was medical, and it seemed to please the family." Dutifully he completed a three-year course and successfully passed the state licensing board examination. But then the school informed the young dentist that an additional three months of study were newly required before he could begin practice. "I wasn't about to spend one more day of study on something I hated," Ash recalled. "A fellow can learn all he needs to know about dentistry in a few weeks, anyway. It's not much better than barbering."

Other things were pressing for his attention—well-tailored clothes from a Canal Street tailor, French wine, the girls from Sophie Newcomb College, the horses running at the New Orleans race track. The doctor's son from the flyspeck town in South Texas was eager to lie down on the softest pillows. He sent word home in a letter that he had decided not to be a dentist. In fact, he was going to loaf awhile and examine his options. Saddened by the report, Dr. Robinson summoned his son to Eagle Lake. He had a surprise.

Did the boy remember family stories about the sugar cane borer, an insect that destroyed Sunnyside Plantation in 1907?

Yes, of course. Often the disaster had been discussed at family gatherings. Most of the plantation owners in central Louisiana had been bankrupted by the devastating insect.

Did the boy also know that his mother had received one sixth of the profits from the forced sale of Sunnyside Plantation, divided between her and five other brothers and sisters?

No, Ash did not realize that his now dead mother had received any moneys from the sale.

"She left you a goodly sum to be delivered upon the occasion of your becoming an adult. I am carrying out my beloved wife's wishes," said Dr. Robinson. He presented his son with a check for $69,000, the extraordinary sum rolling on and on in the flourishes of his father's fine script.

Awed, Ash Robinson held the check and dimly heard his father's coincidental lecture. "Now, son, you didn't earn this money, and you don't know what it's worth. I can tell you that it's more than most men earn in a lifetime. My advice to you is . . . the quicker you get rid of it, the better off you're going to be. Then you'll start finding out what life is really like."

Suddenly, wonderfully rich, Ash returned to New Orleans on the first day of the new year of 1919. By July 4, six months later, he had spent every penny of his inheritance.

"Those damn ponies!" Ash would exclaim decades later, when he remembered the tale. "I thought I knew horses. But I came to find out soon enough I didn't know anything about horses when they were race horses." But for six incandescent months his life was as dazzling as the jewel-studded walking cane he swung on the arm of his hand-tailored suit as he promenaded down Bourbon Street. During his splurge, he made some progress toward a goal that had avoided him during his college years at Tulane, that being acceptance by New Orleans' old guard society. Doors had been slamming rudely in his hick-town face ever since he arrived in a city with more social stratification than Boston. Even his friends at Tulane, delighted to drink the whiskey that his money paid for, rarely invited him to their homes, muttering excuses that, though well couched, did not soothe Ash's ravaged Texas pride.

But with pockets bulging with cash and gold coins, he found his invitations picking up. At one party his eyes fell upon a shy, dark-haired young woman guarded closely by a chaperone. Her name, Ash discovered, was Rhea Ernestine Gardere, and she was the genuine article, a Southern belle with lineage that traced back to the last king of France and a father who, rumor held, owned a fleet of river boats that cruised the Mississippi. He could not have imagined a more perfect object for romantic attention. Rhea Ernestine Gardere had indeed been reared by nannies and chaperones, and she spoke French until she was in her teens. But all she had was a pedigree. There was no money left in her family's bank account. Her father was not the owner of river boats; he was only the captain of one. She would have told Ash this on their first meeting, for she was not a woman to misrepresent herself. The fact of the matter was, she could not get a word in, so overwhelming was Ash Robinson's pursuit. To a friend, Rhea confided, "He talks faster than a tobacco auctioneer and he throws money around like it was confetti. But he *is* good-looking."

Once, when Ash took her to the New Orleans race track, she mentioned that her great-great-great-grandfather had come to America with La Salle and had settled in Louisiana on a 150,000-acre tract awarded him by the French royal house.

"Where is it?" asked Ash, with widened eyes.

"We're standing on it," answered Rhea. Her ancestral home had long ago been lost and had become the New Orleans race track. But as a child she could remember visiting relatives in the great manor house here called Chatsworth, with marble staircases imported from an Italian Renaissance palace, and golden fixtures in the bathrooms.

That night, sitting on the front porch of Rhea's home, a modest place on Chestnut Street, Ash suddenly said, "Marry me."

"Give me some time to think it over," answered Rhea.

"There isn't any time," said Ash urgently.

Rhea wanted to clear up one point. If Ash was a fortune hunter, then he should stalk his game elsewhere. She had less money than the waitress who served them coffee at the old French Market.

"I know that," said Ash. "But it doesn't matter. I love you and I want you."

Rhea looked closely at the restless young man beside her. What would he become? What would he do with his life? He had already told her that it was not his intention to practice dentistry.

"I don't know what I'm going to do," answered Ash frankly, "but I expect we'll have some fun finding out."

Ash Robinson and Rhea Ernestine Gardere were married on July 28, 1919, before a justice of the peace in New Orleans. The groom had ten dollars to his name, all that was left of the $69,000 he had inherited but six months before. By the time he paid for the license and the recording fee, and tipped the justice of the peace, there was one dime left in his pocket. This he used to make two telephone calls, beseeching a college friend to come and fetch the newlyweds and carry them to the boardinghouse where they began their married life.

It became Ash's habit to work out daily at the Elks Club where many of the city's prominent young men gathered to steam away the food from Antoine's restaurant and swim in an indoor pool. A fellow with an alert pair of ears could pick up potentially rewarding information there. During a swim one afternoon, Ash found himself taking laps beside a man named Murphy who revealed that he was going to San Francisco to work in a Vanderbilt family venture. A half century later, Ash could remember what happened:

"Young Mr. Murphy asked me to go along. Said I would get a salary of five hundred dollars a month. Well, in 1922, that was a princely sum of money. And with a name like Vanderbilt behind it, it didn't take me long to say yes. I went home and told Ma we were heading west, to California!" Cornelius Vanderbilt, Jr., was ensconced in San Francisco, preparing to launch sister newspapers in that city and in Los Angeles. Ushered into the dynamic entrepreneur's office, Ash was as subservient as a Milanese peasant approaching the Pope. He had learned to respect money and power. "My entire personal fortune is behind this undertaking," said Vanderbilt. Ash was signed on as deputy to the illustrious man himself, his franchise being the selling of advertisements, the hiring and firing of clerks, and the accommodation of the publisher's smallest whim. He was even permitted to sit in on interviews with actresses and the titans of West Coast finance. Once, during a party on the tenth floor of a building, Ash saw the champagne in his goblet suddenly dance. Then the chandelier swayed ominously. At first he thought it was the effect of the wine, but then someone cried, "Earthquake!" The tremor was a slight one, but it was prophetic for the venture. The newspapers crumbled from weak financing. Ash was ahead of them. Knowing that the empire was about to topple, he fled the city, taking Rhea hurriedly to New York. Someone had told him that only there was real money to be made.

Ash arrived in Manhattan with a small stake of a few thousand dollars, but that was enough for a man on the make. It was 1924, and Wall Street was as giddy and bountiful as the flappers who danced the Charleston at the Astor Hotel. Within a year Ash owned securities worth more than $400,000 and he was not yet twenty-seven years old. Then from the fringes of Rhea's family appeared a "Spanish nobleman," a darkly handsome, thickly accented man in exquisite clothes. He knew his way around the city, speaking whatever language a maître d' seemed most comfortable in, mentioning names like Morgan and Carnegie with such familiarity that Ash was spellbound. The two men went into partnership, opening a firm that dealt in securities and mortgages. Within four months Ash would sadly realize that he had once again picked the wrong coconut shell at the county fair. "We opened an account at the Chase Bank," Ash would remember years later, his voice always taking on a hard edge as he told the story. "And my partner, naturally, had check-writing privileges. I thought everything was going splendidly. I thought it was just a matter of weeks before the Rockefellers would buy us out, or at least have us over for lunch. And then, one day, the bank calls and says our account is overdrawn. Four hundred thousand dollars is gone! And so is my partner. I commissioned the Daugherty Detective Agency to track him down, and they wouldn't take the case without a $500 retainer. I gave them Rhea's diamond ring instead. It didn't take them long. The god damned 'Spanish nobleman' had sailed for Europe on the old *Olympia* steamer, with the Prince of Wales in the next cabin." Ash cabled the ship's captain to arrest the scoundrel and hold him for arrest in France. But upon docking the elegant passenger had a perfect explanation. He had not absconded with his partner's money. It was too bad that their investments were poor, but there was no crime in buying the wrong securities. Tell Ash Robinson better luck next time.

When word soon thereafter arrived that his former partner was setting up a new base of operations in Paris, using the now bankrupt New York office as a reference, Ash decided it was time to leave still another city in a hurry. He booked passage on a Morgan boat bound for Texas and arrived in Galveston with his wife in 1926. He had eleven dollars in his pocket.

"Houston is," a man once wrote the local newspaper, "an overgrown, dirty village, seemingly blundering along without any policy or defined government or management. . . . I am compelled to say that Houston is the most dirty, slovenly, go-as-you-please, vagabond city of which I have knowledge." And though this judgment was offered in 1896, the harsh description was not far off three decades later, when Ash Robinson settled in to try for a third fortune. Twice burned, he had become a suspicious young man, with narrowed eyes that counted his fingers to make sure there were five left on each hand every time he met a new man. It was a time for caution. The city was caught in a whirlwind. Oil leases were hawked on the corners of downtown intersections, great mansions were going up in River Oaks, Cadillacs and Packards crowded the dusty, rutted streets. But no one knew exactly why. There was no real reason for Houston even to exist. Of all the major cities in the world, Houston held slimmest natural promise. She sat inland fifty miles from the Gulf of Mexico, on a relentlessly flat swamp, threaded by muddy bayous on whose banks sunned water moccasins. Her resources were scant; the summer heat was cruel to crops, the earth contained a little oil, but not as much as that to be found in any other direction. Her most valuable asset turned out to be a core of shrewd and ruthless men who literally dug out a place for their city in the world. Although there were a dozen natural ports scattered along those states lapped by the Gulf of Mexico, and three within arm's length of landbound Houston, the city fathers floated a bond issue shortly after the turn of the century to create a channel from the Gulf fifty miles inland to Houston. It was a project approaching in audacity the Panama Canal. But when no Eastern financiers chose to put money into the reckless scheme, then the bankers of Houston did it themselves. To hell with conservative Yankees.

The first week he was in Houston, Ash heard a man say, "A fellow can make ten million dollars here if he wants to run after it. A fellow can make one million dollars just by standing still." But though he could boast of having worked as the personal associate of a Vanderbilt, and of having danced merrily with the bulls of Wall Street, no one would deal Ash Robinson a hand to play unless he had an ante to put on the table.

"I took a job today selling used cars," he told Rhea in the bleakness of their furnished room. "But stay with me, it's gonna get better." His wife nodded cheerfully. She had come to learn that in the roller coaster ride of life with Ash, when the car reached bottom, the next curve was up.

He was, as he would remember, "a helluva salesman. God damn, I sold those cars! I made a two-year-old Packard with its tail pipe dragging as desirable as Napoleon's golden coach." From there, he moved into real estate, joining a firm that hawked raw lots in the south end of the city for $250 each. "I sold out an entire subdivision in less than no time," he liked to say. And then, by stroke of fair fortune, he got into the business that was on the collective lips of everyone. Oil!

A stranger walked into the real estate shack in 1930 and turned a long face toward Ash Robinson. He was in financial trouble. "I've been down that road myself a time or two," said Ash, willing to hear the story. The man had leased a section of land, 640 acres, in East Texas at a dollar an acre, and had pledged that the money due would be paid by the end of the month. The day was approaching quickly, and he lacked funds to cover it. "How much do you need?" asked Ash. "Half of $640," was the answer.

Though skeptical, Ash put up the money and obtained a fifty per cent interest in the lease. And he forgot about it. Three months later the man rushed into the real estate office with surprising good news. An offer had come from an oil company to buy the lease outright at ten dollars an acre. A thousand per cent profit! Ash Robinson did not jump in excitement. In fact, his antennae of suspicion went up. "Had they offered two bucks an acre, I would have sold my part in a Tennessee minute," Ash would remember years later. "But if somebody was offering ten, I figured it must be worth a helluva lot more. I held tight." Two weeks later the offer was upped to twenty-five dollars an acre. Again, Ash declined to sell, though his instincts were waging war against his common sense. Not until the oil company announced it would pay fifty dollars an acre did Ash sell, making $16,000 on an investment of $320.

"At that moment, it is fair to say I became an oilman," Ash would one day remember.

Long before the Spanish kings sent their explorers to pillage Texas in the sixteenth century, the land was awash in oil. Indians had used it for medicine and to calk their canoes. It seeped and bubbled from the ground. The first well was drilled in 1866, but not until four decades later, on a January morning in 1901, did the enormity of the state's natural reserves come to the world's attention. That was the hour of Spindletop, a man-made volcano gushing tens of thousands of barrels of oil into the skies near Beaumont. The discovery was staggering. In 1902, Spindletop alone disgorged 17.5 million barrels of oil, ninety-four per cent of the entire state's production. The price of oil plunged to three cents a barrel.

But Spindletop was only Act One. Act Two began on an October day in 1930, in a stumpy, brushy piece of East Texas land near the village called Turnertown. An eccentric wildcatter named C. M. (Dad) Joiner persisted in pouring money into a territory that geologists of the major oil companies had long since pronounced barren. Dad Joiner was considered the local thickhead. But he not only found oil, he opened up a field so rich that it dwarfed Spindletop. There ensued a hysterical stampede to the farms of Rusk County by speculators trying to buy leases.

Ash Robinson was among them. He packed a satchel with hundred-dollar bills and rushed to the piney woods east of Houston. When a farmer could be found who was willing to lease a few acres, he would not take a check. It had to be cash on signature. And it needed to be consummated that moment, for if a fellow hesitated, then there were four more speculators behind him chugging up the dirt paths to the farm in Model A Fords. Ash met one man who had $50,000 in his satchel ready to scatter among suddenly wary farmers who a month before had been mired to their necks in the Depression. He witnessed promotors shot dead over leasing disputes. Happily he paid fifty dollars to pass a restless night on a cot in a farmer's barn, twenty other hustlers jammed next to one another, clutching their bags until the sun rose. The situation became so frenetic that Governor Ross Sterling declared martial law in August 1931 and dispatched the National Guard to the oil fields to restore order.

Ash became what is known in the business as an "independent oil man," an appellation that has as many shades as layers of rock in an ancient piece of the earth. Many of the greatest Houston oil fortunes were made by such men, who approached their endeavor with the same attitude a stalk of mistletoe has toward a tree. They operated in parasitic fashion. And the principal requirements for success were two: an ability to snoop, an ability to hustle. Ash Robinson was richly endowed in both. An "independent oil man" could hear a rumor over coffee in Houston one morning and by lunch be racing to a place not even on the map, where a major company was—whispers had it —prowling for oil. Often the rumor was as empty as the wind. Once Ash heard on good report that a play was secretly beginning west of Fort Worth, where a major company was quietly buying leases. "I hurried up there and bought two big chunks as fast as I could. And I got there early. Before the week was out, the place was swarming with speculators. Come to find out, nobody knew anything. Nobody made a damn penny except for the farmers, who probably started the rumor in the first place."

It took a considerable amount of money to actually drill a well—$35,000 was the going figure in the 1930s—and at least seventy-five per cent of them came in dry. But major oil companies could afford the risk, operating on the theory first propounded by Queen Elizabeth I. She felt it was worth dispatching fifty ships in search of riches, and if only a handful returned, then the rewards were ample enough to shield her risk. Men like Ash Robinson could not finance the actual drilling of wells, but they devised a way to wiggle in on the profits.

If Ash chanced to hear a guarded conversation in the Houston Club men's room—talk of a new discovery or of one that the Humble Company's geologists felt were promising—he would quickly write the information down. It was further possible to develop contacts within the majors' own executive suites, men willing to tip off speculators in return for one third of the profits, if any. Then it was up to the "independent oil man" to stuff his pockets with cash and search out the farmer whose cornfield might—or might not—be covering a king's ransom in oil. The independent oil man could not just hurry out and buy up the land in question. Not only was this prohibitively expensive, it might so anger the major oil company that it would refuse, out of spite, to drill. The rules of the game dictated that men like Ash should locate a farmer who had *already* leased his land to, say, Texaco. Careful to shed his city manners and replace them with down-home folksiness, Ash would sit down on the farmer's porch and talk a spell. Might be some oil over there. Again, there might not. The odds were overwhelmingly against a gusher raining black gold down on the roof, which, by the way, sure needed patching. Feller might do better for his wife and kids if he gambled, if he took a little profit right here and now, if he signed over one eighth of his potential royalties to Ash Robinson. If Texaco hit it big over there, then the money would flow so lavishly that who'd miss a measly one eighth? On the other hand, if Texaco came up dry, and packed up and went away, and the weeds took over, then the farmer still had this right respectable chunk of cash that Ash Robinson was prepared to pay—that very minute.

In the middle years of the 1930s Ash was a superb persuader, managing to buy "mineral rights," as these deals are called, by the tens of thousands of acres in East and Central Texas. Then, as the decade neared an end, he took two savage beatings. The first almost destroyed his bank account. The second almost sent him to the state penitentiary.

He staked much of his respectable fortune in 1937 on a gamble that oil would burst out of a waste strip of land in Duval County near Corpus Christi. Ash bought several thousand acres of mineral rights. The Humble Oil Company had already drilled part of the area, all the way down to two thousand feet, then pronounced it worthless. But Ash thought he knew better. He had come into possession of a geologist's report and a map of dubious parentage which indicated otherwise. With the fervor of a fundamentalist preacher, Ash insisted oil could be found. But after a year, and after spending $50,000, he sadly realized that the land was arid dust. Not long thereafter, still another independent oil man came to the same spot, sank a well only thirty feet away, and hit the elusive oil. Ash could not even enjoy the irony of his bad luck. He was by this time defending himself against a serious charge, a criminal accusation of fraud and swindle.

While his left hand had tended to the disaster in Duval County, his right had been promoting the exploitation of a 3,000-acre parcel of mineral rights he had leased in Louisiana. Ash was low on cash, and he hustled a man into chipping in $5,000. Only because he was temporarily in need of capital, wooed Ash, would he part with what was surely going to be a staggering bonanza. To back his claim, Ash waved a report in front of his investor's eyes, suggesting that Humble had made a core test on the property and found oil sand of hot promise. And, furthermore, Ash contended that he had turned down a bid from Humble to sell his mineral rights for $750,000! The investor was spellbound; he shoved $5,000 into Ash's hands in return for a promised one thirtieth of the anticipated fortune. But when the months passed and the land belched forth nothing, Ash's new partner began to suspect that he had been sold snake oil. A little research turned up the fact that Humble Oil had neither found oil sand nor offered three quarters of a million dollars for Ash's mineral rights. Complaint was made to the district attorney; Ash Robinson was arrested, indicted, convicted, and sentenced to seven years in the state penitentiary for swindle.

"It was a god damn frame pure and simple," cried Ash at the time, and on every recounting of the experience years thereafter. "Why, the truth of the matter was I had already spent $23,000 drilling the well in question. I was down to 6,000 feet when they got me arrested. I think I know what happened. A lot of independents were being persecuted by the majors, who were after people for getting hold of their information."

Ash did not serve a day in the penitentiary. His sentence was appealed and, the Texas Court of Criminal Appeals deciding that the district attorney's office in Houston had made legal errors in its prosecution, threw out the conviction. Ash may have been chastised by the experience but, if so, it did not show. The cloak of the buccaneer had fallen about his shoulders, and it gave him a raffish, martyrish aura that he relished. Many of the most prominent men in Houston had waltzed across the same thin ice. That Ash Robinson had the misfortune to fall in, pull himself out, dry off, and blast forth in search of new fortune was not damnation. It was 1938. By 1941 Ash was once again a millionaire.

And, more pertinent, his daughter Joan was ten years old, already well embarked on a wondrous life that bade fair to shower him with more attention than had all the oil in Texas gushed at his command. She was the heart of his world. She was the only thing he had done that was special. He would have sold seven eighths of Spindletop just to keep her on his lap and watch her laugh.

3

The circumstances surrounding the birth of Joan Olive Robinson are clouded. Her birth certificate no longer exists in the state records at Austin. The country doctor who delivered her was past ninety years of age in 1975 and either unable or unwilling to recollect the February morning in 1931 when she was born. Nor does it matter much any more, except to shed a sliver of light on the obsession of her father. For that is the word that people would come to use when they spoke of Ash and Joan. *Obsession.*

She was an illegitimate child, born to an anonymous mother and father at a rural hospital near Eagle Lake, Texas, the town where Ash was reared. When the infant was one month old she was carried to the Edna Gladney Home in Fort Worth, Texas, where she was formally adopted by Ash and Rhea Robinson.

Forty-three years later, on a broiling summer noon in 1974, Mrs. Rhea Robinson sipped the thick chicory of her native Louisiana and remembered the long-ago adoption. Or, at least, her version. It was a tale twisted by the long years and shaped by the events that had destroyed her family. On this day Ma, as she had come to be known by all of her friends, was seventy-five years old, and reality was not her constant companion. The haze of the Southern belle still clung to her in wisps, but her memory was like a lace wedding gown kept in an attic, faded, dusty, crumbling with time. This is the way she wanted the story to be put down:

"We had been married for ten years, Pa and I, and it was good. I was always happy with him. We never really struggled, even when we were scraping bottom. Ash always managed to come up with money when we needed it. I would be going along thinking we didn't have two sticks to rub together and then Ash would come home with a velvet box in his pocket. And I'd open it and there would be a diamond ring. That was life with Ash. Velvet and diamonds when you least expected it.

"I couldn't have children, you see. I knew I had always been a little anemic, and I suppose that was the reason. It didn't worry me, because our marriage was so good I didn't need anything else to make me happier. But I did worry about Ash. He wanted a baby—a little girl!—more than anything else in the world. So I went to the doctor to find out why I wasn't getting pregnant. He told me a little correction was needed surgically. That frightened me, and I went home and got up the courage to tell Ash. 'Shall I have it done?' I asked him. He put his arms around me and said, 'I won't push you. It's your decision.' "

The minor operation was performed, but still Mrs. Robinson was unable to conceive a child. Never mind, said

Ash, they could live without one. But at the beginning of 1931, just as he was beginning to make the first of his several oil fortunes, Ash took Rhea out to dinner and chose his words carefully. He had heard of an adoption agency in Fort Worth operated by one Edna Gladney (who would be portrayed by Greer Garson in a 1940s movie entitled *Blossoms in the Dust*). Ash had heard tell that every detail was handled discreetly, that the babies came from the wombs of good girls who had gotten into trouble, that the best families from all over America were finding children there.

"I hesitated," remembered Mrs. Robinson, as she reluctantly pulled the story from her dying memory. "I felt a little ashamed that I could not give my husband a child of our own blood. So I told him I would have to think about it."

In early March 1931 she traveled by train 280 miles to Fort Worth. And at this point her account becomes confusing. Perhaps, charitably, it was a recollection embellished by the passage of four decades. Or, possibly, it had become one of those locked-away secrets that people look at now and then in privacy. If you tell yourself something long enough and hard enough, then it becomes impossible to distinguish between what really happened and what should have happened.

"I went to the Gladney Home with a friend of mine who also wanted to adopt," Ma remembered. "We went in, and we both looked around, and here were all these babies crying and carrying on, and I just wasn't interested. I told my friend that I supposed I just wasn't in the right mood because none of them appealed to me. Actually I was scared, shaking half to death. One little baby boy wanted me, he stretched out his arms to me, and he was the cutest thing I ever saw, but I couldn't bring myself to take him. I went on back to the hotel and wondered how I was going to tell Ash why I was coming home empty-handed.

"Just when I was fixing to leave the next morning, the Gladney Home calls and they say they have this little baby girl I didn't get to see. She had been sick with a cold and they didn't bring her out. So I go back and my eyes behold the most adorable baby I had ever seen. She looked at me and laughed. When I walked away for a minute, she commenced to carrying on. She wanted *me!* I took her in a minute. Mr. Gladney himself drove us to the train station and

he said, 'I envy this child. She is really going to be loved.' "
The prophecy was accurate. Joan Olive Robinson was
showered with love, a tender, quiet, caring kind of love
from her adopted mother, a powerful, crushing, overwhelming kind of love from Ash. Because of this love, it
is perhaps cruel to dissect the story of her adoption, but
there are too many flaws to overlook.

The Edna Gladney Home does not now permit nor has
it ever permitted two prospective mothers to visit at the
same time. Nor does the home have children on display,
like merchandise at a bazaar, for parents to browse over.
The home has always operated under the strictest security,
providing a place for pregnant unwed women to stay during gestation, paying for hospital and obstetrical costs, and
matching an infant with adoptive parents only after meticulous investigation.

Joan Robinson did not learn she was adopted until she
was in her late teens and needing a birth certificate for a
passport. At that moment Ma revealed the family secret,
breaking down in tears as she told Joan. "Don't you see,
honey?" said Ma. "Of all the baby girls in the world, I
picked *you* out to be my own." After that the subject was
never mentioned again.

When Joan was a woman past thirty years old she grew
curious as to the identity of her real parents, as most
adopted children eventually do. Secretly she engaged a
private detective who, after an investigation of several
months, arranged a rendezvous with his client in the parking lot of a Houston shopping center. There he presented
a document that indicated—but fell short of indisputable
proof—that her real father was Ash Robinson and her real
mother a then young woman who had worked in a Houston
office. There was the implication—unproven—that Ash
had paid a woman to bear his child, then arranged to
adopt her.

Joan studied the report carefully, reading it over several
times. Then she ripped the papers into tiny pieces, dropped
them to the pavement, knelt, and set the pile afire with her
cigarette lighter. While smoke rose about her, she murmured, "I wish I hadn't done this. I don't care who my
parents are. My mother is Ma, and my father is Pa, and I
love them more than I can say." Then she kicked the ashes
away and ran in tears to her Cadillac.

The day would come when Ash would be asked repeatedly if he indeed was the blood father of Joan. "No," he answered. "But she was the child of very good people." By this time he would be denying so many other things that it was difficult to choose just which one of Ash Robinson's pronouncements was worth believing.

When Ma stepped off the train that happy morning in 1931 she was met at the Houston depot by Ash, who had yellow roses in his arms and radiance across his face. Immediately he scooped the baby girl from his wife's arms and boosted her high above his head. "Welcome home!" he cried. He carried her like a trophy through the crowded station.

From that moment she was Daddy's girl. "I hardly saw that baby again," Ma used to joke. "I lost her as soon as Ash took her in his arms. There never was a man so smitten with a tiny baby." Ash insisted on fixing the infant's formula. He washed her diapers, rose cheerfully from his bed in the middle of the night to walk her, even carried her off for days at a time to the places where oil was being sought. With geological maps in one hand and his baby girl in the other, Ash would sit in the fading cool of a Texas dusk and talk to an engineer about whether a well was running high or where the abnormalities were hiding in the subsurface of the earth that centuries ago had trapped the oil. Farm wives often rode out with fried chicken and a five-gallon can of fresh coffee for their men. And they would laugh and carry on about the big city fellow with the baby on his lap, but they would also draw back and cluck kindly about his obvious glowing love for the child.

Joan was an exuberant youngster who attacked life full tilt, grabbing it the hour of her awakening each day and squeezing every minute of its value until she reluctantly fell asleep exhausted. And throughout the day she made her father laugh. Not a man of especially good humor, Ash was often dour in demeanor. But at the sight of Joan his face turned joyous. Once the child ran in from a playground and leaped into her father's armchair. "I 'spect I need a good talkin' to, Pa," she suggested seriously.

"Why, honey? Did you do something bad?"

Joan nodded. "Yes, Pa. I just gave Billy a sock in the face." Joan was four; Billy was five.

On another day a religiously committed neighbor suggested to Joan that she attend a nearby Sunday school. "No, ma'am," responded the child politely. "I want to go to hell with my daddy." Ash heard the story and roared, telling it all over Texas.

Joan was as well attended as a czarina. Should a minor scratch appear on her arm from a molesting kitten, Ash would summon a specialist and, if necessary, a medical staff. "I want the best for this child," he always said. Nursemaids, private schools, toe dance teachers—all received his patronage, if their credentials were pre-eminent in Ash's eyes. By 1934 he was in a prosperous period, enough to engage a chauffeur-driven Cadillac, chiefly because he enjoyed going on rides with his daughter and sharing her joy of discovery at the age of three. He did not want to divide his attention between her and the road. Once, while motoring out Houston's South Main Street, Joan noticed an amusement park with pony rides.

"I remember well exactly what happened," Ash would say some forty years later. "Joanie commenced to hollering that she wanted to ride those ponies. I told the chauffeur to stop and I walked over and put her up on the pony. Nickel a ride. I expected her to cry like the other kiddies or get tired and demand to be taken off. But she loved it. That was the beginning. Everything dates from that afternoon."

It is a special moment when a small child connects with something that will dominate a life. Rarely does it happen at such an early age, but from that day in 1934 Joan Robinson was committed to horses as surely as the young Mozart was bound to music.

She began fretting for her nursery school class to end each day so that the chauffeur could drive her to the pony rides. "Hurry!" Joan cried, impatiently sitting in the back seat. Within six weeks she had succeeded in making one of the weary Shetland ponies lope around the track. The manager stood openmouthed in amazement and the other children grew frightened. "You better get this kid a real horse," said the manager to Ash.

Near Houston's Hermann Park was a public stable operated by a man with the Dickensian name of Skaggs. He owned a broken-down chestnut mare named Dot who had borne ten thousand young Houston children on her swayed back. Patient and docile, she seemed void of juices and ready only to lie down forever. But when Joan leaped upon her back, Dot's ears perked and she was rejuvenated. A quiver rippled across the old horse's flanks. Whispering in Dot's ear, Joan dug in her heels and the two were off, bursting from the stable, down a path, into the thick woods.

"My God!" cried Ash fearfully, beginning to run after his tiny daughter. Surely the horse had gone insane and would throw the child, perhaps even trample her.

"They'll be okay," murmured Skaggs. He was not frightened, only astonished.

When Joan returned, with Dot prancing and snorting like a colt, she beseeched her father to buy the horse. "Is she for sale?" asked Ash.

Skaggs scratched his head. He was suddenly a good horse trader. "Well," he allowed, "she's got a lot of turns left in her."

"How much will you take for her?" pushed Ash, taking out his bankroll as testimony to his sincerity. He always carried a wad of big bills, for his trips to the oil country.

"To tell you the truth, old Dot ain't worth a damn," said Skaggs. "But she's the kiddies' favorite. She's made a lot of quarters for me."

Assuming that no deal could be struck, Ash took his disappointed daughter by the hand and led her toward the limousine. Skaggs's words stopped him. " 'Bout a hundred and fifty bucks, I reckon."

"A hundred and fifty dollars?" Ash was incredulous. "That's highway robbery." But his daughter was crying and, to shush her, he counted out the money. Had Joan asked for the Rice Hotel to store her dolls in, Ash would have telephoned his real estate broker.

The deal was struck and Skaggs went over to pat his suddenly illustrious steed. "You're a lucky old nag," he said. "Those other kids just about wore you out. Now maybe you'll get a little rest."

If Skaggs presumed that Joan Robinson, age four, would be like the other rich children, the kind who screamed until their daddies bought them a horse and then ignored the creature in a few weeks after infatuation waned, he was wrong. The spunky child with the light brown hair that flew behind her as she ran—she seldom walked anywhere—fell immediately in love with her first horse. Dot was transformed. She was groomed, scolded, cajoled, fed treats, trained, and generally cared for in the manner of a

Kentucky Derby champion. A society instructor was engaged to teach Joan the fundamentals of riding but could
not suppress a wince at seeing the horse that the child led
out to begin the first lesson. Joan saw the look of dismay.
"Dot can do anything!" she insisted. Within three months
Dot could indeed walk, trot, and even canter on cue. But
only for Joan. She would not respond to any other rider.

When she was five years old and still in need of a step-
ladder to mount Dot, Joan entered the equitation competition at the Houston Fat Stock Show and Rodeo. She was
ready to test her riding ability against all female comers
twelve years and under. Ma and Pa tried to dissuade their
daughter but Joan was adamant. She would enter and she
would win. With drawn breath, the Robinsons watched as
the event began. Their daughter weighed fifty pounds, the
horse fifteen hundred. Together, the imbalance was en-
chanting, clearly the crowd's favorite. Throughout her turn
Joan flashed a dazzling smile, one that would become her
trademark. Dot rose to the occasion, obeying each of
her young mistress' commands, and when the results were
announced Joan Robinson was awarded the third place
ribbon.

"We were both so excited we were ready to bust," Ma
would recall. "But Joan was disappointed and Pa was
angry. They both thought she should have been first." That
night Joan took the white ribbon and tacked it onto a wall
beside her bed. A dozen years later, by the time she had
graduated from a private high school and was enrolled in
the proper Stephens College for women at Columbia, Mis-
souri, the wall was filled with ribbons, mostly blue, and
the shelves sagged from the trophies won in horse show
events across the American South. In 1951 Ash wrote to a
newspaper that inquired about his daughter:

> Joan asked me to write a résumé. It's as simple as
> that—she thinks. But how do I begin to tell you about
> my talented little girl?
>
> She won her first ribbon in equitation when she
> was five years old—a third at the Houston Fat Stock
> Show. She began riding three- and five-gaited horses—
> and winning!—in amateur stakes by the time she was
> seven. She was reserve champion in amateur five-
> gaited stake at the Baton Rouge, La. show in 1938
> (when she was seven years old) on Midnite, a black

gelding. I am sending you a picture torn out of my scrapbook (and please return, it is so important to me). She was first and second in practically all of the equitation and juvenile three- and five-gaited classes from 1938 through 1945. She won the $2,000 championship three-gaited stake at Jackson, Miss., in 1945 on Peavine Rhythm Step, and others at Selma, Ala., New Orleans, and Pensacola—so many on this horse until its death this year.

She sings, plays the piano, swims, works, reads, and is a perfect, wonderful child. Her mother and I adore her. Every minute around her is a treasure. That's about all that I personally know about her—that is, first hand. Yours truly.

When Joan was ten, she wrote a brief composition on the subject "My Father" for an English class. It read:

My father is big and strong. He likes to get his way. He is usually right, Mama says. He is good-looking when he takes his glasses off. He is gone a lot looking for oil. Sometimes he rides horses with me, but I run off and leave him and he gets scared.

He tells funny stories all the time and sits beside my bed until I go to sleep. Sometimes I wake up and he is still there watching me. I used to think he was the sandman. I love my father very much. He gives me everything I want.

The day that a young woman leaves home and goes away to college is normally the day that the umbilical cord is cut. But this was not the case when Joan Robinson left Houston and enrolled at Stephens. Her parents followed her there. Ash leased a suite of rooms at a hotel adjacent to the campus and sent Ma to keep her eye on Joan. He commuted for long weekends, trying to make a little joke about the unusual shadowing of their daughter. "I figured it was cheaper to let Ma move up there than pay the god damn long-distance phone bills," he said at the time. But the truth was that Joan had become the sun for two dulling lives, and neither Ash or Rhea could bear to exist without its warmth.

At Stephens, Joan was a popular, achieving student who made average grades, more interested in rushing from class each afternoon to ride the horse she had brought with her to board, a creature with the lovely name, Song of Revelry. The college was of the old tradition, where wealthy young women could bring their horses and keep them at a campus stable. A classmate would remember that Joan was "the busiest girl on campus." She must have been, rushing from class to stable to her parents' hotel suite, trying to satisfy obligations to all. The same classmate, who later became one of Joan's married friends in Houston, recalled, "Most of us felt sorry for her. She was completely under her parents' thumb. She couldn't even accept a date without checking with them first. The thing I remember most about Joan was how starved for affection she seemed to be. With all that attention, she was hungry for love from somebody other than Ma and Pa."

Briefly, Joan became enamored of acting, and her performance in a college production, along with her regular appearances on the covers of Sunday rotogravure sections from Houston to Tampa, aroused the attention of an MGM talent scout. He offered Joan a screen test if she could find her way to Hollywood. Almost eighteen, she was wholesome, in a June Allyson sort of way, and possessed of a freshness and class that motion pictures might have found appealing. Excitedly, Joan burst into her parents' rooms with the news.

Ash Robinson's face darkened. He was not enthusiastic. "I can't let you do that, Joanie," he said. Too many "good girls" had been destroyed by show business. Dangerous men with salacious intention were lying in wait behind every palm tree in Beverly Hills. It was out of the question.

Joan argued ineffectually. She was not yet strong enough to buck her father. Nor was she sophisticated enough to discern that Pa would not let her go off on her own on any project.

Even marriage.

There were two, in quick order, both disasters. Ash Robinson hovered over both like Zeus throwing thunderbolts down from Mount Ida. The first man was a New Orleans boy named Spike Benton, and their romance flowered the night of the June Ball at Annapolis. "He's from a lovely family," Ma told her husband. "His grandmother was queen of the Mardi Gras, and he's going to be a Navy pilot." Of course Ma had accompanied her daughter to

Annapolis, and had dressed her for the ball, and had watched the handsome young cadets come in dress whites to fetch the girls, and had sat up until daybreak with Joan as she poured out her love for the Benton boy.

Ash Robinson watched the relationship grow serious, and when his daughter's beau came calling to ask permission to wed, he could not even pretend good humor. Joan and Spike were too young, too naïve, too financially dependent on their elders. Who would pay for Joan's horses? Did this boy have any idea how much the hobby cost to sustain? What would Joan do while he was off flying his Navy airplanes around the world? Marriages cannot be impetuous! Go away and let some time pass and come back when they were both mature. Spike Benton had dreaded this scene, but now that it was being played, he realized he had underestimated his antagonist. It was clear that Ash Robinson would sooner tear out his heart than surrender his daughter to another man.

Joan took her father aside and spoke to him in private. She loved Spike Benton. And she wanted him. It was natural. It was the way things had always happened, and always would. She would give up her horses. They were something she had loved as a child, but now she was a woman. She wanted her father's blessing.

Ash Robinson sadly assented. In the family album are wedding photographs revealing a bride of honeyed hair and exceptional beauty, a groom with traditional apprehension, and a father whose smile was forced and tight.

The newlyweds immediately moved to Pensacola, Florida, where Benton would undergo flight training. They were not long left alone. Abruptly Ash "retired" from the oil business, even though he was hardly past fifty years old, and in vigorous health. He was feeling a little weary, he said, and the climate in Pensacola was supposed to be nice. Surely it would be a suitable place for him and Ma to put their feet up, watch the world go by, and visit the young folks now and then. The Robinsons thus moved to Pensacola and took an apartment a few minutes away from their daughter and new son-in-law. Ash found it necessary to begin each day by visiting Joan and drinking coffee. Not unsurprisingly, the marriage of Mr. and Mrs. Spike Benton collapsed within six months. So did the retirement of Ash Robinson.

Husband number two was a young New Orleans lawyer

whom Joan had known since she was a child. His name was Cecil Burglass, and he shared Joan's interest in horses. Cecil's bloodlines were acceptable, at least to Ma, and his proposal of marriage would have seemed an attractive prospect.

This time Ash was not only cautionary, he was adamant. His face purpled. Absolutely out of the question, he stormed. He would not permit his daughter to run from the ruins of one marriage into another one. Rebound romances are as perishable as gardenias. "I will give neither my blessing nor my permission," he said. "And if that is not clear enough, then I *forbid* it. Joan is still a minor in the eyes of the law."

Joan Robinson and Cecil Burglass eloped and were married by a justice of the peace. When Ash heard the news he ordered Ma to pack their belongings. For a time the Robinsons had been living in New Orleans. Declaring that he had shut his disobedient child out of his life forever, Ash moved back to Houston. In less than another half year Mr. and Mrs. Cecil Burglass were separated, soon to be divorced. The Robinson family explanation was that the son-in-law, though charming, bright, and full of promise, was also devoted to the race track.

There was another reason that contributed to the breakup. Joan kept it secret for years, finally confiding in a close girl friend almost a decade later.

"I can laugh about it now," Joan told her, "but at the time it was very strange. In the middle of one night I got a long-distance call from Ma in Houston, and she said Pa had had a heart attack and was critical. It sounded like he was on his deathbed with the arteries spurting blood. So I rushed home as fast as I could."

When she reached her father's deathbed, he was not reclining there. He was, in fact, up and around. If there had been a heart attack, the recovery was swift and miraculous. Ash begged Joan to stay in Houston for a spell. He needed her. Unsaid was the fact that her second marriage seemed so bruised that it would take very little to destroy it altogether.

"Pa offered me a new Cadillac, a mink coat, a diamond ring, and any horse I wanted," Joan told her girl friend years later. "And so I figured, what the hell."

Her luck with men had thus far been poor, with the

exception of one whose love she could depend on. Pa. Joan Robinson returned home. She was twenty years old.

4

Joan Robinson and the city of Houston were metaphors for one another during the 1950s. Both were young, ambitious, restless, wealthy, and tempestuous in an era when most of the nation slumbered contentedly in the bosom of Eisenhower. Both girl and city were eager to establish identities, and both, in their flawed ways, succeeded. In a pale green Cadillac with a rared-up bronze horse as adornment on the hood, a mink tossed around her shoulders, diamonds glinting at her throat, Joan Olive Robinson Benton Burglass dyed her pony tail a hot silver blonde, colored her lips flame red, and began the dance. She became one of the city's first celebrities, prowling its boulevards at night, flash bulbs marking her way. Her needs were both complex and basic. She wanted laughter to surround her, she wanted attention, and she wanted companions to blur the emotional wrenches of two failed marriages. And she found them all, there being no lack of similarly inclined spirits in a town that was a raw-boned country lad who found oil and tried to become a baron in a fortnight.

It was an era of excess and vulgarity, both applauded. Was *anybody* poor? One oilman appeared at public gatherings with a hundred-dollar bill serving as his bow tie, and, if the evening wore well, he took to ripping it off and throwing it to the nearest pretty woman, and clipping on another—and another—and another. A man wrote Picasso in the South of France and sought to buy ten paintings. He specified no color preference or subject, only the size of the wall in his wife's gallery room. The eccentricities of another Croesus were novel, even in Houston. This one kept precisely two thousand silver dollars in racks at his mansion, employing a Negro whose obligation was to keep the coins polished and pristine. The master was given to seizing handfuls for his journeys about the city, throwing them from his open-air Cadillac, laughing like a Roman nobleman as the less fortunate scrambled for his largesse.

While he was absent from the house—which, incidentally, contained fifty telephones—the racks would be refilled to the brim.

Oh, what a lovely carnival it was! How abundant were the stories for Joan to hear and tell! Could anybody not laugh at the account of the two oilmen, Mr. A. and Mr. B., who relished playing practical jokes on one another? Finally Mr. B. triumphed, at some cost. When his friend was away on lengthy sojourn in Europe, he ordered a real roller coaster erected in Mr. A.'s ample back yard. Or what of the terrible fire that destroyed the home of a rich man and his wife? The paper reported that the lady of the house rushed outside in the night to fight the blaze while wearing her mink stole. The very next day her secretary telephoned the city desk with a correction: "It was not her mink she was wearing, but her *marten furs*." Everyone could enjoy the millionaire's wife who always purchased two extra first-class airplane tickets for travels to New York and Paris. Where else would she put her matched poodles, with jeweled collars and chinchilla sweaters?

H. R. Cullen, an oilman who did sensible things like endowing the University of Houston, and less sensible things like insisting that Senator Joseph McCarthy was a voice to rival Thomas Paine, had his biography published in 1954. And he was annoyed that it went largely unread. Therefore he spent more than $200,000 of his own money to mail more than 100,000 copies of his life story to libraries and newspapers across the non-Communist world.

One man used $50,000 vainly trying to keep penguins alive in a refrigerated chamber of his home; another rode lions bareback to greet the mailman. They found oil on the city dump. And at the city prison work farm, too. A Houston lady wrote the Smithsonian to inquire if the Hope diamond was for sale. Property values exploded like land mines. On Main Street lots sold for $2,000 *per front inch*. Skyscrapers shot up like volcanoes raring through the cracks of a massive earthquake. "Was Houston here last year?" asked a visitor in 1955. "Of course," said her friend, the local. "Why?" Because, said the newcomer, looking at the new buildings rising clean and characterless all around her, "it looks like they built everything last week." It was actually difficult to work in downtown Houston because of the noise level. Secretaries stuffed cotton in their ears before descending to the street for lunch. Bulldozers had waiting lists. Steel hammers crashed down anything old. The city became a movie played at the wrong high speed. Newspapers ran regular front-page boxes applauding the number of new residents streaming into the city. "Why did you move to Houston?" asked a reporter of a new resident in 1955. "Because it is a place that is still wide open," replied the man from New York. "Fellow can breathe clean air here." As he spoke he stood within a mile of the Houston Ship Channel, and the air he was prepared to breathe was noxious with fumes from a cauldron—sulpher, oil, petrochemicals, and gas fires—that burned every minute of the day and night, spewing excess into the skies. The city's population jumped from 500,000 in 1940 to 1,250,000 by 1960, the largest growth of any place in the U.S. "I'm One in a Million" read the favored bumper sticker when the city at long last passed the symbolic mark of 1,000,000 souls. Its coming—M-Day—had been measured and anticipated by the Houston *Press*, whose editor actually said, in front of witnesses, "My land, this is a bigger story than D-Day." An urban planner cast worried eyes over the convulsive landscape and predicted that by the year 2000 Houston would be the biggest city in the world. Another study marked Houston in 1950 as the nation's leader in industrial construction with building permits for a three-year period totaling more than half a billion dollars. Never was the "big is good" chorus so hosannahed. Let the Eisenhower recession deeply wound the rest of America; Houston felt not even a scratch.

There was indeed a serious side to the Houston of these years—Stokowski led her symphony, DeBakey and Cooley repaired her hearts, scholars of world rank worked quietly at the Rice Institute, good theater was performed. But though her body public was proud that the Texas Medical Center was throwing up great hospitals faster than mushrooms sprouting in a wet forest, it was more enjoyable to prate of the local boy who married Hedy Lamarr, or the other one, the fellow who wed the Egyptian belly dancer and stuck diamonds in her naval and invited his friends to watch her grind. Houston was an adolescent and behaved accordingly.

Joan Robinson was princess of café society, that slightly ill-mannered relative of the old guard, the principal difference being that the former performed its antics in public with new oil money and the latter stayed at home with dollars stored up from a generation before. Café society even had its official birth date in Houston, that being the evening of March 17, 1949—St. Patrick's Day—when a wildcatter named Glenn McCarthy opened the Shamrock Hotel. It was an indulgence which matched in expense, if certainly not in taste, the Taj Mahal. Eighteen stories high, five miles from the center of downtown Houston, its interior décor slathered with sixty-three different hues of green, the $21-million hotel was a monument to the worst. Frank Lloyd Wright saw it, stared thunderstruck, and was heard to mutter, "Why?" Later, however, he cheered sufficiently to say, "I always wondered what it was like inside a juke box." On opening night, 175 Hollywood stars were brought in as rhinestones, and the ensuing party was as sodden as a banquet at Caligula's court. It would be fictionally celebrated in Edna Ferber's much-loathed (in Texas) novel, *Giant* (one Houston newspaperman always printed the title with a lowercase *g*, and in a type face several sizes smaller than traditional newsprint), and in the ensuing film, which starred James Dean as a McCarthy-like oilman who pitched forward in a stupor as he welcomed his guests.

But, again, never mind. The attitude in Houston was that the carping came from out-of-towners. It's us against them, and we know best. The Shamrock was the Waldorf and the Paris Ritz redoubled in spades. It was the place to go, the place to be seen, the womb for the rich and the restless of Houston.

Joan Robinson in effect set up headquarters there. Tanning beside the "world's largest hotel pool," dancing in the Cork Club, stopping in the lobby and impetuously buying a hundred-dollar sequined sweater on her way to the garage where her Cadillac was washed and waiting, she was one of the hostelry's most admired patrons. Houston's newspapers, eager to establish a sophistication for the city, encouraged their gossip columnists to fabricate a racy dream world of beautiful people afloat on flying carpets of gold. One such, whose Houston *Press* column of trivia was called "The Town Crier," enshrined Joan Robinson. There were weeks when Joan's name and photograph appeared six or eight times. Always she seemed to be "flying off to a horse show" or "winging in from Hollywood where people ogled her at the Mocambo" or "sporting a new diamond from her oilman pop, Ash."

Some sample and actual items:

"The booful blonde in the Shamrock was Joan Robinson, the socialite honey—dateless—but in a crowd. . . ."

"Shamrock singer Dick Kreuger first dated gorgeous socialite Joan Robinson Monday night . . . she forgot to tell her folks she'd be late, so Dick met her oilman Pop when they returned home at 5 ayem. Oh, my-oh-my. . . ."

"CELEBRITEMS—Gay blade builder Eben Locher and blonde socialite Joan Robinson musing with stars in their eyes . . ."

"Shamrock singer Dick Kreuger has no trouble getting suntan lotion spread over his frame poolside these days. All the cuties volunteer. Socialite Joan Robinson especially likes to do it. . . ."

"Glamorous socialite Joan Robinson handholding at the Fontaine Lounge with medical salesman Charley Wagner (and how her list of swains grows and growwws!!!) . . ."

"Joan Robinson was the Troubadorable last night, looking sooooooooo gorgeous, and sooooooo rich. . . ."

These were years tinged with the real abandon of Scott Fitzgerald's imagined world, Joan playing Daisy to a score of Gatsbys. Wasn't that Joan Robinson who was offered a magnum of Dom Perignon to jump fully clothed from the Shamrock's dizzying high diving tower? And they say she refused, only to return that midnight, leaping in compromise from a lesser elevation, in the arms of a suitor, into the deserted pool? And that was certainly Joan who accepted one beau's diamond ring of proposal, only to break impetuously with him and run to the nearest bayou and hurl the modest gem into the muddy waters. Everyone knew of the night when an escort put a fifty-dollar bill down on the waiter's tip tray at the Shamrock, only to have Joan sniff that the offering seemed penurious. Not until the swain put a pair of hundreds into the waiter's hands did Joan smile her favor.

"If she wasn't at the Shamrock, then she was at the Troubador," remembered a best friend, Joan Jaworski, twenty years later. The two Joans were, decided the columnists, "the gold dust twins." Both were slim, blonde, vivacious, given to loud laughter that could rattle a room, and both shared a love of horses since childhood. Fortune blessed them both with adoring and indulgent fathers— Joan Jaworski's would become in 1974 the Watergate prosecutor—whose purses allowed them to decorate the city at night like falling stars that would never fade and vanish.

Always, never far away, a guard dog, was Ash. Each time his daughter's name appeared in print he eagerly clipped it and added to the scrapbooks that now reached from the floor of the closet to his shoulders. With mock complaint he paid Joan's monthly bills at the city's private dinner and drinking clubs, waving them around now and then as if they were the national debt. Still Joan knew her father did not object to her life style. The core of the matter was that each night she returned to his home, not to the bed of another man. Occasionally Joan invited Ma and Pa to join her in an evening's revels, and Mrs. Robinson especially treasured these hours. "I often felt the only real love in my life was Joan," Ma said. "Every time I was out with my daughter I had a wonderful time. She made me feel loved. She called me 'hon.' She'd look across the table and she'd smile and she'd say, 'Are you having fun, hon?' She made me feel *wanted*."

Of the men who flowed in and out of Joan's life like ocean currents, none stayed very long without arousing the attention of Ash. He was not loath to engage private detectives for examination of the backgrounds of men who seemed to have caught his daughter's fancy. One such check revealed that a playboy seen often with Joan was homosexual. Ash found it important to inform his daughter, and she thereafter refused his dates. Another bachelor whose name frequently appeared in the columns beside Joan encountered an assailant as he walked to his car in a dimly lit parking lot. Savagely beaten, he always suspected that Ash had dispatched the pair of knuckles.

During the day Joan spent much of her time around her horses. Her show animals were kept at a stable in Tulsa, Oklahoma, in the hands of a renowned trainer. When Joan participated in a show in, for example, Los Angeles, she would fly there, and the horses would travel separately, in the comfort of a palace railroad car. At home in Houston, Joan boarded a knockabout palomino pony named Danny at the Alameda Stables, not far from where she had kept Dot as a child. Several of her affluent friends kept horses there and it became a clubhouse. "They were wonderful crazy years," remembered a horsewoman named Betty Dorris. "We rode every day, we raced, we had a girls' polo team and we'd get out there and knock the shit out of each other. We even had a drill team and we'd get all gussied up in outrageous satin cowgirl clothes and ride in rodeos. And Joan was the leader of the pack. If she told us to get ready for a ride up Mount Everest, we'd call our daddies and ask for plane fare to Tibet."

Although Joan's group was composed of young women whose ages were generally in their early twenties, one older woman closer to forty hovered nearby. She was not a blooded member of the group, for her social credentials were lacking. But she loved horses and she wore expensive Western clothes and from her lips poured a river of rough talk, so profane that it was artful. It was said that Lilla Paulus could cuss better than a stable hand kicked by a mustang. She also had an attar of the forbidden about her, for it was also said that her husband, Claude Paulus, was a society bookie. Lilla came to the Alameda Stables regularly with her little girl, a spunky child named Mary Josephine whose passion for horses was as great as Joan Robinson's had been twenty years before. Now and again Joan would stop whatever she was doing and give the little girl a pointer in equitation, a kindness that Lilla Paulus noted. There would be a day when Lilla Paulus and her daughter would play major roles in the convoluted drama of Joan Robinson. But at the time no one paid them much attention.

Of the men who orbited around Joan in these vainglorious years, only one endured for more than a figurative moment. She fell deeply in love with Travers Fell. He was, according to Betty Dorris, "the most gorgeous son of a bitch in Texas." His bloodlines were provincially royal, he was heir to a land fortune—one of his antecedents owned great chunks of real estate which lay in the paths of planned freeways—and he knew and loved horseflesh even better than Joan. He also drank heavily and when drunk enjoyed using his ham fists to break up bars and beat up their patrons. His Cadillac sped terrifyingly across the city, sometimes with a loaded .38 under the seat and an open fifth of bourbon on the dash which he swigged like Coke. Legends grew about him. He was the paradigm romantic, reckless Texan. Once he borrowed a dime from Joan at the Alameda Stables to make a telephone call during which he bought a $100,000 race horse.

He was also, according to Ash Robinson, not worth a pitcher of warm piss.

"When Joan and I met," said Travers Fell two decades later, time having cursed him with a face pumped up and reddened from whiskey and a mind tormented by memories, "it was like two magnets coming together. Pow! No two people ever fell in love quite so fast. We could have moved mountains if they got in the way. On the day we met at Alameda Stables, I had two other serious girls in my life, but within forty-eight hours I had forgotten their names. Nobody existed but Joan!"

Ash hated the new man in his daughter's life. When she brought Travers around to the new home he had built on Kirby Drive in River Oaks, the city's most elegant neighborhood, Ash was not even civil. "I could see the hate in his eyes," Travers would one day remember. "Right away old Ash recognized that him and me were two of a kind. Neither one of us would settle for half the hog, we wanted it all! That old bastard leaned on me every way he could. You see, he knew that if I won Joan she'd belong to me. And not to him. I got the impression that Joan wanted to get away from her father, but she both loved him and feared him. I told her I was going to tell the old son of a bitch just what was what, but she warned me off. I remember exactly what she said, 'Pa can be as dangerous as a rattlesnake.' "

Conversely, the crowd at Alameda Stables felt that Joan and Travers were a perfect match, having their love of horses as a common bond, he—if his relatives ever died—having enough money to cover all circumstances. Joan tried to enhance her beau's image in her father's eyes, but the now familiar eruption always occurred. For God's sake, thundered Ash, the man didn't even have a job. Man must work! Man must produce! Man was of the earth and he must give back some small measure!

For years the affair continued with Joan openly dating other men with whom she was publicized in the newspaper columns. But in her heart there was only Travers. She met him secretly at horse shows away from Pa, at the country homes of friends. She nagged at Travers to get a job, any job, even the semblance of a job, anything to prove to her father that the man she wanted was more than a reckless firestorm.

There was another love in Joan's life at the time, one

for which Ash had complete approval, although it placed a strain on his bank account. At a minor horse show in San Antonio, Joan noted a dappled gray mare whose name was Beloved Belinda. The foal of an unknown mare and sire, she nonetheless possessed unusual gaits. "I've got to have this horse, Pa," Joan begged her father. "I want her more than anything I've ever wanted in my life." Ash paid $27,500 for Beloved Belinda, an enormous price for an animal with undistinguished lineage. But to anyone who exclaimed over the sum, he answered, "Look at my little girl's face and tell me if it isn't worth it."

Joan elected to make her debut with the mare at an important horse show in Louisville, Kentucky, a city celebrated for its attention to equine excellence. She devised a secret dollop of showmanship. Normally Joan wore the black formal riding habit favored on the society show circuit. But to complement her new mount she commissioned her tailors in Houston to design a riding costume in *exactly* the same shade as Belinda—a lustrous pearl gray. Even the derby must be the same, she insisted.

When Joan arrived at the Louisville arena she dressed secretly and threw a robe over her costume. She had schemed to enter the ring last, after the other thirty horses and their riders had performed. When the announcer called her name, Joan held Belinda back for a moment of suspense. Then, following a calculated script, she and the great horse burst forth, an exquisite duet in gray, demanding every eye in the house as a pair of superb dancers do when they seize a stage. Suddenly there was no other horse or rider in the ring. At the end of the evening Joan Robinson and Beloved Belinda swept the boards, and the crowd rose in emotional standing ovation.

A newspaperman wrote, "When Joan Robinson rides Beloved Belinda it is one of the most achingly beautiful sights in the world. It is a poem, a waltz, it is the sculpture of Rodin and the painting of Cézanne. My goosepimples get goosepimples." Horse shows tend to be hugely boring to the unsophisticated in that the typical one can last four hours, with endless processions of horses and riders pouring in and out of the ring, with tedious waits for the judges to mark their cards. There is, of course, only so much that a horse can do, and a canter is not that much more invigorating to watch than a trot. But for seven years Joan and Beloved Belinda were like a Roman candle set off in the middle of the preacher's sermon. So accustomed were Joan—and Ash—to winning that, when the ribbon was not blue, a judge could feel their wrath. "Ash Robinson cussed me from hell to breakfast because Joan came in third," one judge remembered. "I told him it was a fair call—the mare was a little heavy in the hock and it showed that night. But Ash said I was a god damned disgrace and I should be thrown out of the horse world."

Joan's temper often rose in concert. Once, in San Antonio, she accepted the second-place red ribbon with no show of pleasure and carried it back to a hotel, the prize wadded in her hand like an unwelcome telegram. When the porter helping her with her bags remarked politely, "Sure is a nice ribbon, ma'am," Joan whirled and snapped, "You like it? You can have it!" And flung the ribbon at the man's feet.

Always Ash was there, just at the edge where the spotlight ended and the black anonymity of the crowd began. Sometimes the lights would catch him, but he made no effort to shield his face from their lovely glare. Always he hurried to the telephone in Louisville or New York or wherever, once the results were in, and he rang the Houston newspapers with his daughter's latest triumph.

He courted the press, sending cases of whiskey and flagons of perfume to favored reporters at Christmas, parceling out "scoops" like choice bits of beef in a stew.

Joan won five world championships on Beloved Belinda from 1953 to 1958, but nothing much else changed in her private moments. Travers Fell remained what he had always been and would always be, the hard-drinking, carefree pursuer of the sweet life. Joan continued as the girl about town, with Ash protecting her, financing her, not closing his eyes for sleep at night until the front door slammed and she was home. In another time and place, perhaps Joan and Travers could have lived together as lovers. Then, perhaps, Joan's music would have always been a waltz.

Too soon began a dance of death.

5

Idly, bored with her own dinner companions, her gaze this autumn night swept across the tables of Houston's rich and those pretending to be, settling momentarily on a young man who looked impossibly out of place. Joan liked to examine strangers surreptitiously and imagine instant biographies for them. What is this one doing at the Cork Club? she wondered. He is definitely a farmer in town for the one big night of his life, she decided. Somebody's cousin from Waxahachie. An Aggie, most assuredly. Or maybe a roughneck who just brought in a well and his boss is buying him dinner. His cheeks were apple pink, almost shining, his suit from the Monkey Ward catalogue with a shirt collar so tight it made his neck bulge, his expression that of a man who has no idea what fork to pick up. If he owns a suitcase, it is cardboard, and if he stood up, his trouser legs would quit three inches above his white socks. Although it did not occur to her at the time, he looked not unlike Travers Fell, who was currently estranged from her companionship. Both had the fleshy, boyish good looks that catch a woman's eye from a distance.

On her way to the powder room later on, Joan noticed that the stranger was in the company of two unlikely friends, one of Houston's most striking couples, Dr. Riley Foster and his wife Maggie. He was a slim, aquiline cardiologist with aristocratic bearing, noted for his patronage of the arts, she an uncommon beauty who so resembled a film star that in the columns her name always contained an identifying afterphrase, ". . . the Lauren Bacall lookalike." Joan knew them both well, for they were very much a part of her crowd, the pack that graced the best restaurants and parties. She could not resist stopping to find out who the bumpkin was at their table.

Maggie Foster smiled and introduced the new man. "This is Dr. John Hill," she said.

"Hi," said Joan, summoning a show ring smile for Dr. John Hill, who rose like an obedient hound dog and pumped her hand enthusiastically. He was almost six feet tall, a well-built man with broad shoulders, thick dark hair, and a wide and guileless face. Joan decided he was worth knowing. She made a discreet signal which Maggie Foster caught. The two friends went to the powder room.

"I don't know much about him," said Maggie. A few nights earlier her husband had called from the hospital and said he was bringing a young intern home for dinner. He was new in Houston, didn't know anybody. Lonely kid, that sort of thing. Supposed to be from some hick town in the Rio Grande Valley.

Good old country boys appealed to her, said Joan.

"Don't fool yourself," answered Maggie. "I opened the front door and here stood this farm boy who is probably the best-looking man I ever saw. He says 'howdy' and 'ma'am' and then he sees Riley's piano and he sits down and plays a Mozart sonata. An *exquisite* Mozart sonata."

Joan freshened her make-up and combed her silvery pony tail. A little cattily, Maggie thought her friend was getting a touch long in the tooth to be wearing her hair in that fashion, but she knew that Joan cared nothing for style. With all that money, Maggie thought to herself, Joan's hemlines are always in direct opposition to the dictum of the season. And she will bounce her grandchildren on her knee with her hair tied back like a college cheerleader.

"I think I want him," said Joan. "Fix it up, Maggie."

In later years John Hill would attempt a modicum of self-depreciation (not much, for he would become a vain and humorless man) by introducing himself as from a town in South Texas so small and so hayseed that "I never even saw a Cadillac until I got to Houston." It was hardly true, for the area from which he sprang was the most fertile soil of Texas, the Rio Grande Valley, a semi-tropical wedge at the extreme tip of the state, with Mexico on one side, the warm Gulf on the other. There the world was lush and steamy, fortunes were made from the grapefruit and oranges that grew in orchards tended by the cheap labor force that crossed the river from Mexico. Among the first settlers to arrive in response to the land booms of the early 1920s were John Hill's parents, who settled in shortly after World War I, at a place that had no name and but one rough dirt road. Within a few years a town was formed and named after the local real estate developer, Ed Couch. That hardly had a progressive ring about it, and looked silly on postal marks, so the decision was made to run the two names together. The town was thenceforth called Edcouch.

Raymond Hill and his wife Myra owned a 75-acre farm where they raised vegetables, cotton, and grain, on what was once an arid desert, made to ripen by the cheap elec-

tricity that pumped in water from the Rio Grande. Theirs
was a prim and businesslike marriage, he being an inquisitive farmer who wanted little more from life than time to
work his earth and tinker with the machines that tilled it,
she a strong, hard-working American Gothic woman with
a passion for religion that lay somewhere between the devout and the fanatic. Early in their partnership an accommodation was reached. Myra had more than enough religion for both of them. Therefore Raymond announced he
would not go to her Church of Christ, or sing her hymns,
or even pay much attention to her biblical quotations,
which were produced for every human occasion from crop
failure in the rare, ruthless winter to the births of their
three children.

The Hills' farm bore so much produce that there was
surplus, and Raymond decided to open a small store at the
corner of the dirt road that ran in front of his house. Mexican laborers began stopping by to purchase tomatoes and
sweet peppers for lunch, and beans and potatoes to carry
across the river to their homes in villages where the land
was still burned and not blessed by irrigation. Quickly the
Hills branched out, adding work clothing, notions, seeds,
and farm equipment to their inventory. Hill's Corner, as
the place became known, soon had a blacksmith, a barber,
and a gas pump, and under Myra's efficient stewardship the
entire stock usually turned over every two months, gross-
ing $1,500 a week.

John Hill was the second child, born in 1931, wedged
between his older sister Judy and his brother Julian, who
appeared one year later. But unlike most youngsters in
the middle, who tend to be quiet and insecure, John was
dominant. His energies and curiosities from the time he
was a toddler were remarkable. Myra grew weary and
exasperated trying to contain both her son and her household. Dishes crashed to the floor when John chanced by,
lamps fell down, once a console radio was dismantled by
the not yet three-year-old, who found it necessary to pull
all the tubes from the innards. While his parents were away
at the Mayo Clinic having Raymond's appendicitis attended
to, John completely took apart a Perfection oil cooking
stove, his mother's pride. Finally Myra Hill took a drastic
step; she literally tied up her son, attaching him to a har-
ness and a thin chain that allowed him to roam about a

carefully prescribed area in the front yard. If he tried to reach the road the chain would yank him back, like an errant puppy dog.

The two brothers grew up inseparable, both fascinated by machines. When their model airplanes and miniature autos and chemistry experiments overflowed their room, Raymond Hill built a small building next to the home to accommodate his sons' hobbies. There dangled planes on wires from the ceiling, with the air redolent of glue and rotten-egg sulphur. The boys were very different, both physically and emotionally. John was the outgoing, impulsive one, with a tendency to overweight. Julian was the quiet son, with a gaunt, almost Lincolnesque face and frame. So somber was the second son that a family friend often wondered, but did not ask, if there was trouble, or pain, within him.

Myra was the disciplinarian, her husband having no desire for the unpleasant scenes that accompanied punishment. He preferred to stay in the fields or behind the store counter, muttering an occasional "Just do what your mother says." The symbol of Myra's discipline was a whip which she once used with vigor, then hung on the wall in a prominent place. When the boys entertained the thought of mischief, all Myra had to do was point at the menacing object, and the reminder was sufficient.

Fervently Myra molded her children into her church, making religion so much a part of their lives at such an early age that they grew to consider it as natural as eating and sleeping. When John was not yet two, his mother began teaching a Sunday school class, and long after he had gone away to college she presided over the same weekly session. Myra took pride in her Bible classes, for she taught not only the philosophies and verses of the book but its attendant history and politics and geographies as well. At home, the children dutifully recited Bible verses as they made beds or washed and dried dishes. On the way to nearby Harlingen to shop, they played car games always revolving around their knowledge of the Bible. "You start a Bible verse with the letter A," directed Myra to one son, and, to the other, "then you follow with a verse beginning with B." By their adolescence, both boys could name every book of the Bible in order from Genesis to Revelations, and the genealogy from Adam to Jesus Christ.

"Religion is not a duty," Myra liked to say. "Religion is

happiness. And ours is not the 'devil's-behind-the-door' kind that scares people into doing right. Ours is joy!"

Both boys became serious musicians, ironic in consideration that their first exposure to song was in a church that forbade musical instruments of any kind. In the Church of Christ, only the human voice is permitted. "We make melody with our lips," explained Myra to her sons when they were small.

Though Myra adhered slavishly to the dictates of her faith, she had no objection to her sons playing musical instruments away from the church house. In fact she encouraged both to study piano, pointing out that musical talent ran traditionally in her branch of the family. A favorite story concerned an uncle who made pianos by hand in Illinois, then vanished from the family bosom for seventeen years, only to finally turn up with a trunkful of music he had composed.

All three of her children thus received piano lessons, with Myra holding them firmly to disciplined practice hours. John was the most dedicated, often sitting for three hours at the bench, rising only to chase his less willing brother about the house and forcefully dragging him to the metronome when it was time to practice duets. He also learned to handle the trombone, tuba, flute, and recorder, the medieval flutelike instrument.

When John became so skilled in music that he transferred to a high school out of his district because a better band program was offered, Myra began to fret. She wanted more for her talented son than to have him play piano for a dance orchestra, he having once made flip suggestion of that as a possible life's work. From his early years, his mother had been pushing medicine. "There are ten doctors in my family," Myra kept reminding John, and Julian as well. "I'd be so proud if my two sons became the eleventh and twelfth."

But John did not seem responsive to his mother's importunings. "I don't know what I want to be," he said. "I haven't made up my mind yet." At Abilene Christian College, an institution sponsored by the Church of Christ, John enrolled in a liberal arts course. There he fell under the influence of an excellent teacher, a biologist, and during Christmas vacation in his sophomore year he gave his mother the gift she had always wanted. He had decided to go to medical school.

His brother Julian announced a similar intent, and Myra prayed exuberant thanks to her God. Never was a mother so blessed, she said. Two fine sons, both gentle, both scholarly, both musicians, both about to become doctors. "They are noble children," she thought to herself, falling to prayer. "They are the gifts of God."

After graduating *summa cum laude* from college, John was accepted at the Baylor College of Medicine in Houston where he completed the four-year course and internship, electing then for a residency in surgery. It was not an uncommon decision for young doctors in this city in the middle 1950s. A veritable factory of surgery was developing under the charismatic leadership of Dr. Michael E. De-Bakey, the flame-tempered Louisianan who was courting world attention by his arterial reconstruction and routing of blood streams clogged by atherosclerosis. At his side was the talented young associate, Dr. Denton Cooley, who was on his way to world rank as a surgeon of the open heart. Their aura and attendant publicity persuaded a disproportionate number of fledgling doctors to choose cardiovascular surgery. So many that John Hill, who liked Houston and wanted to live there permanently, decided the competition in that part of the body was absurd. Heart surgeons were coming out of the walls.

He studied the alternatives carefully and, by the third year of his residency, chose plastic surgery. Several factors worked toward that decision. One was basic. Money. Only ten board-certified plastic surgeons were practicing in this city of more than a million people, and in addition to the native population, tens of thousands of potential patients would be swarming the Texas Medical Center each year as a score of planned new hospitals opened. Plastic surgery would surely flourish with the other medical disciplines. Houston was a city of wealth, brimming with women and men able to pay for face-lifts and eyebag removals. And such procedures could normally be done quickly. The skilled plastic man could schedule six or eight procedures in one day, the potential revenues enormous.

John Hill wanted money. He looked about the city where it seemed to grow like rye grass after a January rain, and he saw the jeweled patrons of drinking clubs where he sometimes played cocktail piano to help pay room and board at the dump where he lived. He drove into River

Oaks and looked at the massive monuments to money
owned by the very doctors over whose patients he labored
as a resident for little more that a hundred dollars a month.
He told a fellow resident, "In my home town, a doctor
might pull down $25,000 a year. I don't see a reason in
the world why a plastic surgeon couldn't make $250,000
a year once he's off and running in Houston."

His friend nodded in agreement. The sum sounded
reasonable. Gossip among the younger men had DeBakey
and Cooley each billing more than a half million dollars a
year in surgical fees. Cooley did open hearts the way other
men ran laps at the YMCA. Ten a day were not unusual.
At $1,500 a pop. In all endeavor, the Houston syndrome
was not so much how good, but how much, and how
many.

John needed money to finance his musical interests, for
the seed that Myra planted in her son when she pushed
him into piano lessons at the age of seven had sprouted
into an unusual commitment. "I'd really rather be a musician," he told a fellow doctor as they sewed up a gunshot
wound at Ben Taub, the city's charity hospital. "But a
fellow can't make a decent living out of it. My dream is
to practice medicine in the daytime and play music at night.
One of the reasons I'm going into plastics is that the
patients don't call you up all night long with bellyaches."
At that moment John had one ear cocked to a portable
radio from which a piano concerto was booming forth in a
corner of the surgical suite.

His reputation in the surgical program was that of a
pleasant, likable young doctor, of potential talent, but one
who was not wholly dependable. A senior surgeon grew
to believe that John also took liberties with the truth. This
cropped up when an indigent drunk with a bad liver
appeared at the hospital with a belly swollen from fluids.

The procedure for alleviating the condition is called
paracentesis, a routine operation wherein the surgeon cuts
a hole in the stomach and simply drains out the fluids. The
only real danger is cutting the bowel and releasing potentially deadly bacteria into the body.

John Hill did just that. When he began the drawing out
of the fluids, he also sucked out feces, clear indication that
his blade had perforated the bowel. It can happen to the
best of surgeons, who must then hurry into an emergency
bowel repair. But rather than own up to the mistake, John

continued draining the fluids, then sewed up the abdomen and bandaged the incision. The patient developed peritonitis and died. In autopsy, the blunder was discovered and Hill was summoned before the senior surgeon. At first he flatly denied knowledge of the bowel perforation, then hedged by insisting that, if such had happened, it seemed so minor that a bowel repair was not warranted. "That guy had a million defenses," the examining surgeon said later. "I let him go with a severe reprimand. He was so charming and so eager that I didn't want to wreck his career over one mistake."

Among those who train students to become doctors, it is said that surgeons find their niche in accordance with their personal characteristics. The orthopedic surgeon is medicine's carpenter—up to his elbows in plaster of Paris —and tradition holds that he is a gruff, slapdash sort of man whose labor is in a very physical area of healing. Away from the hospital, the orthopedists are often hunters, boaters, outdoorsmen. The neurosurgeon, classically, does not get too involved with his patients. Or, for that matter, with anybody. They are cool men, blunted, rarely gregarious. Heart surgeons are thundering egotists, star performers in a dazzling operating theater packed with assistants, nurses, paramedics, and a battery of futuristic equipment which could seemingly lift the room into outer space. These are men who relish drama, who live life on the edge of the precipice.

And the plastic surgeon? He is, by nature, a man of art, and temperament, and sensitivity. "We are the artists who deal in beauty lost, or beauty that never was," said one plastic man at a national convention. "Our stitches are hidden, and so are our emotions." John Hill fit perfectly into this category.

As commanded, Maggie Foster invited Joan Robinson to dine at her home, with John Hill as the extra man. The couple hit it off well, making the tentative explorations and awkward remarks that men and women do when they are interested in one another. As she watched the mating dance, Maggie Foster thought to herself: this is a terrible mismatch. These two people have nothing whatsoever in common except they are both beautiful. She is rich, spoiled, bored, looking for a new husband. She knows horses and night clubs and where Pa keeps his checkbook.

John Hill knows how to play the trombone and make sutures. He is a mama's boy who winces every time Joan says 'god damn,' which is often.

Joan kept the evening merry, her throaty, almost mannish laughter continuing past midnight. She was the kind of woman indigenous to Texas—intensely feminine for one moment, and then, spitting out an obscenity, becoming one of the boys. John Hill was cleaved by lightning. He told Maggie Foster in a bread-and-butter telephone call early the next morning, "She's the most incredible girl I ever met."

Joan Robinson was on the telephone as well, spreading the news among her friends that she had met a "divine new man." One of her horse set pals, a girl named Cleo who was given to blunt questions, asked pointedly, "Did you tell this old boy you've already struck out twice?"

No. Joan had not revealed that news. If things got serious, she would, of course, tell him. With her track record, Joan said practically, she did not think Dr. John Hill had cause for undue concern. "He's just a very nice man," Joan told her friend. "I need one right now."

The young doctor's life underwent sudden and radical surgery. Within weeks he began traveling in a world that he knew existed—but into whose gates he had not anticipated admission for years to come. On their very first private date together, Joan fetched the surgeon at his rooming house, turned over the wheel of her Cadillac to him, and suggested a quiet steak restaurant where they could dine and talk intimately. When the maître d' presented the menu, Joan noticed her escort wince at the prices. Tactfully she excused herself to freshen her make-up. Out of John's sight, she instructed the maître d' to send the dinner check to Ash by mail. She then returned to the table and whispered, "The prices here are outrageous, but order anything you like. They always comp the check. I let them use my name in the columns."

Somehow a relationship developed, he feigning interest in five-gaited horses, she listening politely to Bach quartets. They dined on hamburgers at a greasy spoon near the hospital, they dined on prime ribs at the Petroleum Club where the faucets in the bathrooms were plated of gold, and where models glided softly about in gowns from French haute couture. They danced at the Shamrock, where a resident diamond merchant dropped by their table

and pulled out a handful of brilliant gems and threw them
at Joan like rolling dice. They dressed in togas and laurel
leaves to attend a party of staggering cost where the guests
imitated ancient Romans. They became regular patrons
at a musical theater where the director offered Joan and
John the leading roles in a revival of *Guys and Dolls*.
Declining, Joan roared, "Honey, the only thing I can
sing is 'My Old Kentucky Home,' and people usually
stick their fingers in their ears." Over one autumn weekend, they attended eleven different parties and just before
the sun rose on Monday, when John was due back at the
hospital, they sat on a lonely beach at Galveston, her head
in his lap, he playing the recorder while the sea washed
their weary feet. They posed for photographs at a horse
show cocktail party, and a gossip columnist reported, "Isn't
the new man in cosmopolite Joan Robinson's busy life a
fortunate young surgeon? It is, it is . . . and watch the
other swains sob."

In the beginning, Joan carefully avoided exposing her
new find to Ash. But he knew. He had heard, in fact, of
their very first encounter at the Cork Club, and he had
made discreet inquiries about the boy before the week
was out. And when his daughter began carefully mentioning a young doctor she enjoyed dating, Ash, for a change,
was benign. On the evening that Joan brought John to her
father's home to ask permission to marry, the surgeon was
well briefed what to expect. Pa will lay down five thousand
reasons why the wedding should not take place, Joan said.
Just sit there and listen quietly, she warned. Then let her
take over.

Mount Robinson did not erupt. Ash was charming,
hospitable, and inquisitive. He asked about John Hill's
medical training and remarked on various doctors he knew
and respected. He commented on what a wonderful profession doctoring could be. His own father had been a pioneer surgeon and for a time he himself had considered
medicine. By the way, how much longer did John have in
the educational process?

Six or seven years, he answered. Ash nodded sympatheti-
cally.

Did John Hill care anything about horses? Surely he
knew that they were an integral part of this girl's life.

No, said John. But he could learn. And whatever Joan
liked to do, then he would share her passion.

Finally, did John Hill really love his daughter? She was the most precious possession in his life, and he could not relinquish her to any man if he was not secure in that.

More than that, said John Hill. He worshiped her.

"Then I guess Ma and me will have to fix us a wedding," said Ash in a voice of butter, milk, and honey.

It must have occurred to Ash Robinson as he watched the happy couple drive away that the alliance was, on balance, one that he could live with. Joan was twenty-six years old and if she had to marry somebody, then John Hill was not the worst of choices, certainly more promising than Travers Fell. He was, after all, a surgeon-to-be, and Houston was a city that paid its social dues to surgeons. Ash had never really earned a position in real old guard society, even through his money, his ancestral blood, and his daughter's fame. One of the town's most exclusive clubs had rejected his application for membership, the suspicion being that his conviction for fraud, albeit reversed by the appellate court, made him too much a pirate. He snorted around at the time, saying he didn't give a damn, but the fact that he made application in the first place showed clearly that, in his heart, he did.

It quite possibly further occurred to Ash that this potential son-in-law had several years left to go in his medical education, years that traditionally required sacrifice and careful budgeting. If Joan really went through with a wedding, then Ash might help out with some of the bills, lend a hand now and then to keep the wolf from their door. Why, he could even offer the newlyweds a place to live. No need for them to camp out in somebody's garage apartment. There was plenty of room upstairs in his very own new and spacious home.

And if such help would keep Joan at home, then so be it.

Myra Hill was the more difficult parent to persuade. John dreaded telling his mother that he was even serious about a girl, much less that marriage was on his mind. But, like Ash, she had known almost from the beginning. Julian, still inseparable from his older brother and his roommate at the boardinghouse, dispatched a letter to Edcouch a few days after the couple met. "John is dating a very pretty girl," he wrote. "She is social, charming, and a lovely hostess. And she knows how to ride horses."

Before they became engaged, Joan had revealed the

facts of her two previous marriages. Though taken aback, John Hill responded by saying that what had happened before they met was of no consequence. But he chewed for weeks on how to break the worrisome information to his mother. Myra Hill was completely opposed to divorce. Her religion equated it somewhere on the level of drunkenness and child molestation. One she might be able to accommodate, but two? John elected to parcel out only the first divorce. Later on, long after they were happily married, he might mention the other. "Joan was very young and unready for marriage," he told his mother. "It was over so quick it was almost an annulment."

Nonetheless, Myra Hill voiced strenuous objection. Her son was too young, he had too many years left to go in his training, he possessed limited funds. How would he support a wife? A child, if one came? And a society wife at that who collected diamonds and furs and thoroughbred horses? "We love each other," John answered. "We'll work it out. That's all that matters."

One week before the wedding, as Myra and Raymond Hill prepared to leave the Rio Grande Valley for the long drive to Houston, an anonymous letter arrived at their farm. Myra read the letter over and over again, committing it to memory like a passage from the Bible. The anonymous informant wanted her to know that Joan Robinson had been married not once but twice, and that Ash Robinson had served time in the penitentiary for swindle and fraud. Although the latter accusation was incorrect, Myra was overwhelmed. She rushed to the field where her husband was working.

"Who wrote this?" he asked, finishing the letter.

"I don't know," answered his wife, "but we can't let our son get into a situation like this. He may be destroying his whole life."

Myra hurried to Houston as if on holy crusade, two days in advance of scheduled arrival. During the week of pre-wedding parties, Myra feigned illness, shepherding her strength each day to argue with her son against the marriage. It is not too late to cancel, she insisted. At least delay. Wait! Do this for your mother. Each night she lay awake in prayer, asking for strength to shatter the union.

For the first time in his life, John Hill stood up against his mother. On the day of the wedding, having resisted her exhortations for an entire week, he dressed in his tuxedo and was clipping on his bow tie when Myra entered his small apartment. Her face was as gray as a shroud. She had no more tears, but she made one last, desperate plea. "Your backgrounds are so different," she said. "You live in two different worlds." She reached into her fund of biblical verses to emphasize any point and she withdrew one from Amos. *Can two walk together, except they be agreed?*

"But we are agreed, Mother," he said. "We agree that we love each other and want to get married."

"But Joan's father is an infidel!" cried Myra. On top of everything else, she had heard that he not only disbelieved in God, he blasphemed. "Your father and I haven't raised you as a fine Christian son to let you get into a potential tragedy like this."

With his wedding an hour away, John Hill paced the floor, annoyed that the day was marred by his mother's onslaught. Across Raymond Hill's face was consternation and sorrow. He was a man who rarely spoke, and John knew that he would not buck his wife.

"Mother, I must tell you that this is none of your business," John said sharply. "I have made my decision. Let me be my own man. I'm twenty-six years old."

Never had her son spoken in wrath against her. Myra Hill twisted her gloves. She sank into a chair. "Then," she said quietly, "I just don't think I can go to this wedding."

Angrily, John shot back, "Then I don't think I can ever forgive you."

Myra began to weep. The moment was unbearable. Uncharacteristically, Raymond Hill spoke his mind. Picking up his wife's limp hand, he stretched it out to connect it as peacemaker with his son's. "We'll go," he ordered quietly. "In fact, we'd better hurry. We're late."

Joan Olive Robinson and John Robert Hill became man and wife on a sparkling September afternoon in 1957 beside the swimming pool of Ash Robinson's redwood home. The society pages described it accurately as a storybook wedding, the bride aglow in an elegant white lace gown with pinkish trim and a waist-length veil trailing from her princess cap encrusted with pearls. She had wanted to appear all in white, but her friend Joan Jaworski tactfully suggested that, for the third trip to the altar, a dash of color was more suitable. The groom seemed uncom-

fortable in his rented tuxedo and a severe new haircut that
raised his sideburns above his ears and restored him to the
farmboy look he was anxious to shed. But he was as
proud and as beaming as the first-prize winner at the state
fair.

Myra Hill tried to smile for the wedding photographs,
but her face was a container of worry. Ash Robinson was
a most cheerful father of the bride. In later years he
would say that he knew from the beginning that the marriage was ill fated. But on this afternoon so fraught with
undercurrents, he was paterfamilias, courtly and benevolent.
And why shouldn't he have been? He well knew that after
the honeymoon, for which he was paying, he would have
his daughter living just upstairs with this latest son-in-law.
He could keep an eye on them both. And he would always
be there with money if they needed it, rather like a chain
to keep errant pets in the yard, out of the street.

6

For six years John Hill and his wife lived in the upstairs
bedroom at Ash Robinson's home. While other doctors
in training struggled to keep body, soul, wife, and children
together on the $164 paid to residents monthly for eighty-
hour work weeks, John Hill fared better. He ate food
bought by Ash Robinson and prepared by Ash Robinson's
cook, for he promptly learned upon return from the honeymoon that his wife was not at home in a kitchen. "I can
boil an egg, I think, and make chili, and that's my repertoire," she told him. He drove to work in an automobile
given him by Ash Robinson, or, when it was being serviced,
in a limousine whose chauffeur dropped him off at the
hospital's emergency room entrance and was there to fetch
him at the end of the day. On such occasions the nurses
took to sticking their heads out the window and applauding
or cheering—some derisively whistling "Hail to the Chief"
—as the handsome young doctor stepped briskly from the
Cadillac.

For entertainment, there were catered buffet suppers at
the Robinson home to which John was urged to invite his
medical friends, or dinners for ten at the Houston Club,
and the first nights at supper clubs and theaters where

Joan was always invited by impresarios who knew that her presence would generate newsprint. John Hill became a creature-of-the-columns by marriage, his name appearing with such regularity that a senior doctor took him aside with the warning that the only papers physicians were expected to get their names into were scientific journals. If he continued to hawk his name about town like a male model selling shaving lotion, then the ethics committee might summon him for an explanation. John insisted that he never sought out publicity. Then duck when you see a flash bulb, suggested the older man, with a tiny layer of jealousy to his voice.

And, almost from the beginning, the doctor and his wife went their separate ways. Hardly back from the wedding trip to Mexico, Joan began planning for her spring and summer appearances in a dozen of the nation's major horse shows. It would be Belinda's next-to-last season, and the great gray mare would be shown in competitions at Atlanta, Lexington, Kansas City, Baton Rouge, New Orleans, Tulsa, Oklahoma City, San Francisco, and at Houston's own Pin Oak, a lovely outdoor show in June with tens of thousands of fresh summer roses entwined about the arena.

For each of these shows, Joan was normally away from Houston for five days, from Wednesday until Saturday, and rarely did her husband go with her. His valid excuse was that he could not leave his hospital duties, but the truth was, if he had any spare time, it would not have been spent hanging around a horse barn and waiting for his wife to take home still another cup and ribbon. John's penchant was music, particularly Sunday afternoon gatherings where musicians liked to gather and sight-read chamber works. He usually played piano or recorder at the genteel affairs, held in the company of elderly ladies, the refreshments punch and cookies. These were in decided contrast to the parties at Joan's shows, where bourbon splashed generously in highball glasses, and liveried waiters passed cavier in beds of shaved ice, and the buffet table bent like a sway-back horse under burdens of roast beef and hams.

On the rare occasion when John attended a horse show, he could usually be found reading a paperback mystery while his wife promenaded before him. Once he actually fell asleep in the Robinson box, and when this example of indifferent manners was reported to Joan, she smiled.

"That's okay," she said. "I nodded off during Haydn the other afternoon when he was playing."

During their courtship Joan had explained how much time her hobby entailed. And, as was the pattern of her life in dealing with men, she offered to give up show competition. "You come first," Joan had said. "If anything gets in the way of our happiness, then I'll get rid of it." John dissuaded her from the gesture: she could no more abandon horses than he could surrender music. In truth, both her husband and her father were anxious for Joan to continue her glory ride through the horse world. Ash was repaid in fatherly pride and reflected celebrity, and it gave him the opportunity to rub shoulders with a well-blooded group of people not only in Houston but across America. And Ash relished those weeks when his daughter was with him in Louisville or Atlanta. These were the hours when he did not have to share her with the man whose name she now bore.

John Hill learned that there was a great deal more to successful plastic surgery than a skilled pair of hands, the correct framed diplomas on the wall, a reputation for "judgment," and the ability to withstand tedium and pressure. He could not just go out and open an office and wait for the wealthy to come around for wrinkle removal, or for a referring doctor to send over a patient with a shattered jaw for reconstruction. Like no other medical specialty, plastic surgery depends upon word of mouth, one contented patient telling another potential one, one satisfied GP speaking well in the doctors' lounge of the new boy in town.

Several years after his training was completed, and when he was well established in his profession, John Hill found himself at a medical meeting and during a lengthy dinner he engaged his seat mate in conversation. She was the wife of a junior man, just starting out in plastic work. The woman would never forget what John Hill told her that night, for he seemed to have worked out a guaranteed success formula in the game. Cool and businesslike, he ticked off how to succeed in plastic surgery by really trying:

First, marry well, preferably a wealthy woman who can help you through the seemingly endless years of training. And it helps if she is coincidentally beautiful, because other women will look at her and speculate about whether the husband discreetly plied his trade on her face or breasts.

Secondly, encourage the wife to participate in civic and social affairs. Insist that she serve on committees, raise money for charity, play bridge at the country club. Each affluent friend she makes is a potential client.

Thirdly, live well. Don't be afraid to drive a Cadillac or live in an imposing home in the best part of town. Patients do not worry about their fees going to support such luxuriance. They are, in fact, pleased that "my doctor" is doing well enough to feast that high on the hog.

Lastly, do not exactly run from publicity. True, it is unethical for a doctor to advertise or court the newspapers (a practice often flaunted in Houston, where some doctors are as famous as astronauts and employ aides to book them on national television shows and solicit the cover of *Time* magazine)—but if a man's wife gets into print and, by association, so does he, then so be it.

The wife of the junior man listened attentively to her dinner companion. She would always wonder whether John drew up this remarkable list of specifications before or after he met Joan Robinson.

Beloved Belinda was retired with pomp and grace at Houston's Pin Oak Horse Show in June 1959. The gray mare was concluding a career that had made her one of the most honored horses in the history of the amateur world and a favorite of Houston audiences. Pin Oak was a show closely bound to both high society and to medicine, for it was principally sponsored by the Abercrombie family, one of the city's most prestigious oil clans, and the proceeds went to Texas Children's Hospital, a world-acclaimed institution for pediatric care. Joan Robinson Hill was the undisputed Pavlova of this ballet, and she personally sold tens of thousands of dollars' worth of tickets each year.

On the evening of her horse's last appearance, Joan dressed a final time in the gray riding costume that blended perfectly with the mare. After a fanfare, the lights were lowered and there came the pause of anticipation, the moment of high theatrical suspense. Then, with spotlights dancing on the ring entrance, horse and rider burst forth for one last turn. In the glare, the horse was pale, its mistress almost washed away. There was darkness all around them; they seemed figures suspended in time and space. Joan began to weep, and her tears spilled down her cheeks and onto the bodice of her gray coat. But that did not matter, for she would never wear it again. Six thousand people rose and cheered. Ash Robinson stood at the fence near the riders' entrance, and he cried as he could not remember having done since he was a child. He was transfixed, mesmerized, and he hoped that people damn well knew who bought that mare and who raised that girl.

When she had concluded the last figure eight, Joan dismounted and tenderly removed Belinda's saddle. In its place she put a blanket of fresh red roses. Then, sobbing, she gently led Beloved Belinda around the ring for a solo as the orchestra played "Auld Lang Syne." A black groom standing near Ash Robinson and his wife murmured, "Abe Lincoln hisself didn't have a funeral as good as this one."

When it was all over. Joan led her horse out of the glare and into the barn. People swarmed about her, full of the emotion of the moment. Ash embraced his daughter and kissed her proudly. Ma did the same. Joan looked about for her husband but he was nowhere to be seen. Later she learned that John was in a corridor discussing a musicale scheduled for a few weeks thereafter. He had not even watched his wife in her supreme moment. Joan was deeply hurt, but she did not speak of it. Not this time.

On June 14, 1960, in John Hill's last year of general surgery residency, his wife was delivered of their first child, a son, after a difficult carriage and birth. She had grown frightened during the last month of pregnancy because of kidney trouble, and the pain of anticipation and delivery was great. Her husband had not been enthusiastic over the prospect of a baby, for he was still earning less than two hundred dollars a month and there were two years of specialty training before him. "I don't care if *he's* ready or not," answered Ash Robinson when his daughter revealed her husband's concern. "*We're* very happy." Ash had watched over his daughter and his grandchild-to-be like a benevolent dictator. When Joan craved ice cream in the middle of the night, her father, not her husband, rose to fetch it.

At the moment of the baby's birth John nonetheless was bursting with rare excitement. Known in the hospital as a cool, reserved doctor who displayed little emotion, he shouted, "It's a boy!" as he ran down the hospital corridors informing nurses and patients of his good fortune. He even picked up the phone and told the switchboard operators who so often paged him. One nurse could not shake the impression that John Hill seemed *too* enthusiastic, that he was somehow performing, not living the moment.

The boy was named Robert Ashton Hill, in honor of his maternal grandfather. But hardly was the baby home than he was in Ash's arms. The old man was laughing and tender and he cried, "We'll call you Boot. Boot Hill!"

Ash opened his pocketbook even wider for his grandson. His checks paid for diaper service, formulas, a twenty-four-hour-a-day nurse who was engaged to watch the frail infant during a lengthy period of sickness in his first year. Everything he had done for Joan as a baby he repeated now, three decades later. When Ash announced plans to buy Boot a horse the moment his mother felt he was old enough to be lashed in the saddle alone, Joan laughed. "You are the most outrageous grandpa in the history of the world. You are going to spoil my kid rotten, just like me."

The established physicians who hold faculty positions at medical schools keep a close eye on the men in training, not only to supervise their education and to keep them from carving up patients improperly, but to spot those new men who might be worth taking in as partners. Dr. Nathan Roth watched John Hill carefully over the six years he studied general and plastic surgery. Roth was a corpulent man with a forbidding air about him from a distance, but one who, upon close association, grew both charming and philosophical. He liked to ruminate like a rabbinical scholar, an unusual trait for doctors in Houston, who traditionally are so busy and so consumed that they have scant time for reflection.

Having trained in New York, Roth was considered an outsider in the Houston medical world, and although he was highly skilled in the art of plastic surgery he was, in the early 1960s, having difficulty building a practice. Roth was not a handsome man, which is still another desirable requisite for a doctor who rebuilds damaged faces, nor did he have access to the silk stocking district through marriage or family. And he was Jewish, no advantage in the South despite Houston's large community of merchants.

"When I saw John Hill in the training program," Roth would say in later years, "I beheld a tall, good-looking, broad-shouldered gentile boy, married to a glamorous River

Oaks beauty who knew everybody worth knowing in this town. I also learned that this fortunate young man was living in his father-in-law's home and that the father-in-law was paying all the bills. What an arrangement!"

Roth invited the aspiring young surgeon and his wife home for dinner. He set a good table, poured vintage French wine. On his walls were the beginnings of what would become a distinguished collection of art and sculpture. His library was filled with books on history and philosophy. He seemed a man whose life was in order, whose wife Sheila was attentive, whose children were obedient. John Hill noted all this—the accouterments of the trade—while the older man scrutinized him. The evening went by on a note of pleasantness and good will. John was charming and deferential to the senior man.

"Tell me," said Roth when the evening was nearly done. "Why did you choose plastic surgery?"

John mulled the question. He knew the answer was important. "Because I want to help people," he said. "And because I want to make money."

Nathan Roth nodded contentedly. The answer was what he wanted, and what he understood.

Over the next several days Roth created an imaginary ledger for the man he was considering, assets and liabilities. The former were considerable—Hill's looks, his charm, his ties by marriage, his pair of hands (known to be quick and accomplished in surgery), his WASP air of all-American boyishness. All of these Roth relished and coveted. But he found himself troubled by John Hill's blatant lack of interest in research and the publishing of medical papers. Many ambitious young physicians, Roth himself included, began writing articles for scientific publications while still in medical school. There was also something worrisome—a slipperiness—about John that Nathan Roth could not quite put his finger on: a glibness, a tendency to slide away from an intellectual confrontation, an ability to talk around a subject without really coming to grips with it. Roth fretted about these qualities for a time, but he rationalized that John Hill was young, eager, probably frightened of senior men, and he had years to grow.

Before he would offer John a partnership, Roth needed to discuss two touchy and intimate matters. One was the subject of John's younger brother Julian, a year behind in his medical education and close to beginning his career as a psychiatrist. The quieter of the two brothers, the one whose world was shadowed by the accomplishments of John, Julian was as gaunt as a fence post and his face continually wore an attitude of hidden trouble. He seemed a young man who kept everything bottled up, and Roth worried that someday the cork would blow out from the pressure. And Julian was, if gossip in doctors' lounges was to be believed, sexually confused. While Nathan Roth did not object intellectually to any man's private life, he recognized the potential for scandal. Discreetly, he raised the subject with John Hill. He searched for a euphemism. Was Julian Hill more *interested* in male relationships than female?

John Hill nodded, not in affirmation, but to indicate that he understood the worth of the inquiry. He did not know this to be true, insisted John. Yes, he had heard such rumors, but as far as he knew they were simply that. Julian had many friends in the music world, he being a fine pianist, but for that matter so did John. Julian was not only his best friend, he was a highly intelligent doctor, a gifted musician, and a source of pride and comfort to the family. Of course it was true that Julian had been in analysis, still was for all John knew, but psychiatrists undergo therapy as part of their educational process. He concluded by saying that Julian was perfectly capable of coping with any flaws in his character, *if* there were such flaws.

Nathan Roth accepted the answer, for it seemed loving and well prepared. Now he moved to one last subject with even more tact. He began by speaking of his own Jewishness, of how much he revered a strong family life, of how vital was its harmony in the make-up of a successful professional man. There were rumors in town that the situation at Ash Robinson's home was—and again Roth searched for euphemism—not congenial. One of Roth's friends had heard Ash Robinson remark testily at a party, "Here comes the famous plastic surgeon John Hill, who never even bought his son a jar of baby food." Ash was also reported to be grousing that, although John contributed nothing to the running of the household, he somehow found money enough to buy player piano rolls and old phonograph records.

Carefully, Roth chose his words. He had decided to offer John a partnership on one condition: that the young plastic surgeon move his wife and son out of his father-in-

law's home and set up his own household. "A good partner
is a happy partner," intoned Roth. "If you move away from
your father-in-law, then he will be happy and you will be
happy, and the rift between the two of you will be healed."

John concurred and was indeed eager to accept the offer.
But he did not have the funds to buy his own home, and he
did not want to throw away rent every month. Then, said
Nathan Roth, he would loan John $5,000 for a down pay-
ment on a house. It could be paid back as the practice grew.

Not surprisingly, Ash Robinson failed to rejoice when
his daughter and son-in-law announced that they were
finally leaving his bed and board. He had grown accustomed to having his Joan and her baby but a few feet away
from him at all times. Joan hurried to reassure him. The
house they were buying was just a few miles away, ten
minutes at most by car, and Ash could visit every day if he
wanted to, and, besides. she would be back and forth so
often he would never know she was gone. And the house
was located near the Texas Medical Center, where the city's
major hospitals were situated, and it would be so convenient for John.

"John's got to be his own man," said Joan. "I love him,
too, Daddy."

John Hill joined the practice of Nathan Roth in 1963,
and to welcome his junior partner, the senior plastic
surgeon gave an elaborate party, inviting various doctors,
hospital administrators, and social friends of the young
couple.

One of those invited to the party who did not attend was
John's brother Julian. Although he professed delight at
John's good fortune in securing such a promising partnership, a few days after the festivities, the thin and somber
psychiatrist-to-be climbed to the attic of a friend's home.
There, either out of a convoluted and inexpressible jealousy
over his brother's marriage and fatherhood and advance-
ment into the real world of medicine, or out of sorrow
over a broken friendship with a young man whom he had
been seeing, or acting on the command of some dark
corner of his brain, Julian Hill spread out a cheap blanket,
swallowed a vial of barbiturates, and killed himself.

It was the first act of the tragedy.

7

John Hill was a man in a hurry, his life a blur, a dozen brightly hued balls thrown in the air. And he was, for some time, remarkably adept at keeping them from crashing to earth.

"I never saw a young doctor work so hard," remarked one of the city's famous surgeons. "He was like an industry. Had he asked me to buy stock in him, I would have." And for a time Nathan Roth was pleased, although the new man's very first case with the partnership was troubling. A patient who had suffered a broken jaw presented himself for repair. The traditional method that every plastic surgeon learns is the routine procedure of placing splints on the upper and lower jaws and then securing them with stainless steel wires. On the lower jaw, the wires can be wound around the jaw itself but, with the upper jaw, the surgeon must drill holes on which to affix the wires.

Roth gave John the assignment, as mundane a task as a tyro automobile mechanic being asked to change spark plugs. The operation seemed to go well; the patient went home satisfied. But in a few weeks he returned, concerned over excessive draining from the upper jaw.

Hill was out of the office so Roth examined the patient. He found nothing apparently wrong. He assured him that the draining would cease. A few weeks later the patient had dental work, and X rays revealed that a small tip of the drilling bit had broken off during the jaw repair and was lodged in the upper jaw. The patient burst into Roth's office steaming. "Why didn't that young partner of yours tell me?" he demanded. Roth tried to calm him, assuring him that his life was not in jeopardy, that he could live the rest of his years with the bit in place. Or he could have a free minor operation to remove it.

Roth summoned John Hill and demanded an explanation. It simply could not have been a case of the surgeon not noticing the broken drill. The blunder was in failing to inform the patient. *That* left them open to a lawsuit. "My God," thundered Roth, "it could happen to any surgeon.

I've done the same thing. But I've always told the patient and . . ."

John Hill was abject, seemingly devastated by the scolding. "I'm so ashamed," he said, his eyes downcast. "I was just starting out my career, and I was hesitant to mention this mistake on my very first case."

Roth checked his temper. The mistake was minor; perhaps the patient would not sue. And there was the mitigating factor of Julian's death. It would have been difficult for any doctor to operate on the heels of such numbing personal tragedy.

The patient did file a malpractice suit, but the fates were kind to John Hill. Even before depositions could be taken, the man blew his nose hard one morning. Out flew the drill point. Case dropped. But once more a seed of doubt was planted in Nathan Roth's mind about the new man's reliability.

Nathan Roth was a connoisseur of art. Indeed he resembled a Sydney Greenstreet film character who would pursue a statuette across the Far East to possess it. His office was filled with tasteful paintings and lithographs. John Hill, in emulation of his senior partner, moved quickly to decorate his own office. But his choices were poor. It was as if he said to himself, I am a successful doctor, successful doctors hang paintings on their walls, ergo, I will buy paintings. Roth was aghast to see what John's taste had wrought—cheap oil landscapes of waves crashing against beaches, anonymous cityscapes, lifeless fruits spilling out of cornucopias—the kind of art for sale in Times Square discount houses and peddled by the thousands.

Roth also noted that the one genuinely lovely piece of art that John possessed—a framed photograph of Joan astride Beloved Belinda, a haunting picture with ominous dark clouds above her head—rested on the floor, unhung, for three years. It puzzled him that John would surround himself with atrocious paintings and leave his wife's image on the floor to gather dust.

The average patient who visited John's office would probably not even notice the art, so dazzling was the young doctor's personal style. Particularly if the patient was an impressionable older woman. She would be invited to sit on the sofa while John Hill poured her a glass of wine. There would be small talk of music and perhaps of Joan's latest accomplishments in the horse shows. Then John would move to the piano he had installed near his desk and he would play, perhaps, a soothing Chopin sonata. Finally the conversation would move to the annoying bags that had come so rudely to the woman's eyes. With a thumb so light it seemed made of cobwebs and dusting powder, he would touch the blemishes and murmur his confidence that a quick and easy operation would banish the bags and the wrinkles.

John could perform almost everything he promised. Nathan Roth criticized him now and then for promising too much, but John Hill was not the first plastic surgeon to build a practice by catering to women's vanity. Nor was John Hill the first plastic surgeon to insist on his fee up front, in advance of surgery—in cash. It is one of the financial rules of cosmetic surgery (normally not Blue Cross-able) that the patient is more apt to write a check in anticipation of a miracle than afterward when less than what was expected has been delivered.

He operated with style. While music in an operating theater is not unusual—Denton Cooley, the celebrated Houston heart surgeon, for example, often has a radio tuned to a country and western station—John Hill rigged up a stereo system that he could carry from hospital to hospital. Installing it in a corner, with the amplifier and speakers away from the sterile field, John inserted classical music cassettes. One patient spoke of the experience. "The last thing I remember was this gorgeous doctor bending over me, and Beethoven crashing all around me."

He haunted the emergency rooms of hospitals all over the city, flattering the head nurses, making sure they knew he was able and available should an accident victim arrive in the middle of the night in need of his talents. He attended medical meetings, even the small and unimportant gatherings of country doctors hundreds of miles from Houston, often with his celebrated wife on his arm, shaking hands and dispensing good will and hoping for referrals. He made contact with the Texas prison system, informing the authorities that he was interested in studying criminals and perhaps performing surgery on their faces after they were paroled or pardoned. Some men steal and kill, he once said, because they think they are too ugly to do anything else. "I think I can help them, and society as well." Nathan Roth heard this and arched his eyebrows. He did not believe his junior partner was all that consumed with altruism, but he recognized that John was shrewd enough to realize that ex-prisoners come out of jail and get jobs, jobs that provide insurance, insurance that pays for scar removals and harelip surgery if the hospitalization papers are filled out with sophistication.

Often he operated for free on the children of other doctors, or the sisters of doctors' wives, or the brother-in-law of a scheduling nurse. Again, the practice was not unusual—a young doctor must build up his potential customers—but the zeal with which Hill pursued it was notable. His reputation in the medical community was that of a surgeon with manual dexterity, competent in face work, and particularly capable in the reconstruction of hands. One patient who was a ranked tennis player at a Houston country club suffered a horrible accident at his country house. While cutting firewood, a power saw almost severed his right hand in two. In a series of operations, John rebuilt the hand, his work so exquisite that the patient not only resumed tennis, he won his club's singles tournament within one year of the accident. There were those who felt John Hill was pushing himself too fast, extending his ambition to the detriment of the profession. The day is not long past when nurses were openly hostile toward women who lay in hospital beds awaiting or recovering from cosmetic surgery. The feeling was that these vain patients were taking up space which should have been used by really sick people.

Years later, Nathan Roth had harsh words of criticism for John Hill. But by this time he so loathed his once promising partner that his opinion had to be measured against his bitterness. "John Hill, in my opinion, was an avaricious doctor," Roth would say. "He operated too often. He didn't level with his patients. He assured them, 'Everything is going to be beautiful,' when it most assuredly was not. If a man went through a windshield in a car accident and suffered scars, John would promise to fix them. Three months later, if the patient was not totally satisfied with the results, he would do another operation. Then he would sand the face and do still more surgery. John Hill would operate until the patient was beyond hope of further improvement.

"As long as the patient was willing to lie down on his table, then John Hill would operate—and take his money."

Busy as he was with his practice, he was even more occupied with his music. John rose at 5 A.M., not to make hospital rounds but to practice his tuba in the quiet of his office in a medical building. A nurse who was enamored of her employer rose early as well and was there to greet him at sunrise with coffee, rolls, and just-fried bacon and eggs. His appointment book had two columns, one for medical matters, the other for musical schedules. He devoted at least twenty hours a week to practicing, taking lessons, and playing in several groups, including the Houston Brass Quintet and the Friends of Music, an organization chiefly composed of doctors who played chamber music and sponsored cultural events. Moreover, he was a patron of both the Houston Symphony and grand opera, the principal classical FM station, and—most prestigiously, for it combined both music and medicine—the Heartbeats. This was a band composed principally of doctors (many associated with cardiac work, hence the name) which played at civic functions and at national medical conventions.

Cardiovascular surgeon Grady Hallman was the founder of the Heartbeats, its conductor, and as close a friend as John Hill had, following the death of Julian. The two men had first met when they were teenagers, in 1947, at a Texas high school band convention. Both played trombone and they stole time from the official functions to play duets together. They met again at Rush Day for fraternities at Baylor Medical School in 1952. Each was happy to discover that the other was still pursuing not only music but now medicine as well. Over the next decade or so of medical training, they remained good friends, although it was friendship in the sense of "We'll meet next Thursday," or "Let's play a Respighi," nothing more intimate. Hallman did receive one brisk letter, in 1957, when he was in the Army. "I've met a girl and I'm on the verge of marrying her," John wrote. "You'd like her. She's beautiful and she has an infectious personality."

A musical scholar, Hallman was less impressed with John's abilities than others who had less sophisticated ears. He held his old friend to be a "skimmer" on the piano and a showboat tuba player. John originally asked to become the Heartbeats' pianist, the fellow with many solos. But there was already a capable piano player in the group. The plastic surgeon then became the band's first tuba player,

Hallman glad to have him, for the instrument added a richness to the brass section.

The two musical doctors were much alike, both coming from small Texas towns, both rising quickly in the professional and social hierarchies of Houston. But Hallman could not help but feel he worked harder for his success. During his residency his family lived on furniture made from orange crates, and he ate Fritos and fried pies until his tongue turned red from poor nutrition. It was difficult not to compare this period of hardship with John Hill's limousine and River Oaks existence. Perhaps that contributed to the stand Hallman would one day take, when John Hill was so desperately in need of allies.

On the surface, Joan Robinson seemed very much the model of the busy young housewife and mother, her calendar crowded with civic activity, charitable commitments, car pools, opening nights at theaters and night clubs. More than one doctor in Houston envied John Hill his wife, for she was better than a full-page advertisement in the Houston newspapers. Every Tuesday she put in a full day as a volunteer at Texas Children's Hospital, bustling about the corridors in a starched pink and white apron, her smile wide and white. She dutifully joined the organizations of doctors' wives, attended their teas and luncheons, tried to stay awake during their book reviews. She was a rare commodity, the beautiful girl admired by both men and women. One smitten doctor, the veteran of four failed marriages, summed Joan up well: "She was the friendliest gal in town, natural, affectionate, and warm. She didn't care what she said, and she could cuss like a roughneck. But on her the words didn't seem coarse. She often flirted with a husband and put her arm around him and kissed him on the cheek. The reason other women didn't mind was that Joan didn't give off vibrations saying, 'I'm available.' She obviously loved John Hill. She was a helluva desirable woman, but it wouldn't have occurred to me to try and screw her."

She cared nothing for fashion, and her clothes were the despair of her friends, whose lives revolved around *Vogue*, Neiman-Marcus, and Christian Dior. Her hemlines remained resolutely long and below the knee, at ballerina length after the style had been buried. She saw nothing wrong with a pair of ninety-eight-cent plastic earrings from Woolworth's, and she was delighted to wear a $9.98 dress from Foley's basement to a society tea. In later years, as John's practice grew to more than $100,000 a year, he bought her a full-length mink, only it was from a resale shop in New York and a trifle thin and chewed in places. But it was from John, and she loved it, and she wore it like a trophy.

Her character dictated her taste, or lack of it, in clothes, and this was fortunate, for there never seemed to be enough money. When John went to work in Nathan Roth's office and they set up housekeeping away from Ash, Joan received the sum of $100 a month to run her household. "A hundred bucks a month! You must be kidding!" cried Sheila Roth during a lunch with Joan. No, it was not a joke, insisted Joan. She was hard pressed to buy groceries, pay a part-time maid once a week, cover the utilities, and entertain at John's musicales. "That's madness," said Sheila, still disbelieving. But she was a probing sort of woman and one afternoon, noticing John Hill's checkbook open on his office desk, could not resist thumbing through it. Joan's monthly check was precisely $100. There were, however, checks totaling many times that drawn by John each month to cover musical desires—lessons, records, new instruments.

When her purse was bare, Joan fell back, as she always had and always would, on her father. By custom from the old days in the oil fields, Ash liked to have cash on hand, and he always kept a thousand or two in tens and twenties in a locked filing cabinet in his home. And Joan, who knew where the key was hidden, was given to understand that she could dip into the cache when the occasion arose. Undoubtedly John knew of the dependable supply of family money, although Joan never told him. She was determined to please her husband by staying within the financial limits he had set.

And Ash liked the arrangement. That was one more way he could be assured of seeing his daughter often, and of keeping the leash taut. When he was not away from the city on oil business, Ash normally began each morning at his daughter's house having Louisiana coffee with her and his grandson. *Each* morning.

After the retirement of Beloved Belinda, Joan never found a horse with the same glamor and potential. She owned and showed a few others—Precision Possession and Belle Destiny, and a promising colt named Major Maygar, the foal of Belinda herself. And while Joan won several more competitions with these horses, there was not the electric partnership that had wed her and the dappled gray mare. It had been Joan's hope that Belinda would foal colts infused with the championship blood and inherent equine nobility. But it was not to be. Belinda was not a good breeder. She miscarried often; the colts she produced were skittish and stubborn. The only one of promise, Major Maygar, won competitions due more to the trainer's skill and Joan's distinctive style. Musing on this for months, Joan had an idea which she broached to her father one morning over coffee. How would it be, she suggested, if she bought a small farm somewhere near Houston, a place where she could breed horses, where a trainer could live and work with them daily? Her face lit up as she spun out her fantasies of how her farm could become known all over the world, how it could be dedicated to the classic American saddlebred horse. There could also be a riding school, where children could take lessons, their fees bringing in enough money to cover expenses.

Joan paused, waiting for Ash's response. It came quickly. "Go ahead," he said. "Sounds good. Go look for something.'

"I've found a little place already," she said. Excitedly. "It already exists. Three acres, just west of town."

Ash Robinson bought the small farm for his daughter, paying $25,000, on the condition that he keep the books and hire and fire the staff. Joan was content with the arrangement, for she was hard pressed enough to run her own household.

It was christened Chatsworth Farm, named after Rhea Robinson's ancestral estate in New Orleans, and Joan attacked her new possession with enormous zest. Enlisting her friends, she led fence-whitewashing parties, cut back weeds, mowed grass, planted azaleas and climbing roses. By the spring of 1965 Chatsworth was a lovely place, reminiscent of the Kentucky horse country, with thirty-six horse stalls kept impeccably clean and sweet-smelling, a regulation show ring, and trails that wound lazily along a bayou where the city and its pressures seemed a thousand miles away. Yet it was but twenty minutes by Cadillac from Joan's home.

John Hill tolerated his wife's new passion, for it gave him a needed counterbalance to his own musical avocation.

Early in their marriage Joan had carped at some of his
expenditures for phonograph records—his collection was
already enormous. Now he could throw the stables back at
her whenever a money argument arose, although this
weapon was blunted because Ash was the source of most
of her cash.

John rarely went to Chatsworth, except for the annual
late spring picnic that he and Joan gave—with Ash picking
up the check—for several hundred doctors and their wives.
The affair was famous in the Houston medical world and
valuable to John as a source of good will in his profession.
The show arena was covered with a giant tent, and tables
were set with checkered cloths. Beer flowed from kegs,
barbecue was dished out of steaming cauldrons, vaudeville
acts cavorted on a makeshift stage, and everyone who
entered passed through a brief receiving line, headed by
John Hill's famous wife, who had a phenomenal memory
for names and who could tease and flatter the dourest old
GP into an ear-to-ear grin. The social amenities aside, the
annual picnic not only stamped John Hill's presence and
style on hundreds of potential referring doctors, it introduced Chatsworth to their wives, most of whom had children and would not have objected to their learning to ride
as well as Joan. The week after the party, telephones rang
continuously with mothers wanting riding lessons for their
daughters. And Ash benefited in his way, standing next to
his daughter, catching out of the corner of his eye someone
pointing his way and paying tribute to the lord-in-law of
the manor, drinking to the fullest the cup of power that
was his in these special moments.

The source of John's real dream was somewhere in his
youth. Perhaps it was the music of his church, ringing,
unaccompanied voices praising their God. Or the first
radio he owned as a teenager, with an antenna rigged so
that it would pick up the Metropolitian Opera broadcasts
on Saturday afternoon from the station in San Antonio.

One day in 1965, John came home from the hospital and
told Joan that he had seen a house that was for sale on
Kirby Drive in the very heart of River Oaks. It was located at 1561 Kirby, only a few blocks up the boulevard
from Ash Robinson's home at 1029. The current owners
were embroiled in a turbulent divorce, said John, and they
were anxious to sell—quickly.

Joan knew the house, as did everyone who had the wherewithal to live in River Oaks, an opulently lovely enclave of great houses on wooded estates. Houston's aristocracy settled in River Oaks in the 1920s, and it quickly became a convocation of manor houses whose owners were first citizens like Ima Hogg and Oveta Culp Hobby and Hugh Roy Cullen and John Connally. They dwelt in the city's chief preserve of quiet and dignity and permanence. Their Cadillacs waited on gently curving driveways, like the carriages of archdukes. They lived concealed behind groves of ancient oak and cypress, with thick banks of azaleas hugging their walls and bursting out each spring in sheets of crimson fire. A magnolia blossom did not fall from a branch but a gardener was there to carry it away.

The house that John had found was a dominant one, a powerful and rather forbidding structure set diagonally on an oversized corner lot. The façade was classic Southern colonial, like Margaret Mitchell's Tara. White columns marched across the front and, about it, pines and oaks hung with Spanish moss stood as sentries. The house was both graceful and at the same time arrogant, positioned diagonally as it was, out of balance with the other estates lined up obediently on the famous drive. At first Joan demurred, feeling that such a house was not only out of reach financially but pretentious for a young couple with but one child. And their budget would not permit servants to run the enormous place.

Besides, she had been nursing the idea of building a ranch house at Chatsworth, now that freeways were being built that would loop and whirl about the city, making a country home accessible quickly to any hospital that John needed to attend. But her socially ambitious husband was an ardent salesman. He pointed out the proximity of her parents, two minutes away, built-in baby sitters when she needed care for Boot during her frequent journeys to horse shows. Moreover, he felt the house fitting for a doctor on the rise, one that would suggest a prominence and success that he did not yet have. John's journey from Hill's Corner in Edcouch had been quick and easy. Now he would make the final climb to the top in a compulsive leap.

At the rear of the house was the garage, approachable from the side street, and above that was an unfinished room, probably intended as servants' quarters. Joan hardly noticed it as she toured the huge house, but it was of great importance to John. He did not mention it at this moment, for the culmination of his dream would have to take its place after acquisition of the house and the accumulation of the fees from another few hundred operations. But he shivered with anticipation as he stood in the barren, junk-filled room. Someday, soon, it would be what he knew it could be.

And so it happened that John and Joan Hill bought the great white house for the sum of $95,000, with Ash loaning his son-in-law $12,000 interest-free for the down payment. He would have given them the entire sum in return for having his daughter and grandson so close, on the very same street.

Ash knew the house well. He had once looked at it himself before he built his own home. At the time, he recalled, it had seemed both too large and too cut up, too many rooms.

He had also heard troubling stories attached to the house, dark reports of unhappiness and horror. Besides the nasty divorce of the previous owners, another had died an agonizing death of cancer in one of the bedrooms. And still another had gone up to the top floor and blown his brains out.

But he did not mention these to Joan and John. They were young, they were exuberant. And she was close to him once again.

8

Maggie Foster, the cardiologist's wife who first introduced Joan Robinson to John Hill, was right. They *were* a mismatch, so much so that no child, no success, no mansion could glue together the disparities of their lives. They were more than opposites. They held acutely different attitudes toward the business of running their beings. Joan seemed a creature of daylight, open, unsuspicious, no shadows cluttering her world. She held no secrets; indeed she told all to her friends, unloading her private thoughts on the telephone or at the *Kaffeeklatsch* she assembled each day at the big house. Only the fact that she had been married twice before John did she keep to herself. Few knew that. Out of pain or humiliation, she concealed that chapter of her history. Conversely, John seemed a resident of the night, a man who relished the concealing cloak of darkness. Secretive, uncommunicative, he did not confide in his wife or his friends, for there were none in whom he could invest the torments of a soul. He was a pious man. And stiff, unbending. "You know the funny thing about John Hill?" said a neighbor-psychiatrist to his wife. "I can never remember seeing John in anything but a scrub suit or a coat and tie. I know I must have. He comes over here for pool parties and he undoubtedly wears a sport shirt, maybe even bathing trunks, but he's always wearing a suit as far as I'm concerned."

Joan was the magnet for her crowd, the chairman of the group. For years, she and three other women played a regular Friday night bridge game, but it was always at her house. On occasion Maggie Foster or one of the other women would insist that it was her turn to be hostess and relieve Joan of the responsibility, and Joan would agree, only to about-face during the afternoon hours of Friday and insist that everyone come to her house. "She wanted to be close to the telephone," observed Maggie Foster. "She had so many irons in the fire, so many people calling her, and she was proud of the god-awful house."

It was difficult to reach Joan, for her telephone was always busy. She was either running down her "sucker list" or "angel roster," her alternating terms for her compilation of wealthy businessmen who could be leaned on for a contribution to the children's hospital or the zoo fund or a community theater, whatever her charity of the moment was, or she was gossiping with the girls, or she was trying to reach John, for he had taken to disappearing for hours on end, the excuse being that he was "at the hospital" or "making rounds" or "doing charts." The neighbor-psychiatrist who categorized John as always wearing a business suit felt it strange that the plastic surgeon should sometimes be gone for six or eight evening hours "doing charts" when he, a doctor himself, knew the work could easily be done in an hour by even the busiest physician. But he never mentioned this to Joan.

John Hill was a complex man who did odd things. On one occasion a couple arrived at his home for cocktails before going out to dinner. Joan greeted them with an excuse—John was on his way from the hospital and would be late. In a half hour he bustled in wearing his greens and went upstairs to change. When an hour passed and he had not returned, Joan asked her male guest to go check on him. She was engrossed in an anecdote. In a few minutes the man returned shaking his head. "Your husband," he told Joan, "is standing stark naked behind the bathroom door, playing his recorder."

They spent precious little time together alone. By sunrise John was always gone, practicing his music in his office before the doors opened for patients. And he was rarely home until long after dark, until long after Boot had dined on a tray prepared by the Mexican cook, his mother sitting beside him trying not to fret over her missing husband. When the Hills were together, it was usually out on public view. They seemed constantly on the go. "John and Joan strike me as people always on their way to somewhere else," commented one River Oaks hostess.

"Hell, honey, I'd rather be in the sack with my husband," confided Joan in her earthy manner to a friend named Camille Nichols. "But we don't get along too well in that department, so we go out on the town." In public, with friends, Joan often picked at her husband, but there were rarely signs that her barbs were piercing his flesh. "Sex? What's that?" she snapped when the subject came up from a complaining wife at their restaurant table. John ignored her, as he usually did; sometimes he would dispatch a frosted look that indicated the subject was better discussed in the car going home. The Hills became known in their circle for their quarrels in public, one-sided ones, Joan usually flaring over her husband's lack of attention or his aloof attitude. His response was a patient look, the kind a parent uses with a misbehaving child. John did his nagging in private. He criticized Joan for smoking, telling her that her breath was foul and not enjoyable in a rare embrace. She tried, desperately but unsuccessfully, to quit. He often remarked that she smelled like a horse, despite her baths in perfumed oils and the colognes she splashed over her body after coming home from the stables.

"Their relationship was as fragile as a piece of cooked spaghetti," said a friend, "but somehow they stayed together. Joan loved the man. She adored him, for all of his faults. And I surmise that John wanted for some reason to stay married to her."

Although both inhabited worlds where extramarital affairs were quickly and easily accomplished—John at the hospital, classic fertile ground for casual involvements, Joan at her horse shows where vivid people were thrown together in hotels away from home for four or five days at a time—there was no hint that either betrayed the other during the first few years of the marriage. Joan was known as a one-man woman, always rebuffing any would-be seducer with a kind appreciation for the offer. John impressed those who knew him as a man so busy with his medicine and his music that he had no time for horizontal escapade.

John Hill did not abandon the religion of his youth. Indeed that was another source of occasional conflict between him and his wife. Joan was, after all, Ash's daughter, and she had been raised to the thunder of his atheistic disapproval of the Church and how it imprisoned people. When social conversation turned to religion, Joan fell silent, but John perked up, for he contended it was a dominant factor in his life. He did not swear, he did not smoke, he drank lightly, he felt it obligatory to attend church each Sunday morning, where he often led the singing. And Joan occasionally, though reluctantly, went with him. She did not believe in the teachings of the Church, but she felt they did no harm, and if it contented her husband, then she would sit beside him in a prominent pew. Once it occurred to her that their attendance was not bad for business, because John operated on several members of the congregation.

The partnership between Nathan Roth and John Hill dissolved in bitterness and a lawsuit a little more than three years after it had begun.

From the beginning, Roth held misgivings about the new man and collected grievances against him. The matter of John's record-keeping, for example, drove Roth batty. Hill kept terrible records, scattered over his office, in the trunk of his car, stuffed into coat pockets. Since the two doctors acted in concert on many patients, Roth grew angry when he could not find a certain case history or the bookkeeper could not send out a statement on time. Regular "summit meetings" were held in which he demanded that Hill straighten out his papers. Always John would humble himself, promising to do as the older man asked. Indeed he would try but within a few months the Hill desk and car trunk were once again a mass of unfiled papers.

And there was John's habit of asking Roth to "cover for him," not unknown in the doctoring business, but the senior man felt the junior man abused the practice. "If a man has a legitimate reason to ask me to take over for him in the veritable middle of an operation, I will do it," stormed Roth, "but when that reason is to go play with a chamber music group for a grade school PTA meeting, then the reason is unprofessional." It further distressed Roth that John was not bringing in the carriage trade. Oh, occasionally a wealthy patient would lie down on the junior man's table, but the bulk of his practice was secretaries, or musical friends, or "those god damn convicts." In the beginning, Roth had anticipated that, between him and his attractive partner, "we would lock up this town." But the parking lot checks that the secretary validated were more often for Chevrolets than Cadillacs.

Roth found himself wincing every time he saw the tasteless seascapes on his partner's wall, every time he heard a sonata being played for a female patient, every time he spent a maddening half hour on the telephone trying to find his partner. The original agreement gave John ten per cent of the first year's profits, twenty per cent the second year, and by the fifth year they would split revenues fifty-fifty. In 1967 Roth summoned John Hill into his office and broke the partnership. He would not have the day come when, out of every dollar he made, half would go to a man whom he now considered unprofessional and undependable. Immediately Hill charged breach of contract, that back moneys were due him, that he held a sheaf of grievances against Roth as well. Angrily the two plastic surgeons tore apart the small shreds of respect and friendship that had bound them. They became bitter enemies.

John Hill took an elaborate suite of offices in the same Hermann Professional Building where he had worked with Roth. His new quarters had five patient treatment rooms and an imposing office for the doctor to place his baby grand.

The new independence wrought immediate changes in John Hill. He warmed. He assembled a staff who enjoyed working for him. To straw-boss the office he employed a salty veteran medical secretary named Frances Johnston, whose lay husband was a member of the Heartbeats, the band for which John played tuba. "We ran an incredibly busy shop," she recalled. "John had a heavy case load, he

operated beyond human endurance. But he was trying to
prove that he could be his own man." Although Joan was
now openly complaining to her friends that John was stingy
and never bought her a gift of any sort, he was generous
with his staff. Nurses were paid $700 a month, consid-
erably above average. On their birthdays the boss personally
set up a party table with a linen cloth and cake and, as a
gift, a jewel box from Neiman-Marcus. There were substantial bonuses at Christmas, and when an employee went
away on vacation Dr. Hill gave her a hundred-dollar check
to spend. "Use it selfishly," he instructed, "eat it up or
drink it up. Don't use it on your children or on your
house."

By the end of his first year in practice by himself, John
Hill grossed $168,000, an admirable ledger for a man but
thirty-seven years old and less than five years away from
his residency.

The year was financially prosperous, but it was also the
year in which John Hill's life began to fall apart.

With the money starting to come, with a limitless financial horizon, it was time for realization of John's dream.
Casually he mentioned to Joan one night that he wanted
to create a music room in their home. "Don't we already
have one?" asked Joan. There was a piano in the living
room, recorders in the bedroom, and even stacks of sheet
music on the floor beside the toilet. No, it was his idea to
build a completely new room, in the unfinished servants'
quarters above the garage. It would be soundproofed,
acoustically perfect, with a high-fidelity system built into
the walls. A place to practice and gather friends for
musicales. "How much will it cost?" asked Joan pertinently,
for she was under the impression that their income was
modest. Her husband had expended more than $30,000 to
establish his practice, and the bank loan to cover it was
yet unpaid. And although John had raised her monthly
stipend to $700, she found it difficult if not impossible to
cover the expenses of running the big house with that sum.
Every time she requested more, John had told her that
there was no more.

He already had estimates, said John carefully, and it
should come in for under $10,000. "Where will we get
$10,000?" asked Joan. Her husband's answer was a gesture
down the street, toward the home of Ash Robinson.

Ash refused. He would not lend any more money to his son-in-law, pointing out that he already held a $12,000 second mortgage on the home, the amount he had lent the young people for the down payment. Furthermore, a music room sounded like foolishness, said Ash, whose melodic bent was confined to country and western or Dixieland, if he was in New Orleans. Joan pleaded with her father, but he was adamant. "God almighty," he swore, "I've given your husband the sun and the moon. Now he wants the stars!" Annoyed, John arranged a bank loan sufficient to retire his father-in-law's second mortgage, with $10,000 remaining to commence work on the music room. But that would be hardly enough to buy the carpets for what would soon become a place of palatial intent.

"I want the finest music room since Renaissance Italy," John Hill instructed a sound engineer named Louis Erath. "Since I was a little boy, it has been my dream to build such a room. A perfect room! It will be a room where great music can be played and listened to under superb conditions. Money is no object. The only goal is perfection."

Erath nodded, drawing his breath at the challenge.

"Don't accept this commission unless you can deliver exactly what I want," cautioned the surgeon.

John Hill, remembered Louis Erath long after this first meeting, seemed *possessed*.

9

"Perhaps" is a fragile if not useless word, but the fact remains that perhaps it would not have happened quite the way it did, that perhaps so many lives would not have been torn and wrecked, had not John Hill gone to pick up his son at the summer camp that torrid August day in 1968. He had not intended to make the journey. Operations were scheduled, he had appointments with several craftsmen at work on the music room, he needed to practice a Mozart piece that he was booked to play at a church recital. Driving to Camp Rio Vista in the hill country of Central Texas was not his design. Joan could go get the boy.

But Joan would not go alone. The boy hardly knows he has a father, she snapped. John never took him anywhere, didn't throw footballs with him, or go fishing with him the way other fathers did. The only time he ever saw his father was at those god damn concerts, where the child had to sit up straight like a soldier on inspection.

The Hills had argued earlier in the spring over whether their son should even attend the very proper summer camp. Joan felt that the boy was, at eight, too young. He was frail, slim, quiet, slow to make friends. He seemed to have inherited a small amount of his mother's gregariousness, and much of his father's stiffness. But John had insisted that Boot go off for a four-week session with anticipation that the outdoor life would toughen him. Moreover, it was the thing to do for people in his class; if one lives in River Oaks, one sends one's youngsters off to this expensive camp. Now, on the concluding day, parents were invited to fetch their children and watch them swim, canoe, play softball, and shoot bows and arrows.

"This day is important to Boot," snapped Joan. "Can you remember how lonely it was to be eight years old?"

Stung, John denied his wife's accusations that he was inattentive to their son. But the worry was enough for him to cancel his medical and musical schedules, clearing two days for the trip by Cadillac to Boot's big day.

Another parent drove from Houston that same day to collect her children. She arrived at the wheel of a Thunderbird, and when she stepped out and walked across the campgrounds, more than one daddy temporarily took his eyes off his son's cabin inspection to watch. One husband, a doctor who lived in John Hill's neighborhood, remembered the moment well. "Here comes this old gal wearing a tight T-shirt and hip huggers that showed off her equipment rather well. She was most provocatively attired. And when she saw some kids swinging on this rope out over the lake, she had to try it too. Of course she fell into the lake, and when she got out she was *more* provocatively attired. Bone dry, she was the *femme fatale* of the day. Dripping wet, she was the sex bomb of Camp Rio Vista."

Her name was Ann Kurth, and though she was that day in close reach of her fortieth birthday, she was sexy and lush. Since the day two decades prior when she had been a campus beauty at Southern Methodist University, she had dedicated herself toward enhancing her appearance, and from her collection of paints, powders, oils, dyes, and creams, she daily assembled a remarkable package. People often told her she looked like Elizabeth Taylor, and the resemblance was there—raven-black hair teased and lacquered, eyes accented by purplish-blue pools of color, soft little girl voice, a button or two calculatedly undone to call attention to a richly endowed bosom. Her social credentials were strong as well. The daughter of a prominent Houston architect, she had attended the right private schools and moved in the country club crowd with assurance. Thrice married, thrice divorced, and the mother of three sons, she was uncharacteristically without a husband at the moment she fell into the lake. But she was not without admirers.

John Hill and Ann Kurth would later tell two different stories of how they met and how their curious relationship developed. He would claim that she made the opening play. Conversely, she would contend that he pursued her hotly, with the reckless enthusiasm of a teen-age swain. Whatever, Dr. John Hill leaned over from his lunch table and smiled at Ann Kurth and one of her sons. "I'm Dr. Hill," he said cheerfully.

"I'm Ann Kurth," the woman said, "and this is one of my sons, Grant. Are you a father?"

Yes, he had a son in camp, an eight-year-old boy named Robert, nicknamed Boot, who was at that moment with his mother somewhere off looking at horses.

Later, during an afternoon Indian pageant, Ann Kurth looked across the war-whooping youngsters and noticed John Hill again. Now he was with a striking woman with platinum-blonde hair pulled back into a pony tail. It all clicked. She had paid his name no particular heed before— Dr. Hill was an attractive man, certainly, but only one of many she had seen that day—but she instantly recognized the woman beside him. Joan Robinson! Ann had, in fact, attended Stephens College just before Joan, and they had numerous friends in common—although the two women had never actually met. She looked back at John. So he was the famous prince consort.

Quickly bored with the Indians, Ann took her children and slipped away to the quietness of the lake. They found a canoe and paddled out, the sun cooking their backs. Within moments, one of her boys noted that another canoe was approaching, with a single adult man at the paddle.

"Hello, boys, I'm Dr. Hill," called out the solitary canoeman. John waved merrily at the youngsters and their mother, who recognized immediately that this was not a man out for exercise alone. "Mind if I take some pictures?" he asked, standing up and attempting to steady himself as he began snapping away.

Immediately the canoe tipped and spilled John Hill into the lake while Ann Kurth burst into laughter. Undaunted, Hill rose from the depths with camera held above his head, still clicking pictures. Ann Kurth remembered: "We were collapsing with laughter, but when we saw that he was okay and not drowning, we waved so long and paddled back to shore. Here comes this madman, squish, squish, squish, after us, back to the camp, walking around wet the rest of the afternoon with people looking at him like he's demented. But he's completely saturated and oblivious of everybody else. All he wanted to do was take our pictures."

At evening's end, when the last farewell had been sung, Ann found herself standing next to Joan Robinson Hill, who smiled and muttered, "I can't seem to find my husband."

"Stick with me, kid, and you'll find him," thought Ann to herself.

Back in Houston, before the week was out, John rang up Ann Kurth and said he had his developed pictures and wanted to show them to her. His camera had not been damaged in the capsizing.

"All right," said Ann, "you can come over tonight." And to herself: we'll let this melodrama play one more scene before I pull down the curtain on Dr. John Hill.

The plastic surgeon arrived at Ann's home in the Memorial section of Houston, one rung down from River Oaks in social caste, at 7 P.M. He did not leave until the next morning just before dawn, and only then because he had surgery scheduled at 7 A.M. Before he scrubbed in to operate, he telephoned Ann from the hospital to wish her a cheery good morning. He called again two hours later, after his first procedure. By this moment Ann Kurth was groggy and feeling caught up in an adolescent quest. The next day, at an intimate lunch, John placed, for him, extraordinary cards on the table. As Ann would later recall: "He informed me that, from this moment on, I was to consider my time fully taken up by Dr. John Hill."

"But what of your wife?" asked Ann. That is over, answered John. It is just a matter of time. "He told me," Ann reported to a friend, "that he was trapped in a marriage he had to get out of. Joan's life, her whole life, was horses. His was music and medicine. And he kept telling me that his life was meaningless because he had no one to share it with."

John Hill seemed not an impulsive man, rather one who planned his life carefully, rarely making a decision unless he had circled round and round it like a dog preparing to lie down. Years later his mother, Myra Hill, who would grow to despise Ann Kurth, asked John what he had originally seen in the woman. "She was very desirable," her son answered, "the attraction was physical."

By the end of August, John and Ann were lovers. When Joan returned to the mansion on Kirby Drive after a horse show away from the city, she found a terse note left on her dresser. It was from her husband. "Things are not good between us," it said. "I've gone away for a few days to find myself."

Joan Hill stared at the letter in disbelief. She raced to the telephone and called her husband's office. He was in surgery. She left her name. He did not call back. She called seven times. He did not call back.

For a few days she alternated between tears and anger, keeping the news from Pa each day when he came for coffee. Finally, standing at the stove one morning watching the pot perk, she broke down.

"The son of a bitch walked out on me," she said.

Ash felt the anger swell within him. No one walked out on his daughter. Where was John?

She had no idea.

Well, sir, Ash reckoned something could be found out. A private detective could turn John Hill's life inside out within a few days.

No! Joan did not want a detective set loose on her husband. Not yet. In her hours of secret torment, the idea had come that a temporary separation might warm the marital climate for both of them.

Ash took his daughter in his arms and felt her body jerk and tremble. At that moment he would have knocked his son-in-law against the nearest wall had he come in reach of his fist.

Now that she had told someone, Joan spread the news of her abandonment. Crying, cursing, she rose early and stayed on the telephone until past midnight. Her best friend and across-the-street neighbor, a doctor's wife named

Vann Maxwell, grew concerned over Joan's emotional condition. "She's like a wild woman," Vann told her husband. "She won't sleep or eat. She's like some animal going through the death throes. If somebody called up and tried to sell her encyclopedias on the telephone, she'd tell him first her husband had walked out on her."

Suddenly, after two weeks of silence, John called. Almost formally he requested an appointment with his wife to "talk things over." They agreed to meet at noon in the big house. Excitedly Joan dialed Vann Maxwell and instructed her to be on "standby"—available for immediate counsel on what John proposed.

Promptly at noon Vann stood at her upstairs window, feeling like a spy, and noted two cars drive up beside the Hill home. John emerged from the first car and walked briskly into his house. But who was the driver of the second, an anonymous blue Ford? Vann strained to see, but there was nothing but an inconclusive silhouette. Ten minutes later John hurried out of his house, looking dour, motioned to the second car, and both sped off.

Hurriedly Vann called her neighbor. Joan was in tears. The meeting with John had hardly begun before it blew up in acrimony. "Well, I *think* I saw a woman in a car parked behind his," said Vann. "They just drove off together. Maybe we can follow them and find out who she is."

With the excitement of a high-speed chase, the two women hurried across the sleepy lanes of River Oaks, searching for John Hill's Cadillac with a blue Ford in tail. They drove all the way to the medical building where John had offices, but the two cars were not to be seen. Dejected, Joan asked to be taken home. While stopped at a red light a few blocks from the house, Vann glanced idly at the parking lot of the Avalon drugstore, a famous Houston pharmacy with a clientele chiefly composed of wealthy River Oaks residents. "My lord," she murmured. "I think that's the car I saw." She pointed toward a blue Ford parked among others. Two people—a man and a woman— sat in the front seat. "Turn in!" ordered Joan.

Uneasy now at what loomed as an awkward confrontation, Vann did as her friend directed, finding a parking place twenty feet away. Joan Hill slowly turned her head and looked directly at her husband, caught red-handed in the company of a dark-haired woman. It was characteristic of John Hill that, whenever he was nervous, he began to

sweat profusely. Operating room nurses knew to mop his
brow when a procedure turned tense. At every critical moment in his life, his face was drenched. When he finally felt
his wife's glare and turned to acknowledge her, he was wet
with perspiration and his shirt soaked to his back.

For a moment the surgeon only looked at his wife, then
he nodded, opened the door, and approached. Tactfully,
Vann made an excuse and strode to the drugstore, wishing
she could have been a mosquito in the back seat. As she
walked away, the last thing she heard Joan demand of her
husband was, "Is this the woman you've been having an
affair with?"

From the doorway of the pharmacy Vann watched the
animated conversation, the drops of air conditioned chill
frosting the interior of the car. She could not see the faces.
Then John burst out, slammed the door, returned to the
Ford, and left with the woman.

Vann hurried back to her car. "What did he say?" she
asked, breathlessly.

Joan seemed stunned, almost in shock. "Her name is
Ann Kurth," she said softly. "John said he was in trouble.
He said he was having an affair with this woman's husband,
and that he was being blackmailed."

"Her *husband?*" exclaimed Vann. "Are you sure you
heard it right?"

Joan nodded. "He repeated it twice. What in hell do I do
now?"

Anonymous notes began arriving in the mail for Joan.
They informed her that John was living openly with Ann
Kurth at her home and that they were being seen at
restaurants and concerts together. One note suggested that
Ann Kurth was but one of many women John Hill was
tending.

After a few days of frenetic investigation among her
friends of Ann Kurth, Joan was able to report to Vann:
John had lied about having an affair with that woman's
husband. "In the first place, she doesn't even have a husband any more," said Joan wryly. "And secondly, he's
sleeping at her house every night."

The farce was on. First Joan engaged an off-duty policeman to snoop on her husband. Within a week his reports verified that John Hill was living at Ann Kurth's
home. Filled with jealousy and curiosity, Joan took to cruis-

ing around her rival's neighborhood, shopping in Ann's supermarket, even emerging from a dressing room at a department store where Ann happened to be trying on a dress. Joan pretended she did not know the other woman, but the current between the two was a high-tension wire.

Ann Kurth stood at her window one afternoon and watched Joan drift by in her blue and white Cadillac. A few minutes later, in separate investigation, came Ash at the wheel of his black Lincoln, casting a quick glance at the Kurth home. "My God, it sure is getting classy around this neighborhood," said Ann to John that night. "You wouldn't believe the Cadillacs and Lincolns driving past my house all day." She found the escapade amusing, but unsettling. The phone had started ringing in the middle of the night, with no one in response when she answered it. John put a tape recorder on Ann's phone. Joan put a tape recorder on her phone, but installed it improperly and cursed when it failed to work. Ash put a tape recorder on his phone.

One morning Joan summoned Vann from across the street and announced a plan: "Everything John Hill has— his whole god damn life—he carries around in the trunk of his car. I want to get into that trunk and read his letters." Protesting all the way, Vann nontheless let herself be persuaded to stand lookout for her friend during the caper.

Her instructions from Joan were to stand beside the stairway door that allowed people to enter the basement garage of the medical building where John had his offices. Every time the door opened Vann was to signal, and, on the slender chance that John himself emerged, she should divert him. "How do I explain what I'm doing in his office garage?" asked Vann plaintively.

Joan ran quickly to her husband's conspicuous Cadillac and opened the trunk with her set of keys. It was full of papers, sheet music, letters, and photographs. She began scooping them up, reading them, stashing an occasional document in her purse. At her post, Vann was jumpy. She kept forgetting the signal. Was she to whistle twice or clap her hands if trouble loomed? The door opened several times with people coming for their automobiles, and each time, rather than signal, Vann skipped nervously over to Joan where she hissed at her, "That's enough. Let's get out of here!" But Joan would not shut the trunk, not until she had examined the hundreds of papers.

Finally, her nerves stretched, Vann went to the scene of the small crime and physically pulled her friend away.

Triumphant in her successful burglary, Joan poked over the papers for days, attempting to make sense out of her husband's life. When she discovered a bill from Sakowitz, an expensive department store, for lizard shoes and matching handbag, Joan cried, "The son of a bitch never bought me anything!" She also discovered several checks for a hundred dollars each made out to cash, seven bills for surgery on women marked "Gratis," and a list of nine women with check marks after their names like movie ratings. Beside Ann Kurth were four checks. Somehow her deduction led her to believe that John Hill was having simultaneous affairs with either twelve or thirteen women. How would it be, she said to Vann, if she filed an alienation of affections suit against "Kurth et al."? It would be all over the newspapers, warned Vann. That's how it would be.

As the weeks passed and the year spun into late September, Joan turned occasionally serene; she spoke softly and greeted her friends philosophically. During these periods she professed that John was merely "having a fling." "He's just a country boy from Edcouch," she muttered, more to herself than to her friends, "and he was always kept tied down by his mother and the Church of Christ, and for the first time in his life he's cut loose. I'll give him a little rope."

Then a private detective whom Ash engaged delivered word that John had leased a bachelor apartment in the city's Post Oak area, a community favored by "swinging singles." This darkened Joan's attitude, for it indicated that the estrangement was growing more permanent. Quickly she drove to the apartment and parked outside, watching lithe young people come and go in their sport cars. At thirty-seven, she suddenly felt old and unwanted.

When Joan returned to the big house she found her husband's car parked in the driveway. Joyfully she ran inside, only to find John packing a suitcase with sheet music. He looked embarrassed, glancing at his wife and then mutely returning businesslike to his chore. Angered by his silence, Joan tried first to shame him, cataloging the moneys her father had spent to help finance his surgical training, the loans for cars and houses, the sums spent on Boot. "Send me a bill," he said, "I'll pay it back."

Joan checked her anger and humbled herself. She pleaded with John to return. What was the core of his discontent? Her horses? She would give them up. She would sell the farm. She would do anything he asked. They had a son; they had eleven years together. These were too precious to throw away on a dalliance like Ann Kurth.

The situation was more complex, answered John. He was unable to disentangle himself. Ann Kurth would not let him go, even if he wanted to leave her.

Joan stood at an upstairs window and watched her husband drive away. The one thing she had not done was talk to Ann Kurth herself. This is what civilized people do, she reasoned. They talk things out. Hurriedly she summoned Vann from across the street and revealed her last-ditch plan. How should she act? What should she say? What tone of voice should she use?

Vann disliked the idea. Surely the Kurth telephone was tapped, John being so adept at electronic equipment. Joan might say something rash and regret it later. "So let her tape me," said Joan. "You listen in on the extension for protection."

With Vann as reluctant eavesdropper, Joan dialed the woman who had taken away her husband. Later, Vann would recall the conversation:

"Mrs. Kurth?"

"Yes."

"This is Joan Robinson Hill."

At the other end, a moment of silence, then a warm response. "Oh, yes. My children are making noise and I'm going to change telephones. Just a minute."

From her listening post, Vann put her hand over the receiver and called out to Joan, "Watch out! She's moving to a phone with a bug on it. Be careful!"

Ann Kurth resumed the conversation in a tone of voice both polite and positive. She spoke with self-assurance, as if she were experienced in this sort of awkward encounter.

Immediately Joan blurted out that she was aware of the entire situation, and that her husband *wanted* to come home. But, she quoted him as saying, Ann Kurth would not allow it.

"On the contrary," said Ann sweetly, "I have *encouraged* John to go home, to talk it out with you, to see his son, to make some sort of decision. I don't like this hidden, secretive business, either. I know what tremendous amount of respect John has for you."

At this, Vann winced. She felt that John had no respect for his wife at all. That he, in fact, disliked her intensely.

Joan made a few mumbling remarks and hung up in confusion.

Vann felt the conversation was harmful, that Joan had been bested. "You're no match for this woman," she said. "She's cleverer than you."

And one more thing, cautioned Vann. "This is a dangerous game you're playing. All this snoop business. People have gotten hurt for a lot less."

Joan nodded, but she seemed not to hear the warning. "I love the son of a bitch," she said. "That's what hurts. I'd crawl on my hands and knees across Houston to get him back."

10

John Hill displayed none of the numbing grief that seized his wife during their chaotic autumn of 1968. Rather he seemed proud of the new woman on his arm, as if she were a suitable ornament for a man of his position. Speculation could suggest other reasons for his sudden plunge into the waters of adultery. His life was, by all accounts, an emotionally barren one, shaped by the severe religious ethic imposed by his mother. He was not comfortable in sexual relations with women. Indeed, he had told Joan that he was still a virgin at twenty-six, when they married. And he once remarked to her, in a confession that she repeated to a close friend, that he was unable to really enjoy sex unless it was "illegal or immoral." Joan had responded, "But that's not natural, John." He agreed, but insisted that such was his make-up. "Then you try to work it out," Joan told him, "and I'll stand by you."

And he was approaching forty, the time when a man can feel that his romantic capacities are diminishing. Paramount among his reasons must have been the feeling that for eleven years he had been a possession of both his wife and her father. John had grown to loathe Ash Robinson. He hated his wealth, his power, his control over

Joan. In response to all his frustrations, the surgeon broke out, with a highly desirable woman who would make most any man's head turn.

Perhaps because he was so inexperienced in infidelity, he behaved with a spectacular lack of caution during the period of estrangement. Before a man gets divorced, he normally keeps any new woman in his life secret, for fear of harsh alimony and property division. But John descended on public Houston with what could only be termed abandon. At a popular French restaurant, he made a point of calling out to Maxine Mesinger, gossip columnist for the Houston *Chronicle,* and introducing "my new friend, Ann Kurth." The columnist had heard of his separation from Joan, it having been a prominent topic of gossip in café society for weeks. But she was startled to see the doctor openly dining with Joan's replacement. "That fellow doesn't have any sense," she thought to herself.

The Heartbeats played for a charity gala called the Spanish Ball on October 12, 1968, and John arrived with Ann in an arresting black gown. He introduced her around as "my fiancée." The wives of his fellow band members, mostly doctors, clucked like duennas behind fans. Adultery is not unknown among members of the medical fraternity, but an unwritten rule seemed applicable here: do not bring your plaything to a charity ball.

A few days later John received a telephone call from Dr. Grady Hallman, the heart surgeon who was leader of the orchestra and who had been his friend since they mutually attended a high school band convocation in 1948. Awkwardly, Hallman said that John was being dropped from the Heartbeats.

Stunned, John asked for the reason. Hallman murmured something about his own wife Martha, a deeply religious woman and maternal force behind the group, having asked for the expulsion. And she had the support of other wives. At least until this mess is straightened up, counseled Hallman.

"There is a little hypocrisy going on here," argued John Hill. But he was then and there booted out of the band.

In his absence from the house on Kirby Drive, work nonetheless continued on the music room. Costs had escalated wildly. The original $10,000 estimate was spent in partial payment for contracting costs alone. By October 1968, John had written checks totaling more than $75,000. It must have been in his head that, no matter how the marriage to Joan turned out, he would somehow retain ownership of the house. Sometimes, in bed, late at night, he spent hours telling Ann Kurth how he would someday preside over elegant evenings of great music. He nursed the plan of inviting Joan Sutherland to sing in his home and sell tickets at $1,000 each to raise money for musical charities.

One of John's dreams was to own the most expensive piano built in the world, a Bösendorfer. Handmade in Austria, only a hundred of the instruments are built each year. With no contenders, it is the snobbiest piano in existence. Bill Knight, a salesman for a Houston piano company and a well-known musician himself, telephoned John Hill in late 1968 and revealed that his firm had obtained the Bösendorfer franchise in Houston. Immediately John went to the showroom and ordered an imperial Grand, a massive instrument ten feet long and listed in the catalogue at $15,000. An order was sent to the factory in Austria, delivery promised a few months hence.

In mid-November, Joan answered her front doorbell and was handed a divorce citation. Leaning against the foyer wall, she hastily scanned the paper, then clutched it to her body and progressed upstairs. Midway to her bedroom, she almost fainted. "I had to sit down and get ahold of myself," she told Vann Maxwell.

The allegations were hard and cold, particularly Paragraph IV:

". . . that during all of the time John Hill was living with the defendant (Joan Olive Hill), Plaintiff conducted himself with propriety and treated his wife with kindness and forbearance and has been guilty of no act bringing about or causing the hereinafter described acts, omissions, and commissions on the Defendant's part. But the Defendant, disregarding the solemnity of her marriage vows and obligations to treat Plaintiff with kindness and attention, prior to their separation, commenced a course of unkind, harsh and tyrannical conduct toward him which has continued until the time of their separation and beyond. That Defendant's conduct toward Plaintiff has been of such a nature as to, under the circumstances, render their further living together insupportable . . ."

Joan showed the document to her girl friends. "Can you believe it?" she said testily. "Who exactly commenced this course of 'unkind, harsh and tyrannical conduct' toward whom?"

Before the day was out Joan had telephoned many of her friends to read the humiliating paper. And each, Vann especially, encouraged her not to contest the divorce, nor to counter-file if her pride dictated. "I think you two are better off without one another," she counseled.

But Joan would not have it. She was thirty-seven years old, this would be her third divorce. Her ego and the terrible condition of rejection were involved here, but the overriding factor seemed to be that she still loved her philandering husband. She decided to play a game of stalling, promptly consulting her attorneys and sending John a registered letter stating that she would not consent to the divorce. This, she felt, would tie matters in legal snarls for years.

Ash Robinson had a more direct plan.

On December 9, a few days after his daughter was sued for divorce, he telephoned John Hill at the bachelor apartment, which Ash would later refer to continually as his "love nest."

John listened intently, his face darkening. When he hung up, he told Ann Kurth that something was wrong. He could not make full sense of what the old man was saying, but the implication was that if he ever wanted to see his son Boot again he must hurry to Ash's house.

"Has the kid fallen down the stairs or something?" asked Ann. But John was gone, out the door, tires squealing as he hurried to the house where he had married Joan.

Their conference must have been tense. Ash would later contend that his son-in-law was contrite, desperate for forgiveness, eager to reconcile with Joan. But John later would claim that he had been verbally bludgeoned into signing a most curious letter.

"The letter was one hundred per cent John Hill's idea," Ash would later say. "All I did was copy down his own words as he dictated them."

But the letter was certainly written in the old man's personal hand, on his distinctive stationery that bore his signature as its letterhead, and it contained language more suggestive of an avenging Victorian father than a contritious husband:

Mrs. Joan Hill:

I ask that you become reconciled with me and forgive my transgressions.

I want to come back home and be a good husband to you and a good father to Robert.

In the event of any additional separation between us, no matter what the cause or reason, I will deed you all of my interest in our home at 1561 Kirby Drive.

I will make all payments on same until it is completely paid for; I will pay all taxes and insurance on same until it is completely clear of all encumbrances; I will pay all upkeep on the same during this time also.

I will further give you $1,000 per month for your household and personal expenses. I will take a life insurance policy in sufficient amount to pay off all of the indebtedness on the house at 1561 Kirby Drive in case of my death.

I will place $7,000 to your account at once.

It is distinctly understood that it is not my idea or intention to influence any judicial action now pending or that might be instituted against you or by you.

John Robert Hill, M.D.
9 Dec 1968

Ash took the document, dismissed John Hill, and telephoned his daughter. "He's coming home," said Ash, "if you still want him."

Several things must have been on John's mind when he signed the letter, a document of potential financial destruction, a promise to pay hundreds of thousands of dollars. Perhaps he thought it best to humor Ash Robinson and sign the paper, feeling that it was worthless and not binding in a lawsuit. Or he could have realized that if he did not return to Joan he would never see the completion of the music room, for Ash would demand of his daughter that she ban John Hill from the hearth. Or perhaps he had wearied of his liaison with Ann Kurth, for she was placing extraordinary demands of her own.

Hardly had John begun appearing with Ann in public than he received several anonymous telephone calls suggesting that he had selected an expensive adornment. The office manager, Frances Johnston, would later state that the arrival of Ann Kurth in her employer's life "changed things drastically; in fact, his practice went to hell."

On one occasion after they began living together, Ann appeared at Mrs. Johnston's desk and asked to see John Hill's income tax records. "You ask him for those yourself," said Mrs. Johnston, who, unbeknownst to Ann, was a close friend of Joan's and loyal to her. Much of Joan's inside information about her husband's activities came from Mrs. Johnston.

Turmoil setttled over Dr. Hill's office when Ann began paying regular visits and asking questions about intimate financial details. When she demanded that Mrs. Johnston give her daily copies of the surgeon's operating schedule, and his list of accounts due plus anticipated revenue from surgery, the office manager refused—hotly. Then Mrs. Johnston went to Dr. Hill and said, "Is she running this office or am I?" And in a telephone conversation with Joan, Mrs. Johnston reported, "He's started disappearing on us for hours at a time. Nobody knows where he is. He won't even answer his beeper. I'm worried about him, the patients, and his professional reputation."

When he twice failed to show up at a major hospital for scheduled surgery, a head nurse reamed him out. Operating room time is at a premium, she said, and if he could not keep his schedule straight, then she could not give him precious space.

One close friend, a nurse herself and also the wife of a radiologist, went to the Hill office with a badly cut foot— she had dropped a martini glass and stepped on it—and she endured a painful four-hour wait while his staff telephoned around the city trying to find him.

"Old John," drawled a veteran cardiologist, "has a tiger by the tail, and he can't let go. That woman's turnin' him every way but loose."

After he signed the Ash Robinson letter of repentance, John drove the few blocks up Kirby to the great house where Joan, already alerted by her father, was waiting. There was one last obstacle to a full reconciliation, he said: the matter of his clothes and personal belongings. They were at Ann Kurth's home and he was afraid to go and pick them up.

"Afraid?" said Joan. "Why?"

"The lady has a temper," said John.

Then Joan would engage a protective posse to escort

her husband into enemy territory. She telephoned Clyde Wilson, a colorful private detective and friend of the family. Gruff, blustering, a cigar stump ever growing in his mouth, Wilson was a character from the John Ford stock company. Indeed the only films he ever watched were John Wayne movies. He once was engaged to protect a string of laundries which had been plagued by burglars. Wilson's novel and very Texan solution was to hire an unspecified number of off-duty Houston policemen. They were to lay in wait at the laundries with instructions to shoot unlawful intruders. Coincidentally, he passed word through the Houston underground that, should anyone attempt to rob one of the laundries, that person would be playing a form of Russian roulette. There might, or there might not, be a hired hand with a drawn and loaded gun waiting behind the washtubs. The wave of burglaries slowed dramatically.

Wilson agreed to accompany John Hill to Ann Kurth's home. But once there, the doctor insisted on waiting in the car while the detective rang the doorbell. Unaware of what had taken place between her lover and his father-in-law, Ann greeted Clyde Wilson politely. But when she saw John sitting in the car outside—and when Wilson explained his mission—her demeanor became frosty. She was confused. What the hell was going on? She would not let Wilson have anything unless John Hill himself came into the house and explained matters.

Reluctantly, Hill got out of the car and entered the house where the night before he had held Ann Kurth in his arms. Now he was mute and sullen. The two men gathered up suits, shirts, ties, underwear. Wilson found two guns—a .45 and a .38—under the mattress where Ann and John slept. He took these as well. Beside the bed was a tape recorder with a voice-activating device to record all calls. John collected this and a few cassettes containing calls from Ash and Joan.

The two men left hurriedly as Ann sat on a sofa, both bewildered and furious, her eyes glowing like freshly ignited charcoal on a barbecue grill.

That night, with two other couples, John and Joan Hill held a reconciliation party at Patti's, a new and popular downtown supper club. Owned by a rich divorcee and frustrated café singer named Patti Gordon who, in classic

Houston tradition, built her own place in order to find an outlet for her talents, the restaurant had the atmosphere of a living room, where guests sat on sofas and overstuffed chairs, with dim lighting and attentive black waiters drifting about. During the estrangement Joan had gone to Patti's often, sometimes alone.

Although they were but casual friends, she often confided to Patti intimate details of her broken marriage. "It's that god damned music room," she said. "He doesn't care about me or our son or anybody else. Only that god damned music room. I wish we had never started building it."

With Christmas lights twinkling softly and seasonal greenery all about, John Hill and his wife lifted champagne glasses and toasted one another. Joan was radiant and tender, happy to have her husband back and determined to make the rapprochement permanent.

But Patti Gordon, watching the toast from the bar, noticed a lack of warmth in John Hill's manner. "I don't think he's gotten used to the reconciliation," said Patti to the bartender.

"That's a *reconciliation?*" said the bartender, his eyebrows arching. "It looks more like a last supper. Look at the way he's watching her. He hasn't smiled all evening."

Late that night the telephone rang beside Ann Kurth's bed, a private telephone put in by John Hill. He was the only one who knew the number. Ann let it ring several times, staring at the object with anger, before she answered.

"Hi, baby." It was John.

Ann exploded. "I have no idea what you think you're doing," she shouted, "but you have really screwed up my life royally. I think you've flipped out. Are you the same man who told me you loved me the past three months? For God's sake, John, what is going on?"

John spoke as if nothing had happened. "I'm sorry about the way I handled that," he said. "There was no other way."

"Well, I'm in shock, I can tell you that."

"Let's have lunch tomorrow. I'll explain everything."

Two days before Christmas, 1968, John Hill withdrew his divorce action against Joan Robinson Hill. In celebration, she planned a festive holiday dinner and a party to which their friends would come and see the couple together again. "I think it's going to work out," Joan told Vann Maxwell. "I'm keeping my fingers crossed." She called a baker and ordered a cake in the shape of a grand piano.

On Christmas morning John Hill spent an hour with his wife and son, then excused himself to "make rounds" at the hospital. Instead, he secretly drove out the Katy Highway west of town to a motel where for a week he had been enjoying a separate holiday with Ann Kurth. Over and over he reassured her that his marriage to Joan was still in jeopardy; working it out would simply take more time and thought.

One prank of John's seemed amusing at the time to Ann. When they first drove into the driveway of the motel, John mentioned that he would have to sign the registration book under an assumed name. But the personalized license plates on his Cadillac bore his initials, "JRH." To match them, John invented a curious signature for the desk clerk. He signed boldly, "Mr. and Mrs. J. R. Hyde."

"Dr. Hill and Mr. Hyde," laughed his mistress. "That's really too much."

11

Joan embarked on a self-improvement program to keep her husband from straying again. Desperately she tried to give up smoking, it being one of John's principal complaints against her. Three visits with a hypnotist did her no good. She purchased pacifiers, medication that promised to curtail her craving—nothing worked. Disgusted at her dependence, she took to throwing her package of cigarettes angrily into the kitchen sink and running water on them. There they would sit, waterlogged and crumbly, until an hour had passed and Joan had to put them into the oven to dry and make them smokable again. She compromised by trying to quit daily at least an hour before John normally came home from work, brushing her teeth, gargling with mouthwash, spraying with mint, chewing breath fresheners. Vann Maxwell watched her sit nervously one late afternoon, listening for the sound of John's car, thinking she heard it, running upstairs to the bathroom for a last-minute gargle, then realizing it was not his car, lighting up a cigarette to help her renewed wait, and repeating the process over and over again. Religiously she counted her calories to keep her weight near a hundred and ten. At a post-Christmas party, the hostess exclaimed over Joan's svelte figure and asked what kind of diet she was on. "Nerves, honey," said Joan truthfully.

At the same party was a young woman named Ann Moore, who was the wife of John Hill's junior partner. John had eyed the up-and-coming Dr. Jim Moore in the medical training program and had hired him, just as Nathan Roth had done half a decade earlier. Ann Moore labored successfully to make herself one of the principal scenic attractions of Houston. Compared to her, Ann Kurth was dowdy. Mrs. Moore accomplished complex hairdos, theatrically long false eyelashes, mini-skirts, and enough jewels on her fingers, wrists, throat, and ear lobes to make conversation difficult under bright lights, which she avoided. All of which she set on display in a red Cadillac convertible. Next to her husband's partner's wife, said Joan, "I feel like Grandma Moses' grandma."

Nonetheless, Joan asked her to lunch and midway through an empty remark about a charity project suddenly blurted, "Help me fix myself up, Ann. Give me some beauty tips." Ann nodded, beginning tactfully. It happened that she had spoken with John Hill during his estrangement from Joan, and he had remarked that Joan's "lack of femininity" turned him away from her. "There's not one feminine thing about my wife," he complained.

"So why not change your image?" suggested Ann Moore to her despairing girl friend. "Start by raising those hemlines from below your knee. And that pony tail suited you when you were sixteen, but now women are wearing their hair long and straight." Joan considered the suggestions. "All right, I'll raise my hems," she said, "but I've lived with this pony tail for thirty-eight years and I've had good luck with it." Then she studied Ann Moore's carefully made-up face. Finally, hesitantly, she asked, "How the hell do you put on those god damn false eyelashes?" Smiling, teacher began instructions.

John stretched himself very thin in the opening weeks of 1969, trying to keep his wife happy and free of suspicion —and sustaining a demanding mistress as well. Ann Kurth rode her tormented lover hard, demanding a decision. "Is it me or her?" she pressed. "Make up your mind, Doctor, because I haven't got the time to wait." She was not willing to erect convent walls around herself and wait for a very much married surgeon to pay house calls. "I'm going to go ahead and live my life," she would remember telling John, "and you lead yours—whichever one you find yourself in at the moment. And whenever you get yourself straightened out, then we'll talk."

On February 14, 1969, Valentine's Day, John went to Ann's home for dinner, bearing an enormous box of candy and smaller gifts for each of her three sons. He had bought his own wife nothing. After slices of heart-shaped cake, John was happy and expansive. "This is the way I've always wanted it to be," he told Ann. "I just love my new little family."

The Bösendorfer piano was delivered and installed in the music room. When John encountered it the first time, his attitude was reverential, like a pilgrim approaching the Vatican. He touched it tremblingly, with wonder. The instrument, a magnificent ten feet long, was made from wood so fine and rubbed so lovingly that it gleamed with dignity. "André Previn once encountered a Bösendorfer in Chicago," said piano salesman Bill Knight, "and he locked himself in the room and he played it for four hours."

Joan already owned a Yamaha grand, and the two pianos were now arranged next to one another, for duets. The two men, surgeon and salesman, sat down and played for an hour. "It was some strange sonata," said Bill Knight later. "It sounded like marbles rolling down a staircase, but John knew it well, and he seemed to take pride in playing it better than I."

The music room was nearly completed, and it was, in a word, unbelievable. To enter was to gasp! The size of a hotel ballroom with a double-height ceiling, the opulent color scheme was royal gold and white. On the walls were panels of satin brocade; above, in dominance, chandeliers dangled drops of Baccarat crystal. The fireplace was ornately carved marble from a Louisiana plantation house, and on it were gilded candelabra and an antique clock. The floors were highly polished parquet, bare at one end, where the pianos were placed, and at the other, covered with a thick Chinese carpet, where people could sit on French provincial settees and hear the music. Behind every gold panel, all of which opened by secret silent touch, were intricately arranged shelves—space for two thousand record albums, hundreds of music books, John's collection of musical instruments. The walls contained *four miles* of wiring and 108 speakers. The sound system cost more than $20,000—one of the most expensive privately owned installations in America. A movie screen slid down from the ceiling at the push of a button, and in one of the hidden panels was John's collection of film comedies. He owned several starring W. C. Fields.

When Bill Knight left, John walked around his room, thrilling at what he had wrought from a junk room above a garage. Now it could easily be taken as part of a castle. A king could dine here. A court ballet could be performed here. The great voices could sing here, embraced by the most perfect acoustics man was capable of creating. And John would accompany them on the world's most expensive piano. It would surely happen, he vowed. The room would become famous in the world of people whose souls were stirred by great music. That it had already cost more than $100,000—more than the cost of the entire original house—was irrelevant.

At that moment, Joan walked abruptly in with two women house guests and knelt sarcastically before the fireplace. She crossed herself, as if before an altar. "This is God's room," she said derisively to her friends. John did not find the remark amusing.

It was the second week of March 1969. A series of events were about to convulse the household.

Chatsworth Farm had never approached what Joan intended. No world champion horses were foaled there, nothing much had been accomplished save giving a bunch of little rich girls riding lessons and boarding their ponies. There was no lack of youngsters, Joan Robinson Hill remaining a powerful lure for socially ambitious mothers.

Part of the trouble lay with Ash. One good trainer worked there for a few years, but he found it difficult to get along with the old man. Every time money was needed to purchase a new piece of equipment, it meant prying the funds out of Ash. "It's too much hassle," said the trainer in explanation to Joan, on one of the numerous times he quit, only to be persuaded back by the mistress of Chatsworth. Finally, in 1967, he left for good, angry at a list of broken promises from Ash. And the stables had been without a trainer or manager since his departure. Joan filled in as best she could, hurrying out to the farm at least two or three times a week, but when the Ann Kurth episode commanded her attention, she had little time for horseflesh.

Pa was now threatening to sell the place altogether, for it was not paying its way through boarding and riding lessons. Often he told Joan that he would not underwrite a major program of breeding and training until the ledger was written in black ink. Joan was flustered. Desperately she wanted to hold onto Chatsworth, for it remained a dream as cherished as John's music room. She knew that the potential was there, and through Chatsworth she might leave a mark on her world.

Thus she came up with the idea of hiring an old friend, Diane Settegast, to run the stables, more of a stopgap than anything else. Earthy, rough-talking, most comfortable in jeans long before they became high fashion, Diane was a smoldering Dallas woman around thirty who was proud to reveal that her breasts had been amplified by John Hill's silicone implants. Her companion and roommate was an older woman in her mid-forties named Eunice Woolen. Both were frequent guests at the Hill home.

Diane Settegast knew little of breeding and training show horses, but she could teach the little brats how to keep from falling off their ponies. And, in time, Joan would figure out something else. Anything to keep Ash from selling Chatsworth.

On March 9, 1969, Diane and Eunice arrived at the Hill mansion to spend a day or two and discuss the job proposal. Hardly were their bags out of the car and into the foyer before their hostess greeted them with anger in her eyes. She had just hung up the telephone to conclude a quarrel with John. "The son of a bitch stayed out all night again," she said in greeting. "He promised to take Boot to the car races at the Astrodome, and now he says he can't make it, so I've got to go. . . ."

The visitors were surprised. They had heard of the couple's spectacular estrangement and breakup—gossip had traveled quickly to Dallas where they lived. But now they were under the impression that John and Joan were happily together again.

"And Pa's gone off somewhere, too," continued Joan.

Ash had promised to be present when Diane Settegast arrived, but he had flown instead to Florida on oil business. It seemed that little was going well for Joan at this moment of her life. But soon something struck her as funny, and she was her normal self, warm, laughing heartily, anxious to gossip and show off her house.

"Have you seen our own little Versailles?" asked Joan as she showed her old friends around the house. She led them up the grand staircase, across a theaterlike foyer, and through double-sized doors into the great room. "Jesus God in Heaven," whispered Eunice. Diane stood transfixed, staring at the convocation of gold, white satin, and crystal.

What did it finally cost? Diane wanted to know.

"John's very secretive about just how much," answered Joan. But she knew that the piano alone cost more than the original estimate for the whole room. "And the son of a bitch complains when I need two hundred dollars to pay some groom at the stables."

John Hill came home from hospital rounds shortly after sundown and greeted the two Dallas women warmly. He did not let on there was new tension in his household. To welcome the guests, he suggested dinner at a restaurant called The Stables, one of the city's better steak houses. There the three women and the surgeon ate heartily, with the conversation chiefly turned to Chatsworth and what Joan hoped Diane could accomplish there.

Diane asked if Joan knew what Ash Robinson was planning to offer as salary, and Joan said she did not—only that there was a fixer-upper house available on the premises rent free, and that she would receive a commission on the riding lessons she gave.

Suddenly, in the middle of the conversation, John Hill received a "beep" on his Page Boy apparatus. He went to the telephone to call his service and when he returned he apologized. "I'll be gone to the hospital for a few minutes," he said, "and when I get home we'll talk some more and have some pastries." Diane made a gesture of no thanks, pointing to the heavy meal she had just consumed. "Maybe we'll all be hungry later," said John.

Past eleven on this Sunday evening, John returned from his announced destination—Hermann Hospital—and he was in an ebullient mood. He spoke of how much he had valued the friendships of Diane and Eunice for so many years. Diane warmed to the flattery. She had always liked "ole John," particularly after he performed the breast augmentation procedure on her for a fee of next to nothing. The silicone implantation was so successful that Diane not only enjoyed telling about her new dimensions, she occasionally—if the party was festive enough—even showed them off.

At one such occasion in the Hill home a few months earlier, Diane had unknowingly precipitated a saddening quarrel between John and Joan. During one of John's musicales, Joan and Diane were sitting together, along with Vann Maxwell, and the women were bored by the chamber music being performed on the Hills' patio. The group was playing beside the pool, and the audience of thirty or forty was on rented folding chairs, giving the event the air of a civic outdoor concert. When Joan caught first herself, then the other girls nodding off, she whispered, "Let's go in the kitchen during the next intermission."

There, all the escapees from Bach poured themselves drinks, and Diane Settegast waltzed off to find some mischief, as was her wont. To mark her spectacular new bosom proportions, a friend had given Diane a set of strip-tease tassels, and now seemed a good time to display them. She unbottoned her blouse and put them on her nipples. While the chamber group played, Diane located a picture window through which only the flute player could see. She stood behind the window and, to the tempo of a seventeenth-century composition, performed a slow strip, flashing her blouse open and shut, the effect so hilarious—and provocative—that the musician could not continue. John Hill found the episode amusing, perhaps because the breasts that he had enlarged were the ones causing all the commotion. Joan laughed so hard that she literally fell down on the kitchen floor. A week later, through the devices of an actor friend, Joan borrowed a set of burlesque pasties herself, and one midnight when her husband returned "from rounds," she put New Orleans jazz on the stereo and began a dance that surpassed Diane's in sexual provocation. Joan was proud of her figure, and with her careful dieting—and pursuit of yoga—she looked trim and sexy. "No need to fix these up, is there, honey?" she laughed, cupping her breasts.

John Hill rose, shut off the music, and looked at his wife with ice. "That's shameful," he said.

"It wasn't shameful when Diane did it. You laughed your god damn head off."

"Diane isn't my wife."

Diane knew nothing of this incident, nor did Eunice, and on the late Sunday night as they sat with Joan in the great house's richly paneled den, a fire warming the chilly March night, its flames flickering across the glass of the framed prints of horses, it would seem that the doctor and his wife were somehow holding their crazy marriage together. Joan had spoken gently of him and dismissed his spree with Ann Kurth as "a dumb thing he did, but it's over with." Toward midnight John announced cheerily, "Now let's have those pastries." Eunice Woolen, being the kind of helpful woman who helps hostesses clear dinner tables without being asked, rose to help John with the serving. But he shook his head and gestured for her to keep her seat by the fire. "This is my treat," he said. "You girls keep on talking."

Presently John appeared with a silver tray on which there were four small china plates, each containing an individual pastry. But John did not permit the ladies to choose their preferred treat. As if he were a waiter who had previously taken an order, he handed each of them a pastry. Eunice received a strawberry tart, Diane a chocolate éclair, John the cream puff, and Joan also a chocolate éclair. During the eating, Joan remarked that her husband's cream puff was the most alluring of the treats. "But you like chocolate," said John. "That's why I served you the éclair."

During the snack, John received another page on his beeper. He went to the telephone and came back to the den to report that he had to leave again, on an emergency call. His mission this time was to sew up the lip of some young attorney. Who? asked Joan. He did not know, said John, but the task should not take more that a few minutes. But he left and he did not return the rest of the night. At breakfast the next morning, Joan was furious. She telephoned Vann Maxwell and said, "He's running around again. I think we've both had it." But at midmorning John called, all apologies. The case of the attorney's lip had been a complicated one; he had worked until almost dawn, then he fell asleep in the surgeons' lounge because he had a face-lift scheduled at 7 A.M.

On Tuesday night the three women—Joan, Diane, and Eunice—dined at a barbecue restaurant while the doctor supposedly worked at his office, catching up on patient records. When they returned to the mansion at ten-thirty, John was in his music room, the volume from the stereo *fortissimo*. Smiling, he rose and announced he had another surprise. Just sit down here and wait.

Presently he returned with a tray of pastries, repeating his precise ritual of handing each woman her seemingly preselected plate. Again Joan received a chocolate éclair. On this occasion Joan commenced eating her treat, and after one bite glanced covetingly at what John was eating —a cream puff. "Let's trade, John," she suggested. "Cream puffs are my favorite."

John shook his head negatively. "They're my favorite too," he said. "Besides, I've already eaten half of mine."

The week went from bad to worse. On Wednesday, John and Joan went to a party at the home of a bachelor doctor, and she returned home alone. Once again he had received one of those emergency calls "from the hospital." Joan waited until midnight, then she began dialing around trying to locate her husband, but the Diagnostic Hospital —his destination—could not locate him, nor was he at his office, nor did he answer his emergency number. Angry, she went to bed alone.

The next day Joan rose early, packed Boot off to school, and drove to Chatsworth where she rode for two hours, pushing her horse and herself. A groom noted that she whipped her mount with a crop because he did not perform adequately. It was not like Joan to strike her horse in anger. In fact, the groom had never seen her do it before.

When she returned home, Effie Green, the new maid, an ancient black woman of the Old South, said that Dr. Hill had telephoned. He would definitely be home for dinner. Joan brightened immediately. Her mood swung quickly from anger to happiness. She hurried about the house, dispatching orders to the maid to prepare broiled steak and sweet potato pie, happily informing Diane and Eunice that dinner would be at 7 P.M., *en famille*. At five Joan drove quickly to her hairdresser for a comb-out. Then she put on a new hostess gown she had purchased a few weeks earlier in a fit of anger over John's gifts to Ann Kurth. Both of her house guests noted how desperately she wanted the evening to work. They planned to withdraw to their room as soon as dinner was over, to leave the warring couple alone.

At 8 P.M., when dinner was an hour late, and cold, Joan sadly asked her guests and her son to take their places. They began to eat without John Hill, who had not even telephoned with an apology. Suddenly he drove into the driveway and appeared, full of apologies, a pastry box in his hand. He was late because he had stopped to purchase the treats.

"I'm getting sick and tired of pastries," snapped Joan. "We've been waiting for you more than an hour."

Sorry, said John. There had been another last-minute emergency at his office. No time to call and explain. He would skip dinner anyway because in a few minutes a friend was coming to play duets in the music room. Joan's mouth tightened. She went to bed alone again.

On Friday night of this important week, the Hills were scheduled to attend Houston's annual wild game dinner, a charity affair at which the Heartbeats would play after a meal of venison, boar, even bear shot by local hunters who had been to Alaska. Joan always had fun at this masculine and rowdy party; she had attended for years. The year before she had danced every number with the most attractive men in the hall and had begged the band to keep playing after quitting time at midnight.

In the late afternoon, at a shopping center near her home, Joan encountered Mrs. Dotty Oates, wife of a doctor named Jim Oates who was a member of John's music set and his occasional partner in piano duets. She had not seen her friend in several weeks, and now she exclaimed over how well Joan looked.

"Honey, you look sensational!" said Mrs. Oates. She was a nurse, and she always talked both saltily and with authority, as if ordering a patient to take a pill. "You've lost weight in the butt, but not in your boobs. How the hell do you do it?"

Just trying to keep a wandering husband on the leash, said Joan lightly.

"The way you look," said Mrs. Oates, "any man oughta stay at home permanently." As Joan drove off, her friend noted once again that she looked better than she had looked in months. Within a few days this recollection would loom significantly.

The wild game dinner was not the occasion that Joan

had hoped it would be. She and John arrived late and took seats at a table occupied by Frances Johnston, who had quit as office manager for the doctor, her chief reason being the Ann Kurth commotion. Joan drank lightly, taking but a few sips of scotch and soda from Frances' glass. This, too, would be remembered before another week passed. Joan picked at her plate, nothing more than a few bites of venison. Dieting, she explained. While the Heartbeats played, Frances noted that Joan watched her husband intently, and a wide range of emotions played across her face. At one moment she seemed to adore him. Then a wave of hostility crossed her eyes. But it went away quickly, replaced by tenderness, a memory, perhaps, of a happier moment.

When the orchestra finished its concert, John packed up his tuba, returned to the table, and announced that he and his wife had to leave. He had rounds to make. One of the doctors present in the group glanced at his watch. It was almost ten. Most patients would be asleep. But the doctor said nothing.

Joan started to protest. The evening was just beginning. A rock band would be taking over, and there would be dancing until past midnight. She wanted very much to stay.

"We can't stay," said John firmly.

"Just for a few minutes, honey?" Joan pleaded.

"I've got to go to the hospital, you know that," said John.

Frances Johnston intruded tactfully. "Why don't you stay with us, Joan?" she suggested. "We'll drive you home."

Joan looked at her husband; their eyes locked briefly. Then she shook her head and whispered in Frances' ear, "I'd better do what he wants. I'm still trying to make it work."

On the way home Joan asked her husband if he would be late. He did not know. It depended upon the condition of his patients. Perhaps he would, perhaps he would not. Then, she said, she would wait up for him. They could have a nightcap in the music room and listen to records.

"Don't do that," said John. "I'll probably be late."

At that moment the Cadillac pulled into the driveway of the great house. "Another all-nighter, maybe?" said Joan hotly.

"What do you mean by that?" said John.

"Twice this week you've been out all night," she said.

"If you stay out tonight, then don't bother to come home."

Joan got out of the car angrily. As her husband threw his car into reverse and backed out of the driveway she called after him. She screamed, loud enough for the neighbors to hear, "You've blown it, John! You've just lost your wife, your son, and your god damn music room."

Hot tears falling on her cheeks, she ran into the house.

12

The next day, Saturday, Joan did not rise until almost four in the afternoon. Twice during the day Eunice Woolen grew concerned over her friend sleeping so late, it not being her nature. Normally Joan was up by seven to pack Boot off to school and to attend to her busy schedule. Joan's appointment book was always heavily filled with meetings, parties, and horse activities.

Around noon Eunice opened Joan's door quietly and peeked in. She appeared to be sleeping deeply, curled up and buried under a wad of blankets in the king-sized bed. Around 2:30 P.M., Eunice asked John Hill if there was reason for alarm. Was Joan feeling unwell? Not that he knew, was the answer. The night before, when he returned home from late hospital rounds, Joan had seemed upset over something. They had disagreed over some minor matter at the wild game dinner, and she encountered difficulty in going to sleep. So he gave her a tranquilizer. It was perfectly all right for her to sleep this long.

"When are you girls leaving, by the way?" asked John pointedly.

"As soon as Ash gets back from Florida and we have our talk about the job at the farm," answered Diane.

The two house guests were more than ready to take their leave. The week had been unpleasant, with Joan snappish and cross, John disappearing, both glaring at one another and stalking about the house in elaborate silence and avoidance. "The funny thing," Diane mentioned to Eunice, "is that John used to like to have me stay here. He always seemed anxious for me to be here a few days and keep Joan company because he was so busy with his practice and his music. But this week he's done his damnedest to make me feel totally unwelcome."

When Joan finally rose and groggily descended the staircase, she was embarrassed at having spent the day in bed. The telephone was ringing and she answered it. A friend wanted to remind her of a meeting set for the next Wednesday, the Opera Guild fund drive. "I just did the craziest thing," said Joan. "I slept all day and left two house guests to fend for themselves."

She found Diane and Eunice in the kitchen and apologized for her rudeness. "John gave me some pill last night and it really knocked me out," she said. And, by the way, where was her husband? Diane pointed up, toward the second floor's music room. Joan nodded wearily. If her husband was not out "making rounds," then he was in his music room. His life seemed distilled to these two alternatives. She went in search of him; John had promised to take Boot to the barber for a long-overdue haircut.

During her long sleep a score of telephone messages had stacked up and now, having sent her husband and son to the city's most prominent men's hair stylist, she settled into a chair in the den and began answering them. In the next week she had five meetings scheduled for various charity affairs, and she was making plans to ride in a horse show at Lexington, Kentucky, later in the month. But first she called her mother down the street, who reported that Pa was returning from Florida the next morning and would be able to talk terms with Diane Settegast about the farm position.

Busy as she was with her telephone calls, Joan did not note the passage of time. But when her son returned with his new haircut well past 7 P.M., Joan recognized that he had been gone for more than two hours. Why, she asked the little boy, did it take so long? Boot squirmed uneasily; clearly he did not want to answer. Her curiosity whetted, Joan wheedled an answer out of the child. "Daddy made me promise not to tell," insisted the little boy. "It's just between us," pressed his mother, making a conspiratorial game.

With reluctance, Boot spilled the beans. After his haircut, he had gone with his father to the apartment where John lived during the separation from Joan. "Daddy had to pick up some music," the child murmured.

Joan kissed her son and sent him off to watch television. As soon as he was out of the room, she swore. "God damn!" she cursed, her cry summoning the house guests.

Now she *knew* what she had long suspected. John still possessed the "love nest" and had the gall to take his own kid there. He was probably still supporting Ann Kurth, or some other dame, and the letter of repentance he had signed was not worth blowing her nose on. Patterns of John's recent behavior began to make sense, the absences, the guilty looks. At that moment Joan hated John Hill and his lies. When Pa returned on the morrow she would throw the mess into his lap. He would tell her what to do. He was the only man she could trust.

Joan hurried to the telephone and called Vann Maxwell, her best friend. "Please come over here. I *have* to talk to somebody. Everything's falling apart. I slept all day and I'm nervous and tired and irritable."

Her friend sounded so distraught that Vann canceled other plans and hurried to the Hill house. Joan greeted her and announced that everybody was going to play bridge in the music room. Preparing double-sized highballs for her guests—there being no bar in the music room—she led her friends upstairs in a procession. John was already in the chamber, playing records and walking about checking the 108 speakers buried in the walls.

The four women—Joan, Vann, Diane, and Eunice—began a bridge game at one end of the room, while forty feet away, leaning against the piano, John listened to his music, his head raised almost reverently. The volumn was so high that the situation became lunatic. Diane and Eunice found themselves shouting out their bridge bids.

Clearly Joan had no interest in the game. She was playing another more intense one. She kept beginning sentences that spoke ill of John, then stopping them before completion because she had whetted her husband's curiosity and he had drifted nearer the table to overhear. "I'm going to the lawyer on Monday," she finally said in a voice loud enough to be heard, even over the music. "It's just about over between us."

Uncomfortable in the middle of the combat zone, Vann asked Joan to lower her voice. "He can hear you," she hissed. "Can't we discuss this later?"

"I want him to," shot back Joan.

"Then I'm leaving," said Vann.

Joan pleaded with Vann to stay and complete the bridge game. Vann laid down a condition. "Only if you stop talking about John that way," she said. "He's right here, in this room. At least write notes if you have to say something."

Joan agreed. She began scribbling furious notes to Vann, shoving them across the bridge table, doing it with elaborate strokes so that her husband would see her method of communication. In the notes she told of Boot's revelation about the bachelor apartment, of John's inattention and misbehavior in general.

Vann felt uneasy. The scene was theatrical and painful. She wanted to leave and let her friends argue their troubles out in private. Suddenly John put a slow, romantic, melancholy ballad on the record player. Joan looked up quickly, at the music, at her husband. Perhaps it was a song from their courting days. Tears came to her eyes.

The tension impossible, Vann rose and went to the powder room. In her absence, John came over to the bridge table and hovered behind his wife's chair. Diane broke the tension by suggesting that the couple dance.

When Vann returned she beheld, to her surprise, John and Joan Hill in one another's arms, moving slowly and romantically across the gleaming parquet floor. Joan's head was buried in her husband's shoulder. Touched by the abrupt turn in the evening's weird events, Vann slipped out of the room and left the house. Later she would learn that Joan ran after her, distraught, standing in the driveway and shouting for her friend to return.

Ash Robinson flew into Houston at breakfast time on Sunday morning and he telephoned Joan, as was his custom, to request that she pick him up at the airport. Diane Settegast answered the call and reported that his daughter was still asleep, feeling a little "flu-y." No problem, said Ash. He would take a cab.

As Ash was progressing into the city, his daughter rose and went downstairs in an old bathrobe. Her face was pale and her stomach a trifle upset. But she was cheerful and happy, an air of contentment wrapped about her. She took coffee and revealed to her house guests what had happened the night before.

After their dance, John had led her upstairs, to their bedroom. As Diane and Eunice walked past toward their guest room, Joan had called out to say good night. Eunice had noticed through the open door that John was standing beside his wife's bed. "Joan's feeling lousy," he said. "I think she needs a shot."

"Joan doesn't need a shot," Eunice said quietly. "She needs you." John Hill nodded, as if to agree, and he shut the door.

Now, sipping her coffee and playing with a piece of toast, Joan was anxious to tell of what went on behind the closed door. "He made me very happy," she told her friends. "He told me things I've never heard from the man before in our whole married life. I think it's going to be all right between us from now on."

Listening, Diane noted that Joan was "bubbling over with happiness."

Then a wave of nausea swept over Joan. Her face blanched. She hurried to the bathroom. When she returned, she was weak. "Well, I just tossed my breakfast," she said. "I think I'd better go back to bed."

Joan spent most of Sunday in bed. John checked on his wife several times, and shortly after noon announced to the house guests that he was going to the drugstore to purchase medication "to give her a shot." He asked that Diane Settegast fix Joan a Coca-Cola in his absence. Joan drank part of the cola and promptly vomited.

In the late afternoon Joan went to the downstairs den and curled up with a blanket around her. She said she was very cold and queasy. Her husband felt her forehead and said she seemed to be all right, that it was probably a virus. He felt a little queasy himself, he said. Perhaps it was something they had mutually eaten. Quickly Joan checked back on her food intake for the previous days. The only unusual food was at the wild game dinner, and she had taken but a few bites. Perhaps, she said, whatever she ate did not agree with her.

Several times during the day the telephone rang, and John usually hurried to answer before one of the house guests did. Twice Diane Settegast answered the telephone and on the other end of the line was a woman who spoke in a curious voice. "It sounded very 'put on' and 'made up,'" said Diane later. "It was some strange-sounding woman who insisted on speaking to 'the doctor.'"

Just before 6 P.M. a musician named Ralph Liese appeared at the house to be warmly welcomed by John. Liese, an executive of the Houston Symphony and a veteran musician in the city, was chairman of a brass quintet that played at schools in the city for young audiences. John Hill played tuba with the group and was its star attraction. Not only did the youngsters enjoy the tuba, Hill was exceptionally good at talking to the students, explaining his instrument and answering their questions. On Tuesday, two days hence, the quintet was to play a morning concert at the Montrose Elementary School, where John was scheduled to perform a tuba solo, a debut, in fact, for the piece. The two men went into the music room, and for an hour John played his solo, "Exhibition for Brass." Liese complimented him on how well he played, and John warmed. He had been practicing all week.

When the session was over Liese inquired about Joan, for he had noted her absence. "Joan's feeling a little urpy," said John. "I think she's lying down." He invited his friend out for Mexican dinner, after which they could return to the house and play more music.

"No, thanks," said Liese. "As long as you know your solo so well, there's no need for me to hang around."

John, his son, and the two women house guests went out for dinner and on their way home stopped at a quick food restaurant to purchase a carton of orange juice for the ailing Joan.

Conversation was strained in the group, for Diane had spent an unpleasant half hour with Ash Robinson earlier in the day. He had offered her only two hundred dollars a month salary to run Chatsworth Farm, plus a small percentage from riding lessons. Diane protested that the offer was ridiculously low, but Ash had countered by saying that Joan's farm was a huge money loser and nothing but an indulgence for her anyway. "Well, there's no way anybody could live on that," said Diane. The discussion terminated unpleasantly, and the two women made immediate plans to leave for Dallas the next morning.

When they returned to the big house, John delivered the orange juice to Joan, stood by her bed while she drank it, then excused himself to go visit a musician. He did not return until past midnight, and in his absence Joan threw up several more times.

On Monday morning, March 17, Diane and Eunice rose early, packed, and prepared to leave, wanting to get out of town before traffic snarled the freeways. Diane found John Hill in the kitchen where he was about to leave for

the hospital and an operation scheduled at 7:30 A.M. How
was Joan? she asked. He had been up and down with his
wife most of the night, came the answer, and on his way
to work he was going to stop by the Avalon drugstore and
order medication. Effie, the maid, would be available to
look after Joan during the day and see that she took the
medicine.

"Well, is she all right?" pressed Diane.

"She's got a virus," said John.

The two house guests went into Joan's room to say
good-by. She asked for a pitcher of water, saying her
mouth was parched and she felt dehydrated. While Eunice
went to fetch it, Diane asked if Joan wanted them to stay
longer.

No, said Joan. She would be all right. Effie was there if
she needed anything, and Ma and Pa were just down the
street. She was sorry that the offer Pa made was so penurious, but she was too sick to worry about it now. They
would talk later. Both women kissed their hostess perfunc-
torily and left.

Effie Green and her husband, Archie, had worked for
the Hills less than two months, but they had been accustomed to the eccentric routine of the household. Often
Effie had prepared dinner for the doctor, only to learn
that he would be late. It was her custom to put the food
in a warmer, frequently discovering the next morning that
it had not been touched. She gathered that he either stayed
away on some nights or was an indifferent eater. Both the
doctor and his wife treated her kindly, and Effie grew
quickly fond of her new employers. The Greens lived in
servants' quarters at the rear of the house, but generally
left each Saturday noon and spent the weekend with their
daughter, returning Monday morning.

On the Monday morning when the women from Dallas
left, John Hill instructed Effie specifically about his ailing
wife. Let her rest, he said. Do not disturb her. Do not let
her take telephone calls.

During the morning, when only the two servants and
Joan were in the house, Ash came over to see his daughter.
Effie told him that she was asleep and was still feeling
poorly. Frowning, Ash said he would return later. He went
downtown to watch the market quotations on his broker's
ticker and to visit one of his rental properties.

On this Monday Vann Maxwell waited all morning for her friend to call. During the tense bridge game on Saturday night, Joan had scribbled a note saying that she was going to her lawyer's office on Monday to sue for divorce and to alter her will so that John would not receive anything in case of her death. "I'm chicken and I want you to go with me," Joan had told her friend.

When, by noon, the telephone had not rung, Vann called Joan's house and learned from Effie that Mrs. Hill was resting and not feeling well.

All day long Effie answered Joan's busy telephone, telling callers that her mistress was ill and not able to accept calls. In midafternoon Archie Green told his wife that the situation upstairs "don't seem right." Joan Hill had not summoned either of them on the intercom system, nor had she made a sound all day. Effie told her husband, "You'd better go up there and listen outside the door and see if you can hear anything."

In a few moments Arch returned and said all was silent behind the closed door. Effie then went upstairs and opened the door quietly, disobeying Dr. Hill's instructions to leave his wife undisturbed. Joan was awake. She spoke weakly to her maid. "I'm so sick, Effie."

Effie said that Dr. Hill would be home soon to check on her. Worried, shaking her head, Effie descended the stairs and began watching the clock.

The next morning, Tuesday, March 18, Effie was in the kitchen preparing breakfast for Boot when she heard Dr. Hill summon her. The old black woman hurried upstairs and went into the sickroom. It was dark, the drapes drawn. She could barely make out Dr. Hill sitting on the bed, holding his wife's head in his arms. She seemed limp and unresponsive. "Effie, get busy and clean up Joan's mess," he ordered. John was dressed in a business suit, preparing to leave for the school concert at which he would perform his tuba solo.

The surgeon said he would return during the day to check on his wife. He had one last instruction: Make sure Joan takes her medicine. The instructions were on the label of each bottle. Effie nodded in understanding. She had more questions, but Dr. Hill was in a hurry. Before she could ask another, he was down the stairs and gone.

Effie turned on the bedside light so that she could see. "Let me roll you over, Mrs. Hill," she said, taking her in her arms and moving her across the bed. Under Joan, two white towels had been shoved, and beneath them were feces—soft, perhaps from recent diarrhea. There were also flecks of what Effie took to be blood. The maid was disturbed. It appeared to her that Mrs. Hill had lain in her own excrement for hours. Some of the fecal material was drying, indicating that it had been passed during the night. Her nightgown had not been changed since the morning before, when Effie last attended her.

"I'm gonna clean you up real nice," the maid said. "I ain't going to let you stay like this. I'm gonna change your gown and wash you. Come on, let me help you get to the bathroom."

Joan nodded weakly. "I'm burning up," she said. "I'm burning from here down." She pointed to her neck.

"What is it?" asked Effie.

"I don't know," said Joan. "I'm just so sick."

Effie placed her mistress' arms around her neck and she half dragged her to the bathroom. En route, Joan stumbled and had another bowel movement just before she reached the toilet. Effie, seriously alarmed, noted that Mrs. Hill's face was turning blue, particularly her nose. Now she was cold.

"I don't want to die," gasped Joan.

"You ain't gonna die," said Effie. She stripped the soiled nightgown from Joan and sponged her body. Then she hurriedly gathered up the sheets and put fresh ones on the bed. Helping Joan back into the bed, Effie took her hands and held them tightly, trying to press warmth into them. "You're not going to die," she said. "Let's pray together. God answers prayers."

"All right," said Joan. "You pray for me, Effie."

Effie beseeched the Lord to help her mistress pass through the illness, then she ran to the stairway and called Archie. "Call Mr. Robinson down the street and tell him to come right away."

Archie did as he was directed, but there was no answer at the Robinson home, Effie then went to the telephone and called Dr. Hill's office. The surgeon was not there, Effie was told. Well, she said, he'd sure better come running. "You tell him his wife's terrible sick and he better put her in the hospital. Something wrong's happening to her." Effie glanced at the kitchen clock. It was a few minutes past ten.

At that moment John Hill was on stage at the Montrose Elementary School, engrossed in his tuba solo. When the performance ended, a clerk from the school office handed him a message: Mrs. Hill seemed ill and in need of his attention.

It happened that the plastic surgeon had made a previous appointment for this morning, squeezed in between his concert and his first operation of the day, scheduled for 11:30 A.M. at Sharpstown Hospital, a small suburban institution in the southwest corner of Houston. He was trying to work in a quick pacifying breakfast with Ann Kurth. His mistress had been pushing him hard for a decision on where she stood in his life. For three months now, ever since John signed Ash Robinson's letter of repentance, she had been relegated to what she kept calling a "back street affair." And she was fed up with her state. Ann Kurth was tired of creeping about in shadows.

All during that week the women from Dallas were in his home, and over the weekend when Joan fell ill, John had been slipping out to rendezvous with Ann, desperately trying to buy time. She had thrown an ultimatum at him: either divorce Joan and make an honest woman out of her, or she cuts this off. He had promised an answer on this Tuesday morning.

But so many thoughts were clamoring for John's attention that when he hurried out of the school auditorium to find his car, he was startled to discover Ann waiting for him. Taking her by the arm, he led her to a more private side street.

"Joan's got a bug," he said. "I'm afraid we can't have coffee this morning."

"But when are we going to talk, John?" she pressed. "I'm sick and tired of your stalling around."

"I just can't think right now," he answered. "I'll call you later." With Ann glowering, he got into his Cadillac and drove toward River Oaks, ten minutes away.

Boot Hill had spent the previous night down the street at the home of his grandparents. On this Tuesday morning, Mrs. Robinson prepared his breakfast and Ash drove him to the River Oaks Elementary School where he was in the second grade. Ash then made a quick trip downtown to check the opening stock market quotations, and when he returned home around ten-thirty his wife said she was anxious to visit Joan and see how she was feeling. Ash dropped her off while he went on another business appointment.

Mrs. Robinson was met at the front door of her daughter's home by Archie Green, who led her upstairs to the sickroom. There she discovered her son-in-law, standing at the foot of Joan's bed, a serious expression on his face. "I think we'd better take her to the hospital, Ma," he said.

Up to that point, Mrs. Robinson had no idea how serious her daughter's illness had become. "The news shocked me," she would later state in a deposition. "He said he was making arrangements for her to go to Sharpstown Hospital where she would have intensive care and be treated like a queen."

"Is an ambulance coming?" asked Mrs. Robinson.

No, said John. He was going to drive her personally to the hospital.

It did not seem unusual at the time to Mrs. Robinson that her daughter was going to be treated at Sharpstown, even though it was a new and relatively unknown hospital in the city. Less than fifteen minutes away from the Hill home was the great Texas Medical Center, with some of the world's finest hospitals and every diagnostic facility known to modern medicine. Yet John Hill was preparing to take his wife to a small suburban hospital, twice as far away.

As she would look back on the strange morning, events seemed to move in slow motion. Almost languidly, John Hill helped his wife rise from the bed. Effie found a robe. Mrs. Robinson located white socks to put on her daughter's feet. The group moved out of the bedroom to the head of the curving stairs that led down to the foyer. Effie Green made a move to assist Joan down the stairs. John stopped her. "No," he said. "She can walk by herself." His tone was firm, an order, almost a denial of his wife's illness. Effie would later state that she found it shocking that the doctor would make his wife walk down the stairs by herself. She wanted to put her arms around her mistress and carry her down.

John helped load his wife into the back seat of her blue and white Cadillac, and Mrs. Robinson drew a light blanket over her legs. Just as they were preparing to leave, Ash Robinson drove up in his black Lincoln and got out with a worried look on his face.

"Great God almighty!" he swore. "What on earth has happened to this child?"

John repeated the news that Joan's condition had worsened, that he felt it best she be hospitalized. He had chosen Sharpstown because she would receive "special care" there.

Ash leaned into the back seat and comforted his daughter. "How do you feel, honey?" he asked.

Joan smiled faintly.

"Do you want me to go with you?" he asked.

"I'm going," said Ma.

With that, John started the car and drove away, leaving Ash standing in the driveway, worrying, wondering.

It was approximately eleven miles from the Hill home on Kirby Drive to Sharpstown Hospital. It took John Hill almost three quarters of an hour to progress what could have been done in half that time. "He drove like a snail," Mrs. Robinson would later say. " I felt we were *never* going to get there. In fact, it was almost like he did not want us to get there."

En route, John switched on a classical music tape, and the sounds of a symphony filled the Cadillac. At one point Mrs. Robinson snapped at her son-in-law, "Turn that damn music down, John. I can't hear myself think."

Mrs. Robinson kept asking her daughter, "Honey, how do you feel?" Several times Joan only nodded, but midway, she said, "Mother, I am blind. I can't see you."

Mrs. Robinson turned to her son-in-law. "Did you hear that? What does it mean?"

"She's having a blackout,'" said John. He did not seem concerned. He repeated his previous statement that the hospital was "alerted" and its emergency facilities geared up to receive Joan.

But when the car eased into the driveway that fronts Sharpstown Hospital, no team of emergency medical personnel rushed out to admit Joan Hill. In fact, no one seemed to know she was coming. John Hill got out of the car and went into the hospital. His mother-in-law sat for what seemed like several minutes waiting for someone to help her daughter. Finally John appeared with a nurse who was pushing a wheel chair.

Joan sat up in the back seat of the car, gasping for breath, while her mother pleaded, "Oh, God, hurry!" Joan was lifted carefully and put in the wheel chair and pushed into the hospital. Mrs. Robinson would learn later that the hospital had, in effect, no emergency room facilities at the time. And no intensive care unit whatsoever. The modest suburban hospital was, as one doctor described it in 1969, "a good place to have a baby or get a broken arm fixed— little else."

The sick woman was taken to a private room where nurses descended on her for the admitting process. Mrs. Robinson was asked to leave and did so, standing around helplessly in a corridor for more than an hour. John Hill seemed to have vanished as well, and she could find no one to tell her anything.

Earlier that morning, John had telephoned a physician named Dr. Walter Bertinot who practiced internal medicine at Sharpstown. A capable man, he was nonetheless an unusual choice. Bertinot was not considered one of Houston's many celebrated doctors of world rank, nor had he ever treated Joan Robinson Hill. He had, in fact, only met the woman once or twice, and that was to shake hands at the annual picnic which the Hills gave at Chatsworth Farm.

"Why me?" asked Dr. Bertinot. It occurred to him that perhaps John Hill should be treating his own wife, or that the lady's personal physician might be more suitable to minister to her needs. John Hill's answer was unusual. He said Joan did not really get along with doctors on a professional basis, but she had once spoken well of Bertinot. He made his wife out to be a problem patient, the kind doctors dread. Bertinot, a quiet, colorless, unemotional man with the character of a college physics professor, could handle a temperamental woman.

"What are her symptoms?" asked Bertinot. Diarrhea, vomiting, and nausea, replied John routinely. The Sharpstown doctor asssumed then and there that Joan Hill was suffering from acute gastroenteritis. Or, in lay language, stomach flu. Bertinot was flattered to be asked to treat one of Houston's most famous women, but there seemed no urgency to the matter. John Hill's tone on the telephone was calm and unemotional. There was no mention whatsoever of "intensive care" as the plastic surgeon had told his mother-in-law and the maid.

The first nurse to attend Joan in her hospital bed took a blood pressure reading and was startled to discover that it was 60/40—perilously low.

The nurse was so concerned by the reading that she took

it again, wondering if the apparatus could be malfunctioning. Once more Joan's pressure read 60/40. An emergency call was made to Dr. Bertinot, who at that moment was a block away in a small professional building adjacent to the hospital.

"I dropped everything and went over," Dr. Bertinot would later say. "I canceled out my whole schedule."

When he first encountered Joan Hill, she was sitting up in bed and seemed flushed and short of breath. She did *not* appear to be a woman in shock, but she *had* to be in shock with a blood pressure of 60/40. Moreover, Joan greeted Dr. Bertinot by his first name, "Walter," and smiled at him. All very curious. The doctor ordered IV fluids started immediately in an attempt to build up the blood volume and raise the pressure. The danger here was that the patient would be thrown into terminal shock unless the blood volumn was restored. While the nurses rigged IVs, Dr. Bertinot methodically took Joan's medical history, concentrating on the previous few days. Learning that she had been vomiting, suffering from diarrhea, and complaining of general nausea and malaise, he made a snap judgment that he was dealing with some kind of a dysentery, perhaps salmonella, food poisoning.

Routinely, Dr. Bertinot ordered urinalysis and stool cultures, for if Joan had eaten something that had precipitated food poisoning it could perhaps be determined by studying her feces to see if threatening bacteria were at work there. At this point the condition of his patient did not alarm him, for food poisoning is a common reason for admission to a hospital. But other factors about Joan intrigued him. Why did she seem so rational, when her blood pressure indicated that she was in deep shock? Confounded, Dr. Bertinot summoned a colleague, Dr. Frank Lanza, in consultation. Lanza, a flashy, fleshy young doctor who had once been a professional dancer and who performed a night club act to help his way through medical school, was but two years out of his residency in 1969. And though well trained, neither was he considered one of Houston's most famous diagnosticians. Before many more days passed, questions would begin to arise as to why John Hill employed two doctors of the then lesser stature of Bertinot and Lanza to treat his wife, rather than engage physicians of world rank just across the city.

At this midday on March 18, 1969, John Hill was in

the operating room at Sharpstown, performing an operation for removal of a scar, and listening to a broadcast of classical music.

Despite the IV fluids being dumped into her veins, Joan's blood pressure remained low. Now it occurred to Dr. Lanza that perhaps the woman had septic shock, resulting from a massive bacterial infection somewhere in her body. She had, after all, complained to Effie Green of "burning up" from her neck down. The physician ordered more elaborate blood cultures to search for bacteria, but the trouble here was that the test would take perhaps as long as seventy-two hours. Blood must be placed in agar plates, a gel-like substance, and in this medium, bacteria—if present—will grow.

By late afternoon, six hours after admission to the hospital, a nurse noted that no urine was passing out of Joan's body through a kidney catheter. This indicated kidney failure and was alarming to the attending doctors. They directed that the IV fluids be increased, hoping to stimulate the kidney into producing urine. While this was going on, Ash Robinson popped into the room, promising to bring his daughter yellow roses on the morrow, lingering until the nurses banished him.

Shortly after 8 P.M. her condition became grave. The increased IV fluids had not stimulated the kidney into producing urine, and the blood urea nitrogen level was elevated. A well-respected renal man, Dr. Bernard Hicks, was called in. It took him but a few moments to diagnose serious kidney failure.

"Should we move her to Methodist?" asked Dr. Lanza. A dialysis machine was available at the cross-town hospital that Dr. Michael DeBakey had made famous. Such a machine could take over the work of a kidney, purifying the blood, while doctors tended to other threatening matters in Joan's body.

"No," answered Dr. Hicks. The woman is too sick to move. Instead he would attempt peritoneal dialysis, placing a tube in the stomach and forcing a blood-purifying solution first in and then out a second tube through osmotic pressure. The procedure turns the entire peritoneal cavity into an artificial kidney and can work as well as a dialysis machine.

Dr. Walter Bertinot watched, almost unbelieving. He could not have imagined that this critically ill woman before him was the same who had greeted him warmly ten hours earlier and called him by name.

Dr. Hicks would not begin the peritoneal dialysis without approval from John Hill. Where was he? During the day he had been in out of his wife's room a few times, but now he was home. Effie Green took the call from the hospital and summoned her employer from his music room, where he was sitting alone, absorbed in a concerto. When he hung up, he hurried to the door, telling the maid, "We may lose Mrs. Hill. She is very sick."

But although the call was made at 9:15 P.M., through the hospital switchboard, John did not show up in his wife's room until eleven. When he arrived his wife was conscious and, surprisingly, fairly lucid. A nurse present heard Joan beg her husband to stay with her because she was frightened by all of the tubes and contraptions attached to her body. The surgeon nodded agreeably, read her chart, then pushed a chair beside the bed and propped up his feet.

Dr. Bertinot checked his patient half an hour after midnight and felt there was, if not slight improvement, at least a stabilizing. Blood pressure had raised slightly, and the peritoneal dialysis was working. Since the case was now more or less thrown into the lap of the renal specialist, Dr. Hicks, the physician in charge felt it was all right to go home and get some sleep. "I'll stay a while longer," said Dr. Lanza. "You go on home, Walter, and if anything happens, we'll call you."

John Hill, seemingly satisfied with the care his wife was getting, said he was going to spend the night on a couch in the patient records room, just down the hall.

At 1:30 A.M. on the morning of March 19, Dr. Lanza went home, as had Hicks, the kidney specialist, and Joan Hill was left in the care of nurses and a night resident who was in charge of the patient census. John Hill patted his wife gently and whispered that he would be just down the hall in case he was needed. Drifting now in and out of lucidity, Joan instructed the nurse to make sure that her husband was comfortable. Then she began composing a grocery list for a party she was giving, her mind wandering. The peritoneal dialysis was painful, but she was heavily sedated.

An hour later the nurse noted that her vital signs showed

indications of sudden heart failure. She ran to the doorway and called to the central nursing station to summon the resident with cardiac arrest equipment. At that moment Joan raised her head slightly from her pillow and gasped. "John!" she implored. Frantically she searched for air. Then a torrent of blood raced up from her innards and splashed out of her mouth, staining the pillow red-black.

Dr. Yama, the resident who was moonlighting from his position in radiology at another hospital, raced into the room and plunged adrenalin into the heart. But it was too late.

With that final agonal hemorrhage, Joan Robinson Hill was dead at the age of thirty-eight.

John Hill's grief shattered the predawn stillness of the hospital. "No!" screamed the plastic surgeon, and then again, and again. He rushed into his wife's room and saw horror—her blotched and swollen body, her blood fresh on her face and the linens—and he rocked back and forth moaning. His long-time friend, a nurse named Gail Wholey, murmured consolation to him. "I must call my mother," he suddenly said, and this struck the nurse as odd. Why would John Hill need his own mother before he broke the news to Joan's parents? The plastic surgeon also instructed the nurse to call his friend, Dr. Jim Oates, and request him to come to the hospital. Dr. Oates and his wife Dotty, also a nurse, lived but a few blocks away from the Hill home, and the two men often played piano duets together. Once they had spent six months polishing a Mozart sonata for appearances at a Methodist church.

Mrs. Wholey telephoned the Oates home and told them: "Joan Hill is dead. John wants you to come out to Sharpstown Hospital. Meet him in Joan's room." Dressing hurriedly, still sleepy and confused, the couple drove urgently to the hospital. It occurred to Mrs. Oates en route that perhaps there had been an automobile accident, but no . . . the nurse had said Joan was *in a room*. Had she been killed in a car crash, the nurse would have said the emergency room.

As soon as they entered the back door of the small hospital, Dotty Oates heard John Hill sobbing. His cries echoed all over the building, and on the second floor, patients had come to their doors and were standing outside to see what tragedy had occurred. John was in the doctors' lounge, weeping so hysterically that he seemed near collapse. Dotty Oates went to her friend and held him in her arms for several minutes while he gasped out the story of her sudden illness, and decline, and death. "I can't believe it, Dotty," he said. "My beautiful wife is gone. Why?"

Finally Jim Oates spoke sharply, cutting through his friend's grief. "Okay, John, knock it off. There are things to be done."

By this time Joan's attending physicians, Dr. Bertinot and Dr. Lanza, had been awakened at their homes and had driven back to the hospital. Suddenly the place was full of doctors, and Dotty Oates took the opportunity to slip out and go into Joan's death room. As she would tell it later: "I couldn't believe what I saw. The previous Friday, just before the wild game dinner, I had seen Joan Hill fresh from the beauty parlor and she had looked better than I had ever seen her. But this wasn't the Joan I had seen that day. Often, as a nurse, I have sometimes walked into a patient's room and encountered someone I know socially. But if I did not know this was Joan's body, I would not have recognized her. She was extremely edematous, swollen with fluids. Her superficial blood vessels were ruptured all over her body, making her splotched and mottled purple. On her face was the agony of torture. It must have been a painful and terrible death. Her blood was all over her face and her bedclothes."

Since the death had occurred almost two hours earlier— it was now near five in the morning—Dotty Oates was annoyed that the body had not been washed and cleaned, as is hospital custom. So she did what any good friend would do. "I washed and cleaned Joan. John kept coming in and bothering me, standing by her bed sobbing. It was a ghastly and terrible scene."

In the state of Texas the law required—under criminal penalties—an autopsy to be performed by the county coroner on any person who dies in a hospital within twenty-four hours of admission. The coroner *must* rule on the cause of death before the body is released for embalming and burial. All doctors know this, certainly all hospital pathologists, but in the most curious and bizarre—and soon to be notorious—death of Joan Robinson Hill, the law was either overlooked, flaunted, or deliberately broken, depending on with whom the authorities talked.

In the midst of the discussion being held in the doctors'

lounge shortly before dawn, Dr. Bertinot, who was severely shaken that his patient had so suddenly died, remarked to John Hill that an autopsy must be done.

John Hill nodded affirmatively, murmuring, "Yes, of course." Dr. Bertinot went to telephone the hospital pathologist, a Dr. Arthur Morse, and rouse him from bed to put the post-mortem protocol into operation. But at the same time John instructed his friend Dr. Oates to telephone the Settegast-Kopf Funeral Home and have them come to claim the body and prepare it for burial. At this point the stories become confusing and the sequence of events blurred. But one point stands out: an illegal and puzzling event quickly occurred.

Shortly after 6 A.M. on the misted, fog-draped morning, a Cadillac casket coach backed up to the rear entrance of Sharpstown Hospital and two attendants removed the body of Joan Hill, a chenille coverlet covering her. Then the corpse was transported to the red brick colonial-façade undertaking parlor on Kirby Drive, several blocks away from the Hill home on the very same street. It seemed that everyone was in a hurry this chaotic morning. When one of the funeral home's employees, a Mrs. Verna Bee Cummings, arrived at work at 6:40 A.M.—she is a meticulous person and remembers the time well—she noted that the light was on outside the "prep" room, which meant that inside a body was being embalmed. Mrs. Cummings opened the door to say good morning to the night embalmer, a man named Dick Chalk, and she noticed across the room, on a marble slab, the corpse of a blonde woman.

"You'd never guess who I have on this table," said Chalk, glancing up from his work. "Joan Robinson Hill."

Mrs. Cummings whistled in recognition. That was a big name. It would mean a big funeral. "Probably a goat-roping," she murmured to herself, using the house term for a major event with a full chapel of mourners and probable coverage by the media.

Sometime in the confusing two-hour period between 4 A.M. and 6 A.M., Dr. Bertinot reached the Sharpstown staff pathologist, Dr. Morse, at his home. He would not recollect the exact time, because he did not have a bedside clock. All he could remember from the conversation was that Dr. Bertinot informed him (1) Joan Robinson Hill was dead, (2) an autopsy must be done, (3) the body was being removed to the Settegast-Kopf Funeral Home, and (4) Bertinot had no idea as to the cause of the famous woman's death, other than that he felt she had died of a massive infection, and kidney failure.

Pathologist Morse did not leap from his bed and dress and hurry to the hospital, for he was unaware of the circumstances of Joan Hill's death. He failed to ask how long she had been in the hospital, and he would later state that he "assumed" she had been hospitalized longer than the twenty-four-hour period that legally requires an autopsy by the county coroner. Moreover, he was recently come to Sharpstown Hospital, having been there but six weeks. At his previous place of employment, the Spring Branch Hospital in Houston, it was rigid policy for all autopsies under the twenty-four-hour rule to be cleared with the coroner. Because so many people die from obviously violent causes in Houston—the city's murder rate in 1969 was, per capita, one of the largest in the entire world—the coroner and his staff were kept busy attending to more dramatic deaths and their reasons. The coroner was forced to rely on private hospital pathologists to perform autopsies on routine deaths that fell within the twenty-four-hour rule—provided permission was first granted by the medical examiner's office. Dr. Morse would later testify that he "assumed" someone at Sharpstown—Bertinot, perhaps, or a head nurse, or even John Hill, who was, after all, a duly qualified physician—that someone, for Pete's sake, had touched base with the coroner. But no one had.

It was not unusual for an autopsy to be performed at a funeral home. At the time, Sharpstown Hospital did not even have post-mortem facilities. Dr. Morse was accustomed to dropping by funeral parlors and doing his studies on the embalmer's marble slab before the undertaker did his work.

The young pathologist rose, had breakfast around 7 A.M., and prepared to drive to the Settegast-Kopf Funeral Home where he would slice open the body of Joan Robinson Hill and investigate the agents of her death. But someone had been there ahead of him.

Embalmer Chalk, due to go off night duty at 7 A.M., began his work at a quarter past six, spending several minutes "fixing" the facial features, twisting the jaw and lips into a pleasing expression and stuffing cotton wadding in the mouth to keep the faint smile from slipping. Then he sewed the lips shut and picked up a sharp tool. Making an injection into the femoral artery of the leg, he inserted a clear plastic tube, placing a second tube for drainage in the vein adjacent. Then he turned on a pump, and embalming fluid began flowing through the injection tube, swimming hurriedly throughout every region of the body, shoving out the blood and other body fluids through the drainage tube.

Within forty-five minutes all of Joan Hill's blood was drawn from her body, running through the tube into a nearby sink, to be washed away in the sewers of the city.

When pathologist Morse arrived at the funeral home near 10 A.M. he was taken aback to discover that Joan Hill was already embalmed, her blood and other vital fluids—so necessary for his microscope—forever lost. The nude body was resting on the marble slab, and a note had been dropped on the waxen cheek that had smiled out of ten thousand newspaper photographs. "Hold for autopsy," it said.

In the terrible two hours of John Hill's sobbing and attendant confusion, his friend Jim Oates suddenly asked a pertinent question. "Have Ma and Pa been told?" John raised his head and shook it, negatively. Then it *must* be done immediately, urged his friend. Newspapers find out about these matters quickly. Joan was a famous person. Some early edition police reporter would be calling the Robinson home for quotes. It might shock these old people into their graves.

John agreed. It was obvious to everyone in the room that he dreaded this task. He began to delay, wondering out loud who should preach the funeral, what mourners should be summoned from out of town. Jim Oates took his friend by the shoulders and shook him and demanded that he look him squarely in the eyes.

"It's your duty, John. You've *got* to tell these old people. If you need moral support, Dotty and I will go with you."

In front of the Robinson home, in the fogged dawn, John stood beside his car. Fearfully he approached the front door of the rust-colored house where he had lived for six years with his wife and his son. Just as he raised his finger to press the bell, he broke out in sweat. Perspiration drenched his face. He hesitated a suspenseful moment.

Then he rang and waited for someone in the sleeping house to come and hear.

13

"We've lost Joan," said John.

Ash Robinson said nothing for a moment. He sucked in air and sat quietly on the edge of his bed. Then he rose and prowled the room, his heavy body balanced improperly on his bare feet, the photographs of his daughter smiling at him from every wall like the four corners of his earth.

"I'm sorry, Pa," said John.

"The doctors did everything they could," put in Dr. Jim Oates. Dotty had her arms around Ma, whose face was gray and whose body had no bones.

Finally Ash spoke. "Why?" he asked. "Oh, tell me it's not true."

His son-in-law nodded in reaffirmation of the terrible news.

"But she was all right last night," insisted Pa. "I saw her. They told me she was gonna be all right."

Dr. Oates began an explanation of how Joan had slipped into irreversible kidney failure, but Ash seemed not to listen. He wandered into the living room and sank into his favorite chair. The two doctors in the room watched the old man intently for a few moments to see if he could tolerate the tragedy. But Pa was strong. Abruptly he rose and went to Ma. She buried her face in his shoulder and wept heavily.

John whispered in Jim Oates's ear to give either of the old people a sedative should it be needed. Then he went upstairs to the room where he and Joan had slept in the long years of his medical training, and he stretched out on the bed in his green scrub suit and fell into a light sleep.

Dr. Morse began the autopsy of Joan at the funeral home. He had to hurry, for already a call had come from the Robinson home saying Ash was impatient to view his daughter in death. Family and friends were stalling the old man until Joan was "ready" to be seen.

Immediately, Dr. Morse noted that the corpse on the marble slab was that of an attractive, well-nourished young woman. He checked the death certificate. Barely thirty-eight years old. Then, beginning at the neck, he dissected the body, a direct downward cut like opening the zipper of a winter coat. In the next hour and a half the pathologist severed and removed major organs in the body, weighing each, slicing off little slivers of tissue and putting them in plastic containers for microscopic examination back at his laboratory. In many cases, a pathologist can make an accurate determination of death merely by his gross observations (meaning, what the naked eye sees). But this one was puzzling. There were no visible tumors, no noticeable atherosclerosis, nothing unusual to the eye save a pancreas that was soft, red and mushy. It occurred to Dr. Morse that the woman before him could have died from pancreatitis, an acute inflammation of the pancreas. At 11:30 A.M. he packed up his tools and his tissue containers and informed the undertaker that he was done.

At the height of the affair John Hill had given Ann Kurth a Page Boy, a beeper that many doctors use to keep in touch with office and hospital. He insisted that she keep it on her person at all times so that he could find her whenever he needed her. Sometimes he only had a few minutes between surgery, he had said, and he might want to hear her voice.

On the morning that the news of Joan's death spread quickly across Houston, Ann Kurth was in a boutique trying on clothes when her beeper sounded. She went to the telephone and called home, for that was the custom, and the maid informed her that there were two "urgent" calls —one from a girl friend named Lou who was at that moment sitting under a hair dryer at a beauty parlor, the other from her stockbroker. "Both say it is very important," said the maid. But there was no call from John Hill.

Ann found her friend Lou first at the beauty parlor. Lou came straight to the point. "Did you hear about Joan Hill?"

"Hear what?" said Ann.

"She died. Last night. Everybody in the beauty parlor is talking about it."

"You're kidding, Lou. This is a joke."

"No, she's dead. It's on the radio. What does John say?"

Ann tightened her grip on the telephone. She could not yet accept the news. "I don't know," she muttered. "I haven't talked to him since yesterday."

Quickly she hung up and called her stockbroker. "I guess you heard your boy friend's wife kicked off," he said.

"I know . . . but I don't know anything about it," said Ann. She drove home, confused, wanting to see John but not knowing how to locate him. Surely he would call. Staying at her home was a house guest from Dallas named Joyce. She, too, was full of the shocking news. Ann sat down beside the telephone, watching, waiting. "Oh, God, why doesn't he call?" she said.

Joyce tried to cheer her. "Listen, you've got it made now. Don't get upset that John's not calling you. My God, don't you realize what's happened? He won't have to get a divorce now!"

Dumbly, Ann nodded.

Joan's friends began gathering, not at her house, but at Ash's home. By noon there were fifty people, and by sundown more than a hundred had arrived to pay their respects and offer their condolences.

At midday the funeral parlor began calling, wanting to know what gown Joan would wear in the casket. Should they dress her in one of the robes that were available in stock? A friend of Joan's, a society horsewoman named Ann Lyons, took the call and hung up in distress. There seemed to be no one about capable of making a decision. John was upstairs in the bedroom still asleep. Ash was staring ahead at the wall, in an unapproachable world of his own. Ma was lost to sedatives and whiskey. Someone had fetched Boot from elementary school, but the child had not yet been told that his mother was dead. "Somebody's got to do something!" said Mrs. Lyons in agitation. She noticed John's office nurse trying to be helpful, and she instructed her to go upstairs and wake the surgeon.

Another friend, Yvonne Roper, who had known Joan since both attended Stephens College together, volunteered to go up the street to the Hill home and rummage through the closet to find something for her friend to wear to the grave. The funeral home had given only one proviso: whatever gown was selected must have a high neck to cover the autopsy cuts.

Memories flooded across Yvonne as she went through

her dead friend's closet. She was tempted to select blue jeans and a work shirt, for that was how she remembered Joan—whitewashing fences at Chatworth Farm, leaping onto a horse and riding impulsively across a pasture, laughing, full of joyous life and promise. Then her eyes caught sight of the gold brocade gown Joan had worn at two recent and important occasions—a reception for Dr. Christiaan Barnard, the South African heart surgeon who had come through Houston to pay his respects to Drs. Michael DeBakey and Denton Cooley, and the opera with John. She remembered Joan saying, "I always have a good time when I wear this dress." Moreover, there was a bit of irony attached to the gown, for Joan had bought it in a fit of pique when the department store bills came in, revealing the news that John had bought expensive shoes and a matching purse for Ann Kurth.

Yvonne telephoned the Robinson home and spoke to John, now awake and functioning, and obtained his approval. Then she took the gown to the funeral home and waited until Joan was dressed for the last time. When the work was done, Yvonne was pleased. The gown was right —elegant, chic, and glittery, suiting a woman who had been so often in a spotlight. There would later be criticism of her selection, for some would say that Joan should have worn a riding habit to her grave.

To such, Yvonne would respond, "No, I knew her well, and I remember that horse show times were stressful for her. Joan got so keyed up that she had spasms in her back, and the pain was so awful it hurt to get out of bed."

Now, as she stood over her friend, Yvonne noticed Joan's hands—waxy, swollen, tinged yellow. They were unadorned. Even her wedding ring was gone, having been removed at the hospital. She telephoned John again. Did he want his wife to wear jewelry? John's answer was precise, so firm that there could be no doubting his desire. "No," he said, "the dress is ornate enough. No jewelry."

Ash Robinson and his son-in-law went to the funeral home and quickly chose a casket—the $3,700 blue steel model with a lining of white satin. The old man and the surgeon agreed that it was not necessary to select an outrageously expensive box. "Joan wouldn't want us to spend $10,000," said Ash. And John agreed. The funeral would be two days hence, on Friday, March 21, 1969.

By nightfall Dr. Morse had made preliminary microscopic examination of the tissue slivers from the body. Still the case was worrisome. There was no clear-cut cause of death. Some mysterious inflammation had spread throughout the body, its source and its exact nature unknown. If the pathologist had been able to study the blood and other body fluids he could have made a more scholarly ruling. But he did not come to the corpse until it was already full of embalming fluid. With not much to go on, he decided that a probable cause of death was pancreatitis. He would not bet his home mortgage on it, but it was as good a guess as any. He called Dr. Bertinot and made his report, and the attending physician in turn notified John Hill.

"Pancreatitis?" said Ash Robinson when told the news. "What the hell is that?" One of the doctors who had come to pay respects sat down beside the old man and began an explanation of the small but important gland that secretes digestive fluids and manufactures insulin. If the organ becomes infected and inflamed, it can bring on death. But usually this happens in a much older person than Joan.

On the next day, the eve of the funeral, Diane Settegast and her companion Eunice Woolen arrived from Dallas, shocked at the death of the woman they had said good-by to only three days previously. Although Diane and Ash Robinson had spoken heatedly in their discussion of the chinchy salary he had offered her to run Chatsworth Farm, she was now all comfort to the old man and his wife. Next she went up the street to the great white colonial house to pay her condolences to John Hill. Only three or four cars were parked outside, in comparison to the traffic jam at the Robinsons'. It was as if mourning Houston knew by instinct that the greater loss was Pa's, not John Hill's.

Diane was admitted by Effie, the maid, whose eyes were red from weeping. Dr. Hill was upstairs in the music room. With guests. Effie began to lead the way, but Diane said she could find the room well enough on her own. There was no trouble remembering the unpleasant bridge game from Saturday night. Only five days ago, Joan was sitting in that room cussing John, scribbling notes across the card table, then dancing with her husband. How could death have seized her so quickly?

When Diane pulled open the double doors of the music room she encountered darkness. And, improbably, laughter. The movie screen had been pulled down from the ceiling and a Laurel and Hardy comedy was being shown. John was seated on a couch with a few people Diane did not recognize. Boot Hill and a playmate were on the floor, giggling. Expecting to find a man in deep grief, angered that a slapstick movie was being shown on the night before the funeral, Diane cut jaggedly across the dialogue. "Well, it looks like you're having a good time, John," she snapped, and hurried back downstairs.

But as her feet touched the foyer floor, John was hurrying down the curving staircase after her. Diane spun around angrily. She would remember the conversation that ensued and tell it thusly to many people:

"Why did Joan die, John?"

"She died of pancreatitis. I just wasn't familiar with the symptoms. I wasn't treating her for that."

"Why the hell not? You've been through every god damn specialty there is. Ash paid for it."

"I just didn't know," he said. "I'd give anything I have, anything on this earth, if I could bring her back. . . . I told her that morning when you left that I was going to take her to the hospital. But she didn't want to go. You know how she always was about hospitals."

Diane would remember shaking her head in disbelief. "No, John. I don't know how Joan was about hospitals."

"She didn't like them. Always felt that way. I had to practically carry her down the stairs."

"Then I'd like to know one thing. If Joan was sick enough to die a few hours after she got to the hospital, then why did it take so long for you to decide to take her there? It's pretty god damn strange, John. Nothing makes sense."

Later that evening it would be noted that Diane Settegast returned to the home of Ash Robinson and dropped onto the arm of the old man's chair. The two were immersed in deep conversation for almost an hour. It was also noted that Ash's cheek muscle tightened and his eyes narrowed. A tic jerked his face furiously. He nodded often, taking it all in. Then he rose abruptly, slammed his Stetson on his head, and rushed out alone, into the night.

On Friday, March 21, 1969, at midday, the funeral of Joan Robinson Hill was to be held. And Verna Bee Cummings' prediction of a "goat roping" was accurate. All morning long, attendants set up extra folding chairs in hallways and outside, on the lawns. Florist delivery trucks fought for space at the delivery entrance. More than two hundred floral tributes from all over America, but particularly the deep South, arrived, their combined perfumes of carnations and lilies and roses an almost overwhelming scent. "There's not a rose to be found in Houston or New Orleans," said one florist, and the remark was passed on to Ash, who found comfort therein.

In the two days since his daughter died so abruptly, Ash had scarcely slept. Through the hours of the night he made telephone calls, hurrying out to speak with doctors in all-night coffee shops, with nurses outside emergency rooms, carrying a large envelope spilling over with newspaper clippings and notes scribbled on lined paper. On the morning of the funeral, long before dawn, somewhere in the blackness of 3 or 4 A.M., Ash went to the One's-A-Meal Coffee Shop near his home and spent two hours reading through his scribbled notes, drinking many cups of coffee. One of the regulars noted that he seemed to be wrestling with a decision.

At 9 A.M., when Assistant District Attorney I. D. Mc-Master arrived at his office in the Harris County courthouse, he was informed that a man named Ash Robinson was waiting to see him. And who was that?

The father of Joan Robinson Hill. The society woman who died this week. All over the newspapers. Funeral's this morning. The old man's with Fred Parks.

McMaster whistled to himself. It sounded troublesome. What was the father of Joan Robinson Hill doing in the district attorney's office on the very morning of his daughter's funeral? And in the company of Fred Parks, one of the town's most respected, old-line civil lawyers? It was a lot to digest in the first hour of the last day of the week. Send them in.

Ash went directly to his purpose. "I have reason to believe that my son-in-law murdered my only child." The accusation was not emotional, only cold, the old man locking his glacier eyes dead on with the prosecutor. Ash hurried into his presentation; he had been rehearsing it most of the night. "This is going to sound a little unbelievable," he said. "But it's true." He threw out his facts:

—His daughter was a healthy woman and a superbly conditioned rider of high-spirited horses.

—She fell ill abruptly after eating French pastries served

to her by her husband, John Hill, a plastic surgeon. Two house guests would testify to the curious pastry ritual.

—She ran a fever, suffered vomiting and diarrhea at home, but her husband did not call in another doctor, nor did he allow anyone to enter her sickroom.

—Dr. Hill took her finally to Sharpstown Hospital, where he promised that she would be placed in "intensive care and treated like a queen." Instead, the hospital had no intensive care unit, no one seemed to know she was coming, she was treated by a doctor who had never met her professionally before.

—She died approximately fifteen hours after admission, and her body was "whisked out of the hospital and onto the embalmer's table" before an autopsy could be done. The autopsy, performed only *after* all blood and vital fluids were drained and replaced by embalming fluid, showed she died of pancreatitis.

"I have checked with some of the most prominent doctors in Houston, and they say it is highly unlikely she died of pancreatitis," said Ash.

McMaster listened to the accusations carefully. At first he thought the old man to be "your standard nut case, but important enough to let him get it all out of his system." But by the end of the tale, the random facts were tantalizing. Farfetched. But tantalizing. They could not be automatically dismissed, coming as they did from a man with Ash Robinson's pocketbook, address, and in the company of a silk-stocking lawyer like Fred Parks.

"Okay," answered McMaster slowly. He was the lean, rawboned Texan who spoke carefully, only when it was necessary. "I'll look into it. Call you next week."

Ash shook his head in sudden agitation. He raised his hands and they trembled, clawing the air. "No!" he demanded. "That'll be too late. I want you to get the coroner out there before they close the coffin. Don't you understand? What John Hill wants is to get that girl into the ground as soon as possible."

When the old man left, weeping and almost incoherent, McMaster promptly telephoned Dr. Joseph Jachimczyk, the feisty and highly respected coroner of Harris County. Until Jachimczyk assumed office in the middle 1950s, Houston's coroner system was so primitive as to be beyond belief. Bodies were pronounced officially dead by justices of the

peace who were not required by law to possess either legal
or medical educations. (They still are not, giving certain
criminal proceedings in Texas towns a decided Judge Roy
Bean frontier flavor.) Before the coming of Jachimczyk,
who held both legal *and* medical degrees, many suspicious
homicides were overlooked by ignorant justices. "Without
a doubt, a lot of 'fatal heart attacks' were brought on by
undiscovered ice-pick wounds in the chest," said the coroner at the time, who rapidly moved to institute more modern methods of investigating death.

When Dr. Jachimczyk received the urgent telephone call
from the district attorney's office this Friday morning, it
was the first hint that the death of Joan Robinson Hill was
anything but routine and natural.

"What do you want me to do?" asked the medical examiner.

Go out to the funeral home and look at her body and—
here I. D. McMaster hesitated briefly at the enormity of
what he was about to suggest—if necessary, "Stop the
god damned funeral."

"I'm supposed to tell everybody to go home and come
back another day?" snapped Dr. Jachimczyk. Did the DA's
office really want him to barge into the city's fanciest
funeral home, moments before one of the town's most
prominent women was to be eulogized and buried, and "if
necessary" cart away her body?

"Just go out there and have a look, Joe," soothed Mc-
Master.

Justifiably angry, Dr. Jachimczyk slammed down the
phone and began writing notes to himself. He asked a
secretary to find the news clippings about Joan Hill's death.
Then he called Sharpstown Hospital and spoke to the administrator, a Stanley Hill (no relation to John). The
administrator confirmed that the woman had died in his
hospital, that she was removed to the Settegast-Kopf
Funeral Home, and that the hospital's own pathologist, Dr.
Arthur Morse, performed his autopsy there.

"May I go on record as reminding you that this is a
violation of Article 49.25, the Medical Examiners Law of
the State of Texas, by failing to report this case to my
office?" said the coroner.

Administrator Hill assured him that it would not happen
again.

Jachimczyk hung up and glanced at his watch. It was

now near 10 A.M. He had a morning full of work already
scheduled—three autopsies and a dozen reports to dictate.
How would he find time to drop everything and run out to
a funeral home on the whim of a rich old man?

Next he called Dr. Morse, the Sharpstown pathologist,
a highly embarrassed young doctor. His gross findings, reported the Sharpstown pathologist, had at first revealed
a beefy red pancreas, a good likelihood of pancreatitis. But
microscopic slides revealed this to be post-mortem autolysis
—or a breakdown of pancreatic tissue by enzymes the way
meat tenderizer works on roast beef. The autopsy had further shown hemorrhaging in the esophagus, massive edema
(fluids) in the lungs, and a bladder with not a drop of
urine. The case, all in all, was puzzling but, at this point,
not very sinister. Cause of death? Still unknown.

"What tissues do you still have?" asked Dr. Jachimczyk.

Some pancreas, frozen kidney, liver, and a small amount
of stomach content.

Urine? Blood samples? Surely both were taken upon this
patient's admission to the hospital.

They were, said Dr. Morse. But they had already been
"discarded."

Brusquely the county coroner ordered the Sharpstown
pathologist to turn over all specimens obtained in the autopsy at the funeral home and a copy of his preliminary
report. And one more question, said the coroner. How in
God's name did it happen that the dead body of the famous
wife of a doctor, of all people, was rushed out of the hospital and embalmed before the autopsy was done?

"I don't know," answered Dr. Morse. "It was just a
screw-up all around."

For several minutes Dr. Jachimczyk stood beside the
coffin of Joan Hill and gazed at her remains in the glittery
gold gown. He was making mental notes as to the appearance and condition of the corpse. Bowing his head respectfully from time to time, he tried not to betray the fact
that he was anything but a friend and mourner. Others
were filing by the casket and the chapel was filling up, even
though the funeral service was more than an hour away.
Perhaps no one would have paid any attention to the short,
serious-looking man with the severe crew cut and the thick
glasses. But one of John Hill's doctor friends noted the
presence of the county coroner, and he whispered to his

wife, "That's Dr. Joe. What is *he* doing standing so long over the casket?" The doctor's wife looked hurriedly at the famous pathologist. Her eyes went to his white laboratory shoes, flecks of dried blood on them. She went outside to telephone a friend with this choice piece of news. Within minutes the gossip was dancing around River Oaks that the county coroner was inspecting Joan Hill's body.

Dr. Jachimczyk was satisfied that enough material still existed from Morses's post-mortem to conduct his own autopsy. And from his casual inspection of the fully clothed body in its coffin he elected not to stop the funeral. He slipped out quietly, feeling incorrectly that no one knew he had come to the undertaking parlor with that possibility in mind.

"Here is tragedy in the classical sense of Greek drama," intoned the preacher, the Rev. Pat Harrell of the Church of Christ, where John Hill was a member. "A person, a unique, extraordinary person, falls victim to circumstances beyond human control, but does not merely suffer. In struggling against fate, in recognizing fate, deeper meaning is found.

"Everyone I've spoken to in these last few days, and my own experience would agree, recognized that here was such a unique person, one, to some degree, who seemed out of step with mankind. The truth of the matter is that mankind was out of step with her. For those qualities which set her apart, which we admired most in her, were those very qualities which should be universal in us all, but sadly are not."

The Rev. Mr. Harrell preached to a full house, with every folding chair in the halls taken, and a large crowd gathered in the driveway outside where his words were broadcast on speakers. Two Houston television stations sent cameras, and there were representatives from the radio and newspapers. John Hill sat with his arm around his son, crying softly but audibly enough so that those near him could hear. Ash Robinson had no tears. His face was not committed to any emotion save blankness. He stared continuously at his daughter's coffin, now closed, and only once did anyone see him move his attention. When Dr. Harrell mentioned the grief of Joan's "talented and devoted young husband," Ash Robinson turned to look sharply at his son-in-law.

The eulogy was brief and—the opinion was unanimous among her friends—indicative of Joan. Four qualities were unique about her, said the preacher. "Her friendliness . . . in sharp contrast to the closedness of our society where we build elaborate defenses to keep people at a distance. Her devotion . . . she was loyal, tenaciously loyal, with a special capacity to sustain others, to carry the load for others, to care. We who find it so difficult to move beyond the island of our own self stand in amazement. Thirdly, she gave of herself. She was always busy with civic and charity causes on behalf of others. And, finally, her genuineness. There was about Joan no façade, no pretense.

"Those of us who are fortunate to have faith can even find a deeper meaning in her life. One of the metaphors for death in the Bible is that of a pale horse. That brings back memories, doesn't it? A gray horse. Surely Joan was too accomplished a rider not to leave the wider ring of life without grace and poise and dignity."

Outside the chapel, when the funeral cars were being filled with family members for the ride to the cemetery, Ash Robinson and his wife got into the lead Cadillac limousine and shut the door. When the old man saw John Hill approaching, he said urgently to the driver, "I don't want him in this car. Lock the doors." But John Hill was quick. He opened the door and gently nudged Ma over until he had a place.

At the cemetery, not far from Chatsworth Farm, Ash turned his head away and did not look at the coffin. Instead he burned his gaze at the broken figure of John Hill. And as he walked away, toward the Cadillac, with one arm supporting his sobbing wife, the old man muttered, in a voice strong enough for those nearby to hear, in a voice more chilling than the March wind that whipped about him, the old man said, "If the law doesn't get the son of a bitch, I will."

book two
JOHN

*". . . Behold a pale horse:
and his name that sat on him was Death . . ."*

14

Assistant District Attorney I. D. McMaster was a low-key man of great patience, but a fortnight after Joan Robinson Hill was in her grave, he was fed up. "That damned old man," he told a colleague, "is *obsessed*." Several times each day, it seemed, Ash was on the telephone, with some new and damaging tidbit to report. Finally McMaster told the bothersome caller that nothing could be done until Dr. Jachimczyk released the results of his second autopsy. Until then, there was nothing to investigate. A licensed physician—Bertinot—signed the woman's death certificate, and a qualified hospital pathologist—Morse—did an autopsy, even though the conditions were admittedly abnormal.

Ash would not be subdued, no more than a pot of water would cease boiling when flames licked beneath it. His personal loss was enormous, but there was another factor at work: excitement had been injected into an old and eroding life. A mystery to solve! His home became command headquarters to which Ash summoned first his own doctor, a general practitioner named Ed Gouldin, then others who had been friends of John and Joan Hill. The heart surgeon Grady Hallman was one of the first to come, the Mozart-playing Jim Oates was another. They pored over the Sharpstown Hospital case history and discussed the case. The men of medicine agreed that Joan's death was both tragic and unusual but that, until the county coroner made an official ruling, speculating was not only harmful but potentially slanderous.

Very well. In the meantime Ash would not just sit in his easy chair and wait for what surely would be a bolt of lightning from the medical examiner's office. There was no law against assembling material that might be useful someday. He began telephoning people who reportedly had "information" and he scribbled it all down on the pieces of lined notebook paper that were soon spilling from his pockets. His dining-room table became a blizzard of documents, medical charts, textbooks, scraps with cryptic messages that only he could read.

These were some of the stories that Ash pulled out of people while he waited for the coroner:

"I went by John's house the night of the funeral to pay my respects," said a young widow who had often played bridge with Joan, "and there were just a few people there. John, his mother, Boot, some other doctor and his wife I didn't know. We all sat around drinking coffee, then people started drifting away and it was only John and me left. I made excuses to leave, but he insisted on showing me around the house. We went into that damned music room—most incredible place I ever saw in my life—and I told him that I had already seen it. But he played with all the gadgets and insisted that I sit down.

"There was one straight-backed chair in the middle of the room and he put me there—dead center. Then he puts his music on, some sentimental number about Honey living and Honey dying, and I *begged* him to let me leave. He made me stay thirty minutes, the god damn music crashing all around me. I didn't know *what* he was going to do."

From a psychiatrist who had lived near the Hills: "When I got over to John's the night of the funeral, he was all alone. Right away he started talking about insurance and business matters. He didn't seem to be grieving much at all. In fact, he was smiling. From his attitude that night, Joan's death seemed to have no more impact on him than the Oilers losing a game—and he was certainly not an Oiler fan. He was much more interested in showing me the music room than in talking about Joan's disease. Mr. Ash, we didn't talk about Joan's disease *at all!* And the reason is clear to me. This was a man who had walked out on his wife when she was in terminal shock—and he knew that I, as a doctor, knew it."

From a nurse who passed along a conversation she overheard in the surgeons' lounge at St. Luke's Hospital: "One doctor says, 'I always suspected old John wanted to get rid of his wife. Wonder what he gave her?' And the other doctor said, 'Maybe an overdose of insulin. It's a natural body substance and impossible to trace.' "

And, from several of the River Oaks women who stood in a black-garbed group after Joan's casket was dropped into the earth: "We were all saying how terrible it was the way John neglected Joan when she got sick. It really was a crime, Pa. Negligence!"

* * *

Ash hired himself a private eye, Clyde Wilson, the same
supervirile detective who had been employed by his daughter to fetch John's clothes from under the nose of Ann
Kurth. Wilson owned property near Chatsworth Farm, and
he was an "over the fence" friend and neighbor of the Hills.

His mission was to obtain statements from Diane Settegast and Eunice Woolen, the two Dallas women who had
been house guests in the last week of Joan's life. "We need
to get these girls down on paper before their memories get
stale," ordered Ash. Wilson drove immediately to Chatsworth Farm where Diane and Eunice were staying, woke
them up, and asked if they would write down every single
detail they could remember about the events of the week
leading up to Joan Hill's fatal illness.

Both women agreed, enthusiastically. They stayed up the
rest of the night typing out individual statements which they
signed and left in Wilson's mailbox the next morning. Thus
was the highly inflammatory "chocolate éclair theory" committed to paper. Diane had whispered it in Ash Robinson's
ear the second night of Joan's wake. And she had told it
to others, enough so that the Case of the Poisoned Pastries
was whipping through River Oaks like a plague. Now the
story was on paper, Xeroxed, and beginning to make the
rounds of those whom Ash wanted on his side, as allies in
a deepening war against his son-in-law.

Next Ash sat down with Effie Green and her husband,
Archie, the aged servants who had worked at the Hill
home. Both were frightened, both were anxious to co-
operate with the demanding white man in the tradition of
subservient Southern retainers. Neither had come into contact with the law or with any authority save the Social
Security people in their long lives, and both were anxious
to be done with whatever Mr. Ash wanted. Graciously Ash
sat them down at his table and had his own maid, Carolyn,
prepare them coffee. Already Carolyn had been up the
street talking to the old people and encouraging them to
co-operate with her cantankerous employer.

Ash spoke with the Greens for a few minutes, then wrote
down the following document, typing it himself:

EFFIE AND ARCHIE GREEN ARE SERVANTS IN JOAN'S
HOUSE

EFFIE GREEN'S STATEMENT

Effie came to my home voluntarily in the afternoon of March 26, 1969.

"Mr. Robinson, I am a good Christian woman and I can't stand to see a good woman murdered and not say something. Mrs. Hill was murdered right in front of my own eyes, and Archie will say the same thing.

"Mrs. Hill was in good health and laughing all last week and Saturday when I left. Then early Monday morning Dr. Hill told me, 'Mrs. Hill is sick. Do not go into her room or disturb her all day under any conditions.' Late in the day Archie said, 'Something is wrong up there. Mrs. Hill has not called or moved out all day—no water—no food—nothing. You had better go up and listen at the door.' I went up and listened and heard nothing. I opened the door and looked in. Mrs. Hill was just lying there, but she saw me. She said, 'Effie, I am so sick. I don't want to die.'

"I closed the door real quick and ran down and told Archie. He said for me to stay away or I would be in real trouble; that I should not have opened the door in the first place.

"Archie and I talked all that nite. No one else was there; she was all alone. Dr. Hill came in about 4 in the morning. He called me about 7 A.M. (Tuesday) to come up to Mrs. Hill's room. I went up and he was sitting on her bed holding her face away from me— I could not see her face, it was under his arm.

"He said, 'Effie clean her up and give her all of the liquids that she wants all day.' . . . Dr. Hill left. That was about 7:30 A.M. or earlier. Mrs. Hill did not drink her coffee and seemed to be in a stupor. She didn't seem real. She said, 'Effie, get me all the ice you can. I am burning up inside.' I turned the cover back and it smelled like garbage. The whole bed was covered with watery action and blood. It was not her period— it was POO-POO. It had been there for a long time—it was dry around the corner. He had put towels under her to take up a lot of the wetness. I tried to clean her up and she said, 'Effie, see if you can get me to the bathroom.' I lifted her up and green water and blood just poured out of her. She fell back on the bed and her eyes rolled back in her head and I could see that she was 'Passing.'

"I called Dr. Hill until I got him and told him that he had better come home at once; that his wife was passing. He got there about 9:30 or 10 and went upstairs. In about one-half hour Mrs. Robinson came and they called me up to help carry her down to the car. Mrs. Robinson was crying and asked what had happened to her daughter. Mrs. Hill had told her mother, 'I am blind, I can't see you.'

"We all took her down stairs. (I had the impression that Archie helped, but did not so record.) All the time Dr. Hill was rubbing the back of her hand trying to rub out needle marks between her fingers. He was trying to rub these needle marks out.

"I put pillows in the car and we laid her down in the car."

Abruptly, the document then switched to Ash's point of view.

I asked Effie if she would write all this down in her own hand writing. She said that she certainly would and that Archie would also. "We both saw murder done." As Effie was leaving, she pulled out a small bottle of pills. "See these pills. Dr. Hill gave them to me when I said that I had a headache. I wouldn't take one of them for anything. I know too much and he might try to murder me. When he handed them to me, Boot said, 'Effie don't take those pills. You will go to sleep like my mother did and never wake up.' Dr. Hill grabbed Boot and took him upstairs and whipped him."

At this point the statement seemed to end—unsigned and unsworn—so Ash tacked on an addendum: "Effie did not write all this and I asked my maid to go see her. Carolyn, my maid, has heard most of what Effie said."

And then, in an addendum to the addendum, Ash elaborated on why the document was unsigned. "Effie said that Archie told her they would both be in deep trouble and would not write anything. Archie won't let Effie come back over, but Effie is a good Christian woman and really wants to tell her story. Her conscience seems to be bothering her."

Now this document began to make the rounds ("Read this!" Ash commanded Assistant District Attorney Mc-

Master). But one fact seemed curious to those close to the case. Both Effie and Archie continued to work for Dr. John Hill, odd, certainly, if the old woman was afraid for her life. This statement and the circumstances under which it was written would come under close scrutiny.

Dr. Jachimczyk's report was delivered to Assistant District Attorney McMaster at the end of March 1969, and it was a reeling disappointment to Ash Robinson. Having gone over the original findings by Dr. Morse, the Sharpstown pathologist, and having done his own examination of the tissue specimens that Dr. Morse snipped from Joan's embalmed organs, Dr. Jachimczyk came to a surprising conclusion:

"The cause of death is attributable to acute focal hepatitis." The coroner went on to slap down the favorite "perhaps" being expounded in Ash's living room by the armchair detectives, that being *"perhaps* John put some sort of exotic poison either into the pastries or into the medicine he gave her during her illness."

When Joan was admitted to Sharpstown Hospital, a blood culture was obtained. "The negative blood culture obtained during life excludes a bacterial infection," said the coroner. Moreover, "the negative toxicologic results" from stomach contents taken after embalming "exclude the exogenous poisonous substances." This would rule out arsenics and the like.

"Therefore," wrote the coroner, "it is my opinion based upon a reasonable probability that the cause of death is due to acute focal hepatitis, probably viral in origin."

That very morning Assistant District Attorney McMaster received the report and bowed out of the affair. "The Harris County coroner says your daughter died of hepatitis," he told Ash Robinson, "and that is hard to make a murder case out of."

Ash assembled his medical experts for another session of armchair detection. All were skeptical of the coroner's ruling.

Grady Hallman, once John's closest friend, rejected the notion of hepatitis. He pointed out that Joan's hospital chart did not show jaundice, or an elevation in bilirubin, the standard measure for hepatitis. Moreover, he pointed out, even the most acute viral hepatitis is rarely fatal within two or three days. It had to be remembered that the woman was vibrantly alive and dancing at a ball Friday night before she died on Tuesday.

Dr. Dwight Nichols and Dr. Ed Gouldin concurred. Gouldin even said, "I will stake my reputation that she did not have hepatitis."

The doctors and the old man chewed on the report until well past midnight, developing dozens of possible scenarios.

Ash Robinson was now inspired to do something canny. Had it been possible, he would probably have hired the district attorney himself to prosecute his son-in-law. This being illegal, even in Houston, Ash did the next best thing. He engaged the *former* district attorney, a lawyer named Frank Briscoe, freshly out of public office and into private practice. Here was a man who knew his way around the courthouse, and grand juries, and investigations. No bones were made about the reason for his employment. He was to mastermind a meticulous examination of the death of Joan Robinson Hill and produce sufficient evidence and witnesses to persuade a grand jury to indict Dr. John Hill for premeditated murder.

Briscoe was a handsome, prematurely gray-haired man with an especially kind face. Old women and Little Leaguers would have put their trust in him on first meeting. When he was a prosecutor, jurors often found it difficult to believe that this sweet-looking man would demand with vengeance the death penalty. And usually get it. Briscoe was not opposed to taking old Ash Robinson's money, but he did have one bit of bother. How would a murder charge be possible in light of the coroner's official decision that the poor woman died of hepatitis?

Go out and ask Dr. Joe about that, demanded Ash. His face wore an expression that seemed to say: I know more about this than I am at liberty to say.

On April 9, 1969, Frank Briscoe went to the Harris County morgue and caught up with Dr. Jachimczyk between autopsies. The two men were old friends and could speak easily with one another. Frankly, said the pathologist, he did not believe there was a murder case here. The care that John Hill gave his wife at home was questionable, and his choice of hospitals was unusual, but beyond that?

Is it possible to give somebody hepatitis by injection? wondered Briscoe.

"Sure, it's possible," said the coroner. "But not probable." Dr. Jachimczyk had heard that Joan ate shellfish on a brief trip to Mexico City a few weeks before she died, and she also ate snails at a dinner party in Houston one week before her hospitalization. Possibly hepatitis could have been brought on by one of those ingestions.

Briscoe pressed him. Can a doctor *inject* a patient with a hepatitis-carrying bug of some sort and bring on death?

"Anything is possible," repeated the coroner. "It's probably possible to give somebody hepatitis by giving them poison."

But quickly the coroner shook his head to puncture that balloon. Joan's kidney and liver had both tested negatively for heavy metals (arsenic) and strychnine. "You must remember that the toxological evaluation was negative," said Dr. Jachimczyk. "In other words, we didn't find any traces of poison."

Ma Robinson opened her front door one evening in early April and discovered both her son-in-law and her grandson standing unexpectedly on her front porch. Both pleased and flustered, she ushered them in and went to find a cola for Boot.

John Hill was well aware of the troublesome pot his father-in-law was stirring. Ash, after all, lived but a few blocks away on the same street, and several times in recent weeks John had driven by and noted the automobiles of his friends and colleagues parked in the Robinsons' circular driveway. He had also felt bad vibrations in his profession. A nurse would suddenly stop talking to another one when John Hill appeared in a coffee lounge, or two interns would look at him a little strangely as he nodded good morning on the way to surgery. Even some of the neighbors had been behaving curiously as they came by to pay hurried condolences.

On this night, John came on a mission of peacemaking. Ma took Boot to another part of the house and left the two men together. Ash stared at John Hill coldly.

The plastic surgeon extended his hand in kinship, but the old man studiedly ignored it, letting the proffer fall, unaccepted. Awkwardly John sat down, uninvited. Ash took his favorite chair, under photographs of Joan, throwing one beefy leg over its arm as was his custom. For a time there was nothing but silence.

"I came to see if you and Ma were all right," John began. Maybe they could all go out to dinner together one night soon.

Pa answered in stony non sequitur: "I am not satisfied with either autopsy. I want her body exhumed, so it can be done properly."

John quickly refused the notion. He did not want his wife's grave disturbed.

"Then we have nothing to say to each other," answered Ash. He rose and moved toward the door.

"I'm sorry you feel this way," said John. "I was hoping we could resume our family life together." He called for his son and Ma delivered the child, unwilling to part with him so quickly, knowing, somehow, that she would not be seeing him very often again. Across her face was written the sadness of a lost life. Later, when the two people were together, readying for bed, he in his fading red silk pajamas, she in her worn pink nylon robe, Pa said gruffly, "I sent the son of a bitch packing."

Ma nodded. She, too, had a salty tongue. "The bastard had on dark glasses, did you notice? And it was nighttime. I think he didn't want us to see his eyes. A man's eyes always give him away."

Ash did not answer, so Ma prattled on. "Didn't Boot look good? He's such a fine boy. I just wanted to hold him and keep him."

The old man agreed and got into bed. His own eyes would have given him away at this moment, for they were repositories of loss and anger. Joan had been taken from him, now he would probably forfeit his grandson. His golden years were turning into lead.

Hardly two months later, another surprise event took place, stunning enough to pump new blood into Ash Robinson's faltering efforts to avenge his daughter. In fact, when the old man heard of it, he smiled and said, "Well, well, imagine that." And he actually rubbed his hands together in glee. It was June and his bones were warming.

15

When John telephoned, a very long ten days after the funeral, Ann Kurth feigned coolness. Well, how nice to hear from you. Warm, isn't it? Sorry about Joan. How is the boy? What's new in your life?

"I have to talk to you," he said.

"Do you know what I've been going through for all this time?" Ann shot back huffily. "Not knowing what in hell is happening?"

John issued terse instructions. Meet him in the parking lot of the Meyerland Shopping Center. He was dropping his son off at a movie. They would have two hours to talk.

It was a dreary afternoon with rain building toward the east; black clouds were moving in, streaked with lightning. The two lovers sat in Ann's car, the windows rolled up, the air conditioning belching out cold sheets of moisture. Yet John Hill was perspiring.

"You look awful," said Ann in greeting. "Do you have hepatitis?" The news of the coroner's new decision was freshly in the papers. John shook his head negatively.

"Am I going to get hepatitis?" asked Ann. "Should the boys and I get gamma globulin shots?"

"No," he said. "I'm not going to get it, and neither are you."

"You don't look well," she said. "And you're not going to look any better unless you take care of yourself. Is Robert all right?" Ann had never been able to call the boy "Boot." In fact, after Joan Hill's death, the nickname that Ash gave the boy was never used again. From the moment his mother died, he was called only Robert.

The boy was fine. John's mother, Myra, had come from the Rio Grande Valley. She had taken over the household and it was running by her efficient standards. Ann nodded. She knew what that meant. John had told her how his mother walked around the house with an open Bible, reading verses out loud to whoever might be in the room.

John said he wanted to talk about his dead wife.

"No," said Ann. "It's over. It's a situation that doesn't ever have to be mentioned to me."

"I only wanted to say that she was prettier in her coffin than I ever saw her."

What about Ash and his midnight meetings? she asked. John shrugged, pleading ignorance. So far, Ann gathered, the mischief down Kirby Drive did not worry him. The most vivid memory of that afternoon was John Hill throwing his arms around her and saying very softly, very tenderly, "I just wanna hold you, baby. God, I need somebody to hold onto."

On May 26, less than two and a half months after his first wife was buried, John Hill obtained a license to marry Ann Kurth. They drove to the neighboring Fort Bend County courthouse, hoping to avoid publicity. Then, a week later, while their respective children were touring the Six Flags Over Texas amusement park between Fort Worth and Dallas, the surgeon and his mistress slipped away to a Church of Christ and were wed. They spent their honeymoon night in a motel at the amusement park, with children bouncing happily on their bed and quarreling over domain of the television program.

Hardly had the license been obtained before Ash knew, his source being a gossip columnist who received a tip. And when word came from a private detective shadowing the couple that they had actually gotten married, Ash was outwardly *possessed* with indignation. But blended in was no small amount of excitement. He hurried first to his lawyer, Briscoe, the former district attorney, and urged him to use this new and damaging information as valuably as possible. Briscoe was growing weary of the old man, as was most everyone connected with the situation. But this was indeed an interesting turn of events. Now the motive comes out, insisted Ash. John promised last December, *in writing*, to give up his paramour, but he never did. And when Joan wouldn't give him a divorce, he got rid of *her*.

Briscoe did not see it as crystal clear. A decade in the district attorney's office had taught him that murder was rarely a package wrapped neatly in ribbons. More often it was a collection of loose threads that, when pulled, either formed a snare trap or fell apart and revealed nothing but a wide, empty gap.

But the revelation of John's marriage was enough for him to get in contact with I. D. McMaster, his former junior colleague at the DA's office.

McMaster was a politically ambitious prosecutor who had recognized from the first moment Ash Robinson walked into his office that there was enormous publicity potential to the matter. Now McMaster was beginning to feel that this was one of those events that might be the turning point in a man's career. It was heady company out there in River Oaks, sipping whiskey with fat cat lawyers and society doctors.

"Just how do *you* feel about it?" McMaster asked his former boss.

Frank Briscoe believed only that a few points seemed "a little out of focus," particularly that John Hill had behaved "like an old hound dog" while still married to Joan, and then rewed after an indecently brief period of mourning.

McMaster revealed that he had been spending time researching hepatitis. From a gastroenterologist at the Veterans Administration Hospital the prosecutor had learned that it was possible to give someone hepatitis through an injection, but that it would not usually kill that quickly. Traditionally, hepatitis takes months or years to destroy a liver and cause death.

What about the famous French pastries? asked Briscoe.

McMaster had no answer. All he knew officially was that the coroner's report ruled out poisons, on the basis of studying embalmed tissue. If the lady's blood hadn't washed down the undertaker's sink so quickly, more might be known.

McMaster thus decided—with Briscoe's concurrence—that the best way to satisfy the old man, the community, his own professional curiosity—and ambition—was to proceed with a grand jury investigation. It became over the early summer of 1969 a loose, almost informal affair, rather like a coroner's inquest, with doctors dropping by the courthouse to testify. Lanza, Bertinot, and Morse, the three Sharpstown physicians who were brushed by the case, went before the jury and none had any damaging news that would support "foul play." Others like Hallman and Gouldin—those doctors who convened in Ash's living room to play at Sherlock Holmes—questioned John Hill's choice of hospitals and the length of time it took him to get his wife there. Nathan Roth, the first employer of John Hill, laid spicy testimony before the panel, suggesting that his former junior partner was a philanderer and a would-be seducer of women patients. One witness friendly to John Hill snapped sourly at a newspaper reporter, "I'm here because a rich old fool has influence enough to try and buy an indictment."

John Hill was understandably uneasy about what was

going on at the courthouse. Resolutely he had avoided engaging a criminal lawyer to represent his interests, for he
feared that such would be an admission of guilt. Rather he
went about his practice as ever, secretly desperate because his referrals were dropping sharply. Ash Robinson
had written a letter to the Harris County Medical Society
saying he had "grave charges" to make against his son-in-
law, "who should not be allowed to practice medicine in
this city," and a committee granted the old man an appointment before a disciplinary group. But Ash failed to
show. Moreover, John was getting reports from friends,
each of whom had an ominous Ash Robinson story to pass
on. As he made hospital rounds one afternoon, a nurse
whispered John into a stair well and said she had heard
that Ash was trying to solicit the testimony of a lab technician at the VA Hospital. The gossip was that the old
man was offering $25,000 if she would go before the grand
jury and testify that she smuggled some sort of poison
out of a VA laboratory and gave it to John.

A radiologist called and said Ash was spreading a story
around that John kept a secret apartment where he operated on the faces of escaped criminals, altering their features so that they could elude capture. And a third informed John that Ash was waving around a list of at least
ten women with whom the plastic surgeon was supposedly
carrying on simultaneous love affairs. It also grieved him
that many old friends, particularly Grady Hallman, were
in league with Ash.

All of this John bore stoically. To each of the informants he paid polite gratitude, but to none of them did he
show outrage. Then word came that Ash was even suggesting he was somehow involved in the tragic suicide of
his brother Julian six years earlier, and finally John Hill
took action. But rather than hire an attorney, he rang up—
of all people—Clyde Wilson, the private detective who had
first been engaged by Ash Robinson. Wilson seemed to
be a man for all seasons.

"If I were you," suggested Wilson, "I would volunteer to
take a lie detector test."

"Why?" asked John Hill.

"There are clouds of suspicion hanging over your wife's
death," said Wilson. "A lot of bad talk in this town. Best
way to put the whole thing to rest, and make peace with

your former father-in-law, the best thing would be to take a lie test."

Hill's voice grew tense: "But I'm not guilty of anything. My wife died. I'm sorry she died. But my taking a lie detector examination can't bring her back."

"Agreed," said Wilson quickly. But the water was so muddy at this point that the only way to clear it was through some sort of action. The surgeon might consider going down to the grand jury and giving them a statement.

At this Hill began to protest. That would be tantamount to admitting something was irregular about Joan's death. If he went before the grand jury, the press would have a field day. He wouldn't get another patient for six months. His practice was already falling off.

All the more reason to take a lie test, said Wilson. And don't worry. Such a test would never be admissible in court.

What court? asked John.

Just ruminating, said Wilson. But a properly administered test, with I. D. McMaster sitting there watching, could persuade the district attorney's office that there is nothing to the case save the protestations of a lonely and spiteful old man.

After several days Hill called the private detective and said he had decided to offer himself for examination—but under specific conditions. One, he would not take the standard polygraph test, for he had no faith in its merits. Instead he would agree to Sodium Pentothal injection, the so-called "truth serum." Secondly, it must be done at a hospital, under clinical conditions, not in the courthouse or police station. Three, it must be tape-recorded so that any arguable answer could be listened to at a later date. And lastly, both sides must swear to keep the examination secret from the media.

Wilson took the offer to I. D. McMaster and a bargain was struck. Thus on an afternoon in early June, three months after the death of his first wife and a few days after his marriage to a second, John Hill appeared in a small diagnostic room at Sharpstown Hospital. He selected this institution, he said, because he wished to show his faith in it. Ash Robinson, to be sure, immediately began grumbling that the test would be rigged, as further part of a "conspiracy." He had learned that John Hill owned one per cent interest in the hospital and this was proof enough for the old man that all at Sharpstown—from the administrator down to the mop maids—were clustered around John Hill to shield him.

A young, neutral, and respected Houston anesthesiologist, Dr. Richard Smith, was selected by both parties—John and the DA's office—to administer the drug, although he had never done so for the purpose of examining veracity. Dr. Smith had, however, administered Sodium Pentothal for surgery at least ten thousand times during his career, and was thoroughly familiar with its capacities—and dangers. When he arrived at the room, he professed immediate annoyance at the arrangements. Nothing was available in case of emergency!

"This is a life-threatening procedure," he said. "You don't just give a guy a shot of this and stand back and watch." He would not give the drug unless several things were brought to the room. Quickly he ticked off his requirements: a defibrillator and cardiac arrest equipment in case of heart irregularities, a laryngoscope to look down the windpipe, a drug called atropine ready in a syringe to speed up the heart in case it slowed (the drug also halts production of saliva to keep such from slipping into the lungs), a supply of succinylcholine, a muscle relaxer to facilitate placing a tube in the trachea if needed for emergency breathing (sometimes patients choke during anesthesia as if they were choking on a piece of steak), and—most importantly—an anesthetic machine with positive pressure oxygen and anesthetic gases.

While the equipment was being readied, McMaster watched both the anesthesiologist and the subject closely. It had occurred to him that since Dr. Smith worked chiefly at St. Luke's Hospital, and since John Hill occasionally performed plastic surgery there, then perhaps they had the bond of colleagues, if not more. When asked to conduct the lie test, Dr. Smith volunteered immediately that he not only knew John Hill, he had served as anesthesiologist for the man's surgery on "maybe ten or fifteen operations . . . but none in the past two years." McMaster placed a few discreet phone calls and felt reasonably sure that Smith was an ethical man, and not in league with anybody.

Now, in the blunt, tough way he had people cracking at Sharpstown, McMaster was satisfied that Smith was not on *anybody's* side. This was also the first moment that

McMaster had the opportunity to observe John Hill in the
flesh, and he seemed pleasant enough, not outwardly
ruffled by the ordeal that lay ahead. Certainly he was not
McMaster's kind of man, not the kind to sit next to at a
football game, or wait with for ducks in a blind on a still
East Texas lake. "What we have here," mused I.D. to
himself, "is a rich, spoiled, pretty-faced mama's boy.
Little lacy-britched, too, I'd expect."

The test began with Dr. Smith inserting an IV tube in
the surgeon's arm, starting a drip of water and glucose.
Next he gave John a dose of two per cent Sodium Pentothal, dripping it with the solution. Sodium Pentothal, he
had explained to the prosecutor, is a fast and pleasant way
of going to sleep. The drug also has the ability to remove
any inhibitions a person has about speaking freely. "A guy
will speak his subconscious," said Dr. Smith. And there,
hopefully, reposes the truth. "In theory, the varnish of
lies is removed by this drug."

The anesthesiologist was asked how much Sodium Pentothal it took to accomplish this phenomenon. "Each patient is different," he answered. "A dose that would kill
one man dead might make another lie there and say,
'What time are we gonna get started, Doc?' It is an up-
and-down thing, a cyclical situation. It's sort of like a boat
moving through a heavy sea. You might be in deep water
some of the time, in shallow water at other times. Let's
put it this way: a patient may be way down at one minute, then closer up toward consciousness a few minutes
later."

McMaster watched with fascination. An assistant, T. C.
Jones, was ready with a list of prepared questions. Clyde
Wilson, the private detective, snapped on his tape recorder
and blew into the microphone to make sure it was working. Everything was set and Dr. Smith began the questioning.

Q. How old are you, sir?

A. Thirty-eight years old.

Q. Do you have children?

A. Yes, sir, I have one child.

Q. What is his name, please?

A. His name is Robert.

Q. The district attorney, Mr. McMaster, will begin to
talk now.

Smith thus threw the interrogational ball to McMaster,

who began uneasily, not quite comfortable with the power given him. On the examining table was stretched out one of the city's most famous young doctors, now, apparently, totally helpless, with no defenses, compelled to speak the truth. But there was no feeling of science fiction about it, only a pinprick of bother about invading a man's most private regions. McMaster shook off this worry and began his interrogation. John Hill responded readily, easily, almost casually. Almost *too* casually, McMaster began to feel. It was as if they were in a café, idling over coffee.

Q. When did you marry Joan Hill?

A. In 1957.

Q. And when did she die?

A. Nineteen sixty-nine.

Q. Do you recall the date?

A. March 19.

Q. And the time?

A. I think it was around four-thirty in the morning, or four forty-five.

At this answer, McMaster made note. The death had been an hour earlier. Surely John Hill knew this; why would he alter the time? Dr. Smith increased the dosage slightly, putting his patient in a deeper state.

Q. When did she first become ill, Doctor?

A. She spent the preceding Friday and Saturday laying around, or at least the preceding Saturday laying around mostly in bed.

Here McMaster made a second note to himself. On the last Friday of her life, Joan Hill was radiantly alive. She had drawn a compliment from Mrs. Dotty Oates on how attractive she looked, and she was a vivacious ornament at the wild game dinner. She did not spend that day "laying around."

John Hill breathed heavily for a moment or two, then plunged into an amplification.

". . . I don't know if that was necessarily part of the illness, but I did think it was somewhat unusual . . . but two or three days prior to that she had complained of not feeling well while on a furniture-buying tour for our music room, but I couldn't have called that exactly an illness. Saturday night, prior to her passing, she had quite a bit to drink and went to bed not feeling too well. Saturday, I mean Sunday morning, she didn't seem to feel too well and spent quite a bit of the day in bed, and Sunday afternoon she had some episodes of vomiting and felt like she was going to have a loose bowel movement. Should I go on?"

"Yes."

". . . Felt like she was going to have some loose bowel movements and she vomited so hard it felt like she was going to continue vomiting. She said she felt like everything she put in her mouth she was going to vomit, so I gave her a shot of Compazine. It is a drug to relieve vomiting.

Q. Was this given with a hypodermic?

A. Yes, sir, it was, and I never thought much more about it; it seemed to relieve her of upset stomach, and she did not have any more vomiting until—wait, she complained of some discomfort from chills later in the afternoon Sunday. Sunday evening again, she complained of vomiting and diarrhea . . . and didn't feel she could keep anything on her stomach or take a suppository, so I again gave her another shot of Compazine. It seemed to help her some although she had several more episodes of vomiting and several episodes of diarrhea; she even had one real large diarrhea stool in the bed."

McMaster made a note to the effect that Dr. Hill admitted giving his wife at least two shots of what he *claimed* was Compazine.

Furthermore, it concerned the assistant DA that the answers coming from Hill were more of a *recitative*, a story spun by a narrator, not the terse responses normally given. Sometimes a patient rambles on and on, in and out of fantasies, while under the drug—McMaster learned this in his brief research. But from what he had been led to believe, patients did not lie there coldly and dispassionately and throw off rather well composed speeches. Dr. Smith felt that his subject was too close to the surface of consciousness, so he increased the drip of Sodium Pentothal, and, in the doctor's metaphor of ocean waves, put him once again in deep water.

Q. Did you ever check her fever, Doctor?

A. No, I didn't have a thermometer, but I felt like she had a temperature elevation. I believe, but I cannot say for sure . . . [McMaster to himself: *"Would a man under Sodium Pentothal say, 'I cannot say for sure'?"*] I believe we got a thermometer the next morning, Monday, and checked her temperature and I think her father came over and checked her temperature. I don't remember exactly how much temperature elevation she had, but it was a degree or two.

Q. All right. Monday morning, what was her condition?

A. Monday morning she did not seem to feel well at all. She had a number of diarrhea stools during the night and vomited several times, and she had fever the next morning, and I didn't think she was particularly ill. But I thought perhaps she might have an infection of some sort and that it would probably blow over in a day or two.

Q. Did you leave instructions with the servants at the house that she was not to be disturbed on Monday?

A. I indicated that they should keep a look after her and take care of her and I felt enough concern about her that I ordered some medication from the Avalon pharmacy . . . some [unintelligible] which is an antibiotic. In capsule form. I ordered something for the diarrhea and I instructed the maid to make sure she took the capsules and I asked one of the ladies who was staying in the house at the time, a weekend guest, you might say, although they stayed longer than that, I asked her if she could possibly stay with her, because I was kind of concerned about her, before I went to the office.

Q. This is Monday still are we talking about?

A. Yes, sir, Monday.

Q. Who was that house guest?

A. Miss Diane Settegast.

Q. And did she stay or did she leave?

A. To my best recollection she did leave.

McMaster considered this in contradiction to the statements of Settegast and Woolen, both of whom said they offered to stay and look after Joan on Monday, but that John shooed them off.

Q. Getting back to the time of your wife's illness, Doctor, where did you administer the two shots of Compazine? On what portion of the anatomy?

A. I gave them intravenously because Compazine is very uncomfortable when administered intramuscularly, and I felt that since she hated shots so badly that it would be more comfortable if they were administered intravenously. So I diluted the Compazine and administered it intravenously.

Q. Where specifically?

A. In the arm.

Q. In the forearm?

A. Yes, sir. In the cubital vein.

Q. Did you administer any shots in the hand?

A. No, sir, I did not.

(This was asked in response to Effie's statement that she saw Dr. Hill allegedly rubbing his wife's hand as he took her downstairs en route to the hospital.)

Now McMaster moved abruptly to the doctor's relationship with Ann Kurth, like a man walking a conversational path with another, only to make a quick and unexpected right turn, glancing back to see if the other kept up with him.

Q. Sometime last year, Doctor, you separated from your wife, did you not?

A. Yes, sir.

Q. At that time were you going with one Ann Kurth?

A. Yes, sir, that is correct.

Q. And at that time, were you going to marry her?

A. Yes, sir.

Q. And subsequently you went back to Joan Hill, is that right?

A. Yes, sir.

Q. At the time you went back to Joan Hill, did you have a complete break with Ann Kurth, or did you continue seeing her?

A. I went back with the desire to have a complete break; however, I had left Mrs. Kurth in a difficult situation with her neighbors and where she lived, and so I did check back with her sometime within a twenty-four- to forty-eight-hour period following my reunion with Joan.

McMaster then jumped quickly back to Joan Hill's final hours. John Hill journeyed with him effortlessly, betraying no discomfort at leaving his new wife and returning to his dead one.

Q. Doctor, going back to your wife's illness, on Monday evening, what was her condition?

A. At that time I felt she was significantly ill, but I didn't feel she was deathly ill. She was running fever and still lying in bed and obviously not feeling well.

Q. You were not sleeping with her at that time, were you? While she was ill?

A. Yes, I slept with her while she was ill.

(Later on, Ash Robinson would read this part of the transcript and snort, "God damned liar! He wouldn't sleep with her when she was well, much less in a bed filled with her own excrement.")

Q. On Tuesday morning what was her condition?

A. Her condition was very serious. Early in the morning I felt like she was probably all right and I went and played a Young Audiences concert for some hour and a half to two hours, after which I came back and she appeared to be in shock. I took her to Sharpstown Hospital, much against her desire. She hated doctors and hated shots and did not want to go, but I led her down the stairs in order to take her to the hospital.

McMaster began to press the fact that the doctor allegedly rose from his wife's sick and soiled bed, called the maid to come and clean the defecation on the sheets, then went off to play a concert. Later, he would tell his associates in the DA's office that these answers were the most shocking to him.

Q. And when you called the maid up you went on to the concert? Is that correct?

A. Yes . . . I did. . . . I slept with her and thought that she was all right and asked the maid to see that she took the medication that I had there for her and that she drank plenty of liquids as she seemed to be getting dehydrated.

Q. At this time, Doctor, did you not consider that she was in shock? Tuesday morning, prior to going to the concert?

A. Prior to going to the concert, I checked her pulse and . . .

(Here, for the first time, the doctor's words trailed off altogether, and his answer was unintelligible. Nor did the district attorney pursue it.)

Q. Following her death, did you order an autopsy yourself?

A. Yes, sir, I did.

Q. Did you commission Dr. Morse to conduct that autopsy?

A. I commissioned the hospital.

Q. Do you know what the present result of the autopsies is?

A. I heard hepatitis.

McMaster then asked *the* question of the hour:

Q. Doctor, did you at any time, prior to, or during your wife's illness, cause her to ingest or did you inject anything that could have caused that illness or added any complications to it?

In an almost whisper that the recorder did not pick up fully, he either said, "Do I have to answer that, Clyde?" or "I will answer that, Clyde." He then responded: "No, sir, I did not." Firmly. Positively. No qualifying tremor.

Q. Not in any way, shape, or form?

A. No, sir.

The test consumed an hour, and when it was done, Dr. Smith pronounced the surgeon able to rise from the table and resume his activities—with the suggestion that he go home and rest for the remainder of the work day. First they all went to the hospital coffee shop. McMaster observed that Hill was exhilarated the test was over and kept asking, "Did I pass?"

"The guy's hyperactive," thought McMaster to himself.

Later, in the hospital parking lot, the assistant DA, his associate, T. C. Jones, and the private detective, Clyde Wilson, talked beside their automobiles. Jones spoke first. "Well, I guess he's clean. He passed." The young investigator was convinced of the surgeon's innocence.

McMaster shook his head in disagreement. "Only if you take it at face value. I think he knew everything we asked him."

Later, questions would be put to the anesthesiologist, Dr. Smith, questions seeking reassurance that John Hill was indeed knocked out by the drug and not somehow faking his responses.

Bluntly, is a person able to lie under Sodium Pentothal?

"Well," Smith responded, "it's arguable. There is a bone of contention in medicine. A psychopathic liar who doesn't know the difference between truth and lies might beat the test. . . . John Hill went all the way from being paralyzed by this drug to being, at times, semi-aware. At one point during the test I felt he was not under deep enough, so I increased the dosage. At another point, the guy even stopped breathing, but a little oxygen brought him back."

The anesthesiologist had a brusque comment to make about the experience. "Bullshit," he said. "The whole thing's bullshit. John Hill is innocent."

16

The spring grand jury ended its term in 1969 without acting on the death of Joan Robinson Hill. Assistant District Attorney McMaster thanked the panel for hearing the various witnesses who testified. But he did not even ask for an indictment. Beyond circumstance, there was not a shred of hard evidence. Some of Ash Robinson's medical allies were critical of the manner in which John Hill treated his sick wife, and of the hospital he chose to take her to, and McMaster was not wholly convinced that the truth serum test prodded John Hill's conscience as fully as it was supposed to do. "But I haven't got enough to convict this boy of running a red light," McMaster informed a highly chafed Ash Robinson. The old man thundered to friends with the now familiar storm of accusations and speculations.

"Great God almighty!" cried Ash, invoking a deity in whom he professed no belief. "Just what in hell-fire does it take to bring this man to the bar of justice? He killed my daughter so he could marry his paramour. It's that simple. He took her to a remote hospital where he was part owner and he hired doctors nobody ever heard of to care for her—one of 'em, I understand, used to be an exotic dancer—and when Joan died, they practically stole her body to get it out of the hospital that fast and onto the undertaker's table. Somewhere along that line is enough evidence to convict somebody!"

McMaster had heard all of this before, a score of times before, and he was tired of the old man, fed up with his ravings, worn by the raw thrust of money and power. The prosecutor envied the security of wealth, but at this moment he was full of its abuse. In effect, he told Ash: Show me some evidence and I'll get an indictment. No grand jury is going to indict, and no trial jury is going to convict, solely on the basis of what *you* feel!

Ash telephoned the foreman of the retiring grand jury and asked him for a summation of the panel's attitude. The foreman, Dr. Lancaster, minister of the large and socially prestigious First Presbyterian Church, had already visited with Ash at one of the old man's midnight sessions. This

struck some courthouse observers as bordering on the
ethically dangerous, but the preacher moved and spoke
with such an apparent pipeline to the good and the righ-
teous that no one made complaint. How could there be
criticism of a man who began each day's jury delibera-
tions with a prayer that asked for "divine guidance"?

Dr. Lancaster was willing to make his feelings known
to a reporter after the panel was dismissed. "We just didn't
have enough evidence to indict John Hill," he said. "I recognized the anguish that Mr. Robinson was going through
over his tragic loss, but you cannot indict on anguish."

Considerable testimony was presented showing that
John Hill was—and here the minister grew discreet—"not
a very good husband. . . . We heard and saw a lot of
human frailties and passions, but we were not asked to
return an indictment for adultery."

And the Rev. Mr. Lancaster had one parting comment
which at the outset did not particularly interest Ash Robinson, for it seemed subsidiary to his goal. But it planted
the germ of an idea in the head of I. D. McMaster. "Of
course, we also heard testimony that indicated medical
negligence," he said. "But how can that be proved with a
husband and wife involved? That becomes a very private
matter, a very complex area for the law to enter."

Negligence. McMaster wrote the word down on a yellow
legal pad. And underlined it. A few inches away he wrote,
Murder. Just doodling. Then he drew two lines to connect
them.

In late June, Ash bustled into the office of his attorney,
Frank Briscoe, and announced a new scheme, or, more accurately, the warming up of an old one. One of his medical counselors kept speculating that *perhaps* valuable information could be obtained if the body of Joan Robinson
Hill was dug up and autopsied again. This time, insisted
Ash, "with the best doctors in the world present."

Briscoe was annoyed. Neither coroner's ruling nor the
truth serum examination, nor the grand jury's failure to
indict, nor the district attorney's rapidly failing interest in
the case had dissuaded this old man a whit.

"I want you to get it done for me," ordered Ash. "I already asked John Hill and he said quote I do not want her
body disturbed end quote. Well, that's the first time he was
ever considerate of her."

Briscoe knew the law on this point. An exhumation cannot be done without permission from the next of kin, which, in this case, was the widower.

Ash had done his homework. But a court can order it done! A grand jury could request it, and a judge could sign the paper. "I want the best god damned pathologist in the world," Ash said, "I don't care if he's Egyptian or Eye-talian or on a spaceship halfway to the moon. I want him here, I want my daughter's body autopsied, I want some answers, and hang the cost. I'm paying for the whole god damned thing!"

Briscoe took the new outburst as only the latest in a continuing line of nuisances from his meddlesome client. Surely Ash would find some other street to investigate and forget about this one. But when the telephone began ringing at the Briscoe home before the sun rose, and when the old man began barging into his office with no forewarning, Briscoe called up Dr. Jachimczyk and asked what, if anything, could be accomplished by an exhumation.

He trod carefully on the coroner's ego, for Jachimczyk was a proud man who felt that, as a professor of both legal and medical degrees, he was above most criticism. Recognizing this, from the relationship they had as DA and coroner, Briscoe was canny enough to point out that in *this* exasperating matter, mistakes were made long before Jachimczyk was even notified about the death. Thus any areas of dispute were the fault of other men.

In his long career as coroner, Dr. Jachimczyk had performed several exhumation autopsies, cutting into bodies that had been buried for eight weeks, and others that had been in the ground as long as eight years. Sometimes, the coroner told students, the eight-year internees are in better condition than the fresh-planted ones. "It all depends on the embalmer's art, the environment of the grave, whether it's in a marshy area, or on high and dry ground, whether it's a concrete vault, or whether seepage got into the casket," explained the coroner. "There are just so many variables that you can't predict whether it's worth the time and effort—and anguish—for the family."

Specifically, Briscoe wanted to know, what information might be obtained from an exhumation autopsy? Jachimczyk's answer seemed sensible to him, so much so that he dictated it into his case file: "Dr. Joe feels that nothing would be gained by disinterring the body for further tests except for the very remote possibility of finding needle marks in an unusual place, or from the surrounding area of such needle marks possibly being able to locate traces of some chemical substance. He doubts if anything new would be discovered that was not found in the first autopsy. . . ."

Briscoe repeated this to his client and suggested that the idea of exhuming Joan be dropped. Ash responded by firing his lawyer.

Not at all unhappy to be rid of the old man, Briscoe remarked to a reporter, "Ash has an absolute fixation on his daughter's death. I've never seen anything like it."

In search of succor, Ash dropped in on a crony, Cecil Haden, the prosperous, portly owner of tugboats and oil barges. In his serge suit and vest straining to cover a well-filled belly, in black shoes spit-shined, in unadorned and sensible bifocals, Haden would be cast, in dramatic endeavor, as the banker who says no to the farmer. An elder of the Houston establishment, he engaged a former astronaut to work for his firm, perhaps because he was thus able to display prominently on his office wall a framed dollar bill. "It went to the moon and back," he told visitors. Cecil Haden was a non-related uncle to Joan Robinson Hill, he adored her as much as Ash, and he was not only a pallbearer for her coffin, he wept bitterly at her grave.

From the day of Joan's death, Haden had been privy to the most intimate confidence of his friend of forty years, and he well knew the desire of Ash Robinson to punish John Hill. Haden had even attended one of the armchair detective sessions and listened intently as the doctors scattered about Ash's living room analyzed and dissected the medical information.

Now his old friend was so irritated at his inability either to get an indictment against John or to obtain an exhumation of Joan's body that he grew red in the face and began puffing like a thirsty hunting dog. Cecil Haden bade Ash calm down and collect his thoughts and reduce his blood pressure.

He was angry, explained Ash, because his lawyer would not pressure the district attorney into an exhumation.

Haden nodded in understanding. Did Ash really believe that this drastic act would help his cause?

"You're damned right it would," said Ash. If the best

pathologist in the world turned up in Houston to study his daughter's body, "we'd see some scared rabbits runnin' every which-a-way."

In that case, Haden had a valuable piece of advice for his long-time friend and co-investor in Florida oil and gas ventures. The best way to make the mule go in Houston was to hire a powerful law firm—one like Haden's own attorneys, Vinson, Elkins, Weems, Searls and Connally. The last-listed partner was John Connally, whose name went up and down on the front door between government jobs. The enormous law firm, one of the largest in America, occupies six entire floors of a downtown Houston skyscraper, employed 230 attorneys, and is powerful enough to be, along with another firm or two in Houston and Dallas, an invisible second state government. One of the brightest and most highly respected young fellows in the firm was a lawyer named Richard Keeton, son of the eminent torts scholar Page Keeton. "That boy can do whatever needs to be done," said Haden in glowing recommendation.

Thus engaged, attorney Keeton made a few discreet inquires at the courthouse to learn the attitude of the man whose authority was needed to order an exhumation, he being Carol Vance, district attorney of Harris County, Texas. Unlike previous DAs in his town, Vance was neither flamboyant nor possessed of an ego that required the nourishment of provoking his name into public print regularly. Neither was he considered a particularly brilliant courtroom warrior. His skill lay in administration, like a clever general who knows which lesser officer to fling into battle.

By summer, 1969, District Attorney Vance was fatigued with the non-case of Joan Robinson Hill. Too much time and expense had already been drained from his budget. Had this woman been the daughter of a ship channel worker, and the wife of a garage mechanic, his office would not have spent one hour of investigation after the coroner ruled death from hepatitis.

Yet Vance was not without political ambition, the general assumption around the courthouse being that he would one day run for attorney general of the state of Texas, and thence to the governor's office. Lacking the evangelical fervor that can still stir voters in Texas, a state that likes its politicians to have a little cotton patch dirt under the fingernails and a mail-order wardrobe, Vance was colorless, a lean and rather elegant man who would have to run chiefly on his integrity and his skills as a legal office manager. Valuable tools for any public servant, but not assets calculated to raise a candidate triumphantly to the shoulders of the body politic. Though Vance privately hoped that the Hill case would go away— more than one lawyer connected with the matter counted up the number of years Ash Robinson had walked on the earth and speculated that his biblical allotment was almost up—the district attorney decided he had best keep the pot simmering on the back of his stove and keep an eye on the flame now and then. So he had let his deputy, I. D. McMaster, fool around with the old man.

Now, suddenly, the potent law firm of Vinson, Elkins, etc., had entered the confounded case, in the person of attorney Richard Keeton, and Vance found two new reasons to tolerate further investigation. One was the potential blessing that the enormously powerful firm could award a candidate for high state office, and two—Vance was the protégé of John Connally, former governor of Texas, and the man who had appointed the district attorney to his job. Whether these factors influenced Ash Robinson in his choice of lawyers is speculative, but he missed few other tricks.

It took Ash very little homework among his attending physicians to discover that the ranking world figure in pathology, the dean of forensic medicine in the United States, the *éminence grise* of the autopsy chamber, was Dr. Milton Helpern, chief medical examiner of the city of New York, a man of whom the New York *Times* said, "He knows more about violent and mysterious death than anyone else in the country." Helpern's office publicity releases called him "a Sherlock Holmes with a microscope."

Dr. Helpern's reputation and credentials were so vast that, in listing them, he seemed like a corporation, his statistics an annual report. In forty years in the New York City medical examiner's office, he had personally dissected twenty thousand corpses himself, and had supervised or participated in an almost incomprehensible fifty thousand more. In his examining table had been laid out the bodies of more than ten thousand people who were slain by gunshots alone. He was, with no competition, the most celebrated coroner since the art was initiated in the twelfth century by an English king who wanted to insure that he received bounties due the throne in the case of suicides.

"I focus not on whodunit, but on whatdunit," Dr. Helpern once told a news writer. "My job is to determine the cause of death. I'm not trying to find out who did it. That's the job for the police. But when anyone dies by violence, or suspicion of violence, regardless of whether violence is suicidal, homicidal, accidental, or undetermined, it is an ancient responsibility of government to officially inquire into the death. This is of paramount importance to the administration of justice. If you're going to have a system of justice, we're a very intricate part of it."

Ash requested and received a collection of news clippings concerning Dr. Helpern—a man who did not object to attention from the press—and he underlined two sections of one lengthy interview in a medical publication. The first concerned Dr. Helpern's appearance in more than three thousand courtroom cases as an expert witness on the cause of death: "He has not only been responsible for sometimes determining the guilt or innocence of a person suspected of homicide, but his testimony has decided the distribution of large sums of insurance money—which often hinges on whether a death was natural, a suicide, or an accident."

The second clipping dealt at length with Dr. Helpern's most celebrated case—the matter of Dr. Carl Coppolino. The parallels between the death of Mrs. Coppolino and his daughter's death were tantalizing to Ash Robinson. Coppolino was a New Jersey anesthesiologist whose wife, also a physician, died in Florida. It was officially termed a heart attack. Suspicion arose that Coppolino actually murdered his wife by injecting her with an exotic poison, and a district attorney in Florida asked Helpern to come down to conduct an exhumation autopsy. In the autopsy, he discovered a previously overlooked needle mark in the upper quadrant of the left buttock—and, more puzzling, no sign of heart disease in the remains of the thirty-two-year-old woman. After six months of laboratory work, Dr. Helpern became convinced that there were traces of succinylcholine chloride—a fatal substance—in tissue taken from the buttocks at the point of the needle mark. Dr. Helpern's testimony was the principal factor in the conviction of Dr. Coppolino.

"He sounds like the *papacita* to me," said Cecil Haden.

District Attorney Vance promptly received several letters from Houston physicians at the behest of Ash, each urging that the death of Joan Robinson Hill be further investigated by an exhumation and new autopsy. Ash Robinson would bear all of the expenses, including the considerable sum required to extricate Dr. Milton Helpern from the recesses of Manhattan's Bellevue Hospital and fly him to Houston, all the way down to the $125 required by the cemetery to pay the gravediggers.

Letters and long-distance telephone calls also went out to Dr. Helpern in New York, who responded by ringing up his colleague in Houston, coroner Jachimczyk, to discuss the peculiar situation. Helpern wanted it made clear before the first clod of earth was disturbed on Joan's grave that it was highly unlikely he would discover anything dramatic since the cause of death sounded bacterial, and since the body had been hurriedly embalmed.

He agreed to come, however, if someone in official authority would ask him. Helpern worked out his fee with Ash Robinson in private, and the two men agreed to keep the sum secret. Rumors swirled in Houston that Ash was paying dearly to import the star pathologist. Dr. Jachimczyk told a colleague that he had heard "a six-figure sum" being mentioned. When a reporter asked Ash to be specific, the old man refused to tell. One hundred thousand dollars, he said, was "out of line." But his ego glowed because he possessed the funds and the power to import a medical examiner with a world-wide reputation.

The district attorney, Vance, put the matter before another grand jury to see if they would order an exhumation. The panel reviewed the material submitted to the first grand jury, the one that failed to indict John Hill. They were also given a letter from Ash, an impassioned, inaccurate, and wildly biased plea. Rather than use his own stationery, with his personal signature printed in type at the top of the page, Ash cannily substituted a letterhead from Chatsworth Farm, crowned with the celebrated photograph of Joan Robinson Hill riding Beloved Belinda, one of the most beautiful and *alive* pictures ever made. Anyone reading the letter would pause first to examine the lovely girl and horse, then move eyes down into the terrible message beneath:

I have asked for ten minutes of your time to request your authority to have the body of my daughter exhumed for an additional autopsy. Dr. John Hill refused to give me this permission for reasons of his own. It could hardly be because of his love or sentiment for my daughter because he permitted Ann Kurth to move into his and Joan's home the day after she died and remain there until they were married on June 5.

. . . I hope to learn the cause of Joan's death. If it is not pancreatitis, as they first said, or hepatitis, which so many distinguished doctors do not believe—then what did my daughter die from? In this connection, I have asked numerous doctors for the name of the world's finest and most eminent forensic pathologist and toxicologist. They all said Dr. Milton Helpern, medical examiner for the city of New York. I have-never met him or seen him, but I called him and made arrangements for him to come to Houston and perform an additional autopsy if the Grand Jury will so permit him. There is absolutely no fatal drug that does not leave evidence in the muscle, organs, or bones, and I believe that he can find the same if it is there. . . .

In this case there is certainly widespread speculation and gossip. It should be cleared up to the best of our ability. Then, too, who could object to being proved correct?

Its curiosity whetted, the grand jury voted to let the exhumation proceed.

Until this bit of news reached his ears, Dr. John Hill had not yet hired an attorney. He got one fast, Don Fullenweider, a young lawyer who had represented him in the civil lawsuit that resulted in the angry professional divorce from his first surgical associate, Nathan Roth. The attorney lived across the street from John Hill, and he had kept an idle eye on the comings and goings at the great white colonial mansion. Often Fullenweider saw Ash Robinson prowling around the block in his black Lincoln. Once he noticed the boy Robert Hill playing in the yard. Ash drove by and stopped, watching intently his grandson. The boy glanced up, ran as frightened as a startled deer into the house. "Obviously," thought Fullenweider, "John Hill does not want his son to talk to Ash Robinson."

Fullenweider felt it wise to call in his partner, a colorful, aggressive, and successful criminal attorney named Richard Haynes, one of the city's true characters, known far and wide by his nickname "Racehorse." This appellation referred not to the way he scurried about the courthouse, or the fast way he talked to juries (except when he chose to don the disguise of a down home country boy with figurative stalk of hay 'twixt his teeth), or even his thoroughbred record of victories won. The name harked back to his youth when, playing football, he once attempted to run sideways across the field and shake a herd of pursuant tacklers. "That kid must think he's a race horse," said the coach, and the name stuck, particularly since the short young man had a Napoleonic ego and felt he would surely be governor if not President someday. "Racehorse" was not a bad handle to run a campaign on.

Racehorse Haynes met with the troubled plastic surgeon on a mid-summer's evening at the Fullenweider home. John Hill began by saying he was not sure he even needed a lawyer, but the activities of his ex-father-in-law had progressed beyond the nuisance stage. "He somehow has it mixed up in his head that I am responsible for the death of his daughter," said John. "I want that disproved immediately."

The two lawyers listened as John went over the now familiar tale of his wife's illness, her hospitalization, her sudden death. Haynes did not probe into the matter of the French pastries, or why the doctor so quickly married a woman he had earlier renounced in a signed letter of repentance. At the end of the evening, Racehorse said he would keep an ear to the courthouse and try to learn what, if anything, the district attorney possessed that smelled of criminal trouble.

"More important," urged the lawyer, "get yourself a team of prestigious doctors to stand over Helpern at that autopsy and protect your own interests. You can be damn sure Ash is gonna have *his* doctors there," said Racehorse.

The next day John rang Dr. Jachimczyk and inquired whether it would be a good idea to have friendly doctors in attendance as deputy coroners.

"Well, I'm not in a position to tell you what to do or

what not to do," responded the medical examiner. "But let me put it this way. It all depends on whether you believe in offensive medicine or defensive medicine."

The analogy was clear—and worrisome.

On a damp and overcast Saturday morning, August 16, 1969, at the Forest Park West cemetery, a back hoe scooped away the topsoil from the grave of Joan Robinson Hill and cleared enough earth for a forklift tractor to ease steel fingers underneath the blue steel coffin. With a funeral director from Settegast-Kopf in attendance and operating under the decree of the Harris County grand jury, the coffin was swept of dirt and placed once more in a Cadillac coach and borne to the Ben Taub Hospital. There a remarkable group of doctors were waiting.

Dr. Milton Helpern had flown in the night before from New York, had been met by Ash Robinson, and was taken to a suite at the city's elegant Warwick Hotel. This was a once shabby apartment house which was bought by an oilman who gave his wife a blank check to redecorate it. She flew to Europe and purchased antiques, castle furnishings, and entire flea markets, flying home, it was rumored, $20 million lighter. The Warwick was magnificent, well appreciated in a city that relishes dash and opulence. It was also just the right place for a visiting dignitary.

Waiting in the hallway outside the basement morgue were two teams of doctors, lined up like opponents in a football game, or seconds in a macabre duel. Ash Robinson sent in his regular squad to play for him, those physicians who had met so frequently in his home for theoretical maneuvering. Among them were the heart surgeon Grady Hallman; Ash's personal physician, Ed Gouldin; and even one obese and socially ambitious fellow who, at that moment, held a medical degree but not a license to practice medicine in the state of Texas. But he recognized the publicity value of the event, and he was negotiating to lease Chatsworth Farm, and he volunteered eagerly to serve on behalf of Ash Robinson.

John Hill's squad was far more qualified in the business of the day. He sent forth three genuine pathologists, doctors who specialized in this kind of work, including one, Dr. Robert Bucklin, who was medical examiner for the neighboring city of Galveston. Also present in the morgue were the two Sharpstown Hospital doctors, Walter Bertinot and pathologist Arthur Morse.

All were sworn in as deputy medical examiners by Dr. Jachimczyk, each promising to uphold and defend the Constitution of the United States, though what pertinence this held to the autopsy of Joan Hill no one was quite sure.

Moreover, there was McMaster, the assistant district attorney, who by this time was ambivalent on the subject of John Hill's guilt or innocence ("One day I'm convinced the son of a bitch did her in," he told an associate, "the next day I'm not sure of anything"), plus assorted investigators from the medical examiner's office, representatives of the mortuary and cemetery, and secretaries. "The body is the one lying down," feebly joked one of the doctors as the crowd entered the room.

Realizing the stakes involved and still smarting from the experience with the first autopsy, Dr. Jachimczyk was anxious to make sure that everything was according to form. Before introducing Dr. Helpern to the assemblage, he set out the protocol. Absolute master of the day would be "our distinguished visitor, the chief medical examiner for the city of New York." Dr. Helpern would conduct the autopsy from the initial order to open the casket to the final directive to reseal it. No one could enter or leave the room without Dr. Jachimczyk's permission. There would be no lunch break. "If anyone starts feeling uncomfortable," began Dr. Jachimczyk, with a wave of his hand elaborating on the queasiness that can come in a procedure of this sort, "then he or she may leave, with an escort of my decision." Milton Helpern entered, an amiable but imperious doctor. There was no doubt about his star quality; he was the kind of man for whom others opened doors. He seized control from the moment Dr. Jachimczyk stopped talking. Never once did the sixty-seven-year-old doctor falter, show signs of fatigue, or turn his head away from the grotesqueness of the hours.

A microphone was hung over the dissecting table, and secretaries were on hand to take down his every utterance. "What I plan to do," said Helpern, "is to dictate the findings and the observations out loud, and if anybody wants to comment, whether in agreement or disagreement, or if anybody wants to ask a question, he is at liberty to do so. I am very anxious to have *one* record here. Sometimes these things are done where the pathologist works very quietly and the observer works very quietly, and you don't realize later, from their reports, that it is the same autopsy."

As he spoke, a storm broke over the city and thunder rumbled outside. One of the observing doctors would later say, "The day was written by Edgar Allan Poe. It was a weird and frightening experience."

Dr. Helpern would make three separate sets of tissues and specimens—one for him to take back to New York and study under his microscope, a second for Dr. Jachimczyk, and a third would be made available to the team looking after John Hill's interests. The group nodded in understanding. Dr. Helpern clapped his hands enthusiastically. He was ready to begin. "The body, I am informed by Mr. Todish of the funeral home, has been removed from the cemetery and is now in the autopsy room. It is in a 6-6 steel sealer, 20-gauge, exterior Queen Blue coffin. Is that correct?"

The funeral home attendant agreed.

"Very well," said Dr. Helpern. "Let us enter and begin."

The group took places in a semicircle around the autopsy table, and for the moment all eyes were drawn to the steel-blue coffin. Dr. Jachimczyk approached the box, placed his hand on its cold hard shell, and demanded formally of the mortuary attendant if this was the lawful casket of the decedent, Joan Olive Robinson Hill. It was indeed. "Has it been crushed or damaged in any way?" "It has not." "Very well, then pursuant to the order of the Harris County district attorney dated August 11, 1969, the order is hereby given to open this coffin." The six clasps snapped open easily, and the top half of the lid, like a Dutch door, was swung back.

One of the doctors took one look, sucked in his breath, and shut his eyes. Another, who had known Joan well and had seen her win championships on the great horses, turned away. Death had worked its horror; the cleansing of time was interrupted.

Dr. Jachimczyk studied the body and nodded in affirmation. This was the same corpse that he had viewed in the same coffin at the funeral home six months before. "I remember distinctly this gown," he said, touching his fingertip to its gold glitter. Attendants known as deniers then carefully lifted the body from the coffin and transferred it to the examining table. Dr. Helpern directed that the gold gown be carefully cut away. The naked body was laid forth for him to study.

But something nagged at him. The old pathologist turned

his attention back to the coffin. He brushed his finger against a portion of the white satin lining. He beckoned for Dr. Jachimczyk to move in closer. The two medical examiners bent over the box.

Dr. Jachimczyk shook his head in bewilderment. He snapped his fingers for an aide to come to his side.

The room buzzed. What was happening?

Dr. Helpern broke the suspense. "There is dried mud inside this casket," he said. Old mud. Well-dried mud. Mud not new from the morning's official shovels.

The inescapable conclusion, murmured Dr. Jachimczyk, was that this casket had previously been opened. Someone else had already violated the sleep of Joan Robinson Hill.

17

"This is the body of an adult white woman, appearing to be approximately thirty-five to forty years of age," dictated Dr. Helpern, electing to proceed with his autopsy while lesser figures sought to find out if and why the coffin had previously been opened. He spoke as dryly and as dispassionately as an archaeologist describing the ninth Etruscan vase unearthed that morning. His eyes roamed over the body before he picked up his scalpel.

The over-all state of preservation was good. The silver-blonde hair was still full and in the pony tail she had worn even to the grave. The facial features were mostly intact, save for an abundant growth of black mold that had crept resolutely over the cheeks and nose, as in a masquerade. The nose itself was dehydrated and beginning to crumble. On the torso, almost graceful trails of blackish-green mold grew, easily brushed aside, like an offending cobweb. One hand was covered with the mold, the other was not, and each gleamed with silver nail polish under the bright lights. And everywhere the flesh was softening, soon to pull away from the bones, destined to disappear.

"The fingers," he went on, "are dehydrated and mummified. The fingernails are well manicured, long and loose. . . . Tissues of the upper and lower extremities are soft, and there is maceration of the skin on the lower part of the chin and upper part of the neck, posteriorly, as well as on the extremities of both hands, with separation of the epidermis." Dr. Helpern picked up the left wrist of the corpse, as if he were preparing to take a pulse. He read from a clear plastic bracelet still there, "Joan O. Hill, #23709, Sharpstown General Hospital, Dr. Bertinot." This was the hospital identification bracelet which no one had removed.

"There is a sutured Y-shaped autopsy incision on the body . . . concealed by a strip of white paper gauze. . . . The toenails are painted with a bright red polish. . . . The skin of the feet and legs are macerated with separation of the softened epidermis. . . . Tissues of the extremities and back are very soft with gas formation. . . . There is a mottled bluish-reddish-gray lividity, with some bluish areas in the skin over the left buttock and separation of the epidermis from the posterior surface of the arms. . . . The anus is packed with stained wadding. . . . The tissues around the anus are quite soft and macerated."

Dr. Jachimczyk approached the pathologist and cleared his throat to interrupt. He had been in a corner of the room for several moments, talking quietly but agitatedly with a representative from the Settegast-Kopf Funeral Home. "It has come to my attention," said Dr. Jachimczyk, "that this coffin was opened approximately three days after the interment. A permit was obtained by the deceased's husband, Dr. John R. Hill. Apparently he had the coffin opened so that he could remove a ring from his wife's finger. Or some piece of jewelry. Is that right, sir?"

The undertaker, a Mr. Zernial, nodded. On that March day it had freshly rained, and probably a bit of mud had gotten into the coffin during the reopening. The entire episode was legal, said Zernial. The plastic surgeon had obtained the required permit from the city Health Department, and a representative of the cemetery was present during the exhumation. John Hill was not at his wife's grave for more than a few minutes. Nothing out of the ordinary happened.

But now, the stunning news drenching every imagination in the room, two of the doctors representing Ash Robinson stared at each other in wonder. It tended to confirm their suspicions that John Hill was guilty of his wife's death. Why would he sneak out to her grave and open her coffin, unless he was desperate to view the corpse once again and

see if there was an incriminating needle mark somewhere?
He was, after all, a plastic surgeon, and plastic surgeons
are clever at removing scars and blemishes.

Dr. Helpern punctured the ballooning speculations. It
did not appear that the body has been tampered with, he
announced. The autopsy incisions were closed and intact.
He had seen too many exhumed corpses not to know if
mischief had been done. "Let us continue, gentlemen," he
ordered, bringing the murmuring to a halt. One of the
doctors in the room would later remember thinking at this
moment, "John Hill's goose is cooked. Any second now,
Dr. Helpern is going to pause, shake his head, and announce that he had discovered some trace of an exotic
poison, known only to a remote tribe in the Amazon."

But it was not to be. For another half hour the coroner
continued to remark mechanically on the appearance of
the corpse and its texture to his touch. "The eyelids are
sunken . . . there is some black mold in the frontal portion
of the scalp. This mold and macerated epidermis is very
easily rubbed away. Eyeballs are soft. Jaws have been
wired together with small metal studs. Lower jaw is easily
moved. . . . There is an area of parchment-like drying of
the skin near the inner end of the left clavicle. . . . The
breasts are small, firm, and symmetrical, tissues well
hardened. . . ."

He noted puncture marks, apparent needle injections, on
the arm, but Dr. Bertinot identified these as the sites of the
IV injections. He searched the body inch by inch, looking
for unexplained needle marks, but although several were
encountered—on the buttocks and on the stomach, these
were accounted for by the Sharpstown hospital charts.
The coroner's meticulous search impressed every doctor
in the room. He removed fingernails and toenails and
examined the underlying tissues. He spent a quarter of an
hour on the elbows alone. The eyeballs were probed, the
tongue, inside the ear, the female organs, anywhere that a
needle might have injected a deadly poison. Nothing.
Nothing. Nothing. Again and again, Dr. Helpern shook
his head in negation.

Now he took his blade and opened the corpse along the
lines of the previous autopsy incision, and where the
embalmer had punctured the right groin to pump out the
blood and pump in preserving fluids. Dr. Helpern announced the finding of considerable portions of a brown

substance, "an abundance of petroleum jelly" and cotton wool placed in the body cavity during the embalming process.

As his blade moved through the body, he cut off tiny slivers of the organs, handing them to attendants who quickly placed them in plastic containers and marked the contents. And his narration continued: "The liver, lungs, one kidney and the spleen are detached, showing evidence of sectioning during the prior autopsy. These are now covered with a granular compound which had been placed in the abdomen during the embalming process. The stomach is now being opened and, attached to it, the unopened small bowel and the large bowel are found. . . ."

At this Dr. Helpern paused and pursed his lips. His attitude seemed to say, "Here is a woman who died abruptly and mysteriously of something perhaps ingested—and the first pathologist did not even slice open her gut to examine it!" Opening the stomach, Dr. Helpern discovered an empty region, a gray and foul-smelling organ. The gassy odors of the corpse became so strong that a nurse passed through with an aerosol room freshener.

Nothing significant was encountered there, nor was there any content of note either in the bowel or its lining. Throughout the interior of the body was gray, mushy mucosa material, product of the passage of time and the breaking down of the flesh by nature's forces.

Moving to the chest cavity, Dr. Helpern noted that the aging process had been going on in the aorta, the body's principal blood vessel, but nothing curious about a woman almost forty suffering from narrowing of the arteries by cholesterol and fats. It happens to everyone. Some suspicious-looking black material in the trachea turned out to be the result of terminal aspiration. Lungs were blue-gray in color, soggy, and collapsed. Not unusual.

The pathologist poked around for several moments in the thoracic cavity as if looking for something that should be there. Then he shook his head in mock despair and gestured with his cutting instrument to the place where the human heart normally reposes. The doctors strained to see.

"The heart is missing, gentlemen," said Dr. Helpern. And, just after removing the metal undertaker's clamps that held the scalp in place and further compounding the mysteries of the day, the pathologist announced, "The brain is absent, too."

Dr. Jachimczyk suggested a recess. Ordering one of his deniers to stand guard over the corpse, he led the bewildered assemblage out into the corridor for cigarettes and colas. "Damnedest case I ever saw," said the Houston coroner. Dr. Morse, the Sharpstown pathologist who performed the first autopsy on Joan Hill in the funeral parlor after she was embalmed, approached and requested a moment of privacy.

The missing heart was easy to explain, he said. During his autopsy, he decided to cut out the organ and take it back to his laboratory for study. If he had been working in a large hospital with a first-rate pathology lab, and if he had had access to the body before it was swimming with embalmer's fluid, then this would not have been necessary. A few slivers from the heart would have been sufficient for study. "But I knew this was a case where I couldn't 'go back in' . . . so to speak . . . and I decided I'd better take the entire heart."

A little testily, the coroner accepted the explanation. It is not unusual for a pathologist to remove a heart for study, even though the news is delicately withheld from a mourning family which would not enjoy knowing that the deceased was buried without its most glamorous organ. Sometimes the pathologist takes out the heart, studies it, then at the last minute, before the coffin lid is closed, tosses it back in, wrapped in a plastic bag. The fault this day, felt Dr. Jachimczyk, was simply lack of communication. He was sorely embarrassed to have no answer when Dr. Helpern could not find Joan Hill's heart.

And the brain? Perhaps Dr. Morse could enlighten him about its absence?

Yes. As a matter of fact, the brain was in the trunk of his car at that very moment and he would go outside and get it and bring it to the autopsy room. "In the trunk of your car?" echoed the coroner in disbelief. The Sharpstown pathologist's explanation was that he was currently in the process of transferring several pathological specimens from one laboratory to another, and the container of slivers from Joan Robinson Hill's brain was among them.

At the time of the original autopsy, he had elected to remove the entire brain—a common procedure—because he needed to place it in a liquid called formalin. This "fixes" the tissue after a week or ten days and makes it easier to study microscopically. Brain tissue is usually too soft and mushy otherwise.

Dr. Morse re-entered the autopsy room where Dr. Helpern and the others were waiting. In his hands he bore a white plastic container, similar to the kind women use to store frozen food. Within were several sections of what he said was the brain of Joan Robinson Hill. Immediately Dr. Helpern began examining them with his naked eye. As the visiting pathologist perused the gray and rubbery slices of human brain, Dr. Morse volunteered a new theory for the cause of death. Meningitis. Under the microscope, he suggested, Dr. Helpern would encounter inflammation, specifically an inflammatory exudate consisting of approximately fifty per cent polymorphonuclear leucocytes and fifty per cent mononuclear cells. Dr. Helpern nodded, not in assent but in acknowledgment. He would have no snap comment on this latest hunch as to the woman's mysterious demise—first it was pancreatitis, then it was hepatitis, now it was meningitis—until he could study the brain specimens under his own microscope back in New York. Dr. Helpern's attention returned to the spinal cord and its meninges. "The cord is fairly well preserved throughout its length," noted Dr. Helpern.

At 4:35 P.M., concluding almost seven hours of an emotionally and physically exhausting ordeal, Dr. Helpern put down his blade. If none of the doctors had a further notion, if no one had an idea of some other place to search for nefarious deeds, then he would release the body back to the undertaker for reburial.

As he packed his bag with the officially marked tissue specimens, the mortuary attendants fell to the unpleasant task of redressing the corpse in the glittering gold brocade and returning it to the steel-blue box.

"What do you think, Joe?" asked one of the doctors of the Houston coroner on the way out of the hospital.

"I think it's a classic example of Murphy's Law," Dr. Jachimczyk responded. "Everything that could possibly go wrong—has."

Ash Robinson drove Dr. Helpern to the airport and en route pumped him for the results of the autopsy. The pathologist was reluctant to reveal anything, realizing the volatile character of the vengeful father who was his employer in his matter. But he did volunteer that no unexplained needle marks were found, and nothing dramatic or incriminating was discovered thus far. But most of the detective work would be accomplished in the laboratory, under the microscopes.

Then Dr. Helpern revealed the startling news about the dried mud on the lining of the casket and the tale that the grave had been opened three days after burial.

Ash gripped the wheel to keep the big Lincoln from swerving. Why had John Hill opened his daughter's casket without telling anybody? "That son of a bitch told me he did not want her body disturbed," said the old man angrily.

Racehorse Haynes asked his client for an explanation of the secret journey to his wife's grave. Why was the casket reopened three days after burial? Nothing much to it, answered John Hill, nonplused. During their marriage he had given Joan a valuable ring. And the day after she was buried he could not locate it among her possessions. He looked everywhere, then decided it was probably on her finger. He wanted it back for sentimental reasons. That was all. Turned out it wasn't there. Never did find the thing. Months later, this story reached Yvonne Roper, the college friend who chose Joan's dress for her burial, and she remembered John Hill's dictum: No jewelry. The dress was glittery enough. "My insides started to scream," she told a friend.

One of the doctors who represented John's interests at the exhumation autopsy telephoned him the next day. "I think the whole thing was a farce and a waste of time," the doctor said. "Helpern didn't find anything that wasn't already known. I hope your ordeal is over."

John murmured thanks. He was ready for a piece of hopeful news. Up to that telephone call, he felt his life was disintegrating all around him, like a cliff giving way to the sea.

First his medical partner had left. John had hired Dr. Jim Moore fresh out of plastic surgery training, and the handsome, modish young doctor had eagerly joined the office just one year before. Not only was he skilled—with fast and sure hands—he was a powerful lure for the carriage trade. Matrons would lie down on his table happy just to have him snip their eye bags. And now John needed him for reasons above and beyond his appeal to patients. The notoriety of Joan's death had pared his practice. Referrals from other doctors were down by at least one third. It was John's notion that Jim Moore could keep the money coming in until the hoorah was over.

Once or twice during the grand jury investigation, the junior man went into John's office, shut the door, and blurted out that their relationship was being jeopardized by kooks. "We're getting a lot of sensation seekers coming here ostensibly for consultation, but what they really want is to see the show—us," he said. Jim Moore had hoped that his senior partner, obviously flustered and under enormous strain, would want to talk the problem out. But John merely shrugged. There was nothing he could do about it. "John won't talk to me," Moore told his wife. "I don't think he talks to anybody. How can he keep everything bottled up like that?"

Not only were the curious taking up their time, the office was a mass of continuing intrigue—taping devices on certain telephones, Ann Kurth Hill bustling in and out giving orders to nurses and upsetting them, anonymous threatening calls, patients canceling long-time relationships. When the situation worsened, Jim Moore stopped John in the hallway of their consulting rooms and said, "My patients are starting to look at me in a funny way, John. It's guilt by association. And I can't handle it. I'm sorry as hell. But I'm quitting."

"If you do, I'll never forgive you," said John in a rare moment of public anger.

Later Jim Moore would feel compassion and guilt, but at this moment all he wanted to do was get out. Fast. Moving his case records out in the middle of the night. A medical career could not tolerate scandal, even hints of it.

Next, John learned that he was the vortex of a vicious telephone campaign that was intensifying. The principal of his son's elementary school received a call suggesting that Robert (Boot) Hill's father was a murderer and an intolerable influence on the other children. A dermatologist called John to say that he had just been telephoned by Ash Robinson, who was giving out his ex-son-in-law's private home telephone number with an urging that it be used. He quoted the old man as saying, "Call John Hill in the middle of the night. Pressure him. Make him confess." The Harris County Probation Department received an anonymous call that described John Hill and his new wife, Ann Kurth, as "unfit parents." Even the minister of the Church of Christ which John attended, the religion that shaped his life, was telephoned, and a whispery voice croaked that John Hill's presence in the sanctuary of God was an affront to Christian people.

At this, John was outraged. He would not tolerate slurs on his religion. The next Sunday he asked that he be given permission to make public confession before his congregation. An elder of the church, Jerry Ferguson, commented later that the surgeon was clearly devastated by what was happening to him. "He asked all of us to forgive him for bringing reproach on the Church," said Ferguson. "He said he was sorry that all of these things were happening, and that he needed the prayers of the Church to help him sustain his burden."

Even this painful rite of repentance somehow reached the ears of the district attorney's office. An investigator called the church. No, the DA's man was informed, John Hill did not make any "confession" to his wife's death. He was merely conforming to church policy, which demands that any member who brings notoriety on the congregation must ask for forgiveness from the membership.

Perhaps John Hill could have borne the discomfort of scandal had he found solace in the embrace of his new wife. But Ann Kurth gave him hardly more comfort than had he driven down Kirby Drive and knocked on Ash Robinson's door. "She is driving me crazy," the embattled surgeon told his lawyers at the end of August, just after the exhumation autopsy. "It was the biggest mistake of my life to marry her," he said, enumerating a catalogue of violence—both verbal and physical—that he and his second wife were engaging in. Ann, he said, was possessed of a roundhouse right-hand punch; and during a quarrel she shattered her new husband's nose—no small accomplishment since she weighed less than a hundred and twenty and he almost two hundred pounds. John drove immediately to a hospital where he set the fracture himself, using a mirror, and commenting on the procedure to a group of fascinated medical students who were watching. On another day John's arms were so scratched—from a fight with his wife—that he searched for a long-sleeved scrub suit top to wear into surgery. To a sympathizing nurse, he remarked, "New cat at home."

If John Hill's first marriage to horsewoman Joan Robinson was a mismatch, wedding number two to the ripe peach Ann Kurth was a disaster. From the beginning of the relationship, Ann was wildly jealous of her predecessor in John's marriage bed, and she launched an assault to erase all the ghosts from the white mansion. In one violent *Walpurgisnacht*, John would later testify in a sworn deposition, subject to the penalty of perjury, Ann went on a rampage, shrieking deprecations at her husband, ripping up photographs of Joan, throwing her trophies against a wall, seizing a kitchen knife and scratching the silver cups and platters, hurling paint against a carved stone frieze of horses galloping on a courtyard wall outside the kitchen window. Then she lit a bonfire in an outdoor barbecue pit, threw more mementos of Joan Robinson into the flames, and stood beside it laughing. "I was helpless," John told Racehorse. "I'd never seen a woman, *any* woman, behave that way."

The man who had pursued Ann Kurth so recklessly at Camp Rio Vista only ten months before, the suitor who had fallen into the lake and had come up laughing and clicking photographs, the dashing and apparently wealthy young surgeon who signed "Mr. Hyde" on motel registers and owned one of the most imposing mansions on Kirby Drive, had not turned out in a way to accommodate her fantasies. When Ann Kurth became, legally, the second Mrs. John Hill, she discovered her husband to be a moody man deeply in debt, a doctor whose practice was deteriorating, and a subject of intense scrutiny by lawyers, the DA's office, private detectives, and the fountainhead of all these currents—his ex-father-in-law, Ash Robinson.

After the death of Joan, Myra Hill had come to comfort her son, and she stayed two years in Houston, her stern and pious presence hardly tolerable to a difficult marriage. The two women were, from the outset, as dissimilar as inhabitants of separate planets. "How John lived with that woman as long as he did and maintain his sanity, I'll never know," said Myra years later, when she could speak of that brief convulsion in the long story. "I used to stay awake at nights worrying about it, praying she would not hurt him, or maim his hands."

By the end of October 1969 the four-month-old marriage was a shambles, and John asked his attorney to prepare a divorce action. Instantly Racehorse saw peril. The district attorney still had the death of Joan Hill under investigation. There was no word yet from Helpern in New York, no hint that his microscope had discovered any murderous needle mark or poisoned tissue—but until the report came in, until Ash Robinson eased up his pressure, then a divorce from Ann Kurth was dangerous.

Why? asked the plastic surgeon.

Racehorse would later describe his client as "your typical unemotional doctor, the kind who could look at a liver the size of Chicago and not show any emotion at all." He sat him down and explained the very real facts of life.

Haynes liked to tick matters off for his clients, as if summing up for a jury. Item One: You would be a helluva lot easier to defend if you were still mourning your first wife's death, wearing black, and having nothing more to do with women than escorting your mother and sister to church. Item Two: You rushed into marriage with Ann Kurth in an indecently short time. Item Three: Even if she is making your life one miserable hell, even if it is *intolerable*, then I still urge you to stay married to her.

Again John Hill asked, "Why?"

"John, if you divorce that woman she will join forces with Ash Robinson. And she will come to the courthouse and she will claim things on you—things she will say happened between the two of you—and it'll be up to a jury to decide if she is telling the truth or not. Don't sell her short, John. Ann Kurth is a dynamite woman, smart as hell, and she can make it bad for you."

But already Ann Kurth had been subpoenaed by the first grand jury investigating Joan's death, and her testimony was not harmful, said John. "All she told them was that we had an extramarital affair, which was true, and that she knew nothing about Joan's death, which was also true."

Dr. Jachimczyk, the Harris County coroner, released *his* new findings from the exhumation study. This was the *third* opinion as to the cause of death. In this version, he backed off from his initial ruling of hepatitis. "It is now my opinion that Joan Robinson Hill came to her death as a result of a fulminating infectious process, the specific nature of which is no longer determinable," he wrote. "The immediate embalming and initial autopsy in an environment not equipped to perform adequate bacteriological, virologic, and toxicologic studies precluded pathological determination of the exact cause of death."

Reading the document, Racehorse thought to himself: "In other words, the poor lady died of a bug that caused a big infection all over her body." People die of infections every day and their spouses don't get persecuted for murder. But wait! Jachimczyk was not through. He offered a suggestion:

"It is my further opinion that the exact cause and manner of death cannot be established from the exhumed body autopsy alone. In view of the unusual circumstances surrounding this death and the questions raised following the death, and a review of the hospital chart . . . a thorough Grand Jury investigation is indicated and herewith recommended."

Clearly this was the reaction of a sorely embarrassed public official—chagrined over the first autopsy, and irritated at having the superstar coroner from New York flown in over his head to sort things out. Pilate-like, the coroner was herewith washing his hands of the matter, but throwing the case back to The People to let them get on with a Crucifixion if they so desired.

The pathologists who represented John Hill at the exhumation cheered him about this time by chiming in with their findings. The chairman of the Hill team, the gray-bearded coroner Dr. Robert Bucklin, medical examiner of Galveston County, wrote in a terse report: "I believe the basic lesion and the cause of death is a bacterial meningitis with septicemia." Moreover, Bucklin wrote that he found no evidence whatsoever of poison or exotic bacteria in the slivers of tissue he studied from the exhumation. His two colleagues in the matter, both respected pathologists, concurred. Thus three neutral pathologists, working only from microscopic and laboratory studies, came to the conclusion that Joan Robinson Hill died of natural causes.

But this failed to impress Ash. Weren't these fellows hired by John Hill? he demanded of his allies.

Not surprisingly, John Hill found this development so helpful to his cause that he slipped the results to a reporter on the afternoon Houston *Chronicle*. Furious, Ash called his circle of cronies to complain that John had broken the ground rules. "Nobody was supposed to say anything until Dr. Helpern made his ruling," cried Ash. But when was that going to happen? Four long months had already gone by since the dark and thunderous Saturday when Joan's body was lifted from her grave. At least half a dozen times Ash had called Helpern's office in New York City, but each time he was put off, delayed, promised that the studies were being made. The old man's patience was running thin.

One of those doctors supporting Ash in his case became interested in the matter of Joan's missing brain, and the curious manner in which it was delivered to the exhumation autopsy by Sharpstown pathologist Morse. It occurred to this doctor, who did not have a license to practice medicine in Texas at the time, that if meningitis was found in Joan's brain, then meningitis should have also been discovered in the spinal cord. The two go hand and glove. The doctor thus corralled a respected neurologist, one Dr. William S. Field, professor of neurology at the University of Texas Graduate School of Biomedical Sciences, and led him to the coroner's office to study tissue specimens from Joan Hill's corpse. One week later Dr. Field delivered a brief report. the thrust of which was that he found "cellular exudate" in the brain tissues—but in specimens of spinal cord tissue he found no such thing:

"In the opinion of this examiner, the spinal cord material shows no pathological abnormality, particularly no evidence of meningitis such as is observed in the brain sections. This is, in my opinion, incompatible with the findings of cellular exudate diagnostic of acute meningitis observed in all brain sections. Based on previous experience, I would expect as extensive of meningeal reaction as is seen in this case . . . to also involve the spinal cord. I find it impossible to explain this obvious discrepancy if I assume that all of the material presented to me represents tissue from one and the same individual."

Somehow this information also found its way into the Houston newspapers, obviously planted by the Ash Robinson allies, and the implication was that because there was no evidence of meningitis to be found in the spinal cord of Joan Robinson Hill, then the brain that Dr. Morse produced from his car trunk must have been from another cadaver. Was a "mistake" made?

* * *

Once again, John Hill went to his attorney and said that he could not live with Ann Kurth another moment. He *must* divorce her. She tormented him every hour they were together. John claimed that Ann was so eager to uncover his assets that she even disguised herself as a nurse and went to his office after hours and rummaged through his desk. Moreover, she was bad-mouthing him around town. The plastic surgeon played a taped telephone call for his lawyer in which Ann was heard to say: "His practice has gone down to zero. He's now to the point of removing tattoos and warts to have anything to do at all."

Once again, Racehorse pleaded with his client to stay married, at least until the investigation of Joan Hill's death was concluded. Racehorse read the cards this way: The other side is not going to have any hard medical evidence to link you with your wife's death. The best thing they've got is your affair with Ann Kurth when Joan was still alive, the speed with which you married her, and —God help us, man—the even quicker divorce of wife number two. Juries *do* take notice when a man goes through women like Kleenex.

"Whereas," said Racehorse, summing up, "if you stay married to Ann Kurth—legally married—she can't hurt you. You don't have to live with her, in fact I don't blame you if you split, but you've *got* to stay married. Because if we ever had to go to trial on a murder charge, she could be incompetent as a witness. A wife cannot testify against her husband, etc."

John Hill understood his lawyer well. But he would not obey him. "Hell no," he said. "I understand what you're telling me, but I'm not guilty of anything except choosing the wrong women, and I'm not going to let my life be ruined any more. File the divorce papers. Get her out of my life."

Racehorse sighed and began what he would later refer to as "The War on Kirby Drive."

If ever there was a woman whom a man should have eased gently out of his life, delicately as carrying a basket of eggs across a tightrope, it was Ann Kurth. Yet John Hill put on a catcher's mitt and ski boots for the task. Realizing that it would be difficult to evict the lady from his big house—and John could not bear the notion of moving out himself and being deprived of the music room—he and his lawyer hit upon a scheme that was staggering in its lack of tact and good sense. The plan called for John to feign a new-found affection for his wife and suggest a brief, spur-of-the-moment overnight trip to Hodges Gardens in Louisiana. En route, John would become overwhelmed with apparent passion, park the car in a romantic, bushy spot, and make love. Following that, he would break bad news. His phraseology, according to Ann's later memory of the day, was "Racehorse Haynes thinks he can best defend me if you and I are no longer married and thumbing our nose at the rest of the world." While all of this was going on, a moving truck was backed up to the house on Kirby Drive with men packing up all of Ann Kurth's belongings and transferring them back to her own home in Memorial. John had thoughtfully broken a windowpane at her home to accommodate entrance.

When Ann returned to discover what had taken place while she had been so gallantly romanced, she was furious. Promptly she drove to Ash Robinson's house and spent a long afternoon there. Immediately she became a new and valuable asset in the old man's vendetta.

Referring to the episode of the moving men *in absentia*, Racehorse would later admit, with a tinge of red to his face, "In retrospect, this was not one of our better ideas. But that was the only way we could get control of the castle, so to speak."

On December 16, 1969, John Hill sat for a sworn deposition in the matter of his divorce against Ann Kurth. In his testimony, subject to the penalties of perjury, he set forth a catalogue of grievances against his second wife. Somehow a copy of this slipped out of official hands and became the hottest reading in River Oaks. "Poor John," laughed one hostess. "Talk about your 'out of the frying pan and into the fire.'"

Q. You allege that Mrs. Hill has been guilty of excessively cruel treatment towards you, such conduct being of such an outrageous nature as to render your living together insupportable. Will you briefly describe that conduct to me?

John Hill certainly could: "Well, Ann Kurth had an extreme jealousy of my deceased wife, constantly bringing that up and elaborating on it, referring to Joan in unkind terms constantly, and indicating that whatever I might have done for my former wife, that I should do for her much in excess. As an example, I gave my first wife a monthly allowance of seven hundred fifty dollars, the present Mrs. Hill demanded that I give her a thousand dollars per month plus much more. She ferreted out every single item that had belonged to Joan, that had any sentimentality attached to it whatsoever, and either systematically destroyed it or disposed of it in some way."

Moreover, testified the beleaguered plastic surgeon, Ann "was constantly threatening to take my son down and give him to Ash Robinson if I didn't accede to certain demands. . . ." The woman's wrath extended even into the surgical suites, claimed John. "She was extremely destructive toward my practice, in such a manner as constantly calling the operating room in attempt to dress me down about various things. Sometimes I asked the nurses to simply hang up the telephone, because I was in the middle of surgery. She called back using false names, but the switchboard operator . . . recognized her . . . and started blocking her calls to the operating room because they were so harassing and made my surgery so difficult. She'd do things like hiding my surgical instruments prior to an operation . . . or withhold my keys to the car, making me late to an operation. . . . She kept me awake at all hours of the night so that I'd have very little sleep that night and very little opportunity to rest for the next day's difficult surgery. And the following day, of course, I would be extremely fatigued . . . while she was home resting up for the onslaught to follow the next night."

"How did she keep you awake all night?" asked one of the lawyers.

"By constant talking. If I attempted to sleep, she would jerk the bedclothing off of me and there would be a physical exchange. She would dig her fingernails into me, pull my hair, slap me, anything to continuously keep me awake and harping on whatever she happened to be discontent about at the time."

Ann Kurth gave a deposition as well. She contended that her husband was cold, rude, belligerent, cowardly, hostile toward her and her sons, and that he roughed her up "six or eights times" and tried to kill her twice. Such testimony flows forth a thousand times a day in lawyers' offices across the land, as couples break the ties of marriage.

But in this case the testimony was pertinent to other matters besides the divorce at hand. Ash Robinson read the deposition documents with keep interest. He underlined the key points and asked Ann Kurth to meet with him.

"God knows what they're cooking up," John told Racehorse Haynes. The lawyer restrained himself from saying, "I told you so, Doctor." The broken marriage was less important now than what was going on at the courthouse. Haynes heard from well-placed sources in the DA's office that a third grand jury might convene to hear new evidence in the death of Joan Robinson Hill. Moreover, the Helpern report was due any day, and the word was that it smelled like trouble.

18

The February 1970 grand jury was the third such panel to consider the death of Joan Robinson Hill. Among the twelve solid citizens in this group was one particularly influential member of the community. He was none other than Cecil Haden, wealthy and portly barge builder, lifelong friend to the dead woman, patron of her horse shows, pallbearer at her funeral, and crony and sometime business associate of her father for four decades. Cecil Haden brought to this grand jury scant vestige of impartiality. However, neither the press nor the bar of Houston seemed to find Haden's membership unusual or prejudicial to John Hill's civil rights.

Only the plastic surgeon himself felt a wave of panic as he spoke with Racehorse Haynes. Did Haden have the right to sit on this grand jury? asked John. Here was a man who had attended Ash's late night strategy meetings. Here was a man who had counseled his old friend since the beginning of this mad tea party. Here was a man who had done everything but put his foot on the shovel that raised Joan's body for the exhumation.

Racehorse soothed his client. Two grand juries had already considered this matter and neither had taken action. As far as he knew, there was no new evidence in the district attorney's hands. And the defense lawyer had enough contacts at the courthouse to realize if any "hanging judge" vibrations started emanating from the grand jury chamber. First, Racehorse promised to find out how Cecil Haden managed to merit a seat on the panel. It took him but a single telephone call.

In Texas the grand jury process begins with a district judge who appoints from three to five commissioners. These are supposed to be reputable citizens from a cross section of the county. They in turn nominate twenty grand jurors, from which twelve are selected to sit for a ninety-day term. These twelve jurors consider whether the district attorney has built a criminal case sufficient to be placed before a trial court. The grand jury can either vote an indictment, vote a "no bill," which is a dismissal, or take no action at all. They can also recommend that a succeeding grand jury continue study of a matter. The grand jury has extraordinary power; it can elect to investigate something itself, going above the heads of police and district attorney. It can become a star chamber, but this fortunately is rare. More commonly, grand juries in Texas are but obedient pets of the district attorney, biting whom they are told to bite.

All concerned with the appointment of Cecil Haden insisted that it was "sheer coincidence," and those of a generous spirit might concur. But the coincidence was stunning. One of the five commissioners appointed by the district judge to choose grand jury members was a lawyer named Richard Kolb, partner in the giant legal firm of Vinson, Elkins, Weems, Searls and Connally. This was the powerful group of attorneys who represented Cecil Haden. They also represented Ash Robinson. Attorney Kolb's office was but a few steps down the corridor from that of Richard Keeton, the young lawyer who handled Ash Robinson. Kolb would later insist—and no one challenged his word, for he was considered a most reputable attorney—that it never entered his mind that Cecil Haden would be judging the activities of Dr. John R. Hill.

The oath which all grand jurors must take in Texas swears each member to secrecy and then cautions each against indicting somebody out of "envy, hatred or malice." The oath continues: "Neither shall you leave any person unpresented for love, fear, favor, affection, or hope of reward." But Haden took his seat on the jury anyway and, in the very first week of sessions, proceeded to squirt new fuel on an old fire.

To give him his due, grand juror Haden did not conceal

the fact that he brought a special interest to the delibera-
tions. "I told my fellow jurors that I had known Ash
Robinson for forty years," he would say later. "I told them
Ash was a dear friend, the kind you may not see for
six months, then run into, and pick up just where you
left off. I told them I had known Joan Robinson Hill
since she was in diapers. I said I had no presumption of
anybody's guilt or innocence. It was my proposal that we
consider this situation from its beginning, and cut through
the underbrush once and for all."

One of the jurors, a black man, perhaps a man who
knew how pressures could be brought in Houston, stood
in opposition. He suggested that Haden was unduly prejudiced.

"Maybe I am," answered Haden, as he would recall
the episode later. "But put yourself in Ash Robinson's
shoes. Here is a father who lost his only child; a good
man, a decent man, and a man about to go crazy. We
must take this case up again and settle it forever."

The black juror nodded, convinced. The matter of
Joan Robinson Hill and how she died was once more
on the agenda.

Racehorse Haynes began playing poker. First he laid
down a very low pair, not calculated to win any pot
but potent enough to win a small inside headline in the
newspaper and a brief mention in the evening television
news: "Haynes Demands Court of Inquiry in Hill Case."
The death of Joan Robinson Hill and its aftermath had
become so enmeshed in intrigue, scandal, and mishandling
that the only way justice could be served was through an
open public hearing. DA Carol Vance shook his head
patiently and denied the grandstand play. Whenever lawyers
have time on their hands, they call for a court of inquiry,
something the grand jury was already doing.

Undaunted, Haynes played his next—this a concealed
hand. He filed a ten-million-dollar damage suit against
Ash Robinson—five million dollars in actual damages, five
million dollars in exemplary damages—claiming that the
old man was conspiring to get Dr. John Hill indicted for
a crime he had not committed, that the plastic surgeon's
social and professional reputation was being slandered,
thus causing him to suffer grave financial harm. When
Ash heard of the suit he whistled, almost approvingly.

"Ten million dollars," he said. "At least old John Hill thinks big."

But the beauty part of the lawsuit was that it enabled Racehorse and his associate, Fullenweider, to subpoena everybody in town if they desired, and place them on oath for sworn depositions, under penalty of perjury. Ash Robinson would be giving depositions until Christmas, or until his rear end grew so weary of sitting in lawyer's chairs that he would call off his dogs at the courthouse. Or so Racehorse hoped.

Subpoenas went out—to Ash, his wife, to John Hill, to the doctors who aided Ash and observed at the exhumation, to Diane Settegast and Eunice Woolen, the Dallas women who were house guests the days before Joan Hill died. This was also a very clever way for Racehorse Haynes to discover just what the grand jury was finding out—by subpoenaing their witnesses and asking them the same kind of question. The volumes bound in red leatherette began to grow, and quickly filled an entire closet at the Haynes office. The Joan Robinson Hill case was becoming an industry, with dividends for lawyers, doctors, court reporters, stenographers, private detectives, and purveyors of equipment from telephone bugs to telescopic lenses.

I. D. McMaster, the assistant district attorney, had blown hot and cold on the case since the beginning, when Ash Robinson walked into his office on the morning of Joan's funeral and asked him to stop the service. At first he had been caught up in the glamour of the case, the Cadillacs, the mansions that housed the people he needed information from, the owners whose power and influence could be valuable to any ambitious prosecutor. He had spent tedious hours interviewing neutral doctors, chemists, nurses, checking out almost incomprehensible medical books from the Texas Medical Center library on salmonella and shigella and E. coli bacteria, trying to determine whether it was possible for John Hill to inject somehow one of these deadly organisms into the body of his wife, cleverly killing her. But the case had thus far turned out to be little more than one perfect for the short hours, for dissection late at night in front of a roaring fireplace with a good bottle of burgundy. "Maybe he did thus and so . . ." began the prosecutor in his mind a hundred times, even waking up at night with new imagined solutions, but such ruminations were only entertainment, not sufficient to send a doctor to the penitentiary. Besides, there were nine hundred other active cases in his file, charges more specific, felonies to be traded out, sent to trial, thrown away, forgotten.

One night in early spring, 1970, McMaster dropped by the gloomy old house of one of the doctors who had aided Ash Robinson in getting the exhumation. This doctor lived in a castle-like fortress with thick walls and darkly burnished paneling; even a knight in armor guarded the stone-floored entry hall. All in all, a perfect house for fantasizing murder. McMaster settled into a chair. He was sated by the case. The Milton Helpern report was now six months overdue. Maybe the imperious old coroner had found nothing and was reluctant to send down a negative report. Or, perhaps, he was onto something that just took time at the microscope.

The doctor who was host for the evening nodded. He could well understand the prosecutor's fatigue. He, too, felt that disproportionate time had been wasted in catering to the theatrical furies of Ash Robinson.

There were moments, McMaster admitted, when he started feeling that maybe Joan Hill just got sick and died. On her own. It *does* happen to people.

His host put forth a new theory: Let's say that Joan fell ill with stomach flu. Now John Hill has stated that he gave his wife Compazine, an anti-nausea drug; Kaopectate; a broad-spectrum antibiotic called mystecline-F; and Lomotil, an anti-diarrhea medicine. But what if he slipped in Colace instead, a stool softener, which would *increase* her diarrhea? What if he gave her a diuretic that would drastically step up her urine output? What if these were administered in such tremendous amounts that Joan went into shock?

McMaster followed this train of thought. That Joan Hill was in shock at the time of her admission to Sharpstown Hospital was not arguable. The hospital simply did not know what kind of shock she was in.

The doctor went on. The hospital doctors gave her massive doses of potassium chloride, he recalled, and this brought on a hyperkalemic condition. The woman's potassium level was so increased that an electrolyte imbalance occurred in the heart and it stopped beating. Joan's last potassium level at Sharpstown was measured at 7.4, whereas normal is approximately 4.5. Her chloride level was 116, when normal is 95. These were tremendous elevations, suggested the doctor. Probably they were the actual things that killed her.

But, put in McMaster, this was not a criminal act on the part of the Sharpstown doctors, was it?

Of course not, answered the doctor. They were simply trying to counteract a perilously low blood pressure.

In other words, summed up the prosecutor, a woman turned up at the hospital desperately sick. The doctors gave her too much potassium chloride. So she died. Sad. But not indictable.

Oh well, said the doctor. Just a theory.

Still another friend had been sitting in the room, listening to the host and the prosecutor. He interrupted in disagreement. It had to be remembered that Joan Robinson Hill was not a prisoner in her own bedroom in the big white house when she fell ill. She had a telephone beside her bed. It was not shut off. The wires were not cut. She could have called anybody she wanted to for help if she thought she was dying—even her mother or her father, just a few blocks down the street.

That's true, agreed McMaster. But what if she didn't know how sick she was? Everybody gets the flu now and then. You just stay in bed until the bug has run its course. You do what the doctor *tells* you to do.

And in this case, her husband was her doctor.

Suddenly McMaster grew excited. So did his host for the evening. "Murder can be caused by what somebody does . . ." began the doctor.

"Or by what somebody does *not* do," finished McMaster.

The grand jury contained a suitable cross section of Houstonians, including a lawyer, a postman, a retired schoolteacher, a merchant, and four black people, all upstanding citizens who had never been convicted of a felony or a misdemeanor involving moral turpitude. On their first meeting, a foreman was elected, a retired businessman named Wayne Jones. But there was never any doubt who was the dominant force inside the secret chamber. It was Cecil Haden. While his colleagues waited for the Milton Helpern autopsy report, they could start gathering additional information in the case. If the Helpern report was sufficient to indict John Hill for murder, then whatever the grand jury's investigation unearthed could be served up as garnish for the main course. Haden discovered that his group, if they desired, could employ the investigations of the district attorney's office to run down its various leads, most of which were supplied by Ash Robinson. But secrecy seemed important at this stage of the game, and it was difficult to keep anything quiet in a courthouse where reporters cultivated news sources, particularly in the district attorney's office where young Turks needed reportorial friends for support and sustenance in future political battles.

A previous grand jury had left two hundred dollars behind in a fund for "investigative purposes," but this was not enough to pay a good private detective for two days' work. Haden therefore went to District Judge Wendell Odom, who kept a paternal eye on the jury's activities and who would receive all their indictments and no bills. "I have two requests, Judge," said grand juror Haden. "Can we hire our own private investigators, and, can we put up our own money? I don't want to do anything improper."

The judge was presiding on the bench at that moment, and he asked Haden to let him think on the request. Again, political realities had to be considered, as Odom was planning to seek a seat on the Texas Court of Criminal Appeals. It would not serve him well to make a snap decision in this headlined affair. The intent of Haden was clear. He wanted to spend his own money to hire private detectives to run around the city in the clear hope of finding enough evidence to indict John Hill. And behind Haden stood Ash Robinson. The connection was, or should have been, if it was known, troubling. Nonetheless, as Haden later told it, Judge Odom summoned him the next day and said, "Go ahead. You have my blessings."

When Ash Robinson heard the news he was content. It was the first anniversary of his daughter's death, and before the second one came, the old man felt reasonably sure John Hill would be standing before the bar of justice accused of murder.

The district attorney, Carol Vance, felt discomfort over what was happening in the Hill matter. He knew that a considerable amount of taxpayers' money had already been spent in futile attempts to prove murder had been done, that two grand juries had failed to indict, that it was time to close this melodrama. But his deputy, Mc-Master, was recharged. He was now convinced in his mind that John Hill was *somehow* connected with his first wife's death. And that *somehow* a case could be constructed and a conviction obtained. It would simply take time. And now that private money—Haden's money—was being employed, why worry?

The DA must have fretted, for he then took an unusual step. He summoned his top prosecutor, a legendary assistant DA named Erwin (Ernie) Ernst. Here was a man unique, particularly in Texas where men so often seemed cloned, formed identically from a hundred pounds of bones, forty-five pounds of spare flesh, with a working vocabulary of perhaps two hundred words. Ernst was a romantic, a stocky, loquacious, philosophical lawyer with a common-sense voice from the cracker barrel. Yet he was on intimate terms with Roman poets and Greek philosophers. He had prosecuted hundreds of murderers in a long career and sent many of them to the electric chair, or to life in prison. He was a practical joker, the favorite of the courthouse, and a fellow around whom anecdotes hung like ornaments from a Christmas tree. On one occasion—perhaps apocryphal—in the course of a trial, he had to prove that a young woman was in truth promiscuous—just after she had offered herself to the jury as a virgin. Before trial began that day, the first four rows of the spectator section were suddenly occupied by sturdy young men. A legal wrangle ensued between Ernst and opposition counsel over whether the young woman's reputation was valid in the case. The judge ruled that it was not. Ernst then turned to all the young men and said, "The first four rows can go home. I won't need you now." His point was made. But behind the foolishness and pranks reposed one of the best criminal law minds in the country. Everyone said Ernst should have occupied the DA's chair someday, or a seat on a court of appeals. But it was also said he lacked the gut lust for power. He was content to serve on the next rung down.

DA Vance told Ernie Ernst: "I want you to go into that grand jury room and play devil's advocate in the John Hill case." This was an unprecedented act, sending one prosecutor into the chamber as a rein on another prosecutor's enthusiasm, but Vance was obviously nervous about the involvement of Houston's power structure—medicine

and oil. "I want you to pick that case apart," ordered
Vance, "and if there is still a case left when you are
through, then it can stand on its merits." Vance knew that
if there were nothing to this matter but pride and prejudice and revenge, then Ernst would quickly destroy it.
If there was more, if there was enough to satisfy a trial
jury, then Ernst would nurture it, and eventually harvest
it.

In his first week of becoming acquainted with the evidence and the climate in the grand jury room, Ernst
discovered two factions. The principal one stood behind
Cecil Haden, willing to endorse his every move. If Haden
said, "Let's send our own private detective out to interview Joan Robinson Hill's hairdresser," then the jury
would vote to do just that. And did. But a small note of
contrariness was the presence of a feisty young black
woman who was, at times, rebellious toward Haden. Her
name was Carole Pinkett and she was a Yankee newly
come to Texas, employed by a major oil company as an
executive in the personal division. Well educated, strikingly beautiful in a high-fashion sort of a way, she was
not willing to dance automatically to boss Haden's cadence.
She struck Ernie Ernst as a thinking, reasonable woman,
the kind of deductive mind that any grand jury should
cherish. Haden found her a nuisance, and other jurors
felt she was holding up the progress of the case. But Ernst
liked her. At this point in mid-spring, nothing he had read,
or heard, or seen had convinced him that a murder had
been committed.

On March 12, 1970, one week shy of the first anniversary of Joan's death, John Hill and Ann Kurth were
divorced. Within twenty-four hours Ann was seated in a
grand jury chamber, pouring out tales concerning the
man who had thrown her out. Ernie Ernst listened to the
new ex-wife rant on and he found himself being reminded
of an actress in a solo turn, alone at center stage for an
evening. Her voice rose and fell at moments of peak
drama, her hand sometimes brushed her throat and slid
slowly down across her breasts. It was a swooping, fluttering tour de force. "How much of her can we believe?"
Ernst kept asking himself.

Specifically, Ann Kurth told the grand jury:

(1) John Hill not only killed his first wife, Joan, but

he also tried to kill *her*, the second Mrs. Hill. On three occasions.

(2) John's Sodium Pentothal "truth serum" test was probably rigged. On their wedding trip to Dallas, John went to a medical library where he read up on the drug, searching for an antidote. Later, on the very morning that he was to undergo the examination, she discovered him giving himself a shot in the hip. It was, Ann said, something to counteract the strength of the truth serum. He was thus able to be aware of the questions and provide safe answers. "That's crap," said the anesthesiologist, Dr. Richard Smith, when he heard of this claim. "I don't care if John Hill injected himself with holy water, he was still anesthetized," he said. "There's *no* antidote to the anesthetist's skill and experience, and that's what put John Hill under."

Nonetheless, Ann Kurth made this claim among others, describing her ex-husband as a violent man, chilling the grand jury room like a January norther from the Panhandle. The jurors had questions about her charges, one particularly pertinent one: why had Ann waited until now to tell these things? When she appeared before a previous grand jury in 1969, she had given not a hint of improper conduct on her then husband's part.

None of this had occurred at the time of her previous visit to the grand pury, answered Ann. Prosecutor McMaster pointed out that a wife could not testify against her husband. Only now was she an *ex*-wife. One of the jurors had another question: was the Kurth testimony thus usable in an actual court trial? Or was it privileged? McMaster replied honestly that he did not know.

Myra Hill promptly moved back into her son's house. She was delighted that he had divorced his second wife. "Now that it's all over," she asked, "why did you marry that woman in the first place?"

John gave her a twofold answer, one that Myra would never forget. She even wrote it down on a scrap of paper, to add to the journal of clippings and documents she was keeping.

"If I didn't marry her," said John, "she threatened to call I. D. McMaster and say I killed Joan. And if I divorced her, she said she would commit suicide and leave a note saying I was responsible for her death."

* * *

Ernie Ernst believed that a murder case could not be built around Ann Kurth's testimony alone. A good defense lawyer like Racehorse Haynes would bear down on the fact that she had testified at variance before two grand juries, that she was hostile toward her now ex-husband and still involved in a fight over property settlement and alimony. The Kurth testimony might be useful, but it could not stand unsubstantiated.

"Where the hell is that Helpern autopsy report?" growled McMaster as April 1970 began. This was the grand jury's last month.

If this grand jury failed to indict, then the folder would probably close. There is a fine line between prosecution and persecution, and Ernie Ernst from time to time felt they were falling onto the wrong side of the fence. He telephoned Dr. Jachimczyk, the coroner, and asked him to check with Helpern in New York.

Over long distance Milton Helpern, normally urbane, cool, seemed rather embarrassed. Yes, he was still writing the report. But no, it was not yet finished. Nor would it contain any revelation to hang John Hill. It would be, however, critical of the circumstances surrounding the woman's death.

Cecil Haden and Ash Robinson hatched another idea. With time running out on the grand jury's term, why not import Milton Helpern and have him deliver the report in person? In his very own words? They presented the notion to McMaster, who said it sounded good but that the county lacked funds to pay air fare and expenses. But if somebody else paid the freight, then the grand jury would be happy to welcome the prize package.

Ash Robinson happily wrote a check.

Dr. Helpern was smuggled into town under the wraps of secrecy, installed in the Warwick Hotel in a suite under Cecil Haden's name, and taken into the courthouse through a basement entrance to avoid reporters. With him he carried an 18½-page report on the exhumation autopsy, but it was incomplete, literally stopping in mid-sentence. The explanation was that the trip to Houston had come about so suddenly that his secretary had not finished transcribing his dictation. But never mind. He could deliver his findings to the grand jury verbally, from rough notes.

"This death should have been reported to the medical

examiner's office for official investigation," said Dr. Helpern in his preface, "and this point must be emphasized because the embalming of the body prior to autopsy did interfere with the extent of toxicological study and made entirely impossible microbiological examinations which were clearly indicated in this case on the basis of the entire symptomatology, including an abrupt onset of severe persistent diarrhea, nausea and vomiting, shock and impaired renal function and a rapidly fatal outcome after a short period of hospitalization." Helpern's report was an extraordinary document, containing very little scientific material damaging to the position of John Hill. In fact, Helpern actually cleared the surgeon of many of the rumors swirling about the city.

Rumor: John Hill was up to something more than just searching for a missing ring when he opened his wife's casket three days after burial.

Helpern's finding: "There was no indication that the body of the deceased had been disturbed. . . . When the garments were removed [in the exhumation autopsy], the sutured incisions of the first autopsy did not appear to have been disturbed after the body had been 'laid out.' In other words, there was no evidence that the body had been re-opened, or that any organs had been removed or replaced subsequent to the first interment."

Rumor: John Hill injected his wife with some elusive poison in an unusual part of her body—such as on the back of the hand between the knuckles. The maid, Effie Green, had stated—and Ash repeated it far and wide—that she saw John Hill rubbing the back of Joan's hand.

Helpern's finding: "Careful scrutiny did not reveal any injection sites on the hands."

Rumor: John Hill stole his wife's brain and substituted another one for the exhumation autopsy—a brain riddled with meningitis.

Helpern's finding: "The pathologist [Dr. Morse] who performed the first autopsy delivered a mass of sectioned formalin-fixed brain, weighing a total of 1,020 grams, in a plastic bag. He identified it as being the brain of the deceased which he had removed at the time he performed the first autopsy. . . . The fixed brain did not show any visible evidence of meningitis on naked-eye examination, but later did on microscopic examination. The spinal canal was opened and the spinal cord removed. . . . The

cord was fairly well preserved except for a reddish dis-
coloration which had taken place in the white matter. In
all of the sections, at first glance, the reddish color
appeared dull suggesting the possibility of an inflammation
of the pial layer. The entire cord was then removed with
the meninges for study, and sections were prepared from
the various levels from the cervical to below the lumbar
segments. A smear was made from the inner surface of
the arachnoid. When stained . . . only an occasional
leukocyte was observed. . . . This section of the cord,
when first examined microscopically, appeared to be normal, but on close scrutiny of the leptomeninges, an occasional scattered polymorphonuclear leukocyte and mononuclear leukocyte were found. . . . This evidence of inflammation in the spinal cord was very slight and in most
places absent, entirely unlike the fairly conspicuous microscopic inflammatory cell infiltration in the pia-arachnoid
of the brain. . . . The inflammatory findings in the brain
and cord, although quite different in amount and intensity,
could represent manifestations in different areas of the
brain and spinal cord of the same individual.

"It must be kept in mind that in acute meningitis the
purulent condition of the spinal fluid for the most part
is derived from acute inflammation in the meninges of the
brain rather than in the cord. It is also a fact that in many
autopsies . . . the spinal cord does not necessarily exhibit
the same intensity of inflammation as does the brain."

He thus shot down, for all intents and purposes, the
"switched brain" rumor.

Nor did Helpern discover anything potentially criminal
in the toxicological examinations of the bits and pieces
of tissue he snipped from the body during the exhumation
autopsy. "Portions of the esophagus, stomach, large bowel,
kidney, liver, hair and fluid content in the small bowel . . .
were examined extensively by X ray and emission spectros-
copy. No heavy metals (arsenic, etc.) were found in these
tissues. Further analysis for the presence of fluorides was
also reported negative. Because of the embalming of the
body, it was not feasible to carry out any further toxicological studies.

"The chemical examination, as far as it could be carried
out on the exhumed body tissues, was negative, consistent
with the negative analysis carried out in the laboratory of
the Medical Examiner's Office in Houston on the embalmed

tissues obtained from the pathologist who performed the first autopsy. . . ."

For the first ten pages of his report, Dr. Helpern traveled on professional ground, discussing each organ of the body with authority and in meticulous detail. Then he did an extraordinary thing. In mid-report was suddenly inserted a scenario of how things happened, or how they *might* have happened, if one relied solely on the inflammatory statements offered to Ash Robinson by Effie Green, the maid, and by the two Dallas women, Diane Settegast and Eunice Woolen. None of these statements, save that of Effie Green, was sworn before a public authority under penalty of perjury, or even notarized. Nor did Helpern interrogate these women as to their veracity. Most damningly, the pathologist did not incorporate any of John Hill's position into the report, nor did he interview him, or even request written answers to harmful questions raised by the maid and the house guests. Upon reading a copy of this report, Racehorse Haynes swore mightily. He was not only angry but disbelieving. "Helpern was employed to autopsy a body and nothing else," snapped Racehorse. "His credentials as a Houston homicide cop are not widely recognized."

The balance of Helpern's report read like the synopsis of a terribly complicated, badly written Victorian crime novel. Because he apparently felt it more dignified—or professionally proper—to refer to Joan Robinson Hill throughout as "the deceased," his sentences became not only confusing but unintentionally funny. Example: "The house guest and the deceased's mother went out to purchase chicken for the deceased, the deceased husband, and the child. At that time the deceased was having a drink. . . . It was noted that between 7 and 11 P.M., the guests and the deceased each had about four drinks."

Black humor not withstanding, the report was damning to Dr. John Hill through innuendo. Helpern's document contained phrases such as: "The husband then went upstairs for something and returned to administer the 'shot' to the deceased." By putting his own quotation marks around the word "shot," Helpern gave it ominous emphasis, as if to say, "It might have been a shot of medicine, then again it might have been a shot of something else." Helpern then jumped in his writing to the next day of Joan's life, Sunday, March 16, 1969, and summed it thusly:

"On Sunday . . . the deceased was ill with persistent vomiting, diarrhea and chills, and, one presumed, accompanying fever, although there is no mention about her temperature." Here Helpern engaged in speculation about the existence of fever.

The Helpern report further contained information about the French pastries that John Hill served his wife and guests, the fact that the Hills were in the throes of a deteriorating marriage, and a summation of Effie Green's distasteful account of feces in the bed.

Helpern's document quoted Effie as scolding John Hill for lying about his whereabouts. "A nurse called from the hospital for the husband (Hill) to come because the deceased had 'taken a change.' When the husband came back to the house a few minutes after the call came, she asked him if he had come from the hospital. He said, 'Yes, I have just left.' " The maid said, 'No, you wasn't there. Your wife done made a change and they say come to the hospital right away.' "

Having thus established John Hill as a cruel, uncaring husband who gave his wife a mysterious shot and left her to lie in her own feces, the report moved along to adultery. "The maid indicated that the deceased had told her that her husband had been having an affair with another woman for several months. . . . The maid felt that 'Mrs. Hill ain't just died from being sick.' . . . The maid stated that she never saw the husband inject anything into the deceased, but that she saw a needle prick on the deceased's hand. She got this impression because the husband was rubbing the deceased's hand."

The melodramatic portion of Helpern's autopsy report ended with a heart-tugging quotation from Effie: " 'I don't hate Dr. Hill. The onliest thing is, he just, he didn't do right. He just don't—he just—well, when a husband don't do right and treat his wife right, and wants to treat her like a dog, and when she's humble and nice and sweet and kind to him, it's him, it's no love there. Just—oh, God!—he just don't—like God ain't satisfied with that.' "

Abruptly, Helpern then moved back into areas of legitimate concern for a pathologist. Under a subheading, "Opinion as to the cause of death," he wrote:

"The deceased, a previously healthy, athletic and physically active thirty-eight-year-old married woman and mother of a nine-year-old son, died after an acute illness in which nausea, vomiting and profuse uncontrolled diarrhea with progressive weakness, restlessness, confusion, hypotension, and collapse were the predominant clinical manifestations. Her illness began at home on March 15, 1969, and became progressively worse until March 18 with the aforementioned symptoms. The only medical attention she received was from her physician husband, who specialized in plastic surgery. Despite the severity of her illness at home, she was confined entirely to her room during the latter part of Sunday, March 16, and on Monday, the 17th, and on the morning of Tuesday, the 18th, when she was taken from her home to the Sharpstown Hospital by her husband in his automobile without benefit of stretcher or ambulance. She was admitted to the hospital in a wheel chair on March 18 at 11:45 A.M. and placed in a private room under the care of Dr. Bertinot who saw her for the first time after she was admitted to the hospital. After a vigorous course of treatment during which she did not improve but became steadily worse, she died 16 hours after admission. The admission diagnosis was recorded on the chart as diarrhea. According to Dr. Bertinot's admitting note, the deceased had manifested nausea, vomiting and diarrhea for four days following the ingestion of shell fish. He also stated . . ."

And here Dr. Helpern's report terminated, in midsentence.

To the grand jurors, spellbound by the report, Dr. Helpern now apologized. The press of work in violent New York City had robbed him of the needed time to complete the document. He would deliver the remaining few pages as soon as he returned to New York. But for the nonce, realizing the pressure that the grand jury faced as its term neared an end, he could summarize his findings. But first, he warned the jurors, his opinion was limited by the fact that the body had been embalmed prior to the first autopsy. "This is a procedure which made it impossible to carry out any bacteriological studies and may also have interfered with complete toxicological studies," he cautioned.

He commented briefly on the three causes of death discovered by previous doctors. The first was pancreatitis, announced by the Sharpstown Hospital pathologist, Dr. Morse. "There was no clinical or pathological evidence of pancreatitis," he said bluntly. "This was an erroneous impression of the first pathologist." The second, viral hepatitis, originally announced by Harris County medical examiner Dr. Jachimczyk, was also wrong, but not as wrong as pancreatitis. There *was* extensive liver damage wrought by hepatitis, but Helpern felt the source was not from a virus but only part of a widespread inflammation that ravaged the woman's entire body, particularly her throat, esophagus, and meninges. The acute meningitis announced by the Hill autopsy team was "a terminal complication and not the primary event," said Dr. Helpern. The pathologist also addressed himself to the kidney failure which the Sharpstown doctors tried to treat in the dying patient a few hours after she was admitted to the hospital.

"The acute nephrotic changes observed microscopically in the kidney are best related to the shock and hypotension induced by the vomiting and diarrhea of the original illness and aggravated by overtreatment with intravenous fluids and a variety of medications which were given to combat shock and hypotension, but which unfortunately disturbed the electrolyte balance and caused an irreversible retention of fluid, metabolites and terminal kidney and circulatory failure."

Then what caused the death of Joan Robinson Hill?

"An acute inflammation of some sort," he said, "the origin of which I cannot determine." Most likely, he said, the "portal of entry was by way of the alimentary tract."

One of the grand jurors asked, if it could have been something she ate.

Helpern's answer was non-committal. Possibly. Or possibly not.

Another juror asked if Helpern felt any crime had been committed in this event. "If any death should have been reported in time for an official investigation," he said, "this one obviously should have been."

The jurors had further questions. Was Joan Hill's treatment at home by her husband satisfactory? Was she taken to the hospital too late?

Helpern incorporated the answer to these in his final written report, which he mailed down a few days later. More than anything else, it sealed the case against John Hill. "Failure to provide medical attention at home, and resultant delay in hospitalization for diagnosis and effective

therapy aggravated a situation which proved fatal." Now
the climate on the grand jury was unmistakable. The cries
of the wolf pack rose and the scent of blood was over the
courthouse.

19

The Helpern autopsy report split the medical community
of Houston like a sharpened cleaver. Those faithful to Ash
Robinson predictably hailed the document and lent their
support to its findings. Of the four doctors whom he had
requested to stand over his daughter's corpse while it was
autopsied, three fell quickly into line. "I agree with these
findings and conclusions," wrote Grady Hallman, the
heart surgeon. "I am in complete accord," wrote Ed
Gouldin, the internist on whose home Ash had once held
the mortgage.

But, more pointedly, the only trained *pathologist* Ash
hired to represent him, a physician named Paul Radelat,
wrote an eloquent and thundering letter of opposition to
the report. Not only did he blister Helpern for including
the "internal curiosities" of unsubstantiated testimony
from the maid and the house guests, he wondered why in
the name of fairness a statement from John Hill himself
was not included.

"One would assume," wrote Radelat with pen of heavy
sarcasm, "that he is at least as familiar with the events of
those days as were the female house guests, and a report
from him would have given an opportunity to explain his
own reactions and observations during those ill-fated
days."

His own microscopic studies showed, declared pathologist Radelat, that Joan died "a natural, albeit tragic and
premature death. . . . In my opinion, based on the ana-
tomic evidence . . . Joan R. Hill expired in a state of
shock secondary to gram negative sepsis. In my opinion,
what may well have begun as a relatively mild gastroenteritis deteriorated rapidly and unexpectedly into a severe
esophagitis. . . . Gram negative organisms or their toxic
metabolites gained access to the general circulation through
this site producing sepsis and inflammation most notably

in the leptomeninges, central nervous system, and liver."

In other words, a stomach flu that turned into fatal blood poisoning.

"Examination of the remains of Joan Robinson Hill turned up absolutely no evidence of any poison, drugs, or other injurious agents administered to her either by self or another person. . . .

"John Hill, as everyone knows, is a physician, and physicians are notorious for ignoring the aches and pains of their families, and for practicing less than ideal medicine with their wives and children. Fortunately for us, the end result of this hit or miss attitude is usually not as tragic as what occurred in this case. Everyone has perfect judgment in hindsight, and perhaps had Joan Hill been brought to a hospital sooner, her death might have been averted. But septic shock is a fulminating condition which is frequently fatal even when occurring in the midst of the best medical attention available.

"Perhaps a person not accustomed to disease processes would have reacted more quickly to the early symptoms of Joan Hill's illness, and certainly the emergency rooms of hospitals are filled with many such persons who make unnecessary trips thereto. In a sense, John Hill's medical training may have caused him to view somewhat lightly the initial stages of his wife's illness, but this is no basis for a criminal charge either based on intent or common law negligence."

Dr. Radelat was speaking for many concerned members of the medical profession when he wrote his last sentence: "If criminal charges in this type of situation be appropriate, then anyone whose mate expires unexpectedly after a few days of symptoms, whether from pneumonia, heart attack, or septic shock, should also be indicted."

All of this from a pathologist hired by Ash Robinson! And to add insult to injury, Radelat even sent the old man a $1,500 bill for his services. For a time, Ash flourished the invoice, as if it could somehow dilute the impact of the letter. He need not have bothered. The Radelat letter, provocative as it was, and helpful as it should have been to John Hill, was not warmly received by the grand jury. In fact, several months later, one juror could not even remember reading it. "Perhaps it was offered to us, perhaps it was not," the juror said. "We had mountains of documents to read. Certainly it didn't seem to have any bearing on our decision. Did it?

Suddenly Racehorse Haynes was worried. All along he had felt that the matter would end in a whimper, that Ash would lose interest, or run out of money, or that wiser heads would prevail at the courthouse. Now he picked up the news that even Ernie Ernst had been won over by the Helpern report. The "devil's advocate" had been just that for almost three months of grand jury hearings, remaining unconvinced that murder was done. But when Racehorse heard that Ernst was saying around the courthouse, "I wouldn't let a dog die the way that doctor did his wife," then he knew his client was in peril.

The attorney summoned the plastic surgeon and suggested that he go personally before the grand jury and answer questions. "It's damned risky," cautioned Racehorse. "You go in there without counsel, and they can ask you anything they want. They can even try to trap you and probably will."

Then what good would it do? John wanted to know.

Maybe none whatsoever, answered Racehorse candidly. But it might prove to some of the jurors that there is nothing to hide. And if only four out of the twelve believe so, then there's no indictment. The way the lawyer now heard it, the score stood at eleven to one, but he did not tell his client that.

John readily agreed, for he was now convinced that Ash Robinson had considerably more in mind than simple revenge. The old man wanted him convicted of murder so that he would gain custody of his grandson and, through that accomplishment, obtain control of Joan's sizable estate. Her estate was still snarled in a subsidiary dispute, a matter that never became well known in Houston because of the hot lights that shone on the investigation of her death.

After she was buried, the plastic surgeon routinely filed a copy of her last will and testament for probate. John did not know the extent of his late wife's holdings, other than her ownership of Chatsworth Farm, and a few oil and gas leases that Ash had cut her in on.

"If my beloved husband, John R. Hill, survives me," the will read, "then I will, bequeath and devise to him my interest in all community property jointly owned by him and me at the time of my death." She further instructed that all of her personal property, the farm, the mineral holdings, be given to her son, through a trust administered by John. The will was written in 1962 and on file with an attorney. A quick tally made after her death indicated that the estate was around $400,000.

But before the terms of the will could be carried out a wrench was suddenly thrown—and from a familiar direction. Ash Robinson came forth with the announcement that he possessed a *new* will written by his daughter, and it superseded the other one. In the new will, Joan cut her husband completely off without a penny and left everything to her son, under the financial custodianship of Ash. "Joan wrote this will when she and John were separated, in the autumn of 1968," said Ash. "I knew she put it up somewhere, and it took me a little time to find it. I finally came across it in a folder with her college mementos."

The new will was certainly, to use a word, curious. Clumsily typed, replete with spelling mistakes and language more likely to be used by someone imitating legal terminology, it had the same Victorian flavor of the letter of repentance that John Hill signed in December 1968, before rapprochement with his wife:

"I will, devise and bequeath everything that I own, or have a claim to, or on, or might later own, or have a claim on, to my father, ASH ROBINSON. Should he die before my mother, RHEA ROBINSON, I will, devise and bequeath all of the above interests mentioned above to her. I know that between them they will provide for my son, Robert Ashton Hill. I do not wish his father, Dr. John R. Hill, insofar as my wishes in the matter are concerned, to have anything to do with my interests insofar as they concern my child. He has deserted me and has shown no interest in my son and has not even called him in three months. Hence I do not believe that he has his interest at heart. I nominate my father, Ash Robinson, and appoint him executor of this will and direct that no bond or security be required by my executor."

The will was dated on the typewriter as December 2, 1968. Then someone apparently thought better, for this month is struck out and "NOVEMBER" printed in below, by hand. The witnesses were two long-time friends of Ash, one a horse trainer and former Robinson employee. The signature "Joan R. Hill" bore notable differences from her signature on the 1962 will, which was signed in the presence of her attorneys. In particular, the capital letter "J" in "Joan" was strikingly different. "It's such a blatant forgery," said John Hill, "that it's ridiculous." Ash was furious at the suggestion. He insisted that the will contained his daughter's feelings, language, and signature. At one hearing over the authenticity, Ash did admit that, yes, he had typed out the will for his daughter, on his own portable typewriter. But he presented himself in the role of scribe and nothing else.

John Hill hired three handwriting experts, all of whom cast doubt upon the legitimacy of the signature. He then took the matter to the district attorney's office and asked for an investigation. But as the district attorney was already investigating *him* for possible murder, his plea was not looked upon with great enthusiasm. Besides, Ash had not unsurprisingly found an "examiner of questioned documents" who stated that the new will was genuine. Cecil Haden stepped forward as temporary peacemaker. Put this quarrel aside until the principal one—the death of Joan—was decided. The district attorney's office concurred.

And now John understood that unless he appeared personally before the grand jury, unless he convinced this panel that he was innocent of involvement in his wife's death, then not only would he be indicted for murder, he would then have to pursue the questioned will with the unclean hands of an accused killer, and he would probably lose custody of his son as well. Ash Robinson would win it all. The old man made that hope clear by driving past the doctor's home, thrusting his gnarled and liver-spotted fist out the window of his black Lincoln, and shaking it triumphantly, like a staff of victory.

Dressed in a dark suit, a crisp white shirt, and a neat and narrow dark tie, John Hill came before the grand jury with confidence and that unpleasant attitude that doctors all too often have: Ask your questions quickly because my time is valuable. He was cool, a little condescending. He made comments that were at odds with certain ones previously given the grand jury by earlier witnesses. Nothing of major import was dissimilar, only minor vagaries. But these were enough to trouble the grand jurors.

McMaster and Ernst explained to the doctor at the outset that he was not obligated to testify before this grand jury, that anything he said could later be used or developed in a possible criminal case against him, and he could refuse to answer any question, or get up and leave, now, ten minutes from now, or any time he wanted to. John understood all this. Proceed.

With great deference and courtesy, the prosecutors led the doctor through the days preceding Joan's death. The surgeon confirmed that on the last Saturday afternoon of his wife's life he had taken his son out for a haircut and on the way home stopped by his bachelor apartment.

"This was the one you had supposedly given up, wasn't it?" asked Ernst.

"Yes," answered the doctor.

"And when Joan found out that you had done this—and that you had really kept the apartment in secret—you all had a fight, didn't you?" asked Ernst. John Hill nodded.

Thus established as both a philanderer and a liar in the first moments of his testimony, the doctor slipped further down from there. Words fell too easily from his lips. He had no emotion. Not even remorse. He did not stammer or grope for answers, as most any person would under the pressure of the day. "He was too cold a fish," Ernst would later remember.

Casually, Ernst continued his questioning. "What did you all have for supper that Saturday night?"

"I don't know, sir," answered John. "I wouldn't have any idea."

Ernst seemed startled. "You *never* thought back, 'Maybe she died of food poisoning?' That *never* occurred to you? I should think it might—you being a doctor and all."

John disagreed vigorously. "It never occurred to me. Of course, I was rather shocked and upset at the ultimate severity of her illness and her death, yet it never occurred to me even to consider hiring a lawyer to represent me until virtually up to the point of the exhumation autopsy. Because I felt I had nothing to hide. I just didn't make too much of a mental note . . . of the circumstances immediately preceding and surrounding her death. And so there are a lot of gaps in my information."

Ernst moved along. "Was it your custom to often bring pastries home for Joan to share with you?"

"Yes. I kind of liked them myself and I would—on occasions at least—bring things like that home. A little more frequently when company was present."

"During this week, do you recall bringing tidbits home for the ladies?"

"Yes. Probably on two or three occasions . . . probably some blueberry tarts, a chocolate éclair or two, a sort of cream-filled type of chocolate dessert with crumpled pieces of chocolate on it."

Ernst smiled. He was at most times a very pleasant, easy man. "Were you kind of trying to make her happy, and yourself too?"

John Hill nodded. "We had been through a lot, and it was my hope that one way or another we could effect a reconciliation." But on this particular night, John recollected, there were hot words. "Joan had quite a bit to drink," and there was "a rather heated discussion" over the maintenance of the horse farm.

"Did she ever make the observation," asked Ernst, "something like 'Well, you can find $100,000 for a music room to play music in, and you can't pay $75 a month to feed my horse'?"

John agreed. "She might very well have said that."

"Was there some competition between you two as to the allocation of assets for hobby purposes?"

"In a way. But it had never been a sore point. There was really more competition and resentment over the fact that the things we did sort of took us in opposite directions and caused us to have different friends and different preferences for entertainment and things of that nature. And for a period of time, until I got it off the ground, I think there was a lot of resentment over the fact that I was building a rather elaborate addition to my home, primarily for . . ."

Ernst interrupted quickly. "You call it 'my home.' Wasn't it also your wife and your son's home?"

"Yes, of course. I don't mean to make a distinction there," said the doctor. But Ernst had made a point of greed.

The doctor testified that he specifically requested the two Dallas women house guests to stay with Joan on Monday morning instead of returning to Dallas. Both Diane Settegast and Eunice Woolen had previously told the grand jury a different account of the morning, that they had *offered* to stay and nurse their friend Joan, but that the doctor had indicated it was not necessary.

Another item of contention: John testified that he spent the Monday night in bed with Joan, in her extreme illness, rising often to change the sheets. Effie Green had previously told the grand jury that neither the sheets nor the gown had been changed since Mrs. Hill took to her sickbed on Saturday. Moreover, Effie further testified that, to the best of her remembrance, John Hill came home either not at all, or barely predawn, for his dinner remained uneaten in the stove, and she did not hear his car.

Ernst's next line of questioning—and the answers—disturbed the jurors:

Ernst: "If I were your patient and I came to you and I was unrelated to you, and if I was stooling in the bed and puking all over the room, to put it kind of bluntly, what would you do? Leave me there or send me to the hospital?"

Hill: "Well, that would depend on the nursing care that . . . if I felt you had responsible relatives to care for you and if you could get something down by mouth, I probably would leave you there. I'd probably give you an anti-emetic of some sort to tide you over, and if you had any fever, I would possibly give you an appropriate antibiotic if I felt like that there might be a bacterial problem." This was, the jurors already knew, what he said he had done for his now dead wife.

"Well," continued the prosecutor, "just wondering now, in hindsight, perhaps you would, or could you say, perhaps you maybe *might* have taken her to the hospital right then? In hindsight, of course, Doctor?"

"Well, of course, that's very difficult to say."

"Yes, sir," said Ernst, nodding.

"If I had to rely directly on hindsight, things having developed the way they did, I probably should have taken her to the hospital the very first time she vomited. But this would have been a very abnormal response. Ask any doctor. I don't know of any doctor that treats his family in that manner. And doctors, knowing that most people will get well with just routine bed rest and nursing care, tend to be not quite as much of an alarmist with their own family. . . . Of course, there is a certain amount of psychology which we as physicians want . . . Let me put it this way. If you see a patient, he expects you to function as a doctor, and even if you know full well that if absolutely nothing is done, no medicine given, if you know that time will take care of whatever is wrong, still, you'll give them something for their symptoms. That's what it takes to be a good doctor."

Ernst smiled. "Just a little bull in that, too, perhaps, Doctor?"

The doctor wanted the grand jurors to know that he first mentioned taking his wife to the hospital on Monday morning, when he grew alarmed that she was not taking and holding enough fluids. The problem at that time was dehydration, he said.

"Then why didn't you take her to the hospital then?" asked one of the jurors.

"She was very adamant about not going to the hospital," said the doctor, contradicting testimony from Effie Green and the two Dallas women and Ash Robinson. "She disliked hospitals intensely, and made the statement, 'Well, they'll be sticking needles in me if I go to the hospital, so why don't you treat me at home?' I said, 'Okay, I'll treat you at home, but it's going to be on the basis that you do what I say and get in more fluids, and if you either don't, or can't, then I'm going to send you to the hospital.' "

Two of the most damaging remarks came in John Hill's response to questions concerning (1) the moving of his wife to Sharpstown Hospital, and (2) why he chose that hospital in the first place. The doctor told the grand jury that he helped his wife down the grand staircase of their home, her arms locked about his neck, "sort of dragging her behind me." Effie Green, her husband, and Mrs. Robinson all testified that the doctor ordered Joan to walk for herself.

"What was the primary thought guiding your selection of hospitals?" asked I. D. McMaster.

"I had an operation scheduled at Sharpstown Hospital for, I believe, eleven-thirty that morning. And I wanted to be close to wherever she would be. Also, she had quite a liking for Dr. Walter Bertinot, an internist, and had expressed the thought that if she were ever sick, she liked his manner and thought that he would be a good doctor to take care of her."

"And you respected his ability, also?"

"Yes. I had a great deal of respect for his ability, and I

felt that he would give her good care and would be a person that she would relate to very well, psychologically. . . ."

The jurors compared this remark with what Dr. Bertinot had told them when *he* testified, namely that he had been "quite surprised" on that long-ago morning when John Hill asked him to treat Joan. He barely knew the woman. He had met her only at large parties and had never become friendly with her in any way.

More than anything else, the surgeon's *attitude* gnawed at the grand jurors. One of the women present noted that John's eyes did not even mist—much less spill tears—as he spoke of his wife's tragic death. Any lawyer knows that *how* a witness says something is often more compelling than *what* he says. John Hill for two hours was more like a doctor presenting an interesting case to an amphitheater full of students than a man reaching into an agonizing cupboard of his life.

One of the jurors asked, "Is there *any* regret on your part about the procedure you used?"

"No," shot back the surgeon. "I don't regret the procedure I used, and I don't mean to imply the feeling of neglect. I merely mean to state that I feel the outcome would have been the same—but I would have felt a little bit better about it, and certainly there would be less criticism—the outcome would have been the same if I had taken her to the hospital the first moment she got sick."

Ernie Ernst was dissatisfied. "Suppose you had a dog that you loved very much and the dog got sick with nausea and diarrhea and everything else. What would you do for that dog? Leave it there so it would hopefully get better? Or take it to the vet?"

John Hill sidestepped around the trap. "I'd treat it in the best manner that I could, to answer your hypothetical question, but if the dog was failing to improve, well, sooner or later, I would take the dog to the vet, of course."

"Sooner or later?"

"Yes." John Hill delivered to the room one of the looks that doctors hold a patent on. It said, "We know best."

John was braced for questions relating to Ann Kurth's appearance before the grand jury. Finally one came.

"Did you, prior to taking the Sodium Pentothal test for Mr. McMaster, conduct a study of the nature of that test?" asked Ernst.

"Yes, I did," answered the doctor. "Mrs. Ann Kurth, who became Mrs. Hill over that weekend, and I went to Dallas and took the kids to Six Flags Over Texas. And I was . . . well, I had agreed to go along with something that I didn't really know the nature of, a Sodium Pentothal test, and I was a little bit concerned as to the reliability of the tests and whether or not I might perjure myself or where I might make statements that might be misleading or misconstrued. So I went to a library."

"As a result of that study, did you determine whether or not there was any medication which would tend to off-set the effects of the truth serum drug?"

"No, I did not. I don't think that this would be possible because this is administered by an anesthesiologist, who puts you to sleep, and you are either asleep or you are not asleep, and this is something only he can determine."

"Did you administer any medication, or did anyone else administer any medication to you shortly prior to your Sodium Pentothal examination which would tend to affect the results of that test?"

John dressed his face with an expression of sourness. I know where *that* came from, it seemed to say. "No. Mrs. Kurth indicated that she was going to come down here and allege such a thing if there was a divorce between us. I don't know if you are relying on her information. Anyway, I did not administer any such drug."

"Were you asleep during the test? Under the influence of the drug?"

"Yes, of course. My level of consciousness varied a great deal, I was more alert at times than at others, and I can vaguely remember a question or two at the outset. But the person who knows these things is the anesthesiologist because he is able to measure your blood pressure and your pulse and your respiration and check your pupils and various other responses."

Carole Pinkett had hung back silently during the doctor's testimony, listening carefully, trying to make up her mind about this man. He was a little smooth for her, his answers were too pat. The fact that he sweated profusely, beads of perspiration dotting his forehead and dampening his crisp white collar, was the only crack in his shield.

She asked John Hill how many times he had treated his wife medically prior to her final illness.

"Practically every time she was ill," answered the doctor. "I was responsible mainly for her treatment and that of my son for minor illnesses and also for the medical treatment of the Robinson family."

Ernie Ernst wrote down the answer on his yellow legal pad. Unknowingly, Carole Pinkett had asked the most telling question of the day. Then she moved to an area that had not been touched by the grand jury or the doctor. "Doctor, can you sincerely say that you loved your wife when she died?"

For a moment, a fraction of suspense, John Hill seemed taken aback. "Yes," he began softly in tones less measured than his previous answers. "I did love my wife. . . . We had some pretty serious differences. The nature of my love for Joan was one of respect for an individual with an unusual mind and a very fine personality, great administrative capacity and immense personal charm . . . not necessarily a lot of romantic love." For a moment there, thought Carole Pinkett, he had almost dropped his guard and exposed his real feelings. But then he reverted to form and began describing his marriage as if it were fodder for a medical journal.

"You did care for her?" she pressed.

John nodded.

"Did you *love* her?"

"I was just making a point . . ."

"Is that your definition of love?"

"The character of love that I had for her was not any longer such a romantic, burning love. . . ."

Carole understood. "The honeymoon was over?"

John looked down. "Perhaps that is the way to put it. . . . Everything was over."

He had dreaded the ordeal, but now that it was past John Hill felt elated. He told Racehorse Haynes that the grand jury's questions had been tough but reasonable. "I don't think they're going to indict me," predicted the surgeon. Extremely conservative politically, John Hill held great faith in the legal processes of the American system of justice. Once, before the scandal of Joan's death had wrapped its grip about him, he had attended a forum held by the ACLU and he had sat on the front row, baiting the liberal panel. Only with a rigid, rightist attitude could America survive, he said. No mollycoddling of the downtrodden! At a coffee reception afterward, he told one ACLU member that he held no truck with those who would allow the poor, blacks, and Mexicans special favor under the law, to compensate for the history of their persecution. The system works, he said. Any man can rise to prestige and power—witness himself!—and any man can expect fair treatment under the law.

Racehorse Haynes was no such idealist. Any lawyer who knows his way to the courthouse also knows that the system is majestic and at the same time maddening, corrupt, and pliable to the whims of politics, influence, and money. The next day after his client's appearance before the grand jury, Haynes's attitude was confirmed. The grand jury was requesting a one-month extension of their regular ninety-day term. Had John Hill's appearance before the panel been all that satisfactory, Racehorse knew, then the matter would have been dropped altogether. It was time for another grandstand play. Racehorse called I. D. McMaster—and at the same time slipped the news to a reporter—to say that his client was willing to take a polygraph examination. Because the circumstances surrounding the truth serum test had been sullied by the accusations of Ann Kurth, then the doctor would agree to a test solely administered by police authorities.

"No deal," said McMaster. Not unless John Hill wants to stay in jail for forty-eight hours prior to the test, under constant observation. If a person bombs himself with tranquilizers before a polygraph test, it can drastically alter the results. Racehorse quickly refused, not relishing the spectacle of his client checking into jail for two days and nights. It was certain to be photographed and find a place on the front page of the city's newspapers.

The two assistant DAs, Ernst and McMaster, took off several days and reviewed the case. They reread the Helpern report, the transcript of John Hill's appearance before the grand jury, the summation of Ann Kurth's testimony, bits and pieces from all the others. "There's not a doubt in my mind that the son of a bitch wanted his wife dead," believed Ernst. "In fact, I think he probably did it. But I don't think we've got enough to make a first-degree murder-with-malice charge stick."

He retired to the law library and spent a week searching for precedent to indict, try, and convict John Hill. Never in two decades of trial work had a case so tantalized him. The district attorney, Carol Vance, summoned Ernst and McMaster and asked for a summation of their feelings.

"We *think* he ought to be indicted for murder," said McMaster.

But how would they prove a murder? demanded Vance. That remained the key issue. After all the autopsies by all the doctors Joan Robinson Hill lay in her grave, dead from still unknown causes. Racehorse Haynes would tear apart any accusation that the woman died of possible poisoning, unless there was real proof. There was no margin for speculation in this case, warned Vance. What can be *proved*?

What can be proved? mused McMaster. They could prove that John Hill had a rotten marriage, that he ran around on his wife, that he kept a mistress he wanted to marry, that he signed a financially imprisoning document that would force him to give up his beloved music room if he didn't stop acting like a tomcat, that his wife got sick, that he treated her at home, that she got worse, that he took her to an out-of-the-way hospital, that she died, that he married his mistress before the dead wife was barely cold. That's all they could prove.

Out of all that, said Vance, only two remote criminal possibilities existed. Either John Hill intentionally let his wife die, or he was so grossly negligent in the matter that he hastened her death.

Ernie Ernst asked for another day or two in the law library. He had come onto an obscure possibility. A risky one at best. "But," drawled Ernst, "I just may know a way we can indict this old boy for murder."

20

In 1893 a young woman lived with her aged spinster aunt, who was infirm and unable to care for herself. As the old woman grew more feeble and edged closer to death, the niece "continued to live with her and use her money to purchase food, but she failed to furnish the deceased with said food, provide medical assistance or notify anyone of her terminal illness."

In 1907 a man spent three days with his girl friend in

what the vernacular of the era called "a weekend de-
bauch." During their vivid hours together, the girl took a
fatal dose of morphine tablets. The man, aghast at the
act and its potential for scandal, failed to call a physician
who might have been able to pump out her stomach and
save her life.

In 1923 a man and his wife went out on a bar crawl in
the middle of winter. The night was cold and stormy.
Upon their return home, the woman tripped on the front
steps, laughed drunkenly, and said she was going to rest
a minute in the snow. The man went inside, passed out,
and the next morning woke up to discover his wife dead,
frozen stiff in a snowbank.

In 1935 a distraught woman announced to her fiancé
that she was going to fling herself out the window and
commit suicide. Be my guest, said the lover. She did.

What, hypothetically asked Ernie Ernst, what did these
poor folk all have in common—the ungrateful niece who
sponged off her dying aunt, the rake whose mistress over-
dosed herself with morphine, the thoughtless drunk whose
wife went to sleep forever in the snow, the hapless man
whose girl friend fatally left his apartment via his window?
"They were all convicted of *murder by omission,* that's
what," said Ernst, a little triumphant after his long sab-
batical in the law library.

Murder by omission! In the entire history of American criminal jurisprudence, there were perhaps twenty
cases which could be categorized under this heading.
"They're damned difficult to prove," cautioned Ernst, "and
they often get overturned on appeal." But, to his thinking,
it was the only rap that could be pinned on Dr. John Hill.
Ernst summed up: "The law is fairly clear on this. If you
owe a duty to a person and if you fail to perform it, and
death results, then you are guilty of homicide." If, for
example, you are driving across the Golden Gate Bridge
and you see a potential suicide preparing to leap, the law
does not require you to stop and pull that person down
from the guard rail. But if a man's wife jumps out of the
car and climbs onto the rail and prepares to leap, then
the law says that the man has a *responsibility* to prevent
that death. If he lets her jump, it's murder by omission.
McMaster was fascinated. This was compatible with his
murder-by-negligence theory, but it was stronger.

"A doctor owes a duty to his patient," said Ernst, "and a doctor owes a special duty to his wife if she is the patient."

Can this be murder in the first degree? asked McMaster.

"I think so," answered Ernst. If the state could prove that, through criminal negligence and by withholding proper medical treatment, John Hill caused the death of his wife, then it was murder one, the same as if he had seized a dagger and stabbed her to death in her bed.

The two prosecutors waved their discovery in front of the boss, Carol Vance, who agreed that it was the best of a weak case. Take it before the grand jury, he said wearily, and explain the law, and let them decide.

Grand juror Carole Pinkett was also tired and disenchanted. The idealism she had brought to this secret chamber on her first day of public service was now gone. In college she had studied government and political science, its machinations and intrigue, confident that in the long haul the system was fair. Now her virginity in matters judicial was broken. She listened to Ernst and McMaster droning on, explaining the strange-sounding new charge they had dredged out of old lawbooks, and neither their enthusiasm nor the excitement of some of the other jurors— Haden specifically—bothered her as much as the fact that *she no longer cared very much*. She found herself nodding, almost dumbly, like having explained a mathematical equation that she had not the remotest interest in. She felt now that there was an inexorable end to this drama, one forewritten before she even took her chair on the first day. Certain events and scenes that had nagged at her for almost four months seemed more comprehensible now. At that first session she had been pleased to discover four black faces on the grand jury. At that moment, in 1970, it was the rare panel that contained more than one or two. How fine, she thought, how excellent it was for black people to be assuming civic responsibility in something as basic and powerful as grand jury service! Still, as the weeks dragged on and the John Hill case became a torment to her conscience, she began to fret. She began to speculate that four black people were on this panel because it would be easier to persuade the meek and the subservient to vote in a certain way.

She noticed other things as well. It was worrisome to her

when Cecil Haden became a benevolent white father figure, currying favor with the jurors, sending out for sandwiches and fried chicken—and paying the bill for everybody himself—when it was necessary for the group to continue past the lunch hour. Often she noted Haden leaving for the day with his arm draped pointedly around one of the juror's shoulders, sometimes a black who had never felt the pressure of a rich and powerful white man's touch and comradeship. The sight reminded Carole of a Washington lobbyist strolling down a congressional corridor with a lawmaker in tow. Toward the end of the jury's term Carole encountered difficulty keeping her mind on the witnesses. One thought tore at her: "No matter what I do or say, the stage is set and a script is being acted out." When she rose to attack a theory or a flimsy piece of speculation from the prosecutors, she could sense a collective, if silent, groan from her peers. She began to feel talked down to, abused of her independence, treated like a nigger and a woman and thus twice removed from the possibility of rational thought.

She cared little for John Hill and, during his appearance, felt that he was too glib and cold. But she did not like what was happening to him. "What has the district attorney offered us?" she asked her fellow jurors. "Where is the proof? How can we indict this man? All we have been offered are some shady characters—a doctor who played around, a vengeful father bringing pressure. After three autopsies, we still do not know the cause of death! Can we possibly indict a man on this and refer him to a trial jury?"

The foreman thanked Mrs. Pinkett for her remarks, then passed out secret ballots. "What's the use?" surrendered Carole Pinkett to herself. "I'm tired, everyone else is tired. Everybody's probably thinking the way I am—which is to say, to hell with this. Joan Hill didn't mean a thing to me. John Hill doesn't mean a thing to me. I'll just pass this on to a trial jury. I'll pass them the buck. I'll let them decide if this doctor should go to the penitentiary forever. I'll let everybody go to sleep."

The vote was ten to two in favor of indictment. Carole Pinkett never knew who supported her in opposition to the charge. No one locked eyes with her, or nodded imperceptibly as she studied the jurors' faces during the counting of votes. It did not matter, for John Hill was now formally accused by the People of Texas of murder by omission of his wife.

That night Ash Robinson cried mightily, in exultation!

That night Carole Pinkett uncharacteristically poured herself a large drink and sat alone, in a dark room, wondering at the enormity of the deed. As tired as she was, sleep eluded her.

Racehorse Haynes turned the rare indictment upside down for a newspaper reporter and tried to read it. "It reads just as intelligently this way as it does right side up," he said. The attorney reported that his client's reaction was the same as his, "shock and disbelief." He had never read a document quite like it in his entire career in criminal law.

"But," said Racehorse optimistically, "maybe this grand jury has inadvertently done us a favor. Maybe a no-bill would not have been adequate. Maybe a full jury trial and acquittal are needed to restore Dr. Hill to his rightful place in society."

The indictment was brief:

> On or about the 19th day of March, 1969, John R. Hill was a licensed medical doctor and was the husband of Joan Hill, and had undertaken, and then and there was responsible for the medical treatment of her . . . and the said Joan Hill was then and there sick and thereby in a helpless condition, which was known to Dr. Hill, and the life of Joan Hill was in danger if she did not promptly receive proper medical attention and treatment, and this was known to Dr. John Hill, and the said Dr. John Hill did voluntarily and with malice aforethought kill the said Joan Hill by wilfully, intentionally and culpably failing and omitting to administer to her proper medical treatment, and by wilfully, intentionally and culpably failing and omitting to make timely provisions for her hospitalization and proper medical treatment.

The plastic surgeon was severely shaken by the indictment, but he was reassured by Racehorse's attitude. Moreover, he had a new source of comfort in his life. Her name was Connie, and on the night the state of Texas formally accused him of murdering his first wife, she put her arms around him and vowed to stand by him—whatever.

Connie Loesby was beautiful, a pale, serene, composed woman who resembled a hand-painted cameo from another century. Often she wore her lustrous brunette hair pulled back into a demure bun, emphasizing her eyes, which could look like enormous black opals, polished with a velvet cloth. A man would use old-fashioned words like "genteel" and "ladylike" to describe her. She was the antithesis of both of the women who preceded her in John Hill's life. She seemed a woman who was born to sit attentively in drawing rooms, listening to complex music. The impression was genuine, for music shaped and dominated her life.

Raised in Seattle, Connie was the daughter of a woman who played piano and organ and led a church choir. Connie began piano studies at seven, dallied briefly at ballet, and moved effortlessly into singing in public before she was twelve. She attended the famous Westminster Choir College in New Jersey, taking a master's degree in music, recording the "Missa Solemnis" with the choir under the baton of Leonard Bernstein. For a time she dreamed of an operatic career, and joined an opera workshop in Philadelphia. There she sang the principal soprano roles in *La Bohème, Così Fan Tutte,* even *Madame Butterfly.* Her voice was too sweet and lyrical for the heavy dramatic coloring needed for Cio Cio San, but she was staggeringly beautiful in kimono and taped-back eyes. When a romance with an organist in Philadelphia broke, she joined the Robert Shaw Chorale, touring Europe, cramming as many musical experiences as she could into each week. When she returned to America, she needed a teaching job to sustain her studies, but she found it difficult to obtain such a post. Finally one turned up at a junior college near Houston. She arrived in the city with little money and took a dreary furnished room in the wrong part of town. She fell ill with pneumonia and stomach flu, and during a six-month recuperation a thief stole all of her clothes and possessions. It was not a very encouraging beginning.

On an evening in early December 1969, Connie participated in a musicale at the University of St. Thomas in the old residential center of Houston. She played the harpsichord and later sang a Scarlatti cantata, and, with a partner, two Purcell duets. Afterward, backstage, in the crush

of people offering compliments, Connie was pulled aside
by a flautist friend who wanted to introduce John Hill.
The name meant nothing to her. She was not the kind of
person who read the front page. All she knew was that a
tall, quite handsome, and rather boyish-looking man in his
late thirties was shyly mumbling his congratulations. The
man introduced his son Robert—and the boy also seemed
shy. When they left, father and son, there was a buzzing
backstage, but Connie failed to pick up the cause. Even
when a girl friend complimented her on having caught the
eye of the wealthy and notorious plastic surgeon, Connie
professed never to have heard of him, his dead wife, or the
controversy swirling about both. When John sent an invitation through an emissary that he wanted her to come to
his home for a Sunday afternoon musicale a few weeks
hence, Connie accepted readily. Later she would tell him,
"When you first asked me, I was a little afraid to come.
But I swallowed my apprehension and collected all my
friends in my trusty little VW and arrived. Immediately I
forgot any little bit of worry. Music was the thing we all
had in common, and there is no danger in music."

For a few months Connie attended the musicales in the
ornate room. They were pleasant affairs, with a core of ten
or so professional musicians gathering to play for one another. On occasion John would introduce some obscure
piece of medieval music he had discovered and play it on
his recorder. Or Connie would sing shimmering lieder, or
a visiting performer with the Houston Grand Opera would
present an afternoon of obscure Mozart and Verdi. Afterward there would be champagne punch in fine crystal gob-
lets and polite talk. John Hill was in his element, master
of a palatial room, impresario of splendid music. That he
was also being investigated for the death of his wife seemed
impossible for Connie to believe. Only rarely did she connect the man and the scandal, perhaps when listening to
the classical radio station and hearing the doctor's name
in an intrusive newscast.

Suddenly, surprisingly, for there had never been a moment of intimacy between them—not even private conversation—John called Connie and said, rather stumblingly,
"I have a gift for you." Hemming and hawing, he wondered whether he should mail it or drop it by the doorman
of her new apartment. Connie sensed that here was a man
who wanted to deliver a gift in person. But she was as

shy as her admirer. Finally he blurted, "I would really like to bring it personally." "Then do," said Connie, relieved.

The gift was a recording of Elisabeth Schwarzkopf, whose voice both John and Connie loved. She put it on her cheap portable phonograph, and John frowned at the tinny sound He noted her inexpensive piano. It reminded him, he said, of the one on which he and his brother Julian once played duets. They began to talk of their musical pasts. revealing little bits and pieces of their lives, awkwardly maneuvering toward a relationship.

When John went home and told his mother about the interesting new girl, Myra Hill grew alarmed. She warned her son that it was neither wise nor prudent to be seen in the company of a new woman, with his first wife mysteriously dead, his second wife angrily estranged and so often in the company of Ash Robinson these days.

It was thereby arranged for a charade to be enacted until the storm clouds were blown away. Connie would come regularly to the Hill mansion on the ruse of giving Robert music lessons, after which she would stay for dinner, and then join the master of the house in his music room where they would often sit silently for hours, listening to the classics. The news did not escape Ash's attention for long, because he rang up the district attorney's office in the spring of 1970, just before the indictment was voted, and informed the prosecutors that his former son-in-law had still another woman on his arm. "He's got a whole string of women," Ash said. "He fixes up their faces and they give him free sex." The only trouble with this was that Connie was too lovely to need a plastic surgeon's knife

During the several months that they had known one another, Connie avoided asking John about his first wife's death. After the indictment was handed down, and during an afternoon in which he seemed exceptionally tense and distraught, she brought up the subject quietly.

"I want to know about Joan," she said.

He shook his head, as if there was nothing to tell.

"Please " she pressed,

John Hill shrugged "I made a poor choice of in-laws," he said.

"How do you keep going? It must be very hard on you."

He nodded. "It has been a very difficult time. It's important for me to know that you believe in me. Do you?"

"Yes." Connie's answer was firm. She felt she knew this man, and he was a gentle man, one who could not have anything to do with murder.

One evening a few weeks later, John Hill came into the kitchen where Connie was stirring a cooking pot. He took her into his arms and kissed her and said, "Will you marry me?"

Connie put down the spoon and smiled. "I sure will. When?"

"Whenever you want."

"Tomorrow?" asked Connie.

"I'd better ask my lawyers."

Racehorse Haynes had a piece of paper in his hand and he threw it to the ceiling when John Hill informed him of his plans to marry for a third time. Then just drive on up to Huntsville and spend the wedding night so you'll be close to the state prison, warned Racehorse. His most urgent counsel, said the lawyer, was to wait. In fact, he would rather that the doctor not be seen in the company of any woman save his dear old mother and extremely ugly and well-married surgical nurses. John Hill saw the hard light and agreed to wait.

Though Racehorse was sputtering indignance to the press and tender consolation to his client, he felt exhilarated within. The stakes on the table were, for a change, exciting. Most criminal lawyers spend a career running drunks, addicts, and hijackers past bored judges, all yawning, enacting a scenario prewritten with the district attorney. Texas is no different from any other state in America, wherein ninety per cent of all criminal charges are traded out in advance.

Haynes's heart leaped when he considered this case. It was surely The One. A lawyer could go to his grave waiting in vain for the murder trial where the victim died mysteriously, where the accused was of high professional and social position (and thus able to pay a substantial legal fee) and the opportunity was rich for flair, drama, headlines, and notoriety.

Already Racehorse was being talked about as the heir apparent in Texas to the criminal law kingdom of Percy Foreman, the giant attorney with historic ability to get people off on murder charges, particularly murderesses, but who was, in 1970, in his eighth decade and nearing retirement. Haynes was the archetypal criminal lawyer, possessing a cunning mind with just enough deviousness to sniff out chicanery from the other side—the takes-one-to-know-one principal. His ego was as gigantic as his stature was small, a valuable and admired quality in a city where the most successful men—heart surgeons, astronauts, wildcatting oilmen—did not object when their names appeared in large public print. Moreover, Racehorse was witty, charming, good-looking ("I owe everything to clean living and constant prayer," he liked to say), and a splendid actor, able to summon rage, grief, scorn, or the wrath of the Almighty if it seemed necessary to move a jury.

The best way to understand Racehorse Haynes was to recollect one of his most celebrated events—the Crucifixion Case. He agreed to defend a gang of motorcyclists in a Southern state who were accused of punishing a female follower in a remarkable manner—by nailing her to a tree. Racehorse would come to call this "The Case of the Chick Who Was Tacked to a Stick." He always told the story well: "My clients, whose names were Fat Frank, Spider, Super Squirrel, Crazy John, and Mangy, were upset at one of the ladies who followed their gang because she neglected to follow the first rule of the world's oldest profession—that is, to turn in the money. They elected to punish her, and they nailed her to a tree. She was not killed, she wasn't even hurt terribly bad. But all hell broke loose. It occurred to me that a pimp can burn his whore with a cigarette, or slice her up with a razor blade, or throw her out of a speeding car, or whip her to ribbons with a coat hanger, and nobody gets upset. People tend to think of these things as occupational hazard. But *crucify* one, and the entire Eastern seaboard and Southern states were up in arms."

For his defense, Haynes took the position that (1) the girl in question sort of "volunteered" for what happened to her, and (2) nothing would have happened if the victim's father had not been important. "We told the jury that the prosecution was caused not so much by the rage of the victim but by the anger of her father, who didn't like motorcycle gangs very much. These boys had been roaring around his state for some time, even having the gall to ride into a sheriff's office, put their feet on his desk, and say they were tired of being pushed around."

Haynes won acquittal for Fat Frank et al. and the crucified girl is now, he claims, "quite celebrated around the bars of her area where she shows off her stigmata."

There was, however, one point in the trial at which Racehorse felt his case needed bolstering. He wanted the jury to divorce the emotional and historical wrappings from the act of putting a nail through a human hand and affixing it to a tree. Hastily finding a doctor to advise him in private, the lawyer asked just how painful it was to have a nail driven through the hand. The doctor answered that it was serious but not necessarily life-threatening. "In fact," he said, taking his hand, "there are places where you could put a nail through and barely feel pain." Racehorse suddenly grabbed an idea that made him almost giddy with anticipation. He began to fantasize the scene. On the morning before the closing arguments, he would have his doctor friend secretly inject the top of his hand with a local anesthetic and mark it with a small red dot. Then, in the passion of his address to the jury, in dramatic proof of his contention that it did not hurt the girl all that much to be affixed to a tree trunk, he would slap his hand palm down, withdraw a hammer and nail from his briefcase, and nail himself to the defense table! Sort of an off-Broadway Crucifixion. Law students would surely talk about this defense for centuries thereafter.

"I have always regretted the fact that my case was so strong I was able to win without doing that," Racehorse often said. "Yet I continue to dream of the day when I am cross-examining a witness and my questions are so probing and so brilliant that the fellow blurts out that *he*, not my defendant, committed the foul murder. Then he will pitch forward into my arms, dead of a heart attack."

The John Hill murder case, felt Racehorse, was in that very category.

21

A year of anger and impassioned rhetoric spun by before John Hill was brought to trial. And in this interim Racehorse Haynes became convinced that the state of Texas had—at best—a worthy case of malpractice against his client. "And I doubt seriously if they could win that," he told his law partner, Fullenweider. As much as he wanted to try the tantalizing case, Racehorse leaned hard on the DA's office to drop the charge. His position was this: if John Hill had been a schoolteacher or a bank clerk or any ordinary fellow, he would not be accused of murder by omission, whatever that is. And if John Hill had not been a doctor, and a society page doctor at that, and if his deceased first wife had not been an internationally famous woman and popular friend of power people in Houston, and if he had had any other man on the face of the planet for a father-in-law, John Hill would have been cleared and left alone long ago.

The prosecutors, McMaster and Ernst, paid no attention to Racehorse's exhortations. They were now caught up in the rush to trial, and both had private reasons beyond professional responsibilities and a shared belief that the plastic surgeon was somehow guilty of his wife's death. McMaster had decided to run for a district judgeship, and he knew that a widely publicized performance in this murder trial would win him attention. Ernst planned to retire from public life and slip away to a small town somewhere to teach law and do some writing. The Hill matter would be a satisfactory peak from which to begin a trip down.

The defense considered an all-out pretrial attack on the curious fact that Cecil Haden was a principal force on the grand jury that indicted his client. "It is true that in our criminal law there is no provision per se against the godfather and pallbearer of the deceased sitting on a grand jury that indicts her husband for an alleged murder," Racehorse said sarcastically. "But I imagine the Court of Criminal Appeals would nonetheless find it interesting. And it should scare the pants off the citizens of this town."

But he elected to keep this cannon silent for a time. He could always fire it later on, during the appeals process, in the remote possibility that his client was convicted. Instead he threw a bitter motion before the district criminal court, claiming that the indictment against John Hill was "fatally vague." The crime of "murder by omission" was not even specifically written down in the state's criminal law, nor were there penalties provided for such. And even if it were written down, he argued, there can be no culpable omission unless there is a legal duty. "The present indictment attempts to plead two different duties—that of a doctor and that of a husband, *and* two different omissions

—the omission to administer treatment and the admission to make timely provisions for said treatment—*without* putting the defendant on notice of which theory the prosecution intends to pursue, thus rendering it impossible for the defendant to present his defense." In other words, contended Racehorse, the state had to try this guy as either a husband or a doctor. Couldn't do both.

Most pertinently, the lawyer charged, the indictment did not even allege the cause of Joan Hill's death. What *did* the lady die from? Pancreatitis? Hepatitis? Meningitis? Nor did the indictment allege what treatment John Hill should have given his wife. "What the hell did he omit?" wondered Racehorse sarcastically.

The prosecution fired back with an articulate brief, larded with emotional quotations from legal history:

"It is a general rule that a physician or surgeon who through criminal negligence in the treatment of the patient causes death, is guilty of manslaughter. . . . And in a few cases arising from the negligent practice of medicine, the accused has been charged with murder. . . . Criminal negligence in this respect is largely a matter of degree, incapable of precise definition, and whether or not it exists to such a degree as to involve criminal liability is to be determined by the jury. . . . The courts are generally agreed that negligence exists where the physician or surgeon . . . exhibits gross lack of competency or gross inattention, or criminal indifference to the patient's safety."

And, furthermore, insisted the DA's men, "a criminal liability is imposed upon a husband who negligently fails to furnish his wife with necessities. . . . Dr. John Hill was both the husband and the doctor of the deceased, and as a doctor he became responsible for her medical treatment, and he knew under the law he had some responsibility as a husband; and [he knew] that she was sick and in a helpless condition; and it makes no difference what she was sick with; as a doctor he owes her the duty to properly attend her, regardless of her malady. With malice aforethought, intentionally and culpably, he failed to administer proper medical treatment and failed to timely provide for her hospitalization. . . ."

Judge Fred Hooey, in whose court the case had come to rest, denied Racehorse's plea to quash the indictment and ordered jury selection to begin on March 16, 1971, just three days shy of the second anniversary of the death of Joan Robinson Hill. Angered that his motion was denied, Racehorse nonetheless felt confident on the eve. The state of Texas would have to prove three things to convict John Hill: (1) that he was a licensed medical doctor; (2) that he undertook to be the physician of his wife; and (3) that he deliberately and *with malice* failed to treat her properly and failed to obtain timely hospitalization for her, thus causing her death.

"There's simply no way they can prove anything but Item 1," he decided. Item 2 was an argumentative region of grayness in this husband-wife relationship. If necessary, Racehorse would summon prominent doctors of the city who would testify that, had their own wives displayed similar symptoms, they would have followed the same course of treatment and might have wound up with dead spouses. Item 3, Racehorse convinced himself, was even slipperier. Malice! If a man tells a crowded saloon crowd, "I'm going to get my gun and shoot the bastard who stole my woman," and if he does just that, then murder with malice aforethought is not difficult to establish. "But how is the state of Texas going to convince a jury that John Hill, a gentle, churchgoing surgeon in good standing, deliberately killed his wife through medical negligence?" said the lawyer.

Both sides spent hundreds of yawning hours in medical libraries and in the company of physicians and scientists, trying to comprehend the ways that poisons and bacteria can harm the body. Racehorse decided he could rule out any claim that poison was administered to Joan Hill. She lived too long after she first became ill—more than four days—to have been slipped any quick-acting poison. Moreover, tests for "heavy metals" on the blood first drawn from her in the hour she was admitted to Sharpstown Hospital showed no evidence of such. And none of the pathologists who had autopsied the woman, including the great Dr. Helpern, had been able to discover any unexplained injection site on the body. "Scratch poison," said Racehorse.

But death from *bacteria* was not only a possibility, it was a potentially dangerous opponent to Hill's defense. The state could not *prove* that Joan Hill perished from a bacterial infection of sinister origin, but Racehorse fretted that they could damn well waltz around the idea long enough to make it sound feasible to a jury.

The lesions that the woman suffered were probably bacterial in etiology. The esophagus, liver, spleen, and meninges all had the kind of intense white-cell infiltrations normally found in serious bacterial infection, or, as the disease is also known, bacteremia. True, Dr. Jachimczyk, the Houston coroner, wrote in his very first autopsy report that he would rule out bacterial infection because of a negative blood culture run on blood taken from Joan immediately after her admission to Sharpstown Hospital. But one of Houston's best-known research specialists on this type of disease took issue with the coroner. "We frequently encounter bacteremia even with a negative blood culture," he said. "Maybe one out of six cases, in fact."

The next question was, of course, How did the bacteria get into Joan's body and kill her? One potentially deadly kind of bacteria are called E. coli, and they exist in every human being's body. These are valuable and necessary bacteria because they help produce antibodies that kill harmful organisms that are swallowed and introduced to the system. They also keep intestinal function normal. They live in the colon and are supposed to stay there. But if they get out of the colon they become a deadly threat. A crumb of feces is basically all bacteria and dangerous. Occasionally a surgeon kills a patient by carelessly nicking the bowel wall during an operation, releasing millions of bacteria from feces into the blood stream, and propelling the patient into terminal shock. It is not a rare blunder; John Hill did it once during resident surgery. In one major American hospital there were 860 such fatal cases over a nine-year period. Alas, the grieving family is usually told, your loved one died of postsurgical complications and blood poisoning. Alas, the loved one really died of a surgical mistake.

But, as Racehorse happily reminded himself, Joan Hill did not have surgery.

The other two principal portals of entry for bacteria into a body are ingestion and injection. It would have been possible for John Hill to slip his wife a pathogenic (disease-producing) bacteria by mouth. He could have cultured the E. coli bacteria on an agar plate, a fundamental process known to any medical student, dropped a spoonful of the stuff into a glass of juice or even the cream portion of a chocolate éclair, and given it to Joan. There would not even be a foul taste. No taste at all, in fact.

But it would take a *massive* dose of E. coli bacteria for someone to be killed by swallowing it. Researchers studying the subject at the University of Texas Medical School in Houston have fed volunteers straight spoonfuls of E. coli organisms in a jelly, and the principal complaint is little more than loose bowel movements. It would take continuing doses over a long period of time to kill someone. (A nurse in Houston committed a most bizarre suicide by injecting herself regularly with a solution made from her own parakeet's feces.)

But what about *injecting* the deadly bacteria into a patient with a hypodermic needle? Here Racehorse must have felt a tiny flutter of apprehension. One neutral doctor in Houston who studied the case out of curiosity felt that if you wanted to speculate on murder this was the best place to fantasize. He commented: "I don't think John could have done it orally unless he used a very high-grade pathogen—like salmonella. And this assumes that he knew more bacteriology than we give him credit for. Surgeons are not particularly adroit at this kind of work, and as far as one knows, John Hill never went near a research lab. It is not too difficult to grow salmonella, but first you have to know it is salmonella, and you must go to a laboratory where they have it and get it."

The specialist was a man who enjoyed paperback mysteries and he was willing to concoct a plot: "If you're going to fantasize and speculate and go way out, then imagine that Joan Hill developed acute gastroenteritis on her own. She just got sick with a touch of stomach flu. It might have been something she ate. This began her illness. Now her husband was thinking about getting rid of her, and he took this as an occasion to administer medications intravenously. There is testimony from the two Dallas women house guests and from Effie, the maid, and from John Hill himself that he gave his wife two shots of Compazine. He could have made up a vial to look like any kind of medicine, only it had a heavy suspension of bacteria in it. *Any* bacteria. You would not have to be a trained bacteriologist to do this. You could go out into the yard and pick up a dog dropping. And he could inject this intravenously during the two or three days she was having the gastroenteritis problems. This would bring on the kind of disease she had—massive, overwhelming infection disseminated all over the body.

"And then, of course, the hasty embalming after her death in effect 'sterilized' the body. It removed the culture medium for the organisms to grow in, and it became impossible for anybody to find the fatal bacteria."

But mind you, cautioned the doctor, none of this was provable. It was the stuff of *policiers* and nothing more. Racehorse had no intention of letting the district attorney's office inject any fanciful scenarios into the trial record. He felt there were only two known possibilities of real trouble—Effie Green and Ann Kurth. The maid would once again come out and tell her now famous story of finding Joan Hill lying in a soiled bed. This had the same horror in the telling that the word "crucifixion" had in Racehorse's earlier case. To counter Effie's dangerous testimony, the defense lawyer planned to offer about one half of a mea culpa from his client. He would contend that John Hill slept in the same bed that next to last night of his wife's life, so the feces could not have been all that terrible. And, the lawyer would suggest to the jury, his client simply "misread" the entire situation.

"Let's put this illness in its proper context," he was preparing to say, probably rehearsing his speech while shaving. "Here you have a husband and a wife who did not enjoy the best of relationships. Their marriage was at the breaking point. She was naturally upset over the fact that her husband had been dating another woman. He was, at this point, pretty fed up with his wife. He didn't like her smoking, her personal health habits, her drinking, her nagging at him in public, and the fact that she wouldn't take medication. So when she had the bowel movement he misjudged it. Several things were working on him—the deteriorating marriage, concern for his son, pressure from Ann Kurth, financial problems with the music room. He simply 'misread' that scene that night in bed."

But then there was Ann Kurth.

What had she told the district attorney and the grand jury? What was she prepared to testify? Any conversations that went on between her and her husband during their tempestuous short-lived marriage were privileged and not admissible. But the defense attorney worried that Ernie Ernst was a clever enough prosecutor—even though he would be riding shotgun, in the second chair behind I. D. McMaster—to figure out a way to bend the law and get her on the witness stand and pump the fertile well. A few weeks earlier the lady had dropped a couple of worrisome hints during the taking of a deposition in property division from the divorce. She was talking at the time about how afraid she was of her now ex-husband, her fears having begun when he deliberately tried to kill her in a car accident. Haynes already knew of the event, but as the murder trial neared, he asked his client to elaborate.

Not much to it, said John. He and Ann were out driving late one night, near Chatsworth Farm. A quarrel began. Ann grabbed the wheel and the Cadillac hit a bridge abutment. Both were a little shaken up, but nothing serious. No real injuries.

"Is that all?" pressed Racehorse.

His client nodded. The lawyer studied his handsome face carefully. John Hill was the frostiest man he had ever encountered. Nothing seemed to faze him. Not for one fractional moment since the relationship between lawyer and client began more than a year earlier had John permitted himself any emotion. No despair. No exultation. No tears. Lately, he at least seemed happy, and it was easy to trace. Connie had become invaluable not only to John but to his defense. She was spending scores of hours each week working at the Haynes-Fullenweider office, typing depositions, preparing cross indexes, familiarizing herself with millions of words of sworn testimony so that she could instantly find it should the lawyers need a passage quickly. "She is a most remarkable woman," thought Racehorse. Funny thing about fate, he mused. John Hill should have met this woman first. They should have married and now they would be at home, in the music room, playing Scarlatti duets on the Bösendorfer, living graceful, elegant lives. Instead, he goes on trial for murder next week, and she is walking around a law office with carbon-stained hands.

One other item in Ann Kurth's divorce deposition testimony caught Racehorse's attention. Her lawyer, out of left field, asked if Mrs. Kurth had ever seen some "petri dishes" in the bachelor apartment that John Hill leased during their love affair.

Yes, she had, answered Ann. But the line of questioning was dropped. Racehorse read the entire transcript over again, just to make sure he had not overlooked something. Then he searched for the definition of "petri dish." It can be found in a medical dictionary: "A shallow, circular, glass or plastic dish with a loose-fitting cover over the top and sides, used for culturing bacteria and other micro-organisms, named after R. J. Petri, German bacteriologist."

Racehorse called up John Hill and read him the bother-some portion of Ann's divorce testimony. Did this have any significance?

A moment passed before the surgeon said, quietly but emphatically, "No."

22

Houston is a city whose pulse is quick, and murder trials have a similar tempo. Rare is the case that consumes more than a day or two in jury selection, a week of testimony, and a few hours of deliberation by the jury. If the jurors remain out for more than a day, the worry is that delibera-tions are hung on dead center. The spirit of the frontier is not far back, and there remains an attitude of "get it on, get it over." When a Houston lawyer reads of a faraway trial in, say, New York, where all concerned are in court for six tedious months, the attitude combines disbelief with thanksgiving.

By the end of the second day a jury of eleven men and one woman had been chosen to try Dr. John Hill for the "murder by omission" of his wife Joan. Both sides had come to court not exactly sure as to the kind of juror most desirable to their cause. The prosecution, to Ernie Ernst's way of thinking, had a Sunday tabloid sort of case, with the emphasis heavy on emotion, adultery, lost love, and romantic mischief on the richest boulevard in town. At first Ernst toyed with the idea of putting as many women on the jury as possible, for he felt that churchgoing matrons would respond unkindly to a philandering doctor. Then he began to remember that many women are in love with their doc-tors, one way or another, and that he might blunder by relying on them. "A lot of dames think with their vaginas," he would say later on. "I couldn't run the risk of having them get misty-eyed over that good-lookin' doctor at the defendant's table. They wouldn't vote to convict a good-lookin' doctor for anything." Better to fill the jury box with hard-laboring middle-class white men, the kind who endure from Friday's pay check to Friday's pay check, overly mortgaged, not very content, inclined probably to think that George Wallace might have the political answer, that doctors charge too much money and cover up for each other, that Dr. Fancy Pants who plays the piccolo probably killed his wife.

Conversely, Racehorse *wanted* women. He felt that only females could properly evaluate the testimony of Ann Kurth. "She's the key," he mused. "I suspect she's going to get up there on the stand and tell something horrible on my boy, and we've got to have jurors who can perceive what axes this woman brought to court to grind. The ideal juror for us," reasoned Racehorse, "is a woman between twenty-five and forty-five, who will sit in judgment not so much on John Hill, but on Ann Kurth." He compared it to a rape case, where defense lawyers often accuse the victim of taking liberties with the truth. "Women tend to be very critical of a woman testifying against an alleged rapist," said Racehorse, who had defended his share. "Whereas you put a bunch of guys on the jury and they're ready to hang the son of a bitch."

The defense attorney was not too worried about choosing purple-haired church soprano kind of women who might tsk-tsk moral indignation and/or condemnation toward a philandering doctor. In the first place, the state would have a difficult time getting such testimony into the record, specific acts of sexual misconduct being inadmissible. And secondly, he planned to offer his client as a highly religious, church-going doctor-father-husband. He had members of the Church of Christ laid on to testify about John's devoutness. Lastly, he was not going to hide obvious facts. Sure the marriage had broken down. Sure they had contemplated divorce. Sure she was unhappy. So was he. People's marriages crack and fall apart hourly in this town, like any other town. "But John Hill is not on trial for a bad marriage," Racehorse planned to tell the jury.

Don Fullenweider, Racehorse's partner, was worried about how the defense would cope with the damaging revelation that their client married his mistress just a few weeks after Joan was dead. Simple, answered Racehorse. "We put John on the witness stand, and we let him tell about how this woman appeared in his life, and how, after Joan's death, she made herself necessary, almost vital. She seemed to show concern about his health and his son, and

John needed a surrogate mother for his body. Only after she finagled her way into the new nest did she reveal her true nature, whereupon John's life became hell, and he divorced her."

There are holes in it, suggested Fullenweider to his partner.

Of course there are, said Haynes. But come up with something better and they would use it.

The state spent most of its strikes to knock off prospective women from the panel. Only one, an employee of the personnel department of a Houston school district, survived the challenges. The defense encountered several veniremen who held grievances against the medical profession in general. Having expected that, the lawyer was careful to ask specific questions as to whether a prospective juror had ever had a bad experience with a doctor. He did not want a fellow on the panel whose wife had received a diagnosis of stomach ulcer, then died of cancer.

The eleven men finally selected to join the solitary woman in the jury box were relentlessly middle class, a brewery's assemblage for a foamy commercial to be shown during Sunday afternoon football intermissions. Their jobs were fork-lift operator, airline skycap, chemical plant security guard, paint company foreman, dime store assistant manager, heavy equipment operator. Law-abiding blue-collar citizens, they were men who the state felt would be able to understand deadly shenanigans among the rich. The defense hoped they were sophisticated enough to see through the state's thin case. Their lives seemed to be devoid of frills and poetry and music—common-sense lives all, listing toward boredom. Racehorse felt confident that the events about to take place would hold their attention.

I. D. McMaster opened for the state and was a fine figure before the jurors. Lean, sinewy, his voice rumbled like distant thunder on the far side of the ranch. "We expect to prove," began the assistant district attorney, whose involvement with the case had begun on the morning Joan Hill was buried, "that problems arose in the course of this marriage which resulted in the filing of a divorce petition on December 3, 1968, by the defendant, Dr. John Hill. An answer to said petition for divorce was filed by . . . Joan Robinson Hill . . . making the divorce a contested matter which could have resulted in a court trial.

". . . Realizing that he had insufficient grounds for

divorce and in fear of the adverse publicity in regard to his extramarital activities which might result from a court trial, Dr. John Hill dismissed his divorce case and agreed to a so-called reconciliation with Joan Hill as evidenced by a written instrument which contained, among other things, the following provisions: (1) A request that Joan Hill would forgive her husband's past transgressions, (2) That in the event of a future separation, the defendant promised to deed the home on Kirby Drive to Joan Hill and further to make all payments thereon as well as taxes and upkeep.

". . . Having failed to terminate the marriage legally, the defendant began to formulate a plan to rid himself of an unwanted wife."

As he listened to the accusation, Racehorse looked at the jury intently, studying each face. In two decades of trying criminal cases, he had come to believe that juries sent out vibrations in the opening moments of the proceedings. He could sense either hostility and anger toward a defendant, or courtesy and even friendliness. Unless he was mistaken, Racehorse noted to himself, this jury seemed very much inclined toward John Hill. Beside him, the doctor sat frozen, his face ashen ice. That night he would tell both Connie and his mother that he could not connect himself with the reality of the day. "I kept stepping outside myself and seeing another person sitting there," he said.

McMaster rumbled on with the state's accusations. "The defendant moved back into the house with Joan Hill but continued his extramarital activities. Sometime during the weekend of March 15th and 16th, Joan Hill first displayed symptoms of excessive diarrhea and vomiting which continued and became progressively worse until Joan Hill was completely helpless as evidenced by uncontrolled stools in her bed during the night of Monday, March 17, 1969."

Here Racehorse started to object, for he knew the state would have a hard time proving either "completely helpless" or "uncontrolled stools," but he let it pass, waiting until later to savage the state's case.

"The state's proof is expected to show that the defendant apparently began to act as Joan Hill's physician during the period from March 16th to March 18th of 1969. . . ." Racehorse wrote down the word "apparently" on his yellow legal pad and underlined it. This was an important word, one of the issues to be determined. Was John Hill *ever* his wife's physician? Or was he merely acting as a concerned and caring husband? Certainly he surrendered the responsibility of being her physician the moment he delivered her to Sharpstown Hospital.

"It will further show that Joan Hill was hospitalized March 18, 1969, in a state of irreversible shock and died approximately fourteen hours thereafter. The state's proof is also expected to show that among other diagnoses resulting from autopsies performed on the body of Joan Hill were those of acute hepatitis, acute meningitis, acute splenitis, acute esophagitis, and early bronchopneumonia.

"Further, the state expects to show that the defendant, realizing his wife Joan Hill's condition, intentionally and *with malice aforethought* failed to properly treat Joan Hill and failed to provide timely hospitalization for her in order that she would die."

John Hill shook his head softly, in negation, again and again, attempting to sweep the damnations from his focus. The courtroom spectators, mainly women, eager to hear tales of sex and sorrow, craned to see him. Some agreed with Racehorse that John Hill looked as unlike a murder defendant as any accused who ever sat in a courtroom.

The state began weaving a case based more on style than substance. First they summoned Mrs. Vann Maxwell to the witness stand, she being the beautiful across-the-street neighbor of Joan Hill. Once she had been Joan's ally, confidante, and co-conspirator in tracking the trail of Ann Kurth and in rifling the trunk of John Hill's automobile. With hair streaked beige and silver, a slim body bespeaking the pampering of expensive oils and lotions, she was what the bourgeoisie would expect the aristocracy to be. Even her blouse of modern art on a sheer gossamer seemed designed by Picasso, perhaps woven on his own loom. Had Joan Hill been here to speak for herself, it seemed, she would have offered similar elegance and class. It was easy for the women of the courtroom to imagine the bloodlines being discussed here.

Vann Maxwell, whose marriage to a psychiatrist had ended in divorce not long after Joan's death, was used by the state to introduce the deteriorating relationship between the doctor and his first wife. Telling of the Saturday night bridge game in the music room, with Joan scribbling angry notes and passing them across the table, Vann said, "Joan broke into a crying jag which I did not understand. . . . She said something like, 'I've had it, it's just not going to work out, I can't keep him.'" She said that Joan planned to go to a lawyer on Monday and sue for divorce. "The final thing she said about it was . . . would I go with her?"

On cross, Racehorse casually wondered, "How did she appear to you?"

"She seemed in good health," answered Mrs. Maxwell. This was an important exchange, for the state would have to prove that thirty-six hours later this strong, athletic young sportswoman had become helpless and a prisoner in her own dirty bed.

"Mrs. Effie Green, your honor," said McMaster, and the bailiff led in the aged black maid who had ministered to her mistress in the last hours. A small, birdlike woman, her shoulders bent from a life of hard labor in kitchens and toilets, her hair was steel gray and her hands clutched a handkerchief to dab at moist and teary eyes. It was the first time in her almost seven decades on this earth that she had set foot in a courtroom, and she was as frightened as if she had been told to walk past a graveyard at midnight. I. D. McMaster treated Effie courteously, but businesslike, as superior to inferior, and Racehorse slyly made note of this.

"Did anyone tell you that Mrs. Hill was ill . . . that she was sick on Monday?" asked McMaster.

Effie nodded. "I can't recall now who told me . . . but someone did tell me that she was ill and not to go in the room."

McMaster let this soak in. It was important that the jury accept the portrait of Joan Hill lying gravely ill, with even the maid forbidden to enter the room. At that point something clicked in Racehorse Haynes's mind, and he whispered to Don Fullenweider to find a certain passage in a deposition. The defense lawyers had wheeled an entire filing cabinet into the courtroom, and every word that had been uttered in the case was instantly retrievable. Seldom had a murder case been so excellently prepared.

"Did Mrs. Hill ever call you to come to her room on Monday?" asked the district attorney.

"No, she didn't call me."

At his seat, Racehorse almost put on a smile of contentment. The state was helping *his* case. If the lady was all that sick, why didn't she call Effie for help?

McMaster moved to the next morning, Tuesday, the day that Joan was taken to Sharpstown Hospital. Effie told of making coffee and orange juice "fixed up real nice on a tray" and taking it upstairs to her master and mistress.

"When you went in the bedroom . . . was Mrs. Hill in bed?"

"Yes, she was in the bed."

"Where was Dr. Hill?"

"He was in the bed, on his side of the bed."

Another point for the defense, Racehorse felt. If John Hill was all that negligent and murderous, why would he be in the soiled bed? But the jury had not yet heard that unpleasant part of the tale. John Hill's eyes drilled holes into the old woman. One juror would later say that he thought for a time that the plastic surgeon was trying to hypnotize his former maid. "That man had the coldest eyes I'd ever seen," said the juror.

McMaster prodded Effie to continue her story. "What did Dr. Hill say when he called you to come up to the bedroom?"

"He tell me, 'Effie, come clean up this mess.'"

"What was 'this mess'?"

Effie spoke very carefully here, as if giving testimony before her church congregation.

"I found a bowel movement on the bathroom floor," she said.

"Can you describe it for us? Anything unusual about it?"

"It was just webby . . . just had an odor to it. . . . I can't describe all the color. It had a little greenish-like to it because I noticed when I was cleaning it up."

Later she was summoned by Dr. Hill, who gave nursing instructions. "He tell me to take care of Mrs. Hill and give her medicine and give her all liquids, such as tea and Coke and orange juice and things like that."

In his seat, Racehorse stirred a little happily. This did not sound as if the doctor had "abandoned" his wife to die.

"Where were those medicines? Do you know?"

"They was on the night stand by her bed."

After the plastic surgeon left that fateful Tuesday morning, hurrying to the elementary school where he would play his tuba solo, Effie said she went back to the bedroom of her sick mistress. She helped Mrs. Hill to the bathroom again and, en route, the sick woman swayed, almost fell, and put her arms around the maid's waist.

"I tried to carry her, and she told me, 'Effie, are you going to let me fall?' I said, 'No, I am not. You hold tight to me and I will hold tight to you and carry you in.'"

The maid began to describe how her employer looked and felt. Racehorse rose quickly and objected. She was not qualified as an expert medical witness, pleaded the defense lawyer. McMaster tried to justify it by saying such testimony related to the symptoms of Joan Hill's fatal illness. Judge Fred Hooey permitted the prosecution to continue. Racehorse was worried now, not so much over the explicit testimony as over the climate and spell that the old maid was creating. Though uneducated and not at home in grammar, she was a powerful witness.

"Now," said McMaster, "after you helped her to the bathroom . . . was she able to walk by herself back to the bed? Or not?"

Instantly Haynes was back up. "Your honor, I hate to keep objecting, but counsel is leading this witness and suggesting answers."

Judge Hooey shook his head in disagreement. "That objection is overruled."

"Was she?" asked McMaster again.

"No. I had to help her. She wasn't able to walk by herself. . . . Just as we got in the bathroom into the entrance, her bowels moved again on the floor. . . . I cleaned her up. I asked her to lean herself to the wall, and I got a towel and wet it . . . and I cleaned it up and carried her and put her back to bed. That's the truth: And God knows I tell the truth."

What about the bed itself? wondered McMaster. Was anything unusual there? Effie nodded in recollection. Specifically, demanded the district attorney, was there any sign of bowel movement in the bed?

"It was. Some towels had been put underneath her . . . about three towels." The bottom towel, next to the sheet, "was soiled pretty bad" and "it had a little blood stain on it." Racehorse Haynes could feel the vibrations turning hostile toward his client. He knew that when it was his turn to cross-examine the maid he could damage this part of her testimony. He could confuse her, make her describe specifically the substance of the bowel movement. Hard? Soft? Mushy? Loose? Color? Are you a doctor, Effie? How do you know it was two hours old? Twelve hours old? Ten minutes old? Are you sure they were bloodstains on the sheets? Ever seen rust marks from water on sheets, Effie? How old were these sheets, Effie? You only worked for the Hills two or three months, didn't you, Effie? How do you know these sheets were white and new? Couldn't they have been old and rusted? All of this and more he could ask, until Effie was but a discombobulated fly on the end of his pin. But he would run the grave risk of alienating the jury. Elderly blacks in the South earn a measure of respect. A bit of crustiness is not only allowed but appreciated.

Racehorse Haynes made more than twenty objections to Effie's testimony, all variations on the same theme: that Effie Green was repeating hearsay conversation and that she was making medical judgments on Joan Hill's condition. But sitting beside McMaster was Ernie Ernst, considered to be "the fastest legal gun in the South," and he had quick and winning responses to the defense's objections. A sample:

McMaster: Based on what you saw when she came back from the bathroom—based on what you saw, did you form any opinion of her condition?

Haynes: We would object to that answer. It would be strictly speculative, conjecture, prejudicial, and inflammatory. .

Ernst: May it please the court, it is our position that this witness's opinion . . . goes to the condition of the deceased at that very moment when she was in an *acute* time. Mrs. Green's opinion as to her condition and what she said is evidence of her opinion as to her condition. We must *prove* her condition and her opinion of the condition.

Judge Hooey: All right. I will let her answer the question.

When Racehorse Haynes rose to cross-examine Effie Green he treated her with great respect in the Southern tradition. She was "Miss Effie" in all of his questions, never did he raise his voice disrespectfully, never did he behave in any manner save that of the plantation's eldest son, home from the war, making fond small talk with the woman who perhaps nursed him at her breast. Yet his purpose was to so rattle her as to impeach her credibility as a witness. A fine line to walk. But Effie was sixty-nine years old, and the events she was remembering had happened two long years before.

To begin, Effie could not even remember how long she had worked for the Hills when Joan died. She said she "thought" it was three or four months. In fact, countered Racehorse gently, it was about six weeks. But that was all right. My land, it was such a long time ago. Casually he moved along. Now, about the morning when the two house guests from Dallas left. Effie began to repeat her story, and she began confusing that Monday and the next day, Tuesday, sometimes in the same sentence.

Racehorse sympathized. "I know how hard it is to keep from confusing those days," he said. Effie nodded vigorously, grateful for his support.

"Do you remember on Monday morning that the Avalon drugstore delivered some medicine for Mrs. Hill?" asked the lawyer.

"No . . . I don't rightly remember that."

Racehorse put on a face of mock puzzlement. He referred to a mass of papers on his table. "But, Miss Effie, on that Monday," he said, seemingly in clarification, "you went up to her room, didn't you? And you saw Mrs. Hill sitting in the chair, didn't you, ma'am?"

"Mrs. Hill?"

"Yes, ma'am."

"No." Effie was positive. She did not see Mrs. Hill on the next to last day of her life.

Racehorse hesitated, racing an idea through his head, wondering if it was worth the risk. He deemed that it was. He picked up a thick document from the table and began to read from it. The testimony therein was Effie's sworn statement, taken only six weeks after the death of Joan Hill. Surely Miss Effie remembered the lawyer who questioned her, the nice, gray-haired Mr. Briscoe, used to be the district attorney? The old woman nodded. She remembered.

Well then, on page 11 of this deposition was the following question from Mr. Briscoe. "On that Monday, did you ever go up to her room and see her?" And your answer, "I went up there one time. And she say, 'Just some coffee.' She's sittin' in a big chair."

At this Effie shook her head in vigorous disagreement. "Somebody must've put that there. I didn't say nothing."

"The fellow that took this down put it down wrong, Miss Effie?" asked Racehorse in mock bewilderment. But it was *sworn* testimony. Under the penalty of perjury.

"I didn't give Mrs. Hill no coffee Monday morning," harrumped the maid.

Okay, if *that* was wrong, wondered Racehorse, then how true was Miss Effie's remembrance that she was told—presumably by John Hill—*not* to disturb the sick woman that entire Monday? He read from the transcript, from Effie's words two years prior. " '. . . That Monday, I went up there to her room and I knocked on her door again. And those women [the house guests] say, "She can't be disturbed. She's resting, and let her rest." ' "

Effie shook her head in bewilderment. "That was two years ago," she said softly.

"But it was within a month or so after it happened?"

"I know that."

"So, Miss Effie, your memory may have been better at that time about those little details than it is today."

"I'll tell you I was so upset when Mrs. Hill passed that I didn't know nothing hardly. I really were."

"This leads me to believe that one of those two women told you to let Mrs. Hill rest."

Effie searched for her answer. "I told you . . . I don't recall who did. I don't remember if they did or not. *Someone* told me not to disturb her, and I did not. I didn't ask her about no coffee, because I didn't go to no room."

Racehorse nodded, satisfied. He had scored two points. First, he had cast doubt on the memory of the old woman and her ability to recollect crucial events. Second, and more important, he had shifted the blame of leaving Joan alone in her sick room from the shoulders of her accused husband to, perhaps, the Dallas women.

The lawyer next produced a bottle of Kaopectate from the Avalon drugstore, dated March 17, 1969, with instructions on the label "Teaspoonful after each loose B.M." Then he introduced as defense evidence a bottle of paregoric and a vial of pills labeled Mysteclin-F 250 mg. The drugstore records indicated that Dr. Hill called in the order on March 17 at 8 A.M., the Monday before Joan died. This date contradicted Effie's testimony that she could not remember medicine being delivered that day. But she did verify that the medicine was beside Joan Hill's bed, and this was the same medicine which she tried and failed to administer to an unwilling sick woman. This would further place Effie in the room on Monday.

ASH ROBINSON   He had believed, from the earliest years of his memory, that Ash Robinson was *special*, that he possessed the talent and breeding and drive to climb somehow up the summit and once there claim a place in history. HOUSTON CHRONICLE

RHEA ROBINSON, JOAN ROBINSON, AND ASH ROBINSON Joan Olive Robinson was showered with love, a tender caring kind of love from her adopted mother, a powerful, crushing, overwhelming kind of love from Ash. THE HOUSTON POST CO.

JOAN ROBINSON A newspaperman wrote, "When Joan Robinson rides Beloved Belinda it is one of the most achingly beautiful sights in the world. It is a poem, a waltz, it is the sculpture of Rodin." HOUSTON CHRONICLE

JOAN ROBINSON AND JOHN HILL A gossip columnist wrote: "Isn't the new man in cosmopolite Joan Robinson's busy life a fortunate young surgeon? It is, it is . . . and watch the other swains sob." THE HOUSTON POST CO.

MYRA HILL She was a strong, hard-working American Gothic woman with a passion for religion that lay somewhere between the devout and the fanatic. HOUSTON CHRONICLE

JOAN AND JOHN HILL'S HOME The house was both graceful and at the same time arrogant, positioned diagonally as it was, out of balance with the other estates lined up obediently on the famous drive.

DIANE SETTEGAST Her entire life had orbited around horses, and the manner in which she stalked to the witness box indicated she had ridden up to the courthouse on a stallion, lashed it to a parking meter, and rushed to the trial, with side arms blazing. THE HOUSTON POST CO.

EUNICE WOOLEN Her [Diane's] companion and room-mate was an older woman in her mid-forties named Eunice Woolen. THE HOUSTON POST CO.

JOHN HILL WITH ATTORNEYS "RACEHORSE" HAYNES AND DONN FULLENWEIDER John Hill shook his head softly, in negation, again and again. . . . Some agreed with Racehorse that John Hill looked as unlike a murder defendant as any accused who ever sat in a courtroom. HOUSTON CHRONICLE

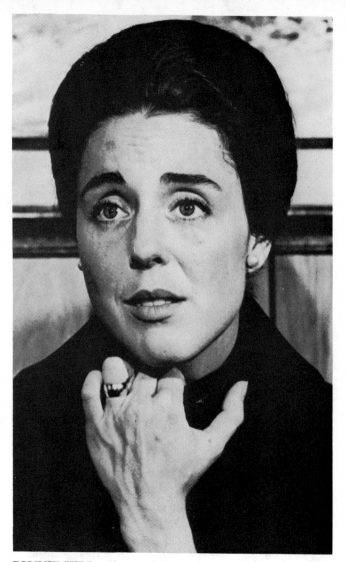

CONNIE HILL She resembled a hand-painted cameo from another century. . . . The antithesis of both of the women who preceded her in John Hill's life, she seemed a woman born to sit attentively in drawing rooms, listening to complex music. THE HOUSTON POST CO.

EFFIE GREEN She was a small birdlike woman, her shoulders bent from a life of hard labor in kitchens and toilets. Her hair was steel-gray and her hands clutched a handkerchief to dab at moist and teary eyes. THE HOUSTON POST CO.

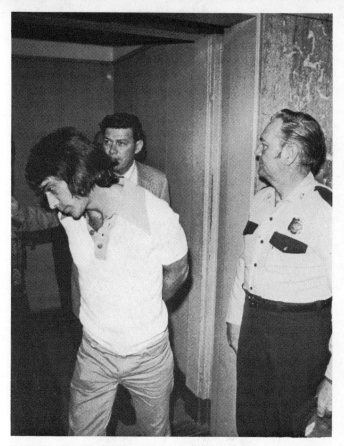

BOBBY VANDIVER The principal of the school auto-graphed Bobby's *Sundial* yearbook with glowing testimony: "To Bobby V.—a good student, hard worker, and fine athlete. Your goal in life should be the very top." But a best friend scribbled his memoir . . . "To Bobby, who if he lives to be 21, will be a miracle." HOUSTON CHRONICLE

JOHN HILL "Lilla Paulus gave me a picture and said this was Dr. Hill. . . . 'You think this mother fucker don't want him dead? Just look how he has the picture cut.' The picture had the corners cut off and it looked like a coffin." THE HOUSTON POST CO.

MARCIA MCKITTRICK   Her colleagues . . . wondered at Marcia's prowess. All they cattily beheld was a slightly chubby girl . . . with a roundish baby face and hard brown eyes . . . and even a few pockmarks on her cheeks. These Marcia alternately explained as either resulting from a severe onset of German measles or as souvenirs of a gang rape in Washington, D.C., by a group of zestful black motorcycle riders.
HOUSTON CHRONICLE

LILLA PAULUS Lilla could cuss better than any whore . . . often carried a pistol with a pearl handle carved like a cameo, and stocked a kitchen supplied with good whiskey, marijuana, and a pot of deer meat chili simmering on the stove. THE HOUSTON POST CO.

MARY PAULUS WOODS Mary Woods was tall and exceptionally beautiful, a prize colt. . . . There was a look of an Egyptian frieze about her. Reddish-gold hair tumbled full down past high cheekbones, past huge eyes—those huge eyes of her mother—dark eyes shadowed by paint and worry. HOUSTON CHRONICLE

LILLA PAULUS WITH LAWYER DICK DEGEURIN In
a severely tailored blue dress . . . hair cut inelegantly and let
go to shades of sleet and snow, she was the woman who has
graded everybody's English Lit exam since education began.
How could the district attorney possibly persuade a jury that
she was mistress to a salon of crime?
HOUSTON CHRONICLE

One more question, Miss Effie. "I suppose you wouldn't hesitate in going back to work for Dr. Hill today?"

"He haven't did nothing to me," said Effie. "I wouldn't mind going back if he needed me. . . . I like him."

Smiling, pleased, Racehorse felt this was the perfect exit line. He sat down.

Promptly I. D. McMaster leaped up and asked to introduce Effie Green's entire sworn deposition. It would not have been admissible had not Racehorse "opened the door" by reading from it to impeach her credibility. "This is the document referred to by Mr. Haynes in his examination of Effie Green, and we offer it in rehabilitation of Mrs. Green," said the prosecutor.

Racehorse objected for a full quarter of an hour, for he desperately wanted to avoid having the jury read this document in full. Though there were discrepancies and inconsistencies, the emotional impact was shattering. Bits and pieces in open court were not too harmful, but over all it was damaging to John Hill.

"I will admit this statement in evidence," said Judge Hooey. McMaster and Ernst were elated. That one victory at the end of the day was worth more than all the previous testimony.

That evening, as was his custom, Racehorse held his own court, in his office, over good whiskey, for the young Turks who liked to drape themselves over the leather chairs and couches and reconstruct the trial session. John Hill usually listened briefly, then dozed on the couch before he rushed out to a hospital and made brief rounds. He was trying to sustain the image of a working surgeon, though his practice had dwindled to very little in the months leading up to the murder trial. In 1968, the last full year of his marriage to Joan, he earned $168,000. In 1971 his gross would be less than one third of that. He had even gone back to his post-resident custom of haunting hospital emergency rooms, hoping to pick up a smashed face from an automobile wreck.

In the weeks before this trial began John had scheduled one minor operation, a nose reconstruction, for the wife of a suburban doctor. Twenty-four hours before the surgery she telephoned and canceled, or postponed, saying she had doubts about the procedure. Pressing her, John learned that she wanted to wait to see if he would be acquitted of the murder charge. "What does that have to do with my ability to do your nose?" he asked. But the woman began to stammer and she hung up quickly. When he was acquitted of this charge, and he felt sure he would be, he would consider moving away. He would take Connie and his son, and they would go to another city. Perhaps Europe. Maybe Milan, where he could go to La Scala every night, and maybe find a chamber group to play with.

While John napped on his lawyer's couch, Racehorse analyzed the day. The question of the hour: Why had he read from Effie Green's old deposition, knowing that the risk was the state would get to put the entire, dangerous transcript into the record, and before the eyes of the jury?

It was, said Racehorse, a calculated risk. He felt it necessary to impeach Effie Green's memory, and the best way to do it, the most gallant way, was to politely point out the grave differences in statements made in the murder trial and those made two years ago, in the passionate weeks just after the death of Joan. Judge Hooey's ruling to admit the entire deposition was in error, Racehorse felt, because the law states that you can only put into the trial record "that part upon which a witness is impeached."

"Not the whole damn thing!" said Racehorse. But he was not devastated by the unfavorable decision. In fact, it could turn out to be an asset. A criminal lawyer in Texas has two ways to win his case. One is to try to prevail before the jury, putting on a performance so dazzling that the twelve men and women will vote favorably on behalf of his defendant. The second, and more tricky one, is to keep an eye on the trial record, hoping for errors severe enough to win reversal in the Court of Criminal Appeals. Haynes called such errors "hickeys." Insurance policies. "I think we got a hickey today," he said. It was the latest in a promising list, the first and most powerful being the fact that Cecil Haden was a member of the indicting grand jury. Racehorse clung to the belief that this alone was "hickey" enough to free his client.

There were more questions from the fascinated young lawyers—they would have had Racehorse entertain them until midnight—but the defense attorney begged off. Tomorrow would be a rather important day. He shook John Hill awake. They needed to talk privately. The subject was Ann Kurth.

23

As the trial entered its tenth day in what it appeared would
be an uncommonly long proceeding, the district attorney's
men were guardedly enthusiastic. I. D. McMaster felt Effie
Green's appearance was, on sum, a definite plus for the
prosecution, and once the jury scanned the emotionally
wrenching deposition that had been admitted to evidence,
they would probably share some of the disgust for John
Hill that the prosecutors had. That the jurors would not be
privy to the pressures applied to Effie by Ash Robinson
was not considered relevant.

Ernie Ernst was more worried about the scheduled appearance of Ann Kurth. Two areas nagged him. The first
was whether Judge Hooey would even allow her to take
the witness stand, for Racehorse was preparing a massive
objection. And even if the prosecution's position was upheld, then God only knew what kind of an impression the
woman would make before the jury. What she had to say
was undeniably dramatic—the press would surely trot out
its favorite term "bombshell testimony"—but her hatred for
her ex-husband was so vitriolic that it would pour from
her lips like smoke from a chemical fusion. Troubling also
was the fact that Ann was so dramatic in phraseology and
gesticulation that she came across as histrionic. Would these
blue-collar jurors buy what she was selling?

Ernst had searched the lawbooks for a way to "open the
door" for her testimony. Texas law, like that in other states,
prohibits a wife from testifying against her husband concerning confidential communications that took place during
the marriage. The laws of the nation are determined to preserve marital union. Moreover, courts have held that even
an ex-wife cannot testify about private talk during the marriage. These are privileged conversations. Just at the point
in pretrial planning when he was reluctantly deciding to
drop Ann Kurth as a witness, Ernst came across an obscure point of law. He took his position before Judge
Hooey, an old friend and colleague from the DA's office.

Ernst had unearthed a case in which a wife *was* permitted to testify against her husband. It was during his trial
for assault on another man. The testimony was allowed into

the record—and upheld on appeal—because the husband in
question made an admission to his wife while he was beating *her* up. "Apparently," Ernst told the judge, "this old
boy was whippin' the shit out of his wife, and while doing
so, he happened to mention to her, 'Oh, by the way, honey,
I also beat the shit out of So-and-So.'"

How, Judge Hooey wanted to know, did this relate to
Ann Kurth's possible appearance in the murder trial of her
ex-husband?

Answered Ernst: The state reads this case to mean that
if an act of violence is committed on a spouse during a
marriage, then the status of privilege is sacrificed in relation
to that specific act. John Hill is being tried for the murder
of his first wife. The state is led to believe that he also tried
to harm his second wife, Ann Kurth. Therefore the state
wants to have Ann Kurth tell about an attempt on *her*
life. Testimony will be limited specifically to the events leading up to and during this particular act of violence.

Judge Hooey considered the request and said he thought
the state's position was fuzzy at best. Agreed, said Ernst.
But Ann Kurth's appearance was *vital* to their posture. Her
testimony would be *res gestae*, a Latin term that means
"the thing speaks." In this case it would refer to an "un-
thinking, unplanned utterance made in the heat of the moment," something John Hill allegedy said to Ann Kurth
just before he committed an alleged act of violence on her.

Judge Hooey agreed to let the woman *begin* her testimony, his clear implication being that if she wandered into
areas taboo under the law he would silence her. Upon
learning of Ernst's maneuver, Racehorse immediately offered a motion in objection, stressing that the prohibition
of a wife testifying against her husband was bedrock—
traceable to ancient law. Judge Hooey listened patiently—
he was at all times a low-key, even-tempered jurist who
never delivered boisterous discipline to counsel—but he once
more gave none too enthusiastic permission for Ann Kurth
to tell her tale.

Freshly forty and not at all happy about it, Ann Kurth
mounted the witness stand with grace, assurance, and a benevolent smile for all, even the stone-faced plastic surgeon a
few feet fore of her whom she intended to carve into ka-
bobs. She had chosen her costume carefully, a simple cream
wool skirt and top and blue panty hose; tailored, obviously
expensive, the ensemble was a tad naughty for a woman her

age and in an era when fashion decreed that mini-skirts were for girls under twelve. But her legs were good, and she knew the men in the jury box looked at them approvingly. Her coiffure for the day was an enormous raven mane, lioness-like, frozen solid by clouds of lacquer. Racehorse eyed her with amusement and caution. She asked to be accepted as a sexy but still proper suburban matron. The defense lawyer wanted the state to hurry with this woman so he could have at her. He had coveted this opportunity ever since one of the divorce hearings between Ann and John. On that day, when the depositions were over, an hour of hard, prying questions, Ann waltzed toward the door, paused for a fragment, and hissed an obscenity between her teeth at Racehorse Haynes. He respected her flair for drama, her intelligence, and her down-in-the-dust love for the brawl. This was going to be the day Racehorse had dreamed about since law school.

Ann Kurth told how she met John Hill at Camp Rio Vista where they had gone to fetch their respective children, and how he pursued her upon their return to Houston.

"Can you tell me when or if your relationship with Dr. Hill ever became one of romance as far as you were concerned?" asked I. D. McMaster. The women in the audience were waiting for this. The living soap opera was approaching its end-of-the-week Friday crisis.

"Well," said Ann in her crisp, positive voice, "on about the third evening I was with him, he asked if I would marry him when he got out of the mess of the marriage that he was in. . . . And I didn't reciprocate the feeling, but told him I would think about it."

"Had you formed any attachment at all for him by that time?"

"Yes."

"Was he charming?"

"Definitely."

"You considered him handsome?"

"Well," said Ann after a few moments of consideration, glancing down at John Hill as if to refresh her memory of his features, "not as handsome as some people I have seen . . . but very attractive."

"When then after that did your relationship with him become that of romance?"

"Oh, in about the next three or four meetings . . . evenings together."

"Did the relationship between you and Dr. Hill eventually come to"—McMaster paused, in search of euphemism—"come to physical love?"

"Yes."

Now McMaster, having established an illicit affair between the defendant and this lush society woman, moved forward to establish motivation for the death of Joan Hill.

"Would you describe what he told you about his feelings for Joan Hill?"

"He hated her. He said he couldn't stand to be around her, that she smoked incessantly and smelled like a goat. This bothered him. He didn't like cigarette smoke."

"All right. Do you smoke?"

"No, sir."

"Was this a single occasion, or was it said on more than one occasion?"

"Well," answered Ann, "when he described this feeling, I cut him short and told him that I felt it was inappropriate for him to say that to me, because if she was that bad, then I didn't want her leftovers."

Here was clearly an opportunity to object, but Racehorse held back. He sensed something unusual happening. He felt that here was a witness who was perilously close to going out of bounds, that the DA did not have her on the leash that prosecutors should have their witnesses on. Of course she had been "woodshedded," that being the custom of all lawyers, who painstakingly rehearse both questions and answers with witnesses. In law school a student has *that* practically tattooed on his forehead. Never Ask A Witness A Question You Don't Know The Answer To. But, Racehorse suddenly felt, Ann Kurth was a woman who was not hewing to protocol. It was mesmerizing to hear and see.

The prosecutor drew from her the news that John Hill deserted his wife, leased a bachelor apartment, and spent most of the autumn months of 1968 either there or at Ann's home in the suburban Memorial district.

"Did you at any time during the months of August, September, October, November, or December of 1968 actually *live* with Dr. Hill?"

Ann nodded helpfully. "He stayed at my house *constantly*." At the defense table, John Hill scribbled furiously in a spiral notebook, ripping out pages and shoving them before his lawyer.

"But he still had the apartment during this time?"

"Yes."

During the March week in 1969, wondered McMaster, did Mrs. Kurth see anything "unusual" at the apartment?

"Yes, sir."

Smelling a dead animal in the walls and trying to get it out before the stench became unbearable, Haynes rose hurriedly. He demanded that the witness pin this date down exactly. This is another defense trick; lawyers like to force witnesses to be specific as to year, month, day, hour, and second when they saw what they did. Since most people stumble, the testimony sometimes comes out a little tainted.

Ann Kurth was unruffled. "It was the week preceding Joan's death in March 1969, approximately Tuesday or Wednesday, sooner or later."

"Go on," said McMaster, happy at the witness' composure.

"We arrived at the apartment together. We each had a key. John said, 'Let me have your key,' because he had lost his and was going to have some others made. So I gave him my key. I held out my hand for the key back, and he said, 'No, I am going to have the locks changed.' And we went in and ultimately I went into the bathroom. And the door had been closed. There was a gooseneck light over the side of the basin, and there were three petri dishes there with red something in them and little dots of something in that. . . ."

John Hill's body tensed and he moved closer to his lawyer. "She's lying," he whispered. "There were no petri dishes." Racehorse started to make interruption. He wondered just how Ann Kurth knew these were "petri dishes" and not bowls of oatmeal or unwashed coffee saucers. The term "petri dish" is not in the layman's vocabulary, and later on it might be fun to pin Ann down on just where she got it from. Ash? McMaster? Did she major in chemistry? But he let it pass. So far the jury seemed unaffected by what she had said. He would wait his turn.

"Was it a liquid, or did it appear to be liquid?" asked McMaster.

"I really didn't get much of a look, because Dr. Hill came up behind me and said, 'Oh, I am doing an experiment and this room is supposed to stay warm.' He had this little gooseneck light over them. He backed me out of there and closed the door, and I didn't really think about it."

There was more to tell. After being escorted out of her lover's bathroom, she said, she progressed to the kitchen and idly opened the refrigerator door. Then, she informed the jury, she beheld two cardboard boxes containing pastries. While she was perusing them, annoyed that John had purchased blueberry tarts, which she did not like, the surgeon came up behind her and said, "Don't eat those. Let's go get Mexican food."

At this point Racehorse objected but was overruled. He sat down angry. Here was a woman who held little if any legal right to be on a witness stand testifying against her ex-husband—Haynes felt sure an appellate court would disallow her appearance—and she was telling things that not only were far and wide of the limits set by the bench, she had been careful thus far *never* to testify about an event in which a third person was involved. It was always Ann and John. To counter, Racehorse would have to put his client on the stand and have him say, "No, no, a thousand times no," to the petri dishes and the French pastries and whatever else was still to come, but it would boil down to which party seemed the most credible. He wished again he had at least two thirds of the jury box filled with hard-eyed women.

She testified that, although John Hill returned to his estranged wife in December 1968, it was only a ruse because he continued meeting her secretly.

McMaster asked: "Was there any time from the day that you first started going with Dr. Hill until your subsequent marriage to him that he did not mention marriage on occasion?"

"Never!" Her voice was a rifle shot. "He was progressively certain that we would be married sooner or later."

Racehorse scribbled a note to himself to explore this area when it was time for cross-examination. This was a harmful revelation. Racehorse wondered if any of the jurors were caught in stale marriages and were picturing what it would be like to install someone like Ann Kurth in a bachelor apartment.

After the death of Joan Hill, inquired McMaster, "did you then take up with—or, shall we put it this way—did you then start seeing him on a regular basis about a week or ten days after the death of his first wife?"

Racehorse objected to the "leading and suggestive nature of the question."

"Overruled," said Judge Hooey, once again favoring the state. The feeling among the press corps covering the trial was that the bench was exceptionally tolerant toward the district attorney's cause. With a theatrical sigh of weariness and disbelief, Racehorse asked for a recess until morning. He needed time to prepare a new motion asking that this woman be thrown out of court. Her presence, Racehorse would contend, was a savage violation of John Hill's civil rights. Moreover, she had been ensconced in the witness box for an entire afternoon, and the conditions that permitted her to be there—"a conversation during an alleged act of violence"—had not yet been disclosed. How many appetizers was the jury going to be served before the main course?

The next morning Racehorse argued with the judge for an hour, pleading that the entire course of Anglo-American law prohibited a situation like the one on display in this murder trial. Of all privileged relationships—doctor/patient, lawyer/client, priest/confessor—none was more sacred than husband/wife. He also contended Ann Kurth "was not worthy of belief."

"Denied," said Judge Hooey, but there was an edge to his voice. Perhaps the judge had second thoughts about permitting the woman's testimony into the record. But he had gone this far, and he would hold firm.

"Then I must move for a mistrial," said Racehorse, citing a grocery list of reasons.

That, too, was overruled. But the judge budged a little. "I am instructing the prosecutor to go into nothing but the 'act of violence' with regard to the period of the marriage," he said sternly. "Now, do you understand?"

Racehorse was not satisfied with the minor crumb. He requested an "exception" to the entire appearance of Ann Kurth.

"You may have your exception," said the judge, throwing the matter into the hands of an appellate court at some later date, if a conviction was obtained.

The story that Ann Kurth was permitted to tell this trial jury, and the story that she had previously told to the district attorney's men and the indicting grand jury were two different things. In essence, they contained the same damning accusations. But, fortunately for John Hill, even the prosecutors felt that this star witness was so theatrical that her act might be difficult for a jury to fully accept. In numerous tellings, Ann had so refined and honed the "act of violence" that it had become a set piece, a gothic monologue, her voice lowering and darkening in the suspenseful moments, then rising and coloring like Portia in the dock.

It was, in every telling, one hell of a yarn.

Ann had first spilled out her narrative before the DA's men after her marriage to John disintegrated. McMaster and Ernst sat and listened, not only stunned, but feeling they were in the presence of a steamroller out to flatten everything in its path. Then, the very next day after her divorce from the plastic surgeon, the ex-Mrs. Hill went before the grand jury and made her startling revelations. This is what she claimed had happened. Or, as one of the DA's men put it, The Gospel According to Kurth:

On the summer evening of June 29, 1969, a month into their marriage, Ann and John dined at a steak restaurant, The Stables. Neither was in good sorts. She was melancholy, for it was the anniversary of her sister's death in a plane crash, and she felt guilty for not being with her parents to comfort them. John seemed in a funk, unresponsive to her feelings. They dined in silence.

John suddenly put down his fork. "I wish people would stop giving me the fisheye in here."

"What do you mean?"

"I can't walk down the corridor in a hospital any more without the nurses whispering and gathering in little groups and pointing at me. That's what people are doing in here."

Ann's eyes swept the room hurriedly. "Oh, John," she would later remember saying, "they're not looking at you. They're looking at your gorgeous new wife and how happy she is."

"No," said John. "They're giving me the fisheye. I'm sick and tired of it. I thought, when I took that truth serum test and went through all the questioning, that people would leave me alone. But they don't."

Ann spoke quietly. "Well, I just wish you had taken it under other circumstances." One week earlier, she claimed to have found her husband in their bathroom trying to give himself a shot in the hip just before leaving for Sharpstown Hospital and the administration of Sodium Pentothal. He told her at that moment it was a vitamin shot and asked her to administer the injection. Which she did, having had previous experience with syringes because one of her sons was diabetic. That night, returning home content after the truth test, he told his wife that he had been conscious enough during the examination to guard his answers to I. D. McMaster's questions. This led Ann to believe that the "vitamin shot" was in truth some sort of antidote to the Sodium Pentothal.

Now, sitting in one of the city's most fashionable restaurants, John Hill began to "shriek" at his second wife. "Don't you ever say that again! How dare you bring that up!" he told her angrily. Later that night, after a visit to a hospital where he left his wife in the parking lot for more than an hour, his mood suddenly softened again. He suggested a drive. A leisurely, after-midnight drive on the edge of the city, where the subdivisions cease and the farms and ranches begin. Ann paid little heed to their direction, for she was accustomed to the capricious behavior of the man she married. The white Cadillac sped through the night, and within the elaborate stereo tape deck played classical music. They drove for more than an hour, seemingly without aim, until it was past two, perhaps closer to three. A week before, John had been in a motorcycle accident—riding with his son Robert, to whom he was more attentive after the death of Joan—and had broken his collarbone. Now he was taking xylocaine shots to deaden the pain, and he was wearing a bandage, but no cast. It occurred to Ann that he must be uncomfortable, driving so long, and she volunteered to take the wheel. No! His refusal was firm. He was the chauffeur. She should sit quietly, listen to the music, and feel the night wind blowing against her face.

But she was tired, and a bit tense. The scene in the restaurant had been awkward, and now, at three o'clock in the morning, they were joy riding around the city limits. She began to nag, wanting to go home. Their sons needed her attention, she was tired, she wanted to go to the bathroom, she felt headachey. Her requests fell against silence. Suddenly, she would later swear, John Hill's face became "a mask." His features became contorted, his voice distorted. As she told it, the transformation of a monster in a horror film came to mind. And then he slowed the car. He did not look at her as he spoke. She would later quote him thusly: "I really didn't want it to be this way. It didn't really have to be this way, but Joan would never have given me a divorce. Ash was going to see to that. So I took every kind of human excretion I could find. I saved feces, urine from patients, pus from a boil off somebody's neck, and I mixed them all together and I grew cultures in those petri dishes. . . . And I first gave her the pastries and that didn't do anything. Then I gave her some ipecac, and she threw up everything but her toenails. . . . And she was so sweet about it. She was begging me to do something for her. . . . So I gave her a shot. I gave her some broad-spectrum antibiotic, and I mixed in some of this culture in liquid suspension . . . and that did it. . . . She was so sweet about it. Just begged me to help her. . . . At the end it was just a matter of time. She had every disease known to man. . . ."

Ann would later claim that "my insides began to crawl and my stomach churned. . . . I was sitting there thinking, 'I don't want to see this man again, I could never bear him touching me.' And then he turned the car off on a gravelly road, and I could hear the crunch underneath the wheels, and the headlights shone on some little sign, and a little white picket fence, and it said 'Chatsworth Farm.' Somehow we had gotten to the entrance of Joan's farm. I was almost screaming, and I said, 'Where are we?' "

John backed the car out of the driveway and prepared to reclaim the small road back to town. He gestured with his head, toward the Chatsworth sign. "That's where someone lived who doesn't live any more," he said. His foot smashed into the gas pedal. The Cadillac leaped crazily ahead. Now the headlights bore down on a small concrete bridge, across a meandering bayou, one of the thousands that thread Houston's salty marshes like the wrinkles on the face of an old farmer.

"And now," he said, "neither do you!" With that, claimed Ann Kurth, her husband deliberately rammed the right-hand side—*her* side—of the Cadillac squarely into the bridge abutment. As she screamed, the crunch of metal against concrete filled the night, and the passenger side of the automobile crumpled like an accordion. "I saw it coming," she told the DA's men, "and thank God I never fasten my seat belt. Because I managed to leap across the front seat onto John's side. Had I been strapped into my seat, I would have been pulverized."

Next, said Ann, John Hill looked at her in disappointment that she was still very much alive. Her account continued: "He had a horrible look on his face, and he reached into his coat pocket and pulled out a needle. I screamed again, 'My God, John, what are you trying to do?' He came at me like a demon, trying to plunge the needle into my chest. I fought him, and he dropped the syringe somewhere on the wreckage of the floor. And without a moment's hesitation, he pulls out *another* syringe. I am screaming, 'Stop it, John, for God's sake don't you know I love you!' " And just as he raised his arm, trembling, to inject her with the second syringe, the lights of a faraway car appeared on the road, behind the shattered Cadillac. John threw that syringe out the window, into a clump of high weeds. The car neared and John threw his hand over Anne's mouth. "Don't say a word, baby," he warned.

The second car pulled up, and a woman and her teen-age son got out to see if help was needed. "We're okay," said John. "My wife is a little hysterical. Could you give us a ride to the closest hospital?" The good Samaritans helpfully drove the doctor and his wife, suffering only from a cut knee and a few scratches, to a suburban hospital. "Sharpstown Hospital was actually the closet," Ann said. "But I figure John couldn't risk having two wives die there, so we went to Memorial Baptist Southwest. I must have been in shock until the next day."

It was not until nine long months later, in March 1970, that Ann Kurth turned up at the district attorney's office to put her grand guignol story into the hopper. At first Ernie Ernst was understandably skeptical. He lashed her with questions.

Did the police investigate the accident?

Yes, answered Ann. After treatment at the emergency room, John insisted they take a taxi back to the remote wreck site. When they arrived, police officers were poking around. John introduced himself and his wife and said he had gone to sleep at the wheel. He had returned to pick up medical papers and equipment. He took Ann aside and in a whisper ordered her to find the hypodermic needle while he talked to the officers. She located it and put it in her purse.

Then why ddin't she say something to these officers about this terrible attempt on her life by a man who had just confessed another murder? wondered McMaster.

Well, sir, she was frightened. She didn't see any other way out but to stay married to him. Her children were at his house, his own son had accepted her and was calling her "Mama." Her money was commingled with his at his bank. John warned her not to speak to anyone of the incident, she said. Not even her own father. And if she tried to run away, he would find her. "I swore a vow of silence," Ann said. It was her only option.

What happened to the syringe?

Toward dawn, when they finally returned to the house on Kirby Drive, Ann claimed she surreptitiously dropped the needle in some high grass near the front door. The next day she went outside to find it, and a gardener had mowed the grass. The syringe was gone. She could not find it.

How could a man with a broken collarbone—taking pain-killing shots himself—and one arm in a sling bandage manage to whip out two syringes so quickly and attempt to inject Ann in the aftermath of a violent collision?

She did not know, said Ann. But her then husband had incredible strength. At that terrible moment, she insisted, "he could have done anything." If the car with the woman and her son had not appeared, Ann said, "I might not be here to tell about it."

But how, how could she continue to live for six more months with a man who had done such a violent deed and made such dire threats?

"I was completely undone from that day on," Ann told a friend, repeating the answer she had given the district attorney. "My weight went from a nice happy healthy hundred and twenty to a hundred and ten, then a hundred and five, within days. I couldn't eat. I couldn't sleep. I just stayed awake and looked at him all night. I waited until morning, when he got up and went to the hospital, before I dared shut my eyes. It became a horrible game: who would fall asleep first? I suspected he was taking amphetamines because he would lie there and watch me in bed, waiting for me to doze off. He tried to make up to me, of course. We would go out to a restaurant and he would try to be sweet and suddenly I would have tears running down my cheeks. I had nowhere to go, nobody to turn to. If I went to the airport and left town, he would have found me. I was just too terrified to make a move."

Ernie Ernst made her tell the story to him so many times that he could have recited it along with her in a declamation contest. He tore at it. He tried to make cole slaw out of it, trying to destroy any part that a jury might disbelieve. Finally he decided that it might not get her into heaven, this story, but it sure oughta keep John Hill out. Only the part of the tale in which John Hill allegedly spoke of brewing up a witches' potion of feces and pus would be held in abeyance. Ernst did not think the jury would believe that. He wasn't altogether sure he did himself, as a matter of fact.

24

"Does the date June 30, 1969, have any special significance for you?" asked I. D. McMaster as Ann Kurth began her second day of testimony before a capacity crowd, ninety per cent of whom were women.

"Yes, sir, it does," she answered in a voice meek and respectful. Ernie Ernst watched her careful. On the way to court he had warned her not to embellish her words with needless gesture and dramatic coloring. The bare bones of the story were strong enough. She had promised to answer simply and calmly.

"On that date were you in an automobile?"

"Yes, sir."

Here it comes, thought Racehorse. The night before he had hammered at his client for hours. Was there anything else about the Cadillac accident the lawyer should know? Was there any hidden word or deed from that night which might leap out and bite them? John Hill insisted that he had told his lawyer everything. To the best of his recollection, he had said, they had been quarreling. Ann began yelling, grabbed the wheel of his Cadillac, and caused the car to smash into a bridge abutment. "I wasn't trying to hurt her," John said. "I wouldn't do anything as crazy as crashing my own car and hoping that only *her* side was damaged." But, the lawyer kept pressing, the police report says John Hill thought he had fallen asleep at the wheel. Was this an error? "It seemed an easier explanation at the time," answered the surgeon. "Besides, it was a one-car accident, and no one was seriously hurt." Her word against yours, old man, mused the lawyer. Who sounds more convincing? Who has less to lose?

* * *

"And were you alone or with someone?" asked Mc-Master.

"With someone . . . Dr. Hill," answered Ann.

"And what automobile were you occupying at that time, the both of you?"

"His car . . . a Cadillac, I guess a '68 or '69 model."

McMaster, satisfied with the crisp, pointed answers, moved deeper into the tale. "Now, on that date, June 30, 1969, what time of that particular day—morning, afternoon, night, is of special significance to you?"

"In the wee small hours of the morning of the thirtieth—two or three in the morning."

"Mrs. Kurth, was the automobile that you and Dr. Hill were driving in that evening or that early morning hour involved in a collision?"

Before Ann could respond, Racehorse was on his feet. "Objection, your honor," he said.

The judge saw nothing damaging in the witness' previous remarks or what she was about to answer. "You object to that?" asked Judge Hooey.

"May we have a running objection to her?" snapped Haynes. A little grandstanding here, for Racehorse had already filed two objections against Ann Kurth's appearance, as well as asking for a mistrial on the basis of her testimony. But the ploy was valuable because it would tend to make the jury suspicious of the witness' worth and relevance to the case.

"Your objection is overruled, counsel," answered the judge.

"To which we except, your honor," fired back Haynes, once again planting a "hickey" in the trial record. There were so many by now that the transcript was as dotted as raisins in a honey cake.

Ann described the accident. "Dr. Hill was driving and came to a stop sign and turned sharply to the right and veered into a bridge and crashed *my* side of the car into a bridge."

"All right. Now, just before the automobile came into contact with the bridge, that is, immediately before, what did John Hill say to you?"

Haynes rose again. For the rest of the morning he bounced upright at just about everything Ann Kurth had to say. "Your honor, we object to the nature of the question as being suggesting and leading."

"That is overruled, counsel." The judge's voice held an edge of irritation.

"Please note our exception," said Haynes, planting another "hickey."

Ann continued enthusiastically. "He pulled up to the stop sign, and glanced to the left, and he had a *horrible*—"

Of course Haynes objected to that. "I am going to object to that part of it as not being responsive to the question, the question being, 'What did he say immediately before the accident?' "

Judge Hooey leaned over and lectured the witness. "Just tell what he said, not how he looked."

Ann looked directly at John Hill. "He said, 'That's where someone used to live that doesn't live any more.' He started the car up, accelerated very fast, turned to the right at forty or fifty miles an hour. He said, "That is where someone lived who doesn't live any more, and now . . . neither are you!' And he slammed into the bridge."

McMaster paused to let the revelation do its intended damage. Ann had told the story well. The crunch of metal and shattered glass was felt. "Now," he continued, "immediately following, did he, in your estimation, once again threaten your life?"

"Yes, sir."

Racehorse popped up with a weary expression. It seemed to say that the jury must share his exasperation with the woman's testimony. "May it please the court there has been no testimony to that effect. We object to it."

"Sustained." The judge looked concerned.

Racehorse wanted more. "And if the court will give a proper instruction to the jury . . ."

Judge Hooey nodded. "The jury will not consider it. Go ahead."

"All right," pressed McMaster. "Immediately after the collision, what did he do?"

Ann moved her right hand inside an imaginary suit coat breast pocket and pulled out an invisible object. Her voice grew ripe with mystery. "He pulled a syringe from his pocket."

Sensing his witness was melodramatic, McMaster cautioned her. "Don't demonstrate. Just tell us what he did."

"He pulled a syringe from his pocket, and he tried to turn where I was and get it into me . . . his hand was shaking . . . he was very nervous, and I was very nervous and shaking from the horrible impact."

"Now, at that time, how was the car lodged? Where was it in relation to the bridge?"

"The side of the car that I was on was slammed into the concrete bridge."

"Could you have gotten out of your side of the car?"

"Oh no, sir. My side of the car was *demolished*."

"Now, at the time that he turned to you with the syringe, would you describe to the jury your position in relation to his position?"

"I had slid over as close to him as I could in seeing that he was accelerating the car at a rapid rate, and I was sitting as close to the driver as I could."

"Were you still in that position at the time he pulled out the needle."

"Yes, sir, I was."

"What did you do in regard to the needle when he pulled it out?"

"I reached up and grabbed his hand and I said, 'John . . .' "

Stunned, Haynes rose to object, more to break the impact of her story than anything else. For this was the first he had heard of the needle John Hill had allegedly tried to stick into Ann Kurth. At the defense table, John Hill was shaking his head in negation of the woman's charge. "Is it understood, your honor, that our objection goes to *all* of the detail of this alleged transaction?"

Judge Hooey nodded, and in his attitude the defense lawyer read a note of uneasiness. Was the bench about to share the defense's position that Ann Kurth was not only an ineligible witness against her ex-husband but one whose taste for high drama lent dangerous color to her testimony?

Hurriedly, McMaster bade his witness continue. A good tale cannot be interrupted too often or the listeners lose the thread of continuity. Ann was eager to go on. She knocked the first hypodermic needle out of her husband's hands, she testified, only to see him coming at her with a second!

"And what did he do with that one, if anything?" wondered the prosecutor.

Ann Kurth edged forward in her seat and pitched her

voice to a pulsating climax. "He tried again to get that syringe into me!" She was Pauline, lashed to the railroad tracks, saved only by the headlights of an approaching automobile.

Now wait a minute, suggested McMaster. Her husband was a doctor, and they had just been in a car wreck. How did she know he wasn't fixing to give her a shot to calm her down, or treat her for something? "Was he attempting to treat you? Or *harm* you? Did you know?"

"Yes, I knew."

"By something that occurred *before* this?" led McMaster. It was a question he would soon regret.

"Yes."

"*Immediately* before this?"

"Yes . . ." Ann hesitated, then she blurted out a shocker. "He told me how he had killed Joan with a needle, and I knew that he . . ."

As a gasp rushed collectively from the spectators, Racehorse rocketed out of his chair. He rushed to the bench and asked for a *sotto voce* conference, out of the jury's earshot. This woman's testimony is not worthy of belief, he hissed. What the witness just slipped into the record is prejudicial, inflammatory, and irrevocable, no matter how many times the bench instructs the jury to disregard these statements. With passion to shake a Chatauqua tent, Racehorse demanded a mistrial.

"Overruled," said Judge Hooey quietly, but he announced a luncheon recess. And he left the courtroom looking troubled.

During the break, the prosecutors warned Ann that she must expect exhaustive cross-examination from the defense. Racehorse would try to pulverize her. She smiled demurely, while newspaper photographers' flash bulbs popped around her. "I can handle Mr. Racehorse," she assured them. She always spoke his nickname with a heavy coat of mockery, often telling how disappointed she was at first meeting with the attorney. "I had been hearing about this man called Racehorse," she once remarked, "and I expected to encounter a fantastic stud. Instead, this little squirt walks in to take my deposition. *Quel* disappointment."

Before trial was to resume 1:30 P.M., Judge Hooey summoned opposing counsel into his chambers. His face was grave. Over the lunch hour he had reviewed the Kurth testimony and Mr. Haynes's motions of opposition to her appearance. "I have decided to grant Mr. Haynes's motion for a mistrial," the judge said.

And suddenly it was over.

Devastated, the district attorney's men urged the judge to change his mind. "We begged, cajoled, pleaded, and cried," McMaster would recall of the moment. "But his honor wouldn't budge." Judge Hooey said he would reset the case for another trial a few months hence. He asked the attorneys to apologize to their other witnesses under subpoena—Racehorse and Don Fullenweider alone had the equivalent of a small hospital staff ready to testify against the state's medical negligence contentions.

When a newspaper reporter asked Ernie Ernst for an explanation of the surprising decision, he said, "It's very simple. The judge just threw our ass out of court." Privately, the two prosecutors came to believe that the judge simply could not accept all of the Kurth testimony. And it had been a mistake for her to quote John Hill as saying he had killed Joan with a needle.

That night the DA's men drank whiskey. They grew rowdy and foolish, Ernst doing a funny imitation of Ann Kurth dodging John Hill's flying hypodermic needles. McMaster laughed, as did everyone else in the room. But in his laughter was the cutting edge of defeat. He knew that the prospects of John Hill being tried again and convicted of murder were lessened now. The state had been blessed with favor from the bench until the trial aborted. Racehorse had made a blunder with the Effie Green deposition, something he would not do again. "We had gotten so much into the record that we could never hope to do again," complained McMaster. And Ann Kurth was their big gun. Now that she had been fired, or *mis*fired, her words would never have the same impact again. McMaster felt certain that the plastic surgeon would now get away with what he had done, *whatever* he had done.

A few blocks away there was celebration in the offices of Haynes and Fullenweider. It was not an unqualified victory, but on the other hand, neither was it defeat. Racehorse had asked for the mistrial mainly to protect the record in any appellate proceeding. But he was not disappointed to be granted one. A certain rhythm and momentum builds in the making of a murder trial, and when it is destroyed by mistrial, rarely can the tempo be regained. Many cases are simply dropped—quietly—or allowed to die from attrition, the district attorney feeling that his obligation to the peace and harmony of the community has been served by the attempt to convict the accused killer in the first place.

John Hill was not happy by the outcome. When he walked out of the courtroom, he told a reporter that he was "extremely disappointed at not being able to carry right on with this thing and get it over with . . . it's been a burden on my shoulders, and on the people around me, for two years now." Two of the jurors walked past him at that moment, and shook his hand and wished him good luck. Later it would be reported that the jury took an informal poll after being dismissed, and the sentiment was overwhelming to acquit the doctor on what had been presented up to that point. One juror said that the testimony of Ann Kurth was not well received. If he really tried to kill her, why had she stayed married to the guy so long? And would a fellow really try to murder somebody by crashing only one side of a Cadillac into a bridge railing? It seemed a rather major risk.

The morning Houston *Post* summed up the mistrial: "Ann Kurth, the 40-year-old divorcee who was the state's bombshell witness, had blown the trial right out of court."

Ash Robinson was furious. He was a man who had constructed a gigantic ship, only to witness its sinking during the maiden voyage. He had spent—he told a friend—hundreds of thousands of dollars in an attempt to see justice done. And now it was money down a sewer.

But there will be another trial, soothed the friend, watching the tic seize Ash's face and jerk the old man's head in a violent pattern.

Ash nodded vigorously. "Well, they damn well better," he said. "They aren't about to let this one dry up and disappear." The friend looked closely at Ash, wondering how he kept his momentum so far into his eighth decade. He was nearly seventy-five. Yet his passion for the destruction of John Hill was still at full flood. What kept him going?

"Hate," answered Ash. "The god damnedest bitter hate that a man can imagine. You see, I am intensely loyal to anything I own. Here is John Hill, a man who married my only child, my beloved daughter. He came to town with a bicycle and a cardboard suitcase. I bought him a Cadillac automobile. I bought him his clothes. I put him through medical school. I even bought him his wife's wedding ring, and it cost me five hundred dollars. I introduced him to people who helped him build a practice. I gave big parties for him. I gave him everything that I would have given my own son. I gave him everything in the world—and he took away from me, in the twilight of my life, the one thing that was dearest to me in the whole world—Joan. Who would have done different than me? I can't slow down, I can't get sick, I can't even die until someone punishes this man."

Racehorse had entertained the idea of hauling Ash into court and trying to toast the old man over flames for at least a few minutes. But he decided it would have been incalculably dangerous to the defense. In Texas, when one side or the other in a trial calls a witness, then that side—be it prosecution or defense—vouches for the witness' veracity, "sponsors" him or her. The defense attorney came to realize that in no way could he "sponsor" Ash Robinson as a truth teller. But it was certainly in his mind to bring up the old man's name often, injecting his off-stage presence so many times into the record, developing the notion that these murder proceedings were largely the result of his avenging hand, so digging at the absent Ash that the state would have been *forced* to call him to rebut. And if the state was predictably fearful of putting the volatile old man on the stand, the jury might well have thought, "Well, *why* didn't the state give us Ash Robinson?" Racehorse was prepared to hypothecate for hours about Ash's participation in the events. He had several witnesses ready to testify about harassment from the old man, even a gravedigger who was primed to tell how Ash stood over his daughter's plot and said: "I have millions to spend, and I will—to get John Hill under this ground."

Throughout the ten days of trial John had forbidden Connie Loesby to attend and she obeyed, knowing that he would have been embarrassed by her presence, even though she was perhaps the most knowledgeable human guide through the entire morass. She had read all of the depositions, documents, transcripts, motions, countermotions, private detective reports, and had even listened to secret tape recordings of conversations between principals in the case. She had prepared a cross index to the thousands of pages of depositions being taken in the ten-million-dollar slander suit her fiancé had filed against his ex-father-in-law. "If that girl can have the most intimate access to John Hill's life," mused Racehorse, "if she can read all of those documents and sift through all of that garbage, and *still* love the guy and believe in his innocence, then that's a feather in his cap as far as I'm concerned."

Now that the trial was over and the second one in the distant future, if ever, John asked his lawyer if he could marry Connie. Racehorse considered the situation carefully. "Well, I'm not going to tell you that this won't be used against you in case of a second trial," he cautioned. "On the other hand, you're a lucky man. Go on. Marry the young lady. And blessings on you both."

John Hill thus took his third wife in June 1971, four months after his mistrial for the murder of his first. But the ceremony was marked by the terrors still loose and prowling about the beleaguered surgeon. The wedding was to be held in Seattle, at the home of Connie's parents, and the preparations were secret. John did not want the gossip columns to trumpet the news until it was a *fait accompli*. The couple planned a honeymoon in Europe where they would drench themselves with the great music of Vienna and Paris and Milan. While Connie flew to Seattle, John stayed behind a few days to arrange his practice for a long vacation and to make the travel arrangements.

Just before he was scheduled to leave, the bank where John had borrowed money totaling $25,000 abruptly called in the loans. Open and unsecured, the loans were subject to repayment at any time. He had originally borrowed the money to pay his lawyers and keep his practice going.

"I'm wiped out," he said to Connie over long distance. He was near tears, the first time that she had heard his voice break in the more than a year and a half they had known one another. He could not prove it, he said, but he suspected the fine hand of Ash Robinson in the bank's action.

"Well," said Connie calmly, "we can still get married, can't we?"

Of course, answered John. But there was no money for the trip to Europe. "I'm so ashamed," he said, "I know I'm disappointing you."

"We'll go to Europe another time," answered Connie. "La Scala is not going to go away. Now hurry up here. I love you." One last cruel act occurred before the marriage.

A packet arrived addressed to Connie's parents. A rough hand had scrawled "Thought you might be interested in these." When opened, the entire tragedy spilled out—newspaper clippings of Joan's death, the investigation, John's indictment, John's trial. Once again, John Hill had a good idea from whence they had come. But they failed to work their intent. Already John had sat down with Connie's mother and her father and he had answered every one of their questions. They believed in him, they said. Even more to the point, they believed in their daughter's judgment. If she loved this man, then they would happily welcome him as their son-in-law.

After the ceremony, before sixty-five friends and relatives, the couple embraced. John brokenly whispered both his love and his happiness. Both of them wept. "Let's consider this our beginning," he said. And for a few fragile months it was that—a world gentle and filled with music.

25

The flat earth of Houston did not crack open nor did public scorn welcome the couple when they returned from the Northwest as man and wife. Actually no one seemed to care very much, save Ash Robinson, who muttered to friends about the latest ornament on John Hill's necklace of women. "I just hope the lady calls in a consulting opinion should she suddenly fall ill," he said. Coincidentally, an anonymous letter and series of telephone calls were made to the Harris County juvenile welfare office, suggesting that someone look into the situation of a child being forced to live with "a murderer and his third wife." But nothing came of it.

Racehorse Haynes had the idea that perhaps an accommodation could be reached with the old man. He opened delicate negotiations through an intermediary, hinting that John Hill would drop the ten-million-dollar slander suit against his ex-father-in-law and, as further token of good faith, permit Ash to visit regularly with his beloved grandson. No more need to mosey around the mansion in the black Lincoln, scaring everybody in the neighborhood. All Ash Robinson had to do was ask the DA to drop the charges. "One word from that old man and I think there would be a unanimous sigh of relief around the district attorney's office," said Racehorse. But Ash gagged on the offer. Implacable, he spat it out like vinegar. "Hell, no," he said. "Have people forgotten that my daughter is dead? I want John Hill to answer for her murder."

The trial was reset for July 1971, then postponed at the request of the defense, later passed again that autumn by the state, scheduled once more for the summer of 1972. When it was delayed still again and set for the following November, Ash was angry. He picked up a rumor that the new stall was at the behest of *another* man named John Hill, this one a politician running for the office of attorney general for the state of Texas. "They tell me he called his friends at the courthouse and urged them to put the trial off so voters wouldn't mix him up with John Hill, murder defendant," Ash told a friend.

The old man resumed bombarding the DA's office with telephone calls, demanding to know if another trial was *ever* going to be held. The response was always affirmative, but in truth there was no enthusiasm to commence the dance once more. Ernie Ernst was retiring after a long and successful career, moving to nearby Huntsville where he would teach law. I. D. McMaster ran successfully for a seat on the criminal court. Cecil Haden hailed the candidate as "a fine young man who will make an excellent judge." McMaster found sufficient financial support to mount an expensive race, handing out "ID" cards with his name and credentials and using the theme in newspaper advertisements and billboards.

The case was passed about the DA's office like an old and unwanted relative, the kind children feel guilty over but would rather stash away in a rest home and forget. Sensing this, Ash Robinson tried mightily to revive the failing fire. He announced that he had uncovered a new "mystery witness" who would be willing to deliver an explosive new accusation against John Hill. His own investigation had turned up a nurse, he said, a frightened nurse from Sharpstown Hospital, who had made confession to her minister. Somehow this confession had reached Ash's alert ears. "She will testify that John Hill gave her two poison pills to administer to Joan," he revealed. "Her conscience finally bothered her so much that she had to tell someone about it." But Ash refused to reveal her name—he was "protecting a confidence"—and the report went into a fat folder at the DA's office of unfounded rumor and "nut calls" in the moldering case.

Racehorse Haynes and Don Fullenweider elected to hold the slander suit over Ash's head as a Damoclean sword, feeling on the one hand that their client was justifiably entitled to financial repair from his avenging ex-father-in-law, but on the other hand not anxious to hurry the suit into a civil courtroom. It was more valuable as a potential roadblock in Ash's hurly-burly path. From time to time the lawyers reviewed the case, dipping into the stack of depositions that spilled out of a closet in their storage room, documents grown taller than a six-foot man. And at each reading they marveled at the enterprise and machinations of old Ash.

But in every sworn word of testimony that he gave in these depositions, Ash brushed off each accusation of chicanery and importuning witnesses. He presented himself as only a grieving father, trying to build evidence against a man who had used his courtesies, then snuffed out the life of his daughter. "God almighty!" he roared at one point. "Would any man who loved his child have done any less? Maybe I am a meddler, but if I didn't meddle, nothing would have been done in this matter."

Racehorse enjoyed his jousts with the old man. Occasionally he felt he caught a glimmer of glee in his opponent's yellowing eyes. He returned to his quarters with juices flowing after bantering for hours with Ash. "He's really incredible," said Racehorse. "And don't ever sell him short. He reminds me of a crocodile. Old. Mean. Thick-skinned. Impervious to injury. He sits there sleeping in the sun, dozing, drowsy, about ready to pass on, or so you think. But just you step on him, and he bites your head off. Snap!"

John and Connie Hill built a quiet but contented life together. She opened the Orpheus Music School where the disciplines of voice, piano, and a few other instruments were taught. He discovered that his medical practice had reached its nadir just before the murder trial, and now that the prospects of a second one were fading, his appointment book was no longer so pristine. One prominent internist wrote the surgeon a moving letter. In it he confessed to having talked bitterly against John in the aftermath of Joan's death, and he had collected each bit of gossip that came his way. "Then, as you perhaps heard," wrote the internist, "my own wife fell ill at home. Normally I would have told her to take two aspirins and call the office nurse if she didn't get better. But after your ordeal, all of us learned a lesson. I put her into Hermann [Hospital] and just in time. She was developing serious problems, but is fine now. I speak for a lot of us around town when I say I am sorry for your troubles, and I devoutly hope they are over." In the next six weeks the doctor referred two cases to the plastic surgeon.

Connie Hill dutifully joined a club of medical wives, and although she did not participate in their meetings with keen enthusiasm—hers was not the character for female tribes—it did her husband good for her to attend. That John Hill could have won the love of a woman as poised and charming as Connie earned him support from the wives, some of whom had never really forgiven him for turning up at the Spanish Ball with Ann Kurth on his arm.

The new couple did not receive many invitations; they were still not accepted in River Oaks' best homes. Nevertheless, at intermissions in the city's concert halls, it was not uncommon to see the Hills in the center of a circle of handsome people, and, off to the side, a group twice as large gaping and trying to overhear. Connie wondered if she should plunge more deeply into the social and political seas of John's medical community. Perhaps hold more parties in the big house for doctors and hospital administrators? John shook his head. Secretly he was afraid no one would come. But he was also tired of playing medical politics. "No," he said. "What we have together is important. When I'm with you, the room is full." Their favorite evenings were those at home, alone, together, in the white and gold music room. Finally it was being used for what John had intended—as an elegant setting to hear and play great music. He enjoyed selecting an evening's concert from his enormous collection of recorded music. Then, sitting blissfully with his wife, head thrown back, eyes closed, he absorbed the power and provocation of the classical repertoire. Their favorite recording remained Schwarzkopf singing Strauss's *Four Last Songs*. Neither John nor Connie ever tired of the soprano's silk and cream voice as she interpreted the final melancholy works of the German master. Sometimes John would snap off the switches and Connie would sing the melodies herself, softly, a capella, just for her husband. It surely did not occur to either that the music they loved best used the metaphors of night, sleep, deepest autumn, and rebirth—symbols of approaching death.

In September 1972 a national meeting of plastic surgeons was to be held in Las Vegas, and the Hills made plans to go. But first they would fly to Seattle where one of Connies' cousins was to be married. John and Connie would play duets on the harpsichord and recorder at the ceremony. Now having been married fifteen months, John was an accepted and popular member of Connie's family. He had especially won the affection of his new mother-in-law, by composing and recording a fanfare that blared a royal welcome when she came to visit the Hills in Houston.

The three days of wedding festivities passed happily; John and Connie played an exquisite Vivaldi sonata at the ceremony. They drove to the Seattle airport for the flight to Las Vegas with a shared sadness over having to leave the warming embrace of Connie's people.

As they hurried toward the departure gate, Connie noted from a flight information sign in the corridor that the plane would make an intermediate stop in San Francisco en route to Las Vegas. Never an impulsive person, and not the kind of woman to crowd her husband with a sudden plea, she nonetheless had a delicious and wicked idea. "Oh, John," she said, "I haven't been to San Francisco in years. Let's get off there and stop just overnight. We can find a cheap hotel room and take buses and eat hamburgers. Wouldn't it be fun! And they'll never miss us in Las Vegas. We can get there a day late and nobody will care."

John frowned artificially, then broke it with a wide smile. He cared nothing for Las Vegas, Connie even less. Her presence in the gambling city would be like a fine piece of Georgian silver sat down on a table of plastic dinnerware. The notion of a secret night in San Francisco was fine by him.

One night stretched into four—the honeymoon they never had in Europe. At the San Francisco Opera, Connie had to nudge John to keep him from humming along with *The Marriage of Figaro*. They dined at the Blue Fox, walked up hills until the backs of their legs ached, grabbed cable cars, ordered omelettes in Ghirardelli-Square, browsed through an outdoor exhibition of Norman Rockwell paintings at Golden Gate Park, retired to the luxury of an expensive but romantic room at the Fairmont. They drank champagne and laughed and made love. On their last night in the lovely city, in a bar atop a giant building, Connie sipped a cocktail and watched an enormous sun drop into the sea, and drapes of violet and black cover San Francisco and carry it into darkness. She felt completely divorced from reality. This was impossibly beautiful, a stage setting. Soon someone would come and shut off the lights and smother the enchantment and close the theater. Somewhere a murder charge was still pending against the man whose hand she held and whose eyes she held in emotional lock. But now, all the furies were banished. For the moment there was no one else, no place else.

In Las Vegas the thin man with the droopy mustache and the dark, shaggy hair sat down on the motel bed and called every major hotel on the Strip. He could not find a Dr. John Hill registered anywhere. He swore. The girl beside him shrugged. Hill was supposed to be here. The thin man called Houston and double-checked. Yes, came the response from their contact. Hill was in Las Vegas. He was attending the plastic surgeons' meeting. "But he's not at the Stardust, god damn it," swore the man impatiently. Then find him, came the order back. At the Stardust, which was headquarters for the assemblage, a woman at the registration desk smiled and helpfully went through the list of attending doctors. Dr. John Hill had not yet checked in. Perhaps he had simply failed to register. Some of the doctors were negligent that way. Maybe he had decided to stay in a quieter motel, or with friends. Would the inquirer want to leave a name in case Dr. Hill turns up? No. The thin man with the mustache shook his head. He grabbed the girl's arm and they spent the rest of the day playing blackjack. When all their money was gone they left town. There would be another opportunity to meet John Hill.

On the flight from Las Vegas to Houston, the plane was filled with members of Houston's plastic surgery community. "If we crash," mused John, "the business is wiped out in Houston." It was a hot Sunday midafternoon when they took off from Las Vegas. It would be even hotter in Houston, where September is the broiling month. Not far away on the plane sat Nathan Roth, the heavy and moody surgeon who had hired John fresh out of medical training. He had gone before one of the grand juries and given harmful testimony about his onetime protégé's character and professional responsibility. The two men were bitter enemies, but Connie every now and then flashed him a mischievous dazzling smile. John knew what she was doing and was amused. Give Connie five minutes with his worst enemy, and she could charm him into a friend. Some of the other surgeons dropped by and chatted with the Hills, grumbling over gambling losses, or speculating on the likelihood of certain Vegas show girls having had breast augmentation.

"Slowly they're forgiving him," thought Connie. "Slowly they're inviting him back into their group. And it's about time!" Before the end of the year, she believed, her husband would be completely accepted by his peers and bear but few scars of his scandal and exile. During the rest of the late afternoon flight John dozed. Now and then Connie nudged him to try out a bit of a speech she was preparing for delivery to a women's group entitled, "Vienna: City of Dreams."

In the taxi home from the Houston airport, Connie snuggled close to John and whispered her thanks for the trip. "Without you, I couldn't have gone to my cousin's wedding, or I couldn't have done San Francisco the way it should be done," she said. Putting her head on John's shoulder, Connie was content. It occurred to her that she and her husband had known each other for almost three years and not one single cross word had been spoken by either. Aside from John's habit of being chronically late, she could find no fault with her quiet husband.

For a few months after the mistrial, she had worried that someone might try to harm him: the hate phone calls kept coming in, and Ash continued his ominous drives past their home. Once, when she went to bed early and fell asleep while waiting for John to return from the hospital, she awoke suddenly at 1 A.M. and found John still absent. Frantically she called the hospital and implored a nurse to search. In the next quarter of an hour Connie paced the great house, imagining that something terrible had happened. Then the phone rang. The nurse had found the plastic surgeon, asleep on a couch in the doctors' lounge. That had been the only disquieting incident in a year and a

half. Their lives had settled into a routine. No one save
Ash Robinson seemed interested in them any more.

At their pillared mansion, Connie sprang out of the taxi
almost before it had parked on the curving driveway. She
was eager to see her stepson, Robert, and tell him of the
trip. The boy was twelve, sprouting tall, and had somehow
managed to survive the tragedy of his mother's death and
his father's murder trial with psyche unharmed. He had
warmed instantly to Connie, and she knew that he would
not settle down for bed until he had visited with his parents.
While John paid the cabbie and attended to the luggage,
Connie rang the doorbell. Impatiently, she pressed her face
to a glass panel beside the door, squashing her features
clownishly, hoping to make Robert laugh. But no one came.
She rang the bell again, thinking she heard the distant
chatter of the television set. Even if Robert was absorbed
in some cowboy program, surely John's mother, Myra,
who had been "baby sitting," would hurry to the door in
greeting.

Then, to her right, through the glass panel, Connie saw a
figure approaching, walking through the sunken living room
and toward the small step that led to the entrance hall.
Connie was not sure, but it seemed that the figure wore a
green costume. She prepared to laugh, for Robert was apparently in masquerade. He had concocted a joke for their
homecoming. What was he wearing? An odd green something covered his face.

But as the figure drew closer Connie sensed in a frag-
mented flash that it was not her stepson. Then it must be
John's mother. No one else was in the house. But what
would Myra Hill be doing with a green hood wrapped
around her head? The door opened and Connie laughed.
"What's this?" she giggled merrily, going along with the
joke. "What now?" Then it registered with her that the
figure was too tall for the boy, too short for the erect
grandmother. She waited for the figure to cry, "Surprise!"
But this was not to be. The person standing before Connie
instead reached out with one hand and grabbed a chunk
of the cream-colored tailored blouse that she wore inside
her suit jacket. Fingers seized a section of the gold chain
necklace that was her wedding gift from John. Like a balk-
ing horse being led by an angry trainer, she was pulled
across the threshold. As she formed a scream, her eyes

saw that the figure held a glistening blue-black gun in his right hand and it was rising toward her, like a serpent preparing to strike. The scream died in her throat.

"This is a robbery," the intruder said, and for the first time Connie recognized him to be a man. All of this had passed in the span of five seconds, and she realized that the taxi had sped away and that John Hill was standing behind her. As she by reflex tried to break the man's grasp on her blouse and necklace, John Hill moved in, pushing her away and confronting the robber. "Now wait a minute here . . ." began John as he pushed Connie out of the way, defending her, freeing her to escape. Hysterically she ran sideways, toward a neighbor's house, afraid to run directly for the street and the help of a passing car for fear that she would be in the path of bullets. Just as she reached the white brick wall that borders the property Connie heard the first shot. Then a second. Screaming, falling, she stumbled crazily to a house two down from hers. "My husband's being murdered!" she cried as the neighbor opened the door. Connie was composed enough to telephone the police, then hung up and dialed her lawyer, Don Fullenweider, partner of Racehorse Haynes. He lived just across Kirby Drive and was dozing after a day of fishing. Seconds after he heard Connie's distraught screams on the telephone, he burst out his front door and hurried across the drive to the Hill home. Already sirens were filling the new night. It was just growing dark.

The white colonial house was eerily quiet. The front door was open a crack. Fullenweider pushed it open and gained entrance. The first thing his eyes found was a vase of yellow mums, fallen onto the parquet floor, smashed, blossoms strewn madly about. And then he beheld a sight that he would never be able to shut from his mind. The child, Robert Hill, was standing over the inert form of his father. Hopping up and down because his feet and arms were bound, the little boy was sobbing, a piece of adhesive tape dangling from his lips as if he were a package newly opened.

"They've killed my daddy," he cried. Scooping him up, muttering shushing reassurances, the young lawyer carried Robert outside to the lawn, where neighbors were gathering. An emergency vehicle from the Houston fire department roared up, and an attendant ran into the house. The attorney led him to John Hill. The plastic surgeon lay face down, the lower half of his body on the foyer floor, his head and shoulders sprawled across the step leading down into the sunken living room. Quickly, expertly, the attendant checked for vital signs. He turned over John Hill. Don Fullenweider gasped. The eyes were sealed shut with adhesive tape. So was the mouth and nose. Blood soaked through the tapes and appeared in blobs about the body. The attendant stood up and shook his head. "I'm sorry, mister," he said. "We're too late. . . ."

Fallen between two symbols of his life—one a brooding metallic bust of Beethoven sitting on an end table, the other a framed drawing of horses galloping through a mist —pale, indefinite horses, hurrying toward a gray and distant horizon—John Hill was dead.

26

They all had something to say.

Racehorse Haynes swore. "God damn it all," he said. "I should have known this would happen. Several months ago I picked up a street rumor that John's life was in danger, but I didn't pay much attention. In this business, you get threats all the time and you learn to live with them. I did tell John that perhaps he should hire a bodyguard, but he just didn't have the money."

John Hill died broke. The strain of more than three years of defending himself against a scandal that devastated his practice drained his resources. When a tally was made, he owed more than $100,000. The Internal Revenue Service was demanding $60,000 in back taxes. Ann Kurth was suing over non-payment of moneys due in the divorce property settlement. A nurse-secretary sought overtime. A music store appeared with a $600 bill for records and instrument repair. There was not even enough money in his bank account to buy a coffin to bury him. The Settegast-Kopf Funeral Home, which staged Joan Hill's elaborate last rites, refused to sell Connie Hill a box for her husband unless she put cash on the table, in advance. In despair, she told Don Fullenweider. An insurance policy was discovered among John's papers that satisfied the mortuary enough to provide a funeral.

Fullenweider felt both rage and helplessness. "Here I had worked for years, for literally thousands and thousands of hours, to help this man extricate himself from an impossible situation," he told his wife, "and then I find him—my client, my friend, my across-the-street neighbor—shot dead and lying in a pool of his own blood."

New Judge I. D. McMaster deplored the violence, in the manner of public figures who are regularly called upon to make such statements in America. But to a friend he later allowed that he was not very surprised. Rather cryptically he said: "When that old boy signed that letter Ash Robinson wrote way back in December 1968, and then reneged on it, he signed his own death warrant."

The child, Robert Hill, watching the attendants carry the body out of the house, seeing the canvas sack that contained the man whose seed had given him life, ran to the arms of his second stepmother, fell into them, and buried his head. "Our daddy is dead," he said. "Whatever are we going to do without him?" At the funeral, private, secret, limited only to the immediate family in attempt to keep the curious away, the child marched at the head of the funeral procession, his spine stiff, his face a mask of whatever emotions a twelve-year-old conceals. He stood quietly and watched his second parent returned to earth. Three years earlier he had buried his mother.

Myra Hill mourned her second and last son. Both had been doctors, both men of music, both wasted. She put herself deep into the consolation of her faith, drawing strength from God, not even questioning the purpose of His ways. If she wept, she wept alone, for no one saw her steely pioneer face dampened by tears. Her major complaint was that she was unable to walk in procession to her son's tomb, for she was confined to a hospital room after the murder.

When the ambulance attendant entered the house and found John Hill dead, Myra Hill was writhing on the floor of an adjoining room, her hands taped behind her, her mouth stuffed with cloth, tape encircling her face. She had heard the shots, heard the final agonal cries, but could do nothing but scream silently into the gag. The killer had kicked her in the throat, and she could not fully tell her story until some days later.

Hers was the best full eyewitness account that the police had to go on:

The day before the killing, the telephone rang mid-Saturday afternoon in the Hill home and she answered it.

"Is Dr. Hill there?" inquired a man's voice.

"No," answered the mother. "He's out of town."

"Oh. When do you expect him?"

"Tomorrow night," she said. "Are you a patient of Dr. Hill's?"

"No. But I need to talk to him very bad."

There was, she would remember in retrospect, a vaguely rough edge to his voice. Perhaps he had a piece of information that could be used in her son's second trial for murder by omission. It was scheduled in a month, and it occurred to Mrs. Hill that this just might be somebody who had something to contribute to the defense. There had been other calls like this.

She asked his name.

"Gleason. James Gleason."

"Mr. Gleason, Dr. Hill should be home tomorrow night around seven-thirty." She was polite, helpful, Christian.

The next day, Sunday, Mrs. Hill took her grandson to church in the morning and church in the evening, and on the way home, around six-thirty, Robert hatched a prank. "Let's go somewhere and fool around for a while and let Mama and Daddy get home first. They'll wonder where we are, then we can burst in and surprise them!"

The grandmother laughed and put down the idea. "No," she said, "we must be there to welcome *them*. How would you like to come home to an empty house?"

The telephone rang again. Once more it was "James Gleason" calling. "He should be here soon, by seven-thirty," Mrs. Hill said helpfully. She scribbled the name down to remember it.

The boy was restless, prowling about the house and watching from the front windows. He had homework to do, but it was unattended on a kitchen table, waiting for the homecoming. Suddenly he wanted to play chess. Myra sighed. She knew little of the game, but perhaps it would content her grandson and pass the hour. She had planned to start dinner but decided to wait and entertain the boy. Probably John and Connie had eaten on the plane and would not be hungry. She glanced at the clock. A quarter past seven. John had called from the Las Vegas airport saying the flight was going to be a few minutes late. She expected them at the front door by 8 P.M. latest.

Suddenly the doorbell rang. With a whoop, Robert ran

to the foyer. Myra followed him. Just as the child put his hands on the knob, his grandmother felt something was wrong. It was one of those vague fragments of apprehension. She was about to call out for the child to wait, but the boy had already flung open the door.

A strange man pushed his way in and stood in dominance. Though in her seventies, Myra's senses were sharp and her powers of observations clear. She would never forget how this intruder looked, even though her heart was rising to her throat. She first noticed his eyes, ". . . wild eyes, like great big marbles rolling about. And glistening like they had a coat of shellac on them. . . ." It seemed he was wearing a sorrel-colored wig, with a strip of greenish cloth dangling about his head. And in his hand, casually held as if it were nothing but a stone picked up at random from a plowed field, was a gun. At this first moment, Myra thought it was a ceramic gun, certainly a toy, but then he raised it and pointed it at the boy, and she recognized it was true steel. A shaft of last afternoon sun from the hot September day fell through an oak outside and glinted against the pistol. For a moment the gun gleamed golden.

"Are you a patient?" asked Myra, trying to keep her voice calm. Perhaps this was a deranged sick person, escaped from a hospital. She had heard tales of distraught men coming to repair imaginary grievances against doctors.

Politely, the man holding the gun shook his head negatively. He was young, thirty perhaps. He swayed in his place unsteadily, as if he were not in control of all of his senses. "No, ma'am," he said. "This is a robbery." With that, Robert sucked in his breath and backed toward the winding staircase. His face was contorted and trembling. The man, fearful that the child would cry out, rushed to him and seized the little boy's face, cupping it in his rough hands. "Be very quiet," he ordered. "Don't say anything. You won't get hurt." At that instant Myra Hill noted that the front door was still open. She could flee into the yard and scream for help. Automobiles were passing outside; people were returning home from weekends in the country. But she would have to leave her grandson alone for such a dash. As she debated with herself, the man whirled and slammed the door, killing her option. He shoved the old woman on the floor and ordered her to stay quiet. As she fell, her shoe came off and she touched it quietly, wondering if it could be used as a weapon, wondering where the heel could inflict the most damage.

There would not be the chance. The man lifted Myra and shoved her into the nearby dining room, the child preceding them. "Sit on the floor," he directed. Myra decided that obedience was best at this point and she sat down quickly, throwing looks of reassurance at her grandson. Now she realized that the gunman's wig, or mask, or whatever it was, had come off, and his face was naked. He had a lean, cruel countenance, with a well-tended drooping mustache, dark, like his shaggy hair. His eyes were aflame. Immediately she assumed that this was surely a drinker, and whiskey was aging him quickly. She revised her estimate. He was older than thirty. Disappearing for a moment into the adjacent kitchen, he returned with a steak knife. Immediately Myra began to pray, throwing her arms about her grandson and trying to shield his eyes, for she felt this was the moment of her sacrifice. But he was not holding the knife as a dagger, rather as an instrument of utility. From his pocket he produced a thick role of adhesive tape, and he began cutting strips, binding first the boy's hands and feet, then his mouth. The child, having seen a similar incident on television, wet his lips just as the tape was pressed against his face. He knew it would not stick, but he kept this secret to himself.

Then, in one of those small side incidents which at the moment seem graver than the actual event, the man pulled Myra Hill's sweater from her shoulders and began slashing it with the kitchen knife. "My beautiful Hong Kong sweater that I bought on my trip around the world," protested Myra, furious that the cherished possession should be so savaged. But her objection could not be vocal, for the man quickly stuffed the strips into her mouth and then turned and did the same to the boy. When he was finished, he became suddenly benevolent, kneeling and looking into the old woman's eyes. "Can you breathe okay?" he asked. Myra nodded. "Are you sure?" he pressed. She nodded again, now certain that he did not plan to murder them. The gag slipped slightly and Myra took the opportunity to blurt out a warning. "Dr. Hill will be here in a minute," she cautioned sternly.

The man nodded knowingly. "That's all right," he said. "I'll be ready for him." And then Myra knew that the man's mission was not robbery, but harm to her son. Her stomach began to heave, but she tried to keep a brave front on behalf of the child. Once more she began to pray. Five eternal minutes more or less crept by, eerily silent suspensions of time and substance. The man had disappeared into the living room, and Myra could not see what he was doing. Then the sounds of a car on the driveway, its doors opening and shutting, murmurs of happy voices. The doorbell! Myra screamed from beneath her gag, "John, don't come in!" With that, the man rushed back into the dining room and brutally kicked the old woman in the throat. "Be quiet!" he hissed. And he kicked the child in the ear.

Now everything happened with speed and violence. She heard Connie scream. Scuffling. Feet scraping. Bodies crashing to the floor. John grunting. The first shot! The second! One last bullet exploding from a chamber! Then the awful silence. The boy spat off his bandage and hobbled to the kitchen telephone. With remarkable presence of mind, he managed to dial the operator and cry for help. "My father's been shot, send somebody quick. The address is 1561 Kirby Drive."

By the time someone came to raise Myra from the floor and peel away her tape bindings, an ambulance attendant had already arrived and was checking John Hill's wounds. She discovered her son propped up against the wall, beneath the drawing of the pale horses, his sport jacket and shirt hitched up and his bare chest splattered with blood. Five pots of mums had been broken and their yellow blossoms scattered about, like offerings.

The mother walked to the body and stood over her son, and the attendant said, "I'm sorry, ma'am. There are no vital signs."

Myra Hill went to a couch and sat down and buried her face in her hands. But she did not weep. Her grief was molested by an intruding thought. Ash Robinson. A few blocks away. She suspected he was somehow the source of her son's death. She thought to herself, "If I went down there right now and shot Ash Robinson—shot him ten times—shot him until his flesh was stripped bare—and then burned the house down, it wouldn't do any good. It would not breathe life into my son."

There was nothing for her to do but sit on the couch and feel the throbbing pain from the kick to her throat and try not to look at the bloodied corpse sprawled forever beyond her reach.

Ann Kurth had moved away from Houston. She had taken a remote house on a lake near Austin, a place approachable only through guarded gates, or by boat across an inlet. She lived quietly with her three sons, relieved to be away from the city of the prior ugliness. Her flashing moments in the spotlight during the murder trial had not been satisfying—she knew her testimony was not well received—and she was apprehensive about Ash Robinson's attitudes, despite the fact that she had borne witness on his behalf.

Near midnight on this late September Sunday, her telephone rang. The number was unlisted. When she answered, a familiar voice was on the line. An old voice, cracking, drawling, unmistakable. "Did you hear about old John Hill?" asked Ash Robinson. "He went and got himself shot to death."

Yes, answered Ann. It had been on the late news. And her telephone had rung several times—relatives and close friends in Houston. It was a terrible thing.

"Yes," echoed Ash. "A terrible thing. Just wanted you to know about it."

As she put down the phone, Ann trembled. She could not be sure, but she thought she discerned in the old man's voice a gloating. For the rest of the night she drew her sons about her and kept the remote house ablaze with lights.

book three
PURSUIT
and TRIAL

*". ... Behold a pale horse: and his name that
sat on him was Death,
and Hell followed with him. ..."*
—*Revelations 6:8*

27

Sunday is a lazy day in Houston, rarely molested by murder. The killings come in one terrible spurt, from Friday sundown when the pay checks go out and are helpfully converted into money and spirits by the liquor stores, until a few hours past Saturday midnight, when the bars close and the radio stations change the tempo from the miseries of lost love to the jubilant shouts of gospel. Traditionally Sunday is so peaceful that the homicide office of the police department has but two pair of detectives on duty—one to answer calls at the station (truant and hungover husbands are the complaint of the day), another out cruising the enormous sprawling city of more than four hundred square miles.

Detectives Joe Gamino and Jerry Carpenter began their field shift at 4 P.M. on the steaming afternoon of September 24, 1972, and passed three hours doing nothing but idling around in the late afternoon traffic, keeping an ear cocked to the dispatcher radio, grateful for the refrigerated calm of their anonymous blue Plymouth. An odd pair who had been teamed for only a month, their relationship was not yet the close one of cops whose professional lives entwine them closer than blood brothers. In fact, they knew little of one another, for neither was the sort who rattled on with shreds of biography.

Joe Gamino was one of the serious men, a look of melancholy often on his face. Stocky, in his late thirties, on his way to overweight like many of the old Mexican men in his family, he had life boiled down to a factum—no one was going to do him any favors. His guard was up; no one got close. He was known to be gentlemanly and polite with those he put under arrest. Never once had he drawn his gun in anger. The only time he ever came close to using it—and he would probably have fired into the air—was to stop one man from strangling another.

A child of the Houston barrio, Joe quit school in the ninth grade and, after a few years of muscle-tearing work carrying plumber's pipes, joined the Marines. The four years he spent in Hawaii and Japan as an aviation ordnance worker were the first really satisfying ones of his life. "The

Marines taught me responsibility," he would later say. "They threw me against men who had education. I even got a little respect for myself, and for two terms I never understood—ambition and direction."

Toward the end of his term, during which he passed a high school equivalency test, Joe was at Camp Pendleton when brochures appeared on the base from the Los Angeles Police Department, soliciting Marines to join the force. The idea held appeal. He was comfortable in a regimented life, with boundaries and discipline, and the wearing of a uniform and its attendant power was further lure. But he had no liking for California and returned home to Houston to apply to the police force. "I never would have dreamt this as a kid," he said. "Cops were always guys who rousted kids and brought news of the men who had been stabbed."

In seven years as a radio patrol officer, Gamino grew maddeningly bored. Hungry for more education, he was spending his spare hours at the University of Houston's night school, and the man who could barely read an English paragraph at sixteen was closing in on a college degree in police science. Yet his police work demanded little more of him than issuing traffic tickets and pursuing peeping Toms. All about him were men in their forties and fifties, still doing the same work, waiting for a pension and a long night's rest. "If I stay in this job, I'll be back to square one," thought Gamino, so he applied to take the examination for detective, crash-studying for a month, trying to learn what other men spent years on—the rules of criminal investigation and evidence. Almost three hundred men took the test, and Gamino placed thirteenth, a remarkable accomplishment. Proud and happy, he shed his blue uniform and went forth as a plainclothes homicide detective.

With a Mexican gold coin dangling from a chain about his neck, with a taste in clothes that favored flaming red ties against matching shirts, with tinted spectacles, with an aura of knowing quite well how to squeeze a hard eight out of a pair of dice, or sweet-talk a reluctant girl into a hurried accommodation, Jerry Carpenter was a hundred-and-eighty-degree turn from Joe Gamino. He spoke "character" talk as well as the gamblers and hookers he busted during several years on Houston's vice squad and, on first encounter, it would be difficult to draw the line between hunter and hunted. For Jerry Carpenter resembled nothing less than a flashy high roller, the kind with no middle initial and ill disposed to rummage in his past. But a façade is the easiest part of a house to build, and within Jerry's private life was uncommon torment and pain.

He, too, had been reared in a house fanatically devoted to God, but his was the fundamentalist deity, the almost primitive kind of hardcore worship. His youth was squirming on the folding chairs in evangelists' tents, shouting helpful Hallelujahs! to faith healers pretending to exorcise devilish tumors from the doomed.

Desperate to leave home and find a measure of freedom, Jerry married quickly, at eighteen, and fathered two children. He found work at Sinclair's enormous refinery, suffocating labor that drenched his senses with the chemical fumes, numbing his outlook. He realized quickly that he had moved from one prison to another. "I was as unhappy as a man can be," he would remember years later. "I had no future, and the world had closed in on me before I was twenty-one years old." His marriage broke, and he was laid off at the same time.

Jerry joined the Houston police force with no sense of calling or notion of glamor. The only reason was that a rookie cop could make four hundred dollars a month in 1961, plus benefits, and it was better than a man with no education, with nothing but a strong back, a restless pair of hands, and two children to support, could do anywhere else. But cop work appealed to him from the beginning, its gift of authority filling him for the first time with dignity that he had never otherwise possessed. "I *am* somebody," he could finally say. He married for a second time, and until 1968, Jerry Carpenter was reasonably content with the way his life was going. Then, in the space of less than a year, his mother, his grandmother, and one of his daughters died. The child suffered for six months from a vicious leukemia that put her in the hospital seven times, draining Jerry of every penny he had and putting him in debt almost $30,000. The tragedies tore him, and he covered his pain with a veneer of almost cocky toughness, but the chip on his shoulder balanced precariously. On vice, he arrested whores and gamblers with diligence but with little enthusiasm, for he felt cops had better ways to spend their time, and, furthermore, he realized that people do things like screwing for money because of personal circumstances that society's laws cannot hope to understand. A life cannot be operated strictly within the boundaries, he reasoned, because parents and religions and diseases that destroy innocent children keep intruding.

But none of this did he tell anyone, nor did his brother officers know that Jerry Carpenter was anything but a solid cop with the best pair of ears to the "character" world of anybody on the force. "I arrested an old whore lady the other day and your name came up," a vice officer told Jerry after he had transferred to homicide. "She says, 'Jerry Carpenter! Why, that son of a bitch is pure character hisself!'" Jerry grinned, accepting the backhanded compliment.

They were eating supper at a cafeteria that Jerry favored, despite Joe Gamino's demur that the food was kept alive for hours past its prime on steam tables, when a cashier called across the room. Headquarters was on the telephone. Jerry took the call. He bolted back to the table and fetched his partner. "Some masked intruder just broke into Dr. John Hill's house and shot him to death," he said.

The detectives could have been anywhere in the city at the moment of the call, but coincidentally they were eating but five minutes away from the Hill mansion. As they drove with sirens shrieking to the house on Kirby Drive, both men raced their minds for memories of the celebrated case. The Houston homicide department had never gotten involved in the death of Joan Robinson Hill, for it had been a project of the district attorney's office from the outset. A medical death that takes place in a hospital with a certificate signed by a doctor does not concern the police. A few routine background examinations had been run by the ID division, turning up no previous blots on the records of Dr. Hill or Ann Kurth, and only the overturned fraud conviction from the 1930s of Ash Robinson. But both cops knew what they had read in the papers and heard in the corridors of the courthouse. The shooting of John Hill came both as stunning surprise and, at the same time, as an almost predictable event.

When they arrived at the great white house, both men were momentarily taken aback. Murders do not occur on boulevards like Kirby Drive in Houston. Stately colonial homes do not contain bullet-mutilated corpses. In police terminology, this was a Good Address. There were, in fact, none better in the city. With no small amount of awe, the two cops—one from the barrio, the other from its correspondent white ghetto—entered the house.

Immediately Jerry Carpenter recognized the handiwork of a "character," his term for professional gangster. It was not the random crime of a dope addict desperate to steal a stereo and caught in the act. The adhesive tape that bound John Hill's mouth, nose, and eyes was a voguish way of extermination in the Texas underworld, the beauty being there was no threat of ballistics identification. Even without being shot three times, John Hill would have died from cruel, horrible suffocation. Assuming command of the scene, barking orders, the two detectives sealed off the house, shooed neighbors from the lawn, and split up the two major responsibilities. Gamino was known in the department as a superior "scene" man, his skill being meticulous examination of a murder setting, observing the position of the body, speculating what might have happened, probing every inch for possible hints and clues. While he worked quietly, Jerry Carpenter performed his specialty—talking to folks. He pulled a witness report out of the sobbing Connie Hill, spoke briefly with Myra before realizing that her throat pained her too much to speak, and questioned the boy Robert for a valuable half hour. The child was composed and able to give a good description of the killer, even down to the observation that he was "probably from Dallas."

"How so, son?" asked Carpenter gently.

"Because he talked like Don Meredith," said the child. Carpenter laughed. The former Dallas football star had a voice like ten thousand other Texas drawls.

From shortly after 8 P.M. until 2:30 A.M. the detectives stayed in the house, roaming about every room, opening every drawer, gaping at the opulence of the music room. Jerry Carpenter was a musician too, playing in a dance band called the Centurions, composed chiefly of cops. He ran his fingers across the keyboard of the Bösendorfer, wondering what it was like to spend a year and a half's salary on an instrument like that. As they worked, the man who had bought the piano was lying nude on a marble slab in the Harris County morgue, being dissected by Dr. Jachimczyk. The coroner had come personally to the murder scene, an unusual appearance for him to make, but he recognized the importance of this death, and he remembered the ruckus over the sloppy autopsy of the doctor's first wife. How long ago that seemed. The coroner withdrew the file on Joan. She had died three and one half years earlier, and now her husband was stretched out on the same table. The coroner located three bullet wounds in John Hill—the first in the wrist, the second in the right shoulder. Neither of these would have killed him, but a third hit squarely in the stomach, tearing into the aorta. He bled to death internally. He probably lasted three to five minutes after the fatal hit. From scratches and bloodied places, the coroner deducted there had been a fierce struggle.

The homicide detectives drove away from the great house of a mind that the murder had occurred as adjunct to botched robbery. John Hill's briefcase and wallet were both missing. The killer had told Connie, "This is a robbery." Connie's best recollection was that her husband had between six and eight hundred dollars in cash on him. Nothing else seemed to have been taken from the mansion. As far as they could determine, the killer had not been in any of the rooms other than those downstairs: the foyer, the dining room, the living room, the kitchen.

Joe Gamino had scant evidence to show for six and one half hours of investigation: a roll of adhesive tape which the child, Robert identified as that used on him and his grandmother, a finger off a cheap brown cotton work glove stuck to one of the tapes that bound the victim's face, and a .38-caliber bullet, spent, and lying on the floor of the entrance hall. Carpenter had compiled a verbal portrait of the killer: a white man between thirty and forty years old, slight, dark hair cut long and vaguely "hippie-ish," droopy Pancho Villa mustache, wearing gray or tan slacks and a sport shirt. The "green something" which Myra Hill had noticed on the intruder's head turned out to be a light green pillowcase, with crude holes cut out for eyes. A grotesque hood, it had been abandoned on the floor near John Hill. The label was still inside and it was new, but it would be difficult to trace.

In the week after the plastic surgeon's death, Gamino and Carpenter put in ninety-six hours of investigation, hardly going home except to change shirts. The initial shot of adrenalin from finding a prominent citizen mysteriously dead in a great mansion was quickly replaced by the grind of textbook cop work: going over the murder house again, and again. Interviewing the neighbors, north, south, east, and west. No one had heard the shots, for the Hill home,

situated as it was in a diagonal position and set far back
on its lot, hid the sounds of gunfire. Irritatingly, none of the
neighbors even saw the killer escaping the house, nor could
anybody remember an unfamiliar car on the block. "This
is weird," said Carpenter. Somehow a gunman managed to
slip into one of the most prominent houses in the city in
the full light of late afternoon, tie up two people, assault a
third, and kill a fourth in what was surely a crashing struggle. And then slip out and away. Neighbors were about that
hour watering roses, raking leaves, riding bicycles, visiting.
It was a sedate neighborhood where people *knew* each
other. A stranger would be noticed. Yet no one the cops
interviewed could recall an unusual visitor in the area.
"We're dealing with a fucking phantom," cracked Jerry
Carpenter.

"I guess we are," said Gamino. The report was back
from the police lab. Nothing. No fingerprints on the adhesive tape, the finger of the work glove, or the pillowcase.

As did the collective attention of the city, their eyes
moved briefly down the street, to the rust-hued home of
Ash Robinson. The detectives did not knock on his door
or even call him on the telephone. They merely drove by
the house slowly, noted its close proximity to the late doctor's house, and wondered. Certainly the old man was not
the actual killer, for he was obviously well known to Myra,
Robert, and Connie. Had he been an ordinary middle-class
citizen, he might have received a visit from the cops, leaning on him for anything he might contribute. But Ash
Robinson was Ash Robinson, a rich, powerful, and important member of the community. In Houston, police did
not barge in on rich, powerful, and important members of
the community with nothing more in mind than a fishing
expedition.

Ash delivered himself of only one public statement,
granting an interview to a news reporter against the advice
of his attorney. He had absolutely nothing to do with the
death of his ex-son-in-law, the old man swore. John Hill's
murder was, in fact, a reeling disappointment to him because he had been keenly anticipating the second murder
trial. It had been scheduled for but a few weeks hence.
"I'd have a thousand times rather see him alive than dead,"
insisted Ash.

In private talk, at the early morning *Kaffeeklatsch* with
his cronies at the Houston Club, Ash was once again the

center of attention. He reveled in it, a whole new mystery to play with! Certainly he had theories. Anybody who sat down at his table could hear him propound possible motives. He had heard "through confidential sources" that John Hill had been secreting large sums of money with Connie's family to avoid paying his income taxes. "I heard tell he was coming back from Seattle with $25,000 in his briefcase to pay Racehorse," said Ash. "That may be why he put up such a fight. The paper says there was a helluva fight between John and the man who killed him." If that possibility did not wash, then Ash had others. "There were a lot of husbands out looking for John Hill," he suggested. "Fellows whose wives had been seduced." And, ruminated the old man, he had picked up gossip that the plastic surgeon had been driven by his failing medical practice and public disgrace to the dangerous business of transforming faces of wanted criminals. "Maybe one of those gangsters didn't like his new face and shot John," speculated Ash. "In fact, there were a lot of people who wanted that man dead. But I didn't do it. I don't know a damn thing about it. I was home watching television with my wife. I was as surprised as anybody else."

The one factor in Ash's protestations of innocence that convinced many people was the fact that the tragedy was played out in front of the eyes of Robert Hill, his grandson. "Do you think I would hire someone to kill that man in front of that boy, and possibly do that child harm?" asked the old man. It made sense. That he loved his grandson even from an enforced distance was beyond dispute.

Jerry Carpenter took the case to the streets, cashing due bills among the snitches. He nursed a considerable stable of informants, rarely paying them in money but in, as he put it, "Brownie points." Word was passed among the whores, gamblers, and characters that Jerry wanted information.

By the end of the first week of investigation, several names had been delivered to the detective. Among them was that of a woman, Lilla Paulus, familiar to vice officers as the widow of one of Houston's most celebrated bookmakers. The informant did not suggest that Mrs. Paulus had anything to do with the death of Dr. John Hill, only that she had acquaintances in that line of work. Jerry Carpenter had a long list of people to talk to, and he added the woman's name to a list he carried around in his coat pocket. But then a startling development got in the way, a break in the case that made him forget about the list for seven long months.

An FBI artist was in Houston on another assignment, and Joe Gamino asked if he would interview Myra, Connie, and Robert Hill to make a composite sketch of the doctor's killer from their recollections. While the artist was seated in the living room of the big white house, an urgent call from headquarters came for the detectives. An eight-year-old child who lived just a block away was looking in a clump of bushes for a lost toy, and he had just discovered what appeared to be Dr. John Hill's missing briefcase.

The two detectives raced puffing on foot down the block, blurring past half-million-dollar estates with ancient oaks hung heavily with Spanish moss and mistletoe. Ahead they heard children's voices, and both men worried that the youngsters would paw the case and disturb any possible fingerprints. The child who had found the case was proud of his discovery and pointed to the place of encounter, a clump of bushes bordering a large brick home. Another half dozen kids danced around excitedly. All of them had touched the briefcase, smearing it with sticky after-school fingers. Inside was nothing but medical papers and documents. While Gamino disappointedly wrote his report, Jerry Carpenter ambled around the area looking for John Hill's still missing wallet. Perhaps the assassin had thrown it here as well.

His eye fell on what appeared to be the stem of a pipe sticking out of a patch of fresh mud underneath more bushes several feet away. Heavy rains had fallen the day before. Curious, Carpenter reached down and grasped the object. It was not a pipe. It was a .38-caliber snub-nosed revolver, rusted from the rain. "Hey, Joe, I think we just got lucky!" shouted Carpenter.

If the lab could prove that the .38-caliber bullet found in the foyer of John Hill's home had been fired from the rusted gun under the bush, then a major piece of evidence would be established. For three days Gamino and Carpenter waited in suspense for the ballistics report.

The science of ballistics was first accepted by a U.S. federal court in 1924, and it is now so recognized that the defense lawyers no longer bother challenging the test results. Sometimes a lawyer will try to disparage the reputation of the expert, but not the science.

The Houston Police Department was fortunate in possessing a technician named Randy Sillivan, one of the ranking figures in the nation, and a man so hard-nosed and proud of his work that he would not testify in a trial unless he was a hundred per cent certain. "If it's only ninety-nine per cent sure," he often said, "then I won't stake my reputation."

Randy Sillivan loaded three test bullets into the rusted .38 and fired them into a half bale of cotton waste. Retrieving each, he placed the bullets one by one next to the slug found in the Hill home. Then he studied them under a microscope. It was his hope that the random markings and identifying characteristics on the bullets would match, like a piece of paper torn in half.

Indeed there were similarities, but not enough for Sillivan to rule that this was the gun that killed John Hill. He was disappointed. The news would be a reeling letdown to the detectives. Just when he was about to call the homicide office and tell Gamino he had the wrong gun, Sillivan decided to run one more test. He had an idea. Although the bullet found in the Hill foyer seemed to be a routine one, like hundreds of millions manufactured by the major weapons makers of America—Remington et al.—there was the slim possibility that it was not machine-made. "Back room" shops still exist in Texas where bullets are handmade. Sillivan found a package of these, loaded the .38, and repeated the process of firing into the cotton bale.

This time, when he put a freshly fired handmade bullet under his microscope next to the bullet the homicide boys had found near the body of John Hill, the markings were identical. The killer had used handmade bullets. Sillivan had this one hundred per cent. "You've got your gun," he told Gamino.

One weak law exists on the federal level that concerns itself with the sale of handguns. In 1968, with the nation shocked by political assassinations, a firearms act was passed by Congress that compels every would-be purchaser of a concealable weapon (less than eighteen inches in length) to fill out a registration form at the gun store, swearing, among other things, that the buyer is not an ex-convict, a narcotics addict, or insane. These forms are sent to the U. S. Department of Justice and stored in a computer, valuable theoretically when police attempt to trace the heritage of a murder weapon. The weakness, of course, is that the law does not relate to the tens of millions of handguns sold prior to 1968, nor does it deal realistically with the private sale of a gun by one party to another. Knowing too well that guns are stolen, and lost, and sold a dozen times after their original purchase and registration, Joe Gamino nonetheless sat down at the teletype and tapped out a description of the rusted .38 and its serial number. Within one hour an answer rattled back from Washington, D.C. The gun had been purchased originally in 1969, at a discount store in Longview, Texas, by a Dr. Orrin Staves.

"Jesus," swore Jerry Carpenter. "A doctor!"

28

Dr. Orrin Staves was not happy to find a pair of Houston homicide detectives in his waiting room. Arrogantly he looked at the rusted snub-nosed .38 and said, yes, it was his, and thanks for finding it, now good-by. The doctor was a heavy-set black man, inclined to the vivid gambler-man suits that Jerry Carpenter liked to wear. A large diamond glinted from one stubby finger; his eyes were hidden by a celebrity's dark glasses. He ran a successful clinic in a small city in the heart of the East Texas black belt, an area first cousin in attitude to the deep South. And in his world, money earned was money displayed. Dr. Staves did not mind telling the cops that he made more than $100,000 a year, drove a number of Eldorado automobiles (he preferred to use the model name rather than the generic "Cadillac"), and openly enjoyed the rewards of the flesh.

In other words, he liked to party, said the doctor. What was wrong with that?

Not a thing, answered Carpenter. But what about this gun? How did it turn up under a bush in River Oaks?

A whore stole it, answered the doctor. His explanation was so rambling, confusing, and unrepentant that Carpenter had to bite his lip to keep from laughing. The good doctor was a man caught in an embarrassing situation, and although the story would later check out, it was not one that he wanted police to share.

In February or March of that year, 1972, Dr. Staves had entertained two white prostitutes from the Dallas-Fort Worth area. After a revel in his home, while the doctor snoozed, the girls increased their fee by stealing one of his Eldorado automobiles. A briefcase containing $2,100 in cash was concurrently missing. Upon awakening, the doctor was justifiably filled with anger at the greediness of his departed guests. He strapped on a .38 and telephoned an air charter service to reserve a flight to Fort Worth where he would go in search of his missing valuables. Just as he was preparing to leave, his story went on, still another "old friend" happened by chance to telephone. This caller was a young woman named Dusty, a traveling whore, and she was in town, wondering if the doctor was in a mood to welcome her.

Indeed he was. The doctor could use the consolation of a friend. Dusty thus hurried to Dr. Staves's home, soothed his brow, suggested that he take a bath to cool off, and while he was in the tub—Stave told the police—the deceitful woman stole the very gun that he was planning to wear on his flight to Fort Worth.

Jerry Carpenter ran the name "Dusty" through his mental file of prostitutes. He knew hundreds of working girls by name, alias, and special effects. But he could not place one named Dusty.

Was that her real name or her trick name? the detective wanted to know.

The doctor shrugged. Dusty was the only name he ever called her by. But if it was worth anything, he had reason to believe her real name was Marcia McKittrick. Something like that.

Carpenter had one more question. Did the doctor know a plastic surgeon named Dr. John Hill in Houston?

"No," said Staves openly and believably. "Never heard the name."

Jerry Carpenter now felt both elation and no small amount of worry. He knew the whore business as well as any cop in Texas. In vice, he had quickly learned the hierarchy. At the bottom in Houston were the waterfront whores, tough, aging women who worked the ship channel bars and specialized in first entertaining, then rolling foreign sailors. "They're so mean we just leave 'em alone," Carpenter told Gamino. "It would take about six very strong men to arrest one of these babes, and it wouldn't be worth the time." A rung up the ladder were the street girls, in congregation daily a block away from the criminal courthouse in downtown Houston. These were prostitutes, mainly black and Mexican-American, who infested hot-bed hotels at the north end of Main Street, an area succumbing to pornographic movie theaters, penny arcades, and cheap emporiums that sold shoddy junk from Taiwan and Korea.

Moving up, the next caste was the traveling whore who worked a circuit in the major towns of Texas and adjoining Southwestern states. And at the pinnacle of the profession were the call girls, many of whom were suburban housewives, *belles de jour* who accepted occasional appointments for fees beginning at a hundred dollars for a brief afternoon encounter. They were busy during large conventions at the city's best hotels.

From what Dr. Staves had said of Marcia McKittrick, it appeared to Jerry Carpenter that she was a member of the traveling category, the "spot" girls, and the most elusive in the trade. A records check in ID confirmed the suspicion. Marcia had been arrested in Houston the year before while working a "spot," the character term for a hotel or motel that offers a hot bed or two in an otherwise legitimate hostelry. The custom is for a girl to spend a maximum of two weeks in a certain hotel whose night manager or chief porter is the entrepreneur of such things, never leaving the room during the period, entertaining customers twenty-four hours a day, and then moving on to another town before complaints result in a bust. The traditional split is sixty per cent for the girl, forty per cent for the hotel employee who handles the situation. Prostitutes in this category carry "spot books" in their purses, that being a valuable list of hotels in various cities that are accommodating. But due to the enormous size of Texas, and the fact that a girl could be working on any given day anywhere from Port Arthur in the southeast corner of the state to Amarillo seven hundred miles north, or El Paso, another eight hundred miles west—or Oklahoma or New Mexico, or even as far away as Las Vegas—made it a frustrating game of cat and mouse.

"Now we look for Marcia," said Joe Gamino. She was their only lead. Both officers well knew that they could spend months chasing the whore all over Texas, only to have it turn out that she pawned the gun the day after she took it from Dr. Staves, or sold it to a sister hooker, or left it under the mattress of a motel in Beaumont. Or she might have given it to her old man, the pimp, a traveling "character" who regularly swung about the circuit, stopping at various "spots" and collecting from the stable of prostitutes he employed. But the cops *had* to find out.

Word quietly went out on the street that Jerry Carpenter wanted information on Marcia McKittrick, and a teletype was dispatched to police departments all over the Southwest. For a month Jerry drove around his old vice squad haunts, visiting madams, both current and retired, rousting pimps from pool halls, menacing bellhops and night porters for information. From police records, the detectives located both a photograph of their quarry and an address for her parents, a small community east of Dallas. The mug shot of Marcia McKittrick revealed a short young woman with heavy breasts and imperfect teeth, with dark hair woven and teased into a coiffure of towering stature, suitable for presentation at the court of the Sun King. The record showed that she was twenty-two years old at the time of the Houston arrest, that she had had a few other minor experiences with the law in and around Dallas, and that she was a suspected drug addict. "You know, I think I know this girl," mused Jerry Carpenter. "I may have busted her once myself." In the photograph were both hauteur and fear, like a girl masquerading at a party to which she had no invitation. Carpenter had seen this bluff a thousand times before. In fact, he wore it himself now and then.

The detectives drove to a rural suburb twenty miles east of Dallas, a place of old and peeling white frame houses set in thick groves of trees. Grandmothers sat on sagging front porches and rocked, noting every strange car that drove past on dusty, pocked roads. Scraggly orange calla lilies tried to bloom outside Marcia's family home, and within, a cheap throw rug of a deer grazing in a meadow was the principal piece of art on the wall. The house was modestly furnished but clean. Marcia's mother was a plump, fast-wrinkling woman past sixty who worked in a hospital as a nursing aide. She sighed over the burden that her daughter had become. Yes, she knew that Marcia was a prostitute. No, she had not the slightest idea where she was. "I haven't seen her in several months," said the mother. A little boy about six with a thin face and a frightened air hung outside on the front porch, trying to eavesdrop through the torn screen door. Often the old woman rose and ordered the child to go down to the creek and find crawdads. "That's Marcia's little boy," she whispered. "She loves him so much. She always turns up for his birthday." Marcia's father, a construction man with a sunburned turkey gobbler neck from outdoor labor, had no news of his daughter either.

"She's basically a sweet, loving girl," said the mother. "Somewhere along the line she just got mixed up with the wrong people. She told me once she met somebody on a hillbilly TV show who got her hooked on drugs. She's never been the same since."

Reluctantly, the parents mentioned two or three names of men whom Marcia spoke of from time to time, and Carpenter dutifully wrote them down. He held little hope that these would be fruitful; he doubted that a prostitute dope addict would tell her parents the truth about much of anything, certainly not the real identities of her friends. In fact, the officer suspected that the parents knew more of their daughter's comings and goings than they cared to mention.

"Hell, I don't really blame them," he told Gamino later. "They're good, hard-working, religious people. They've got the right to protect their kid all they can." This was not a traditional hard-line police attitude, but it was Jerry's attitude. The one thing he could do was identify with poor people in despairing circumstance.

Within a few days—it was now late October, almost a month after the killing of John Hill—the detectives learned that Marcia McKittrick was under the umbrella of a pimp named Clete, out of Dallas. He booked her into various "spots." Hurriedly, the detectives ran a make on the man, but the disappointing news came back that Clete was residing in a federal penitentiary serving a long sentence for theft of interstate commerce, i.e., the hijacking of a truck loaded with automobile parts. Clete had been imprisoned long before the shooting on Kirby Drive. Obviously Marcia had a new manager by now. "Maybe she's free-lancing," suggested Gamino. Carpenter shook his head. "These damned old girls always have a pimp they give their money to," he said. "I never understood it, but it's always true."

Quick enough, an informer passed along the tip that Marcia indeed had a new alliance. He was also a fellow out of Dallas. The name, the snitch thought, was Bobby

Vandergriff. Or Vanderslice. Van-something. A funny, long last name starting with *V*.

Within half an hour a wanted bulletin flashed into every major police station in the United States and Canada, and to Mexican border guards. The presence of Bobby Vandergriff and Marcia McKittrick was desired in Houston by the homicide department. Had Jerry Carpenter made a bet, he would have given short odds that both would be arrested within a month. Fugitives with political connotations might find it possible to survive, through loyal connections, hidden in America. Jerry knew that well. But whores and pimps necessarily crawled on a more treacherous underbelly, every step a potential cave-in. Somewhere soon one or the other would get arrested, and the nation-wide network of police communications would bring them to Houston promptly.

But the weeks became months, and by early 1973 the homicide detectives were like men haunting a mailbox for a letter that never came. They drove thousands of miles over Texas searching for Marcia and Bobby What's-his-name, and once, in March 1973, felt they were close. A report arrived from the West Texas town of Lubbock. Local police had Marcia located at a "spot" motel. "Sit on her," ordered Carpenter. I'll be right there." The detectives broke across the night, over the yawning desolate highways of the empty part of the state, where a car radio is lucky to pick up the music of a Mexican station. In Lubbock they burst into the motel room where, sure enough, they discovered an irritated prostitute and her compromised customer. But she was not the girl they wanted. It would turn out that Marcia had fled town hours before the Houston officers arrived. Already a sister prostitute had taken her place on the sheets. And already Marcia McKittrick was swallowed up in the vastness of West Texas.

Six months after the murder of John Hill, the investigation was nowhere. They could not find Marcia. They weren't even sure of Bobby's last name. The two detectives were weary, cranky, and physically ill. Carpenter at one point suffered what he thought was a nervous breakdown and was hospitalized. But he was only troubled by a tormented stomach and digestive system, enduring as he had been on grabbed hamburgers, fried pies, and too much coffee. Their normal good humor was gone. They had become sour angry cops, under pressure from their captain, from the press, from the public. They kept the case, such as it was, in the trunk of their car, both to shield their investigative reports from press leaks in the office and to avoid having their brother officers know how pitifully scant were their results.

One afternoon, reading the latest in a continuing series of newspaper accounts that taunted, in effect, "No Progress in Hunt for Hill Killer," Jerry Carpenter seized the paper and crumpled it and threw it angrily against the wall. "I want that whore," he said, his eyes sparking fury behind his tinted glasses. "If I have to turn the state of Texas upside down and pour it into the Gulf of Mexico, I'm going to find that god damned whore."

29

Marcia had always been running—from the law, mainly—but also in flight from the constriction of what society dictated was a normal life. "Two things I simply cannot stand," she would say, ". . . to be bored, and to wait." Those who slip outside the fence usually cannot look back and pinpoint the precise moment of detour. Marcia could. Often she did just that, studying her life, closing her eyes and allowing herself a small measure of introspection, even sitting in her working clothes at the bar of a Las Vegas hotel. This was the only kind of waiting she would tolerate, waiting for the trick over there who was winning at the blackjack table, waiting to see how much money she could pry out of him.

For the first thirteen years of her life, there was little to tell and less to set her apart from the others. The sixth of nine children, she was quiet, obedient, helpful with housework, dutiful in attendance at the Baptist church, shy, not even cute in the tradition of most little girls. Truthfully, Marcia was plain, her demeanor and her hair color both mouse, a child given to gaps and silence. Her father was a disciplinarian, in partnership with the Lord in threatened wrath, and so strict, Marcia would remember, that, had he his way, his daughters would not go out of his house unless they were clothed in nuns' habits or the Baptist equivalent thereof. In counterbalance, the mother was overly lenient, shooing Marcia from housework. It was the duty of adults, she said, and soon enough Marcia would be a grown woman with a floor to scrub and babies to nurse. "Go out and play in the yard while you're still young," she often said, like the old women of Tahiti who bid the young girls dance on the sand until the passing years give them their turn to sit, sadly, and watch. In the small Dallas suburb of Mesquite, Marcia was a promising student, so fiercely committed to commendation on her schoolwork that she often sat up until dawn with a homework project. Her mother lost track of the times that she went to wake the child for breakfast, only to discover her still sitting at her desk, building a snowstorm of crumpled papers. "She was a perfectionist," the mother would recall, "and if she got less than an A, she would bawl and squawl."

She became a member of the school choir, the student council, the girls' pep squad. Her figure filled out rapidly and suddenly, and though she could never manage much over five feet no matter how hard she stretched, her breasts were admired and her hips widely coveted. The only source of foul weather on her adolescent landscape was a continuing feud with her older sister, Linda, of whom Marcia was sorely jealous. Linda was more beautiful, Marcia felt, and more popular. In every quarrel, Marcia always lost, for she lacked the temper of her sister. "Leave Linda alone," warned the mother, trying to sustain calm in her household. "Linda would argue with the Devil or a lamp-post."

When Marcia was fourteen her father moved his family from the comforting embrace of a small town to the city of Dallas itself. Marcia was thrown into a new and much larger school. "I'm lost, Mama," she complained. "Everything I had in Mesquite has been taken away from me." *That* move was the turning point in her life, Marcia decided for herself. That wrenching uprooting from familiar surroundings was the moment she boarded the bumper car that her life was to be. She became a friend of another fourteen-year-old girl whose specialty was truancy from school. The first time Marcia stayed away from school for an entire day, her mother sallied forth in search and found her daughter smoking cigarettes in the garage of her new friend's home. Figuratively seizing her by the ear and leading her back to class, the mother grew uncharacteristically stern. What happened to the little girl who would settle for nothing but straight As?

"I don't know," Marcia replied. "I'm just not happy with who I am and what I'm doing with my life."

"You're only fourteen," snapped her mother. "You're too young to worry about the way your life is going."

Marcia agreed, absolutely. Over the next few months, every time she vanished for a day, or sometimes three or four, every time her mother would search for her and find her and lead her back to school, Marcia would agree. Her mother was right. She was repentant, ashamed, full of promises that it would never happen again. But it always did. "That child!" sighed the mother. "I lead her to the schoolhouse door, and she goes inside, and she runs out the back door."

There came a violent confrontation between Marcia and her sister Linda over the older girl's boy friend. Linda accused Marcia of trying to steal him, of parading around the house and yard in vamping larceny. The two sisters screamed and threatened one another for several days.

Finally, in 1964, a few months before her fifteenth birthday, Marcia left home for good. She wrote her mother a poignant letter. "There's something in me I can't stop," she said. "I don't want to go to school any more. I've gotta try things on my own." It was the year after a President was killed in the city where she lived, and it was a time when the young of a nation were beginning to stir. Marcia felt no discernible political flutterings, only an uncheckable passion to run.

Within a few weeks the stumpy little girl who had sung so sweetly in the Baptist choir and twirled the baton so ardently for the Mesquite junior high pep squad was—incredibly!—appearing at Dallas' premier burlesque house, peeling off a borrowed gown to the wailing melody of "Walk on the Wild Side." She had a new name. Sindy Shane. The stunning caterpillar-into-butterfly came about because the first man Marcia met at a party when she left home was a middle-aged Dallas police character named Cousin Morris, a man wise enough to know that seduction of fifteen-year-old girls in Texas was a guaranteed penitentiary offense. But he felt it safe enough to keep a decorative youngster like Marcia around. She made him young and she made him laugh. One night Cousin Morris took his new protégée to the Theater Lounge where he was well known. The owner welcomed the valued patron and made approving note of

his companion, a blossoming young girl in hip huggers.
"With a figure like that," he suggested, "you oughta strip."
How curious, said Marcia, she had been considering just
that.

She rummaged through a backstage wardrobe trunk at
the night club and found a tight emerald-hued sheath with
thousands of hand-sewn sequins that would sparkle and
throb in the follow spots. "It was as if I had been rehearsing
for that moment all my life," she would remember years
later. "I wasn't afraid for one minute. I just got up there
and took my clothes off. And people were clapping and
whistling. For me!"

Marcia's name went up in scarlet paint on posters outside the club, at the bottom of a drawing card that included
established stars like Vikki Joye and Bubbles Cash. She
joined the union at fifteen—pretending to be twenty-one—
and began earning $250 a week, plus "tips" from the cus-
tomers she met after performances and conned into buying
"champagne" in shot glasses. Marcia was the baby of the
club, and the older women mothered her. They all sat backstage sewing on glitter and speaking of worthless but handsome men, and children abandoned to grandmothers. Pregnancy was an ominous prospect, for it could leave stretch
marks across the area most needed for public display.
Nightly, Marcia heard the warnings from the older sisters
of her art: "Tease 'em, take 'em, but, honey, don't let 'em
poke you with that thing or you'll end up at Sears Roebuck
selling cuptowels."

Nearing sixteen, Marcia nonetheless decided to sample
forbidden fruits. She experimented one night with heroin
and fell violently ill, missing several performances. When
her innards calmed enough for her to resume her act, she
swore never to try the drug again. Marijuana was softer,
and, in her crowd, among the characters who came to the
club and sat at the table of her benefactor, Cousin Morris,
smoking pot was as ordinary as drinking Pearl Beer. "I
grew up with these people," Marcia would one day remember. "They were my aunts and uncles and kinfolk. In my
family, I thought all fifteen-year-old girls smoked grass.
It was a part of growing up." Occasionally Marcia heard or
saw items of interest in her patron's home that whetted her
curiosity. Once a man knocked on the door and asked to
borrow a box of bullets and a rope, which Cousin Morris
immediately provided. On another day, she discovered two

men sitting on a bed dividing up more money than she had ever seen. And she knew that the guns resting casually on the mantel or the kitchen drainboard were not the kind that squirted water. For a time she was not exactly sure just what Cousin Morris did for a living. Then she asked. "Let's put it this way," he responded carefully. "I'm forty-six years old and I never got a Social Security card. 'Nuff said?" Marcia nodded. Her education in the character world was blunt. One: don't ask questions. Two: keep silent. "A loose mouth," Cousin Morris liked to say, "causes teeth to fall out." He emphasized this point by making a mock fist and directing it toward the child stripper's jaw.

A girl friend who, at eighteen, was sophisticated in all areas of the furry side of life suggested to Marcia that she could earn extra money with an occasional sexual appointment. The stripper refused, repeating what she had been told about the perils of pregnancy. It would destroy her burgeoning career. Already her name was moving up on the poster out front. The friend laughed and explained that a quick screw was lucrative, usually enjoyable, and not dangerous if precautions were taken. She knew of a car dealer in Fort Worth who liked young girls and would pay handsomely.

In the motel, confronted with her first customer, Marcia did not know how to conduct negotiations. She elected to set a high price on her services, realizing they were fresh and probably valuable. "How long you got in mind, mister?" asked Marcia, noting on her new watch set with tiny diamond chips that it was 8 P.M. on a spring night in 1966.

"Until maybe midnight," said the trick.

"Then that'll be four hundred dollars."

"Four hundred bucks! You must think your pussy's made of platinum."

"It is what it is, mister," snapped Marcia. "And it's one hundred dollars an hour."

Much to her surprise, the man reached into his wallet and handed over four crisp hundred-dollar bills. The rest was, as her girl friend had predicted, lucrative, enjoyable, and not productive of stretch marks. As would often happen in her career, Marcia became friends with the customer and saw him through three wives and four changes of city—though they never went to bed together again. "I have this strange power over men," she told a sister stripper. "They fuck me, then they want to adopt me."

Presently the diamond chips became whole stones, and they adorned her wrist and her fingers. She wore daytime dresses that cost five hundred dollars, smart afternoon suits from Neiman-Marcus with French labels. Once she borrowed Cousin Morris' gleaming silver Cadillac and drove to her old neighborhood, wearing dark glasses, prowling aristocratically around the yards and playgrounds where the girls she had once known—a thousand years ago!—were still clustered on front steps wearing blue jeans and prating of football heroes.

Occasionally she dropped into her mother's tiny country house, settling in for a few hours on clouds of perfume and jewels and money, explaining that her life was rich and ripe with promise. In her wake, a handful of twenty-dollar bills drifted onto the scarred sofa, an offering almost in scorn to the family she had so eagerly abandoned. But there were also nights when she missed them, missed even her sister's screaming tantrums, and when she closed her eyes the motel bed beneath her would turn into the sagging daybed with the chenille spread of her childhood. "Sometimes it was like I was living somebody else's life," she would say years later. "It was like I could step outside my body and watch myself. Sometimes I liked this person. And sometimes I didn't. None of it was really real. It wasn't me, you see. It was somebody else."

The first undoing was, of course, a man. An ordinary man. A fellow with a Social Security card named Lee, and he was nothing more than a punch-clock laborer for the telephone company. But he was strong and slim and cowboy-looking and kind, and absolutely worshipful of Marcia. Somehow his resolute squareness appealed to her as much as her expensive mysteries to him.

Hardly had their relationship begun before Marcia informed Lee that she would never marry him, nor would she bear his children. These conditions were satisfactory. All Lee wanted was her. *That* out of the way, Marcia presently fell ill from recurring stomach pains and went to see a doctor. He diagnosed a stomach malady, perhaps the beginnings of an ulcer. She was also missing her menstrual periods, but these had often been irregular. Not until her stomach began to swell, and not until the customers at the club began making pointed remarks about her poochy belly, did Marcia, not yet eighteen, discover that she was six months' pregnant. When she gave difficult birth to a son named Mikey, she fell into depression. Dejectedly, she studied her still lumpy body and knew that it would not fit into the green-sequined sheath, and even if it did, once she took it off in the spotlight, the ripples on her stomach would turn away customers. She cried for days, holding her baby as if he were a deportation order, banishing Lee from her side. But the hard economic realities of diapers and baby food summoned him back in quick time, and for a year they managed life together as a family. Rarely did Lee bring home more than eighty-five dollars a week, scant offering to a common-law wife who knew neither how to cook nor how to read the right-hand side of a menu.

Cousin Morris professed that he was still her patron and friend, but Marcia sensed his loss of interest when she visited with the smell of sour baby on her shoulder. The other characters who had teased and flirted with her for years now saved their attention for girls who had no responsibilities save painting their toenails purple. For a few months Marcia threw Lee out of their cheap apartment at least twice a week, only to realize she needed him. He was a pier to which she could tie her fast-sinking rowboat. Then Marcia discovered barbiturates, pouring pills into herself, not caring about much of anything once the downs had sedated her. Then it did not hurt so much if the phone failed to ring or doorbells went unanswered after someone peeked out at her through drawn venetian blinds.

She deserted Lee, dropping Mikey with her mother, mumbling something about a job in Florida. Turning a few tricks to renew her union card, shaking off her dependence on reds, and firming up her body to its pre-baby condition, Marcia found work as an exotic dancer in Tampa. Successful there, she moved south to Miami where at Gaiety Theater the reborn Sindy Shane created a sensation as a Tahitian princess being readied for sacrifice, with flaming torches and an oiled, muscled attendant. She commissioned another gown to be made entirely of tiny mirrors. "I want it to be like a thousand prisms," she instructed the seamstress. "It should absolutely hypnotize the audience . . . and me." On opening night, as per her direction, three slender beams of light broke the darkness of the stage, and as the wailing horn behind her began "St. James Infirmary," Marcia began to spin, throwing off infinite sparks of tiny light. She heard first a woman gasp and then a rain of applause for the power and beauty of the act. The only trouble was she did not want to take off the dress. She wanted to stay in the center of the stage and spin slowly, forever, if there would always be someone in the darkness to watch.

But Miami was a city of the old, and when her admirers all seemed to keep their teeth in a glass beside the bed, Marcia bolted. Once again she ran, this time to the North, to Rochester, where a sister stripper named Morgana promised a city of gold. En route, the two girls heard of a rock music festival and detoured. It was August 1969, the time of Woodstock, and for an incredible week Marcia wandered across the rolling cornfields of the Catskills, immersed in the culture of her peers. She was only nineteen, and it was the first time since she had left home so long ago that she was among people who were really her own age. And there were others who seemed just as discontent and restless as she. When one hand offered LSD she took it. When another held out mescaline she took that too. She swallowed whatever was offered her, fascinated by membership in a tribe of half a million youths who sought nothing but to hear music and dance in fields of wild lilac. Only when the others began stripping off their clothes and bathing nude in cold spring lakes did she refuse. "Honey, I get paid for that," she told one boy who beseeched her to join him naked. "Once I made $1,500 in one week."

"Shit, I wouldn't give you a quarter," the boy said, diving in, laughing.

Marcia never got to Rochester. Running out of funds, somehow losing the trunk that contained her gown of a thousand mirrors, she turned back south, to Texas, where she picked up her son, now a toddler. Woodstock had given her a taste for the simple life, and she found her way to the Florida Keys, living in a tumble-down shack, wearing blue jeans, letting the child run naked on the dunes. She built furniture out of driftwood and told herself that this was the way she would spend her years.

But within six months, before 1970 was half done. Marcia was back in Dallas, the child parked again at his grandmother's house. She made a halfhearted attempt at gainful employment, working briefly as a credit investigator, soon realizing that her best possibility for success in the labor force was not in typing. She became a full-time prostitute. "Why not?" she told a retired stripper friend. "Men buy pussy, I sell pussy. I can't think of a more sensible agreement." Marcia was a successful whore who found opportunity everywhere. One night she drove home from an engagement and saw a motorist cursing his flat tire on a quiet residential street. She stopped and with nothing on her mind but good will—she was in fact weary—asked if the poor man needed a ride to the nearest service station. It was at that point around 4 A.M. At 9 A.M., Marcia rose from the motorist's bed, thanked him for the $1,100 he had bestowed on her, and left, noting as she went that his tire was once again leaking air.

Her colleagues in the business wondered at Marcia's prowess. All they cattily beheld was a slightly chubby girl of twenty with a roundish baby face and hard brown eyes, teeth still uneven despite thousands spent in dentistry, and even a few pockmarks on her cheeks. These Marcia alternately explained as either resulting fom a severe onset of German measles or as souvenirs of a gang rape in Washington, D.C., by a group of zestful black motorcycle riders who tied her behind their wheels and dragged her across a gravel parking lot, followed by torture with lighted cigarettes. The way she told it, the tale sounded not only convincing but somehow adventurous and romantic. Perhaps, one competitor reasoned, Marcia was successful because she was so full of bullshit. "That girl!" remarked a sister whore. "She's always going off to Tibet and climb mountains or to Africa and become an empress." One thing Marcia did which no one could dispute was travel to Las Vegas and in her first week there strike up conversation with the proprietor of a small casino. She told him she sought legitimate work. Well, what could she do? "I can deal blackjack," she promised, glancing over at one of the tables where cards fluttered so easily. With no prior experience whatsoever, she thus became one of the club's best-liked dealers, so favored by the customers that when she grew bored in a few months the boss pleaded in vain for her to stay. "Can't do it," she answered. "I appreciate it, but it's time to split. I've dealt myself a bust." She traveled across town to the Strip, positioning herself on a prominent bar stool at the Cleopatra's Barge bar in Caesar's Palace, where in one remembered week she earned $10,000 for services rendered. Promptly she went out and bought the most astonishing ensemble that the city's most ostentatious store had for sale—a brown velvet pants suit, almost naked from the waist up save for two brief cross stripes of cloth, accompanied by an enormous cape with partridge feathers. If the cape displeased her, she could always wear the chinchilla coat and hood purchased by a grateful admirer who felt that Marcia had been largely responsible for his winning $67,000 at craps. She had, after all, stood at his side for sixteen hours as he flung the dice, and her yells had exhorted the winning combinations.

A year later, in triumph, eight pieces of luggage containing the riches of Las Vegas, Marcia returned to Dallas, bearing lavish gifts for her son and her family. She had tales of standing next to Dean Martin at a dice table, of meeting Raquel Welch at a hotel groundbreaking. "That sure is nice," said her mother, wondering what Marcia did to merit her position, but not wanting to ask.

Within a handful of months, Marcia was hooked on barbiturates again, needing so many of the tiny red pills that her closet began losing the partridge feathers and chinchilla; her jewelry box was soon bare of the diamond ring and emerald earbobs. "I'm broke," she told Lee, the father of her child. "And I'm scared." Of course he took her back, but his resources remained helpless to support her needs. On March 25, 1971, both of them were arrested by Dallas police on a charge of passing worthless checks. The checks were not forgeries; the trouble was their account was overdrawn $1,500 at the bank, and they were unable to make restitution. None of Marcia's allies in the character world were available to make bond, Cousin Morris having been unfortunately blasted to death in a high-stakes poker game. There was no one to help but Marcia's mother. So the aging, heavy, tired woman dragged all over Dallas, buying back rubber checks from grocers and five-and-dimes. Even then the police were not content, and the mother was forced to engage a lawyer to represent her daughter. She hired a former assistant district attorney named Charles Caperton, a blond and boyish-looking lawyer with a puppy dog personality and two sets of suits—one from the mail-order catalogue to wear into court and impress folksy, down-home juries, the other of continental cut and modish cloth, better to go with the substantial diamond rings he wore and the image he was most proud to offer. Attorney Caperton persuaded the district attorney's office to put the worthless check charges on the back shelf, knowing that years could go by before someone noticed they were still alive. In the meantime, Marcia and Lee would build a new life together.

For more than two years, from the first week they met, Lee had been urging Marcia to marry him legally. But always she refused. "I just can't get tied down," she told him. "You'd be miserable every time I ran off."

Marcia's mother suspected otherwise. She deduced that Marcia feared the loss of her son to Dallas County probation workers, who would seize the child of a mother with a penchant for criminal activities and award custody to the legal father. But in a common-law marriage, Marcia knew, the social workers were more inclined to leave the child with the mother, particularly if there was a willing grandmother at the back of the picture always able to house and feed a child. And thus it was, Marcia refusing to marry Lee, Marcia continuing to run on indulgent bursts to Denver or Las Vegas or even to Greece as company for a wealthy trick who bought her sea bass and retsina wine at a café in Piraeus and taught her to break glasses on the red tile floor. And always she would return just as suddenly, swooping her little boy into her arms and covering him with kisses and gifts, then hurrying away into the night—alone.

Marcia knew most of the characters in Dallas, they having been her off and on family since she first began stripping at the age of fifteen. One of them, the dashing pimp and burglar named Clete, counseled Marcia one night in an East Dallas lounge. The facts of life in her case were clear, he said. She was twenty-two years old, with three busts on her record—one for shoplifting, one for pot smoking, one for passing worthless checks—nothing major, but the Dallas police were cold, hard, and unforgetful. Best that she not work at home. Better that she fulfill her need for travel by working "spots," these being random two-week stays at hotels in Southwestern cities that allowed discreet prostitution. Clete would set things up, give her a copy of his "spot book," a valuable index of whorehouses in Texas, Oklahoma, Arizona, Arkansas, and New Mexico. The arithmetic in these matters was well established; if a girl earned a hundred dollars from a customer, she gave forty dollars to the night clerk or bellman. Of the remaining sixty dollars, half went to the pimp, who came around regularly to collect from his girls. The system thus awarded but thirty per cent of the proceeds to the person who did one hundred per cent of the work. But Marcia understood that it was always such and would always be. The alternative, Clete suggested, was settling into one of the few remaining permanent brothels in Texas. One was near Texarkana, another outside the central state farm community of La Grange. But these houses enforced rigid discipline on their employees, the girls rarely allowed a single day off in a six-month tour of duty.

Marcia shook her head vigorously. "No way," she said. "I've heard about the one near Texarkana. The old lady that runs it makes the girls get up at dawn and practically blows reveille. I wouldn't last a day until I told her what to do with her bugle."

Then, Clete gestured by making a wide circle with his right index finger, the remaining option is to work the circuit.

She would give the circuit a try. One factor in her decision was a belief that Clete was a singular man who spoke the truth. She had known him since her debut as a stripper. Clete had come into the club one night in the company of Cousin Morris, and Marcia had spent the evening in silent worship of the powerfully built, wide-shouldered, Gary Cooperish sort of man who spoke in wry rumbles. Later, they had a brief affair, she far more enamored than he. Marcia even harbored the secret notion that Clete was perhaps the father of her son. But this she kept to herself. During one of her flush periods, when the diamonds glinted from her fingers and furs swaddled her body, she suggested a more enduring relationship. Clete had laughed at the idea, but it was kind and appreciative, not derisive. "Look at you," he said. "You're got rocks on your fingers, you drive a Cadillac, you own the world. Whatta you wanna get mixed up with me for? The only thing I have a patent on is trouble."

Marcia learned the "spot" business efficiently. The mechanics were simple. "Hello," she would say cheerfully in a long-distance call to a motel night manager in, say, El Paso. "My name is Dusty, and I want an appointment for a couple of weeks."

"What kind of an appointment?" always came the response.

"Well, I sell pussy. *That* kind of appointment." Always, unless it was a prior connection, the employee would sputter ignorance, even indignation, and always Marcia would bide her time until the charade was done, then lay on a name or two of mutual interest. Clete, in particular. Only then would the "appointment" be granted, usually with a warning that the town was hot, the vice were active, and that the split would have to be fifty-fifty due to the pressures involved.

"Uh-uh," Marcia would shoot back in negation. "Sixty-forty. You'll make money. I guarantee it."

· Often the motel manager would ask, "Can you take a bust?" meaning, was Marcia's police position such that she could accommodate a routine, revolving-door vagrancy arrest and fine, or was she wanted on some other charge that would bring grief if visited by the police? "Well, I don't wanna get busted," Marcia usually responded. "But it wouldn't be the end of the world."

She knew that if a working girl could not tolerate a vagrancy rap, then the bellman would automatically get forty-five per cent of her fees, the additional five per cent needed as extra insulation from the police. Marcia was not sure what this entailed—a bribe, assumedly—but it was an old and unchallenged rule of the game.

Working "spots" was a comedown for the girl who had once made $10,000 in a single Las Vegas week, now reduced to setting up shop in motels flung across the American Southwest, and trying to wheedle fifty bucks for "short time"—thirty minutes at most—and wrestling with grunting, laconic old ranchers on thin sheets. But she prospered nonetheless, earning at least five hundred dollars a week for herself, even after commissions were deducted for the various agents involved. The best town was Houston, not for its "spot" certainly, for it was an old and peeling hotel on the fringe of the central downtown district, with urine-smelling corridors, but for the amount of money to be made. During one national convention held at the Astrodome in 1971, Marcia turned fifty-six tricks in five days and earned almost $6,000. At the end of the horizontal siege, she called Clete in Dallas and said she was exhausted —having average 11.2 acts of sexual intercourse per day— and was checking off the circuit for a while. "Don't blame you," said Clete. He was on his way to Houston anyway with a friend. They could all meet at Lilla's house.

Marcia often passed a few days at the comfortable home of Mrs. Lilla Paulus in the sedate West University section of Houston, not far from Rice University. Through her friends in the character world, Marcia learned that Lilla was a hospitable woman in her early fifties who held a more or less continuing salon for those who journeyed on the subterranean paths. The one-story red brick house seemed unlike any other on the block, but once inside, Marcia would later tell a probation officer, "it was twenty-four-hours-a-day non-stop fun and games." Lilla Paulus was a slender woman with high cheekbones that had once framed beauty, and above them were enormous eyes that gave her the look of a startled forest animal. Through her recently deceased husband, Claude, a prominent bookie and operator of a popular downtown "fraternal club" which had gambling in the back room, Lilla had become acquainted with certain men and women whose photographs and biographies reposed in police department files. She herself possessed a minor record, with arrests for vagrancy and investigation of bookmaking. But she could now enter any church in town and, on face value, be mistaken for the spinsterish schoolteacher who had pined a life away in memory of a tragic love affair. Marcia found it amusing that the gentle-looking Lilla could cuss better than any whore she had ever met, often carried a pistol with a pearl handle carved like a cameo, and stocked a kitchen supplied with good whiskey, marijuana, and a pot of deer meat chili simmering on the stove. All of these were antidotes to Lilla's loneliness and fear of advancing years. "When the characters gathered for a party," Marcia would later say, "it was like an arsenal. And when the doorbell rang, nobody opened it unless they had a drawn gun."

Sometime in mid-1971—the date is unclear, because Marcia was fuzzed with a renewed appetite for barbiturates —Clete arrived in Houston with the friend he had mentioned. No introduction was necessary as Marcia had met this old boy in Dallas years before. At the time, she took him for one of the most attractive and devilish men she had ever run across. Right off he called her "squirt," which was not an appellation she enjoyed. Instantly the twin forces of appeal and hostility had sprung up between them. Over the years she had seen him shooting pool and conspiring in the back booths of lounges in Dallas. Once he had even knocked urgently at Cousin Morris' door, seeking to borrow two sticks of dynamite. By repute, she knew him to be a moderately capable burglar whose trademarks were cheap brown cotton work gloves and a ski mask.

His name, she knew, was Bobby Vandiver. "If anything ever happens to me," Clete had said, "Bobby here will take care of you until I get my business straight." Hardly a month would pass before the need arose. Clete was jailed in a Southern state, charged with hijacking, and by the time he was sentenced to fifteen years in a federal penitentiary Marcia was in the arms of his best friend. True, she wept for Clete, but Bobby Vandiver comforted her. He had a terrific sense of humor. He was, in fact, the funniest man she had ever met. And in the dark, when he whispered foolishness in her ear, he sounded just like Don Meredith.

30

Bobby Vandiver was reared in the town of Venus, Texas, whose picturesque name belied a drab community of farmers within graying houses, on their knees in prayer that the sun would spare the summer vegetables from incineration, that the winter wind would not howl away the precious topsoil. Appearing at the end of the Depression decade, Bobby was the second child and only son of a part-time farmer and truck driver who ferried chickens and eggs to market in nearby Dallas. His mother could eke a week's meals out of one fowl, until on the last day there was nothing but bones in the watery soup. But the family endured, due to slavish attention of the father to work, from before each dawn until deep into each night, relentlessly whipping himself with no time for rest save fanatic attendance at the Methodist Church. The elder Vandiver possessed a severe moral code, so devoted to the law that his children made jokes about it. "If Daddy ran a red light," cracked Bobby, "he'd probably drive himself down to the police station and turn himself in." The father worked so hard and laughed so little that his face began to resemble the earth of Venus—thin, gray, weather-beaten. Bobby both feared and respected his father, but only modest rapport existed between them. They rarely talked; theirs was largely a world of avoiding one another. Bobby spent most of his early years alone, his best friends the books he read—Jules Verne and Mark Twain were favored authors—and his dogs. He always had a dog, usually one that would have nothing to do with any other human being save the young master. They all died, these dogs, horribly squashed on the highway. And always Bobby would hold mournful and private burial services, alone, tearfully screaming at anyone who came near the graves, cursing the speeding cars blurring toward Dallas.

His most dependable line of communication was with his sister Virginia, whose vibrant auburn hair earned her the predictable nickname from her brother of "Red." Bobby and Red took to holding "conferences," usually seated on the floor of the locked bathroom, sorting out their young lives. She, being two years older, loomed wise and was tolerant of Bobby's curious ways. "I like you best, Red," he always told her. "You take me like I am. You don't criticize."

It was to Red, his sister, and not his father that Bobby looked for commendation and attention when he brought home a string of crappie from a nearby lake, or a brace of doves killed neatly with the .22 rifle he bought with a coupon from the back pages of an outdoor magazine. The youngster reveled in the outdoors of Venus, sharpening his lean body by running across the cotton fields alone, leaping the neat rows of ripening plants as hurdles in his path. When the family moved to Dallas in the late 1940s, Bobby's life seemed traditional and ordinary. He collected merit badges from the Boy Scouts with ease and filled Red's charm bracelet with the miniature gold track shoes that marked his victories in athletic endeavor. In high school, Bobby's life was heavy with promise. He was vice-president of his class, star athlete, a capable student, and devastatingly successful with girls. They waited by the telephone for his calls, the best girls, the first in an ever lengthening string that would be attracted by his sexual power. The principal of the school autographed Bobby's *Sundial* yearbook with glowing testimony: "To Bobby V.—a good student, hard worker, and fine athlete. Your goal in life should be the very top." But a best friend scribbled his memoir edgd in gloom: "To Bobby, who if he lives to be 21, will be a miracle."

The reference was to Bobby's notoriety with the automobile, burning away unspoken demons by hurtling down highways. He often wrecked his chariots. The first such episode came the night that Red was married. His sister was eighteen, Bobby was sixteen, and he bitterly opposed the man she had chosen. Even as she dressed for the ceremony, Bobby burst into her bedroom and implored her not to marry. "It won't take, Red," he warned. She kissed her brother tenderly and promised that her special love for him would not be diminished by marriage to another man. After the reception, during which Bobby drank several glasses of champagne and glowered in a corner, refusing to congratulate the newlyweds, he took his father's car without permission and roared away, the squeal of rubber heard above the laughter of the hall. Speeding out a quiet street in suburban Oak Cliff, Bobby attracted the attention of a police prowl car, which gave pursuit. He ignored its sirens and flashing lights, pressing the accelerator to the floor, careening wildly, bouncing from curb to curb, slicing across front lawns, sideswiping parked cars, finally crashing into a telephone pole and crumpling the left side of the car so seriously that the vehicle could not turn left. But that did not stop him. Bobby kept going, making a crazed series of right-hand turns, laughing at the dozen police cars lunging toward him, still laughing as he drove into a predicament from which there was no way out but a left turn. Rather than do that, he drove directly into a wall, bricks and mortar showering the car, drowning out his cries of exultation.

His explanation was a rueful memory of too much champagne, but Red recognized the rampage as an act of anger against her marriage. Bobby denied any such thing, but not until Red's marriage broke and ended in divorce within a year—exactly as her kid brother had predicted—did a feeling of good will return to them.

Bobby's father built a good trucking business, enough to buy a series of three new Oldsmobiles, all of which Bobby borrowed, all of which Bobby wrecked. When the elder Vandiver finally had the sense to ban his son from the family automobile, Bobby assembled his financial resources from odd jobs and found a finance company miraculously willing to assist him in the purchase of a Thunderbird. "It's titty pink," he whooped on the telephone to Red. "It's the most gosh damned beautiful car in the whole world!" But the ink on the registration papers was scarcely dry before Bobby went to nearby Mountain Creek Lake for a wiener roast with his best girl, Carlene. There they quarreled over his need for a fuller emotional commitment from her. When she refused to tie herself down totally to the unpredictable boy with the streak of violence, he grew sullen. On the way home, with his Thunderbird crammed with friends, Bobby pushed his car to 80, then 90, picking up a highway patrol car. Noting the tail, Bobby floorboarded the Thunderbird, ignoring Carlene's screams to stop. The pursuing officer clocked the Thunderbird at 120 miles per hour, just at the point when it careened out of control and struck a telephone pole, shearing it in half as easily as a man would snap a tooth pick. The car was demolished, falling broken and smoking into a ditch, and Bobby crawled out, soaked in blood, screaming for help because he was convinced his car contained the dead and the dying. But only he was hurt, the others had been thrown free. At Dallas' Methodist Hospital, attendants had to place the strong seventeen-year-old in a straitjacket so they could sew up the deep gash on his forehead. "Let me alone!" he screamed. "Nobody can touch me unless I say so!"

A few months later, when the cut healed, the scar gave his forehead a raffish look. Once his sister caught him examining his face in a mirror, scowling tough-guy expressions at the reflection.

Retrospective examination of a life must be speculative, even by the one who has lived it. But in the unusual course of Bobby Vandiver's years the first turning point was as obvious as the day Marcia McKittrick fled her home to become a stripper. Bobby married, a few weeks after his graduation day, a girl named Betty Sue who told him that she carried his baby. Because she was known to be generous with her favors, Bobby was not entirely sure that he was specifically to blame. "But I might be," Bobby told his father. "So I guess the right thing to do is marry her." Alarmed at the prospect of his son marrying at seventeen, condemning himself to a life of barren work just as he himself had done two decades earlier, the father railed against the marriage. He spoke of lost dreams, blown away by realities harsher than the winds of Venus. Listening, fascinated, Red could not remember this kind of communication between the two except in the aftermath of the car wrecks. Now they spoke for hours, the man warning the boy that he would be plowing under his prospects for the better life that only a higher education could bring. Already there had been scholarship nibbles from small colleges whose athletic scouts had noted the boy's promise in long-distance running.

"I'd like to go to college," agreed Bobby. "And maybe I will. Things will just have to work out."

Then if his son was not one hundred per cent certain he got this girl pregnant, countered the father, take her to a doctor and be certain. He would pay for it. "It's a lot cheaper than marrying for the wrong reasons."

Perhaps because his father was so opposed, perhaps because he felt a mature responsibility at the immature age of seventeen, perhaps because he was tantalized at the prospect of becoming a father, Bobby married Betty Sue. And within one month she sent him out for Kotex, a coy way of informing her husband that she had been mistaken. But by the end of the first year of a marriage conceived in fraud, a baby son was legitimately born to the couple, and the now eighteen-year-old proud father happily passed out cigars on the loading dock. His work was picking up crates in his thin, hard-muscled arms and putting them into trucks. Six months after that, Betty Sue ran away with a man named Carlos and divorced Bobby. She informed him by letter that he was a no-account common laborer with no prospects for betterment, and that she was going to guarantee that their child, Davey, never had to shove boxes around.

For a few months Bobby visited his son regularly, bearing the child footballs and baseball gloves, tossing him into the air and catching him with delight. Then, abruptly, he resigned his parental responsibility and never saw Davey again after he was two. Only Red knew the reason, or suspected one. Her brother's sorrowful attitude was that the little boy would be better off without knowing that his father was the kind of man Bobby was so suddenly turning out to be.

After Betty Sue's wrenching departure with the child, Bobby began hanging out at a drive-in restaurant in North Dallas, a magnet that drew the kids in their fresh-waxed convertibles, the budding punks with their vacant-eyed ladies, the hookers, the pushers. The carhops wore red and white drum majorette uniforms with dancing fringe stopping high above white boots that displayed provocative flesh. The premier waitress was Maudeen—statuesque, black hair, huge purplish eyes, olive complexion, and a poutful mouth that dispensed easy repartee and profane indignation at cheapskate tips. Not only did Maudeen deliver cheeseburgers and beer to the attentive customers, she was open for business after hours, working under the aegis of a pimp named Preacher, so called because his father was a faith healer. Bobby fell desperately in love with Maudeen, although his desires went unfulfilled. For the first time in his young life a woman feigned absolute indifference to him. All Maudeen did was laugh at his juvenile importunings and wiggle off with the hard-earned dollar bills he threw down on her tray. "Wait till you grow up, hon," she teased. "It takes a bigger bat than you got to play in the major leagues." But gradually, even though she maintained a hands-off policy, Maudeen took to inviting the ardent dock worker on after-curfew rounds with her and Preacher.

When Red began hearing infatuated praise for the incredible creature named Maudeen, she drove to the restaurant and eyed her brother's new treasure. Then she asked a few questions around. It took little effort to learn that Maudeen and Preacher were two-bit police characters, suspected of stealing a little and selling dope. "She's trouble, Bobby," warned Red. It was her turn to prophesy. But Bobby only shrugged. "She's the kind of trouble I'd like to get into, Sis," he answered.

Somehow Maudeen came up with a small printing press. Concurrently, she and Preacher hatched a scheme to print phony company payroll checks, then travel far out of Dallas to cash them with false credentials. They needed a third man, both to help with the driving and to saturate thoroughly the major check-cashing groceries of a distant city in one frenetic late Friday afternoon period. This, Preacher reasoned, was the time of the week when thousands of payroll checks were being cashed, and, moreover, there would be no opportunity to check their genuineness until Monday morning. By that time the travelers would be long back in Dallas, pockets full of easy cash.

For five months the forays worked, just as Preacher said they would. He never printed checks for more than ninety-nine dollars, figuring that any larger sum might catch a clerk's attention. Bobby and Maudeen, curlers in her hair, posed as husband and wife, she feigning impatience to get on with the buying of groceries for a hungry brood out in the station wagon. Bobby's father was the first to note a change in his son's behavior. The boy was still living at his family home in Dallas, and whereas he was previously the

possessor of a good work record on the loading dock, now
he suddenly started missing work, particularly on Mondays
when he dragged in from weekend "fishing trips." Moreover, his wardrobe perked up, and a new gold wrist watch
appeared on his arm. When the foreman at the loading
dock called to complain that Bobby was jeopardizing his
position as "lead man" and was grouchy and full of sloppy
moves, the elder Vandiver summoned his son for a conference. Bobby refused to speak of his behavior. Silently
shaking his head, he walked out.

In the winter of 1961, Bobby and Maudeen successfully
passed three of Preacher's worthless checks at Birmingham,
Alabama, groceries, but on their fourth stop a clerk grew
suspicious. At number five, a few blocks away, police
stepped out from behind the courtesy booth and arrested
the Dallas man and his girl friend, both twenty-one she instantly hurling total blame on Bobby and sobbing that it
was not only his idea, but that he would have harmed her
had she not gone along. Preacher got out of town fast.
Bobby's father received the news of his son's arrest and
immediately flew to Birmingham, spending most of his life
savings on bail and attorney fees. The pair was convicted,
but because it was a first offense both received probated
three-year sentences.

Hardly back in Dallas, Maudeen broke probation by
shoplifting a cheap plastic bracelet at a drugstore and was
returned to Alabama to serve her penitentiary time. From
her cell, she wrote Bobby long and tearful letters of regret,
vowing that only in the shadow of bars could she see her
true love for him. Touched by the revelations Bobby rode
a Greyhound bus through the night, across the pine forests
of East Texas, Louisiana, and Mississippi, arriving at an
Alabama prison bone weary but anticipating an emotional
reunion with the woman of his fantasies.

Maudeen walked hesitantly to the bench and sat down
opposite the dividing rail. She weighed eighty-four pounds.
Her eyes were opaque—empty She looked mostly at her
lap. In six months she had gotten religion She spoke to
Bobby in Bible verses. Then she abused him for his worldly
ways. "But in your letters you said you loved me," pleaded
Bobby. Maudeen shook her head and looked into the middle distance. "That was before I found God," she said.
"When I get out of here, I don't ever want to see your
kind again." She quoted a Bible verse: "There are new

heavens and a new earth that we are awaiting according to His promise, and in this righteousness is to dwell."

Sadly, Bobby rode the bus back to Dallas and tried to forget Maudeen. When she was released from prison she moved to Nebraska, married a banker, and became a prominent figure in church and community affairs. Bobby became a burglar.

The major cities of Texas traditionally rank in the upper echelons of the national crime statistics, partly due to the large populations of blacks and Mexican-Americans among whom such deeds are unhappily a way of life. Dallas has the reputation of being the meanest Texas city, possessing not only large minority ghettos but a historically conservative body politic that reveres the right to own guns. It is also the loose headquarters for a substantial group of thieves and killers which somebody, probably an inventive newspaper reporter, once branded the "Dixie Mafia." The name stuck, even though those to whom it pertained howled at the label. Certainly there was no formal crime syndicate, and no blood oath, such as binds the national Mafia of Sicilian parentage, nor where there territories to divide with organized rackets. The only glue that bonded several hundred outlaws in the Dallas area was the camaraderie of pursuing the same kind of work. The fraternity favored a handful of bars with their custom, and there they bragged of scores made, of women added to their wake, and of helpful contacts should a brother be traveling to a distant city. Principally their callings were burglary, safecracking, narcotics peddling, and pimping. But many of the free-lance criminals had guns for hire, and often they used them on one another. In a seven-year period from 1965 to 1972, thirty were shot to death either by their peers or in battles with police.

One night, in the back booth of an East Dallas lounge, Bobby, twenty-one, was asked to join a group of four older men, in their mid-thirties and early forties. Their plan was to break into a doctor's office and haul away his safe, reportedly full of cash and morphine. They needed a strong pair of shoulders; Bobby, though he still had the body of a runner, had plenty of experience lifting heavy crates. All he would be required to do was stand lookout in the yard, then help carry the safe to a truck. His anticipated share: at least $3,000. On the night of the job Bobby trembled with both cold and excitement. The plan proceeded as schemed, until it reached the crucial point of lifting the 2.000-pound safe and carrying it to the truck. His hands hurting from the bitterly cold January night, Bobby lost his grip and the safe crashed to the sidewalk, mashing his hand and his foot in its descent. Bobby screamed in pain and awoke a neighbor. A porch light switched on. Dogs began to bark. The frustrated thieves drove hurriedly away, cursing their new and bungling accomplice.

The next morning Bobby telephoned his sister and asked her to bring over bandages and medication. He had been moving an icebox, he lied, and it toppled and fell on his foot. When Red arrived, her brother blurted out the truth. "Well," sighed Red, "your foot is broken. I'll have to call a doctor." No! As Bobby quarreled with his sister over the danger of that, an urgent knock on the door interrupted. Two detectives were at the threshold. They arrested Bobby Vandiver on a charge of burglary. Their case was not only airtight, it became a famous and almost laughable one in the history of Dallas crime.

When Bobby dropped the safe, it mashed his hand on the way to breaking his foot. And when police arrived to examine the safe, found unopened outside the doctor's office, they found an indisputable clue. Wedged in a hinge of the safe was a neat and precise right index fingerprint—not only an impression but *the actual flap of skin*. The falling safe had sliced off the tip of Bobby Vandiver's finger. No bungling burglar ever made police work so easy.

"Why?" asked Red quietly, when just before the sentencing they shared a secluded moment together. "I'm not criticizing, Bobby, I told you a long time ago I would never do that. But maybe I could understand you better if you'd tell me why." As she spoke, she brushed away a wet place on her cheek, and the charms on her bracelet jangled, all the mementos of her brother's athletic career. Bobby had no real answer. He was bored, maybe, he said. The plan had seemed exciting, and it *was*. "Until the god damned thing fell on my foot, it was the most terrific sensation I ever had," he said. "And it was something I was doing all by myself. My own decision. Don't blame yourself."

Red nodded. She tried to understand. "Maybe he had to

go out and be his own man," she later told her father. "Maybe we all protected him too much. Maybe we didn't let him grow up. Well, he's certainly a man now." She tried to make light of the impending sentence "It'll only be a few months." she predicted "And at least we won't have to worry about him wrapping his Thunderbird around a telephone pole."

As he stood before the judge, Bobby kept his silence, obeying even as a novice the "character code." He refused to name accomplices. He would have the court believe that the burglary was his and his alone. "You're some man," commented the judge sarcastically. "I haven't met many fellows who could pick up a one-ton safe and carry it off alone. Two to five."

The only person who moaned audibly in the almost empty courtroom was Bobby's father. His face went white. His grief, Red noted, was worse than death. He cried as his son was chained to others who were sentenced, then led out of the courtroom. For the next two years the senior Vandiver drove 250 miles every other Sunday, as often as the rules permitted, to visit his son in the state penitentiary, trying to repair the years when they could not speak. He even ordered a photograph taken with his arm around his son, Bobby wearing white prison work clothes and a sheepish expression, and pasted it prominently in the family album, as if to say he had no shame only love.

Bobby emerged from the penitentiary fit and tanned and full of juices. Red had never seen him so appealing. Not yet twenty-five he was exceptionally handsome and virile. She accompanied him to the East Dallas lounge which was his traditional hangout, and the ladies of the bar flocked about him. He seemed like a lean centurion returning from triumphant battle, ready now for the grapes and kisses due a victor.

Red seized a moment of his time and put a question to him on this homecoming night. "Are you going to go straight?"

"Maybe," he said. "And maybe not. But I'll tell you one thing. Red. Next time, I just won't get caught."

For a time he dallied with legitimate endeavor. When he remarked at a family dinner that he was interested in chinchilla breeding. having read of it in the prison library, the elder Vandiver rushed to fill his garage with a dozen of the expensive and contrary animals. Enamored, Bobby tried to breed them, cursed them, even appeared on Sunday morning television as an "expert" on the business. But within a few months his interest was gone. "I got tired of smelling chinchilla shit," he told Red, "and the little bastards wouldn't screw when I told them to." Then, incredibly, somehow eluding a background check, he even obtained work as an installer of burglar alarm systems, and delightedly seized the opportunity of casing offices as he wired them, returning at nights to relieve them of valuables. When Dallas police arrested him again on a charge of possessing burglary tools, their response was both laughter and embarrassment. "Bobby's the flakiest burglar we've got," said one of the detectives. "And the damnedest thing about him is he always owns up to what he's done. He's almost cheerful in his confessions."

His second penitentiary sentence lasted eighteen months, and once again he was released in fine fettle. "You always look your best when you get out of jail," remarked Red. The only drastic change in her brother was a sudden and ferocious turn against the religion of his youth. Whereas he had once been awarded a ceramic attendance pin with a dozen bars for twelve years of perfect attendance, Bobby now demanded that his sister never mention God or religion again in his presence. When he turned on the car radio and a burst of gospel came forth, angrily he twirled the dial for another station. Driving past churches, he made obscene gestures. And at the funeral of a distant relative, when an old woman beside him murmured, "It's God's will," Bobby disagreed audibly: "God has nothing to do with this. The man is dead. Dead!"

This new attitude worried Red, for she was still shaped by the Sundays of her childhood. But she did not intrude on Bobby's feelings. Their relationship could not withstand criticism, only toleration. By the time Bobby was thirty, Red no longer even questioned the fact that her brother was a burglar. Oh, of course he held jobs from time to time, selling campers, used cars, whatever. But these were only covers to fool parole officers. He stole. He took money and valuables that did not belong to him. He even had a philosophy of crime. "I don't do anything violent," he told Red once as they drank beer together. "I won't even carry a gun. Why risk violence when the stuff is just lying there and so easy to take? It's justified. It's covered by insurance, anyway. Nobody gets hurt."

Now and then Bobby would talk to his sister about his work, but not so much of the danger, or even the potential rewards. He wanted her to know about the day-to-day details of burglary, of how cold it could be while sitting motionless in a clump of bushes waiting for a light to go out inside a target house, or the frustration of trying to quiet a barking dog. Once, he told his sister, he was even taken for a dog and almost killed. He and three colleagues were burglarizing the office of a drive-in movie after the Saturday night proceeds were put in a safe. It had become Bobby's custom, his trademark, to wear both brown cotton work gloves (after the humiliation of leaving his finger-print flap on the safe's hinge in his first disastrous burglary) and a ski mask, both to hide his face and to warm it, for he always complained of the cold night air. In the movie's office, while the others labored to open the safe, Bobby heard a noise and dropped to all fours, crawling toward a window to see if someone was coming. En route he bumped against a box and it fell. One of the other thieves whirled and saw only what appeared to be the brown paws and muzzle of a watchdog and fired reflexively, fearing the attack of a guard dog. Bobby hissed, "It's me, you damn fool!"

Red married again, this time an aircraft worker whom Bobby liked, and the subsequent children of the marriage became his special favorites. Bobby's pattern was to disappear from his sister's life for several weeks, only to burst in again unannounced. If he bore expensive gifts for his sister's family—a tiny teardrop diamond necklace for the little girl, a cowboy suit for the boy—then Red knew well their source. "What can I buy you, Sis?" he once asked. "I never know what to get you."

"All I want is for you to go straight," she answered. "Not square. Just straight."

"Then you want too much," he said. "I can't buy that."

Often Red prepared dinner for her family, called in vain for her children, and then went in search of the neighborhood for them, only to find that her burglar brother had the youngsters under his spell. Once she stood on the edge of a playground and watched as Bobby threw Frisbees, caught footballs, organized relay races, led a pack of ecstatic, squealing little ones up a giant old pecan tree and across its branches—"Watch out for the panthers!" he yelled—mesmerizing his flock. They would have followed his flute, laughing, into the sea. "You should have been a coach," she told him when she finally assembled her family for a cold and overcooked meal.

"I should have been a lot of things, Red," he said. "But I am what I am. Pass the potatoes."

Bobby had the ability to talk on most any level. With the kids he was eight years old, to a pollster calling on the telephone to question political preferences he was an informed voter with knowledge of all the issues (although his prison record denied him his franchise), to the brother characters he spoke the argot more skillfully than any. He was the only one in the family who would bother with a senile grandmother, partially paralyzed after a stroke, condemned to a wheel chair and to continual wandering through the decades of her life. She annoyed her descendants, but Bobby found time to sit by her chair for hours, talking as her friend, her grandson, even becoming her long-dead lover, gently moving in and out of the roles that she assumed in her aging agonies.

For several weeks in 1965, Bobby stayed with his sister in suburban Dallas and rarely went out. He seemed in need of home life, enjoying Red's children and cooking, mowing the lawn, falling asleep on the couch during the late show. Often Sis heard him speak quietly on the telephone, declining offers to go somewhere or do something. A spark of hope caught within her. Her brother was wrestling with some unfulfilled need. Perhaps, she thought, the other life was over, or at least stalled on dead center. She even discovered him reading the newspaper's classified ads in search of work. But then one evening an old friend called and asked Bobby to fetch him at a party; his car would not start. In the gray just before dawn Bobby telephoned Red from the Dallas jail. He was under arrest for possession of narcotics. His story was that he had barely walked through the front door of the apartment where the party was being held when police broke in and took him into custody. "It's a bum rap," he said. "I wasn't holding anything. Maybe it was a setup. I thought it was funny that just as I arrived everybody started leaving." Red immediately thought of some of the "jobs" he had been turning down on the telephone. Maybe this was someone's perverted notion of revenge.

With two previous penitentiary sentences, Bobby now faced—under Texas law—the possibility of a life sentence as a habitual criminal. He bargained for six years' hard time in Huntsville. And bitterly he went away to give at least half a decade to the state of Texas. "The other convictions were deserved," he told his sister. "But the only crime here is a god damned crime against me." The only mercy in it, he said, was that his father was now dead. "I couldn't stand six years of his crying every other Sunday."

But the Vandiver family album did add new photographs, one of Bobby at a drafting table, practicing his new-found craft of design—while in Huntsville he helped draw plans for a new wing of the prison—and one of him wearing striped jailbird pajamas as a gutty participant in the bull-riding event at the annual prison rodeo. This spectacle, held on the four hot Sunday afternoons of each October, is a popular event in Texas, drawing free world crowds eager to see condemned men risk their bones in contests against beasts. In one particularly favored contest, a sack containing twenty-five dollars is tied around the horns of a vicious Brahman bull. Then the creature is turned loose for those prisoners foolish enough to try to snatch the sack, eluding, if possible, the potentially deadly horns. One year Bobby was the winner, and the family album photograph shows him exultantly hoisting his bag of money. But the next year he failed and was badly gored in the stomach.

Due to good behavior and popularity among prison officials—throughout his relationships with police and guards he usually kept in their favor—he served less than three years and was released in 1970. He was thirty-one years old. Almost one fourth of his life had been passed behind bars. In his third homecoming from prison, there was none of the festive air that had marked the others. Now he was sullen, silent, reluctant to speak even to his sister.

He became a pimp, starting with a skinny, tormented nineteen-year-old whore named Reena who quoted poetry and spent most of her hours stoned on mescaline. She adored Bobby and clung to him like a tic to a collie. Whenever Bobby needed money, she drifted away for a day or two, turned a few tricks, and returned with cash in hand for drugs and wine. Soon there were other girls, Bobby learning the "spot" business from his friend Clete and dispatching his employees to the whorehouses of the Southwest. For a time Reena stayed in favor as his principal courtier, and then, when her infatuation turned to LSD and she became unreliable, Bobby cast her out. Later he heard that she had been sent to an insane asylum where, hallucinating, she enacted Mary Magdalene in search of the Savior.

Bobby had no trouble collecting girls who wanted to work for him, but he was not a very good pimp. If one of the whores held back money on him, and he knew it, he would not beat her, as pimps were supposed to do. "I can't get used to hitting women," he told Red. He let his hair grow long and shaggy, and he cultivated a drooping mustache. Red thought he looked disreputable, and told him so —as if he was hoping to reclaim lost prison years by trying to look young and hip. But other women disagreed. His life swarmed with them. Even Maudeen, the repented carhop forger, returned for a brief interlude from Nebraskan domesticity. She lay next to her long-ago lover for a month, then, sated, returned to propriety. Carlene, the childhood sweetheart who had been the catalyst in the wreck of Bobby's titty-pink Thunderbird, reappeared for several months and bore him a child—his second. Then, sensing that it was better for all concerned, she took the baby and vanished.

In the summer of 1971, at a night club in Dallas, Bobby presided over a table brimming with characters. Beside him was a short, full-bodied young woman with an immense hairdo and brown eyes smothered in mascara and false lashes. She dominated the evening, full of anecdotes about the men who had rained thousand-dollar bills and chinchilla furs about her, of the days when she held center stage in a gown of a thousand tiny mirrors. Red, present, took an instant dislike to Marcia McKittrick. "I don't like her," she told her brother. "She's Swiss cheese. There are holes in everything she says."

Bobby shrugged noncommittally. "She's nothing," he said. "She's just a whore who works for me."

For a brief time Marcia occupied the seat next to Bobby at the character gathering places, only to be replaced by a girl named Vicki. "This one's just a little kid," Bobby told his sister. "Doesn't have a lick of sense." It seemed reasonably true. Vicki had fire-pole legs and stood almost six feet in heels, well over Bobby, and there were few curves in a plankish body. She had reddish hair and never said much. When Bobby spoke character talk, Vicki nodded knowingly, although Red recognized that she had no frame of reference for what he was saying. Bobby could have been speaking in ancient Aramaic. Nonetheless, the shy Vicki adored the three-time ex-convict, and something in her naïve freshness touched him Once, years before, when Bobby and Red had sat on the bathroom floor of their parents' farm house in Venus, they had discussed "true love." "It doesn't exist," Bobby had said. "People just make do the best they can." Later, when Red met and became engaged to the man who would become her second husband, she wrote to her brother in prison. "I think I've finally found *it*," she said. "Maybe it does exist."

Now it was Bobby's turn. Shyly he made confession to his sister that he had fallen for Vicki. But, boyishly, all he could manage to say was, "Remember that time, Red, when we talked about *it*? Well, I was wrong." With *it* came ambitious responsibility. Vicki had two children from a first marriage, and Bobby delightedly took them on as instant family, moving everybody into his sister's small, overcrowded tract house. Red was so happy to see the new maturity in her brother—at thirty-two—that she cheerfully made sleeping pallets for the floor and got up a half hour earlier to prepare for work at a factory. "I might be able to get you some kind of job there," she told her brother. "You'd have to run your story down to them up front," she said, using the "character" terminology, "but once you got your foot in the door . . ." She let the sentence dangle, its possibilities unlimited.

What kind of work was she talking about? Bobby wanted to know.

On the loading dock, said Red bluntly. The hardest kind of muscle-knotting labor. She could not articulate her notion intellectually, but somehow she felt it was possible for Bobby to erase—if only symbolically—all the years since his first arrest, by moving back to square one, the same kind of exhausting but honest work that had begun his adult life.

Bobby said he would think about it, and indeed he revved himself up to make application. But then the telephone rang and Bobby spoke in a muffled voice. Disappearing for a few days, he returned to Red's home unshaven and dejected. In his hands was a ski mask. He threw it angrily into a corner. "Everything I try to set up falls apart," he said. "I can't even score enough bread to buy milk for Vicki's kids." All he wanted, he said, was one modest stake, enough money to put aside the old life and live quietly with his woman and his family. For several more weeks he continued going away without explanation and returning in deep depression. Once Red saw him staring at his automobile, a 1950 Ford with stuffing coming out of the seats, as if it were the monument to his life and his despair. He was disgraced that Vicki had to take a job as a cocktail waitress during one of his long absences, and each time she brought home money, he was mortified.

Then Vicki became pregnant and encountered difficulty in carrying the baby. There was danger that she would miscarry unless she stayed in bed and could afford the services of a gynecologist other than the one who so brusquely treated the poor people at the county hospital. In a whirlwind of renewed activity, Bobby burst out of the house each night, bundling up in his sister's blankets and sweaters, in pursuit of midnight money. Red noted him swallowing a handful of uppers; his body seemed stretched like a slingshot. But after several forays there was no money in his pockets. Even his whores moved out on him, for when he became committed solely to Vicki, they were denied the father-lover who was the foundation of their labor. "I'm not much of a man any more," he told his sister.

Then a call came from Houston. Bobby spoke quietly, turning his back so that Red could not hear. When he hung up, he seemed both animated and troubled. He headed for the front door. Then, with an air of fatalism, he turned back and issued a haunting directive. "If I ever die," he said, "just throw my body in a ditch somewhere."

"Don't talk that way," said Red.

"Dead is gone, Sister. It's the end of the string. I don't want any preacher man mumbling God words over my corpse. If you hire a preacher man, I swear I'll come back to haunt you."

Red shook off the macabre thoughts. "Where are you going?"

"To Houston. If I can get that god damn wreck out there started."

"Are you taking Vicki?"

Bobby shook his head negatively. There was no time to explain. Red gathered that he was hurrying to an appointment in Houston that could give him money, perhaps his manhood.

31

As the events would be one day reconstructed by authorities, Marcia McKittrick was staying at the home of Lilla Paulus for a few weeks during the summer of 1972. One afternoon she was luxuriating in a bubble bath when Lilla entered the bathroom and sat down next to the tub. Lilla spoke of a "contract." Would Marcia's new friend, Bobby, be interested in filling it?

"I don't think he does that kind of work," Marcia would remember saying. "But I'll ask him."

Marcia well knew of what Lilla spoke. She had been overhearing murmured talk in the household of an opportunity that existed to kill a man for money. And she further knew that the contract had been "shopped" around her world for several months. When she next saw Bobby and mentioned it, he quickly turned the offer down. Assassination was not his line. Never, in fact, had he been a violent man. Just the other day he had been playing pool and, angry over losing ten bucks, he hit his pool cue against the bar railing. A piece of the tip broke off and flew against his opponent's cheek, causing a trickle of blood. Bobby insisted on taking his barely wounded friend to a doctor who could be trusted for a dab of mercurochrome and a Band-Aid.

Besides, Bobby told Marcia, he had heard from others that this "contract" was fraught with peril. At least two able killers he knew had considered the offer, checked it out, and turned it down. One professional hit man with the chilling reputation of having slain somewhere between ten and fifty men with his busy gun had analyzed the difficulties for Bobby. The target was supposedly a doctor. The fellow worked most of the time in the Hermann Professional Building in Houston, which, during office hours, had hundreds of people milling around the parking garages, lobbies, pharmacies, corridors, and suites. Impossible to shoot someone discreetly there! And the doctor lived in a big house on a wide-open boulevard, on a busy and prominent corner no less, with a wife, a child, and servants. Moreover, the neighborhood was River Oaks, one of the nation's most exclusive preserves, heavily patrolled by private security guards, with watchdogs behind every azalea bush. "You slow down around there at night, and in ten seconds there'll be a radio car asking your business," the hit man cautioned Bobby.

The price being mentioned was $5,000—$1,000 down, the rest on completion of contract. "That's pretty low rent for this kind of work," complained Bobby. Maybe he should at least *talk* to Lilla, suggested Marcia. No. Bobby declined. He felt both apprehension and the uneasiness of a man asked to do a job for which he held no experience.

That night he telephoned his sister in Dallas to inquire after Vicki. "She may lose that baby," warned Red. "She's spotting pretty bad."

The next day he told Marcia that he normally did not kill people. "But I'm ragged," he said. "I'll do it."

Wildly, carelessly, he ran with all the speed of his youth away from the white colonial house, where inside the doctor lay dead. At least he prayed that the son of a bitch was dead. He had kept coming at Bobby, over and over again. The squirrels he had shot on the farm in Venus had always fallen, quickly, silently from their branches. But the doctor fought him until there was no more lead in the gun. His mind spun in hysteria. Almost screaming in fear and exultation, he leaped the sculptured lawns as if they were rows of cotton, weaving across the massive Tudor and French provincial estates, the oaks with their mossy fingers reaching down twisted demon fingers to imprison him. He wanted more of the reds in Marcia's purse to gentle his pounding blood, for he was almost straight after the deed, and his veins were bursting and his position terrified him. There was even blood on his face—he could feel the clammy wetness—and whether it was his own or that of the doctor, he did not know. He wiped it away and dried his hand inside his windbreaker pocket, but at that moment his hand brushed against the still burning gun. His other hand clutched the briefcase that Lilla had said would contain at least $15,000 in cash, maybe as much as $25,000, that the doctor was secretly bringing back to Houston from Seattle. Eight hundred bucks! That was all he found in the wallet, and nothing of value in the briefcase, nothing but papers and medical pamphlets. A police car, siren screaming to break the quiet twilight lull of the lavish neighborhood, screeched around a corner on two wheels, and Bobby quickly lowered his head so that no one could mark his face. Even with a head swimming in barbiturates, he knew that he was as noticeable as a red buoy on a blue sea. He ran to a house and pressed his trembling body against a wall. Ahead he saw a row of thick, dense bushes bordering a house. He ran to them and impulsively threw the briefcase under a clump, kicking it back deep into the growth. And, a few steps away, he threw the gun under some shrubbery, stopping to brush dirt over it. Later, a thousand times he would curse this stupid act, but at the moment he was governed only by fear. He *had* to dispose of the gun and the briefcase, for the night was clamoring with sirens.

Now, freed of these connections to the dead man, he began searching the street signs for Kirby Drive. At least a dozen times he and Marcia had circled these blocks on casing expeditions. He thought he knew them as well as his sister's face. But now, in his desperate flight, they seemed to loop and swirl and dead-end. The carefully rehearsed plan was for Bobby to walk calmly along Kirby Drive several blocks south to the House of Pies where Marcia was waiting with the car. She had promised to stay put, close to the public telephone, in case something went wrong and he had to call. But now he could not find Kirby! He saw a man tending to his front yard up ahead, and Bobby slowed, trying to make his face puzzledly calm, his feet slow, and he asked for instructions. Which way was Kirby Drive? Helpfully the man pointed, smiling, for in that neighborhood it was like asking a resident of mid-Manhattan which was was Fifth Avenue.

Running again, he saw ahead a busy street, heavy with traffic in both directions. He searched for a sign. South Shepherd Drive! Cursing, he ran across the courtyard of an apartment project and paused only long enough to bury the doctor's billfold in a garbage can. He had kept it this long in entertainment of a notion to search the hidden compartments at leisure and keep the credit cards. But there was no time for that. He trotted along Shepherd, imagining himself a jogger and hoping others would take him for one, and when he came to an intersection and another busy drive called West Gray, he whooped happily at the sight of a public pay telephone. He dialed the House of Pies and waited. After two rings, Marcia's familiar drawl answered softly. "There's been a rumble," Bobby blurted. "I'm at a Stop 'n Go market on West Way." Marcia repeated the street, echoing Bobby's mistaken pronunciation of "West Gray." Then ten eternal minutes crawled past. Bobby stayed inside the phone booth, swearing that he would strangle Marcia the moment she arrived. *If* she arrived. She could not be more than two minutes from his spot, and yet she had not shown. Perhaps she had bolted, flaky whore that she was, running off to Tibet as she had always vowed. Suddenly Marcia pulled up and honked, almost merrily. Bobby threw himself into the car and sank down low in the seat. It was done, he said. He had killed the doctor. There was eight hundred dollars in his wallet. He had not intended to kill the bastard, but he had fought. "He kept coming at me!" gasped Bobby.

Then he grabbed Marcia's arm. "You stupid ding!" he shrieked. "What took you so long?" She giggled at the use of his nickname for her, fixed as she was on the twin points of adventure and hysteria.

"Well, *you* got the name of the street wrong!" she said in defense. "You told me West Way. It was West *Gray!*"

Marcia would remember driving crazily to Lilla Paulus' house, becoming lost several times, backing up, making illegal turns, at one point veering into a ditch. Bobby lay on the floor at her feet, worried that he would be arrested for murder because he had put himself into the hands of a retarded prostitute who could not even drive a getaway car. Over and over he screamed at her to keep the car on the road, but she, too, was full of grass and pills, and the route blurred before her. The ten-minute trip took thrice that as the nerve ends of the car's occupants raged at one another. Waiting for them—Marcia would later recall—was Lilla, her serene and composed spinster face suddenly taut and jerky. On the ride, Marcia had not really focused on the enormity of their deed. But seeing Lilla suddenly consumed with uncharacteristic fear, Marcia felt her stomach knot. She ran to the bathroom and tried to vomit.

"Well, I did it, that's for sure," Bobby said harshly, and the deed became even more permanent with his announcement. He hurried immediately to the bathroom, ignoring Marcia's wretching, slashing desperately at his droopy mustache, hacking away the identification. Later, months later, Marcia could not remember the whole night. But there were shards that pierced her awake. Then, sometimes she would even burst out laughing, for the aftermath was not without elements of black comedy.

Marcia would later recall Lilla rushing around her house in a purge, burning any threads that might bind her to the work—newspaper clippings, even an old photograph of her. Marcia, and Bobby, posing drunkenly. She had a clear recollection of Lilla opening a small chest and counting out money to Bobby—$5,000. Then Bobby promptly gave her $1,500 of it back, $500 being expenses, $1,000 being a sort of "finder's fee" for steering him to the job in the first place. She saw Bobby stuff $3,500 into his pockets and then jerk his hand as if the money was acid.

She could remember hearing of John Hill's murder on the 10 P.M. television news and everyone standing in front of the set transfixed. Her recollection was that Lilla began rushing her unwanted guests out of the house, nagging them to be gone. Marcia threw a suitcase into the car trunk and slammed the lid. When, moments later, Bobby was ready to leave, the keys were nowhere to be found. Marcia had locked them inside the trunk! For an hour Bobby struggled with a crowbar, trying to pry open the trunk, Lilla dancing and chattering at the impossible predicament. At one point Lilla contended that it was possible to get into a trunk from the rear seat, and she climbed through wedging her slim and aging body into the trunk, then finding herself unable to either open it or return through the narrow opening. Now, locked in an ovenlike prison, she began to pound in terror. Marcia collapsed on the driveway pavement near hysteria, at the same time certain that any moment a police car would appear and capture them. Finally Bobby pried the trunk open and extricated Lilla. And they were off.

Marcia could not recall the drive to Dallas, other than a memory that the radio played hillbilly music throughout the long night, and that they arrived near dawn, both strung out from amphetamines that worked in contradiction to the afternoon's downs.

The first thing Bobby did was wake up a hairdresser friend and have his hair bleached. Marcia went to visit her son and listened to the six-year-old child read from his primer. Later in the afternoon she caught up with Bobby and burst out laughing. The attempt to lighten his dark brown hair had been disastrous. Four applications of bleach had turned his locks a pinkish orange, and his scalp was festered with blisters from the peroxide. As Marcia was now wearing her hair in an electric red shade—Bobby said it looked like the "Jesus Saves" neon sign atop a Baptist church he once knew—their coiffures were hardly those to aid them in finding anonymity. "Don't laugh at me, you crazy ding," Bobby ordered grouchily, but Marcia could not control herself. Suddenly both burst out and began rolling about the floor of the hairdresser's apartment, the tension of the previous night in Houston momentarily broken.

They decided to separate for a while, Bobby—wearing a blond wig—moving back to his sister's home. The moment he came into her house, Red knew something terrible had happened. Bobby was never clever at concealing his emotions. He lay on the bed blankly, staring at the ceiling, unable to sleep or eat. Red came and sat beside him, not knowing how to help him.

Finally Bobby spoke. "Talk to me, Red," he begged.

"I want to. But I don't know what to say."

"My brain is hurting, Red. Make it stop."

She touched her brother's forehead tenderly.

A week later the news broke in Houston newspapers of Gamino and Carpenter discovering the suspected murder gun in bushes near the home of Dr. John Hill. Bobby heard immediately and telephoned his sister at her place of employment. "I've gotta split for a while," he said. "Tell Vicki I'll be in touch. I'll run it down to you later."

When he picked up Marcia, she was afloat in heroin. She had not used the drug since she once tried it as a teenager. Bobby slapped her across the room. "We've got a big enough load without that shit," he said angrily. "Why'd you start up on that again?"

"They just found your gun in a flower bed," she said airily. "Seems like a good time."

"*My* gun? You're the one who got it offa that nigger doctor."

Marcia giggled. What difference did it make now?

With the $3,500, Bobby purchased a 1970 yellow and white Lincoln Continental, the perfect car for an inconspicuous drive to California, and economical, too, in a period when Americans were caught in a gasoline shortage. But when he sat in the car's luxurious lap, it was better than the embrace of all the women he had ever known. They drove to North Hollywood without incident and rented a neatly furnished apartment. There they lived for a few weeks as recluses. It was a barren life of television and frozen dinners. Then the money played out, and Bobby rang up a contact in his traditional line of work. When he purchased brown cotton gloves and a ski mask, Marcia protested. "You're crazy," she said. "You don't know the territory, and the L.A. cops are heavy. One burst will do it." Pointedly, Bobby brought up Marcia's increasing need for heroin. She was shooting up at least three times a day. Even Bobby had chipped a little on occasion, insisting that he could handle the drug without fear of addiction. If they needed money all that bad, countered Marcia, then she could go out and in one evening's work earn it less dangerously than Bobby in his stupid ski masks. He refused. Their relationship was complex and deep, and although he would never openly confess that he actually loved Marcia, never admitting more than that he was bound to her in exile, he would not permit her to resume prostitution. Marcia well remembered some of the bothersome but at the same time touching things Bobby had done when he once functioned as her pimp. Although she was his principal wage earner, he interfered at every opportunity. Once he burned her spot book, apparently in hopes that she would abandon her work. On another occasion he came to the motel where she was working in North Texas and terrorized the night manager, posing as a vice officer, threatening to burn down the establishment unless all whoring stopped. Her strong suspicion was that he had some quirky, unexplainable attraction for her, and that it was best accommodated by bizarre behavior.

Rather than get into another fight—their months together had been punctuated by frequent brawls, and both bore scars and enduring mementos from the sluggings—Marcia sighed and told Bobby to go out and do his work. The next day he returned with $750 and three color television sets. Los Angeles was ripe, he told her. The Hollywood Hills were full of rich homes hidden in canyons and cul-de-sacs, easy to pluck in broad daylight when the owners were away. Soon there came a day when Bobby revealed that he had been a participant in a bank robbery—the blowing up of a night depository—and the proceeds were $50,000. Marcia clapped her hands in excitement, but Bobby warned her to calm down. The money was not yet in his pocket. It was being divided; his share would be forthcoming. But it never was; his colleagues disappeared.

Frequently, Marcia telephoned to her mother's home near

Dallas and received reports on her son. Once she spoke with the little boy and hung up, crying bitterly. Bobby wanted to know the reason for her tears. "My child," she said, "has just been selected out of the entire school to represent the first grade in a program. He is the best reader on his level." Morose, Marcia shot up and stayed in a heroin fog for several days. When she awoke from a long sleep she found Bobby gone. He was away for almost a week, and in his absence terror mounted within her. She suspected that the Houston police had her name, that the gun registration had been traced to the black doctor from whom she had taken the gun. Now Bobby was gone, and she had no money to run. When he returned, a few dollars in his pocket from a pennyante burglary, she railed at him. "Do you have any idea what it's like to sit in this cheap shit apartment and wonder what's happened to you? You could be in the Hollywood jail for all I know! It drives a person crazy!"

His response was to walk out, slamming the door. Marcia screamed in his wake, "I won't be here when you get back." "Yes, you will, ding," yelled Bobby through the door. "I locked up your clothes." Marcia ran to the closet and yanked at the knob. A new police lock glistened at her. Naked, she sat down cursing and crying.

A few mornings later, when Bobby was out casing a new score, Marcia took the five dollars she had stolen from his pockets while he slept and took a taxi to the Hollywood-Burbank Airport. There she telephoned collect to a pimp friend in Las Vegas who wired her an airplane ticket. The pimp, a black man named Sparks, met her at McCarren Field and expressed dismay over Marcia's appearance. Her hair was unshaped, her face pale, her body stringy from the heroin and the abstinence from most food save candy and colas. "Give me an hour," she said. "You got some working clothes?"

By midafternoon Marcia was wearing a hot pink pants suit and was at her familiar stand, Cleopatra's Barge, in Caesar's Palace. She had been there but ten minutes when a middle-aged man sat down beside her. An hour after that she flew with him to Palm Springs for a sexual matinee, and by suppertime she was back in Las Vegas with $800. At the end of a week she had $6,000. She telephoned Bobby in Los Angeles and taunted him. "Just go ahead and keep stealing," she said. "That's your habit the way some people have dope habits. But don't expect me to sit around wondering whether you're alive or dead."

"Where the fuck are you?" Bobby demanded gruffily.

"Alive, baby. Alive."

But by deep November, Marcia was in despair. Every time a door opened or the telephone rang, her heart jumped. When she walked, she looked both ahead and behind at every step. When she drove, her eyes were riveted to the rear-view mirror. It was but two months after the murder of John Hill, and she knew that the state of Texas was boiling with police in pursuit of her. She had thousands of dollars in gambling chips scattered around her apartment, and a purseful of high-grade heroin, barbiturates, and amphetamines. In her closet were a dozen spectacular outfits. But none of it was what she wanted. She cursed Bobby Vandiver. She wanted him and his droopy mustache and his lean hard arms, and she wanted her son, and she wanted to push back the clock to when she was fifteen—when she decided that all she needed was herself. For most of the day before Thanksgiving she wept, watching her make-up drip off her face in fascinating rivulets. Then she went to the Desert Inn, threw away all of her money on blackjack tables, took the few dollars that remained, and rented a room. There she sat down on the bed and placed seventy-two tiny red barbiturate pills in a neat row around the pillow. Ceremoniously, without hesitation. she ate each of them until the border was bare. Then she injected two grams of heroin into her arm. As the narcotics rushed over her senses, it occurred to Marcia that this was one scene she would have liked to play before an audience. Where was the gown of a thousand mirrors? She should spin and fall in her final exit, feeling the eyes of the spectators locked to the power and beauty of her farewell. Their applause would be the last sound she heard. Stumbling, fighting to sustain a shred of rationality to guide her steps, she left the room and took an elevator to the hotel lobby. The casino was a carnival, spinning and blurring like an insane kaleidoscope about her. She caught a final glimpse of herself in a mirror, and the reflection was that of a fool.

With that she fell to the carpet. "Ace deuce," she murmured, welcoming whatever was in store for her.

32

Bobby stood over her hospital bed in Las Vegas, grinning helpfully. He had thrown away his blond wig and his hair was darkening again, with his melancholy mustache in place. He looked once more exactly as he had looked in the last hour of John Hill's life. "Well, ding," he said in greeting, "you blew that too. Now are you ready to come home?"

Marcia stretched out her arms and pulled Bobby against her chest. "Just get me out of this fuckin' hospital," she said, starting to cry. "They keep coming in here and telling me how lucky I am to be alive. They said by all rights I shoulda died." Her mouth and throat ached, from where the doctors had put the tube down to her stomach to pump out the poisons.

They drove to Palm Springs, where a character friend had offered his house. En route, Bobby filled her in on details of the unsuccessful suicide. "I hear it was the best floor show the Desert Inn had in years," he said. "Sirens, ambulances, dudes runnin' in with stretchers, women screaming. You really pepped up an otherwise dull afternoon."

The other news was that there was no news from Texas. Bobby said he had called Lilla long distance but she hung up on him. And the case was off the front pages, only a little mention now and then.

Bobby's new plan was to lie low here for a few months, collect a little money here and there, and buy false identification documents through an outfit in San Francisco that provided phony passports. Marcia could spin the globe and put her finger on it to stop, and wherever that was, they would find it. Content, and for the moment secure, she snuggled close and told herself that nothing else mattered. She was with Bobby, and what happened yesterday, or what might happen tomorrow, did not count.

In Palm Springs, Marcia regained her strength and announced that she would cook a belated Thanksgiving dinner. This came as startling news to Bobby as he had seen Marcia encounter difficulty in peeling off the aluminum foil from a frozen enchilada dinner. But he bespoke encourage-

ment and waited. For an entire day Marcia domestically
tended the bird, consulting the wrapper that had contained
it and cookbooks, singing merrily all the while. Her major
mistake was cooking the turkey upside down in an ir-
regularly heated oven, and at day's end the bird emerged
not golden brown and juicy but tough, dry, and dead
gray. Bobby laughed, and in anger she snatched up the
spoiled turkey and threw it at him. He threw it back, and
for a time they played an absurd game of football. Finally
Marcia hurled her disaster into the swimming pool, pushed
Bobby in after it, and thus did a much-wanted killer and his
lady pass another day in a sun-warmed city of the old and
bored and rich.

Christmas was a time of pain, for Marcia marked it as
the first one she had not spent in the company of her son.
She telephoned the child at her mother's home outside
Dallas and tried to keep her voice under control. "Mama's
fine, honey," she said. "I have to work out here for a
while, and when I get home we'll go to Six Flags." The
little boy always talked of the day he had spent with his
mother at the amusement park between Dallas and Fort
Worth.

When Bobby telephoned his sister on the holiday he
spoke briefly, then hung up in despair. Vicki had miscarried
and lost his son. He swallowed a few barbiturates and sat
stonily silent for the rest of the day, while carols from the
radio filled the bleak room.

In January 1973, once again in Los Angeles—four
months after the murder—Marcia grew restless and walked
out on Bobby. He was running with a new pack of thieves,
and the risks he was taking alarmed her. She had heard
from a girl friend in Dallas that the two Houston detectives who were looking for her had grown fanatical in their
search, rousting prostitutes from their beds, squeezing
snitches for shreds of information. The relationship with
Bobby was sour; she could no longer bear his moods, his
temper, his wrath when he took off his shoes and his rings
and squared off for a fight with her. He always said he
couldn't hit a woman, but he could sure *wrestle* with
Marcia. She loved him every day, or at least she needed
him every day, but he was in the grip of forces she could
not anticipate or accommodate. "I can't take this shit off of

you any more," she yelled. Bobby made an ushering gesture with his hands, showing her the door.

Hurrying to Las Vegas, she set up shop at a Strip hotel and became reaffiliated with Sparks, the black pimp. His apartment was a treasure cache of drugs. But within a few weeks she fell ill with fever, nausea, and chills. When her eyes turned yellow, she knew it was hepatitis—from injecting heroin with a dirty needle. "If I'm fixin' to die," she told herself, "then it's gonna be at my mama's house." Terribly ill, she flew to Dallas and fell into her mother's embrace. That night, fearful of touching her son and giving him the disease, she bade the little boy sit across the room from her bed and read to her from his primer. She fell asleep, happy.

Marcia refused to go to a hospital, even the one where her mother worked as a nursing aide, for fear that her heroin addiction would be discovered and that in turn would bring the police. She insisted on staying at home, in her old bed, peering out the window every time a car threw gravel on the road in front of the small house. After a few weeks the yellow tinge to her skin and eyes cleared, and she felt her strength returning. She wanted to confide in her mother, for the old woman did not know the trouble her daughter was in, only that the Houston police had come looking for her. But Marcia could not summon the courage to make confession. Instead, she threw herself into an exhausting spurt of housework, as if she needed clean labor, scrubbing floors, washing windows, moving furniture around, promising to pay for a total redecoration once she was able to get out and work. Then, as abruptly as she had come home, she left again, muttering something about a job in West Texas. Her mother protested, but Marcia was gone.

For a time Marcia worked the "spots" in West Texas, staying a day or so in San Angelo, moving on to Lubbock or Odessa. Then she telephoned home and her mother had disturbing news. The Texas Rangers had come looking for her, and the Houston homicide detectives had called to warn that Marcia was in danger of being killed by "characters" unless she contacted them.

"Why don't you at least call them and see what they want?" urged her mother.

"I know what they want," said Marcia. She hung up quickly and packed, running to the bus station, not knowing that within an hour Gamino and Carpenter would be in her very room, cursing the whore who had taken her place in the bed.

In early April she slipped back into Dallas for her son's birthday, and the day before the event, while she was wrapping presents, the telephone rang. It was Bobby. He was still in Los Angeles, he said. He asked if she was all right. And was she ready to come back to him?

"You're really crazy, Bobby," she answered. "We can't make it together. Don't you understand that it's a whole lot easier to be miserable *without* somebody than with somebody? Let's blow it off permanently."

Bobby persisted. But his voice did not have the faraway crackle of a long-distance caller. The connection seemed nearer. Marcia grew suspicious. "Where are you?" she demanded.

"L.A.'"

"I don't believe you, Bobby."

"Why?"

"Because you hesitated before you answered. That always means you're fixin' to lie."

Bobby laughed. And surrendered. "As a matter of fact, I'm about seventeen hundred miles from L.A."

Marcia was startled, and ired. "Then that puts you in downtown Dallas at this very minute. Now I *know* you're crazy. Get out of my life."

The next day, after the children went home full of cake and ice cream, Marcia drove to a nearby grocery to buy food for the evening meal. While there she telephoned home to ask if her mother had thought of anything else the pantry needed. Her mother spoke urgently. Ten minutes after Marcia left the house, a car of Texas Rangers had driven up, demanding to know her whereabouts. They even arrested Marcia's sister and old antagonist, Linda, mistaking her for the woman they wanted. "They know you're in town, honey," said the mother. "They want you real bad. What happened? For God's sake tell me what's going on."

In panic, Marcia ran to a motel and took a room, trying to calm herself. She thought of a hundred solutions, but they all dovetailed back to Bobby. She needed him. And she had an idea how to find him. Wearing dark glasses and a wig, she went to a bar called the Painted Duck the next afternoon. Hardly had she taken a seat in the gloom than Bobby came in. "Hello, ding," he said. "You come here often?"

She told him of the fires licking at her. He shrugged. What else was new? A better idea was to drop by her motel room and talk horizontally. Marcia shook her head in disbelief; the entire state of Texas was bent against her and all Bobby wanted was to attend his crotch. "If you have any notions whatsoever about us getting back together again, then forget it," she said. "I'm leaving town. Dallas is a bad place for either of us to be."

Word was around that the Houston cops now finally knew Bobby's last name. Another snitch had told Carpenter.

"Calm down, ding," soothed Bobby. "Just where you fixin' to go to?"

She could go anywhere, said Marcia, summoning her old bravado. A trick in Denver would send her money. A man in Atlanta would gladly dispatch his private plane. There was a long list of men who would rush to help her. She rattled on, throwing up the false gods, watching Bobby slip into blackness and anger. Finally he rose and said, "Then I guess you don't need me any more." He threw his scotch and milk directly into her face and walked out of the bar. She waited until he was well gone before she found a bar towel to dry her face. But it was hard, for she kept crying.

Bobby had been in Dallas for a few weeks, hiding out at his sister's home. Red still did not know the desperateness of his situation. He had wrapped himself in the security of his family, growing emotional when Red produced long-wrapped Christmas presents from under a bed where they had been kept for months, awaiting his return. After her miscarriage, Vicki had taken a nearby apartment and Bobby spent occasional nights there, still in love but not totally at ease with the thin and quiet girl any more. Red could sense his shame and humiliation at having been away during her miscarriage. The afternoon that he ran into Marcia at the Painted Duck, Dallas police arrested Vicki at her apartment and took her to headquarters for questioning. She refused to tell them anything. The officers also went by Red's house in search of Bobby.

In panic, he called a character friend who could normally be trusted. Bobby needed a hideout. The friend had one, a cabin on a lake near Dallas called Little Elm Reservoir. It was deserted this time of year. No one would find him there. In his flight he took along a girl named Sherry, an occasional prostitute whose arms were full of puncture marks. She had worked for him now and then as a whore, and was devoted to him, and would at least offer the company of another human being.

Captain Joe Murphy of the Dallas division of the Texas Department of Public Safety, the state's crack police force, had picked up a piece of news from a snitch paying a due bill. A dude named Bobby was supposedly holed up at a lake shack near Dallas. The character world grapevine had it that this Bobby No-last-name was wanted in Houston for murder. Not making any important connection, Captain Murphy routinely called Houston. Were they looking for some old boy named Bobby to clean up a murder? Jerry Carpenter grabbed the phone. "If it's Bobby Vandiver, we sure as hell are!" he said. "Have you got him set down pretty good?"

Captain Murphy had no idea. He called the Dallas police and asked if any of their officers could recognize Bobby Wayne Vandiver on sight. Lieutenant A. M. Eberhardt, a Brooklyn-born man who had never shaken his New York accent, spoke up. He certainly could. He had arrested Bobby for his very first offense. "I busted him the time he fell on that safe job," remembered Eberhardt.

The news was passed on to Carpenter in Houston. As much as he wanted to make the arrest himself, the homicide detective knew that he could not gamble on the time it would take to get to Dallas. "Go ahead and run on him," he ordered. "But don't tell him anything about a murder. Just say he's wanted down here for questioning about an old burglary."

It was true. Bobby had been arrested on a charge of possessing burglar's tools in Houston in 1972, and he never turned up in court to answer the charge. A convenient warrant was thus out for his arrest.

The day was gray and cool and a wind made infant whitecaps on the lake north of Dallas. Bobby lay on an old leaky water bed; Sherry was stoned. She had begun to open a can of chili, but the only cooking pot had hardened food from the night before still in it, and the necessity to wash it had seemed overwhelming. She slumped beside the sink, sitting on the floor, trying to read a movie magazine, whimpering, wanting another fix. Bobby would not let her go out, for he had seen a suspicious-looking man walking around one of the deserted cabins the day before.

Then he looked through the window and saw them coming. Three cars. Eight men. All with drawn guns. One Ranger in boots and Stetson even had a machine gun in his hands, stalking the awakening spring earth as if it were the jungles of a South Pacific island. He recognized Lieutenant Eberhardt from a thousand years ago. He smiled ruefully. When the knock came, he took the gun from beneath the pillow and gripped it. "Let 'em in," he softly told the girl.

The officers burst in with their weapons a forest of menace. Bobby, wearing only jeans, barefoot, rose and held up his hands in surrender. Captain Murphy instantly saw the .38 beside his bed and grabbed it, as the others threw manacles on the arms and legs of their prisoners.

"They need to talk to you in Houston, Bobby" said Lieutenant Eberhardt. "How you been?"

On the ride downtown Bobby mentioned that he had briefly considered making his arrest more difficult. "I thought about letting you guys hold court on me," he said, using the character world euphemism for going down with guns blazing. "But I was afraid that skinny old girl would get hurt."

Now it was a prize fight—Gamino and Carpenter in their corner, Bobby in his. Each side spent a day or two sizing the other up, making tentative jabs, withdrawals, no damage done. The cops made sure to obey every constitutional rule, informing the prisoner that he was being charged under an old possession-of-burglary-tools offense and, as this was his fourth felony complaint, it was the ultimate one. Bobby faced a conviction under the habitual criminal statute, which meant an automatic sentence of life imprisonment in the state penitentiary. Under this charge, no bail was allowed; there was, therefore, no question of Bobby slipping from their grasp under bond. He was offered the right to counsel, but he declined. "I can handle myself," he said. The police knew they were dealing with a professional, not one apt to be seduced by salt and sugar routines, with one cop coming on as a Spanish inquisitor, the other as Father O'Malley. The contest was raw and elemental, between two strong forces, neither knowing exactly what strength the other side possessed. Not until the second day of questioning was the murder of Dr. John Hill even mentioned.

Jerry Carpenter, who had been bantering in whore talk almost pleasantly, suddenly asked, "Did you kill Dr. John Hill on September 24, 1972, here in Houston?" Behind his tinted glasses, his eyes were suddenly cold.

Bobby feigned wondrous innocence. Not only did he posses no knowledge of such a terrible deed, he was not even in Houston on that date. Yes, he remembered positively. He was in Dallas then. Relatives and friends could place him there.

"Then," suggested Carpenter, "you won't have any worry about making a showup." Bobby nodded helpfully. He had no objection to standing in a line of men and displaying himself for some witness in a darkened theater.

In the morning showup, Connie Hill studied the faces of seven men but was unable to pick out Bobby as the one who grabbed her blouse and killed her husband. "I'm sorry," she told Joe Gamino. "I only saw him for a split second and then I started running." At that moment, seven months ago, Bobby was wearing a green pillowcase over his face because he had been unable to find a ski mask for sale in Houston in September. At Connie's failure, Jerry Carpenter was momentarily disappointed. But in the afternoon the child, Robert Hill, fascinated at participating in a police drama, watched intently as the prisoners shuffled into line. After a few moments of somber study, the boy narrowed the list down to two. One of the prisoners he pointed to was Bobby Vandiver. And in the evening lineup, Myra Hill was instantly positive. Tight-lipped, she nodded in her definitive fashion. "That's the man," she whispered to the detectives. "There's no doubt in my mind."

This damning information was laid on Bobby, but he would not budge. "She's crazy," said Bobby. "How can I defend myself against a crazy woman?"

Joe Gamino turned philosophical. Speaking gently and easily about his experience in such matters, he talked abstractedly about multiple defendants. The history of such cases is that the one who co-operates first gets the best deal. "It's all a matter of who gets down with us first," he said. "When and if we get Marcia, and she gets down, then it'll be rough on you."

"And by the way," pressed Jerry Carpenter, "where is Marcia McKittrick?" Bobby denied knowing a night creature of that name. "Oh, come on, Bobby," insisted Carpenter, "we know you're her old man. And we know she got the gun from the black doctor. And you got the gun from Marcia and you killed John Hill with it."

Well, it was certainly true that he knew a little of the whore business, allowed Bobby, but he did not know a lady of that appellation. His denial dropped heavily in the oppressive room of interrogation, a lifeless place of dirty blue walls, a barrel desk and chairs, a speaker box in the corner that, though functioning only for public address announcements, gave the appearance of a Big Brother ear, listening, recording.

Carpenter meditated a few moments, then had an idea. A long shot. He suddenly took out his pencil and drew two dots on the face of the desk, each six inches apart. He assumed the manner of a professor illustrating a lecture. "Here's you," he said to Bobby Vandiver, pointing to the first dot. "And here," he said, moving the pencil across to the other mark, "is Dr. John Hill." Slowly, stretching out the suspense, he put two more dots in between. He drew a line of connection between the first dot named Bobby and the unidentified second dot. "This is Marcia McKittrick," he said. Then his pencil hovered over the fourth dot. He pushed down hard, snapping the point. From a corner of his mind he pulled out a fourth name. "And this is Lilla Paulus." With a slashing motion, he linked all four dots, like a child completing a numbered puzzle.

Bobby stared at the desk top. He expelled his breath, sharply. "Oh, wow," he said. "You know *her* name."

Carpenter nodded, hoping that his face would not betray his gamble. Several times during the investigation, the name of Mrs. Lilla Paulus had arisen, the first time one week after the murder. Now and then it had come up again —he knew that Marcia occasionally slept there—but the name was only one among many. As a bluff, a dangerous bluff if it had not worked, he elected to throw in her name in his game of dots; he would later bless the fates that made him win.

"Why don't you get down with us, Bobby?" he said. "Get your business straight."

For a long while Bobby sat silent, staring at the dots. Finally he opened the door, but only a crack. "If I *was* to get down," he tempted, "how much would you need to have?"

"We want it all," said Joe Gamino.

"What if I didn't know it all?" said Bobby, suggesting that names were involved which were unknown to him.

"Then I'd have to talk to the DA," said the officer.

Again, silence. The detectives could watch the forces of torment working within their prisoner's gut. Gamino intruded gently. Would it be worth it to a man to spend the rest of his life in a penitentiary, if that man was not the only one involved in a murder? Now would it, Bobby? Bobby was tired, he wanted sleep. A few hours later, after a shower in the police gymnasium and an uncomfortable meal in the police cafeteria where Bobby sat in a storm of blue uniforms, squirming, unable to eat anything but a package of crackers, he asked to see the district attorney.

Bob Bennett quickly dropped what he was doing and drove the few blocks across town from the Harris County courthouse to the Houston city jail. He was a young assistant DA in the middle thirties, a short, ambitious prosecutor who somehow resembled the formal oil paintings that hang in statehouse rotundas. There was the air of a nineteenth-century senator about him, even in his dark hair that fell in indented layers about his ears. Bennett was respected at the police station, both for the moonlighting weekends he put in advising officers on legal points in cases about to be filed or dropped, and for always making himself available to help them through the maze of courthouse red tape. He had a picture-book wife and children, a pleasing and funny manner of self-deprecation (with the ability to put on various accents and faces), and a very real awareness of the distasteful necessity of negotiating with suspected criminals. Bennett's franchise at the DA's office was organized crime, though Houston was the largest American city without a Mafia family structure. He knew little of the background of the John Hill murder case, but what he did recognize— as had so many others before him—was that here was a case with enormous potential. A man could run for district attorney someday on the power that successful prosecution would net. But he further sized it up as a case deadly with mine traps. Gamino and Carpenter told him on the telephone that they were reasonably sure they had the trigger man in the Hill murder, but if anyone else was to be implicated, it would take some skilled bobbing and weaving.

The two men, prosecutor and killer, had much in common, and from their first meeting a rapport was struck. They shared the same Christian name; both were country boys. Bennett had grown up in a small Louisiana town, son of an oil field worker, and like his adversary in the police interrogation room, he played sports with skill and passion, remarkably scrappy due to his slight stature of only five feet eight inches. A Tulane University football scout had come to see him play and burst out laughing at the notion of awarding a scholarship to a player that modest in dimension. Not only was Bennett the first member of his family to seek education beyond high school, he was the first to lift himself from the restrictions of his social caste. He and Bobby Vandiver could have talked for hours of how to bale hay and of football scores and of the lakes of East Texas where wide-mouthed bass slap against submerged cotton stumps, or—poignantly—why their common roots bore such dissimilar branches. But the business of the moment was barter.

It was in Bobby's mind that, if he confessed, then a suspended or probated sentence might be arranged. Bennett shook that off immediately. "There's no way you're going to get out of this without going to the joint," the prosecutor said. "You're gonna have to do time. Of course, whatever we work out here will have to be cleared with my superiors . . . and when the case gets to a judge, he could well send you up for life. But you know the procedure as well as I do. . . ." Bennett let the sentence dangle, but Bobby nodded to finish it. Both men knew that judges usually follow the DA's recommendation in sentencing.

How much time? Bobby wanted to know. Already he had spoken of Vicki and his love for her. He had told Jerry Carpenter that women had messed him up for the last time. He wanted nothing more than to get his ordeal over with and marry Vicki and disappear.

Bennett had anticipated this question. He had a ready answer. "Twelve years," he said. The offer was generous; Bobby could serve that sentence and be out, with good behavior, in a minimum of two years. Most likely he would stay for five. Unless he was a pain in the ass to all concerned, he would not stay the full twelve. Carpenter and Gamino were both surprised at the district attorney's proposal. At that moment in Texas, some judges were giving thirty years for marijuana possession. But Bennett recognized the basics of the situation. "I knew Bobby Vandiver was a pawn," he would later say, "and I knew he was in over his element. Sure it was a foul thing he did, and sure it was an assault against the peace of our community. But I thought it was an equally foul thing to hire him, and to take advantage of him. I wanted the ones who put him up to it. And if we went for him alone, then the door to those others would be forever shut."

Bobby absorbed the offer, chewed on it, countered with a suggestion that less time in the slammer might make his memory more valuable. Bennett refused. Not even a glimmer of promise was in his eyes. "I'm not fixin' to horse-trade with you, Bobby. That's an exercise in futility. I'd rather try a case any day than plead one. Ask these officers and you'll know I mean what I say."

Late in the afternoon of the third day Bobby made a telephone call to his sister in Dallas. He told her he was in trouble but that he was being well treated. She urged him to get a lawyer. He refused. He was so far content with his negotiations. "I'll run it all down to you real soon," he said mysteriously. Then he thought awhile, chain-lit a cigarette, drank the rest of his now cold coffee, and leaned back in the stiff chair with his eyes closed. Joe Gamino watched him, and in his heart was concern. He knew that Bobby was wrestling with one last demon, the fear that if he told on the others he would be breaking the character code of silence. It was not comforting to the homicide detective that he was offering the benevolence of the law to this skinny, wretched, wasted, but somehow appealing man, knowing that when the cops were done with their work— and Bobby was locked away—then a screwdriver might easily find its revengeful way into his heart one distant night in a dark corner of Huntsville Prison. "What can I tell this kind to calm this fear?" wondered Gamino to himself, and the answer was nothing.

"Well," said Bobby after a time, "I suppose I'd better get down with you boys."

"You did it?" asked Jerry Carpenter.

"Yeah. Now where do you want me to start?"

33

For the next six days, in a marathon that seemed to have
no divisions of day or night—the outside world had in fact
ceased to exist for the hunters and the hunted—the detectives listened and prodded while Bobby led them through
it all. He told of his meeting with Marcia, their brief and
tempestuous relationship as whore and pimp, the occasional
nights spent in the hospitality of Lilla Paulus, the first mention of the contract to kill John Hill, the plans and the
plottings, the trip to Las Vegas in search of the doctor,
the night of death, the flight to California. Often Bob Bennett dropped by, quietly observing, occasionally asking a telling question, anxious that the prisoner's constitutional rights
were protected so as not to have the case break apart one
future day on the altar of the Supreme Court. Now and
then the prosecutor would remind Bobby that he was entitled to call a lawyer, but Bobby always refused. The only
outside person he spoke with was his sister Red in Dallas.
He did not reveal the enormity of his position, but he was
refreshed by his conversations with her.

All three representatives of authority found themselves
somehow liking the wiry man shifting restlessly on the
center-rink tanbark. As he spoke, his tale seemed straight,
wry, unremorseful. It was there—a *fait accompli*, now
wash it and be done with it.

"It was around the middle of August 1972 when Lilla and
I were talking," Bobby said in his statement. "She knew
of a $5,000 contract and asked if I was interested in this
sort of thing. I told her that normally, 'No,' but as ragged
as I was I would think about it. No names were mentioned
at this time. A week later, I called her. She told me
somebody else had taken over the contract. She never did
tell me who this was. The last part of August, I came to
Houston and went to Lilla's. Lilla said the 'other people'
had turned down the contract and she offered it to me
again. I told her I would see what I could do. This was
when she gave me the details.

"She told me the contract was on a doctor who had killed
his wife. And that it was the wife's father who was wanting
him dead. She told me that his name was Dr. Hill, and

that he was plastic surgeon. She said that Dr. Hill had rented a room and that he had grown some bacteria in the bathtub and that he had injected some of the bacteria into some candy that his wife ate. I don't remember if she told me what the doctor's wife's name was. She kept referring to her as 'the doctor's first wife.' She kept referring to the man wanting Dr. Hill dead as 'my man' or 'the old man.' She also said that the old man didn't give a damn what happened to the rest of the people—but not to hurt the youngster. It was while she was giving me some of these details that she took me to the corner of Kirby Drive and Brentwood and pointed out a big white house with columns as being Dr. Hill's house. She told me that 'her man' had pointed out the house. . . . She then took me to some office building out on Fannin Street which was the Hermann Professional Building. She took me into the garage and showed me the doctor's parking area. She also told me that some other people had first taken the contract but that they blew it off because the doctor didn't have a habit as to his hours. She said that the contract had been out on the streets for a couple of years. . . . She told me that she had gotten the money from 'her man,' that 'he' had borrowed it in small sums here and there so that it would not be traceable to him.

"About September 12 or 13, Marcia called Dr. Hill's office to find out about an appointment and how late the appointment could be. But she was told that the doctor would be gone about eleven days . . . to a convention in Las Vegas and would be back around the twenty-fifth of September. Marcia called Las Vegas and found that there was a plastic surgeons' convention and that Dr. Hill did have reservations at the Stardust Hotel. It was decided to do the job in Las Vegas because then it would look like a robbery.

"Lilla Paulus gave me a picture and said this was Dr. Hill, but that she did not know how recent it was. She said to me, 'You think this mother fucker don't want him dead? Just look how he has the picture cut.' The picture had the corners cut off and it looked like a coffin.

"Marcia and I then went to Las Vegas. We checked at the hotel and at the convention center but we weren't able to find Dr. Hill. I think the convention started on the eighteenth of September and we got there that day. We stayed until September 23. During the time we were in

Vegas, we kept calling Lilla from a pay phone out there. She then told us that she had found out from the 'old man' that Dr. Hill had gone to Seattle, Washington, and that he was due back Sunday. The convention was nearly over, so Marcia and I decided to come back to Houston. After coming back, we talked it over with Lilla both that night and the next morning. On Sunday, the 'old man' kept calling Lilla. She told me that he was sure that Hill had been in Washington State and that he was coming back with $15,000 or $30,000. She said that the 'old man' had found this out either from his accountant or from the doctor's accountant or someone that was close to both families. The money that Dr. Hill was bringing back was supposed to be used to pay Dr. Hill's attorney because he was going to trial in November. During one of the times that the 'old man' called, he gave Lilla the doctor's phone number at home. I caled Dr. Hill's home and told them that my name was James Gleason. I was told by a woman that he would be in about 7:30 P.M. or 8 P.M.

"Marcia then called the airline and found out . . . the flight number and what time he was due in. I think it was around 6:30 P.M. Around 7 P.M. I went to Dr. Hill's house. Marcia was driving a white 1967 Olds. She pulled into the driveway facing the garage and I got out and walked to the front door."

After describing how he gained entrance to the house and tied up Myra Hill and her grandson, Bobby moved to the killing itself.

". . . I pulled a pillowcase over my head. I had gotten the pillowcase at Lilla Paulus' house. The doctor and his wife came up and rang the doorbell. They kept ringing the doorbell and I could see the woman looking in through the glass panels alongside the door. So I went to the door and opened it and invited them in. They stood there looking at me as if it was a joke. I reached out with my left hand and grabbed hold of the upper part of her jacket and I had my pistol in my right hand. I said, 'Come on in, this is a holdup.' The woman broke and ran and the doctor said, 'You son of a bitch,' or something like that. He grabbed my pistol and my pillowcase trying to pull it off. We wrestled and he got the pillowcase off my head and kind of stepped back. And I hit him across the face and knocked him back.

"I pointed the pistol at him and I said, 'Hold it!' But he

came toward me, and I shot him. He staggered back a few steps. I pointed the gun at him again, and he tried to grab me again and I shot him a second time. He went down but came up again. He grabbed my gun, and the gun fired again, and I think that it hit the ceiling. I hit him and knocked him back and shot him a third time. When he was going down I hit him in the face a couple of times, and I put my knee on him to keep him from getting up But he wasn't trying to get up any more. I went through his pockets and I got his billfold from his back pocket. I then taped him up around his face from his mouth up around his eyes. . . ."

The detectives and Assistant DA Bennett felt confident that the confession was a solid one, able to stand up to any pressures that the judicial system might bring But if a case was to be made against the others apparently involved —Marcia, Lilla, the "old man"--then more than Bobby's word would have to be offered before a jury. In Texas, a strong law exists relating to accomplices in a crime. A jury cannot convict one defendant upon accomplice witness testimony, even if they believe it to be true. That testimony must be corroborated by other evidence *independent of the accomplice witness testimony*, tending to connect the defendant with the commission of the offense.

If Marcia was ever found, then the murder weapon would be the corroborating evidence needed to convict her, as she could be tightly affiliated with the .38 taken from the black doctor. But Lilla Paulus was another matter. Bobby claimed that he borrowed one pillowcase from her linen cabinet to wear as a mask. More than six months had now passed. Surely she had destroyed the mate But if the officers could figure out a way to get into her house, it would be worth looking for, along with any other bits of evidence she might have missed the night she burned everything in the fireplace.

Ash Robinson at this point was nothing but a vague mention, nothing but "my man" and "the old man." During his negotiations with Lilla, Bobby could not remember mention of the name.

Flipping on a tape recorder and informing Bobby that the reels were spinning, the two detectives took him over and over the territory, trying to find something that might "tend to connect" either Lilla or Ash to the murder. They began with telephone calls, having obtained records from Southwestern Bell Telephone of long-distance charges made to the Paulus telephone.

"On September 16," said Gamino, "a call was made to Western Airlines in Seattle from the Paulus number. Do you have any idea what that call was about?"

"Yeah," said Bobby. "I think it was made to check on whether Dr. Hill had a reservation. He was supposed to be in Seattle or Las Vegas."

"Who would have made the call? You or Marcia?"

"I think Marcia did."

"Here's another call billed to Paulus made to Air West."

"That's the same type thing. Air West and Western are the only two who go from Seattle to Las Vegas. We were trying to locate whether he was leaving Seattle and going to Las Vegas."

Gamino browsed over the list. "Here's one to the Hilton in San Francisco?"

Bobby laughed ruefully. "That was to a chip of mine who was in San Francisco on a demonstration deal for wigs."

On September 15 and 16 two calls to the Stardust Hotel in Las Vegas.

Bobby nodded again. He remembered each of them. "We had contacted Dr. Hill's nurse, or receptionist, probably on the fourteenth, and learned he was supposed to be at this convention in Las Vegas. These calls were to find out if he had reservations or if he was there yet."

Jerry Carpenter perused the list over his partner's shoulder. A call caught his eye. "Here's one to the Atlanta stadium. Probably a football team. These Marcia's tricks, you suppose?"

Bobby agreed. "Marcia has probably got more tricks than any gal in the United States."

"How does she manage it?" asked Carpenter. He had the prostitute's mug shot from an earlier Dallas arrest in his hands. Her hairdo had fallen into despair, her eyelids dropped, her pockmarks showed clearly.

"You tell me," shrugged Bobby. "She used to get on the telephone and call up tricks all over the United States and sweet-talk 'em, and they'd wire her money for plane tickets, and she never went. She had a purseful of valid plane tickets."

If he had to find Marcia this very minute, wondered

Carpenter, where would Bobby look? "Caesar's Palace. Las Vegas. That's her office. If she's not at the bar, then look around the crap tables. Any of the high-rolling places."

As whores went, mused Carpenter, who had as much sophistication as Bobby in this endeavor, he would not mark Marcia as unique. Judging from the mug shot, of course.

"Well, that doesn't do her justice," said Bobby. "She gets her act together pretty good."

"But aren't these scars on her face?" put in Gamino.

"Yeah, agreed Bobby. "She's got scars on her forehead, too. She told me some *bandidos* run over her with motor-cycles and dragged her behind, she got gravel imbedded everywhere. I mean, *everywhere*. She said she and another gal was in niggertown in Washington, D.C., and a bunch of colored dudes got em and put cigarettes out on 'em. She said it was a kinda riot type thing."

Carpenter smiled at the image of Marcia being pursued by a gang of howling blacks in the nation's capital. He did not know her, but already he disbelieved her tales.

"I don't know if it really happened," said Bobby. "It coulda been in Timbuktu on a safari for all I know. One of those man-eatin' cannibals may have had her and turned her loose. That's what I shoulda done."

"You ever know her by any other name than her trick name, Dusty, or her real name, Marcia?" asked Gamino.

"Just Marcia. Dusty was the only trick name she ever used. You know, she might be working spots around Texas. I'd have to find my spot book, and I really don't know where the damn thing is."

"She ever been in a regular whorehouse?" asked Carpenter.

Bobby nodded. "I'm sure she has. But not any more. A regular whorehouse is run differently. She won't go for that. At what's-her name's place in Texarkana, they've got a P.A. system. At a certain time in the morning they say, 'Get your ass outta bed.' "

"When was the last time you saw her?" asked Carpenter.

"In Dallas. Few weeks ago. But I run into a fella the other day who said he heard she was high-rollin' in Vegas. Blowing $1,500 a night. He said he might see her again and did I have anything to tell her? I said, 'Just tell Marcia to keep on truckin'. Win enough for a plane ticket to Outer Mongolia, and keep on truckin'.' "

But Bobby had little to tell about Lilla Paulus. He knew her as a woman who kept her business to herself, who had enough money from her dead husband's estate to live well, and who valued discretion and silence.

"She don't run her head," explained Bobby. "If she ever does tell you about something going on, she doesn't mention any names."

"The way she makes her money," pressed Carpenter. "She never mentioned anything?"

Bobby shook his head negatively. "No. She's just got contacts everywhere. Maybe some coin-operated machines. I think her old man probably left her pretty well fixed. He made some money in this town. Whatever his contacts were, she probably picked 'em up after he died." He fell silent a moment, then he realized what Carpenter was driving at. "As far as names in any of her business, she'd just say, 'My people.' "

"Okay," said Gamino, moving on. "In this statement we took yesterday, you stated that she asked you, 'Are you interested in making $5,000?' And you told us that she kept referring to the person who wanted the contract filled as 'my man,' or 'the old man.' "

"That's right," said Bobby.

"Then, based on this, did you know who was the person behind the contract?"

"Yeah," said Bobby. "Because she said he was the father of the doctor's first wife."

Gamino moved gingerly. He did not want to put words in the confessed assassin's mouth, but once or twice during the interrogations, Bobby had mentioned the name "Ash." How did he know this name?

"It came later on," explained Bobby. "But it was just by accident . . . I think it came from Marcia. She had met him or knew who it was . . . or something. I just remember hearing the name 'Ash,' but I don't think it was *ever* mentioned by Lilla. All I knew was that he was a real prominent, wealthy person."

"Did you ever know his last name?" asked Gamino. "Ever find out?"

"No."

"Not to this day?" pushed Gamino.

Suddenly Bobby said, "It's Robinson, isn't it?"

Excitedly, Gamino asked, "How did you find out?"

"Believe Jerry here mentioned it," said Bobby casually,

gesturing with his thumb toward Carpenter. Gamino groaned inwardly. Modestly embarrassed, Carpenter countered with the notion that perhaps Bobby had read a newspaper account.

"I never did read the papers,' said Bobby. "All I know is that Lilla was worried whether the old man would hold his mud or not when he came down."

Normally adroit at character slang, even Carpenter needed a layman's translation of that comment.

"I mean," said Bobby, "like, if you dudes got him down, would he hold his cool? He was an old man, about half crazy. He don't give a shit, you know. He's lived his life. So the worry was he might not hold his mud."

Gamino harked back to the days preceding the murder. "Did Lilla drive you by and show you Dr. Hill's house?"

"Yeah. In my car." This provoked Bobby to emphasize again that it had not been his intention to commit murder, only robbery. "But like I told you before, I never intended to go through with it."

Carpenter had heard this story before. But he was willing to let Bobby keep telling it, as long as he kept talking about other matters.

"At first, I was just gonna try to get some of the money that the old man had put up . . . beat him out of it . . . but when I actually decided to go to the Hill house, it was just to get some of the money he was supposed to be bringing in from Washington." Besides, Bobby went on, a doctor was fair game. "He probably cheated on his income tax the way those guys do, had money hidden around."

"You knew Lilla already had money in her possession?" asked Carpenter.

"Yeah. I was thinking about ripping her off, you know. I was never serious about wiping him. If I had of been, and if it had just been for $5,000, you wouldn't have me sitting here right now runnin' my head." Bobby's implication was that $5,000 was a far too modest commission for murder.

Carpenter pulled a pack of glossy photographs out of a manila envelope and handed them to Bobby to study. Each showed John Hill in death, in gruesome color. Bobby studied them with no more outward emotion than reviewing album photographs of a long-ago summer picnic. "If he'd-a froze, he wouldn't be dead today," said Bobby. "I told him to hold it. I can't understand to this day why he kept coming at me. I thought maybe he *did* have a large amount of money on him."

"Out of three times you hit him," said Carpenter, "only one was a solid hit. One went in and out of his wrist . . ."

Bobby nodded. "Probably the first shot."

"The next one hit his shoulder," said Carpenter, pointing to the place on the photograph, to a blood-soaked patch on the dead doctor's shirt.

"He went down the second time, but damned if he didn't get back up again. Then . . ." Bobby's voice trailed off and he pointed with a fluttering, hesitating hand to the third and solid shot, a mass of red splash directly in the surgeon's stomach. "Why did he keep coming at me?"

"Maybe he thought he could whip you," suggested Carpenter.

"I've never been foolish enough to think I could whip somebody who had a .38 pointed at me," said Bobby dryly.

Toward the end of the nine-day questioning period, Bobby remembered something of enormous potential in building a case against Lilla Paulus. Gamino thought to ask if, during one of the evenings at the Paulus home when other characters were in attendance, the "contract" on John Hill ever came up?

"Did anybody else hear Lilla mention the contract to you?" Gamino wanted to know.

Bobby thought on this for a few moments, then slowly nodded. "Maybe so," he said. "There may have been this dude named Mart sittin' around one night when Lilla was runnin' things down to me."

And Mart, Bobby had heard, was at this very moment serving time in the North Carolina penitentiary. If Mart would confirm a clandestine conversation between Bobby Vandiver and Lilla Paulus about the plan to kill John Hill, then it would be corroboration from a non-accomplice, a substantial brick. Breaking off the questioning, the two detectives and Bob Bennett flew that same day to Raleigh, North Carolina, and entered the gloomy, medieval fortress that is the state's chief prison. Mart, freshly into a long sentence for robbery, was irritated at the appearance of the Houston lawmen. A few months earlier, at the time of his arrest by North Carolina police, he had mentioned to them that he had information about an important killing in Houston. He wanted to use his information for bartering a better deal. Mart complained that somebody had promised to pass on the tip to the FBI, which in turn was going to inform the Houston homicide office. But the information never progressed along the trail west.

Now he offered nothing but frustration to the detectives. Yes, he did remember a conversation between Lilla Paulus and Bobby Vandiver about a contract to kill a doctor. But no, he would not sign a statement or testify in a court of law. "What good can you guys do me now?" he told Gamino and Carpenter bluntly. Mart was sophisticated enough to know that snitching has a perishable shelf value and that two cops from Houston, despite their pressures and promises, could do nothing to extricate him from a North Carolina prison.

The detectives and the prosecutor flew home with corroboration, but it was not admissible in court, not even worth writing down.

Just before he secretly took the case before a grand jury, Bob Bennett baited a trap for Ash Robinson. The ethics of the matter were shadowy, but in the light of the history of the events, principles were at that moment subordinate. Attaching a tape recorder to his office telephone, Bennett instructed Bobby Vandiver to call Ash Robinson. The conversation was terse and urgent.

"Mr. Robinson? This is Bobby Vandiver. I did a job for you."

After several moments of suspenseful silence, the old man spoke one word, "Yes." But it was not the kind of "yes" that affirmed what the caller was saying, only the kind that meant, "Get on with it."

"I need to get ahold of Lilla real bad," Bobby said, as per his stage directions. "I can't find her. Do you know where she is?"

Another stretch of agonizing quiet. And finally, another unhelpful reply. "No. I haven't seen Lilla in six months and don't know how to get in touch with her." Ash Robinson hung up. He had not nibbled at the bait.

On April 25, 1973, the Harris County grand jury voted secret indictments of murder in the first degree against Bobby Wayne Vandiver, thirty-three, and Marcia McKittrick, twenty-three, and an accomplice to murder accusation against Lilla Paulus, fifty-four. Assistant DA Bennett did *not* ask that an indictment be voted against Ash Robinson, for the state as yet had no case against the father of Joan Hill. His name did not arise during presentation of Vandiver's confession before the panel. The state's case against Lilla Paulus was, in truth, as fragile as onion skin, but the hope was that as soon as Marcia was arrested she would bolster the positions. The cops and the DA were betting on the come.

Joe Gamino had been spending time shadowing the quiet neighborhood where Lilla Paulus lived. He knew that she was often away from home, staying with a man named Meyers of whom she seemed to be enamored. To coincide with the issue of the grand jury indictments, a posse of nine lawmen, including Bob Bennett, who armed himself with a revolver, went to the Meyers home. Jerry Carpenter carried an AR15 Colt rifle, the kind United States soldiers used in South Vietnam. Inside the house, Lilla Paulus was sitting on a couch in the den watching afternoon television. She rose and opened the front door. The first thing she saw was the terrifying long gun balanced provocatively in Carpenter's hand. The first thing she heard was Carpenter reading the standard "blue card" Miranda warning that must be given any suspect before an arrest is made. Lilla Paulus listened almost respectfully, like a civics teacher observing a student deliver a homework project. Indeed, she looked like nothing less menacing than a nice, graying lady of middle years who had permitted herself to be surrounded by a pack of neighborhood youngsters playing at cops and robbers. Soon she would surely clap her hands in mock annoyance and go to the kitchen where cookies were cooling for her tormentors. Then Carpenter threw wrenching handcuffs on her wrists and ordered her to sit mute while police searched about the house. Two loaded pistols and a bit of marijuana were discovered, but nothing to connect her with the murder of John Hill. "I was frightened," she would later say. "Jerry Carpenter told me he was disappointed I didn't go for a gun. He wanted to shoot me on the spot."

Quickly she was put in a police car and chauffeured to her own home on Underwood Street, where Bobby Vandiver claimed the murder plot had been formulated. En route, Bob Bennett hastily scribbled a "consent to search" paper and asked that she sign. If she refused, he contended, then a court order would be easy enough to obtain. Until this very moment, Lilla would later say, she did not know why she was so urgently the object of police attention. "Why?" she asked. "Why am I under arrest?"

Bennett said, "Well, hit her with it."

"You are under arrest," said Jerry Carpenter, "for the murder of Dr. John Hill."

"Who?" asked Lilla, convincingly out of focus.

"Dr. John Hill."

"You must be kidding," she said, in absurd dismissal. Then she signed the "consent to search" as the police car sped across a southwest loop of the city. She did so, she later claimed, because her hands were throbbing from the pain of the cuffs, and she was frightened of the police and their guns.

Jerry Carpenter and his men were unable to locate the mate to the green pillowcase, but they did find, in a back bedroom, a few interesting slips of paper. One appeared to be a partial gin rummy score with a long-distance telephone number on the back and the word "Dusty" below. The second had the name of the downtown Houston "spot" hotel where Marcia McKittrick occasionally worked as a prostitute, plus what seemed to be various airline flight schedules. And the third was a blank check on the account of Mr. and Mrs. C. N. Paulus. Written on the back was a cryptic message: "You had better tell Ash they are trying to subpena Ma." In the depths of Lilla's handbag, the searchers found another scrap of paper with the telephone number 523-3746 written on it. '

And in a kitchen drawer was found a letter written by Marcia McKittrick dated August 6, 1972. Apparently it had never been mailed, and its designee was unknown. The letter had no mention of the Hill murder, but it would tend to place the prostitute in the Paulus home.

That night, after the story broke and confused newspaper reporters were trying to learn what a Dallas hijacker, a fugitive prostitute, and a seemingly respectable widow from a good part of town had to do with the murder of Dr. John Hill, Bob Bennett, Carpenter, and Gamino decided to ride one more bluff. Unannounced, they would visit Ash Robinson. It would be the very first time since the death of the plastic surgeon that the law had gone knocking on the old man's door. Perhaps, Bennett thought, the power of the day's sudden events would so frazzle Ash Robinson that he would let something slip or, conversely, be so sure of his insulation that he would permit a search of his house. The police had no legal right to interrogate him and certainly none to look about his home. But there was nothing to prohibit them from stopping by for a "visit."

Near midnight, the three men drove along Kirby Drive toward the Robinson home. As they passed the white colonial house where John Hill had been shot to death, Bennett noted that it was bathed in floodlights, with others burning inside, as if in readiness for a great party. But the lights had shone every night since the doctor died. Connie Hill had elected to remain in her slain husband's home, raise his son, and sit in his music room where she respected his memory by filling it with the sounds of the music he loved.

Ash Robinson was in his pajamas, but on balance, polite, as he opened the door, presenting himself as a respectable member of the city's most prestigious neighborhood, a bit disturbed that the law would pound unannounced on his door so close to midnight. But he asked the three young men to sit in his living room, and he assumed his favorite armchair, directly beneath a photographic montage of Joan and her social and equine triumphs.

Joe Gamino began haltingly. "We want you to know that we have just arrested your friend Lilla Paulus for the murder of John Hill." He waited for a response. None was forthcoming. ". . . And we think you might have something to do with it."

The old man looked almost amused, as if he knew his opponent was trying to win a big pot by making an outrageous bet on a busted flush. After a very long time of total quiet, after Ash's cold eyes had swept across the face of each of the men in his living room, he shook his head negatively. "Well, boys," he said, "I wouldn't know anything about that."

Bob Bennett noted that on a table beside the old man's chair was a carefully cut out newspaper clipping of the day's indictments and arrest of Lilla Paulus. "If you wouldn't know anything about this, Mr. Robinson," the assistant DA said, "then why do you have those clippings there beside you?"

Ash picked them up, fingered them, let them flutter back to the table. "I'm interested in everything that comes out in the papers about my son-in-law," he said. "The bastard murdered my daughter."

The visitors all had further questions, but Ash rose imperiously. He yawned and gestured toward the door. "I don't believe I should talk to you gentlemen further unless it is in the presence of my lawyer," he said. "And I might remind you gentlemen—and I stress this strongly—that you should be very careful what you say about me."

With the hint of a suit for slander dancing in the crisp midnight air, the frustrated interrogators left. Ash slammed the door behind them. As they drove out of the circular driveway, Bennett could feel the old man's eyes burning through the peephole. Jerry Carpenter pronounced the day's benediction. "That's one cool old son of a bitch," he said.

34

Marcia did not immediately learn of the events in Houston. Something else was troubling her. A tooth. It throbbed so painfully that no amount of aspirin—or the other more clandestine drugs in her purse—could give relief. She could not concentrate on the tricks who were coming to the motel in West Texas where she was ensconced. She flew home to Dallas in late April 1973, anxious to visit a childhood dentist in whom she had faith. After he filled her cavity, with lips still numb and swollen from the novocaine, she telephoned her mother for news of home and sympathy.

"Listen, you'd better buy a newspaper," her mother said. "You and Bobby are all over it. Now do what I say, Marcia. Go to a pay telephone and call the lawyer. Call Charles Caperton. For God's sake, Marcia, for once in your life mind me!"

Marcia ran to a corner and bought the afternoon paper. Police mug shots of her and Bobby decorated a prominent story about murder indictments in the death of Dr. John Hill returned the day before in Houston. Her first instinct was flight. But even as she dialed an airline to inquire about the next plane out to Las Vegas or Los Angeles, she realized the hopelessness of her position. The paper said Bobby was in the Houston jail; somehow the police must have pried information out of him, else indictments would not have been handed down. She dropped the telephone and it dangled from its cord as she sank down in the corner of the booth. "What am I gonna do?" she said to herself, making a song of the words. "Mama-mama-mama, I'm so scared."

Charles Caperton, the former prosecutor for the Dallas district attorney's office and the lawyer who had first defended her on worthless check charges that were still pending in a musty folder in the courthouse, took her call and calmed her down. He was the Pepto-Bismol of lawyers, the very easygoing country boy who knew well both sides of the fence—them and us. Stop crying, he told her. This is only an indictment in Houston, he said. It is not a conviction. They are not making up your bed at the Goree (women's prison). A hundred avenues are still open. But the first, Caperton decided, was an end run around the Houston police force. Enjoying his tactic immensely, Caperton promptly flew to Houston with Marcia cowering at his side, escorted her to the Harris County courthouse—a dozen city blocks away from the police station where Carpenter and Gamino were located—and surrendered the most wanted woman in Texas on the charge of murder. But even as one hand signed the document informing the district court that he was the attorney of record for Miss McKittrick, the other one was making the $15,000 bond set by the judge in this matter. Marcia's parents had mortgaged their home to keep their girl out of jail. Hardly was Marcia in Houston before she was back on a plane headed for Dallas, once more evading the two detectives who had roamed the state of Texas in her pursuit. Gamino had even taken the precaution of appending an urgent note to the documents of her case at the sheriff's office. If Marcia McKittrick should surrender herself, or be surrendered, or somehow show up in the courthouse, then, damnit, immediately phone Jerry Carpenter or Joe Gamino at city homicide, or at home, at any hour of the day or night! But somehow the plea written in red ink was overlooked. When Carpenter discovered that Marcia had once more slipped like a larded piglet from his hands, he stalked about homicide for an hour, cursing like a farm boy who lost out at the state fair.

Charles Caperton told his client to go about and live her life, stay out of trouble, keep in constant touch, and, above all, shut up. "Don't talk to anyone but Charles Caperton," he cautioned. "Not your boy friend, not your

mama, and certainly not to any representative of the law."
She had no obligation to give the time of day to any police
officer.

In Houston, Bob Bennett arranged a life for his star
witness, Bobby Vandiver. It was imperative to keep his
co-operation with the state secret. "If it gets out," Bennett
told Jerry Carpenter, "then they'll waste him, sure as hell."
The lawmen were not afraid that Bobby would run away.
On the day that he signed his confession he told them,
"I'll be glad to get this over. I'm so tired of peepin' and
hidin'."

It was arranged that Vicki could come down from Dallas
to keep Bobby's temperature normal, for he needed his
woman beside him. Bob Bennett found an efficiency apartment at a motel—which the DA's office paid for—and a
job for Vicki as a waitress in a seafood restaurant. The
prosecutor even managed a couple of hundred bucks pocket
money for Bobby, dipping into an informal fund at the
district attorney's office. A token lawyer was engaged to
handle Bobby's court appearances, fully aware of the script
that was to be played out. Bobby would plead guilty, get
twelve years, and then give testimony against Marcia and
Lilla Paulus. As summer began, Bob Bennett felt reasonably secure that the heart of his case was beating contentedly.

How did the turn of events affect Ash Robinson? He
told a friend that he was not surprised at the caliber of
people charged in the death of his ex-son-in-law. That a
thrice-convicted robber, a prostitute, and the widow of a
bookmaker were accused only shored up his long-felt
belief that John Hill had walked on the shady side of the
street. "By his friends we shall know him," said atheist
Ash, using a quotation that though garbled, seemed to him
appropriate.

None of the newspaper accounts were able to provide
lay followers of the case with answers to the most asked
questions: If these three people plotted the death of John
Hill, then why? What was their motive? Money? Were they
hired to execute the surgeon? If so, by whom? Ash? He
remained a principal figure in the public eye. As he stood in
line to cash checks at the bank or waited for his Lincoln to
be brought around at the Houston Club garage, Ash could

see people whispering about him. It did not concern him to be the object of secretive gossip, for he had come to relish being pointed out in a crowd. Still he must have fretted over what was going on in the office of that insolent young prosecutor who had barged unannounced into his home the night those three people were indicted. His lawyer, Richard Keeton, of the town's most powerful firm, kept an ear to the courthouse and so far had picked up nothing that would indicate the old man was in jeopardy. Best to buy a little home fire extinguisher, though, reasoned Ash, just in case the summer heat provoked a little brush fire.

Thus on a June day in 1973, in the New York offices of a lie detector firm, Ash Robinson offered himself for private polygraph examination. No representative of any law enforcement agency was present. After two hours of being hooked up to the machine, Ash emerged with a signed letter:

. . . Davis Ashton Robinson voluntarily came to this polygraph suite for an examination.

The main issue under consideration was whether or not Mr. Robinson was telling the truth when he claimed that he had no guilty knowledge of, nor had he participated in, the murder of Dr. John Hill.

Dr. Hill, who formerly was Mr. Robinson's son-in-law, was murdered on Sept. 24, 1972, in his own home in Houston, Texas. Three persons have been indicted in regard to this murder.

The facts concerning this case were provided the polygraphists by Mr. Richard P. Keeton, who is Mr. Robinson's attorney.

Before his pre-test interview, Mr. Robinson signed two copies of a form stating he was taking the tests voluntarily. One copy of this executed form is enclosed with this report; the other is incorporated as part of our case files.

In the polygraph recordings, there were definite indications of truthfulness when Mr. Robinson was asked the following pertinent test questions:

1. By last Oct. 1, did you then already know for sure who had murdered Dr. John Hill? Answer: No.

2. Did you set up the actual murder of Dr. John Hill? Answer: No.

3. By 7:30 P.M. last Sept. 24, did you then already

know there was going to be an armed man inside the
Hill house that night? Answer: No.

4. In order to have Dr. John Hill murdered, by
7:30 P.M. last Sept. 24, did you promise to pay any
of those three arrested persons? Answer: No.

5. Have you now told me the entire truth as to
what you really know about Dr. John Hill's murder?
Answer: Yes.

It is the opinion of the polygraphists, based upon
Mr. Robinson's . . . examination, that Mr. Robinson is
telling the truth to the above listed questions.

Although lawyer Keeton bade his client to keep the
contents of the letter quiet, Ash could not resist telling
several of his cronies, including former grand juror Cecil
Haden. Of course, for that was the intention, word soon
reached Bob Bennett that Ash had cleared himself through
a lie detector examination. Bennett almost laughed out
loud. "If he's all that innocent," muttered Bennett, "then
why does old Ash have to run all the way off to New York
and get one done secretly? We'll be happy to interrogate
him here. We'll even send a car."

Gamino and Carpenter stepped up their efforts to get
Marcia McKittrick into their interrogation room for a little
talk. The officers desperately needed Marcia to bolster the
skimpy case against Lilla Paulus, and, if the string could
reach that far, against Ash himself. Bobby Vandiver had
mentioned that "perhaps" he had heard the name "Ash"
from Marcia. It was his impression that Marcia had even
met the old man and had seen him and Lilla in conversation
together. The detectives had no clear-cut legal right to
question the prostitute, but they saw nothing wrong with
a bit of extracurricular squeezing. For six frenetic spring
weeks in 1973, Marcia began to feel like the object of a
Keystone Kops chase. "Every cop in Texas is ready to bust
me for jaywalking," she complained to Charles Caperton.
On June 14 the brash Dallas lawyer filed a petition seeking
to make the authorities stop "harassing" his client. "It's
completely outrageous the way these peace officers have been
behaving," he said. "She has the right to remain silent, and
I'm not going to permit the entire might of the state of
Texas to intimidate her." Specifically, Caperton charged
that police were bombarding Marcia's family home near

Dallas with post-midnight telephone calls and showing up with guns menacingly in view at their belts, wanting to interview his client. "On May 17," charged Caperton, "two armed men, representing themselves as Texas Rangers, invaded the home of Miss McKittrick's parents and in a threatening and abusive manner said they were going to talk to her one way or the other, sooner or later, and that they were tired of the whole family's lies about the whereabouts of Miss McKittrick. The next day "*six* armed men, representing themselves as Texas Rangers," repeated the act. But what really made Caperton's gorge rise was Assistant DA Bob Bennett's alleged behavior in the very lobby of the Harris County courthouse. On May 25, Marcia waltzed into Houston and pleaded "Not guilty" at her arraignment. After the brief hearing was concluded, she and her lawyer prepared to leave. According to Caperton, Assistant DA Bennett rushed up, breathing hard as if he had been in hot pursuit of Marcia, and began making both bargains and threats. Caperton quoted Bennett as saying to Marcia:

"Has Caperton told you that I am going to give you immunity if you testify against Ash Robinson? I don't care if we convict him or not, I just want him indicted. He is old and he will probably die before we can get him tried anyway. I just want to tell you that if you don't, not only will I prosecute you on this murder charge, I am going to have the Harris County grand jury file felony indictments against you for failing to pay long-distance telephone calls and I am going to *stack* the sentences that you receive in each of these cases." Bobby Vandiver, during his interrogation, had mentioned that Marcia often used a phony telephone credit card to make her calls.

The very next day, claimed Marcia, she was about to board an airplane at Houston International Airport when two men in business suits appeared beside her, grabbed her arms, and announced they were Texas Rangers with instructions to take her in for questioning. Marcia wrestled with her would-be arrestors and freed herself, running pell-mell down a corridor crowded with approaching travelers, into the lobby, down an escalator, flinging herself onto an underground shuttle train to another terminal. She found a taxi and raced to town where she telephoned Charles Caperton and poured out the tale of the aborted abduction.

With all of this exceptional attention being paid to her

comings and goings, Marcia should have entered a cloister to remain shut away from all those who wanted to speak to her. But on June 12, needing money to pay for her heroin needs, a habit approaching two hundred dollars a day, she turned up at an old stand in a Lubbock motel, eager to turn a few tricks. That same day an informer revealed her presence to a pair of Lubbock detectives who quickly arrested her and then telephoned a delighted Jerry Carpenter in Houston.

The arresting officers handed the telephone to Marcia and she said simply, "Hello, Jerry Carpenter." In Houston, at the other end of the connection, the homicide detective felt a rush of excitement. She existed! She was real! The flaky whore who helped kill John Hill was at long last bound to him by a telephone cable.

Marcia would later claim, in the petition sought by her lawyer, that Jerry Carpenter then urged her to come to Houston "as his protégé," and promised to let her conduct her business of prostitution with no harassment from the vice squad. Her end of the bargain would be cooperation in the Hill case. When this failed to move her, the Houston cop allegedly turned surly, threatening prosecution for her use of a phony telephone credit card. Throughout the conversation, Marcia would contend. Carpenter heaped abuse on her lawyer, suggesting that he was in league with Ash Robinson and was preparing to sacrifice her to the penitentiary to keep the old man at liberty.

None of the importunings disturbed her, said Marcia. All she wanted was to be left alone. Speak to her attorney in Dallas, Charles Caperton. She refused to talk further. One of the Lubbock detectives received instructions from his counterpart in Houston: "Put this girl on a flight to Houston and we will take it from there." Marcia was placed alone on a flight to Houston that made an intermediate stop in Austin. She skipped off the airplane there, and a half hour later, when the craft landed in Houston without her, a furious Jerry Carpenter was ready to dismantle the jet with his bare hands.

All of these harassments are illegal and harmful to Miss McKittrick, said Charles Caperton in his lengthy petition to the court. He demanded that the judge enjoin every single law enforcement authority in the state of Texas— from the chief of the Texas Rangers down to the lowest whistle-stop traffic cop—from bothering Marcia McKittrick in any way. Around the Harris County courthouse, none of the assistant DAs could ever remember a document quite like it.

Bobby Vandiver, living under the code name "Taylor" at the Houston motel, found life tedious. His only activity was to lie around watching daytime television, waiting for Vicki to return from her job at the seafood restaurant. He was forbidden to leave the room, unless escorted by a man from the DA's office. Hearing his complaint, Bennett discerned a hint of shame, for it clearly pained Bobby to depend upon the woman he loved and the DA to pay his way. His trial for the murder of John Hill was set for September 1973, and in early June he asked Bennett to grant a favor.

Vicki's first husband was trying to win custody of her two children, and she needed to go to Dallas and fight him. "She's scared to death of losing her kids," Bobby told his protector. Would the DA trust him to accompany Vicki to Dallas and stand beside her in the troubling matter? "I won't run, Bob," he said. "I think you know me pretty good by now I just wanna get my business straight so Vicki and I can live together someday."

Bennett hesitated. He was not so much worried that his prisoner would flee, but he was deeply concerned that word might have leaked to the "character" fraternity that Bobby was co-operating with the state. Letting him go unescorted to a city where more than thirty of his professional brothers had been murdered in recent years was not a notion conducive to solid sleep. No. Too dangerous. Bobby pleaded. He would not be gone long, only a few days maximum. He would stay with Red, his sister. She was "straight city." He would even check in with Dallas police if Bennett ordered.

Reluctantly, Bennett gave permission. And several days later Bobby telephoned from Dallas. The custody hearing was delayed; it was now necessary for Vicki to stay there and establish a suitable nest for her children. The child welfare people insisted on it. Red had found space in her home. She had even found Bobby a temporary job doing roofing work.

"You staying out of trouble?" asked Bennett.

"Yeah," said Bobby. "I'm so straight I bore myself." No one in Dallas knew of his position in Houston, he said. As far as his world knew, he was simply out on bond in a murder rap. A couple of his character friends had even called to express sympathy over the jam he was in. Bennett, reasonably content that his prisoner's life was in bounds, gave permission for Bobby to stay in Dallas until September, when the trial was to begin.

One of those who called Bobby was Marcia. Her voice slurred heavily on the telephone. She made little sense. Bobby gathered that she was somewhere in Dallas, wrecked on heroin, and living with a character who maintained a legitimate small business to conceal a back-room narcotics operation. When Bobby mentioned that he was living with Vicki, Marcia began to scream. In the middle of her rambling tirade of jealousy Bobby hung up. When the telephone rang again he did not answer. He was done with Marcia.

By late June 1973, Marcia was spending most of her hours in the solace of heroin. Her new patron, Claude, was a gruff, fleshy man with a thick neck and a paradoxical attitude toward dope. He was pleased to sell it to others but he not only refused to use it himself, he railed at Marcia for succumbing to its power. Each day when he left his comfortable home in a Dallas suburb to operate his business, Marcia shredded the house in search of his hidden cache of drugs. Usually she found them, for she now required from six to eight fixes a day, sometimes shooting a frightening eight grams. Her habit was enormous. She passed her hours in basic fashion. She shot up, lay back and, once the drug had worn away, looked around for more. On September 21, after a screaming quarrel with Claude because he had purged his home of narcotics, Marcia unsteadily made exit, stole his Chrysler, a diamond ring, and a book of his manufacturing company's payroll checks. Thirty minutes later she was arrested at the window of a drive-in bank, hands trembling, body near convulsion, attempting to cash a crudely forged $475 check that she had made out to herself on her patron's account. Immediately word was teletyped to Houston homicide that the woman of the year was in the Dallas slammer. Jerry Carpenter, reached at home, was ecstatic. "Here we flat beat this state to death looking for Marcia," he told Bob Bennett, "and she goes and arrests herself."

Carpenter and Gamino drove the 260 miles to Dallas in three hours and finally met Marcia McKittrick face to face. She was pathetic. In the agony of withdrawal, a splash of vomit soured and hardened on her blouse, frightened, angry at her lawyer Caperton because he had not responded to her call, she agreed to go to Houston and get her business straight. For almost a year Jerry Carpenter had conjured illusion of his prey; in his mind she was composed of equal parts of Salome and Houdini. But now, as she slept with her head in his lap, while Gamino drove quietly through the night back to the city where John Hill had been murdered, Carpenter studied her. "She's just a poor old junkie whore," he thought to himself. He knew a thousand just like her. And all of them, once the make-up was rubbed away, had the same sad eyes.

In a later series of court hearings, the accusation would be made that the prostitute made confession only because she was promised narcotic relief by Jerry Carpenter. "That little girl would have confessed to starting World War II, the shape she was in," insisted Charles Caperton. In answer, Jerry Carpenter swore, under penalty of perjury, that he did not dangle an opiate carrot in front of the stick to make Marcia talk. He said that only *after* she made full confession did he take her to a city drug clinic for examination and treatment. The record showed that on a September morning in 1973, while the city of Houston awoke and made ready for a day of work, Marcia McKittrick sat dully in an interrogation room at the city police headquarters where Bobby Vandiver had earlier spent nine days. She made elaborate confession to her part in the murder of Dr. John Hill. She not only bolstered Bobby's sworn account, she firmly implicated Lilla Paulus and threw a weak rope around the neck of Ash Robinson.

The most compelling part of her sworn statement:

In the early part of summer, 1972, I was staying at Lilla Paulus' home. And a heavy set man with thinning hair, in his 70's, was introduced to me as Ash Robinson. Lilla told me that his daughter and her daughter had ridden horses together in horse shows. A short time after I was introduced to Ash Robinson, Lilla told me that he would do anything for her if she would just do him a favor. During the course of the summer, Ash Robinson visited Lilla's house three or four times while I was there. During these visits, he would talk about getting custody of his grandson. He made the statement that it looked like the only way for him to get custody of the grandson was for Hill to be dead, or to be convicted for the murder of his daughter. During the course of the summer, Lilla met Ash two or three times while I was with her. She would meet Ash in the parking lot across the street from Ben Taub Hospital. Each of these times I would sit in Lilla's car, and she and Ash would sit down together nearby or in Ash's car, which was a big, black, new-looking car. I saw Ash hand her money every time that they would meet at this location, but I was too far away to tell how much money it was. About the only thing that Ash ever talked to me about was him wanting to get his grandson, and about how rotten Hill was for killing his daughter. He also talked about the Hill mistrial and about how much it upset him because he knew in his own mind that Hill had killed his daughter on purpose.

Marcia swore that Ash further delivered a diagram of the Hill house floor plan and a batch of newspaper clippings that dealt with the events.

On the day that Dr. Hill was killed [said Marcia in confession], Ash came to Lilla's house in his black car and I watched Ash count out $7,000 in cash, mostly in hundreds and fifties, and he gave this money to Lilla. The best I can recall after he counted the money, he then said, "That about covers it."

Her statement, though not as lengthy as Bobby's, nonetheless matched his in detail that only the two of them would have known. And Marcia had had no access to Vandiver's document. The detectives and Bob Bennett felt certain that this statement would also stand up in court and would be considered as independent of the actual killer.

Off the record, for she passed it on as gossip, Marcia believed that Lilla received $25,000 from Ash Robinson to finance the killing. "Since Bobby only got $5,000, and he gave $1,500 of that back to Lilla, she came off pretty good," observed Marcia.

Early in the afternoon, approximately twenty-four hours after her turbulent exit from her Dallas patron's home in a stolen car, Marcia was put in the hospital ward of the Harris County jail where, having been awarded two barbiturates to help in her withdrawal from heroin, she fell asleep. Not until a week later was she fully conscious and functioning, demanding to see Charles Caperton and claiming that the "confession" had been coerced out of her.

Bobby Vandiver lived quietly in Dallas until this same September, when he was scheduled to return to Houston for his murder trial. A quarter hour before the morning docket was called, he appeared in Bob Bennett's office, holding his toothbrush in his hand. He was ready to play the scene and go to prison that very afternoon. So resolved was he, so seemingly at grips with his situation, that Bennett regretted to tell him that the trial had been delayed for seven months, until the next April. Because Bobby was co-indicted with Marcia and Lilla, their attorneys had requested more time to prepare a defense.

"I'm really sorry," said Bennett. "I know you were ready to go."

Bobby stirred uneasily. In that case, he wanted to go back to Dallas. Every day of his life was precious to him now. He wanted to store up the remaining hours in companionship with Vicki, her children, and Red. The district attorney was apprehensive. It was not comforting to rise each morning and realize that the cornerstone of the most important murder case of the decade in Houston was 260 miles away, completely out of supervision. "I can't let you go back again," said Bennett. "I think you'd better stay here. We'll loosen up a little, let you move around the city."

For a haunting moment, a wild look passed through Bobby's eyes. He had never seemed a cornered, frightened animal until now. Always he had been loose, cocky,. in control. Bennett watched him fumble in his head for a counterproposal. He found one. Bobby pointed out that Bennett's franchise at the DA's office was organized crime. *If* he were permitted to return to Dallas, Bobby could nose around "the boys" up there. He knew a few alleged Mafia names; he could perhaps learn more, probably ferret out some Houston connections.

Bennett shook his head quickly, in alarm. "Don't do that, Bobby," he said. "For God's sake, don't do that. I don't need that now. You might get hurt and I have to keep you as a witness. Right now getting this murder case cleaned up is more important."

"Then," bargained Bobby, "if I promise to stay away from 'those guys' . . . can I go back?"

Bennett hemmed and hawed.

"Please." It was a word Bobby had never used. The very foreignness was eloquent.

Bennett rose and nodded. "All right, get outta here," he said. "But you check in every week. Hear? Call collect!"

Stewing in the downtown Harris County jail for six months, Marcia McKittrick grew bored and her skin turned the color of the mashed potatoes that filled her dinner plate. With her arrest in Dallas on the assortment of theft and forgery charges, her $15,000 bond in the John Hill murder case had been revoked. Moreover, the Dallas district attorney's office had revived the long-ago worthless check charges from her youth. She needed a souvenir program to keep up with the various dramas of her life. Her attorney, Caperton, recommended that the best place for her to be was in jail. Implied was the hint that it was also the safest, for if word got out in the "character" world that Marcia had made confession, she might face harm. By April 1974, however, Marcia was going bananas in a sunless metropolitan basement jail, lacking even an exercise yard. She sent word to Caperton that she wanted him to assemble all of the charges against her—excepting the murder rap—and trade them out for the best possible sentence. "I'd rather be in Goree, where at least you all can come and visit me, and I can see Mikey," she wrote her mother. She was desperate for a visit from her eight-year-old son.

From her sister prisoners in the county jail, Marcia had learned that Goree Women's Prison in Huntsville was not the worst place in the world. The food was supposedly good, the facilities for recreation tolerable, and the work hard but at least it occupied the mind. "If I don't do something fast," Marcia thought to herself, "I am going to start screaming and keep screaming until they put a straightjacket on me."

In Dallas, Caperton arranged a generous trade-out sentence for Marcia—two years in the state prison, with time credited for the months she had reposed in the Houston jail. With a warning that she must remain on guard and behave herself—she would still be standing trial for murder one day soon—Caperton sent his client off to the penitentiary where Marcia promptly landed a sweetheart job

—receptionist in the factory where state uniforms are made. With her vivid tales of gowns made from mirrors and of standing next to Dean Martin while he flung dice across the green felt tables of Las Vegas, Marcia quickly became a popular member of the prison community. None of her fellow inmates were rude enough to ask why, if Marcia had climbed so high on the ladder, she was now at the bottom rung again.

On April 10, 1974, the telephone rang in Bob Bennett's cramped fifth-floor office at the Harris County courthouse. On the line was a familiar voice. "This is Bobby V."

"Hi, Bobby," said Bennett. "We're *on* for next Monday."

"I know. It's really going down this time, is it?"

"Looks like it. You're gonna be here, aren't you?"

"You know it," said Bobby.

"Bring your toothbrush. You're gonna *go* this time," said the prosecutor. "Are you all right?"

"Yeah, I'm all right. I ain't too happy about next Monday, but I'm all right." The two men, now friends, hung up amicably. Bennett fretted for a few minutes. He was not sure, but he thought he discerned a sense of malaise in his star witness. But, Bennett reassured himself, Bobby said he would be here. So far he'd been a man of his word.

On the Monday of the scheduled trial Jerry Carpenter rose early, dressed, and sat beside his home telephone, waiting for a call from Bobby at the Houston airport. Bobby always called the moment he hit town, and the homicide detective did not mind playing chauffeur. No call came. At 9 A.M., with the morning docket about to be called, Bennett sat at the state's table, swiveling his neck every time the door at the rear of the courtroom opened, expecting to see Bobby's lean figure stride in. When half an hour had passed and still no Bobby, the prosecutor made a mumbled excuse of having left something in his office and rushed there, thinking that perhaps his witness was lost in the courthouse corridors. For an hour Bennett sat nervously drumming his fingers, watching his telephone, watching his door. Finally the court clerk warned that the judge was growing impatient, and Bennett returned in bewilderment. Lilla Paulus was now represented by the South's most celebrated criminal attorney, Percy Foreman, and it would be humiliating to stand up against the famous old giant and reveal that the state's star witness was absent.

Fortunately, luck was working for Bennett that morning. Percy Foreman requested a continuance, claiming that his client was suffering from cancer of the cervix, was a doomed woman, and must have further time to rally strength for the ordeal of trial.

Bennett was not exceptionally moved by Mrs. Paulus' medical complaint; in a decade with the DA's office he had grown accustomed to defense lawyers inventing heart attacks and tumors for postponements. It was a famous Percy Foreman tactic to delay, to stall until memories grew weak and witnesses disappeared and prosecutorial enthusiasm diminished. "No client of mine ever went to the penitentiary who did not stand trial," Percy often said. A little perversely, Bennett made noises of disappointment at the delay, he being prepared for trial and all that. The judge ordered a postponement until autumn.

Bennett fairly flew out of the courtroom and began a telephone marathon in search of Bobby Vandiver. He ordered the $15,000 bond revoked, as a lever to expedite his truant witness' arrest should he be off and running again. From Vicki's parents, Bennett learned that their daughter and Bobby had left the Dallas area the night before, presumably en route to Houston for his trial. "God help me," thought Bennett to himself, "he's lying in a ditch somewhere. Somebody got to him and shot him."

Then Bennett telephoned Red, Bobby's sister. She had little to tell, other than that her brother had left Dallas the night before, with Vicki.

"Was he coming here, for the trial?" pressed the DA.

"I think so," said Red. "He was a little mixed up. And upset." At the end of the conversation, somehow Bennett knew that Bobby was safe, not dead, only missing. He had walked to the edge of the water but he could not plunge in. Bobby was running. And the state's murder case to avenge the killing of Dr. John Hill was once more in a shambles.

Red had seen it coming. She had watched her brother examining his face in the bathroom mirror, frowning at the crows' feet and the new worry lines. She knew that he was counting the years that he would have to spend once again in the penitentiary. Twelve years might pass before he could hold Vicki through the night again, and he worried that she might not wait for him. Vicki swore she would. "There will never be another man in my life," she promised. But even this fealty bothered him, for he was guilty over the penalty he was imposing on a child-woman barely twenty years old.

Late one night, when the house was quiet, Red heard soft noises from the living room. She thought someone had left the television set on, and she tiptoed in to shut it off. There she found her brother, crying softly, annoyed that Red had discovered his pain. "You wanna talk?" she asked gently, sitting beside him and trying to take his face in her hands.

"No," he said, turning away. "I don't wanna talk. All I want is a life. It seems I never had one."

Presently the gynecologist gave Vicki sorrowing news. She required a hysterectomy after her difficult pregnancy and miscarriage of Bobby's child. When she told him, Bobby was devastated. He slammed his fist into the kitchen wall. "I'm sorry, baby," he said. Not only was he consumed with guilt over Vicki's loss of their baby—while he was in flight with Marcia—now he had no money to pay for an operation that he considered mutilating, and his fault.

All of this Red knew, but none of it could she tell the helpful district attorney in Houston. Nor could she speak of the cheap pairs of brown cotton work gloves that had suddenly started turning up in the room where Bobby slept, or of the postmidnights and early dawns when her brother came dragging into the house, cold, once again cold.

On the Sunday night that was the eve of his murder trial in Houston, Bobby and Vicki packed to leave in an old yellow Ford that he had purchased for $300, using the false name of J. C. Sheridan on the registration papers. Bobby kissed his sister good-by. He seemed in a hurry to leave. "Are you going to Houston?" she asked, for she saw his torment.

"I don't know, Red," he said. "I just may not be able to make that scene. Not right away." With smoke belching from the tailpipe, the old Ford—Bobby Vandiver's only possession in the thirty-fifth year of an unhappy life—screeched out of Dallas.

35

If ten men were standing in a row, John Raymer would
be the one to whom least attention was paid. With a tendency to flush red when angry or engaged in spirited work,
John Raymer's round face, with a disappearing fringe of
hair at the crown, resembled a hard-boiled egg. A few
more pounds and he would be roly-poly, like a rubber
beach toy that bounces up every time it is knocked to the
sand, but there was little about him to mark him as someone to remember. In the spring of 1974 he was almost half
a century old, short, portly, prudish-looking, and well
accommodated to the fact that he had made but slight
scratches on the face of the earth. Even his continuing
ambition, to obtain a college degree through endless years of
night study, was carried on not in hopes of writing a great
poem or to illumine his relationship in the family of man.
He did not expect to light historic fires at the age of forty-
nine when and if he ever received his Bachelor of Police
Science degree from Tyler State College. All John Rayner
wanted was a shot at a better-paying job, perhaps one with
the Texas parole board or another government agency
that required a diploma. He could use another hundred
dollars a month, maybe to slip a few bucks to the kids and
the grandkids and, if any was left, to sustain his only real
indulgence, the bass rig that bore him into the still, deep
lakes of East Texas. John Raymer was relentlessly small
town in fashion and horizon, and he knew it and would
have it no other way. He considered himself on balance
to be a decent, God-fearing police sergeant who did what
was expected of him, that being observation and eviction
of the "characters" who stayed past their tenuous welcome
in Longview.

In the early 1930s, when Texas was convulsed with the
excitement of tearing open the earth and searching for the
oil beneath, people said Longview would become one of the
world's great cities. It was the capital of the East Texas oil
boom, and it was a rough, brawling town where men
waded through streets of mud to reach the only whiskey
stores within a hundred miles. A richly painted whore
from Marseilles named Marie Claude became celebrated

for so inflaming an ignorant roughneck with a pocketful
of oil leases that he flung a packet of them at her, whereupon she screwed him efficiently, sold the papers for $640,-
000, and returned to Paris where she opened a club called
Le Lone Star. But Longview never grew the way they
said, Houston and Dallas and Fort Worth money and
muscle moving in to lure the bookkeepers and executive
offices away, and by the time John Raymer joined the
Longview police force in the mid 1960s, the town's population stood resolutely at around 50,000. Vestiges of its
violent youth remained, however, for Longview had become a principal rest stop on the I-20 superhighway that
connected Dallas-Fort Worth and Shreveport, Louisiana. It
was also known as a retreat for the big-city police characters who sought a quiet place to hang low for a while.
In his nine years on the force Sergeant Raymer ran some
of Dallas' meanest men out of his town, and he kept a
continuing eye on the comings and goings of Whiskey
Bend, a collection of roadhouses and cheap cafés clustered
like spores of mold around a curve of the Sabine River,
just beyond the city line. If an out-of-town hooker or
robber-lookin' fellow turned up and stayed but a day or
two before moving on, then John Raymer let them be. But
should one hang around town long enough to arouse his
suspicion, John Raymer would find reason to suggest a
quick leave-taking. When Raymer screwed up his face in
a scowl, people usually obeyed. He was not the kind of cop
to argue with.

Because of his quest for a college degree, Raymer
worked the shift that nobody else wanted—from 11 P.M.
until 7 A.M., the short hours of drunks and car crashes and
sobbing women. On the midnight of April 18, 1974, he
made note of a new car in town, a 1969 yellow Ford with
license plates from the Dallas area. Nothing unusual about
this, except that it was parked outside the Continental
Café, née Charlotte's Grill, an all-night joint that smelled of
hamburger grease, spilled beer, and pool-table chalk. Directly beside the I-20, it captured hungry late night travelers and sent them on gulping antacids, and it often housed
for a few hours the kind of folk Raymer wanted to escort
out of town. When the yellow Ford stayed outside the Continental for a few more days, Raymer set out to discover
the owner. He parked nearby and after a wait noticed a
man come out of the café and get into the yellow car. He

was a skinny man in his early thirties, ragged-looking, in jeans and a T-shirt, with a droopy mustache and a vaguely hippieish air. A regular of the café paid a due bill owed to Raymer by reporting that the new man called himself "J.C." and was a fair pool player who hustled a few bucks, and between games seemed enamored of a tall, quiet, flat-chested new waitress named Vicki. Well, fine and good, mused Raymer. But he would have bet half his pay check that "J.C." was in town for one of four reasons: (1) selling dope; (2) waiting for an underworld contact; (3) pimping; or (4) on the lam. The next night Raymer strolled casually into the café—he often dropped in for coffee—and sized up the thin, shaggy man. "J.C." was shooting pool quietly with a black man, still a novel sight in Longview after dark. The town was deep South in racial attitude, and the more redneck of the old-timers would have preferred that niggers be off the sidewalks by sundown.

The way the thin man moved, a little jerkily, and the color of his eyes—streaked with red—made Raymer decide that he was probably an addict, strung out, perhaps trying unsuccessfully to kick. While the cop drank his coffee, the new waitress, Vicki, went over and put her arm around "J.C." She was half a head taller than he, and she struck Raymer as a sexless, vacant girl. "Well, she won't last long with him," Raymer thought to himself. "These old boys swap these girls back and forth like used cars."

Just before he punched out for the morning, as a cheerful orange sun poked its head over the pine forests to the east, Raymer ran a check on the yellow Ford, a 1028 as it is known. He asked Motor Vehicle Division in Austin for identification of the registered owner, and in three minutes the computer flashed back, J. C. Sheridan, Viva Street, Mesquite, Texas—a Dallas suburb. "Okay," thought Raymer, "let's go one step further." He asked the Texas Criminal Information Center in Austin and the national center in Phoenix for any data on a man of that name. From both cities hurried back immediate response that several similar names were stored in their computers, but without a date of birth or additional identification; nothing concrete could be dispatched.

Raymer let it ride for a few days, marking each night that the yellow Ford was parked outside the Continental Café. During the day hours, while the officer slept, another patrolman noted that the car usually moved around various cheap motels in the area. Then Raymer picked up a piece of interesting and troubling news from his informer. The thin man was not really named "J. C. Sheridan." He answered to "Bobby" and the rumor inside the Continental was that he was in some sort of heavy trouble in Mesquite. Moreover, he had been seen carrying a gun.

That was enough. Raymer would question Whatever-his-name-was that very night, and if he had a gun on him, then that was a felony, worth two to five years in the state penitentiary. The Texas legislature, alarmed at the awesome number of barroom killings in the state, had recently enacted a law making it a felony to carry a weapon into a place that sold beer. wine, or whiskey.

On the evening of May 11, 1974, a raucous Saturday night, Raymer collected a brother officer for support and went to the Continental just after midnight. Raymer took a seat at the crowded counter and accepted a cup of coffee from the busy Vicki. A minor commotion at the entrance caught Raymer's ear, and he turned to see what was happening. A querulous, falling-down drunk had detained the other policeman, who now had his hands full. In the next moment, Raymer's eyes swept across the room to the pool table. "Bobby" or "J. C. Sheridan" looked directly at him, across the clouds of cigarette smoke. For a moment of suspense, their eyes met, locked, studied, as if they knew one another's business. Then the thin man abruptly put down his pool cue and almost hastened to a dark rear booth where he joined a table of several people. Raymer sighed. Too much was going on. The joint was packed. If gunfire broke out, a lot of people might get hurt. Best to come back another night and collect this customer. He seemed to be settling down in Longview, anyway.

The weekend passed, and late Monday afternoon, just as John Raymer was awakening after a day of fretful slumber —he had never really grown accustomed to sleeping off-schedule—the telephone beside his bed rang. An anonymous voice barked his name. The voice was youngish, rough, and a new informer. "Raymer," said the caller, "that fellow you've been checking on . . . I believe his name is Vannerman. Bobby Vannerman."

"Wait," said Raymer, trying to clear his head, reaching for a bedside pad and pencil. "How are you spelling that name? V-a-n-n-e-r-m-a-n?"

"Yeah. That's about it." The anonymous caller hung up.

On this night, Raymer had planned to attend his last class in a psychology course called Techniques of Interviewing. But he had already taken the final and gotten a B for the semester, and since the concluding session was to be a party given by the teacher, he decided to cut class. Instead he would pursue "Bobby Vannerman." Raymer sent the name and a physical description to the Mesquite Police Department, as the yellow Ford was registered in that city: "White male, approximately 35, five feet eight inches tall, 145 pounds, black over brown [hair over eyes]." He stayed near the teletype for an hour, waiting for an answer, but at 11 P.M., when it was time to commence nightly rounds, no response had come. "If something turns up from Mesquite," Raymer told the dispatcher, "call me."

In ten minutes Raymer was paged on his car radio and instructed to go to a pay telephone, meaning for him to get off the police radio that is heard by so many citizens with their police band receivers. "Your boy Vannerman turns out to be one Bobby Wayne Vandiver," said the dispatcher when Raymer called in. "The yellow Ford's registered to his sister's address. He's also wanted in Houston on a warrant for jumping bond in a murder case." The message from Mesquite did not mention *which* murder, so Raymer did not attach unusual significance to the report. What he had to deal with was a routine fugitive at loose in his town.

At that moment he was speaking from a pay telephone directly across the street from the Continental Café. He looked through the smoke-stained front window and through it saw Bobby Vandiver shooting pool. "Guess I'll go over and pick him up," said Raymer. But before he hung up, still another message clacked onto the police teletype:

MESQUITE PD TO LONGVIEW PD
Tx05   71600   5-15-74   11:42   CDT
Ref: Bobby Wayne Vandiver
Attn Officers involved in Vandiver case. On 2-13-74 this subject was in Mesquite jail on charges of DWI and no Drivers Lic. Subject advised he would kill the next officer who tried to arrest him. If this need be verified, contact Mesquite officers Duckworth or Westphal. Auth. Sgt. Warren.

"In that case," said Raymer, digesting the news, "send me a backup man," a plainclothes officer who could enter the Continental Café without provocation. If this Vandiver had his gun, an officer in street clothes would have better opportunity to get in close. Raymer would be a second or two behind, in uniform, with a drawn weapon for support.

But Longview's only plainclothesman on night duty was at that moment tied up in a burglary investigation, and all the dispatcher could locate was a twenty-two-year-old rookie in uniform, a boy named Bill Martin. He rendezvoused with Sergeant Raymer down the street from the Continental, and across his face was the bluff of ill-hidden fear. Instantly the older cop changed his plan: he would give the kid the easier assignment.

Everything must be quick; fast, sweeping strokes. Nothing choppy or jerky. "You drive in back of the café and park," ordered Raymer, "and I'll hang around the entrance until I see you coming. They're used to me dropping in for coffee about this time of night. As soon as I determine that you're just a few feet behind me, I'll enter, go directly over to this suspect, arrest him, and if there's any trouble, you'll be right there to help me out. Okay?" The young cop nodded, fascinated by the strategy for his first battlefield mission.

Vicki was tired, her feet and shoulders aching from six hours of throwing cheeseburgers and chicken fried steaks at the customers. She decided to steal a few minutes and go to the toilet and sit down and have a cigarette. On the way, she stopped at the pool table where Bobby was playing with the black dude. She put her arm around him lightly, and he shook her embrace away. It interfered with the shot he was lining up. Vicki leaned closer and whispered, "Hey, baby, your gun's showin' a little." Bobby glanced down; his .38 had ridden above his belt line, its jet-black head glinting in the light above the table. "Thanks, lady," he said, shoving it deeper, out of sight. Vicki left on her errand.

As soon as he saw the younger uniformed cop walking gingerly toward the front door of the café, Sergeant Raymer pushed open the entrance and stepped inside, the feeling rushing over him of intrusion on alien ground. Laughing, animated faces turned hurriedly away from him, staring sullenly toward their cups and mugs. Conversation withered. The plaintive cries from the woman singer on the juke box seemed to swell in volume. The other waitress,

Netta Joe, met the cop at the threshold. She was saucy.
"Whatta you want, John Raymer?" she asked. The middle-
aged officer, suddenly feeling older than his years, sensing
that the clientele was young and strong and mostly drunk,
and dangerous, gestured toward the pool table. "I wanna
talk with that boy who's over there shootin' pool." Raymer delicately moved his hand to his side. He unsnapped
the holster. Then it all took less than thirty seconds.

Unhesitating, Raymer walked to the pool table where a
low-hanging yellowish light illuminated but half of Bobby
Vandiver's lean body. He held a pool cue in his hand. He
was leaning over the green felt when Raymer's words broke
his concentration.

"Bobby?" the officer said. Now his gun was drawn.

Bobby jumped back, perhaps startled at the use of his
real name. Everyone else in the café, save Vicki, knew him
as "J.C."

"What?" he cried, his voice pitching upward. With the
one word, he dropped his pool cue. It fell clattering to
the floor. His opponent in the game, seeing the officer's
threatening gun, backed up prudently against the wall.

The two men, cop and fugitive, stood but two feet apart.
Between them, a literal connecting rod, was Raymer's
service revolver, pointed at Bobby's flat stomach. Reflexively, Bobby jerked out his left hand and grabbed the
gun, trying to shove it away. At the same moment he
snaked his right hand into his trousers and pulled out
his own weapon. John Raymer saw the new gun and did not
hesitate. He fired. Point-blank. But his weapon was still in
the grasp of Bobby's left hand, and the bullet screamed
downward, into the floor, ricocheting up to the ceiling
where it buried itself. The explosion made the gun barrel
so hot, and the powder fumes were so painful, that Bobby
let loose of the police weapon for a moment. John Raymer
fired his now freed gun a second time. The bullet tore open
Bobby's chest.

He sagged to the floor, his arms reaching out like a
supplicant and clutching the cop, pulling him down. The
two men fell to the floor, locked in a terrible embrace. At
the sound of the first shot, Vicki had run out of the ladies'
toilet, and now she saw Bobby writhing on the floor. Then,
quickly, he was silent. She rushed to him and flung her
body over his, hysterically pushing the police executioner
away. She seized Bobby's face and held it in her hands,

kissing his eyes, pressing her full weight against him as if she could transfer her life into his. But there was no need. It was over. Vicki raised her head and howled like a mother animal.

"You've killed Bobby!" she screamed, demonstrating to the room that when she forced open his eyes they fell forever shut again.

Stunned, Raymer backed away. He leaned against the pool table. He had never killed a man before. He pointed at the gun that Bobby still held tightly in his lifeless hand. "You see what he's still holding in his hand, don't you?" said the cop in a voice strong enough for a jury to hear. He wanted support from this crowd. When the ambulance came, Vicki could not let go of her lover. Attendants shrugged and lifted both of them onto the stretcher, carrying the dead man and his mourning woman—as one— away.

The import of the killing in the Continental Café was not learned until the next morning. A brief report found its way into the Associated Press news wire, and a reporter hurried over to the Harris County courthouse in search of Bob Bennett. The prosecutor, in trial on another case, read the item incredulously. Then again. He asked the judge for a brief recess. After a telephone call to Longview for confirmation, Bennett wadded up the news report and threw it against the wall. He was angry—his murder case was devastated and perhaps destroyed. But he also felt curious grief. "I liked him," he told Jerry Carpenter, in similar anguish. "I know everything wrong that Bobby Vandiver did, but I still liked the poor son of a bitch."

Of course it occurred to Bennett that Bobby might have been killed by contract. A lot of people would pass their nights more comfortably with the state's star witness in a grave. But after an investigation was conducted, after John Raymer was interviewed and his simple story dissected, Bennett came to believe that the death was just what it seemed. It is not inconceivable that a Texas cop would accept a contract to kill a character "in the line of duty." But Raymer was not only a respected officer, a grandfather, a devoted churchman, he—most supportive of his story— had enlisted the aid of a brother cop moments before the tragedy. If a lawman wanted to carry out a bounty killing, he would not have chosen an escort, nor would he have done the deed in full view of a café crowded with customers.

"Hell, I didn't know who Bobby Wayne Vandiver was until the next day," Raymer told Bob Bennett. "He was just another fugitive as far as I was concerned. I wouldn't have shot him if he hadn't pulled the gun on me."

But one point nagged John Raymer. How foolish it was for Bobby Vandiver to attempt a showdown in the Continental Café. The thirty seconds were a blur in the policeman's mind, yet he could not shake the notion that Bobby *wanted* to buy a death ticket. Raymer wished he could have heard the fugitive speak more words than the solitary word, *"What?"* Even it sounded—and here Raymer knew he was engaging in fanciful speculation—not unlike the voice on the telephone, the anonymous tipster who first spilled the name "Bobby Vannerman." Could Bobby have informed on himself? Could he have used John Raymer as the instrument of his own death? Did he *want* the law to hold final court on him, as he had told the Dallas posse a year before? John Raymer would never know. He would puzzle over these questions for a long time, particularly during the daylight hours when he couldn't sleep worth a damn anyway.

Bobby's sister had known of the flight to Longview. For a month there was nothing but silence after Bobby and Vicki left her house the Sunday night before his scheduled murder trial. But one morning in early May, around 10 A.M., Vicki called. "Bobby and I are in Longview," she had said. "We're okay. We're just living from hour to hour. It probably won't last, but at least we're together." Red had asked that Bobby take the phone himself. But after a moment of muffled talk Vicki returned to the line and said he was "unavailable." "I understand," said Red. She knew her brother all too well. He was shamed to be once again in flight, the evidence of failure. "Tell him I love him," she said simply. "And tell him I'll always be here if he needs me."

Now she prepared his burial. She remembered his saying so many times over the years that he would not tolerate a religious event. Yet his mother would be devastated if he were put into the earth with no respect for the God he had believed in for all the young, clean years of his life. Red searched for a compromise. After interviewing several ministers, she finally found one who agreed to preside over a businesslike burial, speaking no preacher words, only thoughts of comfort—no warnings and prophecies from the scriptures. At Laurel Land Cemetery, more than one hundred and fifty mourners gathered, some worn and weathered from the farms of Venus, others as vivid and cheap as the prizes of a carnival shooting gallery. The Baptist minister spoke briefly of Bobby Wayne Vandiver, of his deep love for Vicki, and of Vicki's children, and all those who were young, for Red had filled him in on her brother's rapport with youth. He said not to mourn Bobby too much, for he had chosen his way of life. As Red listened to the brusque eulogy she pictured her brother from so long ago, with his face full, his eyes fresh and sparkling, his hair cropped close as in a Marine recruitment poster. Just before the lid was clamped down on the coffin, Red glimpsed her brother for the last time: he had the face of an old farmer, a thin, pinched countenance from the Depression years of Venus, a look of sadness that the cosmetician's art could not push into contentment. His hair and his mustache were long, gray, and melancholy.

The minister suggested that no one judge Bobby Vandiver too harshly, then he closed his eyes. For a worried moment Red feared he would break the agreement and conclude with an automatic Baptist prayer. But then he opened them and smiled at Red and said simply, "Goodby, Bobby."

A matron located Marcia as she walked in a line to the prison cafeteria. "Your fall partner finally did something good," the matron said.

"What's that?" said Marcia.

"Bobby Vandiver just got himself shot to death in Longview," she said coldly.

Marcia fell to the floor screaming. Two attendants were summoned to drag her back to the cell. Later they told her she remained in an almost zombie trance for more than a month.

36

Now Bob Bennett tried to pick up the pieces of his shattered case. "This is the most snake-bit son of a bitch I've ever encountered," he swore wearily. Not a doubt was in his mind that four people had conspired to cause the murder of Dr. John Hill, but by early autumn 1974 he held grave concern that any of the remaining three would pass a night in prison for the crime. Around the courthouse, the coffee shop advice was to let the case slide; wait; delay; tell the reporters that the postponements were being caused by an ill witness or a conflict in scheduling. Finally, after years had gone by, no one would really care or even remember. The man who pulled the trigger was confessed and conveniently dead. If Lilla Paulus really had cancer of the cervix, then she was probably doomed. Marcia was already in the penitentiary on other charges, and when she got out her life style would boomerang her back in. And Ash was nearing eighty. The advice was tempting.

Nevertheless, there was, amid the messy mounds of legal papers, folders, briefs, tape recordings, and bits of a hundred other human dramas, a manila envelope that seemed always to rise to the surface, demanding his attention, pricking his conscience every time the temptation rose to abandon *Vandiver et al*. He shook out four color photographs and glanced once again at John Hill lying bloodied and dead in his foyer. Once again his resolve was renewed.

The young prosecutor had always imposed a severe moral ethic on his life. He was in fact driven by a small wedge of guilt, not the kind that contorts a man into the far reaches of neurotic behavior, but a blip of concern that he had somehow short-changed his obligations. In 1961, Bennett went to the nation's capital, both to attend law school at George Washington University and to answer the lure of John Kennedy's presidency. He was but one of the thousands of strong young men who went to Washington, knowing that it was *their* turn to run the country. Bennett's plan was to obtain a job when he graduated from law school somewhere in the Kennedy circle, no matter how far from the core, and serve both his President and his nation. In the excitement of the Berlin crisis, Bennett hurried to the Naval Air Force seeking a commission. He was rejected as (1) too short and (2) asthmatic. Discouraged, he returned to his studies, only to face the garden-variety Army draft a year later. The U. S. Army certainly wanted him. "Well, to hell with that," said the law student to himself. He won a student deferment to finish his law studies. Then a lunatic in Texas—Lord, why did it have to be in Texas?—destroyed John Kennedy, and all the young men went home. Bennett returned to Texas with his law degree and a season of discontent. With a wife and children, he now escaped military service completely.

"None of it really matters," he used to argue with himself. "I did nothing felonious. The record will show that I asked to serve my country and they turned me down and I obtained deferment." Still he suffered from pangs of conscience. He became a prosecutor, in part, to assuage his feelings of guilt. Most young lawyers who serve valuable apprenticeships in the DA's office leave after a year or two. Bennett had ample opportunity to abandon his oppressive courthouse cubbyhole whose blinds were drawn to conceal dirty windows and a view of decaying Houston—enchilada parlors and bail-bond offices. But he stayed. In 1974 it was his tenth anniversary, and the reason he had endured so long when his classmates were making thrice his salary was rooted somewhere in the old-fashioned, almost trite attitude of responsibility to the community. "And god damn it," he groused to a brother DA, "I may get my ass thrown out of court, but it's unfair to the people of this community, not to mention John Hill, if I don't at least try and prosecute this bunch." Unlike previous prosecutors who had worked this street, Bennett had no emotional ties to Joan Robinson Hill. He neither knew her nor cared about the circumstances of her death. He only wanted to convict those responsible for the murder of her husband.

Of course, principles are not evidence, and Bennett addressed himself to the discouraging prospects of obtaining a conviction against the remaining three. They ranged from bleak to, at the moment, hopeless. Ironically, the strongest of a bad lot was the case against Marcia, and she, in Bennett's view, was the least guilty. True, she had introduced Bobby Vandiver to Lilla Paulus, and true, she drove the killer to the scene of the murder, kissed him good-by like a suburban housewife, told him to be careful, and collected him afterward. But she had committed no personal violence against anyone. Hers was a subsidiary role, hardly murder in the first degree. But because the gun passed through her hands, and Bennett could prove this in court, then it was probably enough to persuade a jury, even if her clever Dallas lawyer managed to quash her confession.

Lilla Paulus was represented by one of the nation's most successful and cunning legal strategists, Percy Foreman, even though he had turned the actual courtroom appearances over to his able young associate, Dick DeGeurin. The old master would certainly be standing in the wings, however, and he had already told one newspaper reporter that the case against Mrs. Paulus was "preposterous." Bennett knew that the Foreman defense would move promptly to throw out both Bobby's and Marcia's statements. And chances were good the motion would be granted. Without those confessions, Bennett had scant corroborating evidence against Lilla. Locked in his filing cabinet was another manila envelope, this one embarrassingly slim. Within were the scraps of paper seized in the search of Lilla's home and purse on the day of her arrest. Could he fling these down before a jury and contend that they linked Lilla Paulus beyond doubt to the terrible death of John Hill? He could more easily grow sunflowers at the North Pole.

And Ash Robinson? Bennett had unleashed investigators from the DA's office to probe the old man's financial affairs, hoping that somewhere along the convoluted line his bank accounts would show enough mysterious cash withdrawals to finance a killing. Helpfully, Racehorse Haynes had already subpoenaed the oilman's records during depositions for the $10-million slander suit. They showed nothing that would even persuade a grand jury to indict Ash, much less a trial jury to convict. Bennett even spent days poring over the intricate transactions of the oil and gas business, entertaining a hunch that maybe old Ash had paid for his son-in-law's extermination by transferring a lucrative oil lease to Lilla Paulus or an intermediary. His search of state records in Texas, Louisiana, and Florida, where Ash was known to hold extensive interests in that state's Panhandle, produced fascinating transfers of revenue-producing properties to several prominent Houstonians, including two of the doctors Ash had enlisted in his original campaign against John Hill. But no lease was traceable to Lilla, or Bobby, or Marcia. By the end of summer, with the trials of the two women near, Bob Bennett

came to the discouraging realization that he had nothing—
nothing!—on Ash Robinson other than Marcia's and Bobby's confessions. The situation outraged him, and he toyed
with the idea of asking the federal district attorney to investigate the matter. Under federal law, no corroborating
evidence is required in accomplice cases—Watergate was
the lighthouse example—and, theoretically, the confessions
of Bobby and Marcia might be enough to convict Ash.
But on what charge? The best Bennett could unearth was
"conspiracy to deprive John Hill of his civil rights by killing him," and that punishment hardly seemed to fit the
crime. Also chafing was the bizarre fact that the general
public still had no idea that Ash Robinson was the pup-
peteer of this grisly show. Houston's newspapers had
treated him with deference since the day his daughter died
(he had, surely, cautioned them against libel as well) and,
as far as the city knew, he was only a sorrowing senior
citizen, a rich and eccentric character of the fiber that built
the great town, and lonely to the point of pity from the
tragedies that had ravaged his twilight years.

For too long a time Bob Bennett had been hearing talk
that held Ash to be some kind of frontier hero. It went
something like this: "I wouldn't have blamed the old man
if he had marched up Kirby Drive with a shotgun and blew
John Hill's head off. And no jury in Texas would have
convicted him." The talk came from lawyers, from cops,
even from DAs who were not privy to the intimacies of the
case.

If he failed in everything else, Bob Bennett promised
himself, he would try to put a few facts on the public
record. Perhaps these would shape a more informative
opinion of the real Ash Robinson. "The truth is," Bennett
could hear himself crying, "Ash Robinson was too *cowardly* to do murder himself. So he *bought* himself a killing."
With these thoughts, he prepared for trial.

In the last week of October 1974 the trial of Marcia
McKittrick for murder and Lilla Paulus for being an accomplice to murder began in the district court of Harris
County. The defendants entered chambers through different
doors and resolutely avoided looking at one another. Free
on bond, Mrs. Paulus used the public entrance and sat
quietly in the front row of the small courtroom for more
than an hour before the press discovered her identity.

She did not seem menacing. In a severely tailored blue dress that enhanced her thinness, with eyeglasses dangling from a silver chain, with sensible black walking shoes, with waiflike hair cut inelegantly and let go to shades of sleet and snow, she was the woman who has graded everybody's English Lit exam since education began. How could Bob Bennett possibly persuade a jury that she was mistress to a salon of crime?

Marcia McKittrick, in handcuffs, came to court under bailiff escort, and she was placed in a cramped waiting corner behind the witness box. On this day she looked less than a battle-scarred whore and more like a frightened white trash housewife, come to court to whisper how a husband had beaten her and abandoned the children to hunger. Prison pallor made her face almost indistinguishable from the wall behind her, and her lumpy figure, filled with institutional food, was contained in a shapeless orange and purple prison smock. On her naked feet and legs were clunky, thick-soled sandals. The romantics among the spectators sympathized, wishing, like Marcia herself, that she could have come for her day of reckoning in the costume of her trade. Marcia was hugely embarrassed to present herself as a pauper; she wanted the paint and feathers and jewels of her art. Nervously clutching and releasing a fistful of the garish sack the matron had ordered her to wear, she sat and watched the people enter the courtroom. It was well past the scheduled starting hour of 10 A.M., and her attorney, Charles Caperton, was not yet in the courtroom.

Percy Foreman wandered in, even though he would not personally represent Mrs. Paulus this day. Matters were in the capable hands of his associate, Dick DeGeurin, busy at the clerk's desk filing new motions to invalidate the confessions of Bobby and Marcia that implicated his client. With Foreman, at least the figure matched his dossier. He exuded star power, a giant with shaggy gray head whose locks tumbled boyishly to his eyes. He had won acquittals for three hundred accused murderers, and specialized in women who shot men. Once he had taken a drawerful of diamond rings collected as fees from these troubled ladies, ordered a pair of opera pumps encrusted with the macabre gems, and knelt before his wife on Christmas morning to slip them onto her feet. As he now took a seat in the front row of the spectators' chamber, people gathered around him, but giving him space, drawing back a little as tourists in Kenya might for an old and celebrated lion. In his eighth decade, the legendary lawyer's court faculties were still machete sharp, but his personal memory seemed to be loosening. Nodding respectfully at Lilla Paulus, he mistook his own client to be Marcia McKittrick. With embarrassment, Lilla corrected him, tossing her head across the room to where the real Marcia sat. Foreman patted the older woman's arm with gentle reassurance.

"Well, nobody would believe this case, that's for sure," he allowed. "All the scandal and subplots, the convolutions, it really outstrips Peyton Place, doesn't it?"

Lilla Paulus nodded, hesitantly.

Then Percy began to talk for the benefit of the reporters clustered about him. "We decided three or four weeks ago that the state had no case against our client," he said. "So we aren't really worried."

Lilla murmured, audibly, but to herself, "I wish they had told *me* that. It's the first I heard of it."

Percy nodded his great head in emphatic affirmation. "I never for a minute had any doubt that it would be disposed of just the way it is going to be. There's no way they could convict Mrs. Paulus with what they have." The Paulus defense had obtained, under disclosure rules, most of the district attorney's case, specifically the slips of paper taken in the search.

If it was all that cut and dried, wondered a young girl reporter, then was there enough evidence to even indict Lilla Paulus?

"It doesn't take much evidence to indict," Foreman lectured. "They could indict you for the murder of the Lindbergh baby, and you weren't even born then. Any DA anywhere can persuade a grand jury to indict anybody for anything." With that, Foreman again patted Lilla's thin hand—it looked like the bone that Gretel stuck out of the cage for the witch to examine—and ambled off. His disdain for the matters of this courtroom seemed to underscore the fragility of the state's condition.

When Judge Frank Price entered to begin proceedings, both women stared incredulously. He further destroyed the business of images. Here was the referee of their destinies, and he looked less like a judge than a postgraduate college student, probably a phys. ed. major. Barely past thirty-five, and having sat on the bench for only two years through an appointment, he seemed impossibly callow to preside over one of the most notorious criminal proceedings in the history of the city. His business suit was modishly Western, the kind a rich rancher would wear to a rodeo cocktail party, and his aviator glasses were from a men's fashion magazine. But behind them was a gaze of friendliness—he warmed the room—and a gentle, caring air. His reputation was that of an exceedingly fair judge who maintained a low-key chamber, not unlike a rookie congressman who recognizes the wisdom of prudent quiet until experience allows crustiness.

The broad-shouldered young judge and both of the attorneys—Bennett and DeGeurin—had all been prosecutors in the district attorney's office. Away from the courthouse, they remained close friends, drinking whiskey together when the occasion arose, dining with wives and dates, and playing handball. Here the judge was the customary winner, not in diplomatic deference to his position but due to his superb condition and his ranking as one of the city's best players. But when the three stood together in a convivial group beside the bench, they seemed boys playing at men's work. The image arose of college law students, allowed to take over the court for a day to hold mock proceedings.

But the day was real, and it could not begin until counsel for Marcia appeared. "Where is Mr. Caperton?" asked Judge Price when an hour past starting time had passed. He was annoyed. He ran a streamlined docket, cutting through the fawnings and formalities, dispensing with morning roll call of defendants and lawyers to cut fifteen minutes and try to speed the snailish path of justice. The court reporter disappeared to make inquiry and returned with the surprising report that Caperton was at this important moment still in Dallas. His office claimed Caperton did not even know his client was going on trial for murder.

"I find this difficult to believe," said Judge Price. "This case has been set and reset, and this time was mutually agreed upon by all of the attorneys with interests here." Both he and the court—not to mention the defendant—were insulted by the lawyer's absence. But the judge calmed himself and issued instructions to the clerk: "Tell Mr. Caperton to catch the next plane to Houston and we will commence at 2 P.M." There was no elastic in his directive.

In the meantime, the judge ruled on a pretrial motion by Dick DeGeurin to quash the confession of Bobby Vandiver as it related to Lilla Paulus' alleged involvement in the murder. "That will be granted," said the judge. Bennett sighed in disappointment, but only slightly, for he had anticipated the decision. The Sixth Amendment guarantees the right to confront an accuser, and it was, after all, impossible to cross-examine the statement of a dead man.

But the judge refused similarly to throw out the statement of Marcia McKittrick as evidence against Mrs. Paulus. Instead, he would hear testimony on DeGeurin's plea. Bennett perked up at this; at least he had a chance.

Full of excuses and apologies, Caperton arrived after lunch, another of the boyish lawyers perfectly cut out to join the handball team. He was by far the flashiest of counsel present, with chunky diamond rings on both hands, and the aura of a professional golfer, down to the tassels on his shoes. His fair face was beet red from running down airport corridors, and his carefully cut blond hair was drenched in perspiration. Judge Price scolded him, and made his displeasure immediately known by coldly denying the first several objections that the lawyer made when testimony began. Caperton was in the unenviable position of having angered the judge at the very beginning of an important murder trial, and even Marcia, sitting beside him, could sense that her position was harmed. But she had faith in her attorney, she called him "my heart," and had he not always managed to bail her out of precarious situations before?

Attorney Caperton, with obvious coaching from DeGeurin, sought to prove that Marcia was in the agony of heroin withdrawal when homicide detective Jerry Carpenter fetched her from the Dallas jail, and that she confessed to the murder of John Hill only because the cop promised her narcotic relief. The defense immediately summoned Carpenter to the stand. Looking very gambler man in a hot salmon shirt with matching tie, Carpenter was skilled at testifying—most veteran cops are—and he delivered his responses tersely, in a twang like a taut guitar string. He did not like Charles Caperton, and the feeling was clearly mutual.

"Was Miss McKittrick sick when you picked her up?" asked the lawyer.

"Yeah. She was sick. Dope sick. Chills, stuff like that."
The homicide detective said he stopped at a café en route
from Dallas to Houston and bought his prisoner breakfast
and gave her two aspirins for her discomfort. But nothing
else.

Caperton made a facetious nod. He did not believe this
at all. If, as the detective had testified, the prisoner was
"dope sick," then did she understand what was happening
to her?

Carpenter nodded. "She's an intelligent girl," he said.
"She understood what we were asking her, and she understood what she was telling us." Marcia did not seem "emotionally distraught."

"Did she understand she could go to the pen for murder?"

"She did."

"Did you make any promises or hold out the hope of a
light sentence . . . *if* she co-operated?"

Here Carpenter hesitated, for what a cop says to a
prisoner and what he hints at by his attitude and demeanor
are two different things. Certainly the promise was in the
air that if Marcia co-operated, things would go easier for
her. "I made no promises," answered Carpenter, "but I
told her I would *talk* to the DA."

The attorney made another look of disbelief. Had there
been a jury, the expressions might have been useful, but
they were not impressing the still smoldering judge.

Caperton demanded to know why Miss McKittrick would
want to talk to the Houston police, since she had spent
months trying to keep them from bothering her, and had
even filed a motion to enjoin every peace officer in the
state of Texas from talking to her?

"Well, she told me she was tired of running and wanted
to get her business straight. In the character world, this
means getting all her legal problems taken care of."

Caperton thrust to the heart of his contention. "Didn't
you make any promises to get her medicine to make her
'feel better'?"

Carpenter glared stonily at the defense lawyer. "No, sir.
I did not." After the prostitute signed the statement, Carpenter and his partner, Gamino, had taken her to the St.
Joseph's Hospital drug clinic where a doctor gave her
medicine for diarrhea and a prescription for Amytal, a
barbiturate useful to help her sleep, thence to jail. With

diligence, Caperton tried to break the cop down, but it was chiseling marble with a toothpick.

Wearily the tired Dallas lawyer put on a parade of witnesses who verified (1) that Marcia was severely addicted to heroin and was suffering from cramps, fever, chills, and diarrhea while in the Dallas jail after her arrest there, and (2) that when she was booked into the Harris County jail following her interrogation and confession, she was passing out. A stout jail matron with purple hair agreed that Miss McKittrick was "semiconscious and had trouble breathing" when Jerry Carpenter delivered her.

"Would a person withdrawing from heroin sign anything—a check, a statement, a confession—to get drugs?"

The matron nodded vigorously. She looked like a missionary who had spent her life among jungle devil worshipers. "Yes, sir, they sure would. They'd do anything to get their drugs."

Then Marcia herself assumed the witness box, her lawyer having laid down ground rules that questioning would be limited to the confession, and exclusive of the alleged murder. Her version was that Carpenter and Gamino not only tempted her with the promise of narcotics, but made alternating threats and promises.

"They told me I wouldn't serve a day in jail if I cooperated with them," she said. And if she refused to sign, "the officers said I would be an old lady before I saw my little boy again. . . . I know that police can do what they say." The entire week that began in Dallas with her arrest in a stolen Chrysler and ended in the Houston jail when she awoke from a drugged sleep was a blank. "Everything is fuzzy. I don't remember signing the confession or even being booked."

Overnight Judge Price perused the testimony and the law, and the next morning he announced a decision that cheered Lilla Paulus and devastated Marcia McKittrick. The prostitute's confession would not be admissible as evidence in the Paulus matter. But it *could* be introduced in the state's case against Marcia herself. The older woman's lawyer, DeGeurin, sensed that the currents of the trial were treacherous, and he had best divorce his client as quickly as possible from Marcia. He thus asked for a continuance in the Paulus trial until the next February, four months away. Judge Price approved.

With that out of the way, the judge turned and directed

that jury selection in the murder trial of Marcia McKittrick would begin on the following Monday—just four days away.

Charles Caperton's mouth dropped open. He began to stammer. He ran his fingers nervously through his hair. He pleaded for a delay. Clearly this was an attorney who was not ready to begin a murder defense. He had put all his money on one throw of the dice—expecting that Marcia's confession would be thrown out. And now he had little left in his pocket.

"I feel this is a total denial of this girl's rights," said Caperton, "if the court makes us go to trial Monday."

The judge was not moved by the lawyer's plight. He was, in fact, further annoyed. Charles Caperton had been Marcia McKittrick's attorney of record in this case for more than a year. He had served her in other matters years before that. This was an important case involving others, and the court—and the community—were anxious that it be settled. The judge would not tolerate further delay. With a suggestion that his patience was stretched as far as it would go, he left the bench.

Violent rain struck the city over the lunch hour and tornadoes danced in the northern regions of the county. People milled about the crowded lobby of the courthouse, unable to go out, watching great sheets of rain assault the building. The midday skies were dark, almost night, as if the forces of nature were out of balance. The setting was grotesquely perfect for the afternoon's drama. Fittingly, it was Halloween.

Charles Caperton decided to try a ploy that was breathtaking in its risk and as potentially turbulent for his client as the storm outside. For two hours he dashed about the building, conferring with Bennett in the DA's quarters, then in the basement jail where Marcia bewilderedly tried to understand what was going on, thence back to the courtroom, now deserted of spectators and press. The attorney believed, or so he said, that he had presented a compelling case to invalidate his client's confession. He felt sure that the state's Court of Criminal Appeals would one day support him and quash the document and either grant a new trial or dismiss charges altogether. Therefore, he hastily plotted a little drama that could be played out in a few minutes and let everybody except Marcia go home. He would come back into court this very afternoon and have Marcia plead "not guilty," then permit the district attorney to present stipulated testimony—roughly the charges contained in the grand jury indictment—and accept an immediate verdict of "guilty" from Judge Price. With his client thus hurriedly condemned, Caperton could return to Dallas and prepare an eloquent appeal, based solely on the merits of the prostitute's confession. And in a year or two, the normal length of time that it took for the high court to rule on such a matter, he anticipated freedom for Marcia McKittrick.

Bob Bennett listened to the proposal carefully and weighed it in his mind. Did Marcia understand the danger of such a move? "Yes," said Caperton. "I explained it to her." The Dallas lawyer seemed fascinated by the machinations of his plot. He also seemed in a hurry to catch a plane back home.

The young assistant district attorney was being handed a plum on a silver platter, and he wanted to make sure there was no chance the fruit was rotten and the container was tin. Did Charles Caperton really mean that he was willing, nay, *eager*, for the court to find his client guilty of the murder of Dr. John Hill, and then have her duly sentenced? "That's *just* what we intend," answered Caperton. Did he have *that* much faith in the merits of his appeal? Yes, he certainly did. Now let them get on with it. Many thoughts swarmed in Bennett's mind, not the least of which was the ulcerish feeling that Marcia McKittrick was not receiving the best legal advice. Here was a lawyer who had failed to appear on the day she went to trial for murder, and who was now throwing in the towel and sending his client off to the state penitentiary as a convicted murderess—with but one avenue of appeal in the distant future available on which to hope for freedom. In a full trial, several dozen matters—the "hickeys" that Racehorse Haynes always searched for—could easily arise and merit appeal, and any one might cause a high court to overturn a decision. There was also the possibility that in a full trial a jury might even find Marcia McKittrick not guilty.

But Bob Bennett was being given the easiest notch on his gun a prosecutor ever got. He could save the community time and money and count an easy win for his side. Failing to put down a queasiness in his conscience, Bennett nonetheless agreed to enact the charade. At midafternoon the storm increased. Marcia was brought into the empty courtroom where she was told to sit at the defense table. About her, the bailiff and the court employees were speaking of the rain and the radio reports that tornadoes were touching down, so far sparing human injury. Marcia's thoughts were on what was about to happen to her. She tried to summon bravado. Over the lunch recess, she had heard from a sister prisoner that the plan was promising. "One of the girls went before a judge and waived a jury trial and she only got a $2,500 fine," said Marcia to the bailiff. He was a big, fatherly man who was kind to the prostitute and was letting her smoke before the judge entered the room.

"What was the girl charged with?" asked the bailiff.

"Assassination," said Marcia. "Of a kidnap victim."

She chain-smoked awhile, listening to the storm. Several times she mentioned to the bailiff that the events about to transpire were "for the best."

"Charles Caperton explained it to me," she said, but there was a tinge of apprehension to her voice, "and he thinks we have a good chance of winning on appeal."

It took five minutes, four of which were used by Bob Bennett to drone stentorially the state's accusation and evidence and stipulated witnesses against Marcia McKittrick for the crime of first degree murder. Charles Caperton rose and accepted the stimulated testimony—with an exception to the disputed confession.

Clearly troubled by the moment, Judge Price instructed the defendant to rise. "I find you guilty of the felony offense of murder," he said, over the rising sounds of the heavy rain. Marcia McKittrick closed her eyes, swayed, and threw her hand knotted against the orange and purple smock to push back a sob. The bailiff had handcuffs ready for her wrists, but, moved by her plight, he took only her arm and almost gently led her away.

Bob Bennett walked out of the courtroom with his eyes to the floor, not even bothering to honor custom by shaking hands with Caperton.

Four weeks later, after presentence investigation by the probation department, Judge Price sentenced Marcia to ten years in the state penitentiary. On the way to the elevator that would take her to the subterranean county jail, Marcia was stopped by Bob Bennett. He wanted to know if she would now testify for the state in the upcoming trial of

Lilla Paulus. Perhaps her situation might improve, he suggested carefully. The implication was that a warm word from the DA's office might go down well with those officials in the penal system who decide when an inmate is sufficiently rehabilitated to rejoin society.

Marcia made to shake her head in dutiful negation. But then she shrugged. "I don't know," she said. "I'm so confused. And I don't feel very good."

He did not blame her. The same taste of ashes was in his mouth.

37

Over the mild winter months that rarely torment Houston with any climatic discomfort save torrential rains and an anemic breeze or two from the north, Marcia McKittrick remained the object of many attentions. She was not transferred back to the state women's prison at Huntsville to complete her old bad check sentence from Dallas, or to begin the new "dime"—as she called it—the ten years decreed for the murder of Dr. John Hill. Rather she was kept cooped up in the downtown Harris County jail where she passed the days reading philosophy, writing children's stories, and looking forward to the frequent visits of a nun named Sister Sophia who did missionary work among the women inmates. Often the nun cheered her by taking Marcia's stories to the outside world and reading them to youngsters in the church school and returning with good reviews. "I always had a vivid imagination," Marcia confided in the sister, "it's just that I never had the time until now to sit down and write it out." It did not seem to be the classic example of the whore obtaining religion and rushing to repentance and redemption. Marcia simply liked Sister Sophia because she made no demands, engaged in no pleading and cajoling, as did everybody else who came to see her. The visits from the opposing lawyers became so commonplace that when the matron roused Marcia from an afternoon nap she would often come awake grouchily and say, "Which one this time? Bennett or DeGuerin?"

Marcia liked Bob Bennett and she told him so. He had no trouble starting up her conversation motor and, once engaged, it spun out merry tales of whoredom and irrelevant anecdotes of life with Bobby Vandiver. Had Bennett ever heard about the time when Bobby burned her spot book? "Oh, and there was that night in Corpus Christi when Bobby and I were ripped, really stoned out of our minds on pills, they practically sold them over the counter at this club, and we staggered out and got on these gocarts next door and went around and around and around!"

The prosecutor laughed, as he always did, and he let out the rope until it was slack and comfortable. But then he always yanked it back. "Are you going to testify for us against Lilla?" was what he wanted to know. It was the reason he always came.

"I can't, Bob," she usually answered, for she was now on a first-name basis with the assistant district attorney. "I can't go back on things I learned when I was a kid."

Once Bennett raged at her. "You and that god damn character code!" he yelled, his voice echoing along the thick-walled chambers of the jail. "Look where it's got you!"

"It's not that," Marcia replied. "It's just a decision I've made. Some mornings I wake up and I wash my face and I think, 'Well, you're a class A fool for not testifying against that woman. . . . But if I did give evidence, then she'd probably get a life sentence. And at the same time, I'd be sentencing myself to die."

Bennett's red flag went up. He lived with the continuing worry that a pair of scissors would find its way into the prostitute's back. That was one reason he was keeping her in the basement jail of the courthouse. The other was convenience. He did not have the time to drive seventy-five miles to Huntsville for his regular bouts of frustration with her. "Have they threatened you?" he demanded to know.

"Let's just say they made me an offer I can't refuse," she giggled. Then she turned serious. "No, I'm kidding you. I just couldn't live with myself if I knew I put somebody else in jail. Listen, Bob, I'm only twenty-five years old. And I've only got a dime to do."

On another day, Bennett discovered Marcia obviously frightened. Her mood was as grave as the shroudlike light trying to work its way through the opaque windows of the jail. Gently, the prosecutor tried to learn the source of her fear. Finally she spoke, her voice heavy with emotion. "If I testified," she said, "I'm scared they would hurt my little boy."

Nonsense, said Bennett, trying to put out this fire. They wouldn't hurt a child.

"You don't know *them*," said Marcia. She once knew a hooker in Dallas who defied the character code of silence and bore witness for the state. Then her four-year-old boy was "mangled" before her very eyes.

"Who are these people?" demanded Bennett. Who was "them"?

Of *them*, Marcia had nothing further to say. Bennett gathered that she desperately feared some of the guests who had formerly enjoyed the hospitality of Lilla Paulus. He tried to dissuade her of that concern. If she was in any way worried about the safety of her loved ones, then the DA's office would bring her child and parents under escort from Dallas, install them in a house, and throw the entire Houston police force around its perimeter as guards. *Then* would she testify against Lilla?

Marcia appreciated the offer, but the answer was still no. "I can't, Bob. I wish I could help you out, but I can't."

The prostitute clung with what seemed unshakable determination to her position over a period of four months. Bob Bennett almost abandoned hope of any co-operation from her. He had no weapons of negotiation remaining. He had called her a dupe and a fool for taking the rap when others were living free. He had held out the tempting suggestion that the state of Texas would look with favor on her co-operation as evidence that she was rehabilitating herself and entitled to rejoin the community. He even tried appealing to her sense of the theatrical; she would be the star! He did not tell her that without her appearance there would be no show.

On the evening of February 16, 1975, a dozen hours or so before Lilla Paulus was due in court to answer the state's accusation that she had been an accomplice to the murder of John Hill, Bennett paid one last visit to the women's section of the county jail. He was in a foul mood, uncharacteristically snappish, tired of fooling around with Marcia, even weary of his job and the system and the city of Houston. An offer had come to him recently from the United States Attorney's office in Washington and the temptation was strong to take it. The eternal John Hill murder case had worn his faith in a judicial process down to a nub. He knew that the next morning a travesty would occur. Oh, he was going to appear for the state and shuffle through the motions of trying to convict Lilla Paulus, but without Marcia, without her nasal little-girl drawl pouring out the tale of Ash Robinson's money and John Hill's blood, then by the end of the day he could probably go home and maybe get the first good night's sleep since he first heard all the names he now so despised.

"It's a god damn shame," he said. His voice was hot. Marcia had never seen him this way. "And you're crazy! You're flat out stupid. Bobby Vandiver, your great friend, did twelve days in the city jail. Twelve days! Ash Robinson, the son of a bitch who put this whole thing together, is sitting out there in his River Oaks mansion and doesn't even have to come down to the courthouse! And you're going to sit back and let Lilla Paulus walk out of here a free woman? It's *insane*, Marcia. You're a smart woman in some things, but you're certifiably crazy when it comes to the most important decision you ever made."

Marcia began her response by saying that she had already made her feelings known. She was *not* going to testify. Period. She had, in fact, just told Dick DeGeurin the news in his most recent visit, and he had praised her for the courage it took to keep her silence. Then, suddenly, she interrupted herself and looked away. A clutch of confusing emotions passed across her face. Bennett wondered briefly if she was ill. Then she smiled, curiously, an enigmatic smile that would have sent Da Vinci for a paintbrush. "Well, who knows what I might do?" she finally said, teasingly. But it was enough to make Bennett sit up. Was there a tiny sliver of hope? "Yeah," Marcia went on, "who knows what I might do if you put me on the witness stand and I see that old bitch sittin' out there in the courtroom?"

"Would you testify against her?" asked Bennett, trying to guard his mounting excitement.

Marcia shrugged. "I told you, Bob. Who knows?"

They all gathered, like kin whose names were written in a family Bible and linked by a great disaster. Jerry Carpenter was there first, arriving at the courthouse long before the starting hour of ten. He had suffered still another tragedy in his personal life; it seemed to reflect the misery of his police work. His teen-age son had been gravely injured in a high-speed traffic crash and the boy's face, shredded, would require years of plastic surgery. If that were not enough to make a man somber, the detective had, just the day before, learned that a "contract" was reportedly out on his life, presumably due to his zealous work in the Hill matter. Carpenter reported the rumor to his superior and was told to take off a few days and stay low. Instead, Carpenter went directly to the courthouse. He would probably be called as a witness in Lila's trial sooner or later but he was so deeply committed to a conviction of the woman that he could not bear to stay at home and wait for a summons. His former partner, Gamino, had been transferred out of homicide, assigned to the training division for rookie cops. He sent word to Bennett that he would be available on five minutes' notice if his testimony were required. "We may not get as far as testimony," cautioned Bennett.

Carpenter sipped coffee in the basement cafeteria and frowned. His mood was so bleak that he could not even enjoy the parade of pretty secretaries, lined up to purchase carry-out breakfasts. "Without Marcia," he muttered, "we might as well hang it up. They'll ask for an instructed verdict, and they'll probably get it." He cursed and threw his empty cigarette pack to the floor. It was fortunate that he did not have to question a suspect on this morning, for he might have slapped someone against the wall. "They must have got to her," he snapped. "Money, maybe. Or threats. She's vulnerable in so many ways. Her kid, her mommy and daddy. And hell, Marcia's smart. She knows she's only serving a dime, and she's probably got less than a year to go." Carpenter had also paid visits to Marcia during the weeks and he had tried first reason, then, failing, a dump truck of scorn. "Ah, hell," he said as he rose to find the elevator and ascend to the sixth-floor courtroom where the others were assmbling, "it's no use blaming anybody. People do what they damn well have to do. The whole city is fucked up."

Overnight a rumor worked its way out of the women's jail and was waiting for Bob Bennett when he arrived at his office. Marcia had been supposedly threatened with death by a sister prisoner if she testified. "I'm sure it's probably true," he told the investigator who brought the report, "but what the hell do I do with it on the morning we begin trial? I don't know how to verify it without interviewing every god damn female in the jail. And they'd all deny it."

Briefly he thought of hurrying down to the slammer and soothing Marcia, but he dared not tamper with that fragile ambiguity from their meeting the night before. Instead he began working on a last-ditch squeeze play in case the whore continued her balk. His plan was highly original and, as best as he could determine through hurried research, at least legal. Its moral ramifications were another matter, and he did not relish putting Marcia in the vise he had concocted. But at this ragged eleventh hour, all he wanted was to satisfy his professional obligations and get every one of these maddening people off the stage of his senses. Normally he was as peppy as a vein full of amphetamines on the first morning of a major trial. Today all he felt was numbing fatigue and the anticipation of humiliating defeat.

Conversely, attorney Dick DeGeurin arrived at the courthouse with Lilla Paulus on one arm, an enormous squat briefcase in the other, and the attitude of a performer about to open in a show that would make him a star. He was careful to conceal his confidence, for he was a cool young man, a patrician lawyer who, it was easy to imagine, had been taught from childhood not to wear emotions for public view, or for the servants in the house. All of his life had been in preparation for this day. Indeed he even remarked to a friend, "When Lilla Paulus goes on trial, *I* go on trial with her." DeGeurin was a short man as was his old friend Bob Bennett—had a plank been placed across their heads it would have balanced perfectly. And he possessed the attendant ego that so often overcompensates small stature. Happily, the ego was reinforced by good looks. DeGeurin brought to mind the playing fields of an Eastern prep school with his blondish hair modishly long and swept back on the sides like that of a Dutch skater on a frozen windy pond. In his Brooks Brothers suit and high-sheen, tightly tied cordovans, he was almost alien, Houston being a city of double knit suits and white patent loafers. DeGeurin was the child of a prominent Austin silk-stocking attorney who detested soiling his hands in the combat of trial. His fees were from society law—oil and gas leases, an occasional divorce. The DeGeurin dinner table rang with talk of politics, of the father's college roommate, John Connally, of Lyndon Johnson's pursuit of the rawest power, of Sam Rayburn's country boy cunning. The child grew with ambitions to become one of these giant men whose handshakes the father knew well, and after law school his path was established. He would season himself with a year or two in the DA's office, then run for the state legislature, then Congress, then, who knew? But unexpected roadblocks caused rerouting. The young lawyer had difficulty staying married; two discordant divorces and a reputation for being exceptionally diligent in the pursuit of comely women was not helpful to an aspiring Texas politician. But he could have probably overcome even that—Texas was loosening its Baptist puritanism in the national sweep of the new morality—had he not spent a discomforting season in Austin as a lobbyist. "I grew up in that town," he told a friend, "and I thought I knew what went on during a legislative session—a bunch of drinkin' and screwin' and ignorance. But I never realized to what extent." The experience caused severe disenchantment with the political process. He abandoned ideas of becoming the United States senator from Texas and turned his attention toward a blazing career in the law, one that would satisfy his father.

After three years in the Houston DA's office where he was recognized as a tough and skilled prosecutor, De-Geurin accepted a position with one of the city's old-line legal firms, a place of thick blue carpets and hushed voices, the kind where the not altogether joking remark was made that only the filing clerk knew the way to the courthouse. From the hurly-burly atmosphere of the DA's office, De-Geurin found himself assigned to work that could have been done by a $600-a-month insurance investigator. "My constant defense position was to deny some poor bastard what was rightly due him from an accident," he complained to a friend. "I am sorely afraid my epitaph will be, 'He devoted his life to determining who entered the intersection first.' "

It happened that a lawyer friend, a fellow who liked to collect weapons, including machine guns, was charged by federal authorities with possessing illegal weapons. Percy Foreman was engaged for the defense, and DeGeurin called up the old warrior and volunteered to help. The offer was accepted, and DeGeurin was quickly overwhelmed by the experience. "To be around Percy was incredible," he would say. "All of our motions were dealing with bedrock constitutional law, the kind of law that has stood for two hundred years. I kept comparing that with what I was supposed to be doing at my law firm, figuring out a workman's compensation settlement for a Mexican with a bad back." Walking home from the courthouse one day, Percy Foreman complimented his volunteer associate and remarked, "Would you rather defend insurance companies or people?" Two days later, the most famous lawyer in Texas made DeGeurin a firm offer which he eagerly accepted. Young Turks would have paid Foreman just to hide in the bookcases and hear the old man dictate. At any given moment the Foreman office carried some three hundred active criminal cases.

But though DeGeurin's trial work was respected by his peers—he had lost only one client to a life sentence—the embrace of public acclaim had not yet enveloped him. He was crown prince to the king of criminal law, and almost no one even knew that the sign on the office door read "Foreman *and* DeGeurin." As he strode confidently into Judge Frank Price's courtroom on the morning of February 17, 1975, he sensed that all this would soon change.

Now it was Lilla's turn.

Since the hour of her arrest, she had wisely remained silent and at the same time sealed off the entrances to her past. Bob Bennett dispatched investigators to rummage through her history, but the ensuing reports were thin-blooded, as frail as the woman herself. She sat now at the defense table, coughing heavily from a long winter siege of bronchitis, her body so thin and her hair so much grayer than at her last court appearance that the skeptics concluded she had deliberately aged herself in preparation for the trial. Would any jury convict its grandmother, particularly when she had obviously risen from a sickbed to answer the state's impudent charge? Lilla's face was set in the cast of a martyr. She seemed one of those anonymous little women with shoulders sagged and rounded, the kind who creeps through life afraid of being heard or noticed, not even spunky enough to tell the greengrocer his tomatoes are rotten. She offered herself as a creature of defeat. She seemed to have accepted her place at the bottom of the heap since the days of childhood, and she had no voice with which to complain. Perhaps the good Lord would note her suffering and make a special place for her.

"How on earth is Bennett going to convince a jury that she's the Ma Barker of our time?" wondered one of the reporters, having heard the courthouse gossip that Lilla had hijackers and hit men as décor in her living room. The same reporter stoped Lilla on the way to the defense table and inquired, "How do you feel about the trial?" And she shook her head and replied, "No comment. I just want to get it over. I'm innocent."

Lilla Paulus was on this day, as she had always been, a clever and purposeful woman. She was coming across exactly as she wanted to, and had she so desired, she could have replaced the St. Christopher medal about her neck with a brace of diamonds, or slipped out of the spinsterly beige wool dress into a hand-sewn, skin-tight Western suit of unborn calf and gold fringes that danced in the wind and were as the marks of vibrance around a sun. Her only daughter, a now grown woman from whom Lilla was bitterly estranged, had given Bob Bennett a guarded and reluctant interview. She made him swear he would never reveal the hidden city in which she lived. "I'm afraid of my mother," the daughter said. "She's a dangerous woman. And one of the greatest actresses of all time."

How similar were all their beginnings! The same words that sketched in the early years of John Hill and Bobby Vandiver and Marcia McKittrick and even Bob Bennett could serve for the opening chapter of Lilla Paulus' life story. She, too, had been born and reared in the same kind of anonymous Texas town where the people worked hard and whose principal purchases in life were a house, a pickup truck, and a tombstone. Lilla was the only child of a devout Methodist couple whose code of living was so restrictive that they forbade their daughter to attend school dances. A pretty youngster with bright blonde hair and a merry attitude, she was constantly threatened with eternal damnation. Years later a classmate would remember that Lilla took a fashion magazine from a drugstore and kept it hidden for months, terrified that her parents would discover the forbidden treasure and inflict terrible punishment, at the same time mesmerized by the beautiful women on the pages. The Depression did not concern these women in marceled hair and clinging satins. They had no worry about hundred-pound sacks of potatoes selling for two bits, or that there was not a spare dime for a hairbrush because the church house needed a new coat of paint and God's needs were always ahead of man's. "I'm going to be

famous someday," said the young Lilla to her friend. It
was not the idle prattle of a child. It seemed at the time
an oath of the soul.

Lilla had difficulty in even getting out of Madisonville.
First she married a local boy, a farmer, and not until she
had borne a son did she realize that marriage had done
little but move her body from one confinement—her parents' home—to another. Abandoning the farmer, Lilla appeared promptly on the rodeo circuit, affixing herself to a
series of cowboys, traveling with the lean, hard-muscled
men and yelling encouragement as they tried to keep seats
atop wild horses and Brahman bulls. Once, to make a little
money, she even stood as the target for a carnival knife-
throwing act. Husband number two was a Dallas man
named Jerry Carpenter would recognize
as a "character." He introduced his shapely blonde wife
around the night spots of Big D as "my beautiful little farm
girl with a face like an angel and a tongue like the devil."
Lilla could shock some of Reynolds' coterie—the kind with
no Social Security cards—by the way she swore. She was
saying "mother fucker" in public before most women were
attempting "damn" in their closets. The police first became
acquainted with Lilla Seay Gibson Reynolds in 1942 when
she was arrested in Shreveport for prostitution, using the
trick name of Molly Rather. That was the first entry in a
file on deposit at the Texas Department of Public Safety
which, by 1949, would have nine more arrests on minor
offenses—"vagrancy" and "common prostitution" were
usually the charges. The file showed that Lilla used several
other names, including Lilla Reynolds, Louise Reynolds,
and Sandra Harris. Whatever the name, the fingerprints
always traced back to the country girl whose parents forbade her to dance. Of these arrests Lilla would later claim
that they were illegitimate, nothing but harassment from
the law because of her alliance with the police character
Reynolds. But they took place in several cities from Port
Arthur at the bottom of Texas to Amarillo at the top, and
it seemed unlikely that the police of such disparate places
would bother to roust a lady so perversely because of her
choice of husbands.

There may have been one or two other spouses, Lilla having once told her daughter that she was married five times.
But the record shows that Lilla wed under her real name
on but three occasions, the last one to a remarkable man

named Claude Paulus. It would endure for more than twenty years and give her a measure of respectability. Claude Paulus was a giant, standing six feet four with wide shoulders and thickly muscled forearms from the work of his youth on the farm of German pioneers in a South Central Texas town called Hallettsville. If someone was needed to toss the beer barrels off the truck at the picnic, or bodily transfer a balky yearling calf from one pen to another, they called on Claude. His parents were well fixed, and his grandmother a millionairess from vast property holdings. When Claude finished high school, his family selected his occupation and sent him off to obtain a dental degree. That earned, the father congratulated his powerful son and gave him $3,000 in cash. This would launch his practice in the awakening city of Houston; a new dentist would be needed in the post-World War I boom. Claude drove to Houston in a Model A Ford. Twenty-four hours later he hitched a ride home on a freight train, his pockets empty. He had been cleaned out—stake and automobile—in a crap game that operated permanently in a downtown Houston hotel room.

Then and there Claude Paulus decided there was more money to be made from shooting dice than filling cavities. He worked around Hallettsville for a few months, assembling a new purse, and returned to Houston as a gambler man. For the rest of his life he was nothing more, but in his way he achieved a modest stature in Houston both as the owner-proprietor of a downtown gambling club and as the city's society bookie. Claude often told his daughter that there had been too many women in his life—"they pained me and drained me" was his way of putting it—and not until he met and wed Lilla did he close his roving eye. Lilla was clearly any man's match.

They met in Dallas when he was well past forty. The six-carat diamond ring that flashed from his finger not unsurprisingly caught the attention of Lilla Reynolds as she sat on a bar stool a few positions down. Lilla deftly worked her way next to the beefy blond fellow and exclaimed over the gem and asked to see it. While she perused its brilliance. Lilla deliberately dropped the ring into an open beer case It took quite awhile to fish it out, and in those moments the couple became acquainted. Soon thereafter they were wed.

Mr. and Mrs. Claude Paulus bought a two-story home

on Sunset Boulevard in Houston, one of the city's most
graceful, and there they and their only child, a girl named
Mary Josephine, lived respectable lives which were not
exactly what the neighbors came to believe. Outwardly,
Claude was in the oil and insurance business, and perhaps
he was, to a modest extent. But his principal position was
operator of the Redman's Club in downtown Houston, a
pseudo-fraternal organization that provided booze, cards,
dice, and a horse-race wire to its brothers. Claude also
owned brothels on Galveston's notorious Post Office Street,
which was to the Texas Gulf Coast what Hamburg was to
the North Sea. Lilla not only faithfully attended St. John's
Episcopal Church, Houston's most socially fashionable, she
turned her attention now and then to the upkeep of her husband's "rent property" in Galveston. Once, her daughter
Mary Jo told Bob Bennett, Lilla had the imaginative idea
of turning one of the brothels into a "House of All Na-
tions." It was her intent to furnish each room in a spectacular foreign décor and install therein a prostitute of the
particular nationality. But the racial color line swept across
that notorious district of Galveston, and Lilla abandoned
her idea once the neighborhood became black and less
popular. Mary Jo carried memories of unusual childhood
summers, one in residence at her father's Galveston
brothel. The high point of the season was, she told Bennett,
when the ceiling of a bedroom fell in on a customer's
head at the prime moment of his passion.

The social register of Houston contains the names of
several women who, if gossip is to be believed, began their
careers as prostitutes. They are a widely appreciated source
of cocktail party gossip and decorative at charity galas.
Lilla Paulus was consumed with the desire to move up
accordingly into the best company of Houston. She became practiced at telling acquaintances in the neighborhood
and church that her husband was in the "oil and insurance
business," but still the invitations with engraved return
addresses never arrived. It angered Lilla that some of the
most prominent men in the city were happy to place bets
with Claude, but their wives did not return her telephone
calls. Thus, like many a parent before her, Lilla used her
daughter as a key to the mansions of River Oaks. For a
time she was a Brownie leader, and a respected one, beaming with pleasure as the little girls disembarked in front
of her home from the chauffeured limousines. And when

Mary Jo announced an interest in ponies, Lilla eagerly attended that whim. She well knew that horses could be an entree to social acceptance. Lilla pried thousands of dollars from her husband's purse to pay for lessons, grooms, and boarding fees at the Alameda Stables, that being a mecca for the "mink and manure" set, and headquarters for Joan Robinson Hill, the epitome of social power in Lilla's eyes. This girl, Lilla decided, was a model for her daughter, a young woman of beauty and great style, with a doctor husband whose practice would someday be lucrative, and a father who obviously worshiped her. Lilla liked Ash Robinson, finding him to be an old rascal who enjoyed a salty woman (which Lilla could always be if she found a use for it) and a man who even knew and accepted Claude's occupation. "Nothing wrong with placing a little bet now and then," winked Ash on occasion. "I even do it myself, but the outgo has always greatly exceeded the income."

As Joan achieved world success and celebration for her talent on an English saddle, Mary Jo Paulus won championship competitions in the Western class, preferring jeans and cowboy boots to the elegantly tailored riding tuxedo and derby. Unspoken between the two parents, but understood, was the fact that both warmed their bones in the glow cast by their daughters. If not completely content, both had nonetheless accommodated their attitudes toward being pointed out as "Joan's father" and "Mary Jo's mother." Occasionally there were times when Lilla would deliberately draw attention to herself. On one memorable afternoon, at the café near the Alameda Stables, Lilla opened her purse to contribute her share of the tab, and the arrogant butt of a revolver poked into view. Several of the young society women sitting around the table made note, but Lilla made no embarrassed effort to shove it back in place. "She seemed anxious for us to see that she carried a gun," one of the women would remember years later.

Lilla Paulus and Ash Robinson shared one further characteristic—an attempt to impose their will on their daughters' choice of men. Lilla was determined that her daughter would marry a socially acceptable man and often lectured Mary Jo: "Make sure he's got money—don't fall in love with a broke." By the time the girl was sixteen, and a bounteous young woman of tall stature and tumbling roan-colored hair, she and her mother were antagonists. From there they fell into deep and bitter hatred. The final rupture came when Mary Jo grew to love Larry Wood. She was eighteen, he a decade older and already the scarred veteran of four broken marriages. It did not take Lilla very long to discover that Larry Wood talked vaguely of being in "investments" and "business for himself," but his real source of income was pimping. He was a society pimp, operating on the upper echelon of Houston whoredom. He kept an apartment in the "swinging singles" southwest section of the city, and in it dwelt three or four expensive prostitutes. Wood dispatched them on call.

When all of Lilla's exhortations against this alliance failed, she took the extraordinary step of taking her daughter to the St. Joseph's Hospital psychiatric clinic and committing her both for suspected drug use and for erratic behavior. Mary Jo stayed in the clinic under observation for three weeks before she managed to slip out and away and into the arms of Larry Wood. They married at once, and Lilla was devastated. Clearly she had counted on a more promising alliance for her child than a pimp, even though he informed his new mother-in-law that he had reformed, given up the old ways, and was going into "Nigerian oil." Because of Lilla's venomous condemnation of the marriage and threats against its existence, the couple left Houston and moved to a secret life in another state.

In his homework for the trial of Lilla Paulus, Bob Bennett managed to track down Mary Jo and interview both her and her husband. The young woman, now twenty-six, was frightened. She was willing, reluctantly, to speak of her mother in confidential conversation, but she refused under any condition to appear at the trial. Until this meeting, Bennett had not realized the strength of the poisoned blood between mother and daughter. If Mary Jo was to be believed, Lilla would stop at nothing in her obsession to destroy the marriage and punish her disobedient daughter.

Mary Jo had grown up knowing that she would someday inherit a substantial fortune from her paternal grandmother. Claude Paulus' mother left an estate of more than four million dollars, but she specifically excluded Claude in her will, frowning all of her Methodist life at his gambling business. Instead, she left one quarter of her fortune to "any legitimate issue of Claude." Mary Jo was the only one. But when she applied to the estate of her grandmother, following Claude's death, Lilla filed suit to block the claim. In a turbulent and ugly hearing at the small Hallettsville, Texas, courthouse, Lilla took the witness stand and denied that her own daughter was legitimate. She swore that she was already pregnant with Mary Jo before she married Claude Paulus, and therefore the girl had no right to inherit the grandmother's clean Methodist money. Lilla had no claim whatsoever on the share due Mary Jo, which could have been more than a million dollars. It seemed instead nothing but a perverse denial of her daughter's inheritance. Lilla's version was believed; the court held against Mary Jo and dismissed her claim on the estate. "That was her way of getting back at me," Mary Jo told Bennett. "When I was testifying, I saw her sitting out there patting her handbag, and I knew she had her gun in it. My blood ran cold with every word I spoke."

Mary Jo's husband, Larry, told Bennett that during their courtship Lilla had visited his apartment. "She came around one night at 2 A.M. She said she wanted to talk to me about my dating Mary Jo. We sat down on the couch, and she pulled a .32 automatic out of her purse and held it. Well, she didn't know it, but I had a gun in my bathrobe pocket. We sat there with the drop on one another. She offered me $5,000 not to marry her daughter. She says to me, 'You're too old, and besides, I checked you out, and you've been working girls.' Hell, I didn't deny it. But that kind of stuff shouldn't have shocked Lilla. I told her, 'You're putting a lot of shit on me, and it's not flushing. Now get the fuck out of my apartment and out of our lives.' "

In 1972 the Houston apartment where Larry Wood and Mary Jo lived was blasted with gunfire. Fortunately the couple was away for the evening. The police report counted fifty-seven bullet holes in the apartment walls and windows.

The kind of work that Larry Wood was engaged in might have contributed to the ferocious attack, but he told Bennett, "That was a wedding present from Lilla. Now do you understand why we left town?"

All of this Bob Bennett wrote down and studied and, eventually, despaired of ever using as evidence of Lilla's character. None of it would be admissible, not even the woman's criminal record, not unless her defense counsel made a blunder and opened one of the peculiar legal doors that allows rummaging around in the locked closets of a defendant's history. But Dick DeGeurin was too smart to do that. On the February morning that the trial began, Bennett glanced over and scrutinized the woman he so desperately wanted to put in the penitentiary. She looked back at him and smiled. A smile! "It's crazy," thought Bennett, "but this woman is enjoying her hour at the center of the public stage." Her childhood vow was now achieved.

Both sides announced ready and Bennett threw his first ball. On face value it seemed a weak pitch, but there was a hidden curve. He proposed that Marcia McKittrick be placed on the witness stand, under oath, and give the court a sort of preview of her testimony. At the defense table, DeGeurin stiffened. What was the district attorney up to? Judge Price, wearing his black formal robes and looking even more like a youngster playing at dress-up, summoned the attorneys to his bench.

"What is the purpose of this?" the judge asked pleasantly.

"I have been given information that Miss McKittrick has changed her mind and will not testify in this case," said Bennett. "This is in direct opposition to her previous commitment. I have been conferring with Miss McKittrick, and her position seems ambiguous. It does not seem to be a definite refusal." In other words, continued the prosecutor, let's put this "yes one day, no the next" hooker on the stand and find out if she is going to testify against Lilla Paulus. If not, then Bennett had no case, and the unspoken implication was that everybody could go home.

The proposal *seemed* sensible, even generous. But De-Geurin smelled trouble. It was not the custom of the DA's office to throw in the towel in the first five minutes of a murder trial. The defense lawyer made strenuous objection. He knew of no procedure under which the star witness could be asked in advance of jury selection just what her testimony would be.

Judge Price chewed on the unusual request for a few moments, then ruled in favor of the state. He was a practical judge, anxious to get on with matters, and if this was a timesaving procedure, then well and good. Bring on Marcia.

She was waiting under guard in a whitewashed anteroom, and when she came into the courtroom and took a seat in the now familiar witness box, Marcia looked out and nodded almost warmly to all the people she recog-

nized—Bennett, Jerry Carpenter, DeGeurin—but her gaze
resolutely avoided Lilla.

"Prior to last Friday, February 14, 1975," began Bennett, "you had expressed a willingness to testify in this matter."

Marcia nodded. Lilla's head shot up, riveting her eyes
to the prostitute in the box. There came a long pause, the
suspense of a balloon blown to its limits and due to burst
with the next push of breath. "Yes," said Marcia, "but now
I don't think I'll be able to testify." Then that was that.
DeGeurin smiled, and Lilla snapped her purse shut, as if the
meeting was over and she could get home in time to watch
a noon soap opera on television.

Bennett nodded, not electing to argue with his exasperating witness. Instead, he reached into a legal folder and
withdrew several copies of a prepared motion, throwing one
down in front of DeGeurin, offering others to the judge
and the clerk. "In that case," said Bennett, "I move to grant
immunity to Marcia McKittrick and *require* her to testify." Judge Price nodded, perhaps in appreciation of a
shrewd prosecutorial maneuver. Quickly DeGeurin devoured the brief document. What he intended, explained
Bennett, was to *guarantee* that the district attorney's office
would never use any of the testimony that the prostitute
might give should the need arise to try her again. This was
a complex offer. It indicated that the possibility at least
existed that the Texas Court of Criminal Appeals might
someday reverse the young woman's murder conviction—
the ten-year prison sentence she was now serving after the
five-minute rush job on the stormy Halloween three and a
half months before. If that happened, and if Marcia was
given a new trial, then the DA promised not to use any of
her testimony in today's trial against Lilla Paulus.

Instantly DeGeurin rose, sputtering with an objection.
This was clearly a denial of a witness's constitutional right
to remain silent, he charged. Moreover, he had never even
heard of such an out-of-bounds trick. Immunity can be
offered to prospective witnesses *before* a trial, but not *after*
a conviction. "Marcia McKittrick has already been prosecuted, found guilty, received punishment, and is now
appealing. We do not think the state can force a person
to testify under those conditions." DeGeurin now felt the
thorn in Bennett's bouquet. If Marcia continued in her re-

fusal to testify, then the judge could hold her in contempt and slap a brand-new prison sentence on that charge against the prostitute. And he could continue resentencing her until the twenty-first century began, or until she saw the light.

Bennett was enjoying the furor. With a mock look of professorial forbearance, he rose to defend his motion. "Our position is that we have removed all future criminal exposure in this case, other than perjury. This is our quid pro quo."

Through all of the harangues, Marcia squirmed silently, not understanding much of what was swirling about her. But then Judge Price turned to her, handed down the unusual motion, and instructed that she read it carefully. When she was done, he carefully explained its meaning— and potential peril. If she did not testify in this trial, then the bench could hold her in contempt and sentence her, and resentence her, until she elected to purge herself.

Fitfully, DeGeurin objected to the judge's "threatening" the witness. With a withering look at his old handball partner, the judge announced, "We will begin jury selection." Marcia was led away, back to the jail, holding the motion in her hand, now faced with Hobson's choice.

38

Forty people were summoned from a central jury pool and herded into Judge Price's courtroom, a place as modest in dimension as traffic court. They filled up the four rows of spectator seats, ten bodies to a row, and waited suspensefully for exactly what the business of the day was to be. Each had been drafted by mail and instructed to return a brief biographical card. Now the opposing lawyers held Xerox copies of the cards and began the crucial task of fleshing out the bare bones contained therein. The procedure—the legal term is *voir dire*—gave both state and defense an opportunity to interview each of the forty, then retire and decide in private which they did not want to be on the jury. Through weeding out by various challenges for cause and strikes, twelve jurors, normally survived. Houston judges do not like jury selection to drag on for days. The generally held attitude is that twelve good men and women can be obtained quickly and fairly out of the original forty. In the trial of Lilla Paulus, the procedure took but three brisk hours. But in that short amount of time, fascinating personalities emerged from the cards. They became real people, creatures of ignorance and sophistication, boredom and intense desire.

Bennett operated gently and easily. He enjoyed the jury selection process, realizing that it was at best a guessing game, that years of investigation and planning led finally to these snap judgments that put people in the box with an attendant prayer that, from the very few pieces of the puzzle the rules of law would permit them to receive, they could assemble enough of the picture to condemn the defendant. The prosecutor usually followed several of the hoary dicta handed down by his elders in the trade—allow no blacks or Mexican-Americans on the jury because the feeling was these minority citizens were programmed since birth to disrespect police authority; and be god damned careful about any women. Here Bennett felt a dilemma: he *wanted* women on the panel, for he hoped to enlist their contempt for the sordid side of Lilla's life (if he could squeeze any such information into the record), but at the same time he feared they might be repelled by Marcia's steamy career. "The best I can hope for," he murmured to an aide, "is that we can find some reasonably intelligent women who can distinguish between an old bad whore and a repented good whore." Bennett addressed the jurors *en masse*. He promised to move along quickly. "I know the mind can absorb only what the rear end can endure," he said. "But there are some fairly complicated legal issues here." The state would try to prove that Lilla Paulus aided and abetted the planned murder of Dr. John Hill, and evidence would be presented that *"tends to connect the defendant"* with the offense. He lingered over the phrase, drawing a line under it verbally for emphasis. These five words would become the most contentious of the trial.

Moving down the rows, Bennett chatted amiably with each of the forty, finding out about their jobs, families, education, previous experiences with the judicial system, and, extremely important, their religions. Judge Price, listening to the process with keen interest, had always been happy to discover a Lutheran on a panel during his years as a prosecutor. "The mere fact that somebody had been indicted was good enough for a Lutheran to vote for hanging," the judge remarked during a recess.

When Bennett began interviewing a grocer, a grandfatherly man with a kind face, the prospective juror said that something was troubling him. He, in fact, held an opinion that might interfere with fair judgment on Mrs. Paulus. Quickly holding out his hands as a traffic cop to stop the man from blurting the opinion—the danger was he could taint the entire panel—Bennett led him before the judge for a whispered conference. Dick DeGeurin hastily caught up. "I think Ash Robinson should be on trial—before that lady over there," the grocer said. "And this would bother me in trying to reach a fair verdict."

Judge Price nodded calmly. He was surprised that Ash's name had not arisen before, since the lawyers had been asking each prospective juror if he or she had read newspaper reports of the enduring case. "I appreciate your candor," said the judge, *sotto voce*, "but you won't be asked to rule on anybody else's guilt or innocence."

"I don't think I could be fair to Lilla Paulus," pleaded the man, "because I think Ash Robinson was the ringleader and the fellow who engineered this whole thing."

Judge Price, with a compliment for his honesty, dismissed the man from the panel.

Bennett's clipboard filled up with people he did not want. He struck one woman because she seemed "sullen." Another was rejected because she had an in-law once convicted of murder. A third was eliminated because she told the prosecutor that she had not read local newspaper accounts of the Hill matter. "I only read the New York *Times*," she said a little grandly. Bennett felt the answer was pretentious and that she was probably "a militant women's libber." She did not fit his needs; he wanted middle-of-the-road people with a sense of community pride and responsibility. The hope was these people would want to cleanse Houston of people like Lilla Paulus.

Defense attorney DeGeurin came on as brusque, a little testy, condescending even, at times waspish—in both definitions of the word. He was a decided contrast to Bennett's rumpled suit and folksy air of feet proped up on the pickle barrel. His was not the best way to begin courtship of a jury. Three major points must be understood, DeGeurin lectured. In Texas, the prosecution had the burden of *proving* its case. "And it never shifts, this burden," said DeGeurin. Moreover, the proof must be *beyond a reasonable doubt.* Most importantly, he stressed, a juror was *required* to believe that Lilla Paulus was innocent. "If you feel otherwise, then you shouldn't be seated in this courtroom," he said. "The law says that Lilla Paulus is innocent, unless the state carries its burden of proof beyond a reasonable doubt."

He scattered a few hints of what was to come. Lilla might or might not testify. "But that should not be a factor in your decision, because it is my decision, not hers." Perhaps, DeGeurin suggested, the state's case would be so flimsy that there would be no need for Mrs. Paulus to enter the witness box. In his place, Bennett smiled. How he would like to get Lilla on cross-examination! Then DeGeurin waded briefly in the murky waters of corroborating evidence. Though he believed privately at this moment that Marcia McKittrick would keep her silence despite the threat of contempt of court, it was still worth getting out the tarbrush. Should a woman named Marcia McKittrick testify, speculated DeGeurin, then "her testimony is not enough for conviction—*even* if you believe her." His tone defined Marcia as the Olympic champion of lying.

DeGeurin also wanted middle-of-the-road people, but he could not live with extreme advocates of law and order. He struck one man because all he did was speak warmly of the Houston police force. Nor could he accept people whose lives were bordered by the Bible on one side and the churchyard on the other.

Finally, at nightfall, the court clerk examined the list of challenges from both sides and drew black lines through the names of those who were not wanted. Five women and seven men survived as the jury that would hear the matter of Lilla Paulus. *En bloc,* they seemed an intelligent and unusual jury in this city. Among them were two master's degrees, an educational plateau rarely reached by jurors in murder cases, tradition holding that neither side wants too much intelligence. There was an oil company art director, a librarian, a chemist. There were also two young, naïve, and exceptionally pretty young women in their early twenties, pleasing both the judge and the lawyers. "The rule of thumb," drawled Bennett while considering his list, "is never knock off a pretty girl unless it is absolutely imperative. Remember you have to look at these people for a week." Even a Mexican-American was seated, breaking the tradition of no minority jurors. This man owned a concrete business, and he struck Bennett somewhat romantically as "being like an Old World craftsman who worked hard to get where he is and he wants the town safe from hired killers." DeGeurin chose him for different reasons, probably feeling that he would be subservient to the will of the others.

Judge Price told the jurors they could go home and urged them to sleep well for the difficult work facing all on the morrow. He chose not to sequester them, a decision he would regret. "They seem like a good bunch," he said as he watched the dozen agitated people leave his chambers. Into twelve ordinary lives a mortar had just fallen.

The judge always relished this moment, seeing how citizens responded to the awesome and frustrating job of dispensing justice. "It's imperfect, this way we do things," he mused. "But it's the best of a bad lot. Somebody once suggested having twelve judges act as jurors, but that would be insane. The defendant would expire from old age before twelve judges could agree on anything."

At that moment he noted both lawyers—Bennett and DeGeurin—rushing downstairs to interview Marcia McKittrick in the women's jail. Hopefully, he remarked, they would not bump into one another.

The state of Texas had to prove (1) that a murder was committed, (2) how the murder was committed, and (3) that Lilla Paulus planned, aided, and profited from said murder. It was easy enough to establish points 1 and 2. The lead-off witness for the prosecution was the coroner of Harris County, Dr. Joseph Jachimczyk, who spent as much time testifying in murder trials as he did standing over corpses with a dissecting tool. On this day, rushing from a dawn autopsy, he had as usual forgotten to change his shoes, and spots of mahogany-colored blood flecked their whiteness. Dr. Joe, as everybody called him, brought a thick folder to court and secreted himself in Judge Price's office to refresh his memory. The folder began with the death in 1969 of Joan Robinson Hill and continued through her exhumation and the murder of her husband. He flipped across the saga and paused in reflection. Six years earlier he had felt that a grand jury should investigate the circumstances of Joan Robinson Hill's sudden death, and his position had been a major factor in the plastic surgeon's indictment. Now the passage of the years had changed his mind—too late to do the dead doctor much good. "From what I had to work with," he said, "there was no murder case against John Hill. Nor could I say in all conscience that there was any conspiracy or maliciousness to cover up her death." He turned back to his folder, perhaps coming across a passage of criticism of John Hill's choice of hospitals, taking Joan to Sharpstown rather than a major institution.

"You know," he said, beginning an anecdote, "doctors do the damnedest things. I consider myself to be a careful man, but once I was sitting in this very courthouse waiting to testify in a trial, and I was chewing on a toothpick. This old judge was quite a storyteller and he delivered himself of a very funny tale. At the punch line I laughed, and the god damned toothpick fell into my throat and stuck there. Tried to cough it up. It wouldn't budge. I got on the stand, and in a few minutes I realized I was in danger of strangling. I apologized to the court and said I had a personal emergency. Well, I got in my car, practically turning blue, and drove all the way over to St. Joe's Hospital, a couple of miles from the courthouse. And not until after they got the toothpick out did I realize that I could have gone to Memorial Hospital a lot quicker. It's only a few blocks and has a fine emergency room. But I was so panicked, I didn't think clearly. Could have killed myself."

His point, the coroner began in amplification, was that perhaps John Hill was so distraught over various events that he made an unwise decision. "It could have been that . . ." he began. But then the bailiff summoned him to the box, and he never finished his story.

At 9:05 P.M. on the night of September 24, 1972, the coroner discovered Dr. John Hill shot dead in the front entrance hall of his home. He was the victim of three .38 bullet wounds, one in the left upper shoulder, one in the right wrist, "and the most significant in the right abdomen, just at the bottom of the right rib cage." This bullet pierced the plastic surgeon's diaphragm, stomach, aorta, and finally stopped in the lower back.

Bob Bennett fished through the pile of documents on the state's table and found the familiar manila envelope that had disturbed his conscience so many times over the years. With meticulousness approaching the rite of cere-

mony. the prosecutor withdrew the four color photographs of Dr. John Hill in death and pressed them against
his bosom to keep them from the jury's eyes. As he approached the bench with the photographs hugged against
his body, each of the jurors strained with curiosity, which,
of course, was exactly what Bennett desired. He moved
to introduce the pictures as state's exhibit one.

Immediately DeGeurin rose in objection. Strenuously
he argued that the pictures were "inflammatory and prejudicial and of small bearing on this case." This was also
exactly what Bennett wanted, for any secret becomes more
tantalizing when someone tries to prohibit its disclosure.
Judge Price calmly admitted the photographs, instructing
the jurors to examine each and pass it on "without comment." The coroner had spent half an hour droning out his
description of the death of John Hill, but his words were
hollow and weak when replaced by the horror of the
camera's eye. The images were awful, each a looking glass
reflecting a juror's face as they passed down the line. John
Hill was to be seen lying on the floor, blood across his features, a strip of tape covering his eyes, as if he had been
before a firing squad . . . another piece of tape had been
pulled away from his mouth and trailed behind him, like a
hangman's rope . . . his nose was cruelly smashed and
broken . . . a wide blob of blood flooded his belly button
. . . his crotch was stained and soiled where he had voided
in the death struggle.

There was not much for DeGeurin to say in cross-examination, but he did ask the coroner if he had autopsied
"Joan Robinson Hill under rather unusual circumstances."

"Yes, I did," answered Jachimczyk, surprised—as was
Bennett—that the defense attorney would open the bottom
drawer of this case. Bennett was pleased that his opponent
had, by error or by curious design, turned the jury's attention back to the long-ago beginning of this tragedy, something that the state would have had difficulty doing.

Now Bennett had to establish the weapon that was the
agent of John Hill's death. He called Dr. Orrin Staves of
Longview, and after the shock of the photos, there was
comic relief. The black doctor had balked in the days before the trial and informed the DA's office that he could
not spare the time to testify. Once he had come to court
under subpoena and had to wait, and in the absence from

his clinic a patient had died. "Well," said Bob Bennett, "I'm sorry about that, and I'm also sorry you got involved with Marcia McKittrick, but you did, and if you don't come to Houston and testify voluntarily, then I'll send somebody up there to arrest you and you can appear in handcuffs."

The doctor took the stand in vivid sartorial ensemble— deep brown pin-stripe suit, hot orange shirt, thick-rimmed sunglasses, jewels flashing at his fingers. His voice was slurred, like that of a man just awakened from a deep sleep.

Bennett went directly to the heart of the matter. Did the doctor know a woman named Marcia McKittrick? Yes, he believed he did, although he knew her under the label of "Dusty."

"Do you own a .38-caliber pistol?" asked the prosecutor.

"Several," said the doctor with an air of boredom. "Two or three. All .38s."

Bennett poked around the pile of envelopes on his table and found a bulky one from which he withdrew a rusted gun, cold and sad-looking. He cupped it in the palm of his hand and bore it to the witness stand for the doctor to see.

"Did you give this pistol to—or was it obtained from you by—Marcia McKittrick?"

Dr. Staves frowned in recollection. "Marcia obtained one of my guns," he began, his words curiously disjointed and diffuse in tone, as if they were coming from several different voice boxes, "but I am not clear at this point in time exactly how. You see, my Eldorado had been stolen and I had a chartered plane standing by at the airport to fly me to Fort Worth."

Bennett interrupted the start of this promising story. "Are you or are you not sure that it was Marcia McKittrick who obtained your gun?"

The doctor nodded. "Yeah," he said. "Because I remember now. She promised to give it back, and she never did."

Satisfied, Bennett handed the offensive object to the witness for identification. The doctor accepted his .38 as a prodigal come home. Examining it quickly, he pronounced it dirty and worn, but definitely his. He had wanted it back, and now seemed like a good time for reclamation. Incredibly, the doctor began to put the gun into his coat pocket. Judge Price threw out a startled arm of prohibition. "Please, sir," said the judge. As the jury laughed, Dr.

Staves shrugged and returned the exhibit to the district attorney, obviously upset that he could not walk out of the courtroom with his weapon.

The best the defense could hope for was that the jurors would find the doctor's social tastes so offensive that his story of the gun would be discredited. With fervor that waltzed perilously close to racism, DeGeurin tried to draw from the doctor the fact that he patronized white prostitutes.

"Did you ever give Marcia McKittrick money in return for her sexual favors?" asked DeGeurin.

Shooting back a look of hauteur, the doctor was insulted. His vanity and his position were not to be abused. "You mean, 'If I give you money, you give me sex,' that sort of thing? No, not that way." The doctor could not even recall if he had *ever* had sex with the lady. The implication was she was but one player in a cast of many.

"Well," DeGeurin moved along, "why does a doctor of your importance need to own 'two or three .38s'?"

Dr. Staves launched into a rambling monologue about "the System," which he employed to take care of missing medicines, to run security checks on employees at his clinic, and to counter any trouble that arose in his life. From the description, it seemed a sort of combine of black muscle, lawyers, and guns.

This gave DeGeurin a wild notion. "Do you deny that 'the System' had Bobby Vandiver murdered in Longview?"

Bennett shot out of his seat faster than a man propelled from a circus cannon. "Objection!" His face was flushed with outrage at the suggestion.

"Sustained," said the judge. DeGeurin was not rattled. The question had come out of left field, and its only apparent purpose—a standard defense maneuver—was to offer the jury a small and mysterious non sequitur, never to be mentioned again.

Returning to the gun, DeGeurin pressed Dr. Staves for details on how it originally escaped from his custody. "The best I can remember," he said, openly belligerent now to the handsome young lawyer, ". . . you see, my *chartered* plane was waiting . . . I *may* have given her that gun and told her, 'I can't take a gun on that plane . . . I'm too mad . . . That *may* have been what happened. I was angry, so I didn't want a gun with me."

DeGeurin arched his eyebrows. "You *might* have used it?"

"I might have used it," agreed the doctor.

"Are you carrying one now?" wondered DeGeurin.

In fury, the doctor glared at the lawyer. "I didn't think I'd need one."

DeGeurin smiled, a point of minor sorts made, and he passed the witness.

With portraits of a dead man and the gun that killed him now firmly etched on the jury, Bennett moved into the circumstances of his execution. He went for emotion, for the power of an echo. "Robert Hill, please." The child of Joan Robinson and John Hill marched erectly into the courtroom with the rigid posture of a young aristocrat. At fourteen, he was just changing from boy to man. His hair was as bright as a sunflower and his eyes were deeply blue. In his crisp navy blazer, he was a startlingly handsome but somber youngster. Later this day a newspaper would publish his photograph on the front page, and Ash Robinson would clip it hungrily, holding it like an icon. From his home in River Oaks, the old man was desperate for news of the trial, and when a friend called him to give him an account of the first day's events, Ash first demanded information about his only grandson. Did the boy look well? Was he well fed? Did he look like Joan? And, finally, "Did he say anything bad about me?"

Robert was a superb witness. Well coached by Bob Bennett, the boy, in firm voice, delivered a chilling account—of answering the doorbell and discovering, instead of his father and stepmother, a stranger with a gun standing on the porch, of being tied up with tape, of licking his lips so that the tape would not hold, of hearing a taxi arrive, of trying to scream a warning from behind his gag. "I heard the man say, 'Now give me your money' . . and then . . . four or five shots."

Wisely, for there was no way to impeach either the character or substance of the child's words without risking anger from the jury—some of the women were dabbing at misted eyes—DeGeurin elected to pass the boy with no questions.

A floor below, waiting in Bennett's office, was Myra Hill, primed to deliver her eyewitness account of the night she lay bound and gagged with strips of her own sweater while her son was murdered in the next room. But Bob Bennett made a snap decision not to use her; she had a tendency to ramble and the prosecutor's worry was that she would tell too much, perhaps pepper her testimony with biblical quotations, and, despite her best intentions, snag the careful cloak of prosecution he was weaving. Instead, the district attorney summoned Connie Hill to the stand. Not only did he want her to tell of her husband's death, but it was important that she establish the hatred between her husband and Ash Robinson.

The third wife of the murdered plastic surgeon was the perfect choice to follow the child. She wore a beige dress of simply cut elegance, with her hair in a modest bun appropriate for a church choir director. Obviously this was a quiet woman of taste and culture, and if Dick DeGeurin ever began using the backhanded defense technique of savaging the reputation of the murder victim, then his task would be difficult. If John Hill could sire a son as poised as Robert, and win the love of a woman as desirable as Connie, then it would be hard to belittle him.

After Connie told once again the story of finding a masked gunman in macabre homecoming, Bennett asked, "Do you know Ash Robinson?"

"Not personally," answered Connie. She had only seen him in his black Lincoln, circling her house now and then.

"Was there animosity between your husband and Ash Robinson?"

"Yes . . . a great deal."

This was the first mention of the old man's name and Bennett turned to see if it made impression on the jurors. One, a matronly, heavy-set woman who lived on the fringe of River Oaks and who, guessed Bennett, has unfulfilled social aspirations of her own, nodded perceptibly. It seemed to say, "I wondered when *his* name was going to come out." But Bennett went no further. The business of the prosecution was to plant tiny saplings of suspicion, then, through shrewd nourishment, hope that they would grow sturdy enough to support a noose.

Now the first day of testimony was almost over and Bennett had fired all of his dependable big guns. He knew that his witnesses had been powerful, but thus far he had presented absolutely nothing that would implicate Lilla Paulus in the gruesome death so emotionally described. His mind raced, his few options tumbling about the weary canyons of his senses. He could ask for a recess, but it was not yet 4 P.M. and he knew Judge Price liked to work a long, full session. He could summon Marcia McKittrick but the risk was that she would only stare at him sullenly and silently, accepting the judge's threat of contempt. The only other choice was to offer the state's "evidence" against the defendant, and he knew that, unbolstered by Marcia, it was as thin and fragile-looking as Lilla herself. Throughout the day she had maintained extraordinary composure, showing not even a raised brow of discomfort at the terrible words raining about her, breaking her silence only to cough, perhaps by happenstance, perhaps by design, for her most fitful sieges seemed to occur during the grimmest moments of witness recollection. Some of the jurors had been watching her with what Bennett took to be sympathy.

"Jerry Carpenter," announced Bennett. Lilla suddenly stopped coughing and turned with her first discernible emotion of the day—hostility—to watch the homicide detective stroll into the room. Bennett wished he could have dictated the cop's choice of costume for his crucial appearance, but Jerry Carpenter was his own man, and if he chose to wear a sunset-hued shirt with matching tie and a gold Mexican coin dangling from his neck, then the jury would have to disregard the fact that he looked eminently capable of flipping the peso across his knuckles. Bennett often worried about police witnesses. He had lost more than one case not because of the strength or weakness of their testimony, but due to the hidden attitudes that citizens hold toward lawmen. Buried among those twelve people in the jury box might be a fellow who got chewed out by a surly traffic cop, or a lady kissed off by a dispatcher when she tried to complain about a neighbor's noisy party. The prosecutor knew that DeGeurin would surely seek to depict Carpenter as a gun-slinging menace who had terrorized his frightened client at gunpoint and had searched her house unlawfully to obtain evidence, and who had tempted the narcotic-hungry Marcia McKittrick to bear false witness.

Bennett need not have worried. Carpenter was not only believable, he was, in a sense, somehow reassuring to the jurors and citizens of a typically violent American city. Here was a tough cop, but he was representative of a busi-

ness where such was required. His voice was deep and solid
gut-bucket Texas. Never did he search for answers. He had
them—fast, direct, lean. No imagination or fancy fell from
his lips. He told of the night he had been called to John
Hill's home to investigate the murder, of finding the briefcase and gun a week later under bushes a block away, of
the pursuit of Marcia and Bobby that occupied him for six
months. Then, locking hardened eyes to Lilla Paulus, a
dozen feet away, he told of arresting her on April 27, 1973.

At this point, DeGeurin rose in objection once again to
the legality of Carpenter's search of his client. In previous
hearings over the past year, the defense lawyer had made
the same complaints. But he needed now to let the jury
know his contention that the search was unlawful. He demanded that the court suppress any of the alleged "evidence," his tone cloaking the word with heavy sarcasm
and disbelief. Dryly, Judge Price noted that his objections
were already in the record, and he gestured to Bennett that
he could continue.

"Did you recover a number of items at the Paulus
home, including pieces of paper?" asked Bennett.

"Yes," answered the homicide detective.

Bennett located another envelope on his table, this one
obvious in its slimness, and withdrew four small slips—
two the size of a memo pad used to jot down telephone
numbers, one apparently a blank check, the last hardly
larger than a postage stamp. Easily concealing them in his
hands, and once again whetting the appetite of the jury,
Bennett asked that they be introduced as a state exhibit.

With permission granted, Bennett paused. It was a good
time to quit for the day. He could sense that the jury was
lusting to know what the slips of paper contained, but he
would let them remain tantalized overnight. Besides, an
aide had just brought him a message that was far more
troubling in its suspense.

Marcia McKittrick had just sent word from the women's
jail downstairs that she wanted to see the prosecutor. Fast!

39

"What is your name?"

"Marcia McKittrick."

"What is your occupation?"

"Prostitute."

"I've reached a decision," she told Bob Bennett the night before, blurting it out, afraid it would stick in her throat and slide back down to the reservoir of fear. "I'll testify. I'm probably crazy to be doing it, but it just dawned on me that every time in my life I had to make a major decision, I always made the wrong one. Maybe it's time to go against my better judgment."

"Did you know Bobby Vandiver?"

"Yes. He was my chip."

"Your chip?"

"My boy friend. And was so until February 1973."

"I've just been so mixed up. When Bobby died, I vowed I would keep silent because he would have wanted me to. But he's gone! He has no claim on my life any more."

"And do you know this defendant, Lilla Paulus?" asked Bennett.

"Yes, I do."

"When did you meet her?"

"In January 1972."

"What type of relationship did you establish with Lilla Paulus?"

"We became friends. I stayed at her house every time I was in Houston."

"Those people have no right to play God with my life and decide who can live and who can die. I don't owe Lilla Paulus or Ash Robinson a god damn minute. I saw that little boy, Robert Hill, when he was waiting to testify today, and my heart broke. You know, I didn't really realize until that moment that he has no real mother or father any more. And I have a little boy just like him who was about to be in the same fix. I should be spending every precious second with my own son. . . ."

Bennett nodded, elated, but not daring to intrude until her declaration was done. He only wished that court was still in session, so he could whisk her into the box before she weakened again. He urged her not to see or speak to anyone, especially not Dick DeGeurin should word seep out from the jail that she would become a witness for the prosecution the next morning. "But I've already told him," she said. "He was really upset. He was so shaken he was practically in tears. He urged me not to testify." Bennett grew annoyed. DeGeurin had no ethical right to exhort this capricious young woman. Marcia saw the discomfort on the prosecutor's face and sought to ease his mind. "I felt I had to tell him. It was a very upsetting conversation. And I told him the same thing I'm telling you. I know how bad he wants to win this case, but he'll have to win it without my silence."

A friend, sympathetic to the drama of the most critical day of Marcia's life, provided a simple white jersey dress for her to wear. Bob Bennett insisted that the blue middy tie be draped modestly across the breasts, for although he had no intention of hiding Marcia's line of work, he did not want her to perch in the witness box like a siren singing on the rocks. She washed and brushed her hair carefully, letting it fall naturally, and with a pale pinkish lipstick borrowed from a sister prisoner, Marcia appeared quite girlish, even demure. Each of the five women jurors scrutinized her carefully, as they would a new arrival at a party, then were clearly fascinated as she led them like tourists into the dark and forbidden caverns of money, sex, and murder. Bennett had warned her that he would be rough, that he—and certainly the defense lawyer on cross-examination—would journey brutally through her private life. He also cautioned her not to look out at Lilla Paulus, worrying that she might falter under the gaze of the older woman. "Don't worry about that," Marcia said, summoning courage, "that moment is going to be worth it all. Oh, I know she'll try to stare me down. She'll try to scare me out of the box. But it won't wash, Lilla. Shut your old ugly eyes!"

"Was Lilla Paulus aware of your profession?"

"Yes." Marcia's voice was soft, thick Texan, covered with the nasal icing of a hillbilly songstress.

In a long series of questions, Bennett asked if Marcia had ever heard of a "contract" that Lilla Paulus was "shopping."

Yes, she had. The "contract" had been around for several

months. Lilla had asked her if she knew anyone capable
of filling it.

"Did you learn who was the subject of this 'contract'?"

Marcia nodded quickly. "Yes. Dr. John Hill." With that
she looked squarely at Lilla Paulus and between the two
women was the ache of a child betraying a parent, the
sorrow of age for errant youth. But if Lilla permitted herself a moment of emotion, she quickly regained her composure and replaced her mask of serene ice. Occasionally
she nudged DeGeurin with an impatient elbow, but the
lawyer was hanging on every word that emerged from the
calm and responsive threat on the stand, and he would not
permit his client to interfere with his concentration.

It was time for Bennett to introduce the great unspoken
name into the proceedings. He pulled a small color snap-
shot from a folder and asked Marcia if she knew this man.

"Yes," said Marcia, glancing at the picture. "This is Ash
Robinson."

Bennett offered the image to the jurors, and each member stared attentively at a benign grandfather—heavy, gray-
haired, prosperous-looking in a dark blue suit, at ease in
his favorite armchair, beneath photographs of Joan.

"Where did you first meet Ash Robinson?"

"At Lilla's house. . . . Ash just came by. . . . He began
discussing Lilla's daughter, Mary Jo, and his own daughter . . . how they had ridden horses together. . . . He was
very upset. . . . He spoke very sadly of the death of his
daughter. . . . He was *obsessed* with the fact that he did
not have custody of his grandson."

Bennett moved cautiously. Marcia was the seamstress
who alone could stitch together the conspiracy. "How many
times did you see Ash Robinson at Lilla's house?"

"Not many. . . . But Lilla told me he was the person
who wanted the 'contract' filled. . . ."

Marcia told of mentioning the contract to Bobby Vandiver in the late spring or early summer of 1972. Bobby
was "disinterested" at first, she testified. But after several
weeks passed, he agreed to speak with Lilla.

"And what was the arrangement?" wondered Bennett. He
was pleased with the manner in which his witness was
testifying—clearly, logically, with no hesitations or embel-
lishments. Occasionally he stole a sideways glance at the
jurors. They were rapt.

"Lilla said he would get $5,000 for the contract . . . and

she would get her money separately from the same source.
. . . Bobby asked me if Lilla could be trusted, and I said,
'Yes.' "

"Did you see Ash Robinson again?"

Marcia nodded. She remembered the old man came once
more to Lilla's house for a meeting while Bobby was asleep
in another room. And there were "a few" meetings between
Lilla and Ash in a parking lot across the street from Ben
Taub Hospital, the city's huge and crowded charity institution. There, Marcia testified, Lilla and Ash would rendezvous, either in her Cadillac or in a nearby park.

"Ash was very leery of anyone else's presence," said
Marcia, explaining the furtive strolls in the woods. But
they did not walk far enough to be completely out of her
sight, said Marcia. "Lilla was handed what appeared to be
money by Ash," she said, boring her eyes once again into
Lilla, suddenly seized with renewed coughing.

Once the bargain was struck between Lilla and Bobby
Vandiver, Marcia said, Lilla helped plan the killing. "Lilla
took us over on Kirby Drive and pointed out the house
and more or less told us Dr. Hill's daily routine, who was
normally in the house . . . that sort of thing." The first
drive-by of the Hill home was three or four weeks ahead
of the crime.

"At this stage of the game," asked Bennett, "what were
the arrangements?"

"There were none," said Marcia, almost cheerful in
reminiscence. She sounded as if the conspirators were such
rank novices at murder—characters from a bumbling Brit-
ish film mystery—that it was miraculous the death actually
occurred. "We couldn't even figure out when he would be
alone. He never was. There were always people around
him."

"How often did you go to the Hill home?"

"I can't count that high. We went at times ranging from
six in the morning to four in the morning."

Bennett skipped ahead in time to the final days of John
Hill's life. He asked Marcia to describe how she and Bobby
stalked the doomed plastic surgeon.

"Ash Robinson told Lilla that John Hill was either in
Seattle or Las Vegas around September 16," she answered.
"I called Vegas . . . but I couldn't locate him. He was lost.
. . . On September 24, 1972, Ash informed us that Hill
would be coming home later on this day and that he sup-

posedly had $15,000 cash on him to pay his lawyer. . . .
Lilla told me that the day before Ash had given her $7,000
on the contract. . . . Lilla had the flight schedule for National Airlines, and there were three flights due into Houston from Vegas. . . . Lilla said she could not find out which
flight the doctor was on She asked me to find out. I called
National and they told me Hill was due in at 6:38
P.M. . . ."

Bob Bennett interrupted, retrieving one of the slips of
paper he had earlier introduced as a state exhibit, offering
it now to Marcia for identification. The slip, seized in Jerry
Carpenter's search of Lilla's house, bore scribbled flight
numbers and estimated times of arrival.

"Do you recognize this handwriting?" asked Bennett.

"Yes," said Marcia. It was the hand of Lilla Paulus.

Quickly DeGeurin objected, claiming that Marcia had
not been qualified as a handwriting expert. Judge Price let
her comment stand, and Bennett moved hurriedly—and
happily—into a newly opened door. How long, he wondered, had Marcia been a guest at Lilla Paulus' home? If
all the nights were added up, estimated Marcia, they would
total three months. Bennett nodded tellingly, hoping that
the jury would make the important connection that Marcia
was very much a fixture at the Paulus home and not just
a rare guest. This would tend to bolster her opinion about
the handwriting, as well as her earlier testimony about the
murder contract being "shopped" for some time.

Finally Bennett led Marcia with patience and gentleness
through the fulfillment of the contract, driving Bobby to the
Hill home, waiting in the House of Pies for his phone call,
the difficulty in picking him up, returning to Lilla's house
for the balance due.

"How much money did Lilla pay him?" asked Bennett.

"Five thousand dollars, whereupon Bobby gave her
$1,000 back for steering him to the job. . . ."

"A commission?" suggested Bennett, dropping the word
heavily, emphasizing the price tag on a human life.

"Yes," agreed Marcia.

DeGeurin was in trouble. Normally he would rip into a
witness of Marcia's reputation, slashing her character, im-
peaching her believability, approaching the task with the
distaste of a man forced to dismantle a blocked sewer pipe.
But Marcia had already owned up to the shaded portions

of her life. Already she had accepted the roles of prostitute, dope addict, assistant murderer. And she sat there patiently, no more fearful of what was to come than a housewife facing a census taker's clipboard. All DeGeurin could do was stomp heavily over the ground, searching for little flaws that might, if gathered together, make a fission in some juror's mind.

"What does 'chip' mean?" demanded DeGeurin.

"Bobby and I were bed partners," said Marcia.

"Did you share your earnings with Bobby?"

"Occasionally."

"Are you familiar with the term 'pimp'?"

"Yes." Marcia's answer was curt, for she knew what was coming.

"Was Bobby your pimp?"

"No." Marcia drew herself up almost haughtily.

DeGeurin made a face of surprise, as if he had just been told that the sun rose each morning in the north. "Then was Bobby a hijacker, a person who robs other people from time to time?"

Marcia agreed with that.

The defense attorney gestured with his right hand at the thin, coughing woman beside him. Then he whirled and pointed accusatorily at Marcia. "Do you deny that you and Bobby Vandiver planned to 'rip off' Lilla Paulus . . . a widow . . . living alone . . . well off . . . an easy mark?"

Marcia almost laughed. "She might be," said the prostitute with heavy sarcasm, "if her home wasn't an arsenal."

The lawyer looked surprised again. "You're inferring that Lilla Paulus' home was an arsenal?"

"Yes," said Marcia firmly.

Prudently. DeGeurin backed away from this coiled and rattling snake as fast as possible. Better that he make a clear distinction between his respectable client and this disreputable whore.

"Isn't it true that in actual fact Lilla Paulus had no real knowledge of your true character?" DeGeurin asked.

Marcia looked amused. "No. She was aware. She even called me at the William Penn Hotel and asked for Dusty." Bob Bennett was silently happy with this answer. Marcia had cleverly managed to slip into the trial record the fact that she worked at the faded downtown hostelry under the trick name of Dusty. One of the four slips of paper introduced in evidence had both the name of the hotel and the pseudonym written on it.

The defense lawyer punched around with unmarkable impact, trying to set up targets—Marcia's addiction to drugs, the charge that she co-operated with the police to obtain narcotics, and—over and over again—that she and Bobby Vandiver were professional robbers, out to steal from Lilla Paulus.

For the better part of two days the opposing lawyers tossed Marcia back and forth like a bean bag, DeGeurin trying to tear her stuffing out as a lying, conniving, junkie whore who changed stories as whimsically as the wind, Bennett seeking to patch any punctures by insisting that his witness was a repentant, truthful, helpful, justice-desiring young woman. Whatever, Marcia emerged, at least to the press and the young Turks who had begun to fill the court-room, as a credible witness and a potent offering for the state.

Significantly, DeGeurin did not attempt to impeach Marcia's graphic narrative of the murder and its planning or Lilla's alleged involvement. The best he could do was hammer at the discrepancies between the testimony she had given at her own murder trial four months earlier and what she was now swearing to—and at the same time rip off the bandages from the sores of her life and display the fes-tering ugliness to the jury. But would this be enough to make the jury disbelieve her? Bennett did not think so. Privately, he was not alarmed at DeGeurin's attempt at character assassination. In his summation, he intended to tell the jury that of course Marcia was a dope addict-pros-titute, and of course Bobby Vandiver was a robber-hit man. You don't hire a preacher to go out and do your killing for you, he would say. Or something like that.

Toward the end of Marcia's second day on the stand, Bob Bennett could not resist pointing out, almost mis-chievously, that if the prostitute's testimony was all that tainted, then why had Dick DeGeurin visited her jail cell and implored her *not* to testify? It was true, wasn't it, that DeGeurin paid frequent visits? And it was true, wasn't it, that he was *not* her attorney in this matter?

Not only were both facts true, she testified, DeGeurin had even suggested to her that Bobby Vandiver was as-sassinated on direct order of Mr. Bennett of the district attorney's office. At this, the young prosecutor's face went hot with anger. The charge was reprehensible, and besides, it made no sense. Since he had worked out a deal with Bobby Vandiver and was crucially dependent on his co-operation to convict the others, why would he order a killing? But all he could do was object vehemently. He could not reveal the delicate negotiations that had gone on between him and a now dead killer. At this point the two lawyers ceased being polite adversaries and bcame bitter antagonists. "Now we get dirty," murmured one of the re-porters.

Scowling at the defense table, Bennett spun back to Mar-cia, searching for a way to get off stage positively before his wrath caused something reversible.

"Have you ever up to Tuesday of this week been a willing witness in this case?" he asked.

Marcia shook her head. "No."

"Then why are you now testifying?"

"I feel," said Marcia, "that it's the right thing to do." At her place Lilla Paulus smiled pseudo patiently, as one would when dealing with a renowned psychopathic liar.

"That's all for now, your honor," said Bennett.

In the court anteroom, waiting for the elevator that would drop her back to the jail, Marcia was invigorated, anxious to relive her appearance, as an actor likes to sit up after the performance and unwind. "It was worth it," she said, a little pride showing, "just to see the expression on Lilla's face. She was always the height of composure. I thought nothing could get to her. But when I told about her meeting with Ash, I thought she was going to fall apart."

Bennett appeared with a compliment for her forthright testimony. And he volunteered a special guard to watch over Marcia in the women's jail that night. No need for that, said Marcia. She was exhilarated and strengthened. "Last night the matron wanted to put me in an isolation cell for my own protection," she said. "But I refused. There's no shower or toilet, and besides, I'm not scared any more. You know the crazy thing, Bob? The other girls said they had been wondering why the hell it took me so long to make my decision." Nonetheless, Bennett quietly ordered that a discreet watch be kept over Marcia, for he had come to know—and fear—the way people who had roles in this case kept dying.

* * *

To conclude, Bennett summoned a Mr. Bolton, "security director" from Southwestern Bell Telephone, who testified about activity on Lilla Paulus' line. During the days preceding the death of Dr. John Hill, long-distance calls were charged to her number and placed to Western Airlines in Seattle, Air West in Seattle, and the Stardust Hotel in Las Vegas, where the convention of plastic surgeons was being held, and which Dr. Hill was scheduled to attend. There was also a call made to Red, Bobby Vandiver's sister, at her home near Dallas, this tending to verify a bit of testimony from Marcia about Lilla calling Bobby there on September 11, 1972, and suggesting that now was a good time to fill the contract.

Even more important, the man from the telephone company testified that, for a short period of time in the autumn of 1972, Ash Robinson took out an unlisted telephone. The number was 523-3746. At this revelation, Bob Bennett produced the smallest slip of paper he had previously introduced mysteriously as evidence. This was a scrap found in the recesses of Lilla's purse on the day she was arrested by Jerry Carpenter. On it was jotted the same private phone number, 523-3746.

With that, Bob Bennett rested his case. It was not the most powerful he had ever presented, but it was, he reasoned, the best he could do. He had given the jury a dead man, eyewitnesses to the crime, a confessed participant, and a few scraps of paper that fragilely bound Lilla Paulus to the role of agent for murder. It would have strengthened his position had he been able to put other people on the witness stand who would testify to having heard Lilla Paulus "shop the contract." There were, he believed, at least three. Perhaps four. He even had their names and whereabouts. The layman would assume that the district attorney possessed the power to subpoena such people and *force* them to testify. Not at all. In one of the pretrial strategy sessions Bennett had fantasized the futility of his position. "I can just see it," he told Jerry Carpenter. "I tell this dude in the North Carolina jailhouse that my name is Bob Bennett and I'm from the district attorney's office in Houston and I *insist* that he come with me to testify he heard Lilla Paulus looking around for sombeody to kill John Hill. He listens and he says. 'Well, fuck you and the horse you rode up on, buddy.' "

Nor was Bennett content with the image of Lilla Paulus that he had presented to the jury. Other than Marcia's helpful remark that the defendant's home was an "arsenal," the jurors had been given nothing to indicate that the coughing gray woman with the haunting eyes lived a life at considerable odds with her image.

As expected, Dick DeGeurin immediately requested an instructed verdict of acquittal. In the privacy of Judge Price's freshly decorated chambers, under a large gold-hued metal weeping willow that dominated the major wall, the defense lawyer imperiously scoffed at the state's case. "There simply is not a shred of evidence that links Mrs. Paulus to this offense," said DeGeurin. "As I see this case, it is much stronger from a defense standpoint than the Chapman case." His reference was to a famous decision in which the appellate court threw out a conviction of a robber who was arrested with a piece of paper in front of him showing how some loot was to be split. That evidence was **not** of sufficient corroboration, the court decreed.

Bennett, still smarting from the accusation that he arranged the murder of Bobby Vandiver, defended his case with passion: "The general test is to look at the evidence other than accomplice testimony and see if it tends to connect the defendant with the commission of the offense. The key word here is *'tends.'*"

DeGeurin cleared his throat to begin a protest, but Bennett angrily plunged ahead. He was bent on tearing down any weeds in his path. "We *know* that Ash Robinson had a motive for the killing of John Hill . . . we *know* of animosity between Ash Robinson and John Hill . . . we *know* there was a connection between Ash Robinson and Lilla Paulus. These do not, taken alone, make a case against Lilla Paulus. But as a whole, considering the evidence, they *tend to connect* her with the commission of this offense."

It was late Friday afternoon, the end of the first long week of the trial. Judge Price asked each of the lawyers to prepare briefs supporting their contentions. He would stop by chambers on Saturday noon after his son's baseball game. "I will rule on Mr. DeGeurin's motion for an instructed verdict of acquittal first thing Monday morning," he promised.

The betting in the courthouse corridor was that DeGeurin would win. Give Bennett an A for effort, they said, but give the defense the gold cup. And if Ash Robinson had

not suddenly and rudely and foolishly injected himself
into the picture over the weekend, perhaps the drama
would have sputtered and died But he did The damned old
man couldn t keep his mouth shut when it was most important

Stretched in sensation across the top eight columns of
the Monday morning Houston *Post* for February 24, 1975,
was a headline that angered Judge Price. ROBINSON DENIES
ROLE IN SLAYING. shrieked the banner, touting a "*Post*
Exclusive' and copyrighted interview with the man everybody in town was talking about:

> Oilman Ash Robinson categorically denied Sunday
> he had anything to do with the slaying of Dr. John
> Hill.
> Robinson said he certainly would not have arranged
> the killing of his former son-in-law, as was testified
> in court last week, before "an audience of people."
> "I didn't want him dead," Robinson said. "His kill-
> ing didn't solve his problems or mine."

And on and on, Robinson using the newspaper as a
trumpet to blast once again his anthem of innocence. He
was breaking his long silence, he said, because he felt it
necessary to respond to the allegations made against him
in the Paulus murder trial. He wanted his grandson to believe in his innocence. The truth of the matter, said Ash
in his interview, was that he *wanted* to get on the witness
stand and—under oath—demolish the lies being told about
him. But his health was failing, he told the reporter. He
doubted if his doctor would permit such an ordeal.

"Bullshit," swore Judge Price when he finished the article,
slamming it down on his desk and wondering if the trial
was now spoiled In retrospect he realized that he should
have locked the jurors up from the moment of their selection. Even though he daily lectured them not to read newspapers or listen to radio and television reports on the trial,
it would have been impossible to avoid seeing this headline, set in a type size appropriate to a Russian invasion of
San Francisco. Newsstands had it clearly visible all over
the courthouse, and his car radio had crackled on the
judge's drive downtown that morning with reference to
Ash's interview.

Ever since the McKittrick-Paulus matters fell onto his docket by chance, the young judge had been fascinated and troubled by the manner in which the dramas were playing out. "It reminds me of that movie *The French Connection*," he had once commented. "It seems to be the kind of situation where the higher-ups insulate themselves and the little people get shot or go to the penitentiary."

Whether the judge might have granted the defense motion for an instructed verdict of acquittal had not Ash splattered himself across the breakfast tables of Houston must be speculation. But there could be no misreading of Judge Price's cold anger when he entered the courtroom and beckoned DeGeurin and Bennett. "Mr. DeGeurin," he said tersely, "your motion will be overruled. May we begin?"

The judge was here following an old and well-traveled route of procedure. He would let the trial continue, hoping that it would finally reach a jury, but if matters got out of hand, or if he developed second thoughts about turning down the DeGeurin motion, then he could at any time grant it and end the state's prosecution of Lilla Paulus.

DeGeurin was disappointed and tired. His smooth and boyish face had new lines of fatigue, and his eyes were as pink as a rabbit's from lack of sleep. He, too, was troubled by the newspaper article, for he recognized that the irascible old man was damaging his defense of Lilla Paulus. He had no control over Ash, despite gossip (which he denied) that he was being paid from Robinson's purse.

At this point, what DeGeurin should have done was quit. Rest his case. Call no witnesses for the defense. Depend upon an impassioned sermon of scorn to wreck the state's feeble case against his client. But all weekend long he had tried theoretically to put himself in the jury box and study just how much damning information was on the record. This is always a challenging task for a lawyer, for when a person lives with a murder case for years, privy to every intimate nuance and detail, it is difficult to distinguish between the few trees newly planted for the jury and the massive forest already growing in the brain.

Had he been a juror, DeGeurin reasoned, trying to be objective, he would have voted for acquittal. The state's case simply did not meet the burden of proof beyond a reasonable doubt. But could the average juror—the heavy-

set grandmother or the vacant-looking young secretary—
distinguish between *real* evidence and the power of colored
photographs of a dead man? Between *real* evidence and
the unsubstantiated testimony of a prostitute trying to win
herself the best possible bargain? Other factors were at
work within DeGeurin. He had prepared a substantial defense. Witnesses were on tap, briefed, ready to respond to
carefully rehearsed questions. Were he to rest the case now
and not call on these people, he would be like a man who
built a cannon and then went into battle but never got to
fire his wondrous contraption. Moreover, the ambitious
young lawyer's ego was caught up in the heady proceedings. Television lights embraced him at every entrance
and exit from the courtroom. However his role thus far
had been in the supporting actor category, interrupting now
and then with a jibe at the district attorney. Only if he became the ringmaster, cracking his whip and bringing on
the acts, only then would he have principal billing. "*I go
on trial with my client,*" he said before the first session began. He had labored for ten thousand hours to prepare
these moments. And he was not content to quit with what
might be a hollow victory. What his reputation hungered
for was a resounding triumph. Like Racehorse Haynes, he
wanted them to lift him to their shoulders and carry him
from the courtroom.

First, he had to do something about those irksome pieces
of paper that the state deemed "evidence." Most troubling
was the scrap found deep in the recesses of Lilla's handbag
the day she was arrested, the one containing Ash Robinson's
private unlisted telephone number. Several routes of attack
were open to DeGeurin, the principal one being his claim
that the search itself was invalid because Jerry Carpenter
and his posse had frightened his client into permission
with their bristling guns. But an extensive objection to this
search was already in the trial proceedings. He would gamble that the appellate court would rule favorably on that
some later day. For now, he called back to the stand one
of the state's own witnesses, Mr. Bolton, the security director for the telephone company. On behalf of the prosecution, Bolton had testified that Ash Robinson took out a
private number in the autumn of 1972, about the time that
John Hill was murdered, kept it for a few weeks, then ordered it discontinued. Bob Bennett had hinted strongly

that this brief-lived number was the communication link between Ash Robinson and Lilla Paulus to plan the killing.

Over a half day of tedious and boring questioning—at least two of the jurors nodded off on occasion as the flustered witness was made to shuffle through stacks of complicated billing invoices that he, as a company cop, clearly had no sophisticated knowledge of—DeGeurin finally elicited the opinion that the unlisted number was installed a few days *after* the murder of John Hill. This hardly seemed relevant to the issue on the table, i.e., What Was Lilla Paulus Doing With The Private Number Of Ash Robinson In The First Place? But DeGeurin growled and snapped so dramatically at the man from the telephone company that perhaps the jurors were mildly impressed. If somebody spends four hours trying to make a point, his hard work seemed to say, surely it must be significant.

For underscoring, DeGeurin summoned one of his prestigious brothers from the bar, attorney Richard Keeton, counsel now and then for the conspicuously absent Ash Robinson. He sat now in the witness box, the very model of respectability, anxious to tell how "agitated and distraught" Mr. Robinson was in the shocking days following the murder of John Hill. In fact, the old man's telephone—the one publicly listed in the directory—was ringing off the wall. Day and night. Attorney Keeton testified that he was occasionally present in the Robinson home during this crisis period and had helpfully answered some of the rings himself. His face indicated that these were from cranks and ill-wishers, out to harass old Ash. DeGeurin nodded knowingly, as if he were glad to get the truth finally out. And the truth, according to the defense, was that Ash Robinson grew so weary over people bothering him that he was forced to disconnect his regular telephone number and have a new and *unlisted* one installed. This he kept until matters quieted down, until the case moved off the front pages, and then he took his old listed phone number back. And had the temporary unlisted one removed. What could be more logical than this? asked DeGeurin.

But there was one important crack in the shield. And Bob Bennett was quick to point it out. It so happened that Ash Robinson had owned, for several years, another private unlisted telephone number. He still did to this day, as a matter of fact. If he was getting crank calls on his publicly listed number, then why was it necessary to have a

brand-new second private line installed? Why not just give
out his long-established confidential number to those with
whom he wished to speak? Why take out a new unlisted
number for a period of a few weeks, and why did it turn
up in Lilla Paulus' purse?

Albert W. Summerford, looked exactly like his name. He
had a precise, prissy face, a twitching white mustache that
behaved like a rabbit's whiskers, and a manner so meticulous that if asked, "How are you, Al?" he would probably respond with his 9 A.M. pulse rate, blood sugar content, and perhaps the exact number of times he had sneezed
since Christmas. He was a handwriting expert, but one
who promptly informed Dick DeGeurin, his patron in this
matter, that he preferred to use the more dignified appellation "examiner of questioned documents." Following that,
he presented his credentials, taking almost a quarter of an
hour to tick off thirty-five years of professional life, including "consultation with the U. S. Secret Service." He
estimated that since 1940 he had participated in from 6,000
to 7,000 cases, and had examined more than 100,000 questioned documents. Obviously Summerford enjoyed deliver-
ing his dossier. He probably did it at cocktail parties. He
had been engaged by DeGeurin to examine the four slips
of paper seized and introduced as evidence against Lilla
Paulus. And, after meticulous study, he "could not positively
identify her as author." To reach this conclusion, Summerford explained, he had dictated nine full pages of random material to Mrs. Paulus and she dutifully wrote his
words down. Then he matched this writing against the
state's evidence. In great detail he described his conclusions, saying things like "Note here that the capital 'Y'
begins with an approach stroke on this page, and on this
slip of paper it does not."

"Well, can you then eliminate Mrs. Paulus as the person
who wrote this note?" demanded DeGeurin, brandishing
the blank check found by police in Lilla's bedroom night
stand, on the back of which was written "You had better
tell Ash they are trying to subpoena Ma."

"I would be inclined to," said Mr. Summerford in a
voice as clipped as his white sideburns. ". . . there are a
number of differences that cannot be reconciled."

And what about the scrap of paper with Ash Robinson's unlisted telephone number?

Summerford hemmed and hawed around this bramble bush. There were both differences—and a few similarities —in the hand that wrote this number and Lilla Paulus' sample writing as he had studied it There was not enough material for him to identify her or eliminate her as the authoress of this telephone number.

In conclusion, he felt that one of the other slips of paper, the one containing airline flight schedule information and a partial gin rummy score, "seemed to be written by Marcia McKittrick."

Bob Bennett rose for cross-examination, and his manner indicated that he put approximately as much faith in handwriting experts as he did in four-year-old kiddies who wore velvet suits, lace collars, and performed faith healing in tents. "Isn't it true, Mr. Summerford," he said, not concealing the sarcasm in his voice, "that if a person is excited or in ill health or . . ." Here he paused. Lilla Paulus was conveniently coughing again, wheezing, trying to catch her breath. He waited for her to complete her beautifully timed seizure. ". . . or *out of breath* that their handwriting is different?"

Summerford shrugged. "A person only knows how to make letters one way," he said.

"Isn't there something called a tremor?" pressed Bennett.

"Yes," agreed the expert.

Bennett glanced at a folder on his table. In it were additional samples of Lilla Paulus' handwriting, obtained by the state months before. To Bennett's naked eye, they seemed remarkably dissimilar to those specimens she had given Albert W. Summerford. He felt Lilla was fooling somebody. The district attorney could have spent a full week attacking the "art" of Albert W. Summerford, for he believed that some experts, once handsomely engaged, tend to be overly helpful in making conclusions favorable to the person who paid the money. But he elected not to whip this horse. Bennett sensed that Summerford was not a particularly helpful witness to the defense. The jury had seemed a little restless, even disinterested in his pompous analysis of Lilla's dotted *i*'s and hastily crossed *t*'s. On a hunch, he passed the witness.

There are two newspapers in Houston, the morning *Post*, and the afternoon *Chronicle*. Both are relentlessly home town in outlook, both are conservative politically, and neither would make a list of the ten best in America. But they are on occasion scrappy in an intramural sort of way, and when the *Post* bannered its "exclusive" interview with Ash Robinson and his denial of all the charges rumbling through the courtroom, the *Chronicle* was clearly scooped. It was hardly one to win even a footnote in the history of journalism, for Ash Robinson had been eminently approachable since the day his daughter died, opening his door with a courtly handshake to correspondents from Europe, New York, even suburban weeklies. Whatever, the *Chronicle*, feeling a little scorched, dispatched one of its reporters to Kirby Drive and once again Ash had something worth a headline. In fact, he had probably held back an appetizing tidbit for the other newspaper, realizing that with his left hand he could dominate the morning edition and with his right command impressive help from the evening competition.

On the next day the *Chronicle* was thus proud to inform its readers in a top-of-the-page scream, OILMAN SAYS LIE DETECTOR TEST CLEARS HIM IN SLAYING. Below was elaborate detail of the polygraph test Ash had bought himself in New York.

The paper hit the streets at midmorning, just as the jury was about to assemble. A copy was put before the judge in his chambers, and if on the day before Frank Price had been angry, now he was furious.

He ordered the jury sequestered from this moment on, instructing the bailiff to make arrangements for lodging, meals, and security guards. And he stalked about his office, the copy of the newspaper crushed in his hand like a club looking for a target. "Why doesn't Mr. DeGeurin call Ash Robinson?" he wondered out loud. "It says in the paper that he is sick, but he isn't too sick to lay around out there in River Oaks conducting press conferences. Hell, he's staging his own trial, which will undoubtedly clear himself since he is the judge *and* the jury."

The young judge was just spouting off, for he well knew that the defense could not dare put the old man on the stand. Not only would it open the door to interminable and ruthless cross-examination from Bob Bennett, Ash would probably invoke the Fifth Amendment. And in that event, murmured the judge, almost perversely, "it would be bye-bye, Lilla." If Ash by silence refused to support Lilla Paulus, he would throw her to the wolves.

A reporter stopped Bob Bennett and asked if the state

planned to subpoena the oilman. Bennett looked almost nauseated. "Do you think I'm going to vouch for Ash Robinson's truth and veracity?" he snapped. If the district attorney hauled Ash into court and made him a state's witness, then Bennett would, under law, be "sponsoring" the old man, and if Ash predictably denied every allegation, then it would destroy the prosecution of Lilla Paulus. The mire was positively Machiavellian, and surely Ash Robinson was reveling in everybody's predicament.

Bennett was walking hurriedly toward the courtroom when he was struck by a new notion. It might just be that his prosecution had been dealt a valuable wild card. With the old man making all of these off-stage noises, surely the jury was going to start wondering why Dick DeGeurin did not summon him to buttress the defense posture. Where the hell was Ash Robinson? The jurors must be asking themselves, Why doesn't the defense get him up here to testify on behalf of Lilla? "This is crazy," said Bennett in a whispered conference with his associate, Bob Burdette, just outside chambers. "But Ash's absence may be the strongest god damn thing we've got going for us."

Dick DeGeurin astonished the courtroom by calling as his next witness Lilla Paulus. The maneuver was breath-taking in its danger, for the district attorney would be beside himself with eagerness to rummage, in cross-examination, through the closets of the defendant's life. But, DeGeurin reasoned, after consultations with the maestro of criminal law, Percy Foreman, the risk was worth taking. There were no felony convictions on Lila's criminal record, nor were there convictions of misdemeanors for moral turpitude. Only a few bond forfeitures, and these were, in the main, from two to three decades old. The state could not bring them up for the jury's consideration. DeGeurin knew that he must be on guard to block every attempt Bennett made to tarnish his client, and indeed, the state might get in a few licks. But, reasoned DeGeurin, there was enormous capital to be made from Lilla Paulus personally taking the stand and, under oath and the penalty of perjury, calmly denying the heinous accusations against her. And Lilla *wanted* to testify. She had, after all, once stood as target for a knife-throwing act. And she had, after all, made it through fifty-six years of an exceptionally flamboyant life. She would not miss the opportunity to enter the place of supreme importance and acquit herself well, in every sense of the word.

Thus prepared to walk across a perilous tightrope, Lilla Paulus raised her hand and vowed to tell the whole truth. She looked like an old bird, ready to peck at the questions thrown at her. Her voice was weak and tremulous. Her eyes were sad, magnified behind thick glasses, great pools of sorrow and burden. Before she could even offer her name, Lilla Paulus began to cough again, pressing her handkerchief to her lips, bending over it in such discomfort that the worry was she might spew out her throat's blood as payment for the cruel ordeal. At first Bennett fretted that the jurors would greet her with sympathy, but then he glimpsed one of the young women on the panel looking a little skeptical at the beautifully timed seizure. *That* was promising.

DeGeurin rushed to the heart of the matter. "Do you know Ash Robinson?" he asked.

Lilla answered politely. "I know of him," she began. "Personally he is not an acquaintance of mine."

"Has Ash Robinson *ever* been in your home?"

"No." The response was as positive as a beat on a bass drum. Her eyes swiveled briefly to Bob Bennett, who was not upset by the answer, only amazed that DeGeurin would permit his client to *completely repudiate* the not particularly damning fact that she at least *knew* the old man. Her total denial was so surprising that Bennett wondered if he could disprove this in the precious few hours left to him. The trial seemed likely to end by the next afternoon. Given a week's recess—an impossibility!—the prosecutor felt confident he could find a score of people who could connect Ash Robinson and Lilla Paulus as old and even devoted friends. Not only had their lives entwined at the Alameda Stables, Bennett had heard a promising bit of gossip that Lilla had even served as the old man's deputy at the aborted murder-by-omission trial of Dr. John Hill in 1971, attending each session, telephoning him each night with blow-by-blow accounts. And Bennett also knew that Ash Robinson had told at least one intimate friend that he had asked Lilla to help him dig up scandalous information on John Hill's character, if such existed, so he could use it as defense ammunition in the surgeon's $10-million slander suit against him. But at this moment all Bob Bennett could do was sit openmouthed, waiting for the next brazenness

from the widow Paulus. He knew now he was up against a
pro.

40

It took Lilla Paulus only thirty-five minutes to present her
life and times to the jury—or, more correctly, the version
she chose to offer on this occasion. And it was so banal and
colorless that the wonder was she had not expired from
boredom years before. She bade the jurors accept her as a
"country woman" who had labored hard all of her un-
frilled life, only to encounter great pain and anguish in
these, her dimming years. She managed to work in frequent
references to the cancer that had allegedly invaded her
frail body. "Let's see, that was *after* my cancer operation . . ." she would say. And there were frequent allusions
to her widowhood. Such-and-such occurred "*after* my
husband Claude passed away from a heart attack." Once
she even combined both cancer and heart trouble in the
same answer, seasoning with a bit of economic hardship
as a bonus. "We bought a smaller two-bedroom house after
I had cancer surgery and Claude had his heart condition."
Death seemed to knock quite regularly at Lilla's door. She
even spoke wistfully of her "sweetheart," a man named
Corley whom she had taken up with after the death of
Claude. Of all things, this beau dropped fatally of a heart
attack while digging a vegetable garden at Lilla's side. At
this Bennett bit the inside of his cheek to keep from
groaning—or laughing. It was too bad about the poor man
dying at such a patriotic pastime, but it was too much, the
way Lilla delivered the mournful set piece.

Then DeGeurin moved to a poignant area.

"Do you have a daughter?"

Lilla smiled, almost sweetly. It was the first ray of light
to cross her face since the hour the trial began. "Yes," she
said. "Mary . . . she's twenty-seven. . . . She went to St.
John's School. . . ." Here Lilla paused for effect, letting the
name of the most distinguished and expensive private
school in town soak in. "I was a Brownie leader and Girl
Scout mother her first two years there. . . ."

Had Lilla here stood up in the witness box, produced
an American flag and, while waving it, delivered both

"The Star-Spangled Banner" and helpful hints for home canning, Bob Bennett would not have been surprised. Clearly this defendant was not going to own up to even the tiniest bit of adolescent mischief. If she kept this up, the jury would accuse *him* of setting a torch beneath St. Lilla of Underwood Street.

Now DeGeurin led his client through a series of demolitions, exploding every major allegation levied against her by the prosecution.

—She denied ownership, authorship, or knowledge of the four slips of paper the state had introduced as evidence. The scrap found in her purse with Ash Robinson's private number? "I did not write it down, nor do I know whose it was. . . ." Perhaps some friend had given it to her for some unknown reason, and she had put it in her purse and forgotten about it. Nor had she ever seen the slips of paper with airline schedules and various telephone numbers relevant to the case and witnesses.

—She denied meeting Ash Robinson in the Ben Taub Hospital parking lot.

—She denied receiving money from Ash Robinson.

—She denied ever meeting or knowing Bobby Wayne Vandiver.

—She denied that her home was "an arsenal," as Marcia McKittrick had implied. "My husband had a 20-gauge shotgun he had owned for years," said Lilla, "and a pistol, and I still have them." That was the extent of that.

—She even denied a minor bit of testimony from Marcia McKittrick that her daughter, Mary Jo, had ridden horses with Joan Robinson Hill at various equestrian shows. Lilla insisted that Joan Hill was a fixture on the "society circuit" while her own daughter was more modestly engaged in rodeos. Their bridle paths did not cross. She would not permit even the frailest thread to bind her to the Ash Robinson family.

But DeGeurin had to introduce information more substantial than that to discredit Marcia McKittrick. He knew that the jurors were probably wanting to know how a respectable widow like Lilla Paulus ever admitted a disreputable prostitute-dope addict like Marcia McKittrick to a household where Brownies and Girl Scouts had once gathered.

"Do you know Marcia McKittrick?" he asked.

Lilla put on a brief face of displeasure. "Yes."

"When did you meet Marcia McKittrick?"

"In the spring of 1972."

"Who introduced you?"

". . . a friend of my husband's."

And then Lilla made a mistake. She was almost across the tightrope when she fell. It could have been avoided. But she did what every lawyer fears a well-rehearsed witness might do—deviate from the script.

Lilla was telling how Marcia inveigled her way into the household. The version was that Lilla, freshly widowed, her own daughter married and living in another city, suffered from loneliness. Along came this girl Marcia, seemingly friendless as well, in need of surrogate mothering, breathing a little vitality and the spring air of youth into the deep, solitary autumn of Lilla Paulus' life.

"Marcia seemed to be a lonely girl," said Lilla, her voice brushed by the sadness of bitter recollection. ". . . she needed a place to stay. . . . I liked her . . . even though you could gather from her conversation that her life was just a little bit different"—dramatic pause—"from mine."

Bob Bennett practically sat up in his chair from electric shock. He repeated the phrase to himself: ". . . *you could gather from her conversation that her life was just a little bit different from mine.*" Had Lilla suddenly lost control? Did she realize that this seemingly innocent remark was perhaps a key to the locked doors of her life?

Incredibly, she went even further. Her tale continued: After Marcia McKittrick had ingratiated herself into the household, she began abusing Lilla's hospitality by bringing around worrisome men of dubious repute. "I told Marcia once that I did not ever want any of her friends . . . those men . . . in my house," sniffed Lilla. "I was a widder woman. . . ."

DeGeurin concluded his questioning with a whiff of police muscle tactics. "Did Jerry Carpenter threaten you? Make any promises?"

Lilla nodded vigorously. "Yes. He told me I would be free of any involvement if I would implicate Ash Robinson."

"What did you say to that?"

"I told Jerry Carpenter I thought the police were supposed to find out the truth. If I testified the way he wanted me to, that would be perjury."

A hush, the kind when an audience waits in the moment of darkness and suspense for the curtain to rise, fell across the courtroom Bob Bennett stood and looked rather courteously at the woman in the jury box How would he impeach what she had said? The feeling in the spectator section was that Lilla had made a powerful argument on her behalf.

The prosecutor began quietly, wondering in his very first question how Lilla's husband supported his family. There must have been a lot of money coming into the cookie jar to buy a house on prestigious Sunset Boulevard and send a daughter to St. John's School and indulge her love of horses.

Well, answered Lilla, she wasn't very good at finances, but as best she knew, her husband had "investments" and "stocks and bonds from which dividends came in" and "there was some rent property in Galveston."

Bennett arched one eyebrow. "Rent property in Galveston?'

'Yes. Some houses on E Street."

Suddenly his voice whiplashed. "Your husband also had an income from gambling, didn't he?"

Lilla put on a face of bewilderment. "No," she said.

"He was a *bookmaker,* wasn't he?"

"Not that I know if," said Lilla, shooting a look at the jury that said the question was impudent and ridiculous. DeGeurin objected, and he had good cause. The district attorney was on thin ice if he planned to impeach Lilla Paulus on the character of her dead husband. With a warning to Bennett that he proceed with extreme caution, the judge let the questioning continue. Judge Price was similarly troubled by the halo Lilla had worn during her testimony, but he could not permit the prosecution to tilt it by wandering off into areas irrelevant to the business of the day, that being whether Lilla Paulus was an accomplice to the murder of John Hill.

Very well, Bennett would drop the queries into Claude Paulus' line of work. But he returned to the "rent property" in Galveston.

"These rent houses were on Post Office Street, weren't they?" asked Bennett, emphasizing the address, for Post Office Street in Galveston was to prostitution what New York's Bowery is to bums.

"Well," said Lilla, giving in a fraction, "E Street is the same as Post Office Street."

"They were *whorehouses,* weren't they?" shot back Bennett.

As DeGeurin shouted his objection, Bennett nodded, knowing the question was out of bounds, but pleased to have made the point anyway. Now he tried to break Lilla down on her blundering aside that her life was "just a little bit different" than Marcia's. Surely, said Bennett, Lilla knew that Marcia worked as a prostitute.

No, insisted Lilla, she had no knowledge of that.

A half dozen ways Bennett asked this question, and a half dozen times Lilla replied that she had no frame of reference for knowing that her house guest earned money in that sordid capacity.

Bennett grunted. What he wanted to do was tear open one of the folders on his table, seize Lilla's rap sheet dating from three decades past, make a paper airplane out of it, and sail it squarely into her lap. Perhaps she could enlighten him to the nature of her own experiences with police, beginning in 1942 and dotted with entries like "Investigation—(hold for clinic)" and "Vag. and common prostitute."

Surely, under the "It takes one to know one" principle, Lilla must have had the tiniest glimmer of knowledge concerning Marcia's work habits. But the law would not permit the district attorney to do this. Only felony convictions and misdemeanors involving moral turpitude were admissible, and Lilla's rap sheet would thus remain as buried from the jury's eyes as the Dead Sea Scrolls.

Frustrated, Bennett passed the witness, but with the proviso that he would perhaps call her back. During recess he went to his office and slumped seething in his chair. He had not pried a molecule of concession out of Lilla's tight lips. "This is a classic example of how the judicial system hides the truth," he said. "I sure would like to ask Mrs. Paulus, 'By the way, Lilla, did you teach all those other Brownies to be whores, like you did your own daughter?' "

A year or so before, in the small Texas town of Hallettsville, Mary Jo Paulus had testified in her unsuccessful attempt to claim the inheritance from her paternal grandmother's estate. She had therein claimed, under penalty of perjury, that her mother, Lilla Paulus, had trained her to be a prostitute. It was all there, in stark and painful black and white, on the pages of a court record in another town. But Bob Bennett could not pass these documents around to his jury, either.

"Why don't you get Mary Jo here and put her on the stand?" wondered one of the DA investigators who had not been involved in the case for the lifetime that Bennett had.

"She won't come," snapped Bennett. "She's scared to death. And, buddy, I don't really blame her."

He returned to the courtroom and ordered Lilla back in the box. There was no more mock courtesy. Was it not true, demanded Bennett, that she had offered the contract on John Hill's life to at least two other police characters, spitting out their names like an Old West marshal nailing "wanted" posters to the jailhouse door?

"No," replied Lilla in a voice of exceeding calm. Her composure was astonishing.

"When you did give Marcia McKittrick a key to your home?"

"I don't know exactly," reminisced Lilla. ". . . spring or summer of 1972."

"By that time you had become convinced, had you not, that her life style was 'a little different' from yours?"

Lilla nodded. "It was quite obvious. I'm fifty-six, and she's in her twenties, I believe."

"Wait a minute," thought Bennett. That's giving me the temperature when I asked the time of day. He asked, "You were talking were you not, about the *life style* as opposed to the age?"

Lilla backed off quickly. For the first time she seemed a little flustered. "No . . . I . . . I . . ." She was stammering.

Bennett rammed back quickly. "You came to suspect that she was a prostitute, did you not?"

Lilla regained her control. "No, I did not know whether she was a prostitute or not. She had never met men in my house."

"So the only thing you knew about Marcia McKittrick that would indicate her life was 'a little different' from yours was that she was twenty-three and you were fifty-six?"

"Well, yes. And she came and went in my house. *She* did not have a home. I *did* have a home. . . . I liked the girl . . . she was friendly."

"That's *all* you knew about her?" demanded Bennett. "That she was younger than you are and she was friendly?"

"That's all I can testify to."

"That's all you *will* testify to," disagreed Bennett.

"That's all I can," shot back Lilla a fraction hotly.

Bennett changed gears "When did you meet Diane Sette-gast?" He introduced the name of the Dallas woman who had been a house guest in Joan Robinson Hill's home the week before she died. She was also the woman who first revealed the tale of the mysterious French pastries and more then anyone else propelled Ash Robinson off his launching pad. Bennett had discovered a curious coincidence: Diane Settegast was also a close friend of Lilla Paulus, had even stayed in the Paulus home during trips to Houston to testify in various proceedings relating to the trial of John Hill. He felt strongly that she was a crucial weld between the old man and the sad-eyed widder woman.

Lilla said she had met Diane Settegast at least fifteen years ago. At the Alameda Stables.

"You were aware that she was a good friend of Ash Robinson's? And of Joan Hill?"

"Yes, sir," Lilla answered cautiously.

"You were aware that she was upset by the death of Joan Hill?"

"Yes, sir."

"You were aware that Ash Robinson, by virtue of your acquaintance with Diane Settegast, was also upset?"

"I did not see Mr. Robinson at the time of his daughter's death, but I assume he was grieved." Bennett hesitated at this answer. The phrase "at the time of his daughter's death" tempted him. If Lilla pretended not to know Ash Robinson at all, then why would she use that curious bit of qualification? Would the jury be smart enough to pick up on this?

"Mr. Robinson, acording to you, has *never* been in your home?" asked Bennett.

"No, sir." Firm. Unyielding.

"So, if Mr. Robinson *says* he was in your home, he is ly—" Bennett pretended to catch himself. "He was . . . in error?"

Lilla paused, perhaps wondering if the district attorney was bluffing—he was—or did he have a trap laid for her? She elected to hew to her line. "Well, he was never in my home when I was in my home."

"He was *not* an acquaintance of yours," said Bennett. "I believe that's the way you put it."

Lilla decided to back-pedal an inch or two "Oh, I knew him . . . just on sight . . . through the horse show circles. But I've never had an intimate conversation or private conversation with Mr. Robinson in my life."

"You never visited in his home?"

"Nosirree."

Tired, angry, unsuccessful, Bennett quit for the day. DeGeurin escorted his client from the courtroom with solicitude for her health and admiration for her performance. He felt she had, to use a phrase, scored Brownie points.

That night, long after darkness had covered the courthouse, after Jerry Carpenter and the reporters had drunk his beer and left his office, after the post-mortems, after the charwomen had come and complained that they could not clean his messy office until he had the courtesy to get out of it, Bob Bennett leaned back in his chair and stared at the ceiling. The day had been an exercise in frustration. "The American judicial system is damn near impotent," he told himself, a little surprised that his moderately liberal nature, forged by the sun of John F. Kennedy, would permit such an archly rightist remark. But the way the trial was going, Lilla-bug was about to fly away home on the wings of acquittal. The offer from the attorney general's office in Washington had never seemed more attractive than at this moment. He wanted to leave his shabby office, get out of Houston, forget about it all.

Then he eyed the telephone. He stared at it blankly for a while. Finally he picked it up and dialed, first a local call. Then, a few minutes later, long distance. They were to be two of the most important conversations of his career.

41

Dick DeGeurin was feeling fine. He had patched the house well against the storm. The only place where the cold wind might get in still was the absence of Ash Robinson. Thus he dramatically issued a subpoena for the old man, slipped the news to a reporter, and the next morning's *Post* carried a major article telling how badly the defense wanted the oilman to appear on its behalf. This was patently false. The last thing on earth that DeGeurin wanted was to face Ash Robinson in the witness box. But he had to *pretend* that he did, and at the same time hope that his mock disappointment at the old man's continuing absence would seep somehow into the jury's cognition.

The process server for Judge Price's court was a gentle and diligent man named Frank Clauder who, in his off hours, performed magic and appeared as a circus clown under the name of "Mr. Misto." An almost legendary figure in courthouse lore, he was reportedly able to serve summonses on the most invisible of men. He failed completely with Ash Robinson. He went to the old man's home in River Oaks and rang the door and stood on the front porch for two hours, waiting for a response. The Robinsons' gleaming black Lincoln was in the garage, lights burned inside the house, Clauder could feel eyes examining him through the peephole. The next morning the process server returned and leaned on the doorbell well before sunrise. Surprisingly it was promptly opened—by Mrs. Ash Robinson. Ma stood on her hearth and was cranky. No, Pa was not home. No, she did not know where he was. No, he could not come in.

"Where is Mr. Robinson?" inquired Clauder courteously.

Maybe he was asleep. Maybe he was sick. Maybe he was away. Ma Robinson just did not know.

Quickly Clauder thrust the summons into the old lady's hands, and instantly she dropped it, letting it fall to the doormat. Clauder returned to Judge Price and informed him that obviously Mrs. Robinson had been instructed not to accept service.

The judge nodded. He was not surprised. He saw through the defense's charade. And he was irritated by it.

DeGeurin was prepared to show the jury why he was unable to get Ash into court. He produced the old man's personal physician, Dr. Edmund Gouldin. The doctor was a short, balding man with a little gray fringe skullcap of hair and a complexion that matched. He had long had an oar in the murky waters of the Joan Robinson Hill case and its tempestuous aftermath. Ash Robinson had used him to pressure the district attorney so long ago for exhumation of his daughter's body. And Gouldin had from time to time counseled the oilman on medical matters arising in the case. Now he was coming to Ash's aid one more time.

"How long have you been Ash Robinson's physician?" asked DeGeurin.

"Since 1946."

"When did you last see Mr. Robinson?"

The doctor seemed glad to be asked that. It just so happened that he had dropped by Ash's home the previous Sunday—four days ago—and during that visit the old man had complained of feeling poorly. Ash said he had awakened in his sleep at 2 A.M., sweating profusely, and, when he was unable to find slumber again, wandered into the living room and tried the couch where he perspired so heavily that the cushions became soaked and had to be turned over. Dr. Gouldin, upon hearing this account, asked his patient to come in for a checkup, and this revealed that the Robinson blood pressure was 174 over 94—"rather high"—and his electrocardiogram showed a "block" from some previous heart muscle scarring.

"I advised Ash that under no circumstances was he to testify in a courtroom setting," testified Dr. Gouldin. He suspected that the old man was suffering from cardiac insufficiency. "I would too, if Marcia McKittrick got up and told the same things on me," mused Bob Bennett to himself. Moreover, Robinson had a hernia of the esophagus, prostate trouble, diverticulosis of the colon, and was considerably overweight.

"I told Ash to lay around a few days and do nothing," said the doctor solemnly.

Bennett could not resist retorting, "Did you tell him to lay around and conduct his press conferences?" Nor could Bennett hold back the desire to illumine the doctor's relationship with Ash a little. Wasn't it true that Ash Robinson once held the mortgage on the doctor's house? "Yes," said Gouldin. And didn't the doctor engage in the oil and mineral business with Ash from time to time? That was also true. But Dr. Gouldin insisted that such financial ties would not constrict his professional integrity.

Dr. Gouldin made a proposition that Ash be allowed to give testimony in "a hospital setting." Bennett scoffed at this, knowing that the session would necessarily have to be conducted out of the jury's earshot, and suspecting that every time he asked a reasonably tough question, the old man would clasp his hands to his breast and have a convenient attack of "cardiac insufficiency."

Judge Price took over the questioning for the first time

in the trial. It did not appear that he was content with the
doctor's testimony.

"I don't really understand the nature of Mr. Robinson's
illness," said the judge. "Was he hospitalized for this heart
trouble?"

"No, your honor."

"Was he hospitalized the *last* time he had a heart problem, which I believe you testified was in 1965?"

"No, your honor."

"Has he *ever* been hospitalized for any of his heart attacks?"

"No, your honor."

"Can he drive?"

"Yes, your honor."

Judge Price's face was a study in disbelief. Dr. Gouldin
rushed quickly in with a bid for sympathy. "Your honor,
how would you feel if Mr. Robinson had a heart attack
and died—right here in your courtroom?"

"I'd feel very bad," said the judge, "just like I would if
anybody had a heart attack in my courtroom. But if Mr.
Robinson can drive, and he is conducting his business
affairs . . ." The judge's voice trailed off, not electing to
conclude his remark. He did not have to. His look of disgust did it for him.

DeGeurin announced he had completed his presentation
of witnesses, but before Bob Bennett could begin his rebuttal testimony the defense lawyer threw down a passionate document requesting a mistrial. His contention was
that the district attorney had prejudiced the jury and ir-
reparably harmed his client's opportunity for a fair verdict
by dragging in inflammatory tidbits about Claude Paulus'
alleged bookmaking business and the "rent property" on
Galveston's Post Office Street.

Judge Price asked the lawyers to come into his private
office and engage in a little debating contest for him.
Bristling, DeGeurin professed absolute "outrage" at the
district attorney's conduct. How dare he attempt to convict
a woman on a murder charge by virtue of her dead husband's business affairs and by snide allusions to rental
property? "His only reason is to prejudice this jury against
Mrs. Paulus," pleaded the defense lawyer.

And if that were not disgraceful enough, pushed De-
Geurin, it was now known that the prosecution planned to

lead off its rebuttal by calling two veteran vice squad cops. Presumably, Bennett wanted them to describe his client as the whore of Babylon. This is not only false, he argued, it is prejudicial and totally irrelevant to the question of whether Lilla Paulus was an accomplice to the murder of John Hill.

Bennett looked a little impish as he rose from the judge's orange suede-cloth couch to answer the charge. "Mrs. Paulus has testified, under oath, that she was the mother of a small child, that she had that child in St. John's School, that she was a big Brownie leader, that she is now a widow lady, that she was unaware of what Marcia Mc-Kittrick's life style was, but that she was aware it was completely different from hers. She has gotten that image and those statements—and alleged them to be facts—all before the jury. It is my position that as a part of rebuttal we can show facts and circumstances which tend to prove those to be untruths. And therefore they are admissible before the jury, not for the purpose of anything other than to impeach her testimony and to show her lack of credibility to the jury."

DeGeurin sputtered a new objection, but the judge shushed him. "Just exactly what will you be up to with this line of questioning?" he asked Bennett.

"Well, we want to show that if she lied in this area of her testimony, i.e., comparing her life style to Marcia's . . . then she perhaps lied in the more important area, i.e., whether or not she hired these killers."

The judge professed that he was uncomfortable with the way this trial was corkscrewing toward a conclusion, like a sidewinder slithering down a dry creek bed. Sighing, he denied DeGeurin's motion for a mistrial. But he cautioned the prosecutor that whenever a potentially sticky area of testimony was about to be presented, then it must be dress-rehearsed with the bench before the jury could hear it.

Bennett frowned at this, but DeGeurin was moderately satisfied. He was now in an alien neighborhood. The defense has a reasonably good notion during the first act of a trial exactly what will be used against it. Under rules of discovery, the defense can obtain access to all of the state's evidence, and by studying subpoena lists learn who will be testifying for the district attorney. But when Act Two, rebuttal testimony, begins, the state can toss surprise witnesses into the frying pan. This is the hour when a de-

fense lawyer's stomach heaves—each time the DA rises
and announces a new name to the bailiff.

Police Lieutenant Allbright, who had spent the bulk of
his eighteen years on the force in the vice squad, was not
permitted by Judge Price to tell the jury his specialty, only
the general information that he was a cop. The word "vice"
bore too notorious a connotation.

Bennett asked if he knew Lilla Paulus, the lady sitting
across the room.

Yes, answered the officer. He had heard her name for
years, and he knew her to be a sometime madam, an associate of thieves, prostitutes, gamblers, pimps, and hijackers. Bennett paused dramatically, letting the new biographical data soak into the jurors' portrait of Lilla. For
the first time there were driblets of black paint splattered
on her robes of white.

"Based on what you know," wondered Bennett, "and on
her reputation for truth and veracity in the community, can
this defendant be believed under oath?"

Lieutenant Allbright shook his head slowly and deliberately from side to side, like a pendulum. "No."

"Mrs. Joanie Worrell, your honor," abruptly announced
Bennett. The courtroom stirred. Here was a new name, an
unknown factor. For a moment even Lilla Paulus went
blank, but then a realization came to her and she bent to
her attorney's ear.

The slim, hardened woman in her early forties who entered the courtroom was chic in a well-cut black and white
suit reminiscent of the riding ring, and she carried the aura
of money. And power. People danced when she blew her
horn. Also on her was the mark of the years, her hair dyed
a not quite believable honey, her eyes set deep in the cobwebs of time and not concealed by expensive potions. In
her bearing was that curious coalescence of the feminine
and the masculine found so often in Texas women—like a
hand soft and creamed on top, but calloused and tough
if the palm were turned over to feel a raindrop.

"What is your name, please?"

"Joanie Jaworski Worrell," she answered, giving slight
emphasis to her maiden name. That was enough. The point
was made. Here was the daughter of Leon Jaworski, the
Watergate prosecutor, a name for years distinguished in
Houston, made prominent world-wide by the tragedy of
Richard Nixon. Now memories were prodded. Now associ-

ations were made. The two Joans! Robinson and Jaworski! The "gold dust twins"! Two decades fell away. These were the graceful young women who rode horses together, drove their Cadillacs across the warm nights with tops down and blonde hair streaming in the wind, danced on the patios of country clubs, stretched out beside the pool of the Shamrock Hotel when it was the Versailles of Houston. They laughed for every camera, competed for whatever desirable man turned up in town. They were the undisputed stars of a city when it was young and brash and new, the symbols of what the good life here could be. Joan Jaworski had been the maid of honor when her best friend married Dr. John Hill. She had also been the first to arrive for the rites of her death, sitting on the arm of Pa's chair and offering herself as substitute child. But she had never believed that John Hill calculatedly murdered his wife, and she had suffered with each new shock of the years. Perhaps, in a way, the death of Joan Robinson Hill had become a symbol of her own unhappiness. For Joan Jaworski Worrell was a woman of devastation—a string of shattered marriages behind her, her only child freshly dead in a car accident, her voice raw with the groove marks of cigarettes before coffee.

After Lilla Paulus swore from the witness stand that she did not even know Ash Robinson, Bob Bennett had plowed through the papers on his desk searching for witnesses who might dispute her. He had spoken to Joan Worrell several times during the investigation, but always she had declined to aid him. "It's not going to bring Joan back, is it?" she had said testily. Once she even slammed the phone down in his ear.

But for reasons only she knew, this time when he called, she listened. She considered his urgent plea. And she agreed to come to court and attack the core of Lilla Paulus' defense.

"Did you know Joan Robinson Hill?" asked Bennett almost deferentially, paying respect due. He needed to keep impressing the jury that this was not a glove clerk at Foley's department store.

"Very well," answered Mrs. Worrell.

"Did you also know her father, Ash Robinson?"

"Too well."

"Have you ever seen this defendant before?" asked Bennett thrusting an erect finger at Lilla Paulus.

"Yes." She glared at Lilla. Her eyes burned like laser rays from behind her glasses.

"Have you ever seen this defendant in the company of Ash Robinson?"

"Yes. Three times." Her memory seemed as precise as the cut of a scalpel. The first was in 1965, at Chatsworth Farm, where Joan rode her horses. The second, in 1969, at the same place, before Joan died. And the third was in 1970, in New Orleans, in a French Quarter restaurant across the street from the Old Absinthe House on Bourbon Street. She spit out the three dates as if they were the years of famous battles memorized for a high school history examination.

When DeGeurin rose for cross-examination, all the lawyers in the audience were glad they did not wear his shoes at this moment. The testimony itself was damaging, and so was the fact that it came from the daughter of Leon Jaworski.

"When did you decide to come forward and make these facts known?" asked DeGeurin calmly.

"Yesterday."

"Did you volunteer?"

"Let's put it this way. I was not subpoenaed. I offered . . . when John Hill was murdered . . . to help in any way that I could."

The defense lawyer begged to disagree. ". . . to do anything you could *to get Ash Robinson charged?*"

She shook her head negatively. "No, that's not the case at all."

DeGeurin pressed her on the New Orleans memory. Where had she stayed? At what hotel?

"The Fairmont Hotel," answered Mrs. Worrell firmly. Bob Bennett felt his heart leap. During rehearsal of her testimony, she had not been able to remember the hotel. Bennett had urged her to reply, if that question came up, "I don't know." Now she was suddenly possessed of recollection. He muttered a silent prayer. Please, God, let her name be on the registration records of the Fairmont. He knew that the moment of the next recess DeGeurin would rush to a telephone and order his office to check with the hostelry.

A case could be lost on something as trivial as that.

* * *

Bob Bennett drew a deep breath and said softly, looking directly at Lilla Paulus, "Mary Wood, your honor."

The defendant's head shot up and she shut her eyes, as if trying to blot out what was about to offend her vision. And when Lilla opened them, her face, for a flashing moment. sagged, melting like a wax doll left out in an August sun. Then she caught herself, and with an attempt at composure that failed to hide terrible hate, Lilla watched her own daughter enter the courtroom. Unbeknownst to Lilla, an armed investigator from the DA's office had his eyes trained on her. Bennett, knowing the old woman's penchant for guns, had worried that in this supreme moment of tension she might pull one from a hidden place and shoot her child dead. It was that bad between them. But Lilla did nothing but move her head involuntarily from side to side, mouthing a silent "No." She had feared that Bob Bennett would do this. She had warned her lawyer, DeGeurin, that the other side might find her daughter, pressure her, tempt her into the courtroom. Now the awful thing was on her, and Lilla Paulus was consumed with panic.

DeGeurin placed his hand over hers and patted it reassuringly. But his own stomach was pitching. What would Mary Wood tell on her mother?

Any other woman would have been proud at the stunning reproduction of herself who was now placing a hand on the courtroom Bible. Mary Wood was tall and exceptionally beautiful, a prize colt, with great long legs in Western pants, and a filmy blouse that covered large high breasts as provocatively as a sculptor's drapes. There was the look of an Egyptian frieze about her. Of ancient nobility. Reddish gold hair tumbled full down past high cheekbones, past huge eyes—those huge eyes of her mother—dark eyes shadowed by paint and worry.

Bennett approached his surprise witness with no small measure of frustration. He knew that she was fraught with fear. He had spent a turbulent hour on long distance with her the night before, beseeching her to come to Houston, promising that deputies with shotguns would meet her plane, guard her hidden hotel room, guarantee her safety in and out of town. She had responded with tears spilled heavily on the telephone. Why did the district attorney need her? Why must he demand that she walk into a courtroom and impeach the character of her mother? This would tear open barely healed scar tissue.

"Because," Bennett answered bluntly, "I don't think I can win this case without you. I can't send your mother to the penitentiary unless you help." He also pointed out that it would greatly assist her cause in the continuing fight over her grandmother's estate if Lilla Paulus were behind bars.

Finally Mary Wood agreed, and Bennett made frantic arrangements for her midnight flight to Houston. And on this morning of her appearance he secretly cleared her testimony with Judge Price. For this was surely a "sticky" area. Bennett sought to use Mary Wood to illustrate a memoir of Lilla Paulus' hidden life. The young woman told the prosecutor she held vivid memories of guns in holsters dangling from the bathroom doorknob, of bedspreads filled with her father's daily take from bookmaking, of police characters who graced her mother's dinner table.

Judge Price forbade all of this. He instructed Bennett that the daughter of Lilla Paulus could be used *only* to impeach specific areas of the defendant's own testimony. Mary Wood could not serve as a clothesline on which to hang out a dirty wash. "Very well," thought Bennett, "we'll do the best we can."

"What is your name, please?"

"Mary Wood."

"And where do you live?"

"In another state." That was part of the bargain. Bennett had promised she would not have to give her address.

"And do you know the defendant? Lilla Paulus?"

"Yes," said Mary Wood. "She is my mother."

A wave of excitement broke across the room. The jurors swiveled from one woman to the other, trying to match the genes and bloodlines.

"Have you ever met Ash Robinson?" asked the prosecutor.

"Yes."

"And where was the first meeting?"

"At my mother's home." The jurors turned again quickly. What was Lilla's reaction to *that*? She looked directly back at them and, of all things, smiled.

"Did you know Joan Robinson Hill?"

"Yes."

"Did you ever go to the Hill house at the intersection of Kirby Drive and Brentwood?"

"Yes. I've been there before. With my mother."

"Was Ash Robinson ever at that location when you went there?"

"He often was. Not always. But often."

Bennett worked quickly. His witness was responding productively, but he noted a tightness at her mouth and a trembling in her hands. She could fall apart at any moment.

"Did your mother ever accompany you to . . . horse shows?"

"She always did."

"Did you ever go to the Pin Oak Horse Show?" asked Bennett, invoking the name of Houston's most glamorous equestrian event, where Joan Hill had starred for almost a decade.

"Yes."

"When you went to the Pin Oak Horse Show with your mother, where did you sit?"

"Sometimes we sat in Ash Robinson's box," said Mary, adding, in emphasis, ". . . Joan's *father's* box."

"On few or many occasions?"

"Quite a few over the years," said Mary.

Bennett did not stretch out the suspense. He set off his detonation. Did Mary Wood remember anything significant about the Christmas of 1970?

"Yes," she answered. She remembered dropping by her mother's house a few days before the holiday, bearing gifts. While there she heard her mother make a startling remark: "Mother and Daddy were talking and Mother said, 'Diane Settegast called and said Ash Robinson is looking for somebody to kill John Hill.'"

And what did Claude Paulus, her father, say to that?

"He had a fit," answered Mary Jo. "And he warned Mother not to have anything to do with it."

Bennett paused. There were a hundred other questions he could ask this witness, but he sensed that revelations she had made were powerful enough to stand without buttressing. But, oh, one more thing. He gestured toward Lilla Paulus: "Is this defendant's reputation such that she can be believed under oath?"

Without hesitation, Mary Jo Wood shook her head fiercely. She looked squarely at her mother and she said, "In *no* way."

Dick DeGeurin now had to climb out of a ten-foot hole

with two feet of rope. He was in the most excruciating of
defense predicaments. His chore was denigration of a witness for whom he was not prepared.

From whatever options crossed his mind, he chose one
that he would soon regret. Logically it seemed the only
thing to do; ram home to the jury the bitter estrangement
between his client and her daughter.

DeGeurin cleared his throat and began. Was it not true
that Mary Wood had a "falling out" with her mother?

Yes. That was true.

"Do you now harbor animosity toward your mother?"
asked the defense lawyer.

"No . . . not animosity as much as regret."

DeGeurin pounced on the word like a hungry lion on a
miraculous piece of meat. "So much *regret* that you would
come here today and tell lies and perjure yourself?"

Mary Wood shook her head sadly. "I have not committed perjury," she said.

DeGeurin threw his hands in the air like a man so disgusted he could find no further words to waste.

Excitedly, Bennett climbed up out of his chair. He felt
DeGeurin had given him a new opportunity.

"Mr. DeGeurin mentioned you had a 'falling out' with
your mother."

"Yes," nodded Mary. "In 1967."

Now DeGeurin tensed. He saw the highway Bennett
was preparing to barrel down at full speed. At its end was
potential disaster for Lilla Paulus. Even as DeGeurin rose
to throw out an objection for roadblock, Bennett was hurrying into his next question.

"Were there several reasons? Or just one?"

"Mainly one," said Mary Jo. But her answer was
drowned out by the defense lawyer's shout, "Objection,
your honor!" DeGeurin hurried toward the bench, words
spilling on the way. "She is apparently going to say something totally prejudicial toward my client."

Judge Price impatiently sighed and led the squabbling
attorneys to his chambers. At least fifty per cent of the
day seemed to pass in the privacy there, where the judge
was glad to shed his robes, always looking even younger
then than the antagonists he had to referee.

"Mr. Bennett, just what are you up to now?" asked Judge
Price.

"I feel I now have the right to explore the entire background of Mary Wood's life with her mother," began Bennett.

"You have no right at all . . ." interrupted DeGeurin.

"Hush! Both of you," said the judge. "Now let Mr. Bennett make his point. He is responding to your objection, Mr. DeGeurin."

Bennett nodded mock gratitude. "Mr. DeGeurin opened the door by attempting to show that there was a harmonious mother-daughter relationship, that the defendant was a sacrificing person who 'laid down her all' for this witness . . . riding lessons . . . Brownie meetings . . . expensive schools. . . . We all know there was another side to this home life."

DeGeurin jumped in again. "What on earth value would be in this . . . this . . . 'girl' . . . saying that five years before the offense charged here, she had a falling out with her mother because her mother 'turned her out to prostitution,' which I take it will be testified. And this in no way has any bearing on whether Marcia McKittrick and Bobby Vandiver killed John Hill, or whether Lilla Paulus hired them, encouraged them, or commanded them to do so. The prejudicial effect of this girl saying these things before a jury, in effect proving some sort of extraneous offense, could not be weighed by any lay person."

The defense lawyer sensed he was in deep trouble. He should not have had his client speak of her daughter in the first place, and he certainly should not have probed the "falling out" between them. The laws regulating a murder trial seem at times like a child's game, not far in dictate from Simon Says. You cannot touch your nose or scratch your elbow unless Simon says you can. Nor can a lawyer examine certain forbidden areas of a defendant's character unless one side or the other makes a mistake.

"I never asked Mary Wood *why* there was a falling out," insisted DeGeurin, trying to put his finger in the broken dike. "If you'll remember, I then went immediately to another subject, without probing, without 'opening any door.' If you let this in, Judge, if you admit what the girl apparently wants to testify to . . . then you might as well admit every enemy Mrs. Paulus ever had before the jury to say whatever they want to say. Because it would have just as much bearing on the case as this girl testifying."

The judge agreed. Mary Wood could not, under the present climate of the trial, tell the jurors that her mother trained her to be a prostitute.

Bennett started to crank up a new plea, but the judge shook his head firmly. He was tired. Everyone was tired. Mary Wood's day in court was over.

If Dick DeGeurin found an hour of sleep during the night, his face did not show it the next morning. His eyes were aflame with fatigue, but his manner was positively exuberant. He sailed into the courtroom with a briefcase full of new tricks. First, he told Judge Price, he had spent hours on the long-distance telephone with the manager of the Fairmont Hotel in New Orleans. There was *no* registration record for Mrs. Joan Jaworski Worrell for the period of time she swore she was in that city and coincidentally espied Lilla Paulus and Ash Robinson dining in a French Quarter restaurant. DeGeurin wanted an emergency subpoena issued and he had a crisp, unused hundred-dollar bill in his hand to pay for the manager's flight to Houston. Next he handed the judge a bulging packet of old hospital records that told of Mary Paulus Wood's three-week stay in a psychiatric clinic in 1967. The defense wished to introduce these, the purpose being to shed a little light on the kind of young woman who had so harshly accused her mother. Judge Price retired to his office and hurriedly persued them. The records were poorly copied and difficult to read, but they were powerful. Lilla Paulus had committed her then seventeen-year-old daughter to St. Joseph's Hospital for treatment of an "emotional disturbance" and possible use of heroin. The young woman underwent three weeks of enforced therapy whereupon she was given a pass to leave the clinic for a beauty parlor. But she never returned. She ran to the arms of her lover, Larry Wood, the twenty-nine-year-old society pimp with four previous broken marriages, and they eloped.

When Judge Price returned to the courtroom, he was disinclined to admit the medical documents. They seemed far afield from the murder charge against Lilla Paulus. He asked DeGeurin for specific reasons why they should be given to the jury for consideration.

"We want to show bias, prejudice, and animosity on the part of Mary Wood toward the defendant," answered DeGeurin.

Bob Bennett made strenuous objection to the idea—the jury at this point had no information that Mary Jo Wood was anything but a beautiful woman who did not like her mother. Her credibility was not tainted. But the prosecutor had his tongue hidden carefully in his cheek. He had to *act* as if he wanted to keep these old documents away from the jury, when in truth he was *eager* for their admission. Once into the record, he could recall Mary Jo to the witness stand and have her begin with memories of the hospital stay, then "tack back" to a remarkably interesting childhood in the home of the widder lady Brownie leader.

Judge Price refused to admit the hospital records. "Then, your honor," snapped DeGeurin, his anger unhidden by legal courtesy, "we move to introduce these records on a bill of exception." This was a slap at the judge. A bill of exception keeps material away from the eyes of the jury, but the disputed information goes into the official trial record that is placed before the Court of Criminal Appeals. That high court can thus determine whether or not the judge was correct in his decision to exclude them.

"That is your privilege, Mr. DeGeurin," said the judge.

But rather than enter the entire package, DeGeurin chose to dictate into the record only choice portions which most tarnished the character of Mary Wood, implying that she was "emotionally disturbed" and a girl who fled from those who were trying to help her.

"Wait just a minute," said the judge. He felt defense counsel was being a mite too selective. There were two sides to this sword. In his quick reading of the medical file, the judge had come across material equally *beneficial* to the reputation of Mary Wood. To balance DeGeurin's editing, the judge pointedly dictated several long paragraphs to the court reporter, one in particular. It had been written by a hospital doctor: "Testing displays no evidence of psychotic process. Patient is in tune with reality. Was told by nurse of mother's carrying gun in her purse during visit to patient. During interrogation I saw no thought disorder. Mother seems to be major problem."

When the judge was done, all of this having transpired out of the jury's earshot, DeGeurin announced a surprise witness of his own. "Diane Settegast, your honor." Into the courtroom steamed the strong-looking woman in her early thirties with a pocked face and eyes that smoldered. Her entire life had orbited around horses, and the manner in which she stalked to the box indicated she had ridden up to the courthouse on a stallion, lashed it to a parking meter, and rushed to stand at the side of her good friend Lilla, with sidearms blazing.

First she fired at Joan Jaworsky Worrell. From September 1968 until February 1969 she had been in residence at Chatsworth Farm and she had *never* seen Mrs. Worrell there except on one occasion after Joan Hill's funeral. This was in contradiction to the testimony that Mrs. Worrell remembered seeing Lilla and Ash there together on two occasions.

"Well, did you *ever* see Lilla Paulus at Chatsworth Farm?" asked DeGeurin.

"Once," said Settegast. "Right before Christmas, 1968, when I invited her out for a drink."

"Have you ever seen Ash Robinson in the presence of Lilla Paulus?"

"Just at horse shows . . . in passing . . . you know, in groups of people, 'Hello, how are you?' that sort of thing." She was "sure" that Ash Robinson and Lilla Paulus did not know one another.

"Have you ever seen Lilla Paulus at John Hill's home?"

"No!"

"Or at Ash Robinson's home?"

"No. To my knowledge she has not been there."

Settegast boomed out her answers in the manner of an oracle with sole possession of the truth. There was no stammering, no hesitant feints. This woman possessed only roundhouse punches.

"In the few days before Christmas, 1970, did you call up Lilla Paulus and tell her that Ash Robinson was looking for somebody to kill John Hill?"

"Certainly not!" The idea seemed absurd to Settegast.

Had DeGeurin quit then and there, he would have walked away winner. But he could not resist one more question, trying to sneak in the fact that Lilla Paulus' daughter had been committed once to a psychiatric clinic.

"When was the last time you saw Mary Wood?" he asked.

Settegast leaned heavily into the microphone. "Before she decided to take up the practice of *prostitution*," she spat, acrid fumes fairly curling around her answer.

From his seat, hearing the stir in the spectator section, knowing he must rise to make strenuous objection, know-

ing he would surely be sustained, Bennett nonetheless felt
a twinge of sympathy for Dick DeGeurin. Diane Settegast,
though well-meaning, had just opened the gates of hell.

42

"I take it, Miss Settegast, due to your connection with the
family, that Mary Wood discussed with you how she
learned to be a prostitute?" Bob Bennett asked, his voice
no longer courtly. Now he was mean. This was a cock-
fight, razors tied to fetters.

"*Practice!*" shot back the witness with heavy sarcasm.

"All right," said Bennett. "Then do you know who began her practice?"

"*She* did."

"And she began it at the interest of her mother, isn't
that right?"

Settegast disagreed with a furious shake of her head.
"Larry Wood was pimping for her . . ."

"I believe the question was . . ."

"No, sir," interrupted Settegast. "That is not where
she *began* . . ."

"Wasn't she first introduced to sexual activity at the
insistence of her mother? Isn't that true?" demanded Bennett.

Arrogantly, Settegast shook off the question. If looks
could kill, she would have decapitated the assistant district attorney of Harris County, Texas. If intent could be
guessed, she wanted to hurl his impudent head out the
window to the chili parlor six floors below. "It doesn't de-
serve an answer. But the answer is *no!*"

"Do you know that to be a fact by virtue of your knowledge of Mrs. Paulus' reputation and . . ." Here Bennett
hesitated; he could not come right out and charge that
Lilla Paulus was once a whore, but he could dance around
the edge. ". . . and the *activity* that she during her lifetime
engaged in?"

Settegast would not budge. "I know what I saw in the
home . . . and I know Lilla spent a lot of money to get
her daughter straightened out."

"You were aware of the income that Mary was bringing in from her prostitution activity, I take it?"

"I certainly wasn't."

"You were aware of the income from prostitution that Lilla Paulus was enjoying, weren't you?"

Settegast drew herself up haughtily. "I certainly was not." Then witness and prosecutor engaged in a cacophonous duet, their voices rising in anger against one another, she shouting, "That is the most outrageous claim I have ever heard in my life," he throttling with "Just answer the question 'yes' or 'no,'" De Geurin shooting up to cry, "I object to Mr. Bennett cutting her off!"

Judge Price was not a gavel-slammer, but now he rapped to separate the combatants. "Answer the question, Miss Settegast."

From clenched teeth, she said, "I have never heard of income coming into that house from prostitution, and I am certain that it never did."

"So you never went to Galveston with her to collect the 'rent' down there?" asked Bennett.

"No, sir, I have never been to Galveston."

Bennett let the temperature cool a moment. He glanced at the jury and caught several of them openmouthed, obviously astonished at the sudden *tempo furioso*. His chief worry now was that too much, too soon was being thrown at them. Could they possibly comprehend the complexities of this human drama? Could they understand that he was trying to prove that Lilla Paulus, Brownie leader from a good neighborhood, was also a woman capable of plotting murder?

He turned back to Settegast. "Are you or are you not aware of the efforts this defendant made to find her daughter, Mary Wood?"

"I am aware that Mrs. Paulus wanted to find her daughter . . . because of her daughter's activities she wanted to give Mary some help . . . as before, when they tried to put her in a hospital and tried to get her some psychiatric help." With that, another plum fell from the tree and tumbled into the prosecutor's lap. Now *he* could bid the jurors to read how Lilla Paulus went to a hospital and visited her daughter with a gun in her purse. Now they could read the passage in the medical documents that stood out as if scrawled across the blue Texas sky: "Mother seems to be the major problem."

"Are you aware," went on Bennett, "that there were

thousands of dollars given to individuals for the purpose
of killing Larry Wood and Mary Wood?"

"I certainly was not," said Settegast.

"Were you aware of the shooting into the apartment
where Larry and Mary Wood lived here in Houston?"

"No!"

With that unelaborated act of violence hanging in the
tense air, Bennett sat contentedly down.

With a forced look of "no harm has been done," De-
Geurin rose in attempt to rehabilitate his witness. All he
could try to do was get Settegast to denounce once more
what the district attorney had alleged, and save his remaining strength for summation.

"The breakup of Mary Wood and her mother, Lilla
Paulus, did that come about because of Larry Wood?"
asked De Geurin, trying to smudge his client's daughter's
husband a little.

"Yes."

"How many times before had Larry Wood been married?"

Bennett, of course, made objection to that, but Settegast
beat him to the punch. "Three or four," she said triumphantly, as if that answer alone were enough to acquit
her friend. In her desire to help the defense and lay waste
to the prosecution, Settegast was so prejudiced a witness
that the jury knew it. But for the moment she was all the
defense had to rebut Mary Wood's catalogue of horrors.

"Mr. Bennett has inferred that Lilla Paulus ran a house
of prostitution. Your answer in that regard is what?"

"Ridiculous!" And at least one lawyer in the spectator
section wondered why DeGeurin was re-emphasizing a
point best left alone.

"Mr. Bennett has inferred that Lilla Paulus hired people, and put out money to have her only daughter killed?
Your testimony in that regard?"

"Ridiculous!"

"When was the first time you heard this claim that Mr.
Bennett has made that Lilla Paulus had men fondle her
daughter? . . ."

Settegast laughed sneeringly. "That's the first time I
ever heard of it. It is sickening . . . and it is not true . . .
and it is a lie by whoever said it."

Bob Bennett rose and could not resist one modestly perverse maneuver before he would let Settegast off the stand. He withdrew a police mug shot from a folder, carefully cupped it in his hand to shield it from the jury's eyes, and handed it to the witness. The photograph was of Lilla Paulus, taken when she was arrested in 1956 along with her husband on suspicion of bookmaking. This was a vastly different Lilla Paulus, a full-bodied, hearty woman with one thick blonde pigtail down her back. Settegast stared at it dumbly; of course she recognized her friend, but she was loath to say so. DeGeurin came to her rescue with an angry objection and asked for a mistrial. It seemed like the eight hundredth such request.

"Your honor," he cried, ". . . this puts me in the position where the jury may think I'm trying to hide something from them. Mr. Bennett knows . . . or *should* know . . . that this is so prejudicial and so inflammatory . . . a deliberate attempt by him to prejudice the jury."

Before the judge could even rule on the motion, De-Geurin—weary and anguished to the point that his words were glued together—threw out a non-stop barrage of other requests. He asked that the bench rebuke the district attorney, that the jury disregard the photograph, that the jury make note of Mr. Bennett's unprofessional conduct, and—petulantly—that the judge step down and be replaced by another. The last motion, rarely used, was an enormous insult. DeGeurin backed up his demand by suggesting that Judge Price was "smirking" during parts of the Settegast testimony.

His face as icy as Lilla's, the judge coldly snapped, "Overruled," to each of the motions. There was now deep rupture between the two men.

It was necessary, DeGeurin decided, to throw Lilla back on the stand. Her testimony this time was but a hurried denial of every allegation made against her by Joan Jaworski Worrell and by Mary Wood. Lilla denied having been in New Orleans since 1961. She denied *ever* having been in the home of Dr. and Mrs. John Hill. Her denials came wrapped in a new meek and tiny voice, as if she had been stepped on by bullies and there was hardly a breath left.

Judge Price grew so fascinated by Lilla's dramatic change of voice that he leaned sideways in his chair to observe. At this, DeGeurin made truculent complaint that the judge was making "faces," influencing the jury, and necessitating a mistrial. The expression Judge Price bestowed on the defense counsel as he snapped, "Denied," was one of patience wearing not only thin but out.

The judge decided it was necessary to declare a brief recess He went to his chambers to cool off. "I've never been asked to excuse myself before in the middle of a trial," he told his court reporter, stalking into his office and tearing off his black robes. "But I'm not going to let myself be goaded into giving Dickie a mistrial. He's made some mistakes and he's getting desperate. He should have rested his case the moment Bennett did."

Bennett's business during the break was to find a phone and call the hotel where Mary Wood and her husband were packing to leave. His worry was that the couple might have already checked out. He dialed frantically. He had to use a coded password before the deputy sheriff with a 12-gauge shotgun who answered the hotel room phone would put Mary on the line.

"I need you over here again," said Bennett. "I'm sorry. I know what a strain this is on you."

"I've already been through hell once," she said. "I suppose the second time around can't be so bad."

Mary threw open her suitcase and found another pair of riding pants and a blouse. She dressed quickly. She knew that now Bob Bennett was going to push her cruelly back to a past that she had spent most of her adult life running from. As she bent over the mirror to put on makeup, waiting for the unmarked car to arrive and take her to the courthouse, one of the young investigators from the DA's office asked how she felt about what was going to happen. He had grown to like Mary and he had seen the pressures on her. "Frankly I'm paralyzed," she answered. Then why go through with it?

"Three reasons," said Mary, staring in the mirror at her long, tumbling auburn hair. "Number one, she did it. Number two, I'm not vindictive, but I'm tired of hiding from her She's dangerous; if she gets out of this, she'll be invincible. And number three, I didn't like living through some of the things I'm fixing to testify about. I couldn't let them get away with putting Lilla on display as a Brownie leader who raised me with a lollipop in each hand."

This time when Mary Wood entered the courtroom, Lilla Paulus put her head on the counsel table and did not raise it until well into the testimony. Thus she did not see her daughter pause, breaking her stately rolling gait, stopping to find her mother and let her know by the expression on her face that it was the hour of revelation. But Lilla felt the awful gaze of her child, and she trembled. Her hand shook as she found a handkerchief and put it to her face.

Immediately, Bennett asked Mary Wood when she had married. In August 1967, came the answer, three weeks after she was trapped into going to a psychiatric clinic. She had run away from the doctors. She married Larry. And they stayed married. . . .

"Did you go to St. Joseph's Hospital of your own free will?" asked Bennett.

"No . . . wait, in a way. My parents thought I was on heroin, and if I could prove that I wasn't—then I could get married. When I got there, they had me locked up."

"Did your mother come to visit you in the hospital?"

"Yes. For a period of time. . . . Then she came up there with a gun and was waving it around . . . and a nurse saw it." Mary stopped her answer. And Bennett paused. When there was a drum roll, he wanted the echo to last as long as he dared.

"Had you ever see your mother carry one before?"

"To my personal knowledge, I never saw her without one." At this, Lilla's head snapped erect and her eyes bore malevolently at her daughter.

All right, thought Bennett to himself, on to the grand finale. "During your lifetime," he began gently, "have you ever engaged in sexual activity for money or other things of value?"

Mary Wood did not hesitate. She nodded and said quietly, "Yes, I have."

"When did you *first* enter into sexual activities in return for favors or money?"

"The first I can remember . . . was when I was about four years old." The gasps that Bennett anticipated swept the court. One of the women jurors threw her hand involuntarily to her mouth. One of the men looked at his lap, as if embarrassed to hear the rest of this story.

"Where was that?"

"At my home."

"Who else was present at that time?"

"My mother was in the house."

DeGeurin, hoarse from his day of harangues, objected. Once. Twice. Ten times. He finally settled for a running objection to every word that came out of Mary Wood's mouth.

"Was this a male person?" asked Bennett. "How old?"

"Yes. . . . He was in his sixties."

"What prompted you to engage in some sort of sexual activity with that sixty-year-old person?"

"The first time I didn't understand really what was happening and I told him to leave me alone. When he left, I told my mother I didn't like him and didn't want to be around him. She said for me to be nice to him. He gave her money."

"Did you ever see him give her money?"

"Yes, I did."

Lilla Paulus seized a pencil and wrote on her lawyer's yellow pad. "LIES!" She pressed so hard that the lead broke and her fingers fell against the paper in despair.

"Did this engaging in sexual activities for money continue after that?"

"Yes."

"Was it intermittent, or was it continuous?"

"One person came two or three times a week until I was about eleven." Mary Jo Wood continued for some time, speaking in a flat, dry voice, as if she was reading from the pages of someone else's diary. The day before, Bennett had feared that she would disintegrate emotionally. But now, in an excruciatingly poignant hour, she was calm. She told of her mother becoming a sort of manageress by the time she was sixteen, of how Lilla would make appointments for her, sometimes even answer the telephone and fake the daughter's voice. Lilla also set fees, the young woman testified. "I had hundred-dollar tricks."

"Objection!" DeGeurin continued to plead. But he could have been making his cries in sign language for all the power they carried against Mary Wood's stark and painful recitative.

"When you were growing up, did you ever have occasion to visit Galveston?" asked Bennett.

"Yes, to collect the rent. And rob the juke boxes. That means taking the money out of the juke boxes and counting it and splitting it with the owners of the place. . . . Mother owned four buildings."

"What kind of houses or establishments were these?"

"Houses of prostitution."

"How did you know?"

"I was there quite often," said Mary. "It was obvious . . . and I spent one summer there."

DeGeurin tried one more time. He was on a teeter-totter between outrage and supplication: "How long will these lies go on? This is incredible. To allow this kind of testimony. It has nothing to do—*nothing*—with the facts of this case!"

But Bennett would not cease. He had too many griev-ances against all of these people. "Were you going to the St. John's School at the time?"

"Yes."

"Was your mother a Brownie leader?"

"Yes, she was."

"Were the other Brownies made aware of what your mother's activities were?" Bennett asked not uncruelly.

"No."

"Did you leave Houston after you married Larry Wood?"

"Yes."

"Why?"

"Threats made on my life."

"That's all, your honor." Bennett returned to his chair and sat down quietly. He knew that DeGeurin would not meddle with the girl any more. It was over. Tomorrow the two lawyers would pound their chests and sermonize in summation. But in the end it would boil down to this: would the jury believe this girl? Or had he gone too far? Would they perhaps be so sickened by tales of blood and money that they would run confused toward the clean air of their own lives, and set Lilla Paulus free?

That night DeGeurin walked Lilla arm in arm across the city's streets to his office, as was their custom. Normal-ly she talked animatedly of each day's session, adding and subtracting from her cause. But on this night she put her head down on DeGeurin's desk and she wept. The lawyer had never seen the tough old woman cry before and he knew of no way to comfort her.

In the courthouse, in Bob Bennett's office, waiting for the car that would take her still guarded to the airport, and a hurried flight to her secret home, Mary Wood sat with a face of ivory. Then *she* broke, sobbing uncontrol-lably for a quarter of an hour, until the deputy came.

"I'm sorry," she said, fishing in her purse for cosmetic relief. "Is there a word for when you've just exorcised your own mother?"

43

No time was left to wait for the manager of the Fairmont Hotel in New Orleans to make an appearance. Therefore Judge Price allowed the opposing lawyers to share a conference long-distance telephone call with the man, as the court reporter transcribed the conversation for the trial record. The import was that his records showed no mention of Mrs. Joan Jaworski Worrell during the period of 1970 when she testified to having been registered at that hotel. But this did not absolutely exclude her presence there at that time, for the manager admitted that his records were not perfect, and that occasionally, when a guest paid cash, the documents were filed incorrectly or not at all.

DeGeurin felt it was a helpful lift to the defense, and he planned to make use of the discrepancy in his summation.

Now, fourteen days after the trial had begun, they all assembled for the last time, like characters in a mystery play, waiting in suspense for the chief inspector to reveal the denouement. The rule that keeps witnesses out of the courtroom except during the period of their own testimony was now suspended. All could come and hear the final arguments and await the verdict.

Connie Hill took a seat directly in the front row, next to Myra Hill. The widow and the mother of the murdered plastic surgeon had insisted on coming, even though Bennett had cautioned them that the experience would be painful. He intended to re-create the death of John Hill with all the ugliness he could summon. "I know that," said Myra, "but I wouldn't miss this for the world." She was disappointed that the prosecutor had not used her as an eyewitness to murder. Moreover, she had never seen the living flesh of Lilla Paulus, only newspaper photographs and those bleakly lit television sequences of the defendant scurrying in and out of chambers.

Now, as Lilla entered the court on the arm of DeGeurin,

Myra Hill scrutinized her like a germ on a slide. All of her life she had tried to be an example of the Bible that she read for at least two hours of every day, but at this juncture she possessed no Christian charity.

Jerry Carpenter squeezed in a back row, amid an excited gaggle of lawyer wives and courthouse secretaries. He had encountered Lilla in the hallway outside, had even nodded politely at her, but she had cut him dead and turned quickly away. The homicide detective, having followed every twist of testimony, was enthusiastic over the state's chance for conviction. But Bob Bennett had dampened his optimism. Overnight he had grown despondent. "This may not be *the* sloppiest murder case I've ever tried," he told his wife, "but it is certainly close." Well after midnight, he rose from his bed and went outside and sat beside a tree he had recently planted, cursing it for its lack of growth.

By tradition, the state opens and closes final arguments, with the defense sandwiched between. The theory is that the defense possesses many advantages during the trial itself while the state has the burden of proof; thus the jury retires with the last words in their ears coming from the prosecution.

Bennett delegated his associate, Bob Burdette, to commence the proceedings as an opening act. This was the first time that the younger assistant district attorney had opened his mouth during the trial, and the jurors were surprised to hear the strength of his argument. A little thick in the hips, he nonetheless darted about the room with style, stopping behind Lilla Paulus' chair to accuse, "Here, ladies and gentlemen of the jury, here is our Brownie leader widder lady who totes a pistol in her handbag. . . . You're finally going to be able to consider the fact that she also owns whorehouses in Galveston, that she went on runs to pick up bookmaking money, that she brought up her own daughter to be a prostitute. For two weeks these facts were kept away from you. Now, *only now*, do you know them. The jury box is on the same side of the courtroom as the witness stand, and there is a reason for that. The reason is so that you can look intently and closely at the witnesses and determine for yourselves who is telling the truth and who is lying."

Then it was DeGeurin's turn. He had not slept much the night before either, sitting for a long while in a steaming tub, sipping an iced tea glass of fine whiskey, entertaining a modest degree of paranoia. He felt that the entire experience was unfair to both him and his client. He had not counted them up, but his snap impression was that the judge had overruled at least eighty per cent of his motions During Marcia McKittrick's days in court, he had even discovered the prostitute rather happily sitting in Judge Price's private office, munching a fried chicken box lunch that the bench had provided. Where were the ethics of a judge buying lunch for the state's star witness? DeGeurin asked himself. He still harbored the idea of filing a complaint about that, alleging further that the judge was advising Marcia what to do. And then there was Mary Wood. Lilla had sworn to him that the girl was lying, that she had dreamed up psychotic fantasies as revenge for her defeat in the matter of her grandmother's estate. Whatever, the inequity of her appearance for the state was as devastating as a grenade lobbed into his bath. Jerry Carpenter paraded back and forth across his consciousness during the long soak. The lawyer had never believed the detective's version of how Marcia had suddenly abdicated her previous position of silence to so rapidly make confession. The way he saw it, Carpenter squeezed the little whore until her eyeballs rattled, shoving out a paper of confession with one hand, figuratively holding a syringe of heroin in the other. He would light up the detective's "diligence" with 1,000-watt bulbs in his summation.

Now, as DeGeurin stood and nodded good morning at the jurors, he elected to speak with softness to turn away the prosecution's wrath. DeGeurin was eminently capable of slapping the table and playing the organ of his voice with all stops pulled. But he sensed that this had to be an interlude of quiet logic, of low-key persuasion.

"I know I'll be able to sleep at night," he began, "for I have done the best I can. If in representing Mrs. Paulus I have been overzealous, I do not apologize for that. If, in attempting to get the facts to you, I have offended Mr. Bennett, I do not apologize for that."

He had ordered a giant, bulletin-board-sized blowup of Ash Robinson's telephone records made, and he dwelt for ten tedious minutes on the matter of the briefly unlisted private telephone number. It seemed crucially important to him that this number was installed *after* the murder of

Dr. John Hill, and not *before*, as the prosecution had suggested.

Then he moved to the people of the tragedy. "The prosecution has asked you to vote a conviction, in effect, on a dispute between this woman and her daughter. Mary Jo Paulus Wood is a girl who hates her mother so much that she would bring lies before you—and that's what they are, lies." Marcia McKittrick? "I feel frankly sorry for her. I don't think she has much future. I don't think she can live with herself after what she did. When she first had the opportunity to implicate Lilla Paulus and Ash Robinson, she wouldn't do it. Then she was offered immunity—she was offered freedom—if she would say what Jerry Carpenter wanted her to say." Heavy scorn now came to his voice. "Marcia McKittrick was almost *comatose* when Jerry Carpenter got through with her."

He sought to wreck Joan Jaworski Worrell. "Oh, by the way, why did she use her maiden name when she was sworn in? How many of you women jurors still use your maiden names? Why didn't she use some of her other married names—Moncrief? O'Connor? . . . It took some work, but we finally found out that Joan Worrell lied. They keep records at the Fairmont Hotel, thank God! They prove what Joan Worrell said was just a hoked-up lie. Hoked up in the hopes that you would believe it." This was boldness; he was accusing one of the most prominent names in Houston—and daughter of one of the nation's most celebrated lawyers—of perjuring herself.

He gestured at the folder containing the color pictures of John Hill murdered. "They're terrible!" he agreed, his voice rising for the first time. "Awful! But you can look at these until the moon drops out of the sky and you won't see a clue to connect Lilla Paulus with this terrible death. . . .

"With every ounce of energy I have left in me, I beg you not to be blinded by the prejudicial testimony. I beg you to judge this case on the evidence. Please give Mrs. Paulus that chance. You are her only chance. You are the only thing standing between her—and Mr. Bennett and Mr. Carpenter. If you have that doubt, that *reasonable doubt* that you must have, then that doubt belongs to Lilla Paulus. Even though it is in your mind, it is her property. The law gives her that doubt. She is entitled to that doubt. For God's sake, don't surrender that. She is *not guilty* of this offense."

Bob Bennett saw no need for calm. He wanted a storm to rise and build and rage until it shook the walls of the jury deliberation room.

"The only issue at trial here," he began, "and has been from Time One, is whether Lilla Paulus aided and abetted the murder of John Hill. And this is murder particularly foul, when you shoot a man until he is dead, and then go back and collect money from a defendant like this." He thrust out his arm in condemnation of Lilla Paulus.

"On September 24, 1972, John Hill ended his life as a very brave man. He ended his life by saving Connie's. Like any life, there was good and bad in John Hill's, but he ended his life with courage!" Quickly Bennett looked out at the widow and the mother of the dead man. Both were crying softly. It did his case no harm to turn a kind phrase in memory of the victim. It was time someone in this town did.

The prosecutor ceremoniously picked up one of the bullets and the revolver he had introduced as evidence. "This was fired through the barrel of this gun because Ash Robinson wanted it done, and because Lilla Paulus wanted it done for profit. The contest here has not been over the death or, in essence, the motive. The contest here has been whether Lilla Paulus *knew* Ash Robinson, and whether Lilla Paulus *knew* what Marcia McKittrick and her life style were all about. . . ." He paused, realizing it was time to defend Marcia against DeGeurin's denigration. "If there was one iota of difference in what Marcia's statement was—and in what she testified before you—don't you think Mr. DeGeurin would have jammed this in your face a thousand times?" This was a worth-while comment. The defense attorney had not attempted to soil Marcia's account of the crime—not a line of it—only the manner in which she was arrested and gave confession.

As long as he was propping up people, there was Jerry Carpenter to defend. "And you bet Jerry Carpenter's vigorous! You bet he stayed on this case. So did Joe Gamino. And aren't you glad! Would you have wanted them to quit—sometime late on the night of September 24, 1972? If you hold his diligence against Jerry Carpenter, then hold that against every honest cop on the force." The prosecutor's eyes swept the jury hurriedly. Were there

any faces before him which stared back with hostility
for police? He could not tell, but the worry still nagged
him. Perhaps he should have left the detective out of his
summation altogether.

Bennett did not dwell at length on the evidence that
he had submitted. He well knew that the four slips of
paper were not, to use the phrase that had suddenly
become voguish in the wake of Watergate, "a smoking gun."
But he did reduce the issue of the private telephone
number to basics. "The significance of this is that it 'tends
to connect' Lilla Paulus with Ash Robinson. It was found
in her purse on April 25, 1973. There's no question and
no dispute that it was private, unlisted, and found in Lilla's
purse. Lilla had it because she wanted to get in touch
with Ash Robinson. She had it because they were designing
the annihilation of John Hill."

Bennett bobbed and weaved as he talked, bringing to
mind a welterweight boxer. He spoke extemporaneously,
and his thoughts tended to become jumbled, clauses
tangling hopelessly, but there was no misunderstanding the
depth of his convictions. He moved quickly to the subject
of Mary Wood, noting that his hour was almost done. He
agreed that her testimony was shocking, perhaps incredible.
"But you take her testimony . . . in the light of everything
that has happened to her . . . and you read those hospital
records . . . and you see how her main problem quote
seems to be her mother end quote . . . and in the light
of all that, her testimony does become credible. And it does
lend you some assistance, I hope, in deciding upon . . .
what kind of person it really is who participates in the
killing for money of someone else."

He returned to the phrase that had so delighted him
the moment it slipped out of Lilla's mouth in the witness
box. "Well, I wouldn't be able to recognize Marcia McKittrick as a prostitute," he paraphrased, mimicking Lilla's
tiny, tremulous, old woman's voice, "*her life is a little bit
different from mine.*"

Bennett nodded. For a moment he seemed to endorse
the quotation. Then he roared with scorn: "It really was
different, ladies and gentlemen! It was *worse* than Marcia
McKittrick's! Oh, there were some similarities. They each
had a history of criminal conduct. They each were married
or living with law violators. They neither one of them
were strangers to violence. And both were involved with

prostitution. . . . But the similarities ended there, and Lilla's got worse. *She's* the one who profited off of the proceeds of people like Marcia, and from 'turning her daughter out.' "

DeGeurin jumped up and broke into his opponent's summation. "Objection, your honor. There's absolutely no evidence of that. It's a complete falsehood and I object to it."

Judge Price overruled the complaint. "The jury heard the evidence," he said tersely.

Bennett nodded in gratitude. "Yes, they *did* hear the evidence. And the evidence is there. There's no falsehood about it. . . . And I tell you something else that's different from Marcia McKittrick's life style and hers. Marcia McKittrick has at least shown some signs of reform. One of the last questions asked of her was, 'Well, why are you testifying?' And she answered, 'Because it's the right thing to do.' There's *no* sign of reform in this defendant."

The weary prosecutor searched back through what he had said. Was there any point of business left unattended? This was his last shot, the dying moments in the forum where he could seek not only conviction but a purge for his system. His attention lodged against the father: the man who wasn't there. "Oh yes," he cried, his face more vengeful than his own wife, sitting in a back row of the courtroom, had ever seen him. For a moment she was alarmed.

"Where's the guy who's *most important*, and who *could* have been called as a witness?" Bennett's tone made it clear that the lack was not *his* fault. "Who is missing most in this case thus far? If there was someone who could refute the allegations made against his friend, Lilla, it is Ash Robinson. . . .

"The coffin picture! Remember that? Does that show you what Ash Robinson thought and how his mind works? Cutting the picture of John Hill out in the shape of a coffin and giving it to her for identification purposes so that the killers . . . would be able to recognize the victim. Ash said, I guess to himself, 'I will not leave it to the law to decide John Hill's fate.' So he and Lilla Paulus together played some supreme being. They decided, '*Ye* shall live, but John Hill, *ye* shall die.'

"Now, ladies and gentlemen, that is what is very wrong in this case. There will always be murders of passion, and there will always be people who may go crazy and berserk and shoot other people . . . but you, as members of the government, must take a stand and cry. 'There cannot be people who are playing God and decreeing when an individual must die.' When that happens, people like Lilla Paulus cannot make their profit off it. . . ."

The prosecutor interrupted himself. He noticed the pile of murder photographs turned face down on his table. Snatching them up, they gave him his final shot of fuel. "And Mr. DeGeurin says these are 'not material.' Mr. DeGeurin says these are 'prejudicial.' Mr. DeGeurin says, of me, 'Mr. Bennett just put those in there so the jury would get mad at Lilla Paulus.' Well, if that's what effect these pictures have, then fine! Is it not *material* when a woman participates in annihilating another human being, with *these* as the result?"

Bennett fanned out the pictures, as if performing a macabre card trick, in one hand. "Look at these," he implored, "and see what Lilla Paulus did! And she couldn't even do it with her own hand. She had to hire some depraved ski mask bandit . . ."

With an abrupt softness, he then asked that the jurors convict Lilla Paulus for hiring the death of John Hill. And, with a silent thought sent to Bobby Vandiver, wherever he was, in small apology for his choice of adjectives, Bob Bennett sat down exhausted.

Less than five hours later, at 7:35 P.M., just when Judge Price had been dealt a sufficiently promising hand to bid a grand slam in bridge, his bailiff interrupted the game in his chambers to announce that a verdict had been reached.

The judge reached for his robes. The courtroom was almost deserted. Snail trails of suspense and worry were marked across the faces of the opposing lawyers. The amount of time spent by the jury in deliberation was puzzling. Had they returned within an hour or less, then Bennett would have felt confident of conviction. Conversely, they had not remained out long enough to stir a fire of hope within DeGeurin. When a jury stays behind locked doors until the hours outside become almost unbearable for those waiting, then tradition holds that the panel is confused, contentious with one another apt to report back hopelessly split, or so anxious to break out of their sequestration—it was, after all, Friday night—that their votes go to the defendant in contradiction of their feelings.

"Would you rise, please?" instructed Judge Price in a voice of kindness.

Lilla Paulus obeyed promptly. She commanded her body to an erect position of dignity. Her lawyer gestured a hand of help, but she shook it off. In her was contained the strength to confront this moment. She had even put on fresh lipstick, and against her drained face, pale and white and empty of emotion for the public to see, it was as vivid as a river of blood on the full moon.

The judge opened the folded slip of paper that had been delivered to him by the foreman, a newly widowed man in his middle forties who was the superintendent of a factory.

He read the words once, hurriedly, then shut the paper and leveled his gaze at the old woman standing before him: "We the jury find the defendant *guilty* of the offense charged."

She was sentenced to thirty-five years in the state penitentiary with the anticipation that, given the condition of her health, she would perish there.

Within the hour, Ash Robinson heard the news. He received the verdict in a telephone call from a well-placed source at the courthouse. The old man had cultivated alert ears for more than six years. It was his belief that very little took place in the DA's office that he did not quickly come to know about.

Then the doorbell rang. Ash looked through the peephole. A friend had come to dissect the day's surprising events. The old man was pleased to talk to someone, and he found a half cup of thick coffee left from the dinner pot. The two men settled into chairs and sipped. Clippings were scattered about Ash as if he were a Father Christmas whose stuffing had come out.

"Well," asked Ash, "I wonder what it all means?"

The friend shrugged; he had no answer.

"I suppose that bastard Bennett will keep tryin' to get something on me," Ash went on. His tic jerked his face violently, and he threw his hand to his chest, perhaps to gain reassurance from the beating of his rusted heart. He chuckled ruefully. "You know, it *could* be that Lilla and them made up this story to blackmail me," he suggested.

"Man makes a little money in his life, and he's lucky if there's enough left to bury him once the vultures eat their fill."

Oh, he knew Lilla all right. He would own up to it, even if she would not. For a few rambling moments he wandered erratically through their association, and during his journey he became a man who walked to the very brink of confession. But he did not plunge into its purifying waters. "All I ever did—so help me!—was ask Lilla to find things out on John Hill," he wanted his friend to know. At the time, three or four years ago, there had been critical need of malicious information concerning his ex-son-in-law to use as defense against the ingrate's $10-million slander suit. "Lilla told me she could find out everything about John Hill," reminisced the old man. "I offered to pay her all right, but she told me, 'Mr. Robinson, I loved your daughter. Joan was so good to my own child, Mary Jo. Joan put Mary on her first horse. Mr. Robinson, I wouldn't take a nickel off of you. I just want you to get justice.' "

The friend looked at his watch. It was past ten. He knew that the old man traditionally went to bed early. Already Ma was asleep on a couch in the den. The drone of the television was her sedative. But Ash did not want to be left alone with the terrors of this night. He found a sliver of cheesecake and insisted that his friend stay and talk some more. Ash eased his heavy body back down into his chair and put his feet on the throw rug below. On it was woven the faded, almost invisible portrait of a pale horse. Threadbare, soon it would wear away to nothing.

Now the old man tilted his head back and closed his eyes. The friend wondered if he had drifted off to sleep. Perhaps it was best to leave, silently. But Ash jerked back. He had only been peregrinating in his memory. "I went up to the Houston Club this morning," he said. "We have this round table for breakfast. Well, I admit it was kind of macabre, but some of the men there, some of the biggest men in town, mind you, they all gathered around me and they put their arms around my shoulders and they said, 'We don't know what you did or didn't do. But you should have killed the s.o.b. years ago.' "

The friend raised an eyebrow but did not ask the obvious question.

"I know what you're thinking," said Ash, "and the

answer is no. *Hell,* no. If they had one iota of evidence against me, they'd of indicted me faster than a Tennessee minute. It's just a bunch of fellas down at the courthouse with political ambitions."

The friend rose. He knew that Ash would, if allowed, continue his meanderings until the sun took away his night fears.

"It's water off a duck's back, anyway," said Ash. He seemed in the courtroom suddenly, defending himself, throwing out his long life for all to see and approve. "I've never had a bill I didn't pay. I don't have to worry about money. Did I tell you about the gas well that came in yesterday?" He searched about his papers for an envelope, found it, opened it, read of tens of thousands of cubic feet of natural gas spewing from the earth and into his pockets. "Ma and me won't be going on the public tit any time soon," he said, as he walked his friend to the door.

In another part of the big house, a telephone was ringing. But the old man did not let it interrupt. He was deep into his own mortality. "They tell me," he finally said, "that at the temple of Abu Simbel, in Egypt, at a certain time in the early morning, for maybe fifteen minutes, the new sun shines through this little hole and it lights up the face of old Radames II. For this little moment of time, there is a golden light. Always has been, always will be. Ain't that a hell of a thing!"

The friend agreed. The image was remarkable, coming as it did on a night when it was time to count bodies and wasted lives and the brutalities of abused power. Ash's money had bought him nothing but tragedy. Even the great horse, Beloved Belinda, had perished in a bizarre accident. After the deaths of Joan and John Hill, the mare broke out of a barn during a thunderstorm, ran into a field, reared up pawing and screaming at the elements, was struck down fatally by a bolt of lightning.

Now, just as the friend took his leave, turning the knob of Ash's front door, grateful to leave as a theatergoer would be to depart the house of Lear, he ventured a rude question. What would Ash have them write on *his* grave?

"Oh, hell, I don't know," said the old man brusquely. "Something like—'Here lies Ash Robinson. He lived and he died and he didn't give a damn what people thought of him.'"

The friend got into his car, but Ash called after him.

He had one more thing to say. "You know that son of a bitch John Hill didn't even want to buy my Joan a tombstone! A week before his murder trial, he finally runs out and orders one, just in case it came up in testimony. And have you seen that marker? It's a *crime*."

How Ash Robinson hated that tombstone that memorialized his Joan. In life, she had always been "Joan *Robinson* Hill," and it was thus in all the newspaper accounts, etched on all the silver and gold trophies that were now darkening and unattended on the shelves of his room. They shone no golden light on Ash's face. But in death, the granite slab did not even bear her father's name. She was for the rest of time the chattel of the man Ash hated most—John Hill.

Some night he just might change that. Some night when it was very dark, when men could do their deeds without the glow of stars, the modest monument might topple and split and need to be replaced. That was on the old man's mind. Failing that, it might even be necessary to lift his Joan once more—one last time—raise her from the earth, from the lonely, barren, sunburned grave that her husband had chosen, and carry her to a cool and green place, perhaps under the benevolent shade of a great oak at Chatsworth Farm, just around the bend from Beloved Belinda Walk. In a place like that, Ash could ease his heavy body down beside her. And there, with Joan at last able to sleep at the side of the only man who really loved her—and proved it—only then would their story finally, mercifully, be done.

EPILOGUE

But the story was not yet done. In August 1977, the events that began with the death of Joan Robinson Hill and were continued for almost a decade thereafter, were once again replayed. This time the setting was a tiny civil district court in Houston where Connie Hill, her stepson Robert (Boot) Hill, and Myra Hill jointly sued Ash Robinson for $7,550,000 in damages. Their contention was that the old man caused the death of Dr. John Hill and that they, as survivors, were entitled to civil damages. The suit, an unusual one, was called a "wrongful death" trial, and for seven weeks the front pages of Houston's newspapers were filled with familiar names. Marcia McKittrick once again refused to testify, but, threatened with contempt by the bench, she repeated her now celebrated tale of how Bobby Vandiver filled the murder contract on John Hill's life. Lilla Paulus took the Fifth Amendment and resisted all efforts and threats to pry further testimony from her lips. Myra Hill and Connie told of the night that John was murdered before their eyes. Robert Hill, now a poised and strikingly handsome youth of seventeen, told the jury with remarkable composure that he felt his grandfather, Ash Robinson, caused the death of his father.

Ash Robinson's defense was constructed on two principal building blocks. The first was a savage attack on John Hill's reputation. He was represented by various witnesses as a poor doctor, an adulterous husband, and a man who seduced his patients. Dr. Nathan Roth, the murdered plastic surgeon's first partner, gave extremely damaging testimony, calling Hill a "psychopath," and dropping the spicy revelation that he had once discovered Hill making love to a woman patient on the office couch.

But the most powerful element of Ash Robinson's defense was the old man himself. Nearing eighty years of age, he took the stand vigorously, his heavy body supported by a cane that he rapped on the floor crustily when he could not hear a question; and he looked his grandson directly in the eye for the first time since they had become estranged after Joan's death. And Ash swore: "Boot, I had no more to do with the death of your father than you did. . . . I did not want him dead . . . death—murder—doesn't solve any problem on the face of the earth. I was deeply embittered against your father because I thought he had killed your mother, a dear person whom everybody loved . . . you were the greatest thing in her life as well as you were in my and Ma's life. . . ."

The jury deliberated for the better part of two days before they brought in a stunning verdict. Although the jurors believed that a conspiracy had existed to assassinate John Hill, and that damages of several hundred thousand dollars were due the Hill family, they did *not* find Ash Robinson to be responsible. He was *not liable* for the murder of John Hill. Ash considered it to be a verdict of not guilty, even though the trial was not a criminal one.

The verdict was an enormous disappointment to the Hill family, and they vowed to appeal it. Several other lawsuits continued to swirl like the winds of an enduring dust storm. One weary lawyer said, "These matters will go on as long as Ash does. And Ash Robinson will outlive us all."